Getting the Bull by the Tail

The Best of Bruce M. Kennedy

Sage Publishing Co.
Cody, Wyoming

Sage Publishing Co. Cody, WY 82414
© 2002 by Sage Publishing Co.
All rights reserved. Published 2002
Printed and bound in the United States of America
ISBN 0-9713662-0-9

Library of Congress Control Number: 2001119044

First edition 2002

Edited by Brian Kennedy and Betty Kennedy

To Bruce Kennedy's faithful readers
who shared his life through his column.

Table of Contents

About the author vii
    A brief biography of Bruce M. Kennedy.

Foreward by Brian Kennedy ix

Introduction by Brian Kennedy xi

Getting the Bull by the Tail 1
    The best items picked from more than 36 years of columns and organized chronologically.

Bruce Kennedy's Favorite Photos 277
    Eighteen Kennedy pictures from the pages of the Greybull Standard. Prize-winning favorites include feature, news and sports photos.

Pages from an Editor's Notebook 485
    A national-award-winning single-topic column published in the 1960s written in addition to Getting the Bull by the Tail.

Index of Names 507
    Find all the names appearing in this book.

Bruce M. Kennedy

Bruce McKenzie Kennedy was born March 13, 1929, to Gilbert V. and Leila McKenzie Kennedy in Basin, Wyo. He grew up in Basin where his father was an insurance and real estate businessman, secretary-treasurer of the Big Horn Canal Association for 45 years and secretary-treasurer of the Tillard Canal for 25 years. Gib had moved to Wyoming from Omaha, Neb. in 1920 after two years of college at the University of Nebraska and service in the Army. Leila was raised on a ranch on the Powder River near Miles City, Mont. After graduating from the University of Montana in 1924 with a degree in Library Science, she moved to Basin and was Big Horn County librarian from 1925 to 1928. She and Gib were married June 10, 1927, in Miles City, Mont. Gib died in 1979 at age 83.

Bruce graduated from Basin High School in 1947 and enrolled at the University of Nebraska where he studied journalism. His interest in newspapering began in high school when he wrote a column for the Basin Republican-Rustler.

At college, he joined the Alpha Tau Omega fraternity, the same fraternity where his father and two uncles had been members.

When he was a sophomore at college, his mother became critically ill with cancer. She died May 6, 1949, in a Billings hospital. She was 47. Bruce couldn't attend her funeral because he had been hospitalized in the same Billings hospital with a ruptured appendix.

Bruce met Betty Green at college and they worked on campus publications, he on the Daily Nebraskan newspaper and she on the Cornhusker yearbook. He was editor of the newspaper his senior year and she was associate editor of the yearbook.

Bruce and Betty were married on March 18, 1951, in Lincoln, shortly before graduating with degrees in journalism.

He enlisted in the U.S. Army in August 1951 and began two years of military service during the Korean War. He was stationed in Tokyo, Japan with the Quartermaster Depot as public information officer. After his discharge July 14, 1953, he worked at the Neligh, (Neb.) News and then the Wyoming State Journal at Lander. In August 1956, he became editor of the Greybull Standard and wrote his first column for the Standard in December. Three years later – on April 1, 1959 – he and Betty bought the weekly newspaper from Lynn Severance.

They continued publishing the Standard (except for 1974-78) while expanding their ownership into other Wyoming newspapers. They founded Sage Publishing Co. and he was co-publisher or publisher and manager of several other newspapers: the Wyoming State Journal in Lander, a semi-weekly, 1967-82; the Gillette News-Record, a daily, 1970 to the present; the Cody Enterprise, a semi-weekly, 1971 to the present; Green River Star, a weekly, 1975 to the present; the Hungry Horse News, a weekly at Columbia Falls, Mont., later owned by son Brian Kennedy, 1978-87; the Whitefish (Mont.) Pilot, a weekly, 1978-99; the Dillon (Mont.) Tribune, a weekly, 1979-89; the Douglas Budget, a weekly, 1984 to the present.

Three new weekly newspapers were established during his management and under the guidance of the Wyoming State Journal and Green River Star. The Dubois Frontier and the Bridger Valley Pioneer continue today as independent newspapers. The Jeffrey City News served a boom town of several thousand residents who worked in the uranium mines. When the mines shut down, so did the newspaper.

Sage Publishing Co. also owns the Business Center in Douglas.

Bruce was a private pilot with more than 700 hours of experience and flew his Beechcraft Bonanza for business and pleasure. He also enjoyed raising quarterhorses and riding in the mountains. Other hobbies included running, skiing, tennis, gardening and travel.

He was a member of the First Presbyterian Church of Greybull and the Wyoming Press Association. He served on the Wyoming Travel Commission 1963-67 and was a director of the First National Bank of Greybull.

He died June 12, 1992, in a one-car rollover on the Horse Creek Road near Shell. The Kennedy family established a memorial scholarship fund for young journalists after Bruce's death. It continues to benefit college students pursuing careers in community journalism.

Bruce's family carries on his newspapering legacy. Betty lives at the family home on Greybull Heights where she serves as president of Sage Publishing Co. and the Gillette News-Record Inc.

Brian continued to publish the Hungry Horse News until 1999 when it was sold. He lives in Columbia Falls, Mont. with his family. Ann Kennedy Franscell is editor and publisher of the Gillette News-Record. Bob is CEO and business manager of Sage Publishing and oversees all its Wyoming operations which now include one daily newspaper, three weekly newspapers, two shopping guides and one office supply business.

There are six grandchildren.

Foreward

Bruce Kennedy wanted to publish a book like this someday but he was so busy writing new chapters for it that he never got the chance. His column writing ended with his death in 1992, but his dream of this book did not.

It's been nearly ten years since he died and his family at last has completed such a book. Readers will find all their favorite columns here, and probably a few they've forgotten. First, however, a few notes of explanation.

From its beginning, "Getting the Bull by the Tail" was a column about different subjects. Some items were a single line, while others required several paragraphs. Separating each item required typographical solutions. The column evolved from alternating bold face paragraphs, then asterisks or dashes or spaces between paragraphs, and finally to capitalized words before each new item. Throughout this book, we've retained the same formats he used for separating column items. That's why the columns in 1958 look different from those in 1963, and 1970 columns don't look the same as those in 1975.

Sharp-eyed readers will remember a Poor Richard saying from Ben Franklin's "Poor Richard's Almanack" at the top of each "Getting the Bull by the Tail" column. This Kennedy tradition started in May 1958 in the Greybull Standard and continued until September 1982. Each week a different Poor Richard quote appeared over the column although a few of the better sayings were rerun over the years. Except for the first time one was used on May 8, 1958, we didn't include any Poor Richard sayings with his columns in this book. That collection can be found in any bookstore.

"Getting the Bull by the Tail" was more than a year old before its unique artwork became a fixture at the top of each column. Archie Pendergraft's cartoon of a man hanging on to the tail of a snorting buffalo was first used on March 6, 1958. Pendergraft was a game warden who once lived in Greybull and was a talented Western artist. His colorful drawing was with each column until 1974.

Except for August 1974 through April 1978 when the Kennedys didn't own the Greybull Standard, his column always appeared in the Greybull newspaper. During that period it was printed in other Wyoming newspapers he published.

Using many local names was a trademark of the Greybull Standard when the Kennedys edited and published the newspaper. This carried over to "Getting the Bull by the Tail" columns where just about everyone in town was mentioned at one time or another. We thought it would be helpful to have an index of the 1,250 names used in this book so readers could more easily find items about people they know. Readers should note that husbands and wives are listed together in the index, although only one may be mentioned in a particular column. We also recognize that some who were couples then aren't together any longer.

Every column he wrote is not included in this book. To reprint all 1,857 of them – totaling more than 940,000 words – would have required four books this size. While his family will keep every word of each column he wrote, we don't wish for readers to wade through them all. Neither would he.

This collection is only Bruce Kennedy's best work, the favorites from a columnist who always gave his readers a memorable ride. You'll find "Getting the Bull by the Tail" is just as good the second time around.

Brian Kennedy

Introduction

Compiling this book of my father's columns has been one of my most enjoyable achievements as a journalist, and one of the most rewarding in personal satisfaction.

Looking through years and years of "Getting the Bull by the Tail" columns was a nostalgic journey through Greybull's past. Recognizing familiar names and remembering funny stories from those days was like growing up in the old hometown all over again. What fun to read once more about Reuben Reifschneider, Red Michaelis, Jack Williams and all the other personalities who made Greybull special.

This project began a few months after Bruce Kennedy died when reading and retyping his old columns was tough. Emotionally it was too soon to work on the book because we missed him so much. Managing my own newspaper until a few years ago also delayed its completion.

Time hasn't dimmed his family's belief in this book, however. We wanted his words remembered.

Chosen from 1,857 columns spanning more than 36 years, the writings in this collection reflect Dad's love of the West and his joy of living in a small town. From the first column he wrote in 1956 to the last, published the day before he died, he captured the beauty of Wyoming and the spirit of its people.

He combined his considerable journalistic talents with an outgoing personality and love of conversation to write columns about many subjects. Ice going out on the Big Horn River was a certain topic every March. Flowers, weather, politics and local history were other favorites. Sharing his family, his friends and his experiences, he touched readers throughout Wyoming.

Exploring everyday life in a humorous, yet sensitive way made him many friends over the years. People linked only by his column sent him letters about his comments they'd read. A Cody woman once sent him a bouquet of marigolds after he wrote how much he liked them. Another stranger had saved all his columns in a scrapbook she kept in her store. Sen. Al Simpson had two framed Kennedy columns hanging in his Washington, D.C. den.

One of Dad's favorite columns to write was his Merry Christmas column, a tradition started in 1980 and eagerly anticipated by his readers. Each holiday season he wrote greetings to those who had been part of his life the previous year. Many Greybull readers looked forward to the last paper before Christmas to see if their name was in his column. All but one of his dozen Christmas columns are included in this book.

Also inside are some of his favorite pictures he took during his years as editor of the Greybull Standard. He was a pioneer in using good pictures and photography was important to his newspaper. Many of these pictures won state and national awards. His newspaper frequently received honors in national contests for its use of photographs.

His columns also won awards. The National Editorial Association judged his 1964 Editor's Notebook column the best one-topic column in the 50-state competition among weeklies and dailies.

The "judges" who mattered most, however, were his readers. It delighted him when strangers came up and took out a column they'd clipped and saved in their wallets. Those rewards he cherished most.

When Green River Star Publisher Adrian Reynolds died in 1982, Dad wrote, "... Pens won't write forever. We all know that. But many a newspaperman hopes to do like Adrian Reynolds, to go right to the very end of his career, keeping on writing and writing, sharing thoughts, filling your one part of the paper. And that's what Adrian did so well for all those years."

And that's what Bruce Kennedy did too — kept on writing and writing, filling his one part of the paper right to the end. When he died in June 1992, he was Wyoming's longest continuous column writer. And one of the most popular.

This book is a collection of our favorite columns that helped us appreciate life a little more. They made us laugh. And cry. And be thankful all over again that we knew him. He would be thrilled to know his words touched us once again.

Brian Kennedy

Getting the Bull by the Tail

By Bruce M. Kennedy

1956

December 6, 1956

Hard work will not kill a man but it almost scares some men to death.

* * *

The pictures on today's front page are examples of what can happen when you pose as a clerk in Larry Probst's Western Store. The dozens of people who came in the store Saturday afternoon to see if the No. 444 checked with their own number had no idea they were being photographed. Bet many of them will probably remember the "clerk" who stood around back of the counter and wasn't too helpful.

There is a lot of luck in getting pictures like these. Invariably the people came down the wrong aisle and approached our pre-arranged focus point wrong. No matter which way you turned the number someone would always look at it out of camera range and there were some eagle-eyed kids who could spot the number from the doorway.

Some people knew something wasn't quite right about the set-up. And they must have thought the clerk Larry hired for the Christmas rush was pretty green at the game. In fact we only got one chance to show how good we could sell clothes the entire afternoon. That was when some lady asked where the size 33 trousers were and we didn't know!

For those camera enthusiasts who might like to know, we took the pictures with an Argus C-3 35mm camera at 3.5, 1/50th of a second exposure and focused at about 6 feet. They were developed in DK 60a for 5 1/2 minutes.

* * *

Old Archie Moore just didn't have it against young Floyd Patterson in the heavyweight championship Friday night. Patterson's leaping "Kangaroo" punch, according to the announcer, helped do the damage to the aging ring gypsy Moore. Some sportswriter for the Associated Press must have felt kind of foolish the morning after the fight. He had written in Friday's story preceding the fight that Moore was the "pick here, especially if Patterson leaps off the floor with his 'Kangaroo' punch."

* * *

Another sportswriter in Worland probably would have known just how he felt. In the Worland Daily News several weeks ago after the Warrior-Torrington state championship game, some writer penned: "Although the score might tend to make this sound like a one-sided affair (it was 46-12) it was actually a very close contest up until the time the opening whistle blew."

December 13, 1956

John Paris down at DeLane's Cafe said there was a counter full at his place about 3:30 a.m. Sunday when the flood was stirring up the north end of town. But most of the excitement for the rest of the town was the next morning when people began realizing how close it had been.

* * *

"Red" Michaelis, whose house was one of the worst hit, was not among the late risers. And he doesn't have to wonder how close the water was. In fact he can tell you it's quite a sensation to open the front door from the outside and have about six inches of water beat you in!

December 20, 1956

Every year at this time in our house we go through the argument of whether the tinsel looks better carefully strung on every bare branch or whether you get the same effect by standing across the room and throwing it on. For years now the matter has remained a deadlock. But this Christmas we found a willing, although erratic helper, in our 18-month-old son, who thinks throwing anything is the greatest of sports.

1957

January 17, 1957

The Lloyd Groseclose's beat the stork to the new hospital by six minutes the other day when Lora Jean was born. For those expectant parents who would like to know, driving at 50 miles an hour, it takes exactly five minutes flat to make the trip from the traffic light in Greybull to the front steps of the new hospital.

February 21, 1957

If you don't believe in gremlins, ghosts, elves, pixies and all the rest, you haven't worked on a newspaper. Because after so long you can't find anything else to blame for the mistakes. Take last week for instance. In our "Greybull Shopper" which we print every Thursday morning for distribution in Basin, we usually reprint the hospital notes.

Last Thursday afternoon Clint Core stopped us and asked how we knew Julius Nelson would be in the hospital March 1. We grabbed for a "Shopper" and sure enough, mixed in with the hospital notes were all the dates and names of the farm sales scheduled clear up until March 7.

So to Elmer J. Harper, John Fink Jr., Bill Schmidt, Jay McGuffey, Julius Nelson and Tom Riley, we apologize and hope our prophecies of hospitalization are only mere whims of some printer's gremlin.

* * *

One thing this younger generation of drivers who learn on Dad's automatic transmission will miss is the awful embarrassment all of the beginning drivers of years back had when they let the clutch out too fast. We remember one time it happened to us on the main street of Basin. The old Chevy choked and jerked and sputtered its way down half a block before we got it and our senses under control. It's pretty hard to try to hide behind the steering wheel and still see over the dashboard.

March 14, 1957

Now that the ice has gone out of the Big Horn river, we are going to have to find something else to look at when we drive over the river bridge on the way home every day. For months now we've kept a watchful eye on every little crack and change of condition of the ice. Looking at just plain old water won't be half the fun the ice used to be.

* * *

We met an old friend the other day. It was the old 1941 Chevrolet which served as the family car for almost nine years. Oscar Larson is driving it now, says he paid $50 for it and still runs fine. We learned to drive on that old Chevy and helped put it over the 100,000 mile mark until it was finally sold. We thought we had recognized it several times before but it wasn't until the other day we were positive. For still stuck on the back window since we put it on in 1947 is our old college sticker.

May 2, 1957

You just never know when being a printer will pay off for you. Take the other day, for instance, when George Johnson had to read a serial number on a trailer house motor. Since the number was in an inaccessible place, George got a mirror to find out the number. But the problem still wasn't solved because the numbers were all upside down to anyone but a printer. So he called on us and we obliged.

May 9, 1957

This could only happen in a small town. Last week someone on Main Street gave us back our LIFE magazine of two weeks ago. It had been put in our post office box by mistake, they explained, but since they knew we were on vacation, they just went ahead and finished reading it until we got back! That's something a guy from Chicago would never understand.

May 23, 1957

Why is it that some little kids can't say water without mumbling "wa-wa" or radio without it coming out "oy-oy?" And yet pronounce with the most amazing clarity a full vocabulary of cuss words.

May 30, 1957

This incident of last week kept us chuckling for several days afterward. A woman in her middle thirties who was trying to look like a girl in her teens was observed on Main Street, complete with a pony tail, pedal pushers, sweater and girlish shoes. After the usual looks were sent her way by interested menfolk, one of them was heard to remark: "Now there goes a pony tail on an old horse."

June 6, 1957

At our son's second birthday party the other night we lugged the camera home and took the traditional picture of him blowing out all two candles. Last year we took another one of him on his first birthday, but so far we have never gotten around to printing it up so we still don't know what it looks like. And then people wonder why the wife chokes up when someone says: "Oh, how nice to have a photographer in the family to take so many pictures."

June 13, 1957

The pony tail which bobbed into our column of two weeks ago created some protests among the women readers. One of them informed us that pony tails on "old horses" were no worse than "crew cuts on old men!"

June 20, 1957

The judges and parade committee were still trying to learn the identity of the person driving the oxen-drawn covered wagon which won a $25 prize at the 49er parade Saturday. Maybe he was just passing through!

July 11, 1957

It is a tribute to the ingenuity and resourcefulness of American engineering that they can make enough different automobiles so a populace the size of Greybull's can distinguish each other by the model and color of car everyone drives.

* * *

The best tourist story to date is this true one which happened last week in Greybull. A 40-year-old man from Chicago, standing about six feet and weighing at least a healthy 190, came in to Penneys. He was wearing chin whiskers, a beret, a Hawaiian print sport shirt and a pair of Bermuda shorts with a buckle in the back. A pair of argyle socks falling down over size 12 crepe sole brogues completed the outfit. He asked Jack Williams for a pair of trousers. "Like the ones you have on?" Jack asked. "No," the man said. "I'm getting rid of these. They were too cold up in the mountains this morning; I'm too hot in them now. And besides," he added, "all the cowboys are whistling at me!"

July 25, 1957

Stepping on the kid's balloon just barely full of air, while you're wandering around the dark house barefooted is enough to send a person screaming into the night. Our household hasn't settled down yet.

August 1, 1957

When a newspaper reader doesn't expect an editor to comment on his wife's having a new baby girl, somebody is a tremendous optimist. So for the record, our daughter, Ann, arrived at 1:05 p.m. at the South Big Horn County hospital, weighing in at 6 lbs., 11 oz., and is probably the cutest little tyke we've seen in quite awhile.

* * *

When a newspaper editor's wife has a new baby, it is a new addition to the family . . . or is it an edition?

August 8, 1957

We're getting a complex about our comfortable (and paid for) 1951 Chevrolet we are nursing over the bumps. But it's getting close to the time to turn it in, we suppose. At least we got quite a shock the other day when we picked up the paper and noticed a caption about "Jalopy Struck By Train." It looked surprisingly like the vintage of an auto not far from the '51 class. We always thought jalopies were Model T Fords.

* * *

Five-year-old Donnie Schultz (our old friend from the Thanksgiving turkey picture of last year) was the first one to tell us about our aging car. And he was undoubtedly the frankest. He informed us the other day that "we have a fancier car than you do."

August 15, 1957

We know a woman who instead of "reconciling" her bank statement, always "rationalized" it. Maybe she was closer to being right than the rest of us.

* * *

A good samaritan on the highway isn't always news. But when a Good Samaritan helps another Good Samaritan it should get some mention. Seems Heinie Meier was towing some tourist with car trouble down the mountain. Outside of Shell Heinie had a flat tire. And no jack in the jeep! So the tourist gets in the act, fishes out his jack and helps Heinie take the flat off, thus qualifying as a Good Samaritan himself.

August 22, 1957

It is a husband's lot sometimes to suffer through the wife's cooking without a murmur. With the new baby, the canning and the usual hectic mess around the house, we tried to overlook the hard cookies we got for supper the other night. But it was too much to keep a straight face when our little boy took his small wooden mallet to one on the floor to break it up into eatable pieces.

August 29, 1957

We saw our first little boy in a football helmet today, heralding for sure the coming of the football season. He wasn't exactly giving up summer though – for he was still wearing his Little League baseball jersey.

October 3, 1957

Whenever you fall into the bad habit of talking baby talk to your kids, you run the risk of spouting it in public. And somehow even your friends look queerly at you when you sprinkle your vocabulary with such gems as "hanies," "nite-nite," and "toot-toot."

October 10, 1957

Boys will always be boys. At the Elks hamburger feed for all the newsboys in Greybull and Basin, one of the Elks helping serve the lunch asked one 12-year-old if he wanted another hamburger. Here was his reply. "No, I couldn't eat any more. I've had four already. I guess I shouldn't have eaten before I came."

October 24, 1957

Out at our house we shouldn't be afraid of burglars. Anyone who can make it across our living room floor in the pitch dark without stepping on a toy truck, a handful of marbles and maybe some of mother's spools of thread deserves the sterling silver.

* * *

Bill Ford doesn't know whether to be grateful to the guy who pulled him out of the mud in Antelope Butte area the first day of elk hunting or not. When Bill's 1955 Chevrolet station wagon got mired in the mud, he got a pull from a man from Sheridan driving a Model A Ford!

October 31, 1957

Too young to be a student of geography or to own a compass, John Copenhaver's youngest son has no trouble finding his way around. Main street, he says, is the street where you pay all the bills.

November 28, 1957

Linda Shortt has the right idea but it isn't exactly the King James version. After hearing her sister practicing the 23rd Psalm for Sunday School, Linda's version at the breakfast table the other day was: "He maketh me lie down in green pastures, and he don't tell no darn lies, either."

December 12, 1957

We don't know who is going to have more fun seeing George (Conoco and Santa Claus) Scott a week from Saturday – our little boy who is on his first trip or ourselves who will be on our second!

December 26, 1957

Debbie Paustian is only seven but she's a woman! When informed early Monday morning that she had won the bicycle at the Big Horn Drug and could she come down for a picture, she replied: "I'll have to fix my hair first!"

1958

January 23, 1958

The wife reminded us that when someone says something nice to a man he feels 10 feet tall – when it's said to a woman she feels like she weighs 110 pounds.

January 30, 1958

A woman in the office the other day buying a pencil sharpener said she didn't want too expensive pencils: "They won't last long around our house now," she explained. "My kids are at the pencil-sharpening age!"

* * *

Eighty-three-year-old Oscar Hoback of Manderson, the Spanish-American War veteran who attended the VFW dance in full uniform last Saturday night, told several of us that he was the last of six good friends who ran around together "in those days." "I've been a little concerned the past few years," he chuckled. "They may be thinking I've gone the other way!"

February 27, 1958

We overheard two parents at Friday's basketball game saying: "It's a fine idea to kiss the children goodnight, if you don't mind waiting up till they come home."

March 6, 1958

Heading today's column is the artist's conception of what it entails to "get the bull by the tail." In writing to him about such a cut, we suggested maybe incorporating a little dignity into such a cut. But he replied, and quite correctly: "Trying to get dignity into a cartoon is a pretty tough chore at best, and when the subject matter involves grasping a bull's tail, human dignity is quite unattainable!" And so it is.

* * *

And from the little boy side of the ledger comes this true story: Mike, a five-year-old Basin boy was playing with an older friend. His parents overheard the following conversation:

Friend: "Say, did you know that I'm half Italian?"

Mike, hating to be outdone, pondered a moment and then answered: "That's nothing, I'm half Indian and half cowboy, myself."

March 13, 1958

The winter of 1958, when the river hasn't even frozen over, would certainly be a "drought" year for the old icemen like Stanfield and Alderdice, Henry Jennings and Henry Staggs. We now rely on Pacific Power to do the job these men in collaboration with Mother Nature and the Big Horn river used to do.

March 20, 1958

Mrs. Gottlieb Marcus helped us celebrate our birthday last week in royal style. Mrs. Marcus (whose 87 angel food birthday cakes for her family was a feature story in The Standard Jan. 9) surprised us by baking our birthday cake. And surprises like angel food cakes from Mrs. Marcus' oven just don't come any nicer. We wouldn't blame the Marcus grandchildren at all for trying to figure out some way to squeeze at least one more birthday into a calendar year.

March 27, 1958

We saw Miss DeAnna Brown and two of her third grade pupils on Main Street Monday night but we didn't realize the full news value of such an event until Bobby Evans pointed it out to us. "If I give you some news will you put it in the paper?" Sure, we said. "Okay, then put this news in: 'Corky Williams and Bobby Evans walked around main street with Miss Brown Monday afternoon.' That's news, isn't it?" Sure, we said.

April 10, 1958

The biggest thrill of the entire trip to Lander was in the Wind River canyon when we met the train on its way to Greybull. We owe a debt of gratitude to No. 29's engineer or fireman who answered our son's wave out the window with two short blasts on the whistle. He's still talking about the train that "honked" at him.

April 17, 1958

Conversation overheard on main street Monday between two Greybull teenagers, one wearing a pair of shorts and the other a more seasonal pair of jeans. Girl without shorts: "I was going to wear mine, but I thought people would make remarks." Girl with shorts: "Don't worry. They do!"

April 24, 1958

Having the most fun at the track meet between Greybull, Manderson and Basin were a half dozen fifth and sixth grade boys who stood behind Starter Bertel Budd . . . and pretended they were shot every time the gun went off!

May 8, 1958 (First time Poor Richard quote was used at the top of a column.)

"Wink at small faults; remember thou hast great ones." – Poor Richard.

May 15, 1958

The first thing we looked for (after we looked to see if our name was spelled right) in the new telephone books was to see if Mr. and Mrs. Claude Spencer's new phone was listed. Last year the family and friends chipped in and had a telephone line installed into their house for their 50th anniversary. And it's there all right. It's No. 339 at Shell.

May 22, 1958

Trying to make conversation has its pitfalls. We "fell" into one of these last week when we conversationally asked Nick Smith of Manderson "how he liked it down there." "Well," he replied, with just the barest trace of grim humor, "I've been down there long enough to have made up my mind – I first settled there in 1890!"

* * *

Nick had one story about the Allens on Paintrock creek and the Baders on Tensleep creek. In those days, according to Nick, there weren't many other families in that area and when a couple of strangers would meet, one would ask: "Are you a Bader?" "Nope, not me." "Well, then you must be an Allen."

* * *

Folks on the Sheridan side this week discovered another old timer. A farmer who was cutting down an ancient cottonwood to make room for the windbreak, discovered a wagon wheel imbedded in the trunk. The tree was forked and had grown completely around the wheel, hiding it and the story of how it ever got there.

May 29, 1958

With every fire whistle that ever blew (and Tuesday morning's was no exception) our first thought has always been: "It's our house for sure."

* * *

But luckily enough for all of us, Tuesday's whistle was a false alarm. Coach Adolph Zellner couldn't quite understand why so many people had come out to help his Little Leaguers burn off weeds around the baseball diamond. Then someone broke the news that the crowd had come to PUT OUT the fire, not START one.

June 5, 1958

John Copenhaver can never be called short. In fact his 6-foot, 5-inch frame is downright tall. His two boys think so too. The other day downtown they said it was easy to find him on the street. "You're always up above everything!"

* * *

Jack Williams, who took his 14-year-old son, Johnnie, to the Town Council meeting Monday night, told him, "It will be good experience for you, actually," Jack told him, "it's really a poor man's boys state!"

June 12, 1958

One of the little conveniences of life you have to give up when your city converts to dial telephones is not being able to call the operator to find out where the fire is. Basin residents found this out last week (as Greybull people did a couple of years ago) when they swamped the Worland operators with calls asking where the fire was. (All dial calls go to Worland now.) Ah, progress. Now Basin is just like Greybull . . . you have to chase every fire instead of sitting at home and chatting with the operator about it!

July 3, 1958

The one service in town that will give you more for your money than it did ten years ago is Carroll Durkee's penny-for-your-weight scale in front of the Big Horn Drug.

* * *

Calories aren't a problem for our little three-year-old nephew. But saying a mouthful like "breakfast" is. Much to the consternation of his parents he continues to make "breakfast" sound like anything but "breakfast." Recently, after a session with his Mother at trying to pronounce it correctly, he announced: "Can't say breakfast, Mama, let's have lunch."

July 17, 1958

"It's a dog's life" certainly doesn't fit Slim Brewer's dog. No one else we've ever seen enjoys riding in the back of a pickup more than this dog does. And who else – even among we humans – can call (or bark) all our pet names at fellow dogs from such a safe perch!

July 24, 1958

We were told not to print it, but we think this is too good to keep. When the Calgary Herald photographer snapped a picture (and published it) of the seven Greybull Girl Scouts during their stop on the recent trip to Canada, he wasn't aware just how clever some livewire American girls can be. The regular Girl Scout uniforms were donned for the picture . . . but underneath each girls' trim, good-looking outfit were their usual traveling attire – good old western jeans, carefully rolled up out of sight!

July 31, 1958

If you're inclined to s-s-s-stutter every time you try to say your esses, you'd have a s-s-s-specially hard time s-s-saying the roster of the Junior Legion baseball team. S-s-six of the 12 boys' names s-start with "S" – Spangler, Sehorn, Sills, Sommerville, Schutte and Schuyler. Also on the team are: Randy Clark, Rich Clark, Larry Clause, Kurt Holland, Dan Hunter and Tom Wilkinson. (The team, managed by Adolph Zellner, finished the season 12-0 and won the Big Horn Basin championship.)

* * *

Newspapermen just can't resist the obvious sometimes. We noticed a movie review in a Nebraska newspaper had one-word cutlines under pictures of two forthcoming movies. Under a picture of Ingrid Bergman and Cary Grant, it had "Indiscreet." Under adjoining picture of Tarzan Bob Baker and his girl friend, Jane, was "Indejungle."

August 7, 1958

Amos Small carries around an old 1907 dime (worn nearly smooth) which he tells us is just the right size to measure the sparkplug gap.

* * *

This authentic story should be among the tops for the 1958 summer. Seems two of the "tourists" who ride the rails jumped off in Greybull a couple of weeks ago. They went into a Greybull grocery and purchased two bottles of lemon extract. While their purchase was being wrapped, one of them turned to his partner – and with an elaborate air of nonchalance to show everyone this was a legitimate purchase – exclaimed: "That ought to be enough to bake a cake hadn't it?"

August 28, 1958

A faulty carburetor forced down Wee Collingwood Monday while flying the pipeline. He landed without trouble on a gravel road west of Deaver and right behind a guy in a pickup. We'd like to have seen the double take the guy must have pulled when he casually glanced in his rear view mirror and saw an airplane trying to pass him.

September 11, 1958

We wonder just who put the historical pieces in the Basin High school cornerstone which was found last week. In addition to the regular newspaper issue, a history of the school district, etc., someone slipped in a pair of dice!

* * *

Somebody burned an "O" in the Greybull football field Monday night. Unless somebody comes up with a Wyoming school we've never heard of, the finger of blame points at poor old Otto!

* * *

"This is some town," Jerry Patterson said as he watched us trying to get a picture of the runaway hog Monday, "when a hog is news."

September 18, 1958

The mystery of the burned letter "O" on the football field turned out to be no mystery at all. Someone showed up the following night and finished making the letter "B".

* * *

There is a little boy in town who, when his foot is asleep, says he has "dots" on it.

* * *

And there was another one who cried out in frustration against this grown-up language: "No, I don't want a hot dog. I want a wiener."

September 25, 1958
Latest addition to the Standard window is several ears of many colored squaw corn grown by Henry Fiene on the Martin Fiene farm. Another squaw corn grower in the area is Jonathan Davis of Emblem who has 20 acres of it. But his hogs get his crop and really go for it. Jonathan believes "They must think it's real pretty."

* * *

Clarence Ortman says he wonders how_____(we won't tell who) is handling all the vagrants Clarence sends up this way. Seems every time some transient comes in for a hand out, Clarence gives him the name and address of this particular businessman. Which all made for a wonderful joke until someone asked Clarence, "Did you ever wonder why YOU get so many?"

* * *

Cullen Fletcher has an interesting souvenir of the shooting of Glenn Coxen several weeks ago. The day after the shooting, Cullen found one of the spent slugs from Coxen's gun lying in the middle of the street.

* * *

This is like the story of the sailor who had never been to sea. Vern Smith, who has had many, many hours of flight time and was recently accepted as a co-pilot on Northwest Airlines, received a pass from the Airlines to fly back to Minneapolis for his examinations. It was his first flight on a commercial airline!

October 2, 1958
Say what you will about George Johnson's whistle on the Greybull Shoe store, everyone in town is quitting work by it!

October 9, 1958
A calf we got recently (for a little beef later on) finally got a name. We're calling it "Hamburger" under the assumption that no animal with a name like that can ever become too much of a pet for the kids to see readied for the freezer.

October 16, 1958
Someone asked one would-be hunter where his red cap was: "In the car," he replied. Where's your red shirt? "I'm not going that far up."

* * *

Peyton Patterson had a red shirt all right. But someone thoughtfully (?) stencilled a five-ring target with a two-inch bullseye on the back of it.

* * *

And then there was the reformed drunk of a couple of years who told one Greybullite: "They haven't put out a good song since I stopped drinking."

November 6, 1958
Drinking the old well water Monday reminds us of those old days before the line to Shell when Greybull's horrible tasting water was a subject not dis-

cussed. Carroll Durkee always remembers how he used to put a glass of the stuff before a tourist and then watch as the tourist took a sip. "They used to get a look on their face just like someone slapped them!" he recalls.

December 4, 1958
The roads over the weekend were full of Thanksgiving holiday traffic. But there was only one family we knew for sure who had been eating Thanksgiving with the folks. That was the car we passed with a high chair strapped on top!

* * *

Art Peterson knows now which button it is that blows the fire whistle! Painting with his brother, Chuck, in Parker's cafe Tuesday night, Art accidentally hit the fire whistle button, which blew the whistle, that called out the firemen, who cussed one Art Peterson.

December 18, 1958
Down in Mrs. John Minnis' first grade room at least a half dozen kids are just at the age when they start losing their front teeth. Which makes it darned hard to say, for instance, "Mrth. Minnith."

December 25, 1958
Hap Crain of Hyattville is wearing a western string tie with a tiny thermometer on the clasp. It was registering 80 degrees when we read it.

* * *

"I'll make a deal with you, Grandmother," one of Mrs. Mildred Call's grandchildren whispered to her the other night. "I'll tell you what are in your presents if you'll tell me what is in mine."

January 8, 1959

Last year we reported Mrs. Gottlieb Marcus baked 87 angel food cakes to give to the many members of her family on their birthdays and anniversaries. This year she's topped the 1957 record with 110 in 1958.

January 15, 1959

Our sincere thanks to Greybull's volunteer fire department for answering the false alarm fire at our house Sunday. Although we felt like crying when we saw them coming, we will always be impressed with the prompt, efficient way they answered the call.

And the firemen tell us – since Sunday we know more of them – that although the Junior police treasury is pretty low right now, you can expect to see a sizeable increase soon.

Tommy Wilkinson is proud as a peacock about the fancy hat he sports around. Someone was admiring it on the basketball trip to Lovell Friday night and Tom replied he'd "sell it to you for ten bucks." "Heck," said Kurt Holland from the back of the bus, "I'll sell my car for ten bucks."

February 5, 1959

All ex-GI's would have welcomed a needle like the kind Dr. Jack Lester wields for rabies vaccinations. There's no prolonged agony when he does it. The needle is in and out in half a second. "You learn not to be slow," he explains "after the first couple of 'patients' turn around and take a bite out of you." Which is one hazard Army corpsmen don't have to face, we admit.

"Lavern Shortt found his new dog lapping up gas the other day," Ken Jones was telling the Ortman Drug coffee crowd, "and the dog started running around and around the garage. Finally he just laid down."

"Did it kill him," Slim Nielsen wondered.

"Oh, no," Ken said, "he just ran out of gas."

February 19, 1959

The picture we should have gotten Tuesday was at the highway intersection near the Community hall. One of the two "Danger" signs put up to warn cars away from the deep holes in the pavement had toppled over into one of them . . . and toppled clear out of sight.

March 5, 1959

The Rah-Rah boys from GHS at the Greybull-Basin game brought down the house with this yell the other night: "Go, Basin, Go. Go, Basin, Go. Down the floor and out the door, Go, Basin, Go."

March 12, 1959

Coach Henry Eckroth's instructions to the ball team before Friday's game with Riverton were explicit: "Bring a suitcase and be prepared to stay overnight. Greybull could lose to Riverton and have to play Saturday morning. That means staying overnight in Thermop." But the only two who showed up in Thermop with suitcases were Coach Henry Eckroth and Assistant Coach Jerry Hickman. The players explained they never figured on losing!

April 2, 1959

At least one family was prepared for the usual rainy Easter weather. The father of the household was around Greybull businesses Saturday looking for four raincoats – "one for each gal in the family who has an Easter outfit," he explained.

Dale Chamberlain who was helping out at the hunt had his shirt stuffed full of extra sacks of eggs. As he walked around the park, he'd drop a few every so often. Then he looked around. Some little girl had been following him all the time, filling her Easter basket.

April 9, 1959

When they tore down Birdie's Cafe Sunday they found 20 cents and one Indianhead penny the floor sweeper must have failed to find.

April 16, 1959

One Greybullite – whose job demands much tact and diplomacy – gave us part of the secret of his success. "You can't drive people to do anything," he says, "but you can haze them into doing most everything."

April 30, 1959

Having babies and putting out newspapers all at the same time is one hazard of the game they never tell you about. (Our son, Robert, arrived at 4:45 a.m. Friday). But for the third time in a row, our family has managed to have their new members arrive on Friday, the day after the paper comes out – an attribute that is every bit as attractive to their father as their happy smiles and those sturdy little legs.

Of the three men on the five-man Big Horn County welfare board all three are named John (Flitner, Picton and Welch.) That's not quite as bad, though, as the Odd Fellows bowling team where there are three Bill's (Simpson, Kunkle and King) and two Harry's (Gillett and Neeley.)

May 7, 1959

Last week in mentioning "same names" we overlooked the three doctor's wives (Dr. Forsyth, Dr. Gregg and Dr. Rogers) in the Greybull-Basin area, who are all named Betty.

Ted Olson told us the other day it looked like our beard was "hailed out."

May 21, 1959

Our mathematics are fouled up somewhere. It has taken us eight weeks to get out 40 pages of the special 50th anniversary edition and we have about 25 more pages to print in just two weeks. Feed that into your IBM machine and see if you come out with the same answer we got by staying awake last night.

June 18, 1959

Tables were turned on us Friday night. In over 10 years of newspapering it was the first time we ever had our picture taken for our own publication. Our thanks to fellow photographer Harry Roe for recording for posterity the winners in the Days of '09 beard contest.

Ours actually wasn't a "winner." Getting the award for having the "poorest attempt" at a beard sounds like the booby prize to us. Oh well, in another 25 years we'll give it the old college try again.

And it wasn't all whiskers that came off the bearded men around Greybull. A lot of years "disappeared" too.

July 2, 1959

Saturday wasn't our little boy's best day he's ever had. How can you call it anything but catastrophic when your Teddy Bear is left up at Shell and you have to spend one whole night with your arm around a limp, inanimate pillow. But thanks to Jack Douglass at the Wagon Wheel who found and kept good care of "Teddy", the sun is shining brightly once again on the four-year-old level.

One woman tourist on her way to the West Coast to get her parents, stopped in at Harold's Standard Service when he still sported his beard. Coming back again this week she told her parents, "Now when I stop at this Standard station here, I want to show you the whitest beard you've ever seen." But alas, the razor had made a quicker trip and beardless Harold had to explain why he couldn't have left the white whiskers on for just one more week.

July 9, 1959

Someone methodically placed two strings of firecrackers on Police Judge Riley Wilson's front porch Saturday night and lit the whole works off at once.

The din which followed woke up the neighborhood. Riley described it the next morning: "I've been charivaried."

July 16, 1959

Chuck Unterzuber, one of Greybull's outstanding athletes, was back in Greybull visiting over the weekend. No one could ever accuse Chuck of being puny, but he has lost some weight since his football days. In fact, he says he weighs just 10 pounds more now than he did when he was in the 7th grade. But he's not wasting away – even in those grade school days he weighed 177 pounds!

The straw hats the Core Chevrolet crew are decked out in, of course, have an ulterior purpose. Inside the hat (which they'll be glad to show you) says: "I can save you a hatful of money on a new Buick today." The hat's a fine gimmick, says Clint Core. But it's tough when the wind blows. Hat sizes only run in two sizes: "Large and larger."

July 23, 1959

It's too bad future generations can't be here now to see the wonderful things we are doing with their money.

Easily the most ambitious people in town are the five mothers – Mary Gormley, Beverly Hankins, Roberta Bullinger, Freda Tolman and Donna Moberly – who formed the "Knobby Knees Bicycle Club." Active membership requires a ride every Tuesday and Thursday mornings. Time of departure: 5 a.m.!

August 27, 1959

They aren't giving mosquitoes letters this year for being "out" for football. But just the same they're reporting for the night practices by the hundreds of thousands.

Michael Fricke, 7, son of Mr. and Mrs. Jim Fricke of Bellevue, Wash. spent a couple of days with his grandfather, O. E. Olson of Billings (who regularly tunes many Greybull pianos). Seeing the sights in Billings included Michael's first Shrine circus and first big baseball game. After one particularly exciting day, as Michael was getting ready to go to sleep he looked up at "Grandpa" Olson and said: "Grandpa, this is sure living, isn't it?"

September 6, 1959

A little boy in Shores Shoes the other day answered everyone's question on how he hurt his finger with: "I cut it square around."

Coach Buck Eckroth is fond of telling people who ask about the size of the football team that the "Biggest man is Small". That's Homer, who weighs 225 and is a tackle.

September 10, 1959

There was a woman at the bottom of the trouble with the highway sign that got knocked over. That's what the boys at Lloyd's Super Service report. According to them it was a young man in the car all right. But he was looking at some girl in shorts across the street!

September 24, 1959

And we asked an eighth grader out for Junior high football, what position he was playing. "I'm out for end," he said, and then pausing reflectively, he added: "And I'm just about the end, too."

Andy Long, manager of the Greybull Drug, and Lois Shortt who works there, will never forget this incident. And neither, probably, will the lady involved, who walked up to Lois and asked: "Are you Mrs. Long?" "No," replied Lois, "I'm Mrs. Shortt."

October 22, 1959

In the pure bedlam that reigned in the cafe where the Cody junior high team was eating after their victory over Greybull Saturday, one impish boy told the waitress he wanted: "A hamburger, a beer and a pack of cigarettes!"

November 29, 1959

Harry Moberly says the worst thing in the world is getting up in the middle of night and stepping on your little girls' jacks with your bare feet. Everywhere you jump, says Harry, there's another jack.

December 3, 1959

Nothing touches our heart quite so much as seeing the phrase, written in the large block letters of a little child's writing, "I love you, Santa."

December 24, 1959

Down at Thermop during Greybull's recent wrestling match there fans saw the ultimate. In the midst of a heated bout, a Greybull wrestler's pants started to slip down. But the Thermop boy (who was on top) reached down and gave a very gentlemanly hitch up on his opponent's britches. And then very ungentlemanly went ahead and won the match.

December 31, 1959

It must be the time of the year. In today's want ads, Standard readers are advertising as lost, a red pen, a white tailgate and a green parakeet.

January 7, 1960

A Volkswagen owner always does things different. We saw one the other day that had its license plate (an out-of-state one) pinned on to the car with a clothespin.

The most startling sight of the week was at the Legion Hall Monday night during the first practice of Greybull's wrestling team in their new quarters. Tucked over in the corner out of the way but not out of earshot from the shouting, whistle-blowing, exuberant wrestling boys were the members of Girl Scout Troop 444. "Do you meet here every Monday night," we asked one who was like the rest of her little friends, half turned to hear the meeting and half turned to watch the boys. "Yes," she said and pointing to the wrestlers, "are they going to be here again too?" We said we were sure they would be. She looked up with big bright eyes. "Oh, goody," she bubbled over.

January 14, 1960

We assume that a song rated high on the "top tunes" list requires repeated playings and demands throughout the nation. It isn't surprising then that Bobby Darin's "Mack, the Knife" has been up there. It takes that long to finally figure out what the words are.

You could tell last Saturday was the Senior Ball. Every high school girl we saw had her hair put up.

January 21, 1960

We went to the press convention last weekend in Casper and driving into town Sunday p.m. we were reminded of what Vic Larson said after he returned from his 3,000-mile trip. "The Mrs. and I drove 3,000 miles," he told us, "and the roughest roads we hit were the four blocks south of Greybull's main street."

January 28, 1960

We'll be anxious to know how many accurate replies the Wyoming Game and Fish department gets from its latest questionnaire on the 1959 big game kill. There's a space to fill in on the type of "dear" license purchased.

February 4, 1960

When Gary Deveraux begins his practice teaching in the ag department of

Greybull high school next week, he'll be following right in his Dad's footsteps. After graduating from the University of Wyoming in 1941, O.J. Deveraux's first position was as GHS ag teacher.

February 11, 1960

Because so many people have asked about it, we wish to call attention to the Justice Court news wherein our name appears on a failure to display the license plates we purchased in December and which had been on top of the refrigerator ever since.

But if we're $9 poorer because of it, we are richer in experience for having gone through Justice Court. "Are you in a hurry," Judge Riley Wilson asked when we walked in. We allowed that we were. "It'll be $9 ($5 and costs)," Riley said. "Don't we get a chance to plead guilty," we asked. "Can if you want – fine is still $9."

February 25, 1960

Miss May E. Palmer, whose obituary appears in this week's Standard had a strong family tie with the Andy Hurst family. Mrs. Ira Sherard and Mrs. Flora Lawson remember that Miss Palmer, in her first year of teaching, taught the two older Hurst sisters in their first year of school. Then years later Miss Palmer came to Greybull and taught their children!

Our receding hairline and general lack of hair bothers our little four-year-old son. After a long hard look the other day, he asked us: "Did God forget to put hair up there?"

March 10, 1960

At the coaches' noon dinner Friday given in Gillette during the tournament, the Gillette Lions club passed out little square envelopes to all coaches. Inside were three or four tranquilizers.

March 17, 1960

It's no coincidence that Don Tew has license number 9-2222. His father, Merrill Tew in Lovell, had the number since 1949. Then Don picked it up in 1959, to keep the twos in the Tew family.

Boots Cochrane is enjoying all the double takes and side glances he's getting from the local populace since he started driving Pruett Cleaner's old delivery wagon. No, he's not working for Mel and Martha – he just bought their old panel truck and hasn't yet painted out the "Let Pruett Do It."

The teachers aren't saying who it is but there was one little boy who figured out what he wanted to give up for Lent. It was school.

March 24, 1960
There was no doubt about last Thursday being St. Patrick's Day at the Smokehouse Bar. Cleo McKinney and Leonard Jennings stayed up the night before putting green cake coloring in all the tap beer. Result: A Kelly green beer to serve the astonished customers the next day.

April 7, 1960
Our kids know us better than we think. In Lander a car crashed into the house late one evening, demolishing one of the rooms. One of the little girls in another part of the house woke up in the clatter and told her sister: "Daddy's home."

April 28, 1960
Oscar Shoemaker has an "aisle runner," a long cloth that's put down the aisle during weddings. He rents it out to wedding parties and then has it cleaned each time. The last time it came back from the laundry the ticket read: "One tablecloth, long, long, long . . . 50 ft." Sumptuous dinners, they must think, Oscar has.

May 5, 1960
While Mrs. Ed Gillis was back at the Mayo clinic, she was given a particularly bad time by a patient (from Texas) who just couldn't figure out "why one of those Wonderful Women From Wyoming" had to have a medical checkup. Standing it as long as she could, Mrs. Gillis finally told him that last fall she just couldn't run down an antelope out in these wide open spaces so husband Ed figured it was time she went back for a checkup. The conversation ended.

May 12, 1960
You've heard of the guys who slap a "friend" on the back only to find out the "friend" is an utter stranger. Maurie Logan in Lander went even better than that. He was sitting in a Lander bar when he thought he recognized a man who just came in. So he got off his bar stool and gave the guy a good swift kick in the pants. Then the guy turned around and Maurie didn't know him from Adam. That's how to win friends and influence people!

Naming a "her" cat with a "him" name is commonplace. Down in Riverton a family solved the problem when their cat named "Ben" gave birth to four kittens. Now they just call the mama cat, "Ben Her".

Watching Red Michaelis pitch a softball game Monday night reminded us of the last time Red and ourselves played on the same Basin softball team back in the 1940's, that was smothered by the All-Negro Kansas City Ghosts. The astronomical score they piled up was bad enough, but more humiliating yet was the fact they played most of the game with just their pitcher and a catcher. The rest of their team just sat on the bench and watched.

May 26, 1960

In Lander plans for the new hospital first put a Room 13 in and then took it out. People are too superstitious about being sick in a room numbered 13. South Big Horn County hospital doesn't have that problem. Yet, anyway. Number 11 is the last room number out there.

Yellowstone Park traffic is being routed through the new tunnel while the old canyon road is being repaired. Cody residents by the car-fulls were driving out Sunday just to go through the tunnel, turn around at the damsite and go back through again.

And just plan on your kids being spoiled for life with tunnels, once they go through that one. Being as long as it is, all the rest of the tunnels around here are mere pikers. And don't think the kids don't know it.

Seeing a group of motorcyclists in town the other night reminded us of the two brothers around here who once donned black jackets and straddled the two wheelers. At night their favorite trick was to ride side by side, just the same distance as the usual car headlights. From a distance the two headlights looked exactly like a car to any poor approaching motorist. But then about a quarter of a mile away, the boys on the motorcycles would start weaving in and out simultaneously – which would first bring the lights close together and then far apart. They used to keep track of how many cars came to a dead stop. Whether in this generation or the last, we "elders" don't stand a chance.

June 9, 1960

It is safe to say that there are more magpies than people in Big Horn county. Last year's magpie contest by the Elks turned up 10,536 pairs of legs, (the 1960 census turned up 11,886 people) and there's still a lot flying around, magpies, that is.

The old fire bell brought memories back for Bill Harbaugh, too, who remembers the racket Greybullites made with it when the false armistice came over the wire in 1918. Clanging on the fire bell touched off quite an all-night celebration. He also remembers one fire it rang for down in the east end of town. "Three houses burned before we finally found the fire hydrant in the dark. We did save the lot, though," he says.

June 16, 1960

Some cowboy at the Days of '49 rodeo asked our five-year-old son if he thought he could ride some of those bucking horses. "No," he said, "I can't even reach the pedals."

June 30, 1960

Cleo Lazaros' parrots went to the Park with her the other day. One of them was looking out the window, she relates when one of the bears reared up, putting his big ugly face next to the window. "Diablo," screeched the parrot (Spanish for the Devil) and fled to the other side of the car.

July 7, 1960

Ralph Haley was up a couple of weeks ago from Basin to take his granddaughter, Jillray, fishing in the Beaver creek reservoir. Net catch for the day: Old fisherman Ralph – none; Jillray – a three-pound, five-ounce beauty that was a first prize winner for that week in the Olson Brothers Big Fish contest.

Dr. David Gregg's car has always sported the little sign on back, "I'd rather be flying." When the car was in for servicing the other day, Lloyd Groseclose tacked on some more "flying" stickers. They were two airborne storks, each loaded with a bundled up new baby.

July 14, 1960

Small town curiosity has its good sides, too, you know. Ernie Hershberger, who is starting up the rock shop in town, tells of a tourist who walked into his new Greybull location just a few hours after Ernie did Monday morning. "I asked at the drug store if there was a rock shop in town," the tourist told Ernie. "Some other customer said there was one unloading down here last night. So I came on down." Ernie says the guy bought something, too.

Most helpful person we talked to all week was six-year-old David Anderson. We telephoned looking for his dad, Rev. Jack Anderson. "He's not here," David said. "But my sister is here, my brother is here, my grandma is here and my grandpa is here."

July 21, 1960

Two tourists that stopped at Fletcher's Standard Wednesday morning figured out how the mountains were named. Just as they were stretching their legs, Cullen said, the 7 a.m. whistle blew. "Yes, sir," said one. "There it is, the Big Horn."

August 4, 1960

After one of our frantic attempts to be funny at the dinner table, our oldest paid us the ultimate in compliments with: "Gee, Daddy, you're just like the Three Stooges." (He meant the one without any hair, of course.)

A newspaper reporter can always tell when these high school athletes reach adolescence. It's when they request you to leave the "y's" and "ie's" off the Johnnys, the Timmys and all the rest.

The Minnesota couple and their daughter who made a wrong turn and ended up within three miles of the Paintrock Lakes instead of Sheridan (see front page story) really threw Joe Auckenback who was working on the forest service road. The Easterners (who believed they were on their way to Sheridan) asked Joe how far it was to the next filling station. Joe stared at them awhile, pushed his hat back further on his head and said, slow-like: "Well, now, that'll take a little consideration."

August 11, 1960

At the Cody night rodeo there's an aptly named Indian riding the broncs. He's Pete Bruised Head.

Jake Piercy insists it isn't rumor but an actual fact that his neighbors in the drought-stricken Burlington area are losing livestock in the cracks in the ground.

August 25, 1960

The hardest task right now in football practice is trying to figure out which boy is inside the pads and guards and paraphernalia of a football suit. And invariably when you ask who it is, the voice inside says, "It's me."

A Greybullite says she has a pair of nephews who wanted to play cowboys and Indians, but they were having a time figuring out who would get to be Roy Rogers. They solved it finally with the cold, calculating logic of little boys: One would be Roy and the other would be Rogers.

September 1, 1960

Cleo McKinney, who called us about the cowboy "parking" his three horses on main street Tuesday, said he wanted to make sure that everyone realized Greybull wasn't just a one horse town!

September 8, 1960

One little boy with a malted milk in one hand and a fudgicle in the other, ran up to his mother on main street the other day saying: "Look, Mom, I bought a bellyache."

September 22, 1960

Pitt Berry and Al Lindell went down into Shell canyon Sunday to bring out the salvable pieces of the Michelena pickup. They report someone had already tried to steal two of the tires but evidently couldn't get them off the rims!

September 29, 1960

Lessie Sims was giving a polio shot to a jumpy man the other day. "Are you gentle?" he asked nervously. "I'm not gentle," Lessie told him, "but I'm awfully kind."

October 6, 1960
   Oldtimers left their mark and their names on creeks, peaks, rivers and lakes all over the Big Horn mountains. But not always. Take Scojen Springs, for instance. Forest Service officials said they thought for years that it was named after some old boy who discovered the area. Then they found out that two surveyors of recent years left their stamp on the official map. Their names: Scott and Jensen from whence came the "Sco" and the "Jen."

   Ever hear of a red fox in this country? The Metz Smith family almost ran over one the other day on the county road near their farm on Lower Shell creek. The fox raced alongside the car for several hundred feet before turning up into the gullies and washes leading back of the golf course. There was no mistaking it, the Smiths said, big bushy tail and all.

October 20, 1960
   Rev. Herb Donovan was the center of attraction for awhile on the field Friday night. While running the chain with Jim Core, Herb got interested in one of Greybull's long runs. When enthused Jim took off down the field, for the first down, the chain wrapped around Herb's ankles . . . and the vicar went flying!

November 10, 1960
   The braying of the donkey that someone had in back of the parked truck on main street was good for a lot of laughs this past week. Tired of waiting, the old boy let out a "hee-haw" that shattered the morning quiet of main street in a thousand pieces.

   And caused one man to holler across the street to a friend: "Aw, stop your griping, John."

   And Cleo McKinney went to the door of the Smokehouse and hollered out: "Shut up out there – we've got enough in here already."

November 17, 1960
   One parental risk Dr. Spock says nothing about: Singing your children's early grade songs at work particularly embarrassing ones like, "I'm A Little Teapot, Short and Stout."

   One want ad we were happy to kill out was Logan Hoover's ad for his lost watch after Saturday's football game. The watch was a special gift from the VFW the night before. Logan had worn it just that first day when a pin came loose in the band. He missed the watch after the game but couldn't find it. Jerry Ewen, son of Mr. and Mrs. Maxson Ewen of Shell, discovered it though on the field and turned it in to the school, who contacted Logan.

November 24, 1960
  The losers Saturday at Jim Crawford field weren't too gentlemanly about it either. When they announced that the trophies would be awarded in a few minutes, one Evanston woman fan stopped in midfield, shook an angry fist in the air and screamed toward the PA system: "Give one to the referees, too."

  One small boy told Bill Simpson before the game that Greybull would win all right if "we can just keep our resistance up."

December 1, 1960
  Tom Hubbard and Ray Bristow and the cold weather were right on schedule with the lights. Every year it's the same. After days of bright warm sunshine, the day when the boys put up the town Christmas decorations, turns out to be the coldest darn day of the year.

December 8, 1960
  For the record, John Bass sang tenor in the All District Choir.

December 29, 1960
  As customary, the dude ranch hand was nonchalantly displaying his dexterity rolling cigarettes one-handed. One duly impressed Easterner expressed his admiration for the skill involved. "Actually, rolling them don't take much," the cow hand allowed, "it's getting the filter in that's the trick."

1961

January 12, 1961

Said one little kindergartner when Miss Maxine Meadows walked in with some perfume on: "I smell something pink."

Workmen tearing down a shed in the rear of the Republican-Rustler building at Basin came up with a board inscribed thusly: "Anyone sees this board drop me a card. This board was nailed on by B.L. Harrison, Oct. 5, 1906."

January 26, 1961

One thing about a railroad town – any train trip you take, you're not apt to get lonesome for some hometown company. Thursday on the trip down to the press convention, we talked with George Scott and Del Hughes. On the way back Sunday, L.J. Senstad was on duty.

Several people have remembered the old coal mine still burning on Greybull river operated up until the 1930's. Frank Bellamy said: "A man and his wife ran the coal mine during the depression days. It wasn't a thick vein – only 18 inches or so. But they could make a little money and a lot of people around here went out to get some of it. Only cost $3 a ton as I remember. Wasn't a good grade of coal, but it would keep you warm."

February 23, 1961

Mrs. Mary Welch, whose ninetieth birthday was reported in last week's Standard, was telling us about a group she was at recently. "Most of the ladies there were 50 or 60 and I thought to myself as I looked back: 'I was just a chicken then.'"

March 16, 1961

The bum lamb on the front page last week reminded someone of a rancher down on the Sweetwater who wound up with two lambs to one old ewe. He didn't know if the ewe had twins or what, but he did know he didn't want to be nursing any bum lambs. He remembered that ewes identify their own offspring by smelling them, so he had the bright idea of spraying both lambs and the ewe with his wife's hair spray. It worked. The ewe took care of both lambs.

March 23, 1961

Spring makes a difference when it comes to shots. All the boys in the lower grades told Mrs. Ernie Kovacs, the school nurse, they didn't want the shots in their "marble arms."

No late delivery of oysters was going to deprive Ray DeSomber of oysters at the Misnamed Oyster Feed at the Elks the other night. Ray stepped over across the alley, stirred up some oyster stew and brought it back to the hall to eat – the lone oyster feeder, among the rest of the roast beef eating Elks.

March 30, 1961
The Norris Hotel fire scorched Doc Chambers' bull fiddle. Doc claims it has a "charcoal tone" now.

April 6, 1961
It's being said around town that the reason the ice is all gone at Boysen lake is because ice fishermen Howard Unterzuber and George Wright bored so many holes this winter, it all just caved in.

Here's one six-year-old girl's definition of a newspaper: "We need them so we can know who reks and who drownds and who shoots somebody. And who wants a house or who dies or gets a baby. It tells if your dog is lost. They are good on shelves and to make bond fires. They also do good under a baby's plate an to keep dogs offa things. You can wrap potato peelings in em. You can put one when you defrost. They tell about shows and how much things are."

To which you might add: They also are good to swat things with, like flies and public officials and things.

April 20, 1961
Asked Jonathan Davis what old Dry Dout had to say about this rainless spring weather. Jonathan said he hadn't seen Dry Dout lately but he did chat a while the other day with his brother, Blow Dout.

Sometimes we're sure Lessie Sims could do a better job of writing this column. Her latest about needles and nurses: "The secret of shots is in a sharp needle," says Lessie. "I'd rather be shot with a dull nurse and a sharp needle than a dull needle and a sharp nurse."

April 27, 1961
Someone jumped down our neck this week and it reminded us of that classic cartoon we'll never forget, of the man saying to his psychiatrist: "I said I don't seem to get along with people. Open your ears, fathead."

May 11, 1961
They turned some of the Shell creek reservoir water loose this past weekend to alleviate some of the water shortage along Shell creek. Just in time, too, Colonel Noyes believes. "We were just about going to have to teach the fish how to walk," he said.

May 25, 1961
Doc Chambers' niece (Julie Ann Hindorff of Cody) won a beauty contest at Colorado State College. "Now that is really having Beauty and the Beast in the same family," pointed out Doc, who was Greybull's 1959 Ugliest Man.

Amazingly enough, tourists are still coming through Greybull who remember Doc on the Art Linkletter show and who ask for his autograph or picture.

June 1, 1961
The dead bullsnake somebody coiled right by the police car the other night had its desired effect on Policeman Schafer. It would have been more effective, though, says Schafer, if it could have buzzed just a little.

June 22, 1961
If you're wondering how the Western Television corporation got the Cable TV line across the river (they're putting cable TV on the Heights) ask Ray Bristow. He limbered up his bow, tied some fish line to an arrow and shot the darn thing across. Then the TV crew tied the fish line to the wire and the Big Horn was bridged!

June 29, 1961
Every family must have had this happen once to them. Our little girl loves to pick flowers – any kind of flower just so long as it blooms, like dandelions, weeds, all the petunias off one bush, rosebuds. Our latest bouquet on the dinner table – a big bunch of potato plant blooms!

July 6, 1961
There's two entrances to the Norris Hotel's Bar of Music, you know. One through the side door (to the Piano Bar) and the other at the main entrance. Frank Norris says the other night a woman hollered down from the main entrance: "Is my husband down there?" And four guys left through the side door.

If you saw Plet Avery digging in her flowerbed the other day, she was burying her dog's bones. It's true! Seems the Avery dog was picking the flower bed as the most likely bone cemetery. So Plett dug them all up, moved them to another part of the yard, reburied them and now the dog is just as contented as ever . . . and the flowers aren't in danger of their lives.

July 13, 1961

The Bantam chickens at Babe Wilkerson's are turning out to be great hitchhikers. "They love to roost on car axles," Blanche says, "and people drive off without knowing they're underneath." The chickens are scattered everywhere. In Emblem, around Shell; one old black rooster got off at the Greybull main street intersection. Latest bunch of hitchhikers were a little red rooster and a little white hen who rode down from Wilkerson's underneath the Oral Harvey car.

Dr. Lewis Hay sent the coffee crowd into hearty laughter the other day when he said he was just recovering from a toothache. But good sport Doc could see the humor in a dentist having a toothache. "Got a taste of my own medicine, I guess," he said.

July 20, 1961

Hap Crain took us out to the curb to see his "Dutch Cadillac" as he called it. It turned out to be a black Volkswagen.

"Welcome to the club," George Nelson told Dick Burkhart the other day after Dick and his airplane got tangled up out in the hills in a small ground wreck. "What club," asked Dick. "There's two kinds of pilots," George explained. "Those who are going to crash and those who already have. You've just graduated to the second one!"

Ouryoungsonsaidgracetheothernightaboutthisspeed. When he finished he added: "andInevertookabreath."

July 27, 1961

Jim Wilkinson of Jim's Texaco, who is not noted for shy and soft-spoken ways on the softball diamond, says he'll be glad when the season is over. "I figure I lose ten customers every ball game," he says.

August 31, 1961

It was just about three years ago that Policeman Glenn Coxen was shot by the California couple. George Olson was remembering the revolver sales he made the day after the pair was loose all night, keeping half the town awake. "We sold three or four revolvers the next day – gun business was never so good," he said.

September 28, 1961

The Brent Leavitts who are visiting from Denver got one Greybull Standard this summer in terrible condition – tattered and torn, yellowed, dirty, in a deplorable mess. "Whatever are they doing to the paper," Mrs. Leavitt wondered. Then she opened it up and found it was the Christmas issue mailed from Greybull back in December and just getting to Denver by July. Well, the stage has been running late!

October 12, 1961
The Tim Grahams, who are building the area's first fallout shelter, were also the first in the telephone exchange when it came through. It was a little different than fallout shelters though, Graham points out. "We had our phone all right, but we couldn't call anyone else until they got theirs!"

One of the Frank Norris Jr. little girls had a special interest in the World Series this year. She excitedly asked her mother if she knew that "Yogi Bear" was playing on the Yankees. She still isn't convinced even now that there is any difference between the ball player Yogi, who wears the pinstripe uniform and can't talk straight, and the Yellowstone Park type Yogi who cavorts over the little folk's TV programs.

November 2, 1961
Down at the Lander ball game there was the wire fence fans had to look through. It got in the way of Dr. A.S. Rogers and Skip Anderson who had to get together over Skip's dislocated finger. But instead of taking the time to go around, Skip just jumped up on a bench, dangled his arm over the fence while Dr. Rogers fixed it up, and back in the ball game went Skip.

November 23, 1961
One thing about Frontier Town marshals, there wasn't much trouble about "fitting" on a horse – they either got on or got off. Nowadays, it's a different story if the police car is a Buick Special and the "Marshal" is tall and man-sized like Mandy Mohr. He just sort of folds up when he gets in and out of it.

The football player at our house is sadder but wiser and two stitches (on the side of his head) richer. He missed a fellow first grader who had the ball, but executed a perfect tackle on one of the playground posts.

December 7, 1961
The Lavern Shortt family were out at the hospital visiting the newest addition here several months ago and in front of the nursery there was a feather lying on the floor. Lannie, 12, saw it and exclaimed: "You can sure tell the stork was here!"

1962

January 4, 1962

Justice of the Peace R.S. Woodward, who married Mr. and Mrs. Harry Schafer 50 years ago Tuesday, carried a frequent ad in the early Standard which read: "Nuptial knots tied with diabolical promptness." And the Schafers have proved he tied them securely, too.

The Schafers are, we believe, the first people celebrating their 50th anniversary, to have been married in Greybull and still reside here.

January 11, 1962

Mel Christler brought a "special delivery, air freight" package to Greybull the other day. He delivered two tiny Siamese kittens to the Wee Collingwood kids. The air ride didn't bother the kittens at all – they were just as pert and saucy as could be.

January 18, 1962

Latest mode of transportation on the ice at the skating pond harnesses some willing "dog" power. The kids get on one end of a long stick, the dog pulls on the other, and away they go. One old brown dog likes it so much he just sits and waits for someone to come skating.

January 25, 1962

Rev. Thomas Adam asked us the other day if there wasn't something we could do about turning off the cold weather. Well, we got the sun shining for a change again, we said. "Oh, no, you can't claim that – that's my department," he told us.

The Chuck Harndens had animal trouble, too, with their little boy, just like we do with the lion out our way. But they solved it by putting him in the top bunk "where the animals can't get up to." Never a bit more trouble, they report. We're going to try it.

February 1, 1962

We just found out Lessie Sims' maiden name was O'Kelly. Which explains much about her zest for life. We should have known there was some Irish behind her ability to make the rest of us smile a little bit more.

February 15, 1962

People all over the United States "knew" more about the flood and evacuation in Greybull than all of us did right here. A nephew of Mrs. Ernie Rice called from Rhode Island less than an hour after the evacuation to ask how everyone was. He'd seen it on TV back there. Mrs. Roy Lee Cline in Washington, D.C. called Clint Core on the same question. On the other side of the United States, at Long Beach Calif., Tuesday Cleo McKinney's mother called to tell Cleo that the dike washed out and the people were under water. She'd heard that report on television. Cleo said he was glad to finally hear "something definite." And there were probably dozens of other just such calls.

One passenger on the ice Monday night that got more than he bargained for probably was a skunk near the ball park. Darrel Hanson watched him go out on the dike, out over the ice and finally got on a chunk that was moving. The last Darrel saw was the black and white traveler heading down river.

And Glory Be, for the weekly newspaper fraternity . . . the excitement actually happened BEFORE the paper got out.

Red Lindsey had his boat ready by the door all day. He said he was going to put a new name on it — "Noah's Ark."

Bentonite price delivered to the business district at one time Tuesday morning was 25 cents per sack if you don't use it, $1 a sack if you do. At the Wyo-Ben mill, the sacked bentonite was free for flood purposes if you hauled it yourself.

First thing Irvin Werbelow saw as he was driving home after the whistle blew was the big puddle of water between the depot and Foe-Saunders. His first thought — "it's here already!"

February 22, 1962
Your flood-riddled nerves are back to normal again if you can let the nine o'clock curfew whistle blow without jumping slightly.

Many Greybullites felt like Mr. and Mrs. Oscar Heywood after the flood was over. "We decided we'd just saved $1,900," Oscar said, "so we splurged and called the kids to tell them we were okay."

Dutch Bricker should receive special credit for showing up Denver's boast of the longest steer horns. He spotted the original Rocky Mountain News article and got things rolling that eventually established the Elks club pair of horns as the largest.

Ann Bass wrote her folks that one member of the Carroll College ski team broke his leg skiing recently. He was the ski club president!

The Standard really had a run on last week's papers at various times. We kept running out when we'd least expect it. One time Max Coleman came up from Lee's to pick up a bundle of 45 papers we'd saved for the newsstand down there. It was the last bunch we had left. So he stood outside the Standard office and sold 12 before he could get into his car.

March 8, 1962
Coach Tony Vinnola didn't need a cake to celebrate his birthday Saturday. His basketball team gave him two wins, a berth in the state tournament and a gold-plated third place trophy instead. It was a joyous bunch of boys who crowded around him in the locker room at the Thermop game Saturday night and "wished him happy birthday."

March 29, 1962
The George Hauns had twin black and white lambs born this year that were nearly identical. Both had the same markings, same white streak on the forehead, same white tipped noses.

Stevie DeRoche caught a pheasant on main street Tuesday afternoon. It apparently blew in from the railroad side of town and when the dust cleared, found itself in the middle of main street. It's back in the sagebrush again now, shaken, but worldly wiser.

April 12, 1962
Did you hear about the lumber company that couldn't sell an overstock of birch lumber? Couldn't peddle it anywhere. No one wanted it. So they investigated current lumber trends and found a demand for outhouses. They started building outhouses with their birch logs, found someone to peddle them and then incorporated the whole outfit into the Birch John Society.

Track Manager John Bass doesn't set exactly the right kind of an example out at track practice. He's got a motor scooter he rides back and forth between the supply room and the practice area. Only John would think of something like that!

Jack Karhu had a friend in Red Lodge who borrowed $5 way back in 1927. Twenty years later he stopped through Greybull and borrowed $10 more. Monday Jack got a letter in the mail from the guy. Inside was $15!

April 19, 1962
One of the problems of Park Manager John Loveland: whether to clean the park up now or wait until after Easter Sunday. Several years ago the park crew got busy and cleaned up the park before the Easter Egg hunt . . . and then caught you know what because there weren't leaves and tall grass enough

to hide the Easter eggs!

April 26, 1962
That wasn't the Easter Bunny you saw the other day. It was Miss Dorothy Ankrum's poodle dog dyed a bright Easter egg purple.

The three kids at our house may see through the Santa Claus myth one of these years, but this business about the Easter bunny will die hard.
Sunday's home-grown Easter Egg hunt in our front lawn fixed that. It all happened when they were looking through the window trying to spot the Easter eggs (which their sleepy old man had broadcast like wheat a few hours earlier.) Suddenly the eldest cried: "Look, there's the Easter Bunny!"
And sure enough there was this cotton-picking rabbit leisurely hopping around all the Easter Eggs. What a success that Easter Egg hunt was!

May 3, 1962
If you're amazed at the speed which the Dr. A.J. Kelly building is going up, don't be — there's enough sidewalk superintendents down there to "boss" a dozen or so jobs.

May 10, 1962
Lloyd Eaton said at the Sports Banquet he went to a town once to speak, but a blizzard cut the crowd down to a solitary rancher. Eaton said he didn't know what to do but the rancher pointed out that whether he had one cow or a herd he always fed them. So Eaton said he gave the rancher a 40-minute briefing, showed a film and then gave a fiery speech on athletics. When he finished he asked the rancher. "Well, how was that?" The rancher allowed it was all right but "when I only found one cow in the pasture I didn't feed her the whole load."

Another addition to Wyoming's wonderful women department: Last week when Mrs. Dale Hill's car stalled in front of the Standard office she just got out, took off her shoe, lifted up the hood and pounded away inside. Then she got back in and roared away.

May 24, 1962
Jack Stockwell drove out to the salesbarn two weeks ago to see how the horse sale was going and raised his hand at the wrong time: net result, one little donkey. But he took it home anyway and tied it up in the front yard. "Your Mother's Day present is outside in the front yard," he kidded Mrs. Stockwell the next morning. "It was so late last night when the kids and I realized the next day was Mother's Day the only place open was the salesbarn!"

May 31, 1962
When National Guardsmen Steve Rogers and John Williams left by train

for six months training Sunday, the kids flocked down to the depot. "It looked like an assembly," one person put it.

United Press International (and later Reader's Digest) carried this item which is worth a laugh or two. Posted on a fence in Montana is this sign: "Powderville, Mont. Population 1, Mayor Joe Hodges, Chief of Police Joe Hodges. Fire Chief Joe Hodges. Drive carefully – the life you save may be Joe's."

June 14, 1962
Several old timers are back visiting in the area this summer. Fritz Winzenreid of Salt Lake is visiting here. "I have to come back every so often to these old hills where I grew up," he told us. Mr. and Mrs. George Kershner of Bozeman stopped in Monday. Kershner and Herb Smith of Shell have been in this country longer than any one else. Smith arrived in Shell in 1886, a year earlier than the Kershners.

The tornado that hit the Arnold Wamhoff's farm Tuesday, in typical choosy fashion of all tornados, demolished the chicken house, ripping the roof off, scattering boards and chickens in all directions. But it didn't break one egg inside!

June 21, 1962
If your kids ever left anything in the last town during a trip, you'll appreciate the dilemma of an Iowa tourist family whose little boy left his shoes in the city park. They called back to Greybull from Cody, and Policeman John Boyd found the shoes in the park. Shores shoes wrapped them up and they were sent on back to Iowa.

In Riverton Saturday we gave a service station attendant our credit card, he looked at the address and said consolingly: "You've heard about the tornado in Greybull today haven't you – thousands of dollars worth of damages." "You're kidding," we said, our stomach down around our shoe tops. "No, sir, just heard it – thousands of dollars worth of damages." With an image of a leveled town before us, we called back to Greybull, finally got Jack Kvale on the phone at the Big Horn Drug. "No tornados here," he assured us. Come to find out the service station guy had heard a bit of radio news about the Arnold Wamhoff tornado which the Standard carried last Thursday. Now that's being a victim of your own story, isn't it?

June 28, 1962
Shores Shoes was swamped with requests to turn the whistle back on. Mothers missed it, so did kids and businessmen. Even the Shores stayed open an extra ten minutes the other night, waiting for the thing to blow!

July 5, 1962

Add to the Small World Department: John Gahley who joined the Big Horn Drug as a pharmacist this week is a relative of Walter Fisk who ran the Fisk Pharmacy in the same location until selling to Carroll Durkee in 1931.

That horse in front of Probst Western store sure gets the attention ... even from the other horses! The other day a horse went through town in a horse trailer and cast a covert look. Tom Foe who was standing in front of Probst's nickered and darned if the traveling horse didn't nicker right back!

July 19, 1962

One of our kids woke up from a bad dream the other night and in the consoling and comforting conversation that followed we asked what had happened. Well, he'd got into big long fight with the bear. And they'd fought and fought. "Well, who won," we wondered. "The bear," he quavered.

July 26, 1962

A tourist stopped by the Smokehouse and was telling the boys there how wonderful he'd found the fishing in Shell canyon. "Caught four," he told them proudly. "But when I was cleaning them at the motel I lost three of them down the drain. But they were dandies." Sounds like it.

August 2, 1962

We have made our mistakes in the past, but none can quite compare with the recent purported experience of a North Carolina daily newspaper. A man with a sewing machine to sell places a classified ad in the paper. The following series of ads appeared: "For sale: R.D. Smith has one sewing machine for sale. Phone 958. Call after 7:00 p.m. and ask for Mrs. Kelly who lives with him cheap."

Next paper: "We regret having erred in R.D. Smith's ad. It should have read: For sale: R.D. Smith has one sewing machine for sale. Phone 958 and ask for Mrs. Kelly who lives with him after 7 p.m."

Next paper: "R.D. Smith says he has had several annoying phone calls because of an error in his ad. His ad stands corrected: For Sale: R.D. Smith has one sewing machine for sale. Cheap. Phone 958 after 7 p.m. and ask for Mrs. Kelly who loves with him."

Next paper: "Notice: I, R.D. Smith, have no sewing machine for sale. I smashed it. Don't call 958 the phone has been taken out. I have not been carrying on with Mrs. Kelly. Until yesterday she was my housekeeper."

Ted Anderson walked in the Norris Hotel the other morning while Frankie Norris was having a hamburger for breakfast. "A hamburger for breakfast," Ted said amazed. "What do you have for dinner, Shredded Wheat?" Frankie feigned equal amazement: "Doesn't everybody?"

August 9, 1962

Wes Thorley, Forrest Shores and Slim Smith of Basin went to the ball game last week in the Thorley car and Wes took one of Butch Sommerville's softball home runs right through the windshield. So the next night they took Slim's pickup and another softball went through that windshield. The next Tuesday night they asked Shores if he wanted to take his car. "Nothing doing," Shores said. "Let's walk."

August 16, 1962

When Vic Larson was working on Chet Whaley's new house this spring, he was driving some nails and missed the same nail twice in a row. Up piped Chet's little daughter who was watching all the time: "My daddy's got a hammer like that and it does the same thing!"

August 23, 1962

We asked one farmer whose place looked clean and neat and well-kept, "How do you do it?" "Well," he told us, "we don't get any bedsores."

Mrs. Mildred Avery can always tell when the town fills up with tourists and there's no motel rooms left. She gets calls to rent her front bedroom. She goes to the back bedroom. On some nights she gets calls to rent that too, so then she says, "I end up on the davenport."

August 30, 1962

A young motorcyclist from Buffalo, N.Y. (who stopped in Shell on his way home) wrote back to tell the folks in Shell he arrived okay. He addressed the letter: "Sam 'Bud' (wife runs gas station in town), rancher aged 50, Shell Wyoming." Mr. and Mrs. Bud Scharen got the letter okay.

Funniest sight of the week was the inebriated fellow (celebrating the end of summer we suppose) who tried to ride, break, shoe, rope, and make friends with the fake horse out in front of Probst's. Larry finally had to chase him away.

September 13, 1962

A couple of fourth grade girls jumped us about the Who's Who contest. "I hope I won because if I did my daddy said I could take the money and make a down payment on a horse." "A horse," exclaimed the other girl. "Who wants a horse! I want a boy!"

It'll never be summer again department: The George Clements and the Gerald Williams went skiing over the weekend up on the Big Horns.

September 20, 1962

The kicking tee, which came sailing out of the game after a Greybull point-after-touchdown, sailed right into Assistant Coach Terry Tonn conking him on the back of the head. "Do you want a headgear, coach," Coach Buck Eckroth joked. "I don't know about a headgear," Tonn replied, "but send me in the game – it's safer."

An uncle of ours thought Custer's Battlefield was the most interesting part of his 4,000-mile trip through the Rocky Mountain West. In fact, he thought so much of it, and got so interested he planned to make a talk on it to his professional group when he got back home to Omaha. We wonder if those Omahans listening to a speech on Custer missed the irony of it all though – our uncle and all the men he was speaking to were Life Insurance Agents!

September 27, 1962

Did you know there's a Greybull avenue in Cheyenne. There probably isn't another one in the world!

A salesman stopped in at Ed's 66 Saturday morning and told Eddie he never saw such a dead town as Greybull the night before. "Where were all your young folks last night," he wondered. Eddie replied: "If you wanted to see our young folks you did two things wrong. First you didn't look over the board fence in the back of the high school. And secondly you must have gone to bed before the game was over."

October 4, 1962

Two prisoners from the state prison farm at Riverton didn't feel like carrying the heavy backpack water pumps filled with water during a recent forest fire in the Wind river country. So they blew up the collapsible pumps with air to make them look full and walked around that way until some of the authorities wised up to it.

October 11, 1962

Rev. and Mrs. Tom Adam's three-year-old daughter, Shari Leonard, who was here to watch her Aunt Ruth get married apparently thought everything about the wedding was all right except the part at the last "when they threw gravel at Aunt Ruth and chased her out of town."

One thing you learn on a bus carrying the victorious football squad home is that there are a dozen or so pitches, keys and tunes to every song. The only song everyone got right was Rain Rain Go Away which the boys sang gloriously whenever there was a lull.

When you're sighting down your gun barrel at a pheasant this year thank men like W.J. Jones, Howard Unterzuber and his father W. F. Unterzuber, Dan Rogers and C.F. MacKenzie who brought pheasant eggs into here in 1917 and 1918 and used Banty hens to hatch out the first pheasant eggs.

Duties of a football squad manager the book doesn't cover: Holding a small transistor radio (like Manager Mike Spencer did) close to big tough Bill Werbelow's ear while he stretched out his full length on the floor in that tense pre game waiting period. "It helps me relax," Werbelow explained to the coaches.

October 25, 1962
Little Julie Norris was sitting on Doc Chambers' lap the other day at the hotel, and asked him, "Doc, if you shaved off your mustache, would you still be Doc?"

November 1, 1962
The one word you don't use around the Greybull football squad and coaches is "Mumps." Half the team's never had them, there's just two more days until the last game of the season and the thought of anyone missing the Buffalo game this year is unbearable. Rich Douglass' ulcerated tooth (which swelled his jaw and looked like the mumps) caused one heart after another to skip a beat.

Plans are being made to assure Mrs. Mary Welch of voting in this election. At 92 she'll undoubtedly be the county's oldest voter.

George Hoffman is making a hit handing out pocket combs which read: "George Hoffman, candidate for County Treasurer." George always explains: "Can't use them myself."

November 8, 1962
The Jim Clifton kids made a production out of this Halloween. Dressed appropriately they mounted their horses and rode around to the neighbors as Headless Horsemen.

And isn't there a difference in what grade you teach when it comes to your reaction to Halloween trick or treating? The beginning grade teachers get a tremendous lift out of treating their kids on their nightly excursion. Jittery high school teachers several blocks away would just as soon never see a kid around their houses.

Our kids made the stop at Larry Probst's on Halloween but they knocked and knocked and no one answered. Finally the door opened slowly and there in the dark stood a big, big Indian. The kids didn't know whether to laugh or cry or run away. When the suspense had just about gotten the best of them, Larry whipped off the mask and handed out the candy. Our little three-year-old son was telling us about it and he wound up with: "Boy, that funny."

November 15, 1962
It was Jim Crawford "day" on Sunday's televised pro game between Boston and Denver. Announcer Curt Gowdy, himself a Wyoming grad had a happy time pointing out Crawford's play during the game and reminding the viewing audience that Jim was a rodeo hand from Greybull, Wyoming in the off season. Incidentally, did you read where the jubilant players awarded Jim the game ball in the dressing room after the game?

A young stunning brunette tourist who stayed overnight at the Norris Hotel, decided the next day to get a pair of saddle pants. She asked Doc Chambers where to buy them and Doc told her he'd show her himself. So they walked uptown, she got her Wyoming cut outfit and after they had walked back to the hotel, she told him: "You sure have a lot of friends, Doc." "I don't' ordinarily," Doc chuckled.

November 29, 1962
The Junior High School newspaper staff (Carol Johnson, Rosalind Riopelle and Wally Dalbey) stopped in at the office the other day to ask what we did about "those horrible spaces left over at the bottom of the columns". There is no good answer kids – newspapermen since Gutenberg have had four or five lines left over at the bottom of column after column.

At Burlington, though, they have solved it! In their last school paper (at the bottom of the page of course) was this little gem:
To dear old Phillip,
We dedicate this space
To Phillip Who?
To Phillip Space!

December 6, 1962
Remember several years ago when the baseball team had nearly half its members' names starting with "S". This year's basketball team is liberally sprinkled with Ricks (Minter and Daley) and Rich's (Douglass and Leavitt.)

The mail must get through department: Orville Stockwell sent a letter from Denver addressed to the Greybull Standard on one line; then on the line below: "Near-White Gentleman-Cow, Wyoming." It came right through!

December 13, 1962

The old number "8" hasn't lighted up on the GHS basketball scoreboard very many times. Friday when the Buffs topped the 80-point mark against Buffalo, Timer Hillman Snell wasn't sure for a minute the "8" would flash on or not when he punched it. But it did!

The letters to Santa made quite a hit at our house but our second grader son was wide-eyed about one thing: He hadn't realized, he told us, "That our paper went clear up to the North Pole."

December 20, 1962

Advice to fathers of inquiring little boys who still believe in Santa Claus. Don't take him up on the roof to help put up the outside Christmas decorations. You're courting catastrophe when he peers down the dinky hole in the chimney and asks how Santa will ever get down through that? (What do you say anyway?)

George Scott and his helpers did a fine job at the Community hall Saturday during the Chamber of Commerce's annual visit by Santa. Someday we're going to take pictures of Momma and Poppa's faces instead of the kids. Sometimes they're as enthralled as their youngsters. It's a happy time for everyone.

December 27, 1962

The Big Horn river was still trying not to freeze over as this column was written. But as Bob Foe pointed out: Don't worry about the river freezing over – it's the thawing out that brings the gray hairs.

We're keeping a list of the salesmen, peddlers, dropper-inners, introduced strangers and downright bums who've asked with a wink if we're related to the Kennedy in the White House . . . and the number just passed 1,067.

Our youngest dropped and broke one of his plastic toys already. And now he has it "hided away" so Santa Claus can't see it.

1963

January 3, 1963

The New York Sun wrote to little Virginia about there being a Santa Claus, but Glen Shores, 7, got to see the real thing. Glen hasn't been sure all year there was a Santa Claus. In fact, he'd just about believed those stories kids are bound to hear from their elder playmates. ("I won't believe it until I see him.") So the Shores family got Tom Thorley, Glen's uncle, to dress up in a Santa Claus suit and come to the Shores house while Glen was still awake. Glen was enthralled. ("It's really him.") He shooed the family out into the kitchen ("We don't want him to see us.") and then he peeked out the door while Santa arranged the packages, put some more under the tree and did all those things Santas are supposed to do. So by the time Santa left there was one little boy who's certain there is a Santa Claus.

January 10, 1963

This is the time of year when we'd like to find some lefthanded friend who has a drawerful of still good right hand gloves who'd trade us for our drawerful of still good left hand ones.

January 17, 1963

The longest distance between two points on our lane: a boy's tracks in the snow between where the school bus lets him out and the front door.

Jack Douglass, the Shell area's one-man Chamber of Commerce, called the other frosty morning to remind us the temperatures at the Wagon Wheel were 10 to 15 higher than ours down here in shivering Greybull. He keeps not one but three thermometers just so no one can accuse him of aiding and abetting the mercury.

February 7, 1963

Floyd Farr is sure getting a warm welcome as the new fire chief. Within a week after his election there have been three fires, including two in one day!

February 14, 1963

Miss Edith Scott, who was honored as the Teacher of the Year, has taught many, many Greybullites, including one third generation family: Mrs. E. Brown (at the Kane school) and Mrs. Brown's grandchildren Linda and Larry Collingwood. Her daughter, Ina Collingwood, was in another fifth grade room at the Greybull grade school but her brother, Don, was in Miss Scott's room.

Here's a basketball fan for you. Mrs. Frank St. Jermain walked all by herself to the basketball game Friday night, and then walked by herself home afterward. She's over 80 years old.

One of the reasons they are switching to all number dialing was guys like Bill Wood who had some land on Bear creek east of No Wood. He set out one day to make a long distance telephone call to his brother on the old crank and holler type of phone at the now defunct No Wood store. He got the operator, told her he wanted to talk to Jim Wood at Riverton. She wanted to know who was calling. "Bill Wood," he replied. Where was he calling from? "No Wood," he answered. And the disgusted operator promptly hung up on him.

February 21, 1963
Oscar Heywood stopped us on the street the other day and told us we missed the picture of the year. "Last night," he said, "I had my arms around the entire GHS graduating class of 1919!" (He was talking about Reba Williamson Schoeggle of Kirkland, Wash. the solitary graduate from Greybull in 1919 who visited Oscar and Gladys Heywood recently.)

March 7, 1963
Leo Knudson parked in front of the bank and started to put a penny in the 12-minute meter. But the coin wouldn't go in. It wasn't until he laid the penny on top of the meter that he noticed eight other pennies up there, too . . . put there by eight other honest people who had tried it and found out it wouldn't work.

We pulled this want ad out of the classified section in order to explain it further: "Will the party who left the green Army gas can with the initials "H.T." on it in front of the Pete Chroninger house, please claim said can at the Greybull police station. Also one rubber hose." (The inside story: Mrs. Chroninger heard a noise outside and when she opened the front door, she thought she heard someone run off. She called the police who found the Oklahoma credit card materials exactly where someone had dropped them: the piece of hose still sticking out of the tank and the initialed gas can nearby.

March 14, 1963
Ken Casey, who always gives the Standard staff a bad time about the lack of news in the paper each week, had to admit last Thursday that once in awhile there's something in it. Like the item last week about the green Army gas can with the initials "H. T." on it. The can turns out to be Casey's which someone swiped from him awhile back. He reclaimed it at the police station after the paper came out. The "H. T." incidentally, stands for "high-test," says Casey.

March 28, 1963

Jimmy Avery soloed the other day on his 16th birthday . . . which, by the way, is the minimum age permitted for soloing. Bob Foe was his instructor.

April 4, 1963

Have you wondered about Old Toomy, that 38-year-old horse at Dan Straight's. Well, he made it through the winter and Mrs. Straight said over the phone the other day that "He's fine and eating good. If anything he's put on weight." The men filed his teeth even and he may make it through several more winters.

April 11, 1963

A tramp came into the depot the other night when Don Olson was working the night shift, and spent considerable time alone in the empty waiting room. Don could hear him talking to himself at a steady clip, jabbering and chatting away. Finally the bum got up in a huff and announced: "It's too noisy in here for me," and stalked out.

We've been trying to explain life's tragedies and hard knocks to our kids and we've overworked the phrase about "that's just the way life is." The other day our oldest (he's 8) and our youngest (he's 4) were playing Cowboys and Indians and the youngest was tired of always having to "be killed". He was getting a stern lecture from his older brother who was admonishing him that Indians had to be shot and they had to fall over dead. He wound up with: "That's just the way life is, you know."

A bit of Greybull "local color" . . . the telephone number the kids dial more than any other is the Bob Tolman residence. The kids take to that 2 3 4 5 business!

April 18, 1963

Ginny Core said she thinks any trophies for the Days of '49 beards should go to the WIVES!

Greybull glimpses: bunch of boys in a noisy baseball game in the vacant lot across from Reilly Motel and the star pitcher — barred from Little League games, of course — a real cool, baseball-wise Raelene Kelly.

April 25, 1963

We had a lot of fun taking the second grade Brownie Scouts through the Standard office Thursday, showing them how the paper is printed each week. But we make this off hand observation to other newspaper publishers. Don't have your second grade son emptying the office wastebaskets at the same time. There's a certain clash of interests there!

May 9, 1963
The only time the kids were quiet on the return trip Sunday afternoon on the steam engine ride was when the masked "robbers" burst into the car. The kids took one look and sat down — right now — especially the little tykes who were sure it was for real.

Young Bill Shelledy, one of the train "robbers," poked a gun in our four-year-old's stomach and snarled through his mask: "Want to get your name in the paper, kid." Our boy is still talking about it.

Irvin Wilkinson was at the depot to see this last steam engine go out. Irvin saw the first one come into Greybull back before there was a town here. His wife, who came into this area in a wagon with her father, Uncle Johnny Borner and lived in the old cabin in the park, had never seen a train. So they went up on the bluff east of the river, Irvin said, and watched that first one come in.

They were kidding Bill Harbaugh about his bald head and he told them that was "overwork of the brain, fellows." When they laughed and scoffed, he told them: "Did you ever see hair on a woman's chin. Overwork of the jaw, boys, overwork of the jaw."

May 23, 1963
When you live in a small town you take it for granted that a guy named Red Brown can have a White car.

We left a wake of smiling people in our dash last week to catch Frontier's evening flight home from Cheyenne. And we decided that people just naturally laugh at a guy who's late and trying to catch a plane . . . that is we thought that until we got home and found three inches of shirttail trailing out of our suitcases! We thought that sort of thing only happened to the Keystone cops.

May 30, 1963
Vic Larson tells about the old timer around Greybull who was just a born pessimist. He just never felt good. "The best you could ever get him to say was, 'Well, I was worse yesterday.'" Vic says.

Of course you've seen the rodeo street sign at the east end of Greybull Avenue. "Who hasn't?" asks Larry Probst. (Instead of 49er rodeo it's 48er rodeo and the dates are a day late.) "But it's the best mistake we've ever made — I've got phone call after phone call about it and the rodeo," Probst says. The mistake was the sign company's. They'll change it before too many days go by.

June 6, 1963
Guffy Groseclose is hoping to get four mules pulling an old wagon in the parade. But he still has the wagon to finish and the mules to break. "We'll see you in the parade, Guffy," we told him. "I don't know," he replied. "You may have to look awful fast."

The waitress gave our just-out-of kindergarten little girl a menu along with all of the rest of us who could read. After she left, our daughter leaned over and whispered: "She must have thought I was in the first grade."

June 13, 1963
The Dan Straights at Hyattville have finally found out how old the old gray horse Toomy is. He is 39 years old, write the Merritt Mills family of Ethete. They had the horse first (and called it Corkie). When they moved away from Ten Sleep they left it with the Vern Rices. The rest of the story was printed last fall in the Greybull Standard. That same story, incidentally was reprinted in the Western Horseman magazine (June issue) and the Straights say they're getting letters from people throughout the United States.

The western rodeo fever got to Mike Hill who delivers newspapers on Greybull Heights. When his motor scooter broke down he promptly switched to his horse and rode into town every morning to get his papers and made his route up on the Heights horseback. Wednesday morning we saw him on his bike and asked, "How come?" "Too slow on a horse," he said.

June 20, 1963
The Elks magpie contest passed the 6,000 mark last week. Kids are bringing them in by the basketful, George (Conoco) Scott reports. But there's still 4,000 to go to meet the annual 10,000 goal the Elks get every year. That many magpies just proves what every Westerner has known for years. There's more magpies than people out in these parts.

One picture We Wish We Could Have Taken: Tom Hubbard, called away from an Elks doings Friday night to restore power in the north end, and climbing a pole in his tux!

Fourteen-year-old Chuck Snyder put off doing what his mother told him to do Friday . . . and this once everyone was glad he did. When it started to rain his mother asked him to go outside and close the car windows. Chuckie decided to wait until the present television scene was over and then go out. In the meantime a lightning bolt hit just outside in the front yard where he would have been if he'd gone right out.

June 27, 1963
Tom Swift Passes Thru
We can't resist any longer. We give in to the Tom Swifties (those sentences written in the style of the old Tom Swift stories but with the modern twist of the adverb at the end forming a pun) and report this overheard conversation:

"Are we in Greybull yet?" she said buffaloed.
"Oh, yes I see the neon sign now," she said brightly.
"While you're stopped can I check your tires?" he asked airily.
"Yes, I want no trouble," she said flatly.
"Are you going far?" he said distantly.
"Only to Yellowstone to see the geysers," she said gushingly.
"Then you'll go by Cody and through the tunnel," he said darkly.
"How is the road?" she asked smoothly.
"There's some construction," he said gravelly.
"I just came from Mount Rushmore," she said facing him.
"Through Gillette?" he asked sharply.
"Yes, and Sheridan," she said generally.
"How did you like the Big Horns?" he asked sheepishly.
"The flowers were beautiful," she said wildly.
"And I even went rock hunting," she added stonily.
"Be sure to see the Tetons," he said pointedly.
"I want to see the Rockefeller lodge," she said Happily.
"And I'll stop in Jackson, too," she said gamely.
"Goodbye, have fun, see it all and enjoy Wyoming," he said wonderfully.

July 4, 1963

Our second grade son is fast growing up. After a weekend trip through the Park, he came back home and penned this note to a little friend of his. "We saw eight bears, six moose, one elk, two deer, and 18 pretty girls!"

One of the "victims" of the flood at Krueger Brothers place was their new Smith Corona portable typewriter. Gabe Hirsch dug it out of the mud, and it looked hopeless. But he hosed off the grime, greased it thoroughly and faithfully for several days, stopped in at the Standard office for a new typewriter ribbon for it . . . and presented it to the Kruegers. And it works, compliments of Gabe.

July 11, 1963

Cleo McKinney topped Lloyd Groseclose's count on the number of tourists met on the road from Emblem to Dry Creek. The other day Lloyd counted 83 . . . last week Cleo had 109.

July 18, 1963

Chuck Harnden "caught" a Tupperware container full of lettuce when he went fishing a few weeks back. It came floating merrily down the creek. A few days ago, casting out by the Big Rock, he hauled in a half grown mink who had taken his lure! Chuck finally got the mink off and went back looking for the fish.

August 29, 1963

A letter from Frank Norris at the Travel Commission office in Cheyenne had this written at the top: "How do you like this Tom Swifty: 'This is Mr. Norris,' he said Frankly."

We rode up to Shell with tourists and before dropping down the hill into town we were explaining that Herb Smith, who has lived longer in this area than anyone (1886) lived right here in this little town. We had no more than said it than we passed Herb walking by the Shell store. So we could point out: "And there he is." And we didn't even rehearse it, Herb.

Jonathan Davis was driving his John Deere self-propelled combine through Greybull and he was wearing a sun helmet with the International Harvester IH symbol on it. We told him: "Only Jonathan Davis would drive a John Deere outfit and wear an International hat." "Whatdayamean", he exclaimed and turned his hat around the other way. On the back were the gold letters of JOHN DEERE.

September 5, 1963

The man on main street the other day, enroute from the freight to the bars and back to the freight, had developed as Oscar Shoemaker pointed out, "a slight tendency to yaw."

September 12, 1963

The comment on the old orchard on Beaver Creek brought this letter from Frank St. Jermain: "I was there when the trees were about four or five feet. They were planted some 50 years ago. They are all bearing except two or three yellow transparents which couldn't take the droughts and the hard winters of 50 years. I helped Mr. James Davidson build that old log cabin. The orchard is known as the Davidson orchard."

September 19, 1963

At the Buff's opening game at Cody last week we didn't think we were too shook up. But after we developed our pictures we found we had TRIPLE exposed one negative. Not double but triple! Don't ask us how we did it.

September 26, 1963

Jack Williams succumbed to the temptation every do it yourself painter has at one time or another. He took all the remains of every can of paint he could find and mixed them all up. And surprise! Instead of a dull gray or an icky blue, it came out a pretty peach. Drive by his garage sometime and look inside!

Jim Bohl was trying to buy a rain gauge the other day and couldn't find one. "You're asking for the wrong thing in this country," someone told him. "Ask for a dust gauge and they'll know right what you mean."

October 3, 1963
It took the entire neighborhood to consume the big 40-pound watermelon of Mrs. Adamy's pictured in last week's Standard. Even the rind was put to good use – in watermelon pickles.

At the University of Wyoming football game we followed Tom Wilkinson's playing so hard (and thought it was so faultless) that someone leaned over and asked: "Are you yelling for the Wyoming Cowboys or for Tom Wilkinson?"

The Best Deed among the Good Deeds last week in Greybull: Dr. Rogers took his combination camper to the hospital Friday night, picked up football fans Skip Anderson and Tim Paris and the three of them went to the GHS Homecoming football game.

October 10, 1963
"I wish," said my little boy's mother, "that our kids would go rock hunting and never find a rock."

Jack Williams is the latest victim of Gumperson's law which says that if you go to all the trouble to empty all the paint cans around the place to get enough paint for the garage, you'll win four gallons of paint as a prize at Olson Brothers Hardware opening. And Jack did.

"Why did you have to put that awful story in about the Junior High getting beat 35 to 0? said Chris Kelly and some of the Junior High football boys. "Well, I thought the Standard was real kind to you . . . we didn't put in about the five Thermop TDs they called back or it would have been 65 to 0," we told them. "Yeah, we know," Chris said, "but we thought maybe you could put something in like 'the game is still in progress as we go to press.' "

October 17, 1963
Football fans at Gillette got a kick out of the radio announcer when the Buffs tangled with the Camels of Gillette at Gillette Friday. When Rich Douglass made his two long TD runs, the announcer said: "Well, there goes Douglass: he's the straw that broke the Camels' back." So the team tagged Rich old 'Straw Douglass' now.

October 24, 1963
　Saturdays are busy days for Marvin Clause down at the barber shop. Especially these football afternoon Saturdays. He keeps two radios going all during football game time: one of them tuned to Tom Wilkinson and the University of Wyoming football game; the other turned to Son Larry Clause and the Rocky Mountain College game!

November 7, 1963
　Jack Williams is miffed at somebody who sneaked down in his basement and took all the shot out of his shotgun shells. At least that's the way he's explaining all those misses on the first day of bird hunting season.

November 14, 1963
　"We heard you were naughty at the free show Saturday?" Solemn, five-year-old eyes looked at me. "Is that right?" The little head nods. "I heard you shot your cap gun right in the show. Is that right?" The head nods again. "Who in the world were you shooting at?" "I shot at the witch." "You mean the witch in Snow White." Another nod. "But why did you do that?" "Daddy, I don't like witches."

November 21, 1963
　When they were pouring the new concrete floor over at the county jail, George Warfel wondered: "Maybe we ought to stand all the prisoners in it until it dries and then we'll know for sure where they all are."

December 12, 1963
　Frank Casey, watching a TV commercial about those new pull off tabs for beer cans, pointed out: "Now there's two more things to pick up alongside the road instead of one."

December 26, 1963
　One of Art Collingwood's grandkids spent a long time whispering very confidentially to Santa Claus at the Community Hall Saturday morning. When he got finished, Art asked Santa what the little boy had told him he wanted. Santa gave a big chuckle. "He said he couldn't remember."

A picture too dark to get Sunday: "The post office pickup coming back from the depot late that afternoon! Piled up at least four sacks above the cab was one mail sack after another. Sacks were in the seat. On top of the cab. Another one was on top of the hood. Ken Jones had to crane his neck to see out the right side when he made the turn into the post office and on the back, arms stretched out, holding down as many of the wobbly sacks as he could, was Art Peterson. A real pickup load of Christmas! Santa's sleigh couldn't have held any more.

1964

January 2, 1964

Clint Core said it was quite a thrill for "a small town boy" to see the 60,000 people packed into the stadium to see the East-West game. "And then to see them all file out after the game, thousands and thousands of people. Of course, me being a small town boy, I tried to speak to all of them."

January 9, 1964

Unless Jake Piercy has let them melt, he's still got some of those hailstones that fell on his place up Burlington way last summer. Was going to keep them in the freezer to show people how big they were.

"Daddy," said our young son with all the innocence of a four-year-old, "were you bald-headed when you were a little boy like me?"

February 6, 1964

Happiness. . .

Happiness actually comes in small doses.

Happiness is being 10 and getting a valentine from your favorite.

Happiness is getting a flower and garden seed catalog on the coldest day in January.

Happiness is finding a parking place in front of the post office.

Happiness is dialing the radio past all the rock and roll and finding some station who plays a whole hour of Glenn Miller records.

Happiness is reading about some successful personality who didn't amount to anything until he was past 50!

Happiness is guessing who Time magazine's Man of the Year will be before that year-end issue comes out.

Happiness is coming home from a weekend trip and having a flat tire in the garage.

Happiness is finding an old Saturday Evening Post in the attic, about 1948 vintage, and reading once again what a real magazine was like.

Happiness is turning on the switch and presto! The Old Press works!

Happiness is going to the dump and coming back with more stuff than when you left the house.

Happiness is being a Democrat and reading about a Republican being indicted for graft.

Happiness is discovering the bank made an error on your statement.

Happiness is still being able to get into your old Army uniform.

Happiness is the first batch of peas from the garden in the spring and the last batch of sweet corn in the fall

Happiness is bacon frying for breakfast.

Happiness is getting the week's pictures on Friday, the sports written on Saturday and the editorial on Monday.

February 13, 1964

Mrs. Gertrude Shotwell writes about coming to Greybull in 1910 to qualify for a Fifty Year Club: "We arrived on March 17, 1910 St. Patrick's Day and I am sure, had St. Pat been here that very warm day he would have roasted." She also adds that she thinks it would be "interesting to get together and reminisce about the so-called 'good old days', the days of gas lights, backyard pumps, no trees or lawns, almost no sidewalks and the usual Friday afternoon dust storms after we had given the house a thorough cleaning for the weekend."

This week was the second anniversary of the big flood. Did you remember to go down and give the old dike an affectionate pat?

February 20, 1964

Many comments and letters have been received from those people who've been in Greybull for 50 years or more. One of them from the Chester Mercers in Hyattville was interesting. Chester Mercer has been here 50 years and in fact has another record we don't think will be topped. He is still living in the same house he was born in 50 years ago (the Asa Mercer house) on Thanksgiving Day, 1913.

And Fred Conners came in this week to point out that "You had all the kids' names in last week." Fred came here in 1899 when he was 18 years old.

February 27, 1964

There's nothing new under the sun. Look at the Beatle haircut. Old Mo in the Three Stooges has had one for 20 years!

And there's a sign down at Bill Hanson's barbershop in Thermopolis: "Beatle Exterminator Inside."

March 12, 1964

Mrs. Mary Reeg's 100th birthday celebration last week has reminded many of Uncle Sim Cockins of Basin who just missed a similar century celebration by one day! He passed away the night before his 100th birthday in 1937, living 99 years, 364 days.

More names for the 50-year club published last week:
Mrs. Anna Blakesley, 1907
Mrs. Myrtle Good, 1907

Band members have been enjoying a little stray pooch (who has now found a home apparently for he hasn't been back in several days) who regularly came in each morning during practice, went straight to the podium and curled up under Director Chuck Rutherford's feet. There he slept the day through . . . while the band played on!

March 19, 1964
John Boyd and John Loveland's "shamrocks" you noticed them wearing Tuesday didn't come from Ireland. But from the Western Floral and Gift who gave the boys each one (and pinned it on) when they were out in front cleaning up main street's last bit of ice. Bright green they were.

Mrs. Wayne Adamy and son Fred who's in the service have their own code for smuggling food from home past all of Fred's hungry buddies. Mrs. Adamy puts up a big box of cookies and candy and then hides all the real good stuff in a small box wrapped in Greybull Standards Fred hasn't seen yet. Fred grabs for the Standard-wrapped box and leaves all the rest of the goodies for his buddies. Then he goes off with the choice morsels and catches up on his hometown reading at the same time!

My sister who is teaching first grade in Malta, Montana, had the kids make shadow silhouettes of themselves and then had the rest of the class try to guess who each one was. Just for fun she made one of herself, and slipped it in with the rest and had them guess hers, too. One little boy's decision: "George Washington."

March 26, 1964
More members of the 50-year club:
Charlie Howe 1912
Mrs. Gertie Forbes 1906
Mrs. Carl Peavler 1908
Harry Schafer 1912
Mrs. Harry Schafer 1912
John Menzel 1903
Mrs. John Menzel 1906

April 2, 1964
Our boys lost a kite Sunday when the string broke and for a while it looked like it would make Lovell with no trouble. The boys had bigger ideas though, the oldest thought it was going into orbit and the little tyke was sure "it was

going into heaven." But the kite gave up long before either destination and came down over Cy Dorn's place. So the day . . . and the kite . . . were both saved.

April 30, 1964

Chuck Peterson's boy was up on a stepladder and happened to glance down on Papa's shiny dome. "Is baldness hereditary, Dad?" "Sure is," said Chuck. Silence from the boy for a moment and then: "Oh, Oh."

May 21, 1964

We drove down the street last Wednesday just before dark and never saw so many kids playing outside! They were on every block, in the yards, the streets, on the porches. Kids everywhere. Now that's unusual we thought. Something's wrong. It sure was. The high winds that afternoon had knocked out the town's TV!

May 28, 1964

This could happen only in a small town! The post office got a letter from Centralia, Washington addressed to:
The Low Dark Brick Motel
3 blocks down from the Parker Cafe (opposite side of street)
Greybull, Wyoming.
The post office delivered it correctly to the Yellowstone Motel where the woman had left a pillow she wanted returned.

June 4, 1964

That little blockhouse down by the river near the Wyo-Ben plant kept pulling a slow disappearing act and no one could figure out why it was looking different. One day it just went pffft! The people at Wyo-Ben checked it and found it had been carted away, block by block!

June 11, 1964

An old gent was passing an intersection when a large St. Bernard ran by and knocked him down. A moment later, a Volkswagen skidded around the corner and inflicted other damage. A bystander helped him to his feet, and someone asked if the dog hurt him.

"Well," he answered, "the dog didn't hurt so much, but the tin can tied to his tail nearly killed me!"

June 18, 1964

A tourist stopped in at Parker's Cafe early Sunday morning after the rodeo and asked if there was an "early morning Mass here." The waitress, not understanding, replied wearily: "We have an early morning mess here after EVERY rodeo."

If every rodeo goer would make as much of an effort to get to the rodeo as Steven Jennings did, the grandstand would be full every year. The fourth grader rode his bike all the way from Lovell to Greybull Friday afternoon because he didn't want to miss the annual celebration. He started at 2 p.m. and got here around 7:15 p.m. and the trip included one flat tire which a service station man fixed for him in Lovell free after the little boy explained his "trip" His 13-year-old cousin, Max Jennings, accompanied him!

June 25, 1964
They say you always try to save your most valuable possession when fire strikes. Take John Bass for instance, who was among the Greybull boys who got burned out of their trailer in Jackson. John saved a T-BONE steak his mother had just sent down!

July 9, 1964
Here's a switch on the dog-bitten postman. Jess Nance's boxer goes along with Ken Casey on his rounds. What a body guard! Now the boxer takes after all those molesting dogs and Casey walks up to the porch without a toothmark. The Nance's who just moved here from Douglas (he is the new lessee of the Conoco station) say the dog follows postmen but nobody else and has been doing it for some time.

Substitute carrier Leo Hoflund on the other hand could have used the dog last week when he was subbing for Casey. He got bit twice!

And one more dog and postman story: When Leo was just starting at the post office and came home one noon for lunch, carrying his mail sack, his own dog took after him!

July 23, 1964
J. G. Davis of Emblem, after being grounded for 90 years, finally got airborne last Wednesday when he took his first plane ride. He accompanied Morris Avery in the Avery Aviation helicopter on a weed spraying job . . . and "enjoyed every minute of it!"

Our kids took off on a trip with their granddad to visit their cousins for a few days this week and the goodbyes, as always, were varied. The boys were boys and matter of fact both inside and outside; the mommy and the daddy were matter of fact on the outside only; and the tearful little girl, not matter of fact at all inside or outside!

August 6, 1964
Another advantage of living in a small town: Jill Leonard McIntosh got a letter addressed in her maiden name (with a check enclosed for the 1944 Class

reunion) The mailman delivered the letter promptly and the bank cashed the check without question! And it's been 19 years since she was Jill Leonard. Try to do that with the New York Post Office system or the Chase National Bank.

Lessie Sims and Kay Keller went on a vacation together recently, each visiting relatives, Kay in Sacramento and Lessie in Reno. On the way they stopped in Idaho at the Crater of the Moon . . . and sent post cards to everyone, signed: "The Moon Maids."

August 13, 1964
When Earl Reilly sold the Reilly Motel to the Russell Kimbros last month he also "retired" as Greybull's "oldest" resident in years on main street. Earl would have been in business in Greybull 42 years Aug. 1, first in the Elevator and then in the motel.

Bill Harbaugh holds the current record, incidentally, for being the "oldest" businessman in years in the same business.

August 27, 1964
Cullen Fletcher at the Standard station whose forefinger lost a battle with a pulley belt is all bandaged up still. When people ask what happened, Fletcher just says he "wore it out pointing towards the Park."

September 3, 1964
School's started for sure now. By Tuesday Martin Fiene had already counted five baseballs tossed up accidentally on the grade school roof!

"I never thought school would get here," the little boy told us on the playground Monday. "Neither did I," his mother whispered to us.

September 10, 1964
If you noticed fewer kids running around at the football game Friday night than usual give credit to a frantic jackrabbit which led half the youngsters in town an exhausting chase around and around inside the football field. The kids finally wore Brer Rabbit down, turned him loose and spent a quieter than usual rest of the evening getting their wind back. Note to all the rest of the jackrabbit population: Avoid the football field on Friday nights.

September 24, 1964
Many Greybullites who can look back over a successful summer of keeping the lawn green and the flowers blooming and the trees growing, may appreciate the story A.W. Coons once printed in his column in Basin. A favorite of Dr. Chester Harris', the story was about Mike who had spent every extra hour out trying to get his place looking nice. At the end of several summers it was

truly a magnificent sight. Nice trees, big, green lawn, flowers everywhere. One day the preacher came by and remarked: "My what a fine job you and God have done with this place, Mike." "That's true," said Mike, "but you should have seen it when God was trying to go it alone."

October 1, 1964

We've been smiling for weeks at Joe Emrich's want ads to give his cats away. First they were "kittens;" now they've progressed to "half-grown." They're "integrated and variegated." And now this week: "at Joe Emrich's Cattery at Shell."

October 29, 1964

Second grader Liesa Wilcox saw her first football game Friday night and after watching the several huddles, leaned over to her daddy, Oren, and asked: "Daddy, what's the secret?"

November 5, 1964

The Standard story about the bell in the stone schoolhouse being gone and the Fun Valley directors not having a bell for their ski school brought quick results. John Allen on Shell creek saw the story and contacted Director Jim Horn about a bell on the Allen ranch from the old Whaley school house. So now that old bell will toll for students again though this time they'll be on skis.

Young Johnny Collingwood has the answer to all those bowlers who are having a bit of trouble with their game. Last Saturday morning while competing in the Bantam league he told Mrs. Virginia Leavitt that he knew what was wrong. He'd found a ball that could "knock down only nine pins."

November 26, 1964

Morris Avery's rescue of another group of lost hunters adds to a growing list of services and accomplishments by Avery Aviation helicopters. We've often wondered what the area did without them before.

December 3, 1964

Tom Hubbard and Ray Bristow who have always put up the big Christmas trees every year were comparing those real ones they used to put up at the east end of main street with the artificial one at the west end this year. At least with this new one, they point out "we don't have to put the branches back on."

Mrs. Barbara Golden really got the lesson across to our kindergarten boy about keeping his report card clean. Everyone in the family had to wash their hands before they could look at it!

1965

January 14, 1965

This year will mark 58 years since the first store building appeared on what is now Greybull's main street and 56 years since the incorporation of the town in 1909. Keep these in mind when you think about what you can do to help promote this year's historical and rodeo celebration and the Wyoming Centennial.

January 28, 1965

Sign of these January "summer" days: The Russell Bonds were out burning weeds along the ditchbank last Friday.

February 4, 1965

We parents shouldn't complain about rock and roll records the kids buy. They're so economical. When they wear out you can't tell the difference.

They have continual music piped outside at the Antelope Ski area and last Saturday someone slipped on a couple of Beatle records. Skiing and Beatle records. Now that's a combined experience. Yeah, yeah, yeah.

February 11, 1965

Anita Shores, daughter of Mr. and Mrs. Forrest Shores now in Miles City, has gone all the way through school (she's a senior now) without ever missing a day – until last week! The measles laid her low for a week.

February 18, 1965

When the kids at school had their dental checkups the other day, Sean Kelly came home from kindergarten terribly worried. He told his mother he was afraid he was going to have to go to the dentist!

Jack Stockwell has a good story about a Cody couple who run a horse ranch outside of town. Jack was up hunting in the Cody country and ran out of feed for his horses. The town of Cody was bare of rolled oats, so Jack started down the farm roads, asking at each place. He came to this one ranch, knocked on the door and asked the lady who answered if she had any oats to sell. "Nope," she said firmly. "Gosh that's too bad," Jack said "Sure got some hungry horses up in the hunting camp." The lady turned and hollered back over her shoulder, "It's for some hungry horses, dear." Jack got his oats!

February 25, 1965
Jake Marcus is going to have tulips blooming at the Gottlieb Marcus place yet. Mrs. Marcus said she thought the tulips would bloom if you could get them into the ground now so they could freeze. So Jake got them planted this past week. Even the frozen ground didn't stop him. He just got out his electric drill and drilled the holes in the ground!

March 4, 1965
Floyd Farr gets along okay with the Number "13." His Sweetheart bread truck license is 1313. He's salesman number 13. And he's been with the company 13 years.

March 25, 1965
One thing for the snow — it covered up all the leaves, the debris, and the old weeds, the remnants of three months of winter that we were supposed to clean up during the last good Sunday. Now, out of sight, out of wife's mind.

Our five-year-old asked us and we'll ask you: Can witches fly without their brooms?

April 15, 1965
Ted Anderson Jr. holed out a Par Four hole at Worland on the second shot the other day. The ball landed on the green and disappeared. "I think it went in," Ted told golfing partner Clint Core. They walked up to the green and Clint walked over to look in the hole. "No ball in here," he deadpanned. I've really overshot it then, Ted thought. But just to be sure he went over for a look too. Sure enough, there was the ball — right in the cup!

April 22, 1965
The kids are getting pretty sharp at this Easter egg hunting at the city park. One little girl apparently figured that if the Greybull Standard photographer stopped alongside a pile of leaves he was waiting to get a picture of someone finding some eggs there. (She was right) So she just followed right along with us. Every time we'd stop so would she! And the leaves all around us would just fly.

Take it from one who's had a sneak preview of what the Can Can girls very excellent routine looks like — it's going to wow 'em all over! Without a doubt, it will be the big hit of the celebration and wherever else it goes.

May 6, 1965
If you think the mistakes were bad that got into the paper last week, you should have seen the ones that didn't get in! Like the one we caught about the "First Notional Bank." And then the cap "S" didn't fall all through the Shell news and that, my friend, is a real — hell of a mess!

June 3, 1965

A first-born son who reaches 10 ages by just one more year. But his father suddenly feels as if he just added all 10 more!

June 17, 1965

"Now there's a horse a cowboy should have," said Rodeo Announcer Kenneth Adkins Friday night as he pointed out one of the roping horses. "You can rope on him, dog on him, team rope on him, girl on him . . ."

Lloyd Groseclose and Harry Gillett "swept up" the tail end of this year's parade too, a job they've done voluntarily for years. It wouldn't be a 49er parade without them.

July 1, 1965

If you're a human and get lost, always go downstream. If you're a little dog belonging to a postman named Chuck Peterson, go to the nearest post office! The little Peterson dog rode over to Basin with Mrs. Peterson to get a driver's license at the highway shop a few days ago. But he jumped out to sleep awhile under the shade trees there and the Petersons went off and forgot him. They didn't miss him until late that night. But the next morning Town Treasurer C. H. Walton called to say a dog with his dog tag number was at the Basin post office. And sure enough, he was. He'd headed for the one familiar sight and smell in a strange town, howled mournfully all night and part of the morning until some of the Basin post office crew went out and looked at the dog's tag, called the Town of Greybull and the Peterson "family" was reunited again!

Life is what happens while you're making other plans.

July 15, 1965

When Bonnie Bluejacket went down to see the Girl Scout special train Tuesday afternoon at the depot she wound up with a big sack full of letters and post cards the girls asked her to mail for them. They wanted them postmarked "Greybull, Wyoming" they told her.

July 22, 1965

When Neal Thorn and Orvie Olson took a trip down to Old Mexico, Neal got a shoe shine. He asked the boy before he started how much it would be? One peso, the boy replied. When he got done, though, the boy held up two fingers. "Two," said Neal, "I thought it was one." The boy pointed first to one shoe, then to the other. One peso – one shoe!

July 29, 1965

Griff St. Jermain, 93-year-old timer of Greybull, says you'll notice a change in him now. He didn't want to spruce up until leap year was over so as not "to give the girls an unfair chance."

In the middle of the press run of orange ink for those Can Can Orange Garter Days, our old press "threw a rod" and quit for a couple of hours of repairs. Which just goes to show you even an old piece of a machinery can go to pieces over those high kicking Can Can girls.

August 26, 1965
A discourteous bunch of tourists were giving Park Custodian John Loveland a bad time the other day. They kept asking for information and then making sarcastic remarks about it after he gave it. Whatever John said they had some smart retort to make. Finally one of the men asked: "By the way, what do the bears eat in Yellowstone Park?" John leaned over confidentially and whispered: "Tourists."

September 2, 1965
Andy Schmidt missed the intrasquad game Friday night. Said he had "a grand opening in my throat . . . a tonsillectomy."

September 23, 1965
One farmer who decided to quit and do something else, offered this explanation: "Too many 'ups' for me. First you have to wake up, then you have to get up. Then you have to wash up, feed up and hitch up. Next you have to catch up and keep up. When you check up, you find you've barely enough to pay up. That's when I gave up." He could have added in this past week that he had to "dry up," too, around here!

If only we had a camera to follow everybody. Chuck Peterson was making his rounds in the middle of the snowy mess Thursday morning. As he walked along, head down, sorting mail for the next stop, he walked into one of the open pits the gas company was digging! He almost disappeared! "Boy did old Chuck come awake in a hurry," he says.

October 7, 1965
The Big G store picked the perfect day for their first day of business – Saturday morning after the Greybull-Powell Junior High game. The place was jammed from one end to the other with kids!

October 14, 1965
A couple of mothers of junior high football players who hear a lot of talk about football at home were at the recent Greybull-Powell junior high game. Looking out at the mass of running kids, the plays and the formations, one of them remarked: "It doesn't look at all like the salt and pepper shakers and knives and forks on the kitchen table."

It'll be two cakes and one birthday at the Jim Crawford house. Week old Lee James was born Oct. 6 — on the same day his sister, Judy, was born a year ago!

October 21, 1965

Red Michaelis had a sign on his barbershop: "Out to Lunch. Back Tuesday." Which in hunting season jargon means "I've gone to get my elk." Reminds us of the sign Reuben Reifschneider put on his shop door in 1959: "Closed for Hunting Season so my customers can go hunting."

November 11, 1965

You pheasant hunters trying for the long feather record might be interested in knowing the Nebraska record is 30 5/8 inches held by a Norfolk man who brought down the prize rooster in 1962.

The mayor of Douglas tells this story when his town was recently flooded with hunters. A little old lady tourist who was passing through came in to tell him what a nice town Douglas was, and how impressed she was with Wyoming and Douglas. And she added: "This is also the only place I have ever been to that they make the drunks wear red shirts!"

November 18, 1965

Jimmy Porter (visiting at our house over the weekend) said he'd heard that pretty soon they're going to add a daddy doll to join Barbie and Midge and all the rest, a baldheaded Daddy at that, which sent all the Kennedy kids (who have such a daddy) into gales of appreciative laughter.

November 25, 1965

Radio announcers will have a time keeping the Smiths straight on Greybull's basketball team. There's Marcel Smith, Paul Smith, Robert Smith and coach Don Smith!

December 16, 1965

Mandy Mohr claims the Christmas tree out in front of the motel is getting middle-age — a lot of spread around the middle which takes an average of one extra string of lights every year.

December 23, 1965

This wrestling is tough on the spectators. As John Spargur remarked after Saturday's match with the Worland "B" squad, each wrestler has just one match "and the spectators have to wrestle all 12!"

1966

January 20, 1966

We've been having a tough time finding some Ben Franklin's Poor Richard sayings which we haven't used before during these past eight or nine years at the top of this column. Our little book of them is about used up unless we start on the repeats. But our little first grader told us we shouldn't have to worry about it. "You can always get another one of those books at the Benjamin Franklin store," he told us.

Frank Dunning who is recuperating from surgery at SBHC hospital heard a baby crying late at night and was sure he recognized the cry. He got up and went down the hall to see. Sure enough, it was his one-year-old grandson, Stevie Dunning, who'd been brought in during the night.

February 24, 1966

In a railroad town I hesitate to repeat this but Doc Chambers used to call the local passenger, the C. F. and B. M. (Cowley, Frannie and Back Maybe.)

Not everyone plays basketball this time of year. Our first grader announced at the dinner table: "I'm not going to play Batman anymore. I skinned both of my hands today." This learning to fly does take time.

March 10, 1966

To give you some idea of the traffic on the road between Greybull and Basin, the average 24-hour volume for January was 1,595 cars. This was the HIGHEST number of cars on any stretch of road in the state except those around Casper and Cheyenne and two places on Highway 30.

Greybull and Lovell athletes have dominated the Wilford Mower trophy presentation with Don Black's recent honor. Through the years the award has gone to three Greybull athletes, Jim Schuyler, Tom Wilkinson, and Don Anderson; two from Lovell, Black and Roy Despain; and to Mark Higdon of Lander and Everett Befus of Riverton. That's five out of seven for these two Class "A" schools.

Thoughts from a beginning middle-aged skier — You get awful tired of having your fifth grader son ski up behind you all the time asking anxiously, "Are you all right, Dad?"

March 24, 1966

The ice in the Big Horn river went out so quietly we forgot to mention it last week. On March 10th. Right on its annual schedule. Through 50 years of Greybull Standards you can find most of them record the ice going out of the Big Horn between Mar. 10 and 15.

March 31, 1966

When Jonathan Davis flew back to Washington on business for the Agrarian canal, he didn't pay much attention to the guy across the aisle from him who got on at Milwaukee. But about an hour later Jonathan glanced over, did a double take and looked again. The man reached out his hand. "Yep, I'm who you think I am" and Jonathan and Richard Nixon shook hands across the aisle.

April 7, 1966

Why Parents Get Gray Department: "I got 100 on my tests at school," shouted our third grader girl home from school yesterday, ". . . a 60 and a 40!"

When Ken Jones was digging up some sod around the post office, Dick Burkhart came by and asked: "What are you going to do with that sod . . . buster?"

April 28, 1966

When some tourist asked John Paris at DeLane's Cafe how come the eggs were high priced out here, John deadpanned that it was because they were mountain grown.

May 19, 1966

The Otto school kids visited the newspaper office last Thursday and unknowingly were among the last of our readers to see our old letterpress way of printing Greybull Standards. We owe them another tour one of these days to see the new way.

Is the 1966 graduating class motto any indication of the Vietnam times? It reads: "It is fatal to enter any war without the will to win."

May 26, 1966

One of the real stories behind William Harrison's rescue after he had to land his plane in the Dubois country was Sheepherder Joe Walsh's long walk out to tell people the Sheridan man was safe. Walsh had walked some 15 miles rock hunting that day. When Harrison came to his sheep wagon, Walsh went on to Dubois for help, another walk of 25 miles at night in the snow and mud. Then shunning offers for a ride, he turned around and had walked another 10 miles back before finally giving in to riding the rest of the way. Incidentally, one of those who finally talked him into riding on home was Greybull's Dave Mobley who's stationed over there with the Game and Fish commission.

June 9, 1966
One of the disadvantages of being an amateur gardener living on Greybull Heights is that you have to drive by Jesse Hein's flowers and vegetables every day.

June 23, 1966
Our youngest out-of-town subscriber is 12-year-old Debbie Kvale who is out in California. She told her folks to send her the paper – she didn't want to miss what was going on back home!

August 4, 1966
The water's short enough around the area that more than one irrigator knows what Irv Davis of Shell means when he says he's been "irrigating in my bedroom slippers." No boots needed!

The Silver Spur is back at the Silver Spur! Missing since last Christmas, the pure silver spur which the Ray DeSombers kept in their bar, has been to California and back. Someone lifted the spur during the holidays; someone else told the DeSombers they knew who had it and they'd get it back. That was months ago, but sure enough this week, the spur was brought back. Now it's bolted back down in place again.

August 11, 1966
The son of the man who built the Alamo Hotel stopped through town last Wednesday. He was John D. Schaffer of Chino, Calif., son of Melville Roy Schaffer who died in 1962. In his later life, the elder Schaffer talked much of the old days in Greybull, the son said, so he decided to stop by Greybull and see the hotel. "It looks just like the pictures Dad had of it," he said.

Talk about selling refrigerators to the eskimos . . . Cub Collingwood and Jess Black sold a trailer house to a tourist Monday afternoon! The guy was tired of camping and wanted something more comfortable. So now he's driving one of the Collingwood Motors trailerhouses through Yellowstone Park!

September 8, 1966
Note found under a windshield wiper: "I have just smashed into your car. The people who saw the accident are watching me. They think I am writing down my name and address. They are wrong."

Guffy Groseclose took his coon dog hunting and the dog got two skunks and one porcupine . . . but no coons!

September 22, 1966
Overheard a tourist telling Red McIntosh (after coming down Shell canyon) "I've felt safer on that mountain road than I have in Times Square."

Ted Anderson Jr. was guiding in the Thoroughfare country and was successfully calling in a bull elk for his hunter with a bugle call. The bull would bugle and then Ted would bugle. They could hear the elk rattle his horns and pretty soon he stepped into a clearing. Ted called him again, the bull answered and made straight for them. The hunter, a man from California, exclaimed as the bull came closer: "I hope I don't have to separate you two!"

October 13, 1966
I thoroughly enjoy Lusk Editor Jim Griffith's column and quite shamelessly quote from it regularly. His latest remark: "When I play golf I usually play in the low 70's. If it gets any colder than that I quit!"

The three-year-old son of Mr. and Mrs. Guy Hibbert after listening to a family discussion of political affairs, announced to a newcomer on the scene, "My daddy is a demacrack and my grandmother a repelican."

October 20, 1966
When Junior High Coach Brad Moon came up short a tackle (three on the sick list) Seventh Grader Randy Preston, a center, went home and learned all the tackle plays. The next day he told Coach Moon that he could fill in at tackle if he needed him. And that's where he played Saturday morning against Powell. "Did a good job, too," Coach Moon reports.

November 3, 1966
A Nebraska editor's wife heard a fearsome noise in her washing machine and called the serviceman. He came when she was out and left this note: "Do not wash nails. Use them dirty."

Chuck Peterson (and the rest of the post office crew) who handle hundreds of Greybull Standards every Thursday, didn't appreciate the big black bear on the cover of last week's front page. Such a bear takes a lot of ink which finds its way to the postal clerk's hands, face, clothes, etc. "Next time you take a picture of a bear," Chuck advised us, "make it a polar bear."

December 8, 1966
You see all types up skiing but the coldest soul Sunday was a dachshund dog. He couldn't keep his long tummy off the ground! And he waddled around all day with snow all over his underside!

You always hear talk about the world needing a new mousetrap. Don't believe it. Paul Kinnaird sells one at the Co-op station that is the darndest mice catcher you'll ever see. Doesn't even take any bait. Our kids put it down among the rolled oats and cracked corn sacks and got 14 mice in two days!

December 15, 1966
"What do you think your sister would like for Christmas?" the mother asked the little boy. He thought for a moment. Then he brightened. "How about a truck?" he asked.

Watching Santa Claus come downtown a couple of weeks ago made it a big night for little Jody Meeker and his parents, Mr. and Mrs. Bob Meeker. But after watching Santa around talking to the kids, Jody was obviously disappointed. Finally he asked: "But Mommy, when's he going to dash!"

In the Boy's Home Ec class there are four members of the wrestling squad, seven members of last season's football squad and two members of the basketball squad!

December 22, 1966
When the sacked candy failed to arrive for last Saturday's visit by Santa Claus, Ray Bristow got candy and sacks and took them home to his family and those good citizens stayed up late sacking all the candy themselves.

A homemade sign in a little cafe in Cheyenne we saw over the weekend: "Our credit manager is Helen Hunt. If you want credit, go to Helen Hunt for it."

December 29, 1966
A Lander cowboy came in the dress shop to buy his wife a pair of hose. He didn't know the size, but he told the clerk "she wears 33 inch chaps."

1967

January 19, 1967

One of Greybull's teachers played some long haired music for some of the grade school music classes and then asked them to draw a picture of what they had heard on the records. But that classical stuff didn't reach one sixth grader. He drew out his picture and labeled it "City Dump."

February 9, 1967

Thermop holds the Big Horn Basin distinction of the town producing the most coaches. Bill Bush, Jack King, Joe McKethen, Tritz Jurovich, all who coached at Lander one time or another; Moe Radovich at Sheridan college; Phil Crouch, assistant Greybull coach, to name some of the list.

February 23, 1967

The Elks hall is only a couple of weeks old but it's already a popular spot. In the last five days about 250 farmers and ranchers attended the Farm and Ranch Day there; the Lions had a dance that night; and Monday nearly 200 were at the Boy Scout Award dinner.

March 9, 1967

There's quite a local tale about March 5 birthdays. Kenneth Bryant, 13, and Ricky Bryant, 10, sons of Mr. and Mrs. Jim Bryant, both have birthdays on the SAME DAY, March 5. That's enough of a coincidence. But it's even more so when you figure that the two girls of the Harry Barnetts, Stacy, 4, and Jama Leigh, 11, were also born on the same day and IT WAS MARCH 5 TOO!

March 23, 1967

His mother and I are embarrassed about this but our Bob insists on wearing his new T-shirt with the "S" (for small) tag still on the front. He says it stands for "Super."

April 6, 1967

Russell Bond pointed out Wednesday that the date could be written: 4-5-67. He also sat down and figured out that this sequence wouldn't happen again for 11 years, one month and one day.

Those quintuplet lambs of Martin Howe's are still "doing fine," the Howes report. All five as healthy as can be.

April 20, 1967
    Did you know that in the old days of Greybull, the town called itself: "The Biggest Little Town in Wyoming," the same slogan that Frannie uses now.

The Fun Valley Board of directors were supposed to have a meeting Sunday (during the private opening of the area for the ski patrol, directors, personnel. etc. who worked on Antelope Butte last season). But there was too much steak and good snow (nearly a foot of new powder) and they never did get around to holding a meeting!

April 27, 1967
    When Kris LeDuc ran the two mile against Lovell a week or so ago it was his first attempt at that distance. He did a creditable job of reaching third place about halfway around, too far behind to catch first and second place runners, but far ahead of the rest of the field. So he stopped and walked awhile. When fourth and fifth place runners started to catch up, Kris would go back to jogging! And he still finished in third place.

Happiness is having the sun shine and the day turn off nice on your eight-year-old son's birthday party . . . just when you thought everyone was going to have to stay inside!

May 4, 1967
    "Let me write on your cast," Art Sylvester told our girl with the broken arm. After several minutes of scribbling, he said "There, that will make it work better." Right at the elbow, Carpenter Art had drawn a perfect hinge!

June 1, 1967
    Our youngest takes longer to tell a story than anyone I've ever known. We've learned at our house never to ask him "what the show was about." An hour later, he'll still be going. He's the only storyteller I know where the synopsis is longer than the movie.

June 8, 1967
    The best horse race of the season won't be re-staged during the Days of '49 although if the 49er board wanted an extra attraction that would be it. Marvin Hankins and Dick Reed raced their quarter horses on the airport straightway recently. The bet: $25. The winner: Reed's horse by a length and a half.

June 15, 1967
    Rodeo aftermath – more people were interested in Fifth Grader Curt Kinghorn's roping at the rodeo Saturday and Sunday than in all the rest of the events. Curt's been hazing the steers and calves back to catch pen for several rodeos now. This year he added a rope of his own which he swung with gusto

– and accuracy. He used a breakaway so when he set his horse the loop released; he didn't have to get off his horse and the calf never had to stop. Consensus of the crowd: Give Curt a few more years and he'll give all the old hands a run for their roping money.

There's always a lot of people who help with the rodeo whom the crowd never sees. Helping with the stock and the roping chutes this year were Charles Blakesley, Leonard Good, Ron Dalin, J. D. Perkins, Tom Rodman, Walter Lynam and Frank Porter.

Our thanks to John Good, Joe Molaskey, Steve Bristow, Kevin Probst and Jeff Tolman for helping at the kids races, and to Dick Burkhart for his usual able assistance.

Oscar Shoemaker and Guffy Groseclose both teamed up to give the best announced parade and Saturday morning activities for a long time.

June 22, 1967
It wasn't exactly the Jim Crawfords week. Jim suffered three broken ribs over the weekend. Tuesday night at the first night rodeo Mary Crawford suffered a bruised leg when her barrel racing horse hit a gate pole.

June 29, 1967
Out of the 1965 Greybull High School graduating class, 32 boys are now in the armed forces.

August 3, 1967
A month ago Chuck Williamson at U-Smile, as he was trying to lock up, had a tourist come in for a can of beans. The tourist had forgotten his money so Chuck just gave him the beans. This week he received a letter from Muncie, Ind. which read: "Think back and you'll remember a traveler, who ran into your store as you were trying to get away on July 1. You were kind to give me a can of beans for chili when I had no change and you were late. I got your name from the Standard Station man and am now sending you a quarter to pay for the beans. Thanks again for your kindness. It is people like you who make people remember certain towns they passed through on their travels. Signed, M. Julian."

August 17, 1967
Does anyone watch the road anymore? The gang at Collingwood Motors is sure they don't. Wednesday after lunch, they took an old beat up billfold that had been around the place, stuck a dollar bill in it and laid it carefully out in the middle of the highway in front of the garage. But no one was tempted. About 400 cars whizzed by without ever stopping . . . and by 3:30 presstime they were still running over it . . . and over it . . . and over it.

August 24, 1967

A Worland guy – some good Wyoming driver with his eyes on the road – spotted the planted wallet in front of Collingwood Motors last Wednesday evening. He whipped around the block, stopped to pick up the wallet and then went on down the road south.

Danny Michaelis went swimming in Ewen's reservoir last month and forgot to take off his glasses, and one pair of glasses went to the bottom! But a couple of weeks later, the Ewens drained down the Reservoir and Mrs. Wayne Adamy found the glasses in the mud. They had Danny's name on the frame and the boy and the glasses were soon reunited.

August 31, 1967

The cooks at the GHS football camp worked harder than the boys. Mrs. Esther Hansen said, "We couldn't keep them filled up. All the boys gained weight and I lost four pounds."

You can tell most of the kids who went to the camp by their sunburns ... on the backs of their legs between where their football pants ended and the tops of their shoes started.

September 14, 1967

Clyde Douglass, Tom Foe and John Clark all made New York City together last week. And New York probably won't be the same again.

Isn't it too bad that the people best qualified to run a newspaper are engaged in other activities?

Police Chief Mandy Mohr's dog net may never be the same again. He had to use it to capture a porcupine who wandered down North Sixth street about 6 in the morning recently. Bob Severy saw it while driving down North Sixth. He drove back to tell the police about it. Mandy caught up with it in back of Lee's Grocery, netted it and gave Mr. Porcupine walking papers out of town.

When the John Haleys were showing their champion Jerseys at the Billings fair, about six beatniks came up to the stalls. They looked over a pen of calves John had fixed up and then at the big Jersey bull alongside. One of them finally pointed to the bull and asked John: "Is that mamma of dese calves?" "No," John replied, "it's the poppa, but I'll be glad to explain it all to you if you stick around a minute." The beatnik fled.

September 21, 1967

Isn't it great to get old! Those two senior candidates for Homecoming Queen were FIRST GRADERS when this photographer took his first Greybull Standard Homecoming queen picture.

September 28, 1967

Randy Preston, eighth grader veteran on the Junior High team, showed up to take the bus to the Worland game Saturday wearing a cast on one arm. But before the horrified gazes of team and coaches, he took it off. It was just a fake! No wonder coaches get gray.

And there's another good football story about Hector Good. Two Fridays back he was mowing the lawn before going to the Douglas game. He shut off the motor for a minute and could hear them playing the Star Spangled Banner on the football field. He ran in the house, dressed, tore up to the football field . . . and nobody was there yet. It was only quarter to seven. The band had just come up early to practice.

October 19, 1967

Third grade talk at the school lunch room: Young John Anderson from Shell says sauerkraut "tastes like silage."

October 26, 1967

Some out-of-state hunter went through Greybull with his horse all loaded up. But he wasn't taking any chances. Right on the side of the horse was painted: "H O R S E."

November 30, 1967

The Christmas tree on main street was hauled down from above the Ranger Station by Ray Bristow, Howard Norskog and Ed Rech. It will be decorated as soon as the lights arrive.

We wondered last year how many bulbs the Mandy Mohrs had on their Christmas tree in the front. Mandy counted them this year. There are 228.

December 7, 1967

Third grader Sean Kelly was wondering the other day: "When you slam your finger in the door, I wonder what your finger looks like on the other side."

December 28, 1967

School vacations aren't particularly made for parents. (Do you parents have that horrible feeling that this is the way your kids may act at school too?) As our littlest one told me: "Dad, we just like to fussterate you."

February 1, 1968

The Greybull first grader said he had gone ice fishing over the weekend. "What kind of fish did you catch," asked the teacher.

"Ice fish," he replied.

February 15, 1968

When we called for the temperatures at Marathon Pipeline, Matt Pavlus reported last Saturday's temperature as a high of 36, a low of 6 "and the fish were biting." (He caught 10 on flies in Tensleep Creek!)

February 22, 1968

One of ours got his math paper back the other day. He got a "B" on his part of it. We got a "D" on ours.

They rodeoed Sunday at the Greybull arena. Had to shovel a four-foot drift away from in front of the bucking chutes, but they could rodeo in February anyway.

April 4, 1968

One of the joys of small town living. Richard Baugh called his mother, Mrs. Art Baugh and told her to make an appointment with Red Michaelis for 10 a.m. Saturday. He was coming home and wanted one of Red's haircuts! Baugh was in Alaska at the time!

April 25, 1968

WO Jerold S. Ewen had a short Easter Sunday. He left Travis AFB at 10 p.m. Saturday, Apr. 13 and arrived at Qui Nham, Vietnam on Monday, Apr. 15. It was an 18-hour trip including stops in Hawaii and Philippines. But with the time zones, etc., his Easter Day was only THREE HOURS LONG!

May 2, 1968

The new museum won't lack for Art. There's Art Sylvester who's doing the building of the new display cases. There's Art Smith who is doing the electrical work. And Art Baugh who is doing the painting.

May 16, 1968

Bud Ridenour, Greybull's band instructor, showed up at the concert the other night with flowers in each lapel. He explained to the crowd that he'd already had a boutonniere and then someone met him at the door with a rose so he put that on, too. He said he was explaining all this "so you people won't think I'm a hippie."

May 30, 1968

Paul Peterson never knows what his mailbox at the Chamber of Commerce office will bring. Each day is Surprise Day. Once he had a request from a woman who was looking for a monkey. The other day he had to go out to a Greybull River sandbar and dig up some sand for a guy back in New Jersey with a sand collection. The guy wrote that it had arrived okay so now back in Jersey city there's a spot that will be "forever Greybull."

June 27, 1968

The kids in the Little League think it's hilarious when Manager John Good calls roll, and hollers for "Jack" (son of Mr. and Mrs. Dale Wright). Jack always answers "Right."

July 4, 1968

Went through the old Basin grade school the other day and there were many memories among the halls, even though Russell Holtz is in the process of tearing the old building down. That one fountain near the first grade room seemed awfully small. I remember it as being much, much taller than that.

HOW TO MAKE A MILLION DOLLARS. Find something no one else is doing. Sell it. Work hard. A couple of Greybull would-be millionaires are following this formula. Sean Kelly and Jack Wright, both 9. They've set up a concession this summer to wash people's dogs for them!

July 18, 1968

A tourist knocked on Dr. A.S. Rogers' door the other day. She asked if she could use the telephone. She wanted to call a doctor.

July 25, 1968

Our house has been peculiarly quiet the past few days since our fourth grader son had his tonsils out. Don't know where all the noise has gone! But while he could still talk he confided that he hoped Dr. Rogers would save his tonsils for him. (Is there a Tonsil Good Fairy?)

One of the most prevalent sights on most farms anymore are the three barrels for barrel racing practice. It used to be the basketball hoop over the barn door.

August 1, 1968

When sixth grader David Haller was in the hospital several days ago he put one of those creepy things on the end of his bed stead, just where the nurse would put her hand when she came in. Y-e-o-w!

August 8, 1968
There was more than just a good buy in the cash register Clarence Walton purchased during the Fletcher's Standard closeout sale. Some sentimental reasons were involved too. Walton had bought that same McCaskey register in 1932 or 1933 when he had the station! The Town of Greybull will use it now in the Town office.

August 15, 1968
Football season starting reminds us that it's the end of an era for Skip and Edna Schuyler and the Greybull schools. This will be the first school year since 1955 that either Jim or Don or Tom wasn't playing some kind of Greybull school athletics. All three boys are now in the service.

August 22, 1968
No one believes us when we tell them we saw that moose near Dry Creek on the Cody road last week. And one of the tourists who stopped to look at him said they'd driven all through the Park and hadn't seen one. When we told him he could drive for a million more miles and never see a moose on Dry Creek in Wyoming, he looked very skeptical as if we were pulling his leg. So he didn't believe us either. You can't win, either way.

September 5, 1968
A big laugh amid this year of politics is the action by the University of Colorado students to rename that school's student union, Packer Hall, after Alfred E. Packer who was convicted of cannibalism. In fact, the old boy ate five of the seven Democrats in the county!

September 26, 1968
Pat Good of Greybull Heights who is the secretary at the Basin High School has two small flags on her car's radio antenna. One reads: Go Bobcats. The other says: Go Buffs.

Even the cheerleaders didn't know the numbers of Junior High kids when they played Meeteetse Saturday morning. When one of them got the wind knocked out of him (it was Stanley Horton, No. 21) the girls sent the manager out on the field to see who it was before they could holler: "Yea Stanley, Yea Horton . . ."

October 3, 1968
The Chamber of Commerce has sent five pounds of John Haley's Wyoming honey to Vince Lombardi and the Green Bay Packers. Paul Peterson

noticed in Look magazine the Packers use honey on their training table for "quick energy." And it might also change their luck!

Peaches are getting to be another good Wyoming product. John Schmer on the Greybull River route got about 20 peaches this year. Last year was a better Wyoming peach year, though. He got three fourths of a bushel then.

October 17, 1968
That article about the Chamber of Commerce sending some of John Haley's honey to the Green Bay Packers wiped out the Haley honey supply. Many people around the Greybull area must have figured: "If it's good enough for the Packers, it's good enough for me." And they bought all the rest of this year's crop!

November 7, 1968
A couple of weeks ago we carried a story about Seaman Mike Scott and his ship putting in to dry dock at "Yakasuki" which is what "Yokosuka" sort of sounds like to those of us not so familiar with it. Jim Whipps noticed the item, wrote back and asked: Was this supposed to be Yokosuka maybe? And then adds the postscript: "Shades of Heroheetoe."

Another Navy man, Wayne Harnden, was walking down the streets of Seattle with a Greybull Standard rolled up and sticking out of his back pocket. Walking behind him a few steps was Reginald Johnson, who graduated around 1957 from GHS. He recognized the Greybull Standard, hurried up to see who was a Greybull Standard reader and he and Wayne recognized each other. They'd been in school together.

A rancher in the office the other day to buy No Trespassing signs said the trespassing violations were getting worse. People's disregard for the property of others reminded him of the story about the elderly Ten Sleep man who had let people fish and hunt on his place for years. He came home one day to find a bonfire going about 10 feet from his granary. The granary had about 2,000 bushels of grain in it. It made him mad enough to go down to the creek and tell the fishermen to leave. The more he thought about it, though, the madder he got. So he drove to Worland to the guy's house and started a bonfire on his front lawn.

November 14, 1968
Three of Avery Aviation's B-25's have been sold on the West Coast to be used in a movie about those World War II vintage planes. The movie is reported to be "Catch-22" so when it comes around at least three of the planes will have spent part of their life in Greybull, Wyoming.

December 5, 1968

Postmaster Ted Anderson, Assistant Postmaster Bill Wilkinson and Clerks Pat Tomlinson and John Haley have a total of 110 years at the post office between them. (Anderson 28, Wilkinson 38, Tomlinson 23, Haley 21.)

December 19, 1968

By Betty Kennedy

With apologies to Poor Richard whose immortal sayings will have to be skipped this week since I can't find the book . . . and Poor Bruce who is taking the week "off" with the flu.

Illness, of course, does come to every family. But some way or other in a newspaper family, the mere thought of illness on WEDNESDAY brings with it visions of downright disaster.

Anyone who's made it through this flu knows what disaster is, though. Knowing the old flu remedies of 7-Up, chicken noodle soup and blackberry brandy isn't enough. We need home cures now for dry cough and runny noses and sheer panic.

Someone pointed out to us that Eighth Grader Jim Reilly even suffered some absenteeism this week – the third time in nine years he's missed school.

One bright spot in the week: the Hector Goods and the John Goods both had babies Monday at SBHC hospital. Fathers are usually ignored at this time. But this was remarkable. These fathers are cousins, and both are managers of Little League teams.

And with scissors and paste-pot, we note: Some modern girls can dish it out, but they can't cook it.

Which reminds me of what one wag said when he heard Bruce was sick (two of the Kennedy kids have also been home sick): "Don't ask me to eat YOUR cooking."

December 26, 1968

It isn't necessarily so "great" to be back in the harness again this week after being home with diseases, but you can't stay away from an editor's chair too long and still be indispensable. The staff and the wife of the publisher didn't appear to miss anyone too much in last week's paper. As Dr. Rogers pointed out: "You'd better get back while you still have a job."

1969

January 30, 1969

Heard on the radio the other night that if you wrap a piece of string around your head three times, then cut the ends so they just meet, that will be your exact height! I guess if it goes around more than three times then you're obviously a fathead.

February 20, 1969

I haven't paid much attention to whether the drive up telephone by the Reilly K-bar motel gets much use. But for one local boy it's an okay deal. Saw him stretched out in the front seat of his car, with the heater going (and the radio, too, probably) and the phone trailed in through the window. Calling his girl with all the comforts of home. And best of all, utter privacy.

February 27, 1969

One of the most memorable moments of the Junior High tournament: When a Lovell player came over to try to take the ball away from Blaine Welling, the Basin eighth grader easily passed it off to someone else, then turned around and stuck out his tongue at his astonished opponent!

Our youngest got one of those traps that catch 'em alive. We went down to the river with him Sunday to see how he made out and while we were gone, a newspaper friend from another town called. He asked our daughter where her dad was. "Down at the river checking the traps," she told him. "By golly, I didn't know the newspaper business was that bad yet," he exclaimed.

March 13, 1969

Reuben Reifschneider has the distinction of having watched both 300 games at the Big Horn Lanes. He was there when Mel Green rolled his five or six years ago and last Wednesday watched while John Preis did it.

Incidentally, Preis took an awful ribbing from the bowling alley crowd when he bowled his next game at the lanes. It was a 148!

And it was Wayne Wright who kept score for Preis.

April 3, 1969

When the picture of the new calf on the front page of the Standard came out a couple of weeks ago, Sylva Smith went through all the papers the high school gets and carefully penciled in her dad's brand on the left flank. It was his calf, all right, that posed for us!

June 5, 1969
I wish that fragrant Russian Olive tree outside the bedroom window would bloom all summer long. Waking to music is supposed to soothe the day's troubles. Wonder how psychologists would rate the perfume of a Russian Olive... or a flowering crab.

June 26, 1969
Carving initials used to be the "in" thing in Yellowstone's trees, guard rails, wood benches. We noticed a new twist last weekend. On Sylvan Pass people have started to spell out the names of their states. They take rocks and imprint them in the snow!

Bill Boyle's picture with Eisenhower just before D-Day is one of the featured pictures in this week's issue of the National Geographic. It nearly covers one centerfold. The same picture has appeared many, many places. In the pocket edition of "The Longest Day" the men in the picture are identified by name.

July 10, 1969
Vaughn Roberts, if he makes the Class of 1939 reunion as he plans to do, already has the coming-the-longest-distance prize cinched. He will have to come all the way from Libya.

Something else that came from a long way back are the set of leg irons, made in 1882, that Sheriff George Warfel found in the county jail. He has loaned them to the Greybull museum.

The weather balloon that drifted over Tuesday morning caused considerable comment. Jack Douglass saw it early from his Wagon Wheel court at the Big Horns. He said he called the airport and they told him it had a sign hanging down: "Get your Cleaning Done at Pruett's."

July 24, 1969
John Collingwood, who broke his arm in a bike accident the other day, has obviously had to answer a lot of questions about his cast. His stock deadpan answer now is: "I fell out of a tree raking leaves."

It seems many, many years ago, but the news of Homer Small's appointment to the Wyoming Highway Patrol at Lander brings back memories of his football career when he was the biggest boy on the Greybull team. Coach Buck Eckroth was fond of saying: "The biggest man on our team is Small!"

July 31, 1969
Thank Cleo McKinney for all those new trees you see at the golf course

(there's 40 of them in all!) He's responsible for getting them all planted.

September 11, 1969
When you say in a story that Jay Wilkinson, the new Safeway manager, has lived all his life in Greybull you can go back even further! He is one of the very few fourth generation Greybullites. His great grandfather, Johnny Borner, built Greybull's first house, the old cabin in the park.

September 18, 1969
Lloyd Groseclose, who spends a lot of time on the phone, leaned over to Mrs. Elva Clifton, longtime telephone operator at the "B" squad game Tuesday night and remarked: "If we're here, who's on the phone!"

September 25, 1969
One of those Meeteetse kids was so little his pants came clear to his ankles (instead of his knees) and his helmet fit so far on his shoulder pads that it looked like a space helmet. But he played hard and gave it all he had. After the game, one of the Greybull boys came all the way over from the other side to shake his hand and I heard him say to the little tyke: "You played as hard as all the big boys." There was one little boy who went home on a cloud.

October 9, 1969
Frank Bellamy said they finally had to let him out of the SBHC hospital "because they couldn't stand for my singing."
And he says to keep that Greybull Standard coming out to the hospital. "Your paper made the best fly swatter of them all," he said slyly.

October 16, 1969
Over the sheriff's radio the other day, some operator in another part of the state was giving a description of a wanted guy. It went "Brown hair, blue eyes, five feet six inches, beer belly!" Now how's that for an identifying feature! You fugitives – keep in shape if you don't want slandered over the airwaves.

October 23, 1969
The Great Western sugar company has spent thousands of dollars helping in the development of better seed, chemical fertilizers and weeders but haven't changed the method of unloading beets for over 30 years.

October 30, 1969
Did you get shot at up there hunting season, we asked Frank Casey who stays up at the Forest Service cabin. No, but "I generally stay in the basement that first day."

November 6, 1969

Some sports notes before we quit the football scene . . . That gentleman in the striped shirt refereeing at the Basin-Byron game that may have looked familiar to you Greybull fans was Ox Zellner who coached here in the late 1950's . . . Jack Williams has not missed a home football game at Greybull in 20 years. Can anyone else top that one? . . . By the files it was just 10 years ago in the next to last game of the season when a football player by the name of Skip Anderson scored three touchdowns against Cody. He was a freshman!

December 25, 1969

You know that tape the basketball boys wear around their wrists? It's supposed to keep the sweat from running down into your hands. Well, the other Saturday morning the fifth and sixth grade ball players found some old pieces in the locker room and the first thing I knew here was about half a dozen little boys all with tape around their wrists! Real big time!

And speaking of basketball, the biggest scene stealer was when one of the Gillette boys lost his contact on the Greybull floor Saturday night. Everyone was down on their hands and knees in the awkward find-the-contact stance. The Greybull pep squad started a chant: "Look Harder, Look Harder".

And when one of the referees got down on his hands and knees for a look, too, Lawrence Good, who was sitting behind us, cried out, "Don't let the refs look – they haven't seen anything all night!"

January 8, 1970
We're indebted to Slim Brewer and Orville Stockwell who discovered this picture and decided that "Bruce Kennedy finally did get a bull by the tail!"

February 5, 1970
At the German Club banquet Tony Beirith, who is construction superintendent of the First National Bank building, told of the time he and his wife went to the movie. In front of them was a big hulk of a guy you could hardly see over. Said Tony's wife in German to Tony the equivalent of: "If that big meathead would move, we could see the show." The man's wife started to laugh, turned around and said, in German, too, "He sure is!"

February 12, 1970
Offering real contrast to the hectic game of basketball Friday night, as Bill Shelledy remarked, was watching all the little fourth, fifth and sixth graders pour out of the "hole" in the west end of the gym. They came in from the wrestling room, looking like an Invasion of the Mini People for sure.

- - -

People got a great kick out of the sign in front of the Elden Sanders home his week (they adopted a new son) which read: "It's a boy. Welcome Home."

February 19, 1970

We were looking through the 10 years ago files and found the picture we took way back then of Kelly Michaelis and Becky Tomlinson on Valentine's Day. We set it up so it looked like they were two shy kids holding a valentine in back of each other ready to exchange them if they could only work up enough nerve. They were only third graders then. At the time I remember people saying I made one mistake, though, with that picture. Said one mother: "I've never known Kelly Michaelis to be shy!"

- - -

Stopped in Shoshoni to fill up with gas the other night and two cowboys inside the station were talking about their troubles. Said one: "You either got to go to the preacher or the banker for help, don't you?" "Yeah," said the other one, "but it seems I go to the banker a damn site more than the preacher."

February 26, 1970

The Absarokee cheerleaders had a little dance routine they did Saturday night at the basketball game. Bruce Hanson picked up the rhythm on the drums and drummed out a good loud beat for them. It tickled the girls so much they turned around after they'd finished and gave Bruce all the applause!

- - -

Incidentally, we're going to miss that boy next year in the pep band!

- - -

One little AAU wrestler asked Coach Dick Claycomb the other night at wrestling practice: "Coach, can I go home," "Sure you can," Claycomb said, "is there any special reason." "I'm tired," sighed the little tyke.

March 5, 1970

If you don't think this is spring already, consider the fact that the girls softball team has already practiced for this summer . . . and Mary Batenhorst has a broken finger suffered in one of them. Now that's surely a Wyoming weather record. A broken finger from playing softball in February!

- - -

The new calves are just starting . . . the rest are waiting for the next big storm.

March 26, 1970

The March lamb got mixed up and came in February it seems. But you could fly a kite in some perfect weather earlier in March. Bob Brinkerhoff and Chuck Williamson got a kite up in back of the U-Smile grocery and it took nine balls of string. It was just a speck up there.

April 2, 1970

When the police were first trying out the dog trap there were several dogs who just wouldn't stay in. At one time in the north end the police kept catching this dog and he kept getting away. Over behind the fence were three little girls who were watching the whole thing. Everytime the dog would get away they would dance up and down and hug each other. It was a little like standing on the hill above the Little Big Horn and cheering the Indians!

- - -

When the Cub Scouts visited the Big Horn County jail, Jake Piercy took a look at the little tykes and promptly dubbed them "Mini Scouts."

They solemnly toured everything and when they got to the basement one of them asked Jake: "Where is the Gas Chamber?"

"We don't kill them here," confided Jake, "We just torture them."

April 9, 1970

That school fire had many funny moments. Some of the littler girls got outside, one teacher said, and began the usual chant of "I hope it burns down, I hope it burns down." Then the smoke rolled up and horrified, they cried: "Oh we didn't mean it, we didn't mean it."

- - -

Let it be known for the record that it was Mark Powers who punched the box to turn in the fire alarm. He wanted me to tell you this!

And it is some distinction really. Mark Powers is the only Greybull student who has turned in a real fire alarm in the grade school for a long, long time.

The last fire people can remember in the grade school was when Miss Margaret Wallace was making taffy apples on a camp stove and it flamed up out of control. Burned the camp stove but didn't get much else scorched except Miss Wallace's pride. There probably wasn't even an alarm then either, though. They kept this pretty well hushed up. After all, the school principal making taffy apples in the office . . . !

That must have been between 1930 and 1933.

April 16, 1970

Mrs. John Haley wished for the Standard camera for awhile Friday morning. Three elk came down in her yard in Shelltown and one old cow was quite taken with a three-week-old jersey calf, probably wishing she could take it back home with her in the Big Horns.

- - -

Cub Collingwood, who cleaned up the wrecked auto yard in back of Collingwood motors said he should announce "that the Midnight Auto Supply is closed."

May 7, 1970

The Wyo Ben stripping crew out at the old golf course has consistently found golf balls as they work across the old course. Bill Lynam says it's hard to tell now what was fairway and what was rough, but "It's a real rough now!"

- - -

That Tempest Cub Collingwood is advertising this week that "has been driven very carefully by a nice young grandma for only 46,000 miles" belonged to his mother-in-law!

June 4, 1970
The material for the Rapid City band uniforms that didn't show up (they were lost in the shuffle someplace in shipment) were the main topic of conversation for this week. Especially in Williams Department store. Jack Williams has been telling everyone that they're going to set up a sewing machine in back of the bus and "sew all the way over."

- - -

Tim Schutte was responsible for a triple play in Little League the other night. He caught a fly, went over and touched second to catch one runner and then caught a runner off third. Out. Out. Out. Better sign him up.

June 11, 1970
Can't say there isn't a western flavor to this town's bars. We have the Silver Spur . . . the Branding Iron . . . and the Hanging Tree!

- - -

The kids really like those old band uniforms. At Rapid City, the band played selections like "Over There," "She's a Grand Old Flag" and "Give my Regards to Broadway." Said one of the high school girls: "We're playing World War I music to go along with our World War I uniforms."

June 18, 1970
Did you miss Lloyd Groseclose in Saturday's parade . . . that's the first time he's missed since the 49er parade started over 20 years ago . . .

- - -

If the petunias can last through the Days of '49 celebration without being pulled up, trampled or drowned in beer, they'll surely last through summer heat.

- - -

The crowd got a big charge out of Sheriff George Warfel and Greybull Police Chief Elvin Saul leading the parade neck and neck down main street. The two will be "running together" again in the August primary.

- - -

It's not every day that a printer in Greybull, Wyoming is asked to print a Japanese business card. In fact, we don't expect to again. But Dick Claycomb who is headed with the Wyoming wrestling team for the tour of Japan this week, had the Ondo family in Worland make the Japanese lettering and we ran these cards (front and back) off for him.

June 25, 1970
Before this rodeo gets too old let us also acknowledge the contributions – year after year – of Oscar Shoemaker in many ways but particularly for his

announcing for two and one half hours Saturday morning beginning with the Kiddies Parade and winding up with the Kids Races.

Did you see the name of the company who is doing the bridge painting job on the Manderson bridge? Spiller's Paint Company. How's that for a name!

Darren Burrows decided to go downtown early the other morning and caused quite a sensation in his pajamas. Walked right out of his house about 7 a.m. at 516 1st Avenue South and wound up having coffee with a tourist family in Parker's before the police . . . and his dad . . . caught up with him. He's only two!

July 2, 1970
You could get a lot of volunteers for the highway clean up if you could guarantee everyone would be as lucky as Terry Davis, 10-year-old son of Mr. and Mrs. Bill Davis of Basin, who found a $5 bill. He picked it up among all the "litter" in the borrowpit across from the hospital. If all litter could be so green!

July 9, 1970
Tony Good, 12-year-old son of Albert Good of Greybull, is the one who thought up the name for Cub Collingwood's camper court. He heard everyone talking about a name one day and he piped up: "I think you ought to call it Cub's Camper Court and put a picture of a bear on the sign." And that's just what they did.

July 16, 1970
If you're wondering why Frank Casey didn't have his fish pond at the Ranger station this year, it's because Frank got discouraged with all those "great" fishermen who used to "fish" it when no one was looking.

July 30, 1970
The Father and Son Little League game was great for the kids, but kind of tough on the old men. We played so badly that several people thought the fathers were throwing the game in favor of the kids! We love our kids but even parental devotion balks at getting beat 23 to 1.

Red Lindsey and Jim Core contributed their announcing talents again to the affair. Red is a longtime veteran of handing out microphone abuse to the old men. I went down to file a slander suit but there were so many ahead of me the courts will be clogged until next spring.

August 13, 1970
A tourist with North Carolina plates on walked back from parking along

Shell creek above the Wagon Wheel and Jack Douglass noticed he was soaking wet. "Did you fall in?" Jack wondered. "No," replied the man, "I'm an ordained minister and my kids have never been baptised. When they saw this stream here they decided that this is where they wanted to be baptised so I just finished. That water was sure cold!"

August 20, 1970

Slim Nielsen had a long-haired couple drive up to camp overnight at his camper court and one of them asked where the showers were. The men's is over there, Slim told him and then he turned to the wife and said, "the ladies' is over there." A deep masculine voice answered: "Thank you." You just can't tell with this long hair, Slim.

September 3, 1970

Did you see that story going around about the student hitchhiker out of Bozeman (after the cannibalistic story of the two Sheridan hitchhikers) who stood on the road with his thumb out and carrying a sign reading: "Vegetarian".

The annual fall invasion of the skunks seems to be on. Red Michaelis said he opened the door the other night and there stood a skunk, eyeball to eyeball with him. Police Chief Elvin Saul's wife woke him up and told him, "There's a skunk running down the street." "Is he running away?" the chief wanted to know. "Yes." "Well then let him go," Saul said.

September 24, 1970

Do you ever get the feeling that they like red Volkswagens at the Basin post office? It is possible to have five (5!) of them around in the parking lot all at the same time: Postmaster Red O'Neill has one; so does Fred Ellis. And then carriers Bob Harvey, Mrs. Mary Tolman, and K.C. Baker all drive up in one! All five are red Volkswagens.

October 29, 1970

At the Newcastle game the other night, Jim Michaelis, a former resident of both Greybull and Basin, spent the game on the Greybull sidelines. He had more than just an old-times-sake interest – he also had two nephews, Barry and Dan, playing for Greybull.

December 31, 1970

The sign was propped up behind the counter where you couldn't help but stare at it over your coffee cup. All it said, in neat block letters, was YCHJ-CYAQFTJB. One guy couldn't stand it any longer. "What's that sign supposed to be," he asked the waitress. She went over and pointed to each letter: Your Curiosity Has Just Cost You A Quarter For The Juke Box. He paid up!

1971

January 7, 1971

We liked Helen Turner's remedy for covering your bald spot. It's a mixture of persimmon and alum, Helen says. You spread this generously on your bald spot. It doesn't make the hair grow but it shrinks your head to fit what you have!

February 11, 1971

I was a printer a long time before I was a publisher and during the hectic press day at Lander last week trying to get out the fire edition, I put the old printer's apron back on again. One of the newsboys picking up his papers glanced over my way once and turned to the kid next to him. "Gee," he exclaimed, "they're getting all sorts of new guys around here!"

March 4, 1971

Several local people made "the news" this past week or so. George "Conoco" Scott was one of the featured persons in a recent Conoco trade publication. George retired during the past year. One picture in the article showed George and the Cody pilot who flew over the 1929 ice jam and successfully bombed it loose with dynamite.

March 25, 1971

Minnie Woodring remembers in her "Mini Notes" in Lander about one watermelon swiping foray when her date ditched her for another gal . . . But Minnie says she had the last laugh anyway. The other gal spent an hour in the doctor's office "getting the buckshot picked out of the place that went over the fence last."

April 29, 1971

EARTH WEEK: Time to take a clod to lunch.

May 27, 1971

MIDDLE AGE is when you never make a list anymore of all the things you are going to do this summer because you know Labor Day will arrive again with most of them undone . . .

THE CHET HUNTLEY dinner reminded how long the slogan "Big Sky," floated around before anyone picked it up . . . A.B. Guthrie's book, "The Big Sky," came out in 1946 . . . and it wasn't until the early 1960's that it caught on as Montana's slogan . . . the irony is that it could have been Wyoming's slogan just as easily . . . it is still one of the best phrases that sums up this great Western country.

THOSE DON'T GET OUT OF BED DAYS — A couple of Lusk ranchers spent the day getting a windmill put up . . . got it all done . . . climbed in the old pickup and started for home . . . They didn't know a chain was still hooked from pickup to windmill . . . looked back to see the brand new mill following along behind! . . . That's another day shot!

AT THE HUNTLEY DINNER . . . Chet Huntley made a reference to the Japanese-American 442 Combat Team, the most decorated unit in American military history. Huntley might be interested to know that the most decorated individual of the 442nd is a fellow journalist . . . Ben Kuroki . . . who started his weekly newspaper career in York, Nebr. . . after graduation from the University of Nebraska in 1950.

There was always a great story connected with Ben Kuroki's first issue published.
Nebraska publishers and editors from all over the state came down to York and pitched in setting type, selling ads, writing news to help Ben get started.
And this was in the early 1950's . . . You young people note: 20 years ago the Establishment had heart and feelings, too.

June 3, 1971
THAT GUY who took his brother's place in the Army in Vietnam said it was easy to pose as a GI. All I did, he was quoted as saying, was salute whenever anyone else did and the rest of the time acted stupid . . . yes, that is the Army I knew.

ALL OF THIS wet weather and rising Big Horn river reminded Pat Michaelis of Greybull of the flood and ice jam in 1962 at Greybull . . . The family evacuated the house when one blast from Morris Avery's dynamite-dropping helicopter shattered a window . . . The Mrs. grabbed the youngest, a can of coffee and a jar of peanut butter . . . "Guess she figured that's all she needed," Pat remembers.

June 10, 1971
ARE THERE MANY HOMES that do not have a lilac bush growing in the yard someplace? . . . When you drive around town this spring time of year, you just seem to see one after another . . . In the old days, it used to be yellow rose bushes. Every house had a yard full of cottonwoods and a yellow rose bush.

A GIRL whose surname was Cain popped up in the news the other day in Billings . . . and our family tried to guess her first name without looking at the story . . . picked "Hurri" and "Sugar" but both were wrong . . . Her parents had named her "Candi!"

THE MELLERDRAMMER play cast at Greybull had finished a dress rehearsal last week and were standing out in front of the theatre in their long dresses and crazy outfits . . . a young teenager who had just moved to town drove by, took a quick second look, drove around the block, came by again, looked some more and finally parked. He walked over and asked real quietly, "Say do you suppose one of you guys could get me a six pack of beer." He thought he'd stumbled on to the darndest bunch of hippies he'd ever seen.

June 17, 1971
A BOX IN A service station in Gillette had a sign printed on it, "Baby Rattlers" . . . I knew better than to look but couldn't resist finally taking a peek . . . sure enough, that's what was inside . . . baby rattles . . . the plastic kind that make a great noise when you shake it in your chubby little fist . . . I looked around to see if anyone had seen me get stung so badly . . . but no one had, thank gosh.

DO LITTLE BOYS still try to sell tourists cockleburrs for porcupine eggs . . . or was that just in my generation?

THE STANDARD'S PETUNIAS, after the Days of '49 celebration, have the distinction of being the beeriest petunias in town . . . everyone who went by dumped a glass in our petunia pot! . . . AT THE BAND CONCERT before the Canada trip noticed that Lynn Bullinger is playing the saxophone . . . Her grandfather Fred Gould would certainly have been proud of this.

July 1, 1971
IN "The I Hate to Housekeep Book" it advises housewives: "If it's loose, pick it up; if it isn't, dust it; if it moves, feed it."

AT PAHASKA they're keeping a "Post List" in the Texaco station . . . keeps track of how many tourists hit the post near the station. Friday the list had 26 marks on it. Last year the total was 89!

July 15, 1971
IS IT TRUE all wine tasters just slurp the stuff around without actually swallowing it. Would have to, I guess. Otherwise it sure would shorten your working hours. You couldn't last long! "Where does your daddy work?" "He's a wine taster. He works from 9 in the morning until they carry him home just a little before noon!"

THE MIXED GROUP of skinny dippers at a Flaming Gorge campground recently drew two audiences . . . one outraged group of campers who threatened to shoot . . . another group with binoculars who wanted the "swimmers" to stay . . . you can't please the world . . . DO YOU THINK the world has changed? It hasn't. In the 1921 Greybull Standard this month the town was in an uproar over the skinny dippers in the Big Horn river near Greybull . . . Fifty years ago . . . and the mayor was threatening some kind of legal action to stop this degeneration.

THE RINGSIDE SEAT at the Endurance Race will be occupied by Slim Brewer who is taking a folding chair up to his Elk Springs hunting camp this week (which is right alongside the endurance ride route) and watch the race . . . so you contestants wave when you go by.

MRS. LOIDENE (Groseclose) Williams wound up with a second place in the goat tying at Lovell's Mustang Days last weekend . . . "That's not bad for a daughter of an old goat tie-er like Dad," she pointed out. "It's hereditary," Father Lloyd says.

July 22, 1971

AGE is when you have to keep moving the car seat forward because your son's legs are about five inches longer than yours . . . and he can't stand to drive with the seat "pushed up like that!"

FOR MANY YEARS now our family has been in love with an old boxer dog that we rescued from the dog pound when he was just a pup. He's gone through our individual and collective lives like no other force. He's been the main character in dozens of hilarious situations that have all become family jokes. He's survived a bobcat trap, innumerable losing bouts with skunks and one horrible afternoon on how-not-to-be-a-hunting dog. He's affectionate beyond all right to be; doesn't know how to be mean; barks seldom; laughs often; is a big, beautiful colored dog with the largest mouth on any animal outside of an African game preserve. We've always wished for "some pups out of old Butch." But now he's getting old and we're afraid he's going to be leaving us before that ever happens. If anyone with a female boxer would like to make a "deal" we're ready to listen. Surely the world could use such progeny.

SOMEONE WROTE for a Sunday edition of the Standard . . . guess I'll have to come down Sunday and mail her one.

July 29, 1971

THE SHOW, "Tora, Tora, Tora" reminded me of the time I sat through John Wayne's movie "Iwo Jima" . . . in a Tokyo theatre . . . Eerie feeling . . . the predominate Japanese audience would yell and clap when the Japanese were ahead . . . stare stonily ahead when old Duke was winning . . . Me? . . . I just slouched down in my seat with a wadded up bag of popcorn . . . Longest show I ever saw.

DESERVING A PAT on the back for their continued volunteer efforts with kids' programs . . . like last Saturday night's Father-Son game, were umpires Bob Hallcroft, Larry Bullinger, Hector Good and the Art Schuttes who always help . . . and I can't forget Jim Core who always announces and who, it seems to me, is fascinated by my lack of hair . . . he keeps mentioning it over the air . . . did you ever notice it's always the guys with hair who pick on us bald-headed guys!

August 5, 1971
AS NICE as we like their dollars a tourist does some of the strangest things . . . In front of Brown's Furniture the other day one guy got out of his out-of-state car and dumped two ash trays full into one of the town's petunia pots . . . Don't know what he thought the flowers were doing there . . . anyway it must have been the prettiest garbage cans he'd ever dumped in!

August 19, 1971
MEANT TO MENTION a couple of weeks ago the Cody Little Leaguer who was coaching third base during Cody's first game at the state tournament against Greybull . . . The score was already up past 12 to nothing for Cody and it was evident how the outcome was going to be . . . The little guy – he wasn't very big – turned around to the Greybull dugout and pointed out: "And we went swimming this afternoon, too!"

September 2, 1971
THE COMMA was left out of this headline in Gillette and it read: SORRY POOL CLOSES EARLY.

September 9, 1971
OVERHEARD a conversation about a fire in a Wyoming town that had apparently started when the housewife left the iron on . . . The fire looked suspicious, though, and despite the wife's insistence that she must have left the iron on, insurance adjusters took another look . . . Sure enough . . . The ironing board was charred and half burned up . . . all except right under the iron . . . That was the only place the gasoline didn't reach!

MISS SEEING that old cabin on Irv Davis' place on Shell creek . . . that cabin had a long history . . . a man from Jackson, tracing his grandfather's diary, stopped there once and found the old boy's initials inside.

SLIM BREWER, John Anderson and George Scott returned from the

Thorofare country after a five-day pack trip . . . were trying to find an old bear trap George used up there years ago . . . but they were greeted with eight inches of snow! . . . and never found it.

September 16, 1971

JERRY GEBHART, an ex-GHS football guard watching football practice the other night, remembers how he enjoyed pulling out and running those power sweeps . . . "Gosh, it was great to get your nose out of the dirt and up into the sunshine again," he sighed. "I used to go back to the huddle and tell them: 'Let's run a power sweep, let's run a power sweep.' "

I HAVEN'T seen this myself but tourists coming into Greybull from Shell must have done a double take when they saw Bob Meeker and his dog, Josh, riding the Meeker Honda. Or was it the other way around? Josh, an English-Setter, sits in front of Bob with his paws on the handle-bars! . . . doing the driving?

September 23, 1971

WHEN Greybull and Basin junior high teams met Saturday Greybull coaches Koch and Haiman gave a good pep talk to the kids about the attitude on the field . . . You should go out and act like football players, look like football players. Be tough, look determined, be aggressive and so forth . . . The boys took the good advice and hit the door with a burst, ran out toward the field, teeth bared . . . grrr-ferocious looks, the works . . . and there wasn't a single soul there yet!!! No other team, nobody in the stands, no pep squad yet . . . an empty house.

September 30, 1971

DURING GREYBULL'S junior high game with Powell, Greybull Coach Lonnie Koch called to one of the boys to take a play in. The boy ran from the sidelines out to the huddle, gave the quarterback the play . . . and then promptly ran right back off the field again!

ONE OF THE MOST graceful sights is a paddle wheel, whether it's on a river boat or a hay windrower.

October 7, 1971

NOW THAT NASA has about wound up the Apollo moon flights, I have several problems I hope they can work on . . . one being a system whereby I do not have to get out of bed at 5 a.m. to let the dog out . . . then at 5:15 to let the cat out . . . and then at 5:45 to let the dog back in again . . . and 5:50 to let the cat back in again.

AS A KID in our home there was a small cat-sized hole built into the outside basement entrance for our cat to go in and out . . . It worked like a charm . . . until all the cats in the neighborhood found out about it . . . There were times when our basement sounded like a Roman Amphitheatre.

GORDON GROSECLOSE was in his room at the Cody hospital when in came Robert Shepard for knee surgery. He told the nurse: "There's my neighbor!" (in the north end of town.) A little while later Dave Lindsey came in the same hospital and again Gordon told her "There's my neighbor." (Out on the Groseclose farm.) "Gee, you sure have a lot of neighbors," she exclaimed.

October 21, 1971
THERE ARE TWO things out of state hunters won't believe: that the bad weather doesn't last long, (it almost did!) and that there aren't too many deer around here . . . When I told one out of state hunter that one spring I had taken a picture of a ranch at the foot of the Big Horns with over 400 deer in the field, I know he thought I was out of my mind.

SAW AN OLD FRIEND on television the other night again . . . Henry Morgan . . . and I can never see him without remembering that he was one of the first movie stars I ever saw in person . . . way back in those college days . . . We were in the same Denver bar and he was holding court over a long table in the middle of the room . . . He'd been there for some time apparently . . . and every so often he would stand up, rap for attention, and announce to the group: "I suppose you're all wondering why I asked you here tonight" . . . and then he'd sit down to gales of laughter . . . only to jump up again in a few minutes and grandly announce: "I suppose you're all wondering why I asked you here tonight" . . . I don't know how long it lasted but his staying power was amazing.
The other night when I glanced at the screen and saw his mouth start to open, I was sure for a minute, just absolutely sure, that he was going to say: "I suppose you're all wondering . . ."

MADE THE SAME COMMENT A YEAR AGO – Nothing like harvesting sugar beets with all the latest equipment . . . and then coming in to use a pre-World War II dump.

THAT SUGAR BEET pile at the Greybull dump has turned into the greatest wind break football fans have ever had!

October 28, 1971
I CALLED up the FAA people at the Worland airport the other day and told the guy: "I've just received a new barometer and need to have you tell me where I should set it." "Well, on the mantle I guess," he said . . . very funny guy!

MY GRANDMOTHER died in Miles City the other day after being in the Powder River country of Montana for over 75 of her 95 years.

She came to Montana before the century turned joining my grandfather on the ranch on the Powder river. And they were a part – without ever really knowing it – of the Old West that came to mean so much to American heritage. Her funeral in Miles City was a reunion of many old timers from the Powderville country, mostly sons and daughters of people like herself, who had spent their lives in the country.

Those were different times. When my mother was born on the ranch they sent word to the doctor in Miles City but he arrived by buggy a day and a half too late . . . so he just stayed a week and went hunting!

November 11, 1971

NOTICE that the Highway department is still tearing down many of the billboards along the Greybull-to-Cody highway . . . These are the ones which have been abandoned by the owners . . . and there's more than you think.

THEY WERE BURNING some of those old signs alongside the highway Tuesday . . . take down the pollution from the road sides and send it up in polluted smoke!

THE PEACE sign is painted on more places than any other symbol or word . . . it is starting to appear everywhere . . . on buildings, water tanks, almost any flat surface . . . in fact there was a gigantic one out in the snow in our front yard for a while . . . tramped out by a pair of busy little feet! . . . But that one washed off!

SCRATCH ONE RED FOX who thought he was safe near our chicken house . . . a big ole devil . . . 16 pounds and 4 1/2 feet long from nose tip to tail tip.

THOSE new Eisenhower dollars have all the heft and feel of a pool hall hickey!

November 18, 1971

WISH TO REPORT that our family's glee with having knocked off that "Godfather" fox in our chicken yard was short-lived . . . the next couple of nights his whole family must have come back . . . so now scratch five of our chickens . . . The Mafia has struck!

November 25, 1971

HATE TO SEE Jim Crawford's football rushing mark broken at the University this year . . . That record had stood for 14 years . . . But the tie with Greybull is still there to some degree . . . Frosty Franklin of Powell who eclipsed Crawford's old mark is the grandson of Mrs. Helen White of Greybull.

December 2, 1971

THE BURLINGTON TRAIN was so long at the crossing in Gillette the other day (45 minutes) that one woman we know ran out of gas while she was waiting!

December 16, 1971

THAT GAZETTE headline writer who called artificial turf (on football fields) MOD SOD sure is with it.

OUR CHRISTMAS CARDS this year are really gems of originality . . . They tell everyone we are fine, there's snow on the ground, come and see us, Brian is 16, Ann is 14, Bob is 12 . . . LAST YEAR we wrote that we are fine, there's snow on the ground and come and see us, Brian is 15, Ann is 13 and Bob is 11.

December 30, 1971

THE OLD MAN at this house is the only one who likes mincemeat pie . . . and out of deference to my age, I guess, I get it twice a year — once at Thanksgiving and again at Christmas . . . But I am finding out, as I get older, what Mark Twain meant when he said: "I have learned not to frolic with mincemeat pie any more!"

YOU KNOW, if you turn down the volume on KOMA in Oklahoma City, it's not a bad station . . . at our house I seldom hear it at any less than 80 decibels.

1972

January 6, 1972

AGAIN THIS YEAR, watching all those flashbulbs go off in the Orange Bowl, I couldn't get over how misinformed people are about the use of light in taking a picture . . . Hundreds of bulbs must have gone off during that spectacular halftime show – you could see them light up in the crowd constantly . . . Yet the light from that flashbulb not only didn't make it down the field, it didn't get much further than that baldheaded guy three rows ahead!

January 20, 1972

JACK DOUGLASS has dubbed a friendly big horn ram that comes down close to the Wagon Wheel, "The Colonel" . . . Always sharp, that Jack.

January 27, 1972

IT'S SO COLD that all the noises from across the river floating over to our house are magnified dozens of times . . . the switch engine sounds like it is backing up to the garage . . . If I stood on top of our garage and hollered over to the Nielsen's to tell Slim I only needed three quarts of milk this morning, I'm sure he'd hear it!

February 3, 1972

SOME WISE GUY CALLED the Greybull post office after the appointment of Peyton (Pat) Tomlinson and asked Pat "If this was Peyton's Place."

February 10, 1972

LEW MERRIOT of Thermopolis, who watched me grow up next door to his house in Basin, was reminded of those days from last week's Greybull Standard. He writes: "My wife and I often talk of the kids that lived in our neighborhood. I noted by a recent paper where Jeanie Palmer has been appointed to an important job as head of a nursing school. I remember when I used to watch her through our window when she had a sucker and would take a lick and then give her dog, Jiggs, a lick!"

WE GOT A LETTER addressed to Greybull Standard, Greybull, Wyo. Inside the first sentence read: Dear Mr. Standard:

February 17, 1972

THE NEW WYOMING license plate colors of yellow and brown are still the best . . . why can't we just alternate every year between yellow letters on brown and brown letters on yellow . . . would be so much simpler and would keep those good UW colors.

I DREAMED the other night that I stopped the On-To-Oregon wagon train I was on from annihilation because I decided if we put that plastic foam packing (the same as they make those cheap coolers from) all around the wagons the arrows couldn't go through . . . it worked of course . . . but the wagons looked like a bunch of fat doughnuts wallowing across the plain, arrows sticking out all over . . . Can't remember whether we saved the horses or not, but the wagons all came through . . . I don't know why the pioneers didn't figure that out!

NO ONE has mentioned our new Greybull Standard sign out front . . . but then no one mentioned we didn't have one up for a year either!

February 24, 1972
IS THE ICE any thicker and the winters any colder than they used to be? . . . CLAIR STEARNS remembers pushing 600 head of cattle across on the Big Horn river ice on Thanksgiving day years ago . . . and he couldn't have done that on many Thanksgiving Days of recent years.

March 2, 1972
The "X" rated movie in Greybull the other night . . . was preceded by a Donald Duck cartoon . . . which I thought incongruously hilarious.

March 9, 1972
BOB HARVEY and Laurence Roehrkasse took in both the Class AA and the Class A tournaments over the mountain . . . The two men had a grandson Lennie Roehrkasse playing for Laramie at the Sheridan tournament . . . and then they drove back to Gillette to watch the basketball action there . . . I WISH someone would have kept track of the basketball games Bob Harvey has watched in his lifetime . . . There isn't anyone who has seen more games than he has . . . junior high . . . junior varsity . . . varsity . . . Greybull games . . . Basin games . . . tournaments . . . You can see him at all of them . . . There's no better basketball fan.

GEORGE SCURLOCK who has been in 40 states in his lifetime says Greybull is the cleanest town in the U.S. for its size.

MARCH WINDS about blew the state down . . . and brought one inch of topsoil from Emblem to Greybull's main street . . . together with a very poor crop of weeds from the Dry creek area.

March 16, 1972

THE FIFTH AND SIXTH graders wound up their Saturday morning basketball . . . and I always look back on having learned more than the kids did . . . It is amazing, continually, to watch how much a youngster that age can absorb . . . He learns as he is having fun . . . and when he becomes proficient at it, a good dribbler or a good shooter or good rebounder, he takes a pride in it that is bigger than all his 75 pounds! A boy in the fifth or sixth grade actually learns an awful lot about basketball . . . It is a mistake to think he can't . . . I was watching junior high basketball practice in another town last year and the coach and I got to talking about teaching kids to shoot. He told me: "You know shooting is a lot using your wrist. But these eighth graders' wrists aren't strong enough yet and they won't learn this until later on." I didn't say anything but I could have said, come over here to Greybull, Wyoming and I'll show you some FIFTH graders who are popping their wrists just like they should be!

March 23, 1972

OUR ENTIRE FAMILY had to try the chair-up-against-the-wall trick (women can do it, but men can't) that Archie Bunker tried to do on his Sunday night show . . . You know, you back up three shoe lengths away from the door, then put a chair close in front of you, lean over it and touch your head against the door; reach down and grab the chair and lift it up; then straighten up from the door . . . The women can do it – but the men can't . . . Someone's got to explain this to me . . . I'm as bewildered as Archie was.

ARCHIE BUNKER has belligerently shoved his way into American life in an amazing short time. It has to be because there is a little Archie Bunker in all of us. This doesn't take much psychology to figure out, of course – we are all prejudiced about something; we are all instinctively against change and we lash out at it when it begins to threaten us. What we don't understand we seem to be against.

So Archie – or at least a part of Archie – is you and me and the guy down the street and isn't that a shame in a way. Isn't it a little sad that we are honoring a bigot as a typical guy. Well, maybe the typical person is an Archie Bunker but this is a little like the ancient battle of good news and bad news and only the good is supposed to be printed. Only the good is supposed to be our national example. But I won't climb on the soapbox over this. To attempt to legislate Archie Bunker off the air waves because he is "bad news" would be folly!

Besides I keep running into him at our house. The other night the kids had the most monotonous drum record on I've ever heard. I thought the needle was stuck for 10 minutes straight. But no, it turns out the guy was just hung up on that beat. When I complained about it, they implied I didn't know good drumming, and, in a very pointed attack at my age, said "you never had good drummers back when you were growing up." Which naturally sent me into a long, angry speech about the likes of Buddy Rich and Gene Krupa and Dave Brubeck's "Take Five" and how the young today were just as big a bigots as they claimed we old people were because they didn't accept anything that had happened before 1960 as being any good at all.

And in the midst of all this tirade, I suddenly thought, "Old Man, you are sounding one heck of a lot like Archie Bunker." And I don't think I shut up before someone else thought of it, too!

"WE'RE here to help make the entire state of Wyoming a national park," said a couple of young environmentalists in Greybull the other day.

"Where are you guys from," asked Chris Paustian.

"New Hampshire," they said.

"Well, why don't we make New Hampshire a national park?" Chris asked.

"But that's a crazy idea," they exclaimed.

"Yeah, isn't it."

March 30, 1972

COWS CAN'T talk like humans but they sure do take on some very human traits . . . a friend of ours from Shell was saying that he could almost find everyone of his neighbors along Shell creek among the cows in his herd, the same personality traits and all . . . to which some smart aleck downtown said: "Boy, it's been a long winter for you!"

"A WOMAN can do everything a man can do and when she does, she should get equal pay for equal work," announced our daughter in the midst of a family discussion about women's lib . . . "Okay, then," said her little brother, who isn't too happy about his spring work, "how about you taking over hauling the manure."

April 6, 1972

I HAVE DECIDED that I had better learn the metric system . . . if I start now maybe I'll be prepared for that inevitable switch from inches and pounds to centimeters and grams . . . It's a good switch . . . None of us ever remembered the other ancient English system very well anyway.

WHICH leads me to a story and incident I haven't thought about in years. It happened at a Greybull city council meeting years ago when one of the town's old men (I won't tell you who!) came to the Council with a complaint.

It was an old man's irrational complaint that was out of place and not too important to anyone but the old man. He stated his case in his old man's voice and he said all the usual things that rile up a council of much younger fellows. It was almost impossible to reason with him, and I remember sitting there on the sidelines feeling sorry for him. The times had passed him by and he couldn't understand something that seemed so outrageous to him was being shrugged off by the Council.

But he took his lumps gracefully (I thought) and before he sat down he asked if he could just sit and listen to the rest of the meeting. Of course he could, so the Council told him, although you could see they hoped he wouldn't say anything else. The meeting droned on and I can't remember how it came up but someone suddenly asked how many square feet in so many square miles or something like that and they got out the pencils and started figuring.

The old man suddenly perked up at that and asked what the question was. Someone told him and without hardly a pause the old man rattled off the answer from the top of his head. One of the councilmen who was figuring with a pencil, said "hey, that's right."

"Of course it is," the old man said. "I learned that a long, long time ago."

And he had. He'd been drilled in it probably, remembered it, used it, practiced all those tables and all the combinations until he could recite it perfectly. It was a piece of education that the rest of us had not bothered with.

But he remembered it and he could tell you right away what the answer was. Without a pencil. That night or any night.

Now, somehow, he didn't seem to be the old, cantankerous guy he'd been before. That was his little triumph. The Council knew it; I knew it; but I'm sure he didn't. It didn't seem to bother him one way or another. But I was happy for him just the same.

April 20, 1972

ONE GREYBULL grade school class brought scorpions to class and the teacher put them all in a plastic pail over night. All ten escaped! The janitors had rounded up seven at last report . . . but the rest were soaking up learning in some dark corner.

THE THINGS LITTLE BOYS dream up to scare the girls is a constant source of amazement to me . . . The criminal mind is certainly fertile! . . . Some boys I know in junior high were playing with lizards at school, much to the fright of one girl . . . They pretended they were going to put the lizard on her arm when she wasn't looking . . . Instead they put a rubber band which has the same crawling, rubbery feeling . . . EEOW! . . . Great fun. They did it again, same rubber band . . . Only a slight reaction . . . Again when she wasn't looking, same rubber band . . . Old stuff by now . . . But on the next time, when her attention wandered again, they put the lizard on . . . She looked down to brush off that silly rubber band, and . . . EEOW! EEOW! EEOW!

PEOPLE around the state are impressed with Greybull's efforts to obtain a new swimming pool . . . In the five years I've been on the road this is one of the first positive comments people have had to make about the old town.

April 27, 1972

I DON'T KNOW what you think of the new silver dollars but it seems to me some of the old charm has gone out of these new ones . . . I cried real tears when that part of Wyoming living disappeared . . . now I'm ashamed to admit I'd probably carry around paper, given the choice.

MANDY Mohr of Greybull was remembering years ago when he was a young man and had headed for California from Iowa. He and a couple of buddies were driving down a street early in the morning looking for the Biltmore hotel where one of the boy's dad was a chef. They were driving an old open Model T Ford and looked about as penniless as they were.

Not quite sure of their directions they drove up to a policeman on the corner and asked: "Is this the road to the Biltmore Hotel?"

"It is," he said, and looking them over carefully, added, "But they don't put the cans out until 7 o'clock."

May 18, 1972

It's about this time of year, when the sun gets warm enough to put the top down, that I'm sure that a person never really gets over convertible fever, not entirely anyway. It seems to hang on, like they say tick fever does, to re-occur on days of warm sunshine and big, beautiful skies full of white clouds when you wish you could hit the button and bring it all in to the seat beside you. I think once bitten, you're a victim for life and even when sober judgment tells you to drive an old man's car, you still think about convertibles every so often.

I told Cub Collingwood once, years ago, when he had an old Pontiac convertible to sell, that I'd sure like to buy it and "get this convertible thing out of my system." Cub said, I remember, that he couldn't see a convertible. "It would be just like going to a dinner party in my shorts," he told me.

But I went ahead anyway and took that convertible on our family's first open air tour of Yellowstone Park via Red Lodge and Cooke City and the north east entrance and Fishing Bridge. And by the time we floated down the Northfork to Cody and home, after a day of absolutely perfect, still weather, of beautiful sunshine I knew I was hooked for good. Three convertibles later we finally went back to sanity and bought a car with a top that wouldn't rattle and one that miraculously kept the dust out, the cotton out, the June cold out, the October leaves out. Nothing is as cold as a convertible; nothing is as hot. But then no trip up the Big Horns is ever the same again either. It's absolutely perfect driving at times. The birds sound louder, the pine trees smell stronger, the air is sharper, more exhilarating.

For awhile during this convertible fever, I was sure my hair was growing back! But it was only a convertible illusion, brought on by those long, sleek unmatchable lines of a convertible and all those great trips in them.

But the wind punishes those in the back seat. Our family ended up many trips home either all five huddled in the front seat (when the kids were smaller) or someone hiding down on the floorboards. Wind lost a convert in our girl, too, who couldn't take that constant windblown hair. And the cold is at times unbelievable even in the middle of July. Those people bundled in coats and hats with the top down may look crazy but they're at least warm.

But still there were great times . . . beating out a light rain storm with the airstream lifting the rain over the top of you and everyone hilarious over being dry in the middle of a rain . . . the trip when everyone seemed so friendly on the road until the old man realized all three kids were standing up in the back waving, waving, waving . . . what a joke on old Dad . . . Drifting alongside the Tetons one brilliant summer day . . . memories that set the hook very deep indeed . . . even after you know you'll probably never drive another one again.

May 25, 1972

THEY WERE PITCHING horseshoes in the old swimming pool last week . . . the pool has been filled with dirt now for some time . . . and it might as well be used for a horseshoe pit!

SPEAKING OF DIRT . . . you can tell who lives on Shell creek (or who drives to Shell creek) by all the mud on their car . . . that gumbo stuff on the new road construction reminds you of the old days of wet springs with no gravel, no pavement and no fun!

BUT THE ROAD is going to be a dandy . . . I won't be sorry to see that old road go . . . AND I'M GLAD they didn't cut down that old cottonwood by the late Jim Moberly place . . . that's a beauty . . . PROBABLY should make a "picture turnout" by Chester Whaley's place . . . you see more and more people stop near there to take a picture across the valley and on up to the Big Horns.

June 8, 1972

RODE BY a not-very-old calf elk Sunday, hidden away in the sagebrush with its head and neck stretched out against the ground like they do . . . the only movement you could see was that big, wide eye following you by.

THE WOMAN TOLD US: "Well, I know what people are doing in town, but I'm just buying your paper to see who gets caught."

June 15, 1972.

THE TOURISTS must have thought Greybull folks were sure a clean bunch . . . there were two garbage cans right in the middle of main street early Sunday morning of the 49er rodeo celebration.

WHEN JAKE PIERCY was a youngster in Greybull, he and his young buddies found out where the Ku Klux Klan was meeting and memorized all who were there . . . then when the kids would meet the guys on the street the kids would go: KLUCK KLUCK KLUCK KLUXERS like a hen clucking sound . . . and then run and laugh . . . You can't beat the kids! . . . No matter what generation.

June 22, 1972
MY BOY figured out, finally, how not to lose pocket knives . . . He bought one for 25 cents several years ago and still has it . . . If he'd paid $3.95 for it yesterday, he would have lost it this morning.

WE HAVE a front door cat and a back door cat . . . and the twain only meet in a mass of flying fur and yowls . . . It's just been lately, when his manners improved, that the backdoor cat ever got into the house for very long . . . and when he does he's been getting into the habit of climbing up on the highest spot in the room . . . the table, or the desk, like an Indian on a hill . . . The other night he sneaked into our bedroom and curled up without any of us noticing on top of the bed headboard, next to the telephone and spent the night there. I didn't know he was there until morning and it was light . . . thank gosh for the light . . . I shudder to think of the shambles had I reached up for the phone in the dark and put my hand on something warm and furry instead.

July 6, 1972
PAUL PETERSON is one of Cody's oldest oldtimers . . . he went there in 1903 . . . and there wasn't much in Cody, Wyoming in 1903!

NOT MANY PLACES in the Big Horn Mountains show much originality or color in the names of creeks, buttes, peaks and lakes, but Belly Ache Flats is descriptive enough!

July 13, 1972
THIS COUNTRY has become so automated that it is almost impossible to get a glass of weak iced tea without explaining to the waitress how to make "the machine give you weak iced tea." Invariably the waitress will say: "I can't make it weak because it comes right out of the machine." . . . and then you say: "Well, how about filling it up only half full out of the machine and fill the rest of the way up with water." . . . and then she says: "Say, that's about half smart!"

ON THE LAKE SOLITUDE trail last weekend part of us wanted to stay at the lake to fish and part of us wanted to ride on up country so we tied one horse across the trail right at the lake's end.
It was at the place where the lake is on one side of the trail and the sheer rock cliff on the other with a couple of trees just barely growing alongside, and no room for anything else. The horse just filled up everything across the trail but then there's not much traffic up there.
But we created a traffic jam at that because coming back again we ran into a backpacker from Princeton who had to get by that big, old buckskin some-

how. (Imagine a traffic jam at Lake Solitude!) And without untying it, it must have been some trick.

We apologized for messing him up. We didn't know he was anywhere around.

"Oh, that's all right, I got by all right. I just petted him so he wouldn't kick me!"

July 20, 1972

THE KENNEDYS HAVE lived in the country for 16 years, and Tuesday was the first time in all those long, long months that we've ever found a rattlesnake on the place . . . Am trying to find some kind of an omen in that!

July 27, 1972

WHEN BILL MOBERLY was pouring hot tar in the sidewalk cracks in front of the Carey buildings he had to take considerable ribbing from passerbys . . . The reason: He was using a coffee pot to pour the tar out . . . which prompted Blondie May to remark: "That really must be bad coffee. It's the first time I ever saw anyone pour it out on the sidewalk."

August 10, 1972

LAKE SOLITUDE is beckoning more and more people . . . In the old days it was quite a trip . . . now the Forest Service approach roads are better, more accessible . . . RED DEVERAUX was remembering one Solitude trip when he took 18 FFA boys in on a ten-day excursion "back in the old days!" . . . Eighteen boys, and 32 horses! That must have made quite a string up the mountain.

August 24, 1972

A STEER WITH acute stage fright finally got through the Big Horn County fair but not without a lot of work for its owner, Gary Collingwood . . . Gary's steer, sweet and gentle on the farm, went into a frenzy when he took it to the county fair. Back home again with the steer. Sweet and gentle. Give the fair another try. More wild-eyed tearing around Basin. Back home again. Finally Doc Lester gave it a tranquilizer. Serenity settles in. The steer is back to normal. As docile as Ferdinand in the flower patch. It's worth remembering — next time you get uptight, Doc Lester has the cure.

August 31, 1972

A GUY was telling me about another guy he didn't like: "Why that guy is just iggerant," he said.

I MADE A VERY BAD BARGAIN way back in May when I said that I would take over the irrigating again right after school started . . . But the first day of school seemed like an eternity away back then . . . Now I have that shovel back on my shoulder again and the boys say they don't miss it at all!

September 7, 1972

    THAT OLD RACCOON who has had the same old meal of sweet corn around our place, hopefully, is tiring of it . . . It is also true that he is fast running out of it!

    Wish someone would trace the evolution of Wyoming's raccoons for me. I'd never heard of a coon in this country until about 10 years ago. Now you hear about them all the time.

    Were there coons around in the old days?

    Are they an import? Are these Nebraska coons? Kansas coons? Missouri coons? Or just damned coons?

    OUT ON SHELL CREEK Eighth grader Morris Smith put out some traps for the Shell creek coon population and caught one coon . . . and two men? (His dad and the hired man!)

    BOB WALTON made that long walk down into Box canyon where Cedar creek comes in and waded across the creek to get to the other side ("I don't know of any other way to get across but to wade," he says) fished for awhile, turned around . . . and there was Game Warden Terry Cleveland!

September 14, 1972

    A COUPLE OF YOUNG boys were fishing down by the river near our place and one was having one heck of a time with his reel. It wouldn't feed out the line right. It would jam in the middle of a cast. The drag was wrong. The line would foul up. All those usual symptoms that fishermen know so well. After several frustrating attempts to make it work, including a long session of taking it apart, the boy quietly took the reel off his pole, set it down on a rock, picked up another big rock about the size of a basketball . . . and brought it down SMASH right on top of the reel.

    I ASKED a rancher the other day if any of his growing boys were athletes. "I hope not," he replied, thinking ahead to all the hours those "hired men" would be away from the irrigation ditch, the hay baler, the back of a horse.

    THIS FOOTBALL TIME of year always brings back memories of those boys who played great football around here . . . THE PLAYER who made one of the most memorable impressions was Chuck Unterzuber . . . I WAS at a basketball game at Columbus several years ago and the guy in front of me turned around and said: "The last time I can remember Columbus playing Greybull was when Unterzuber just clobbered us . . . AND ANOTHER time at a fancy dinner at the University the middle-aged Riverton lawyer across from me asked where I was from. "Greybull," I replied. "You know, whenever I think of Greybull I think of me lying there in the dust on a football field with Chuck Unterzuber running over the top of me."

September 21, 1972

THERE'S BIG fish in the Big Horn if you're a fisherman with the talents of Bob Garland . . . He got a five to six-pound pike the other day . . . measured about 24 inches!

PICKED UP a young hitchhiker on the road the other day, violating a long standing rule I've always had against it . . . but it was a beautiful September day, the week was about over, things had gone right, and I just decided to celebrate with someone . . . so he got an unexpected, unprecedented ride.
But he "paid" for it by telling me, "It was really something last night to see the stars in the sky. That's something I haven't been able to see traveling back from the East. The skies are never that clear other places."
I think he was a psychology major . . . how did he know I was a sucker for all nice things said about Wyoming.

September 28, 1972

BASIN'S football field is one of the best around . . . Very well kept compared to others . . . A good stand of grass . . . I remember when it was straight gravel, rocks and all . . . Not saying those old days made greater men than there are now, but let me tell you it took something extra to throw a downfield block in the middle of a pile of gravel.

October 5, 1972

HAD SKIP ANDERSON come down with the Billings team as an opposing coach Friday night, he would have been the first Greybull player to play on the field, coach for Greybull and coach against Greybull . . . JIM CRAWFORD is the only other one who would have but his Lovell team that year hosted Greybull at Lovell, as I remember.

THERE IS A BOY named Will Wood on the Lovell football roster . . . That's like having a player named Shell Creek for Greybull.

REV. SHANNON RODMAN who loves to play practical jokes on people, was standing by himself in a corner of Safeway the other day and one of the Safeway crew got on the loudspeaker and in a deep, deep voice beamed at Shannon, intoned: "Reverend Rodman, This is the Lord."

October 19, 1972

AN OLD COLLEGE buddy was on the phone the other night and told me: "I have a six foot daughter and I've lost all my hair!" He didn't say in what order this chaos arrived!

WHEN BRETT DEWITT, Greybull seventh grader, walked into the Cody Medical Center Thursday night for sixteen stitches in his right eyebrow he must have caused a little sensation . . . He'd just come from the Cody football field across the street where he'd been injured in the Junior High game. He was still in his football uniform, clomping cleats and all . . . That's really battlefield casualty treatment.

THE CODY JUNIOR HIGH football players have their names taped across their helmets. When Scott Arney, Greybull's tough, aggressive center lined up across from his man, he noticed he was a "McGee." Scott grinned maliciously across the line and began chanting loud enough for everyone to hear, "McGee for Me, McGee for Me, McGee for Me."

November 2, 1972
DID YOU EVER notice what a deep silence there is at the dinner table when the kids ask: "What did you do on Halloween, Dad?" And Dr. Spock says to tell your kids everything!

November 9, 1972
I LIKE chocolate sundaes, Mr. Goodbars and cheeseburgers . . . not necessarily in that order . . . but the new calorie counter the family has says EACH one of these delightful things are over 400 calories? . . . How can all the good things count so much . . . If I didn't know cottage cheese was low in calories I could have told you just by the way it tastes.

MY UNCLE, a White Russian who escaped Russia some 50 years ago and came to America, had some marvelous stories about his early days in this new country. Eventually he married my aunt, became one of the scientists in the Bell Telephone Laboratory in New York and worked on early day television in the 1930's and radar in the 1940's. But there were lean, hard years before all this success.
After attending school on the West Coast he hopped a freighter and went through the Panama Canal to New Orleans. There he ran into a fellow White Russian who was promoting an impossible scheme and wanted investment money. My uncle had only enough money to get to New York – this was in the 1920's – so he turned down the venture.
His countryman who offered him the investment was Igor Sikorsky who died this month. His scheme that he needed money for was the helicopter which he did finally successfully build.

November 23, 1972
ONE OF THE MOST interesting raffles in a long time is the one the GHS students are conducting to see which student gets to be the first in the new swimming pool!

WHEN EARL MADSEN and Anthony Manager Ron Elliot were putting up the Anthony sign on the new company building I tried to make a joke and tell them the "S" was backward . . . but they didn't think that was very funny . . . I guess it is only a printer's joke anyway . . . You cannot make an "S" backward, no matter which way you turn it . . . And all young printers (in those old days of letterpress) had to go through the initiation of learning that.

I remember over 20 years ago, working as a printer's devil for Hi Anderson at the Basin Republican Rustler when fellow worker Fred Gould told me that I had an "S" backward in the form. I took the form out of the press, took the "S", turned it right side up, put it back in the form, and back on the press. I printed a sample. "You still got that "S" upside down," Fred said exasperatingly. I looked. It sure did look backward. So I did it all over again. And again. Until somewhere the light dawned.

November 30, 1972

IT WAS LATE WHEN I came down to the office the other night and I was fumbling around with a pair of cold hands and a balky key trying to get the front door open. I heard someone call my name . . . I looked over toward the depot. No one there. Looked over my other shoulder at the bank. Someone called again. I sneaked a look over at Oscar Shoemaker's. Still no one. Then the voice said: "This is the Lord." I looked up and there on top of the Carey building, taking a time exposure of the Christmas lights, was Bruce Hanson.

December 7, 1972

THE TYPE PROCESS of "old type" such as we use now in offset printing is just not as reliable as that old "hot type" or Linotype we used for so many many years . . . The Linotype had its share of Wednesday exhaustions, but you could talk that thing back into operation if you knew what you were doing . . . The Standard still uses Linotypes for part of our composition . . . In fact, the machine Lynn Severance still operates has been at the Standard operating EVERY week for the past FIFTY-SIX years! It was put there in 1917 . . . Any plows around that old and still plowing?

BLESSED SNOW, you have covered up all of my mistakes, the weeds I never cut, the leaves I failed to burn, the junk I never picked up . . . Now I won't have to look at it again until next spring.

COUNTY CLERK Ellen Whipps finally had to buy a box of paper clips the other day . . . What's so unusual about that, you say? Well, it's the first box in 25 years she has had to buy! All this time she has saved the clips other people send to her!

"DEPOT" is a word seldom mentioned in conversation anymore unless you're a railroader or a railroad family . . . No passenger trains, no Western Union, no mail.

"CAN YOU heat up our baby's bottle for us," a tourist asked Paul Kinnaird at the Co-op station last summer? Paul dug up an old tester for thermostats, stuck the bottle in it, got it to the right temperature and handed it back to the woman . . . Now that, my friends, is a service station.

December 14, 1972

THE CODY JUNIOR HIGH eighth grade team is TALLER than Greybull's high school team! . . . One boy is six foot, the young Flannigan boy is 5' 11" and Al and Ann (Schroll) Simpson's son is in the 5' 11" neighborhood.

SPEAKING OF BASKETBALL height, someone should do a survey some day to find out what's in this Shell creek water we drink to cause such shortage of tall, tall boys.

In the past 15 years Greybull hasn't had more than a half dozen of those tall boys that help a basketball team so much. Bob Reed in the past five years was just about the tallest GHS ever had. Several boys like Don Kawulok, Barry Hunter, and Roland Smith didn't reach their full height or potential until they were out of high school. There have been several six foot ballplayers but no one of any big size. When Greybull won the 1959 Big Horn Basin championship Larry Clause was the mainstay under the basket and he was only six foot.

At the same time Basin had Davis', Masseys, Eckerdts, Ellis', Herdts, Lewis', all good-sized and talented boys.

December 28, 1972

AT THE POOL dedication, the architect said he was thinking that if "everyone here has brought their swimming suits today, this is going to be the wettest party in the history of Greybull." . . . MARK POWERS and JODY MEEKER carried off their "first in" status with poise and aplomb . . . They were the first official High school and Grade school students in the pool . . . That was a clever idea.

FRANK COPP'S contribution to the pool (though he wasn't at the dedication) was rightfully recognized . . . He was one of the first to advocate the pool be located at the high school . . . and he was saying and working for it at a time when no one else was.

1973

January 4, 1973

THERE ARE more "old faithful dog" stories than any other subject . . . Another one in the Reader's Digest this month reminds me of this . . . Reason must be that there are so many old faithful dogs, and each one to each family seems such a unique experience, such a heart-warming period in their lives that they tell it as if it had never happened before. In reality, nearly every family who ever had a dog has had exactly the same feelings for it, the same long associations, the same kids growing up while the dog grew old, the same dog growing feeble, the same old head barely lifting up when the master comes in and finally the long, sad trip to the veterinarian's.

Every family knows the feelings, and every family is sure its dog, like its kids, have special qualities. Which makes some of these stories the best you'll ever read.

January 11, 1973

HAVE SOLD OFF all our cows and calves and this year during spring we won't be playing nurse maid to all "those expectant mothers" . . . I'm going to miss that calving, I told my old army buddy, Fred Hageman at Douglas. "Come on down to see me this spring, then," he said. "I'm going to have 50 two-year-old heifers calving!" Sorry, it's not THAT much "fun", Fred.

January 25, 1973

I HAVE MADE my debut splash in the new swimming pool and let me report it is a magnificent pool . . . I have also determined that a 44-year-old man can go from the men's dressing room to the edge of the pool in 25 steps while holding his breath and attempting to look flat-stomached!

LAST WEEK we wondered what "QT" stands for as in "on the QT" and we got this delightful letter from J.T. Borders in Casper who wrote: "QT stands for quiet – QN for question – QK for quick – and so on. In the 'Old' days, when all news wire service was carried by morse telegraph the telegraphers adopted a code known as Phillips Code which had a short for almost every common word. The reason for this was that any good telegrapher could copy faster than it could be sent by hand – even with a vibroplex (bug). Phillips Code operators were in an exclusive society of telegraphers and were really envied by the ordinary boys. Some of the old timers may still have copies of the Phillips Code – I do not.

"TT was that, TY they, ccn correction, gg going, pous President of the

United States, gth go to hell; just mention any word and they had a code for it. Just ask old Roy Neeley or Jim Blackwood – they can tell you more about it."

February 8, 1973
   THE SNOW IN GREYBULL Tuesday was my fault . . . Sunday I decided it was getting warm enough to shovel off the foot of snow on the basketball court at our place . . . That was a mistake! As my family pointed out, cleaning off the basketball court in the winter is the same as washing the car in the summer . . . either one brings on more moisture.

   I DON'T KNOW what this means in terms of old friends and school ties and belonging to a country, but I was delighted to shake hands with Orville Wright after the Greybull-Basin basketball game Friday night . . . the same Orville Wright who was superintendent and started me out in the first grade at Basin and now was watching my son, a senior, wind up his basketball career.

   THERE'S ONLY one pancake flour, you know. That's Aunt Jemima PLAIN WHITE not buttermilk or buckwheat, but white . . . I've tried every kind there was for 25 years and nothing tops it . . . It makes that melt-in-your-mouth kind of pancakes and waffles . . . Really there's no equal . . . But it's scarce . . . Stores just don't stock it in competition to the more advertised brands . . . So after months and months of not having Aunt Jemima regularly, our family insisted that The Cook order it special . . . We now have a case of 12 three-pound packages of the stuff . . . The Kennedys are bullish on Aunt Jemima!

February 15, 1973
   GORDON GROSECLOSE wears a size 14 shoe! Consider that Wilt Chamberlain only wears a size 13 1/2!

March 1, 1973
   READING AN OLD Cody Enterprise the other day, I came across a picture of a hunting party at the Sunlight Ranch . . . and a sign over one cabin read: "This may look like hell to you, but it's home sweet home to me."

   IF GREYBULL, WYOMING was Greybull, Missouri and the year was 1846 and the town was getting up a wagon train to go to Oregon, which members of your community do you think would be on it? Try to put 20 families who live in Greybull right now in those 20 wagons . . . Some of your final choices will surprise you . . . Our family had a lot of fun with this one.

   WHEN the Greybull wrestlers wound up the last competition at the state wrestling tournament, they went out and bought 49 pounds of groceries at some all-night grocery outfit . . . and ate it all up!

WHEN the Greybull pep club were supposed to drive to Basin to meet the homecoming wrestlers, they got as far as the Unterzuber hill and stalled out with a flat tire . . . Undaunted they waited there for the bus and when it showed up down the road they hurriedly spread this big WELCOME HOME paper sign across the highway and the startled bus drove through it. That there was no oncoming traffic coming the other way to break it at the wrong time was taken care of by those special gods who look after cheerleaders and pep clubs.

REUBEN REIFSCHNEIDER was chosen Wyoming's Ugliest man years ago in a contest sponsored by Art Linkletter and Reuben has always had a lot of fun telling people about his "hard earned title." . . . When he was back East for his daughter's wedding in 1970 and the wedding photographer was getting ready to take the traditional pictures Reuben cautioned him about "making this a good shot because it could be your last one." . . . "Listen, I've been taking pictures for years and this camera hasn't broken on a face yet," the guy said. "Yes," Reuben replied, "but you haven't ever taken a picture of the Ugliest Man in Wyoming." Pow! the guy snaps the picture . . . and promptly burns out his strobe cord!

They had to hold up the wedding an hour and a half until the guy went back to his studio and brought back another cord!

March 8, 1973
SOMEONE ASKED where all those Poor Richard sayings come from at the top of this column . . . I get them from a little leather-bound book my grandmother had in Omaha . . . published about 1898 as a facsimile to those little original Poor Richard almanacs . . . The book is still full of sayings not used yet . . . some of the more earthy ones I guess you'll never see . . . Ben Franklin didn't pull punches in those days either!

March 15, 1973
CAN YOU remember back 10 years ago when all of us were ridiculing the Beatles, not only for their long hair (which is short by today's standards!) but for those horrible sounds? If that's music (we used to say) . . . The only people who liked them were all the "degenerate" young folks . . . Now the Beatles are recognized for their musical genius, their songs are playing everywhere by the Mancini's as well as the Groups, their hair style is "in". The other night I made the mistake of asking who wrote that good song? "The Beatles," they said . . . And right then I realized how old I was getting.

April 5, 1973
I CAN REMEMBER one Sunday several years after our first lessons, when Don Kurtz and I rode the tow together – it wasn't a lesson, we just moved into line together and we naturally talked skiing and I said I was having troubles, probably picking up bad habits . . . So Don said: "Ski on ahead of me and let

me watch" . . . So I did and about halfway down I waited for Don to ski up. "There's only one thing wrong with your skiing," he told me, and I said "What's that?" . . . and he pointed his finger right at my stomach, just about above the belt buckle! I got the message immediately because I'd known it all along! No G U T S.

April 26, 1973

FRANK CASEY being gone from the mountain this summer will be a drastic change . . . Frank had become almost as much a part of the Big Horns as the trees.

May 3, 1973

THAT WOMAN who wrote in the Reader's Digest about finding all sorts of things in the bird's nests around her place started me looking all over ours to see what we had.

She described an intriguing list of things she'd found: Some of her daughter's blond hair, bits of plastic. Our birds aren't that imaginative. The most common ingredient in those nests at our place were several shades of horse hair! You could have woven a blanket with all the gray, black and white horse hair that is hanging in our trees. But there was little else very exciting. One bird would use nothing but ragweed stems; another would pick up grass.

Yet even without the sophistication of those Eastern bird nest builders, it is still interesting to see what a bird might find to put into a nest.

I can remember a nest building robin giving me one of the true surprises of my life early one morning. I was out of bed half asleep at about the same time the sun was half-asleep in the east. As I glanced outside – without my glasses on yet – I noticed a large piece of blue suddenly take off straight up from the ground. I thought the Martians had landed for sure! But after I frantically got my glasses back on, it was only a robin flying up to a new nest with a piece of old blue Kleenex. Now there was a bird that showed some class.

May 10, 1973

THAT STORY about Gordon Groseclose winning distance races in Montana while running for Northwest Community College reminds me that Gordon has been running a long time . . . Back when he was in the seventh grade he never did get initiated into the junior high lettermen's club during the annual picnic . . . When it came time for the initiation he just outran everyone! No one ever did catch him.

May 31, 1973

THAT KOMA radio advertisement about "WhiteWing" coming to Greybull, Wyoming at the "City Auditorium" makes the old Community Hall sound sumptuous . . . We will be lucky if all those "great sounds" don't tumble down the old log walls!

DAVE GRABBERT in his Valedictory said in closing that he "ain't what I should be, I ain't what I could be, but I ain't what I used to be!"

AND ALUMNUS Frank Norris who gave the main address ended with: "And there Ed Friesen, Ethel Lindsey, Edith Scott, Dorothy and Jim Quigg et al is my reflection of what you've taught and, good or bad, it doesn't need a grade!"

June 14, 1973
NEVER GET OVER that good quality of those old, old pictures . . . they reproduce as if they were taken yesterday . . . Look at the picture of the Alderdice and Stanfield livery barn in the Standard's 49er edition last week if you don't believe me.

WHEN THE STANDARD printed that 50th anniversary edition in 1959, George Strickland dug out some old negatives for us that he had taken as a young boy around Greybull . . . I put them in the enlarger and blew them up to all sizes and they came out as good as if he had taken them the day before . . . What was even more interesting to me was that George had developed and printed the pictures himself way back then with one of those early-day-develop-it-yourself kits.

SOME OF THOSE Indian writings I looked at the other day in the Buffalo Bill Historical Center, I had looked at several times as a boy . . . Back then they were on that old sandstone cliff on the John Tillard place south of Greybull . . . In the last decade they were carefully cut out of the cliff and taken to Cody for preservation . . . Otherwise they probably wouldn't be here today.

AND LET ME ASSURE you that there must have been an 'old grey buffalo bull' at one time way back when . . . There's a picture of an albino or grey bull at the historical center . . . He's in a herd with some others in Montana in a picture taken by the museum director himself, Dr. Harold McCracken, back in 1942.

June 21, 1973
I TRIED TO TALK Slim Brewer into running his old Army truck in the 49er parade next year . . . His must be the oldest running Army vehicle in the state . . . It deserves to be recognized officially!

June 28, 1973
I THINK I MAY have stumbled on to why the kids at Shell would rather go to the Shell school than come in to Greybull. I was talking to young Joe Arnett last week and he told me: "You know, Greybull not only has bossy teachers but they have a principal to send you to!"

July 5, 1973

A PRESENTATION ceremony for buckle winners at the Gillette rodeo was scheduled for Sunday night after the rodeo was over . . . but only three out of the 20 winners showed up . . . Where were all the rest? . . . Well, someone had got up a jackpot roping after the regular rodeo was all over and all the winners were out for the ropin' instead of the presentin'.

THE ONLY TIME I've ever really experienced the feeling of getting the bull by the horns is opening that new door of the Big Horn Federal Savings and Loan.

July 12, 1973

THE VISIT A WEEK AGO of Buck Eckroth and his family was a pleasant trip back in football memories for a lot of Greybull people.

The Eckroths were here for a few days to say hello to a community that a dozen years ago was in athletic heaven. And the man who helped put it there was Buck Eckroth.

As he said last week, "we had an awful lot of good kids" which is true of course and there haven't been that many good athletes in a span of three or four years since.

But neither has there been another Buck Eckroth and without the coaching you don't have it, no matter how many kids are out on the field.

Eckroth's record will probably stand for a long time in Greybull. His 1959 basketball team won the district championship; two of his football teams were title contenders and another one shared the mythical state title with Laramie. And his track squad won the Class A track championship.

Most of all he built a sense of winning and gave the community a school athletic program that didn't have the loser's image. The importance of this winning pride is indisputable when you look back over the past 12 years since he left, particularly the great inadequacies of the last two years. The entire school is affected and the town just plain gives up.

But, to those more pleasant thoughts of yesterday, when Greybull's own Two Dozen Horseman ran together, there are as many different great stories to tell as there are people to tell them. And the Eckroths spent many hours reliving some of those happy times.

Eckroth went on to coach additional successful years in North Dakota before the ulcers got too bad; now he is out of coaching, in administration.

But some of his most intense memories of athletics and good times were at Greybull. He's still a subscriber to the Standard; his "boys" like Tom Wilkinson and Larry Clause still keep in touch.

When you talk about the "good old days" now those days were really good ones! And it was great to visit again with the guy who helped make them that way.

AFTER DEE PERKINS lost his wallet on the trail to Lake Arden over the Fourth, he asked Robert Walton to keep an eye out for it when he went up later . . . sure enough Walton found it. It had been found by someone else who took out the money and tossed it alongside the trail.

July 19, 1973
I'M NOT TOO SURE the Wyoming Republican Party realizes that Watergate is not something to do with irrigation.

LAKE SOLITUDE, over the weekend, was blessed with beautiful clear weather, NO mosquitoes, NO horseflies, NO flies of any kind, NO people.

But what people were there had one thing in common. Everyone had brought along his dog.

One bunch of backpackers had a wooly animal that looked like Slim Brewer's old dog.

Another group from out of state near Grace Lake had two just plain dogs hanging around camp.

Another girl fishing on a rock as we went by had a little pooch of some kind that barked once at the horses and then scurried for cover.

And another had a poodle-type that she gathered up in her arms as we went by.

Apparently people don't go to the hills unless the family dog is along.

But the thing that startled me were the hikers from Casper who brought along their cat. "Daisy" was its name. You could hear the girl calling it clear across the lake one night. She called it "Daisy" and her husband called it "Kitty." Now there's something out of place in the wilderness country of Lake Solitude to hear someone calling their cat. You're up there with a three-day growth of beard, you haven't been near a water faucet, a shower head, or a comb for some time, you're living off the land so to speak, roughing it, getting away from civilization . . . and here's some guy calling out: "Here, Kitty, Kitty, Kitty." In that high-pitched voice you use when you call cats . . . "Here Kitty, Kitty, Kitty."

July 26, 1973
TOURISTS ARE ALWAYS amazed at the friendliness of the West . . . Overheard a couple talking as they walked along Greybull's main street Wednesday and the husband was saying to his wife: "In a town this size everyone treats you differently, don't they? They're all very friendly."

And when I went over for a cup of coffee the tourist next to me was also caught up in this friendly reception he'd been having on his trip and he told me what a nice trip he was having.

"In fact," he said, "we are from Kentucky and a friend of ours stayed here in Greybull three years ago and recommended it to us. But we couldn't quite make it last night so we decided to drive here to have breakfast. Greybull is a very friendly place."

And when he paid his bill he told Chuck Shirran "this was the best breakfast we've had yet."

Outside, they stopped to talk to two more local people before they got into their car and headed back to Kentucky where not all the people are so friendly!

Another family won't forget Greybull, either, but in a different way. They were the ones who drove off from Dale's Standard Saturday and left their eight-year-old daughter behind.

After they didn't come back right away, Police Chief Elvin Saul drove out towards Cody with the little girl and sure enough, met her parents on the airport hill, coming back to get her.

August 2, 1973

TOURISTS are still beating a path to Reuben Reifschneider's blacksmith shop this summer . . . but not for any iron work . . . Instead they want to see what the "Ugliest Man in Wyoming" actually looks like . . . Since that first story came out in BIG Wyoming at the start of the summer, Reuben estimated over 500 people have stopped . . . One day last week "there must have been 20 people in the place at one time," he said . . . One guy had seen the original Art Linkletter show when Reuben was chosen . . . Another tourist had to meet someone in Buffalo at 1 p.m. and it was already noon . . . he called up and told his friend: "I can't make it at 1 p.m. I'm talking to the ugliest guy in the state of Wyoming!"

THE IDEA for the Ugly Man contest was dreamed up by Frankie Norris in 1959 for the Greybull 50th anniversary.

August 23, 1973

THAT MOSQUITO FOGGER does too do some good . . . it's bound to run over some.

HEAR BY THE RADIO that the oldie, "My Prayer" is back over the air waves . . . I never thought I'd hear the ancient tune again . . . When the CCC camp at Basin broke up years ago I was scavenging among the ruins and came across an unbroken Jimmy Dorsey record . . . with "My Prayer" on one side, sung by a quavery-voiced gal I can still hear . . . It was the first record I ever owned . . . I must have played it 5,000 times . . . And I can tell what was on the flip side, too . . . That was the great sentimental favorite: "Columbus Discovered America in 1492 . . . but I Discovered You." . . . My kids are right . . . Our music was as far out in left field sometimes as we think theirs is.

September 6, 1973

DO YOU REMEMBER when we had Pat Hubbard who was only a couple of years old then, draw the football picks for the week out of a hat? Then we pitted Pat's fearless predictions (by the draw) against Frank Norris Jr., Bob Tolman and Frank Copp (by scientific picking) . . . That first week Pat beat them all. Now Pat is almost out of high school down at Lander . . . I'm getting very, very old when I succumb to mentioning things like this!

September 13, 1973

THOSE PESKY raccoons seem to be taking over the country . . . but they're in shorter supply up Beaver creek . . . At the Elevator the other day they said Martin Frank Michelena had trapped 54 (fifty-four!) of them this year.

CLEANED OUT the place a little the other day and ran across this historical tidbit:

"Shell Creek –

"At a time prior to any settlement along the Shell valley, Fred Whitney, Dick Shell and others were rounding up cattle for J.D. Woodruff in through this part of the country. Dick Shell fell in love with the country and said he was going to come back and take up land at the head of the creek.

"The following spring they were again rounding up cattle in that neighborhood. They asked Woodruff how far he wanted them to go to look for cattle. He grinned and told them to go as far as (Dick) Shell's creek. They afterwards always referred to this place as Shell's creek until it gradually assumed the name of Shell Creek.

"Many believe that Shell Creek took its name from the shells found along its banks but this is erroneous." – Stories of Early Days in Wyoming by Tacetta B. Walker.

September 20, 1973

I HESITATE to mention this for reasons which will be obvious . . . but it may be safe, now that the frost is here, to report that in a petunia planter in front of a Colorado newspaper office, someone sneaked in some marijuana seeds . . . which grew mightily and conspicuously this summer . . . all the while the editor was writing mighty editorials against marijuana . . . until someone pointed out to him that he had his own pot in the petunias.

I'M GLAD I'LL be able to tell my grandkids that I watched Secretariat race . . . Why do you choke all up when you see some magnificent animal perform like that?

I THINK the raccoons have pushed us all too far in this country . . . I predict a reduction in population all over the county come next year . . . CHOT SMITH at Shell is smarter than the rest of us corn growers . . . He used an electric fence and ate sweet corn all summer . . . We did get one crop out of our patch . . . it was good . . . both bites.

IN THE LAST Junior Varsity tackle pot (the winner is the one with the most tackles) there was 25 cents and 10 IOU's!

September 27, 1973
THE KIDS put a lot of work into this year's Homecoming activities . . . Harley Wilkerson and Bob Harvey who rode in the parade played football for Greybull on a team 51 years ago . . . That's a ways back!

October 11, 1973
BOB EVANS' fine picture of the horse yawning was snapped just at the right time . . . There was another photographer years ago, back East someplace who was trying for the same kind of picture and couldn't get the horse to open his mouth at the right time. It was a picture of a police horse tied up to a parking meter and the photographer was trying to show boredom. But the old horse wouldn't cooperate. The guy went into the drugstore, bought some taffy, slipped a piece of it to the horse, and in the ensuing bout between horse teeth, jaw and taffy, got a picture of a very yawny horse!

November 15, 1973
THE TOM CLARKES of North Hollywood spend their summers in Shell and after Clarke and Stan Davis shared some fishing holes this past summer, Clarke invited Stan and his son, Corky, out to see the final Dodger-Giant series in Dodger Stadium in September.
About halfway through the game the stadium scoreboard flashed to the 43,000 people attending: "Dodger Stadium Welcome to Stan Davis and son – Corky – Greybull, Wyoming"

November 29, 1973
Rev. and Mrs. S.T. Rodman celebrated their 66th wedding anniversary Tuesday! Now that's a long time together. I told Shannon I thought Mrs. Rodman was the one who deserved the most congratulations for having to put up with him for so long.
Shannon had it all figured out that they had been married 24,000 days.
She had served at least 72,000 meals.
They had been married 576,000 hours.
And this grand couple are still going!

December 6, 1973
A GUY CALLED me all the way from Florida last week to ask if that leaning building (the one in the Standard's prize winning picture of last year) was still standing . . . Darn, he was disappointed when I said it wasn't . . . I don't know what he wanted to know for . . . he never said . . . I forgot to ask . . . Too busy thinking about how far a picture or a word can go . . . From Emblem, Wyoming to the tip of Florida.

NOTHING has quite the power of Black Type . . . Whenever people say to me how much more the world knows now than it used to, I've learned not to argue about it . . . Too much science statistics and all that, they throw at you . . . But the basic Humanities haven't changed much at all . . . Black type of hundreds of years ago is still as strong and as powerful as it ever was. When I was a high school student, eager and determined to enter the world as a journalist, I made a trip over to see A.W. Coons, the longtime editor and newspaperman of the Basin Rustler and then the Republican-Rustler. I asked the usual young man's question: "What should I do or read to be a good newspaperman?" He offered only two books, the same two books he said an old newspaperman told him to read: All the works of Shakespeare and the Holy Bible. Between these two, he said, is the education and the inspiration of black type and the human race.

December 13, 1973

WYOMING HAS more antelope than any state in the union, reports the Wyoming Wildlife, 200,000 of them. The closest other antelope-populated state is Montana with 95,000. The total of all antelope in North America is only 435,199; Wyoming has almost half of that. That's where all our people went — to antelope.

THAT'S THE Wyoming dilemma which all of us fight at one time or another: As individuals choosing to live in Wyoming we want to keep Wyoming as much like it is as we can, unspoiled, unpopulated, untrampled, ours alone. But as businessmen, parents, professionals, to keep building the state, increasing the tax base and economic climate so we can enjoy better schools, business districts, farms, better jobs and standards of living. The two goals are always at odds with each other.

BILL HARBAUGH used to be the senior member of the Greybull Chamber of Commerce . . . he had belonged longer than anyone else . . . Got to thinking . . . I'll have to conduct a search among Ruth Meier, Clint Core, Larry Probst, Dale Foe, Oscar Shoemaker, Joe Carey, the Minters, Skip Schuyler, Paul Kinnaird, Ed Huddleston, Jim Haycock (Have I missed anyone?) . . . to see who is the "senior" member of the Chamber now.

1974

January 10, 1974

THAT GHS TEAM of 1969-70 basketball was the last one to produce consistent winning. The streak of two wins put together by that team included the game in Big Piney where Bob Reed played with his prescription sunglasses on (he had lost a contact lens the previous night.) What a cool one, that Bob! And what a ballplayer!

SPEAKING OF BALLPLAYERS, I still can't get over that Otis Beach played on a high school team in Ogallala, Nebr. and he was the shortest player on the starting five . . . at 6'4"!

January 24, 1974

DON'T KNOW whether Thermopolis was up to its usual basketball par when it was dumped by Lovell the other night, but they had one heck of a time even getting to Lovell . . . First, Tony Christler missed the bus and had to catch up in a car . . . When he climbed on the bus, the driver inadvertently shut Christler's hand in the door . . . Back to Thermop for X-rays, hand was okay . . . Another start . . . Bus broke down outside Thermop. Back for another bus . . . Second bus ran out of gas . . . Wait for someone to bring them gas . . . Another start . . . Got as far as Greybull, second bus breaks down. They borrow one of Greybull's buses . . . Finally get to Lovell.

January 31, 1974

I COUNTED UP seven fathers and sons in business on Greybull's main street.

February 14, 1974

NEVER THOUGHT I'd see two real estate offices in Greybull . . . four cafes "uptown" . . . or no parking spaces in our block between the stop light and the depot.

SPEAKING OF CAFES, Gladys Heywood wrote on her Christmas card that she remembers when people ate Sunday dinners at the Alamo! "I am glad they are using the Alamo again. In the early days we considered it such a nice place, when I was a girl. Going there for Sunday dinner was a great pleasure. For me especially as I didn't have to cook it. That was at the time we were learning to eat grapefruit and Mrs. Nelson always dressed it up with a cherry in the center. When we had it that way other mornings later on, I thought of Mrs. Nelson."

THAT NEW GYM scoreboard (provided through the Larry Shepard Memorial) has certainly been an improvement over the old one.

February 21, 1974
THOSE TWO HORSES tied up at the Yellowstone Motel the other day looked like they had found the only green grass in the country . . . Mandy's putting green! . . . but that plastic stuff doesn't have much nibblin' to it . . . bright color, but not too chewy!

OUR OLD HORSE decided that the grass must really be greener on the other side . . . and ("encouraged" by another gelding higher up the pecking order) jumped two legs over a wood gate and left the back two on the other side . . . A good picture . . . if I had been in the mood.

March 21, 1974
STREAKERS are sure in the news . . . I don't know whether you people who criticize our newspapers for printing only the bad news would say that streakers are "good" news or not, but you've got to admit, it's different news! Sometimes, it's hilarious news. I liked that one about the skier at Steamboat Springs, who streaked down the ski slope there two weeks ago in only his skis . . . and then came out of his bindings! . . . And landed splatt . . . into the snow . . . That was surely the week's only blue streak.

March 28, 1974
SOME GREYBULL college kids heading back to Laramie pulled in behind a highway patrolman just outside Shoshoni and followed him at 55 mph for the next 100 miles . . . when they pulled into Casper there were 18 cars in the caravan behind them!

April 4, 1974
Monday, April 1, was Betty's and my anniversary of 15 years of owning the Greybull Standard. Back in 1959 on that date we bought the Standard from Lynn Severance on the most generous and liberal terms two kids ever got for their first venture.

On this same Monday, April 1, in the morning's mail was the first copy of a book I wrote on Community Journalism.

I have to think it wasn't a coincidence.

No two things were ever tied more closely together than this book and the Greybull Standard. What I put into the book was mostly what I learned being editor and publisher of the Greybull Standard. My life has been journalism for a long time, but I never newspapered more intensely than I have here in Greybull and what I learned from the pages of the Standard went into the pages of the book.

There are other pages from other towns, too – from Neligh, Nebr., and

Basin, Wyo., and Lincoln and Lander and all those other places where I spent time learning the profession of weekly journalism. I came into weekly newspapering as a printer's devil first, a teenager who was fascinated by the print shop. But it was the end of the era when this apprenticeship was necessary. Letterpress was dying out. That ritual of putting hot lead to newsprint was ending. I helped bury it on my own newspaper later, and embraced the new offset eagerly. But letterpress or offset, the real profession of weekly newspapering is the same. I have spent all my adult life living and preaching and believing in weekly journalism.

The book is an outgrowth of these feelings.

You cannot be objective about your own book. You lived with it too long. It was over 10 years from its beginning to this past Monday. I can tell you exactly when I started it. The week after Maurice Thompson went back to Mississippi after spending a few days in 1963 around Greybull and Shell and Horse Creek. Places he'd spent one summer as a boy with Tom Olney. It was Maurice Thompson who knew how to encourage me to write this book. He inspired me to start. And I did, in less than a week. And I was able, as I went along, to put down in black type the feelings and opinions and advice I had to anyone else who might want to follow in these journalism steps.

It is not an accounting of the experiences I had in Greybull as a newspaper editor. That is another story for another time. It is rather a book that explains weekly newspapering. I hope it is better than a "how-to" book. And hopefully it won't be considered a stuffy academic one either. It is for young people and old people who want to live life in a small town as a weekly editor . . . who want to know the thrills I have . . . who want to feel the adrenalin flow from one Wednesday to the next. It is my philosophy on ways to accomplish this on your own "Greybull Standard" somewhere.

June 6, 1974

PAUL KINNAIRD when he retired as manager of the Big Horn Co-op Service Station last month, had been in the service station business longer than anyone else in town. He began to work for the Co-op in 1937 and worked there until 1945 when he bought a half interest in the old Short Stop service station with Henry Minnis.

In 1955 he went back as manager of the Co-op and worked there until May 1, 19 more years.

He gave service to thousands of guys like me and I always got a great deal of enjoyment talking to him. He'll be in Billings now, with his son and daughter, Bob and Betty.

To put his service to this community in perspective, when he went to the Co-op that old building was so small they couldn't get the long cars in . . . and ended up enlarging the building two more times.

June 20, 1974

YOU KNOW, taking care of a yard is just about the first job a man has . . . and the last one.

IF I HAD to pick one color Wyoming has that I like best, it would have to be the red dirt around Shell and Hyattville.

THAT FAMOUS picture of Eisenhower talking to the 101st Airborne paratroopers before the Normandy invasion drop has been republished many times. But on the 30th anniversary of the invasion, the National Observer went a little further and tried to find out what some of the men in the photo were doing 30 years later. Their search brought them to Greybull to talk to Bill Boyle, one of the pictured paratroopers. They contacted three other paratroopers from the picture – one in Washington, D.C., one in Saginaw, Mich., one in Fargo, N.D. and Bill Boyle in Greybull. And they ran a big spread in the national weekly with the headline: Ike's Paratroopers Ponder, D-Day and Today.

July 4, 1974

FIRST OF ALL, Tom Wilkinson makes a heck of a lot more than $10,000 per year as we had in last week's Standard . . . Make that $100,000 instead! Now that sounds more like what the top quarterback for Edmonton in the Canadian League should be making.

There's a lot of us who take a great deal of vicarious pleasure in seeing Tom make that kind of money . . . and doing something that he still must consider fun. I have watched, taken pictures of, read about, heard about Tom Wilkinson playing football in EVERY one of the 18 years I have been in Greybull . . . from the eighth grade, through those state championship years in high school . . . the record-breaking years at the University and then on to Canada football.

What was always Tom's strongest asset was not his physical talent, his ability to pass a football. Instead it was intense desire – a contagious desire – to win. There are and will be many athletes with greater ability, but he has few peers when it comes to excelling in winning.

"It's not how big you are, but how tightly you are wound," has always applied to Tom Wilkinson.

August 22, 1974

Betty and I are closing out our Greybull newspaper careers with the sale this week of the Standard to Sally and Paul Massey. So this will be the last "Getting the Bull by the Tail" column I will write in the Greybull Standard. I don't know that you should write a Swan Song in a Bull-by-the-Tail column. That may be a mixing of too many animals. Essentially, though, this is a swan song, an ending piece about how much we've enjoyed this newspaper life in Greybull, how many memories it holds for us, how much pride and accomplishment we have taken with the paper.

We have owned the Standard longer than any one else has. This is our 16th year. We thought we would own it forever. We bought it on a shoestring, raised our kids on it and with it, started our life here, grew "old" here. But time and circumstance change and we must change with them. Part of the change is today's sale of the Standard.

And with the sale, of course, comes an end to this column which has been a part of this newspaper career here from the start. The column has gone through several changes of format. The content has been revamped a little as time went on. At one time it was one of three columns I was writing for the Standard, all going at the same time.

We never agonized over a name. I've had some columns I never could get the right name for. But somehow, this one just fit in a town that was named after an old grey bull. And we thought it better to get an old grey bull by the tail than the horns! Actually, the only bull by the tail I ever saw was the picture of one over in India that Slim Brewer and Orville Stockwell sent me. Sure enough, there was a guy who had a bull by the tail.

It was enough for us trying to hang on to where the column took us over the years. I went for one stretch of nearly 12 years and never missed an issue. Betty filled in for me once when I came down with the mumps which was a humiliating way to break a record. But the rest of the time it was there week after week, part of the paper we referred to generally as "The Standard."

The best picture I ever took — "best" being that picture which generated the most reaction — was the March Lamb. Thelma Smith got her lambs out for me on their lane and helped me get that one.

The hardest we ever worked was the anniversary edition of 1959. Ninety pages of letterpress history — an unheard of number for such a small paper in those days. On Sunday night, three days before press day, we had only 36 pages done and worked on almost no sleep to produce that final 54 by Thursday morning.

The ice jam story of 1962 was our best reporting, but so was Glenn Coxen's getting shot by the California couple a few years earlier, and the flooding of the Greybull river in 1967.

The most informative story we ever did was the four-page series in 1960 on the financial structure and condition of the Town of Greybull and its water line.

In fact, town government became a hobby and at one time I had attended more council meetings than anyone else in town. My "term" started before Clarence Walton was treasurer and went from Mayor Oscar Shoemaker, George Hughes, Frank Dunning, Earl Madsen, LeRoy Balfour, Frank Copp to Mayor Bill Murdoch.

The pig that got away and trotted down a startled main street in the early 1960's was the most fun I ever had doing a story. That one wrote itself. And that picture of Jim House, John Boyd and Clair Stearns carrying it down the street is still in the files someplace and indelibly in my mind.

The historical series I wished I'd done would have been to spend an afternoon with K.K. Kimbro up Beaver creek; John Loveland up Trapper creek; Dan Cropsey at McDonald's Ferry; Herb Smith all over Shell creek; and Fred Conners over his old mail route over the Big Horns.

I wish I had dug deeper into that story years ago when the county official had to resign.

I wish I had written something that would have contributed to Dresser's putting on that filter years before they did.

There is just no end to the memories of these years since 1956 when we came to work for Lynn Severance on the Standard staff. I can't look anywhere anymore without seeing a story I once wrote about. You touch an amazing number of people when you newspaper right in a town. There is a name and a face to every story I ever wrote, every picture I ever took. It was about all these years at the Standard that I wrote in my book: "When I look back on it, I see many words I'm glad I wrote, some pictures I know I'll never get again, some friends that are still around. I flip through the bound files and see all those Wednesdays of the past, all that newspapering; and I can feel the old adrenalin flowing again."

We were right about getting the old bull by the tail rather than the horns. For it's been a great, great ride!

Thoughts by Vonnie

By Vonnie Harnden

August 22, 1974

When the Standard crew called to see if I would help put the paper out this week, I consented almost without thinking. Hanging up the phone I thought . . . Good Grief! What in the world possessed me! It has been a whole year since I've participated in the hectic process of grinding out the weekly sheet. I'd probably be in the way, goof it up, botch the job . . . be a real hometown Edith Bunker. Type sizes, fonts, ad lay-outs, proofreading, were a thing of the past . . . I thought.

But after a few hours on the job, I discovered, much to my simple-minded amazement, the whole thing returned. It's much like riding a bicycle after years of non-riding. Only easier. You ought to see my pedal pushing "expertise" these days. Pretty wild.

Several main street merchants seemed surprised Monday when I charged into their stores and plunked my clip board down to take their ads. It was great to be back, though; they made me feel like "Queen for a Day".

We're sorry to learn this week is the last of Bruce Kennedy's "Bull column", and all the other things he has made so interesting and alive for us over the years.

Through his excellent newspapering, commonplace small town events became important happenings. Important, not because the participants of the events were "big wheels" in the community, but rather because those participants were you and me, the guy on the street.

It didn't matter whether the man coming in the front door of the Standard was a senator, the garbage collector or the gas jockey on the corner. That person was given the same consideration whether he was peddling political views or just bringing in a tremendous turnip grown in his back yard that season. Each was important in his own right.

Kennedy editorials were classics. He believed in taking a stand on an issue and fighting tooth and nail for what he thought was right, whether it was a popular concept or not. He angered some and overjoyed others. What good editor ever did otherwise? But if he was proven wrong, he had the same guts to admit it.

His editorials were leaders of men, yet his enthusiasm for sports, kids and scholastic ability was, I'm sure, a factor that sparked many youngsters to better themselves along those lines. He and that extension of his right arm, the camera, were there for great shots of Little League, science fair winners or the insane tangle of thighs, elbows and jawbones of a football game. I remember watching Bruce once at a high school wrestling match. His camera lay ready but momentarily forgotten on the floor beside him as he was vicariously caught up in the struggle of those two boys on the mat. You could tell by the body English and agonized contortions of his face that he was mentally trying to help each kid pin the other guy!

Speaking from an employee's standpoint, we could never have asked for better employers than Bruce and Betty Kennedy. In 10 years of working at the Standard, I never once got "bawled out", though I had it coming many times. And when one of us made some glaring error in a merchant's ad, or forgot one completely, Kennedys took the blame themselves, never saying, "Well that was So-and-So's fault."

We were guided, encouraged and stimulated into doing our work right. But never berated and put down.

Bruce and Betty provided a new challenge, a new inspiration every day to do it better than we did yesterday or last week. We were made to feel we were not just employees to be "bossed" or yelled at like so many lackeys; we were an actual part of that paper and we wanted it to be the best we could provide that week.

Bruce was always trying to make the Standard a better paper for his readers and advertisers. He was continually visiting other newspaper plants and gleaning new, better and faster methods of getting things done. Every time he was out of town, we knew that on his return we'd be singing "There'll Be Some Changes Made Today". Many times I wished he'd just stop going to those places and bringing home all those great ideas to change us. But that's what progress is all about . . . new ideas, better ways, change. That's a Kennedy . . . and we are proud to have been there.

With the sale of the Greybull Standard, "Getting the Bull by the Tail" was no longer printed in the Greybull newspaper. The column continued to appear in the Wyoming State Journal in Lander where it started in 1967, the Gillette News-Record beginning in 1970 and the Cody Enterprise starting in 1971. The Green River Star began using it in 1975 and the Douglas Budget in 1985. In these other newspapers, the column was titled "Some Thoughts."

August 28, 1974

A TOURIST CAR in northern Wyoming the other day had its back seat loaded with . . . (I bet you think I'm going to say Coors beer) . . . nope, not Coors beer, but tumbleweeds! Now what in heck will people do with a back seat of tumbleweeds . . . In the first place, how many tumbleweeds can you get in a back seat . . . Four? One thing about saving tumbleweeds for the tourists instead of elk antlers is that tumbleweeds are a lot easier to find!

DURING THE GOVERNOR'S race, Malcolm Wallop knocked on one door in a house-to-house canvass of a Wyoming town and the housewife came to the door topless! . . . "Don't be disturbed," she told him, "I go around the house like this all the time."

September 5, 1974

IN GILLETTE when you want to fly commercially in or out you ride a three-time-a-day shuttle flight to Casper . . . called "Antelope Airlines" which always raises a chuckle from those more sophisticated big city people who come out this way . . . But I submit that there's more zest in that name than a Frontier or a Western.

A PAIR OF DENVER businessmen rode it the other day and were talking with a fellow passenger . . . "What do you do in Gillette," they asked? . . . "I'm the TV repairman for Gillette," he replied . . . Now those city folks just couldn't get over that, either, the fact that they were in the company of the only guy who repaired TV's in the town . . . They must not run into anyone in Denver who says: "I'm the plumber for Denver."

SUPPOSE YOU already knew that the song about the yellow ribbon and the old oak tree is a true story . . . There was a guy just out of prison who told the waiting wife to tie a yellow ribbon, then he told the bus about it and then there was a block of yellow ribbons . . . Reader's Digest carried it several years back . . . I choke up every time I hear it, but then I seem to be choking up about something all the time anymore!

GREYBULL'S FOOTBALL team will have to play its home games on the Basin high school field while the Greybull field is being replanted . . . Which means those visiting teams won't be without a tremendous cheering section . . .

Rival Basin WON'T be rooting for any Greybull success!

WE WERE OFF to the side of the trail in the Big Horn wilderness area when the two backpackers went by and it wasn't until after we looked back at them that we saw they had ripped off two Forest Service signs (the ones that say "Middle Paintrock Creek") . . . Even then it didn't soak in fast enough that they must have unbolted those small signs and actually tied them on the back of their packs and were going back to civilization with them . . . I will hate myself forever for not going back down the trail and at least trying to get those signs back.

September 11, 1974
WE GOT OUR first pullet egg the other day . . . The way I have it figured that egg cost us $64.58!

I THINK WYOMING pickups should be sold with a gun rack already mounted in the back window.

September 18, 1974
MY FAMILY HAD fun with this typewriter doodling that Addison Bragg had in his column . . . I'm borrowing it from him in case you didn't see it:
Type a line of lower case "o".
Go back and type the ampersand (&) over the "o".
Do the same with the slash (/).
Space down one-half space and type capital "W" underneath each figure.
Space one-half down again, type a quotation (") under each.
Finally, tell the men to fall out and get back to work.

IN PAST WEEKS, during a transition of one president to another, Americans saw again the greatness of the Constitution. And from everywhere in the nation we marveled that a group of men 200 years ago could devise so great a document. But we are a materialistic country now, in this 1974, and we tend to forget our beginnings as a people, the heritage and the faith, the ideas and the ideals. We are materialistic now, but the Constitution is not a rocket that can put a man on the moon. It is not a refrigerator that can make ice cubes. Or a car that can be air-conditioned. And if it cannot be put together physically, we modern Americans as a people really do not understand it. Actually, we may suspect it.
But our forefathers didn't know about the technology, the industrial magnificence, the corporate might America would have. They were not preparing for that. The education then was not a scientific one. Or a business one. It was

the study of the Humanities, the Law, the Classics, the Histories, the Religions, the Literature. And it taught one very important precept – there is nothing new under the sun. That a man given a certain set of circumstances was going to react in an almost predictable way. You gave him the opportunity to soar to his greatness; you protected his followers and subjects in case he failed.

They wrote the Constitution for human beings, not for a physical country. And it will endure and give hope and inspiration for as long as there are people.

October 9, 1974

DON'T VOUCH FOR THIS story from the Gillette area, but the talk around there the other day was about an alleged out-of-state antelope hunter who waited to dress out his animal . . . until he was in his room at the fanciest motel in town . . . and dressed it out in the bathtub.

October 23, 1974

BECAUSE I HAVE taken pictures for a living, people are always asking me technical problems about photography, but the questions miss the point . . . Good photography is not dependent upon what developer you or I use or film or camera or any special kind of equipment or process . . . It is rather how YOU TAKE the picture . . . This point seldom satisfies my questioners. They want gadgets and modern technology to solve their photography problems . . . I have the urge to dig out my old Speed Graphic and hand it to the next questioner and to tell him, "Use this for a month, take all the pictures you can think of, and see at the end if you're not concentrating on the picture and not the camera."

OUR FAMILY has a big yellow dog who is insecure and full of doubts and he barks a lot to keep up his courage . . . I question his intelligence actually . . . He will even bark if he is on the outside of the house and someone knocks on the inside . . . Modern dogs are getting as neurotic as their owners. The old boxer we had before this one couldn't bear the sound of a door slamming somewhere in the house . . . especially when he was alone . . . If you came home and he was still behind the big chair, you knew a gust had come up and slammed a door somewhere . . . The wind purposely teased him into an early old age.

He was harmless really, but the ugliest, meanest looking dog ever and he had a list of people who never came near the place without checking first. A friend who worked on our house once ran out of gas near our lane, but he chose to walk an extra half-mile to the neighbors to call for help. He said later he didn't want to face the dog. The joke really was on him, though. Our old Butch had been dead for six months by then. But how he would have laughed if he'd known his spirit was still guarding the place.

October 30, 1974

IF I HADN'T realized I was on a college campus at Laramie Saturday I should have known from the announcements about the two raffles being held ... One prize was a waterbed. The other was a 16-gallon keg of beer.

November 6, 1974

OUR HENS, after weeks of steady laying, dropped off drastically one day and then picked back up the next ... Puzzling ... Sudden weather, I guessed ... Or a late hibernating skunk. Neither one, old man. Look at the date, Halloween Eve ... The family egg thrower needed ammunition!

A NEBRASKA FOOTBALL fan ran into the head ticket manager outside the UW stadium. "Geeze, Jim," he says, "I sure wish I had brought my piano with me." Why's that? asks a bewildered Pittenger. "Because my tickets are on it."

November 20, 1974

DISTRICT ENGINEER Pat Brown, who's responsible for the Wyoming Highway Department in the Big Horn Basin and Fremont County, says the road system is in its best shape in 13 years. And several current projects are making it better. He has work going on in five or six areas, including the Riverton to Hudson stretch which has to be the worst 12 miles of road in Wyoming. Cody west to the forest service boundary will receive work; Cody east from the Oregon Basin turn-off to Eagle Pass and from Eagle Pass to the county line will be done. The new Sage Creek bridge is already under construction. And so is the new bridge and approach at Worland on Highway 20.

Brown has been particularly effective in bringing the Shoshoni to Frannie highway up to present traffic standards. "That road is the lifeline of the Basin," he says. It carries traffic south to Casper-Cheyenne-Laramie-Denver and also to Fremont County and Salt Lake. It's the main road to the north. And it's in far better shape than it was.

Remember those horrible 10 miles of old road from Shoshoni north, including that underpass? That's all gone, now. The tunnels in the canyon have been widened; the approaches on both sides of Thermop are wider and easier, and three-laned on the north end; the highway from the reformatory to Worland is a dream now; the old "black hill" on the Lovell road is gone.

It's a smoother, wider, better ride, even if we're still only supposed to go 55 miles per hour!

December 4, 1974

CENTENNIAL, the new James Michener book, is the only major book I've ever read where I knew people in the "Acknowledgments" ... a lot of familiar Wyoming names in that book.

IF THE POST OFFICE is "being run like a business" now, God help the capitalistic system.

December 11, 1974

A BUSINESSMAN friend of mine had a phone call from a customer asking about the price of a certain item . . . When he gave it to him, the customer blew up and shouted over the phone, "You robber!" . . . Which brings up the tragedy of present inflations and recessions . . . Neither can control it or prevent it. The merchant is in an even worse position than the customer. He not only is a customer himself of all other services except that which he sells, but he is at the mercy of the wholesalers, freight shippers, warehousemen, corporation presidents who take a cut before the item ever gets to his shelves. Yet no one feels the customer's ire like the merchant who must actually sell it at the retail level. The corporation president pockets his profit before he sends it to the wholesaler, who in turn takes his share before passing it along to the shipper, who brings it and gets paid for his service. Then only does the merchant have it to hand to the customer who screams at him, "You robber!"

OUR BIG YELLOW dog was guarding the empty house with some ferocious barking when Oscar Shoemaker came to make a delivery the other day . . . Oscar knew the delivery had to be put inside so it wouldn't freeze, but how to get past the big, mean dog? . . . Finally Oscar opened the door just a crack and in a stern voice said: "Now you go over there around the corner." And that's what the big, yellow mutt did, went right around the corner and out of sight, cowering under the bed, I suppose, with his paws over his eyes.

1975

January 8, 1975

THE BIG HORN RIVER is a month late in freezing over . . . It usually lets the ice take over in December . . . But Monday morning when I went over it was still open . . . The only year it never froze over at all was way back in the 1960's during that one balmy winter . . . Otherwise it's ice from December to March.

MY FAMILY has reached the stage where they have memorized all my stories.

Apparently I am conditioned, like Pavlov's dog, to react to the same stimulus with the same story. And when, like in this last holiday season with everyone home, I started to tell a story, I could see by the looks I was going over old ground.

At my age I'm too old to learn all new material. Frankly, I didn't realize before how much "old" material I was collecting. Until this year. And now I see that some of my tales have been around a long, long time. Of course, I still enjoy the hell out of them. But my audience is weakening. They've been polite, bless them. Patient and polite and understanding. But they're getting awfully squirmy now when it's my turn to talk.

I should have started numbering all those stories long ago. So I could say, Do you remember No. 38, (That could be the one from overseas.) Or No. 14, that could be the high school play one. Or No. 24, the one when we burned the shed down!

February 5, 1975

PUBLISHER Don Schmidt in Gillette, who has a friend Modene who works for the Social Security people, told about the old Indian who couldn't write. So instead of endorsing the Social Security check with his signature, he simply made an inked-up thumb print on the back of the check . . . it was all legit. But for some reason somebody got to comparing his thumb print on the cancelled checks that he'd endorsed over a period of years. Modene said it looked like the same print . . . but then again it didn't. Seemed to be getting sort of blurred. So someone went to visit the old fellow. But he wasn't there. Had been dead for years. All that was left of him was his thumb . . . in a bottle of formaldehyde.

MY IDEA of happiness is watching the Boston Celtics play basketball.

February 19, 1975

DID YOU SEE where the old 10 cent stamp won't be with us much longer . . . the Post Office needs more money to take longer to get a letter to you . . . One of the baffling parts about this downhill slide of the national postal service is that the local postal employees I have contact with are the most accommodating people you run into . . . They do their jobs – and more . . . but someplace else the whole system is bogging down.

March 5, 1975

THIS IS THE TIME of year when I just can't stay away from the trees around our place.

I never can get over how much they grow. They can grow as fast as your kids, a small sprout of a thing one week and taller-than-you the next. Five years on a tree turns it into a giant sometimes, especially after those first, slow getting-started years. There's a Scotch pine in one corner of the yard we used to put Christmas tree lights clear to the top. Now it would take a 30-foot ladder and more lights than you could ever get together. The row of Lombardy poplars we set out, the spindliest four-foot things I ever saw, are now visible for miles and last fall made a solid wall of gold that was unforgettable.

So I putter around, lopping off a branch here and there like the book says to do in February and March, probably looking just as foolish as that guy in the Homelite saw commercial. Actually, I haven't cut a tree down in years. If you're a tree on our place you have a long life ahead of you!

March 12, 1975

I RAN INTO A STORY in another Wyoming city, a couple of hundred miles away, but it carries such a universal message to all newspaper people that it ought to be pinned to every journalism school wall, stapled on every editor's calendar pad.

Let me share it with you.

It was about six months ago and the young woman reporter was in the mayor's office for her usual interview. She had written a lot of copy about the mayor and the problems of his city. Although she was just a beginning reporter, a first year stringer for a daily newspaper, she had had considerable stories printed.

Today as she sat across from the mayor to begin yet another interview, the mayor suddenly reached over and took her pencil out of her hand. He broke the pencil in two and threw the pieces in his wastebasket. Then he reached for his own pencil and handed it to her.

"Why did you do that?" the flabbergasted girl asked.

Replied the Mayor: "I just wanted to see if my pencil would write what I say."

April 2, 1975
   WYOMING is a state when many times there's not enough snow for a white Christmas but enough to cover up your Easter eggs.

   WHEN THE THREE-YEAR-OLD son of a friend of ours pulled his dad's car out of "Park" and sent it careening down the hill, the little boy went to his room and promptly pulled the covers over his head. No one knew the car was far down in the ditch. But he just stayed under there, quiet, comfortable and safe. Finally he got up, went out in the front room and told his Dad, "I've got $20 in the bank and it's all yours!"

   THIS DIDN'T HAPPEN in Cody but it did in another Big Horn Basin town. Apparently the town cops got a tip that there was a continual pot party in progress in a house, supposedly put on by junior high school kids.
   So the police got permission from neighbors to use their garage for surveillance. The first thing that police did in the garage was put up curtains. Curtain? In a garage? That's what the kids wondered. So, being kids, they went over to the garage to see what was going on behind the curtains. Alas, the cops' cover was blown. In a small town you don't put up curtains in a two-stall garage.
   Moral: Try to be smarter than the kids.

April 9, 1975
   FRIDAY at the Greybull-Basin golf course it was dusty playing golf . . . By the next day the fairways were ankle deep in snow . . . HAVE YOU EVER noticed people traveling on rough, wintery roads like these of the past several weeks always wave more often to each other, as if to say, "I think we're both crazy to be here."

   WERE YOU among those "oldtimers" who said goodbye to Gene Dobbins this past week? He was 78 when he died Mar. 26, and Fred has been dead for 18 years, but a lot of us will remember all that dance music he and his partner, Fred Gould, produced in the 1920's, 30's, 40's and 50's. No two people ever produced more. It's been amazing to me since to realize how much music came from one short, happy little guy on the piano, Gene; and one very talented saxophone player, Fred. They played for proms, Saturday night dances, Thanksgiving dances, Christmas dances, for New Year's and rodeos and the Elks and anyplace else where people wanted to dance. Many, many times, just the two of them. I have a vivid picture in a countless number of dances of Gene moving his head back and forth to the rhythm as he played, and Fred, sitting with one thin leg crossed over the other on that inevitable folding chair. The big band sound from a very little band.

April 23, 1975
THOSE GUYS in the Marlboro ads never haul hay or never build a fence . . . All they do is get on a horse and ride . . . Or get off a horse and sit by the campfire . . . The non-smokers must get to do all the hay hauling and the staple pounding.

THE FARMER never gets credit enough for stewardship of America's land.
For generation after generation the land has produced and produced. It is probably in better shape now than ever before. There is no law to make him protect it or replenish it. There is no tax to pay if he doesn't. He has been his own steward and taught his heirs to do the same. It has been his responsibility and he has carried it well.
The land has been good to him and he has been good to the land. And we all have benefited.

May 7, 1975
THEY ARE TAKING some of those Vietnam refugees to Fort Chaffee, Arkansas – are we trying to welcome them or sentence them! . . . Fort Chaffee, Ark. (or Camp Chaffee, as I knew it once) is the bottom of the world as far as I am concerned.
I lost five good months of my life there in the U.S. Army and I found it to be a place you send your enemies to, not your friends. It was so hot when I hit there in August, 1951, that they cut out all doubletiming. No running. You could barely walk! You couldn't sleep for the humidity. The first sound I heard as we lined up in the street by the train depot was the guy behind me keeling over from the heat. And that wasn't the hottest! In September they had a heat wave. Two months later it was so damned cold you couldn't stand it.
Walter Winchell, in the middle of that heat wave, had an item which read: "Write to the boys in Korea, but pray for those in Camp Chaffee, Ark."
A couple of years later there was a bill in Congress to change the name to Camp Truman which I found hilarious. But they never did. They gave it some stature with the "Fort" in front, but believe me you would have to reshape the earth to make Camp Chaffee, Ark. into anything.

May 28, 1975
COORS BEER says they're going public with 1.4 million shares which ought to make a lot of beer drinkers – and non-beer drinkers – happy . . . There'll be many people who won't be able to resist that one.

WHICH LEADS ME into a reported conversation between a bunch of girls who were discussing the "proof" labels on alcoholic beverages . . . Said one, who claimed to have it figured out: "If it says 50 proof, that means that if there are 100 people in the room, 50 of them will be smashed." No, young lady, that's not quite how it works.

June 4, 1975

I STOPPED at a service station in Montana and the girl who checked the oil, washed the windshield and pumped the gas had given up trying to keep her hands clean . . . They were greasy, dirty black – but she'd painted her fingernails the brightest red I ever saw!

July 2, 1975

THE TEMPERATURES say it's getting to be July . . . I think the frost has finally gone out . . . and the mosquitoes are back, rejoicing in the knowledge that I am still good eating.

THE PURE SOUND of a meadowlark is as much Wyoming as our blue sky. A summer morning would not be the same without it. But I am fascinated by the long, complicated, double-noted song of the brown thrasher. If you had a yardful of brown thrashers and a field full of meadowlarks, what a symphony.

STILL THINKING about reunions and summer get-togethers . . . Someone always gets a prize for "changing the most." But really there aren't many changes. Some people blossom out after school days. All of us grow up, of course. And a hidden talent develops and sends us in a new direction as adults.

But basically none of us change. We're still the same people as adults as we were as kids. I run into people every day that I've known since we were kids 40 years ago. The wrinkles are there and the hair isn't. And there's thinness and fatness and sags in places we wish weren't. But underneath it's the same gal, same guy. The mannerisms are just as I remember. The smile or the frown. Even the words and expressions haven't changed. More important, how they think and judge and approach life is from the same mold as it was around Boy Scout campfires or in high school classes. And I am to them, too. We're just the same people, I don't care how many years go by.

August 13, 1975

SATURDAY, Aug. 9 there was a six point bull elk 100 yards from the highway, standing in the middle of the badlands five miles out between Lovell and Greybull . . . Figure that one out.

August 20, 1975

I KNOW OF A public swimming pool in Wyoming, (no, not in this town!) where the older women's swimming class made a deal with the male lifeguards . . . so that the male lifeguards are never around when the self-conscious women go in or out of the pool . . . The men are in the lifeguard room when the women are out of the water leaving and entering, so all they ever see of their pupils are their heads!

I HAVE ENJOYED immensely flying over the Oregon Trail this summer on flights between Lander and Green River.

There must be a dozen roads out in that South Pass country, but there is only one Oregon Trail. And it is unmistakable. It took me awhile to know what to look for. But there are three characteristics that separate it from all the other roads and trails and modern marks on the land: 1) It has to be near the Sweetwater or bend back towards it; 2) It is never straight, more squiggly and wandering; 3) and it has a wide roadway, a "borrowpit" if you will, that extends on each side of it for many, many feet.

The breadth of the "borrowpit" is the thing that gets to me. There is an active, traveled road in the center, still today. People drive along it, either knowing or not knowing they are riding on history. But the "borrowpit" is ancient. There's a definite width to it, wider than any road, cut into the ground by horses and cattle and wagons out of line, and thousands and thousands of walking feet. The ruts of one time were not necessarily the ruts of another, though the direction was the same, and all this cut a swath across that Wyoming land that you can see mile after mile in either direction.

Knowing the Oregon Trail is down there is a thrill for me. But even greater is seeing that deep mark going on and on.

August 27, 1975

NOW THAT THE KIDS are all back at school, this house seems awful empty. Just a weekend ago we were all in each other's way . . . The last tennis game of the summer . . . the last day of work . . . the last day of the two-a-days at football practice . . . the last clothes-buying spree . . . it's all behind us.

WHEN I WENT TO THE DOOR there were three little boys – grade school age – standing outside, with fishing gear and canteens and their clothes soaking wet like they'd just come out of Shell creek which they had. They wanted to use the phone . . . "It's too far to town to walk," they said. We herded them in out of the chill of a Wyoming evening and we wondered how come they'd gotten so wet. "Well," said the biggest, "after we got done fishing we just went swimming. What else can you do when the next day is the first day of school?"

A PHONE BOOTH is an irresistible force to a little boy . . . I've watched . . . and raised two . . . and it is impossible for little boys of about 8 to 10 not to check the coin return "just in case" someone forgot to pick up the change.

A WYOMING resident of 56 years, John Martin of Greybull, said the other day that "we've got the best climate in this state, but I get where the winters take an awful bite out of me."

TO KEEP THE SWEET CORN for the Kennedys and not the raccoons I decided to try that radio-playing-at-night bit. (And so far it's worked!) But the coons had made one raiding party before I got hooked up and the patch looked like a truck had gone through it in one place. I strung wire anyway to an old radio and turned it on and jacked up the volume. And here comes on Peggy Lee singing in that big voice of hers: "Is That All There Is?"

I was crushed.

September 10, 1975

SOMEONE CAME IN to see an automobile dealer friend of mine saying he thought there was something wrong with the transmission in his car.

"How old is your son?" the dealer asked.

"He's 16."

"That's what's wrong with your transmission!" replied the dealer.

Maybe only we parents who have sons who drive can appreciate that one.

THE GUY HAD advertised his trailer for sale for $45 and he left instructions with his wife to sell it if she could. This is what he told me last week anyway. I only have his word for it. But the wife did sell it all right. To the first guy who came to the door. There was only one hitch. The trailer had a $400 homemade camper on it. The camper wasn't supposed to go with the deal. But the wife didn't know. And the other guy didn't ask more than once. So the whole thing went for $45! When the husband came home he was speechless . . . for awhile.

ACTUALLY we men make a lot out of this "it's-the-wife's-fault bit." I've touched on this before. It's a game both sides play. If I don't tell you that the camper doesn't go with the deal, you're supposed to know it. Any dummy would know that. On the other hand, if you forget the can of peas at the store, it's my fault because the car was being washed, and besides it was Thursday, and the kids don't like peas anyway!

ONE THING WIVES and husbands do agree on, though, is that the wife "keeps company" better than anyone else can. Wherever you go, you can see wives outside keeping company with their husbands while he does some chore. As I drive along a half dozen different highways in Wyoming every month, I see women outside just talking to their working husbands. He'll be fixing a tractor and she'll be sitting on a box alongside. Mowing the grass, painting the boat, working the horse, whatever he's doing, the wife is keeping him company. I've seen it hundreds of times. But last week was the first time for this one: The husband was roofing the new house, a two-story affair, and sitting cross-legged right on the roof with him, was the wife! I predict that marriage will last.

AN OLD FRIEND who I went through high school in Basin with, Denny Roush, is now a brigadier general . . . and I wrote him a letter the other day and told him he was the only general I ever got into a fight with!

September 17, 1975

WE HAVE TWO NEW CATS at our place . . . They just showed up one morning, hungry and yowling, one on one day and the other a couple of days later . . . and now because we gave in and fed them they're making themselves at home . . . I suppose they'll stay. We're too soft-hearted any more. It is my experience that cats just don't wander on to a place usually . . . Someone has dumped them out along the road near a farmhouse, hoping that they will end up with a new life. This is humane enough treatment for the cat, but it's hell on the farmers!

PEOPLE ARE ALWAYS remarking on the rabbit recycling, but I think cats can recycle almost as fast. George Warfel, the present sheriff of Big Horn county, lived down the road from us years ago, and Mrs. Warfel told me one day she had 16 cats around the place. I thought that was awfully funny, a good joke on the Warfels. But I went home and counted the cats around our place at that time, and we had 13! People who have cats should never laugh at other people who have cats.

THE FIRST THING I do when I get in the car and turn on the key is to try to start the thing. The first thing my son does after he turns on the key is to turn on the radio.

September 24, 1975

WHAT THE WORLD needs is a raccoon that will eat up all the old squash you don't want, clean up the overripe cucumbers, knock down all the dried up cornstalks but leave the sweet corn alone.

JUST READ DOUGLAS MACARTHUR'S farewell speech to the West Point cadets and wish it could be required reading and study for every high school student . . . Which reminds me to ask, if you were put in charge of setting up the school curriculum what would you change? If I could make one major change I think it would be to require ALL students to take one or two years of speech, even a year in the grades. Fear of audiences and the lack of basic communication skills affects a tremendous number of adults. Dale Carnegie found that out. Being able to speak your thoughts in front of other people is of immeasurable help in getting ahead.

The world is in awe of someone who can make a speech.

PAUL SCHUBERT of Shell once wrote an article for the old Saturday Evening Post about women and he entitled it "Wyoming's Wonderful Women." It appeared in the mid 1950's – way ahead of its time, Women's Lib was years away yet. It said women are proud of their contribution and men are more aware of it than we always say. I think Paul was right, too — Wyoming women are special!

BANKER BERT HARRIS of Greybull asked Dan Hawkins of Hawkins & Powers Aviation as they were flying towards the Big Horn mountains, how much clearance do you have to have to get over. "About two feet," Dan replied.

October 1, 1975
PUBLISHER JACK Nisselius, on a trip the last couple of weeks, wrote back to the rest of us photographers that he had run "into lots of rain — about f/2 at 1/30th".

SAW WHERE Red Fenwick, the Denver Post columnist who had such a wide audience in Wyoming, has announced his retirement. Red started to newspaper on the Greybull Standard in 1931 for $18 a week, before moving on to Douglas. I came to work on the Greybull Standard in 1956 for $75 a week. There was an advertiser on Greybull's main street who had given ads to both of us — to Red in 1931 and then me in the 1950's — and he always reminded me of it. "Look what this job did for Red Fenwick," he would say.

LANDER EDITOR Bill Sniffin reports this story out of the One-Shot Antelope Hunt by Gov. Jim Edwards of South Carolina. Edwards said his friend, Sen. Strom Thurmond is in his 70's, married to a girl in her 20's and they are expecting their fourth child. Thurmond was having trouble with his bulls and cows. No results! But then everything got all right again.
"How did you get the situation taken care of," Edwards asked Thurmond.
"Well, the vet used this big white pill on the bulls," Thurmond said.
"What was in the pill?" Edwards asked.
"I don't know," Thurmond replied, "but it tasted like peppermint."

October 8, 1975
A TELEPHONE has very bad manners.
It has become so deeply ingrained in our culture that we allow it, when it rings, to take precedence over everything else.
It will bring you dripping out of the bathtub, from underneath a car, down off a ladder. You leave the baby crying, the meat burning, a warm bed to answer it. It seldom rings more than three times before you pounce on it.
No matter what the conversation, a phone can stop it momentarily. If the man you want to see has a string of people waiting, you can step to a phone, call him and get right to the head of the line.
You can tell all your family not to bother you for an hour while you concentrate, yet you'll take a phone call from a complete stranger, immediately and without question.
We have given in to it completely!

FROM A PERSONAL point of view, I believe that milk toast is a perfect indicator of how well you are getting. When milk toast starts to taste bad, you're well.

October 15, 1975
ONE OF THE BEST WAYS to learn history is to read biographies . . . They place the person and the time in perspective . . . His or her participation in a given moment in history remains indelible . . . I wish my history teachers had assigned me 10 such books to read and forget all the memorization of those dates – which I don't remember anyway.

NO ARTIFICIAL HIGH can equal that precise moment on a cloudy day when the sun first comes out and burns off all the gloom. What a lift of spirits. In the Forties, out of high school and between-times, I was hitchhiking along the Billings to Bozeman road which is now Interstate 90 on the gloomiest, cloudiest day. And I was getting more and more discouraged. I had to walk all the way through town. But just as I turned one corner – and I could take you right to it today – the sun burst out and the whole world changed! Hello Sun! Hello Blue Sky! Hello World! I've liked Bozeman ever since.

October 22, 1975
WHEN YOU ADD UP all the hunting costs this year, that Hereford steer I should have tied up in the corral and hit over the head with a 2x4 gets cheaper and cheaper.

HAVE YOU EVER NOTICED how everyone always gets a dry doe or a dry cow. There hasn't been a wet doe or a wet cow killed on the mountain in 40 years!

AT OUR HUNTING CAMP I wanted to hang a sign that said: "Welcome Visiting Elks" . . . but no one would let me.

October 29, 1975
DID YOU SEE WHERE the comic strip, "Peanuts" is 25 years old now? When Charles Schulz says that Snoopy would take over the strip if you would let him, you know exactly what he means. That pooch has his hooks deep into me.

November 5, 1975
IT WAS Benjamin Franklin who thought the turkey was such a noble and American bird that it should be the national emblem, not the eagle. The turkey was an American bird, an original North American creature; it was a permanent part of American culinary tradition, widely respected in early colonial days, Franklin pointed out. But he didn't get his wish. In fact, he'd be shocked today to hear modern Americans say: "Get off my back, you turkey."

AS YOU WIVES KNOW, you can tell hunting season is over if the Levis in the corner are standing there with no one in them.

I'M STILL FASCINATED with the constant use of the expression "old boy." You hear it everywhere. I used to think it was a Western expression, but it's even cropping up in print from all over. "There was this old boy down home," or "That old boy took one look" – I heard both of these the other morning.

DON'T KNOW IF the Halloween pranks around your neighborhood were more or less than usual. But did anyone around you have their back door bricked up? That happened to a favorite schoolteacher in our town once. The kids got a load of bricks, backed up in the alley and then had a 20-kid bucket brigade, laying on the ground, passing bricks up the line. The guy on the back porch carefully piled up the bricks, one by one, layer by layer until the entire door was solidly walled. Happy Halloween, teacher!

November 19, 1975
A NUMBER OF YEARS ago I spent some Saturdays with fifth and sixth graders who wanted to play basketball. At the end of the season I typed up a prediction of what kind of player each boy would make in his later years.
I based the predictions not only on his athletic ability which was just beginning to show at that age, but also on his personality and character and how he was as a person. Actually it was not as much his ability as it was the other. They all had learned how to shoot, but had they learned to play? There is a difference and it has little to do with pure athletic ability.
I bring this up because I was thinking about those predictions the other day while I was watching these grown-up boys practice basketball. The predictions way back in the grades were still true today.
You can pick out what a boy or girl is going to be as an adult when he is just a youngster. His weaknesses then are his weaknesses now unless someone comes along to compensate or correct them for him.
He needs the help not only on how to shoot but how to live. And this is the basic fault of most coaching. Not many look past the shooter to the boy or the girl. Or if they do look, they misjudge what they see.
You coach people, not teams.

I'LL KNOW WOMEN'S LIB is here to stay when the cook of the house stops eating all the overdone eggs and the burned pieces and makes the rest of us take our turn.

December 3, 1975
THE ONLY TIME a car is human is during this below zero weather. They

become the worst creatures I know, balky, crabby as heck. Nothing works right, and they complain, complain, complain. And they never want to go. It's no wonder California has so many cars. Think how glad they must be to be there instead of suffering through a Wyoming winter.

I NEVER GET INTO a cold car in the winter without wondering how awful it must have been to try to conquer Russia in a German motorized unit.

MY FRIEND Connie Craft, who is going to school in Spearfish, said while she was home this Thanksgiving that one of her days last fall was so bad she cut the entire date off her calendar!

I WAS TALKING ABOUT Women's Lib the other day and I think it's really catching on more than we men realize. I was waiting behind the woman in the post office and the postal clerk said it would take a little while to make out a money order. "Oh, that's alright," the woman said. "I don't have to be anywhere right now except to make lunch at home." She paused a little bit and thought about that. "But I don't need to be home," she said out loud. She turned to me. "Let him fix his own lunch. If he gets hungry there's enough stuff around there for him to eat. I don't need to fix it. I've been fixing his lunch for 47 years. Let him fix his own!"

December 10, 1975
STARLINGS DON'T go south because no one else wants them either.

THIS IS A TRUE story about a "five-year" senior at the University of Wyoming who had decided early going to school was going to be more than just books for her. So Debbie had a great time, a lot of parties, some classes to take over and here she still was, in Laramie, after five years, still waiting to graduate. When Deb moved in with her new roommate this fall, the new roommate was lamenting how she was now a senior and "all I've done is study, study, study, books, books, books. I haven't done anything else." "That's okay, honey," Debbie told her. "I've done enough playing for both of us!"

December 17, 1975
I SHUDDER to think what will happen when Christmas toys arrive with metric instructions . . . It's always been bad enough those Christmas mornings when the instructions were still in "American."

ACTUALLY MIDDLE AGE wouldn't be such a dread if you young people would just realize that you someday get old enough never to have to assemble a Christmas toy on Christmas morning . . . that someday there is a place where there are enough screws, hexagon nuts, directions, batteries and father to go around!

I WAS IN THE school parking lot one foggy morning last week, and kids being kids, I noticed an abundance of cars with their lights on and the "drivers" in the school building. So I got out and went around turning off all I could see. I felt like I was doing my good turn for the day for all fathers who raise children who drive cars. But knowing kids, I'm sure the kids were probably saying to each other, "Who's that crazy old guy turning off the lights in the parking lot?"

December 24, 1975

I LIKED THAT cartoon in the paper the other day where the little boy was saying: ". . . and a Frisbee for Aunt Nancy and a harmonica for Grandma . . . " . . . IN OUR FAMILY we call those "trucks" – getting something for someone that you'd like to have yourself. "Trucks" stem back to the time years ago when we asked the little boy in the family what he thought his sister would like. "I think she'd like a truck," he told us.

BUT WHETHER YOU BUY a truck or not, I'll bet your family is like ours and the package is wrapped and tied with a recycled Christmas ribbon...Those very prettily-tied ribbons never get thrown away, but are "recycled" for another year. This has been going on long before Coors ever did it with a beer can.

I TRY TO WARD OFF oncoming age by jogging every so often and when I stopped off at the barber shop the other day I asked Barber Pat Michaelis: "I've got my running shoes on. Do you want to come up with me and run around the gym, Pat?"
"ALL around it," he asked?

December 31, 1975

IT'S GETTING INCREASINGLY hard to find any radio station at night that plays what must now be called "old people's" music . . . That mellow sound of the Forties and Fifties is becoming as ancient and extinct as the Dodo bird . . . My kids remark that they grew up with KOMA Oklahoma City. I grew old with it!

A COUPLE OF STRANGERS standing in a line behind me, both young college age kids, were discussing their high school football. They had grown up in rival towns on the other side of the Big Horns. Said one, "I never did understand how they could insist you were never playing as hard as you could, when you always felt like you were." Said the other: "I know what you mean. I could never take all the competitive stuff. How could people, growing up in the same environment, the same heritage and culture, hate each other so much when it came to high school athletics?" It made me wonder, as I listened, who are the adults and who are the kids?

1976

January 7, 1976

FOR MANY YEARS I was too young for New Year's Eve . . . and now I'm too damned old!

January 14, 1976

EVERY GENERATION believes its music is the best. I wouldn't want to change that. The impression that music makes on the young at heart is life-lasting. No music will ever sound as great again. The beat does go on – indefinitely – no matter how many other beats come along.

FOR CHRISTMAS my son got me a blue sweatsuit with a red and white racing stripe (racing?) down one side . . . Very classy . . . I went out the other day in it, and flashed along the road by the neighbor's cows – and stampeded the whole bunch!

January 28, 1976

I HOPE THOSE people in UFO's from outer space who are watching us and our government can make more sense out of things than I can.

WENT OUT OF TOWN and bought some lamps and when we went to go into the motel I decided we had better carry the lampshades inside, anyway, to remove the temptation for someone else to walk off with them. The problem with that is walking out the next morning carrying lampshades from the motel room. I felt I could hear someone looking out his window and saying, "My Gawd, Maude, they're even carrying the lamps from that room."

A GAL WAS IN THE SKI LINE complaining bitterly about its length and having to wait. She was blaming it on the GLM skiers, those people who learn on short skis and progress rapidly from beginner to intermediate skiing. She felt, though, there were too many people on short skis who were "cluttering up the slopes." She missed the whole point. GLM has enabled hundreds of people to ski and to ski better, and brought skiing to where it should be, an enjoyable sport. Ten years ago the teaching methods took years longer and the suffering of beginning skiers on long skis has not been accurately measured! A plague on that gal! May she always ski on rocks and ice and very wet powder!

I HAVE DONE MY SHARE of complaining in ski lines. It's not GLM that gets me, it's those line breakers. It's those people who never go to the end of a line, but find someone they know in the line ahead and crash it.

Kids are the best at this. Two kids are in line. Two more ski up. The first two divide and zip! Two more places. It's like a bunch of amoebas. One Sunday Miss Popularity, about 16, divided five times while I stood in the same place. I had the feeling maybe the whole hill was going up ahead of me.

That doesn't do much for a middle-age disposition. I muttered bad things under my breath. Then I get louder and tried to remember all the things we used to say in Army chow lines.

And then I thought, you crabby old man. What's the hurry. You need the rest. You're not going to ski all day anyway. And you've been around kids enough to know you don't teach them manners by yelling at them in public. Whatever you say now, they'd resent. And with justification. It's serious to you but a game to them. So you glower and snarl and make a fool out of yourself and the line ahead is still going to divide, divide.

So let's forget it, I told Betty, let's forget it before someone breaks a ski pole over our cranky old heads!

February 4, 1976

DOWN SOUTH in Georgia someone wrote a newspaper article about watching workmen move a Confederate soldier statue (they always face north to keep out the Northern troops). It was moved on a large truck. At every turn in the road, they would stop and turn the statue so that it always faced north. When it was finally placed in its new spot in front of a hospital, it did not face the road at all, but it still faced north.

February 11, 1976

WHEN THE GREYBULL basketball team bus took a wrong turn trying to find the Rock Springs Holiday Inn, some of the players in the back end of the bus had a portable CB and called back to another CB'er cruising in back of them for directions. "I'll show you," the Rock Springs CB called back and pulled in front to lead them on into the Holiday Inn parking lot. Later that evening the team got a telegram wishing them luck on the game that night. Signed by their CB Scout of that afternoon.

February 25, 1976

OVERHEARD A GUY with his hair turning gray say to another: "I don't care if it turns gray, as long as it doesn't turn loose."

ON AN ELECTRIC blower-type hand dryer in the Denver airport is a very small sticker above the button. Printed red and white, it says: "For a message from Governor Lamm, press button." And of course, all that comes out is very hot air.

DID YOU HEAR ABOUT the guy who was teeing off at the first marker of a golf club. But he was standing about 10 feet in front of where the shot should be fired.

Now standing nearby was the president of the club. And he was angry beyond measure at this infidelity. "Hey, there," he hollered, "you aren't supposed to tee off from there. Get even with the markers."

The golfer calmly walked over to the president and said: "I have belonged to this club for three years and you are the first person who has spoken to me, and I appreciate it. But if you insist on talking to me, I would like for you not to do it while I am preparing to shoot. It disturbs my concentration. This happens to be my second shot."

March 10, 1976

COULD THOSE COLONIAL SOLDIERS shoot very well? The American Legion magazine says so . . . It quotes: "When the Revolutionary War began, there was no American army, but the country was rich in skilled shooting men who had fought the Indians for a century with a steadily improving rifled-barrel gun and hunted food with a hungry eye. Many marksmen could hit the head of a man at 200 yards. Early in 1775 so many men came out of the Virginia mountains to enlist that a sharpshooting match was held to see who would qualify for the quota of 500 men. A board one foot square with a chalk outline of a nose was nailed to a tree 150 yards away. It is recorded in John Harrowers' diary that the first 50 shooters cut the nose entirely out of the board." – American Legion magazine.

March 17, 1976

DURING HIS SPEECH Sydney Harris told a story about a young boy who asked his parents about sex. After Harris finished the story, my wife and I turned incredulously to each other and said at the same time, "But that is exactly what happened to us." We, too, were sitting around our house with our very, very young son and out of the blue he asked: "What is Sex?" It was our first encounter with the question and I was stunned. I faltered around and made a couple of agonizing false starts and was just beginning to put the birds and the flowers all in the same sentence when I had the presence to say (oh so casually) "Why do you ask?"

"Well," he said, "I am filling out this card in my new wallet and there is this blank that says S E X."

March 24, 1976

ONE OF THE THINGS I-always-wanted-to-do-but-know-I-never-will is to publish something on what weather to expect in Wyoming week by week . . . Don't laugh, I think it is more predictable than all of us think. The proof of it is to look back through 50 years of newspapers and watch what the weather is in any one week. It is amazingly the same. It is also amazingly different at times and this is what we remember the most. Those snowstorms when it shouldn't have, those 40 below weeks, those winds that blow and blow at any hour, are what confuse us to the normal week by week weather. Given these exceptions and the failing of the human mind to remember life in any sequence produces the feeling of unpredictable and fickle Wyoming weather.

But if you would spend some time going back through the issues you'd see a consistent pattern of weather, section by section. The ice in the Big Horn river below my place has gone out around Mar. 10 for decade after decade. This year? Right on schedule. It's just playing the percentages.

I know what you're thinking. Thus guy has lived too long in Wyoming's weather. It's addled his brain. But the next time it storms between September 12 and 20, remember what I said.

April 7, 1976
THE SALESBARN GOES THROUGH the same ritual every week: the stock comes in one door, goes through the ring, is sold and goes out the other door. And the stockyard's loudspeaker, pointed across the river to my place, blurts out the sorting pen information, "Pen No. 4." "Pen No. 2." Every Saturday afternoon for years and years, the same sounds have drifted over, the same voice over and over, "Pen No. 15." "Pen No. 2." That's why I was startled the other Saturday to hear the singsong rhythm broken with what was either a very bad day or a very new helper. For across the way came: "No, Goddammit not in that pen, in the other one."

May 12, 1976
SOMEONE TOLD ME the other day that it looked like to her that I was shrinking! How's that for openers, in the middle of the street, on a bright sunny day? But she'd known me a long, long time and she always did say her mind. Just the same, I measured myself the other day and discovered in horror, that in the past 30 years since high school days, I have "grown" 1-1/2 inches closer to the ground! It's a natural catastrophe at my age, everyone now tells me — compression of the backbone and all that — but I had little enough height to spare and none to lose! I wonder if they make a three-inch elevated shoe in a 50-year-old style.

I TOLD ALL THIS TO a friend of mine who is even shorter than I am and he exclaimed: "By the time I get done with all that I'll look like a basketball."

THE MOORS OF SPAIN are said to have had a belief that the most beautiful sound in the world was made by water . . . so they had fountains and waterfalls all over. In Wyoming, irrigating water makes the same sounds.

YOU HAVE TO BE an irrigator to really appreciate the beauty and wealth of water . . . and to also know its drudgery.

May 19, 1976

A YOUNG FRIEND was figuring out he and his wife's bio-rhythm and he came to the conclusion that since they had been born 14 days apart, the cycle of 28 days was going to put them forever on an opposite up and down, up and down. Young man, I told him, you have been married a year and a half and you have just discovered one of the mysteries of wedded bliss. 14 days apart, 14 years, 140 years, it doesn't matter. You'll be amazed to find when you're up, she's down. When you're down, she's up!

THE ABOVE COMMENT has nothing to do with the fact that the wife said the other day she thought I'd probably had an overabundance of column items about Angie Dickinson.

May 26, 1976

A SLEEPLESS MEADOWLARK outside my window Saturday uttered his first song of the day at exactly 4:17 a.m. . . . That's early, even for the birds, it seems to me. Anyway, if he couldn't sleep, he had company. Neither could I. Apparently we both had insomnia, but he was the only one willing to sing about it.

HOW DID I KNOW it was exactly 4:17? By that incomparable digital clock of course, which has to be one of the best inventions of the past 100 years. Pretty soon clocks will be as digital as transmissions are automatic. And you people with little kids won't have them asking, "What time is it if the big hand is at 3 and the little hand is . . ."

June 2, 1976

ONE OF THE CHANGES in these changing times is how much of a status symbol the pickup has become among the younger people . . . Add this new glamour to the pickup's already traditional workhorse role as a second family car in Wyoming and you have some of the reason why pickups are now figuring high in the traffic statistics . . . I wonder among all the statistics we keep if there is one that shows how many miles Wyoming pickups travel in a year . . . I think it would startle us.

JUST THE OTHER DAY I wanted to use the pickup to go to town, but when I went to get in it, the daughter had it . . . which is not exactly the kind of a statistic I wanted put on it that day . . . I was still scowling by the time she got home, but she had a very logical, clear and perfectly frivolous reason why she didn't take her own car. Hers was only four miles away from turning over all 00000's at 100,000 miles and "I didn't want to waste that occasion on just a trip to town!"

I WISH IRIS BLOOMED all summer long . . . I ALSO WISH there were three Mays in every year and only one week of January, one week of February and two weeks of August.

June 9, 1976

SOMEONE'S BUILDING a small shed for his horse on the highway between Greybull and Basin . . . and he's not quite done – still working on the sides – but that hasn't mattered to the horse. It's been inside the shed since the roof went up. They have to shoo it out to get anything done.

THAT HORSE DOESN'T have anything on me. I've moved into more unfinished houses than finished ones. Looking back, I don't think I've ever lived in a finished house. It always had something left to do. A friend of mine who had put up his own house, and had already moved in (like the horse) was questioned about how long before it would be all done. "I give it about 15 years," the friend sighed.

June 16, 1976

I WAS OUT TO THE nursing home and told one old friend how good he looked. With a twinkle in his eye, he said: "How come if I look so good, I feel so bad?"

HE'S BEEN IN WYOMING a long time, over 70 years, and another friend down the hall reminded me that she'd come to this town of ours in 1907. So she was an oldtimer, too.

It used to be quite a milestone to have lived in Wyoming for 50 years. Twenty-five or 30 years ago that would have put you in the state prior to 1900 and those oldtimers were disappearing fast. In 1959 I ran weekly a list of all those who had been in the community for 50, 60 and 70 years and you knew everyone on the list. Run a list like that for 50 years now and it would fill columns.

Because an entire generation is now approaching and passing that 50-year mark. All of us who grew up in the 1930's and 1940's in Wyoming are almost there! Fifty-year Wyomingites. It's hard to believe.

ONE OF THE CONSISTENT points the oldtimers always made about settling Wyoming was that there were no "old people." The country was too young, and it was settled by the younger generations, and the grandpas and aunts were back home someplace in Nebraska. The older people who did come here had affectionate names in many cases. In my town there was Daddy Payne and Daddy Stout and Uncle Sim. And they looked old enough when I was growing up to have been here for 150 years! But even then, even they hadn't been in Wyoming 50 years yet. Now I've been here almost 50 years – and try not to look in the mirror any more than I absolutely have to.

JUNE 14 AND FLAG DAY and probably several people like Lucy Batenhorst of Basin whose birthday is on that day, and whose husband said: "I always knew it was Momma's birthday because all the flags were flying."

June 23, 1976
ONE THING ABOUT petunias – they give you your money's worth . . . And so do marigolds . . . And so do cottonwood trees. Those old, old cottonwoods give you more. They give you bales of flying cotton to battle this time of year. Which reminds me to mention that the oldtimers must have hooted at the modern times when Wyoming made the SEEDLESS cottonwood the state tree. They must have found it hilarious that we had to first sterilize and hybridize the cottonwood to our modern tastes. Flying cotton in June is as much Wyoming as the blue sky. It's a wonder someone didn't ask the meadowlark to change her key.

GIVING AWAY FLOWERS and trees gives you more than one garden, because you're just as proud of "your" flowers in the other garden as you are those in your own. In fact, so are the new owners. In our lawn, the flourishing bunch of daisies we still call "Heywood's Flowers," after Gladys and Oscar, and "Coleman's Iris" just stopped blooming.

July 14, 1976
MY DAD, WHO WAS 81 years old last March, says this heat has been reminding him of Little Rock, Ark. He served there in the Army in World War I "and I've been trying to be good ever since."

THE ONE PART OF the Bicentennial I wish I could have seen were the tall ships. I would have gladly traded a couple days' view I have of the Big Horn mountains for a couple hours of spectacular watching along the Hudson River. That had to be the most daring and most successful of all the Bicentennial ideas.
But all things are relative I guess. One of my relatives who is a New Yorker said the family didn't watch it. Too much hassle getting in and out of New York. Too much traffic tying everything up. The getting there for them was more than the being there. Out here in Wyoming, we never worry about the getting there. It's the being there that counts! That's the difference in living in a state where there are only 375,000 people and living in a city with millions and millions. Mind you, I didn't say I wanted to trade my view of the Big Horns for a view of the Hudson forever, but only for a couple of hours!

IN THE WHIRL OF ALL the Bicentennial celebration in Greybull, they dedicated a new metal buffalo statue and unveiled it with proper ceremonies. The next morning there was a big, longstemmed red rose in its mouth. I suspect the class of 1946 (which was bringing in the next 100 years with a class reunion that day) left another memento!

July 21, 1976

AN OLD GRADE SCHOOL friend called up from Sacramento Saturday night to talk about Wyoming. (He says he's never really left the state – he just lives somewhere else.) And we got to talking about our ancestors and the Bicentennial and all. We had one thing in common: Both his and my Scottish ancestors who came to New England in the 1600's moved on to Nova Scotia when the Revolution started. Tories to the end, they didn't want any part of their independent neighbors.

"It's embarrassing in this Bicentennial year," my old buddy said, "to look back at your ancient relatives and find they thought the King was right!"

THE BICENTENNIAL generated a lot of this searching back for roots. The talk was in the past, the thoughts back in those years of beginning, your own family's beginning as well as the country's. But the reverse also became true. It really didn't matter how many generations your ancestors had been in America just as long as they were here! You and I don't need eight generations to be an American. Less than one will do! Betty's grandfather was raised in Indiana and when someone would ask him: "Are you German or English?" he would invariably reply: "I'm a Hoosier." That was the important thing. To be a Hoosier, in America, with the future all ahead of you.

It has never been as important to know where you came from as it has to know where you are going. That has always been America's promise: Its future. And we Americans celebrated as much this hope for our future as we did our pride of the past when we watched those tall ships sail by.

July 28, 1976

YOU CAN TELL THE various weeks of summer around our house by watching the robins. First they eat all the cherries as they set on. Then they move over to the first crop of strawberries. When these are gone, they hit the dogwood and then the small Chinese cherries and maybe a few raspberries. Now it's chokecherry time and they'll beat heck out of the apples before too long. And then more strawberries. Next it'll be the plums and the grapes if we don't get out there. Their summer is over when it's all wiped out. The rascals. When you talk about fat robins, you're talking about those waddling around our place.

IF ADULTS would show better manners TO kids, we would see better manners IN kids. No group is more rudely treated than kids are, in restaurants, in stores, in public. The adult sees the youngster as loud, silly, scheming, intent on mischief and destruction. The youngster sees the adult as stubborn, bigoted, cold, critical. Both are strangers to each other. The adult should know better, but he forgets his own youth and forgets to keep understanding. It is only briefly, when and if he raises his own kids, that he even comes close to understanding and patience towards youth. And even then if he succeeds, he loses more and more tolerance as he and they both grow older. And the vicious cycle continues, each treating each other badly, from one generation to the next.

REMEMBER WHEN "spaced out" was something you put between letters?

THESE SUMMER REUNIONS remind me of one I took pictures at years ago, when there were so many kids and uncles and grandkids that they filled up most of the Big Horn County courthouse steps. When I finished that picture (using all the negative of that old 4x5 camera), they wanted "just Mom and Dad and the six kids." So the original family got back up on the steps to pose. And all the kids and in-laws moved back of the camera to watch. By comparison with the previous picture, the small group up there now wasn't very big and it made an impression on one of the in-laws. Because she called out very loud, "Boy, without us, you're nothin'!"

August 4, 1976
THE THREE OF US were jawing up at the airport and the young man among us said he sure would like to be a pilot on the airlines. He thought that would be a great life. Well, my friend who is very knowledgeable about airplanes made some negative technical point about the job of flying a commercial airline plane. And I said it would be like driving a truck after awhile, I supposed. But the young guy said he still thought it would be a lot of fun. "I'd love to wheel one of those around," he told us.

And of course, he was right. Afterwards, thinking about it, I knew us old fogies were all wet. He had the enthusiasm and the dream and the excitement. Where had our fire gone? Diluted by years, I guess, years and other dreams and plans. But his was still fresh and still exciting. His whole world is ahead of him yet and if he chooses to fly in it, wheeling around the sky in a monstrous jet, I rejoice with him.

August 11, 1976
ON MY WAY HOME every night I go by Grandma Baker's old house, but I hardly recognize the place any more. She's been dead a number of years now, but while she was there she had it fixed up as good as she could for a woman in her eighties. She kept the lawn green with a pump her son fixed up for her out of the ditch. The grass never was much, as sparse as an old woman's hair, but it was green and cool. And she had several big old cottonwoods for shade. She always had some flowers, not many, but some; and the inevitable lilac bush on one side of the house. When you went by she was dragging that old hose from one end of the place to the other, but it was going and it was green and it looked like someone lived there.

After she died they sold the house to a family from out of state who moved in right away that fall. By next spring, though, they didn't hook up the pump and never watered the lawn once. That was dead by mid-summer. There weren't any flowers, and by the next year one cottonwood had died. Then another one went. The place looks like something out of the depression pictures, now, with no trees, no shade, cars parked where the lawn used to be. Weeds and bare ground and dead trees. An eighty-year-old woman who cared made a home out of that little house. It's just a place now, and a poor place at that.

I don't look at it any more. No, I said that wrong. I can't look at it any more.

August 18, 1976

MY CORN IS GOING to be late, but old friend Frank Casey's came early enough – just in time for the coons to get it. Frank ended up down at Worland buying corn from a luckier farmer.

"Did you ever try that trick to keep coons out of corn by playing a radio all night?" I asked Frank.

"Aw, they just dance to it," he exclaimed.

Well, I'm still with the radio, Frank. And it sure sounds awful funny blaring away out there in the corn patch. Last night I went out to make sure it was still on and some gal was giving a poetry lesson at 11:30 at night. Poetry in the corn! Maybe that will work. You can't dance to poetry!

THE FIRST OLD HIGH SCHOOL buddy I met when I went to the class reunion Sunday said: "You're just like me – putting on a lot of weight," which wasn't exactly the kind of initial impression I had wanted to make after 30 years. And especially not so when I thought he looked overweight as hell! But it was a start anyway and somewhere between that first handclasp and the last one I had a marvelous good time.

Several classes were there – it takes a couple of years of Basin graduates to make a crowd – and they came from the usual faraway places. But we'd lost track of each other so much in the years between that I was embarrassed to have someone tell me he "just lived over in Powell" . . . and another who had "been in Cody for 26 years." Thirty years ago I couldn't have imagined that happening.

Someone who had been to reunions on the 10th and the 20th and the 30th years made an astute observation that the tenth was all babies; at the 20th all jobs and teenagers; and at the 30th all grandkids and middle age. I could understand that, for reunions, like the old high school days, are just reflections of the times.

And the times we had. I can't remember all the hours we lived over or the stories we laughed about. But in this horse country of Wyoming I got a kick out of hearing again about old Bryson who was telling us about the big horse his uncle had. Old Bryson who didn't know anything about horses himself. He said his uncle's horse was the biggest horse in that county. "It weighed 700 pounds." When everyone started to laugh, he knew he had something wrong with that horse. So he quickly said, "Or was it 7,000!"

Well, there were a lot of big horses in those days. Big horses, big stories, many big laughs. You never can go home again, Thomas Wolfe was always saying. But he didn't mean that to include a Sunday afternoon in the old town park with the veterans of the Battle of Basin High School!

August 25, 1976

THE TEAM WAS OUT IN PADS and jerseys going through pre-season drills last week.

A car outside the fence stopped and watched awhile. Then the guy leaned out and hollered over at the boys, "Hey, No. 71."

No. 71 looked around. "What?"

"Wear that number with respect, boy," the alum said and drove off, away from the past.

September 1, 1976

I TORE UP THE LIST of things I was going to do this summer and have made a new list of Things To Do This Fall . . . which will be torn up sometime around the first of November . . . and a new list started for Things To Do Next Spring . . . which in turn will meet a similar fate. I either have to get more efficient — or stop making lists.

THE TEACHER WAS remembering the incident of the football player who was down in his grades, but anxious to play. So he asked for permission "to do a little extra" to get his grade up. That was okay with the teacher; so the youth came in and the teacher handed him several books and some assignments. The youngster hesitated, looked at the books in his arms and said wistfully: "I had something else in mind, like scrubbing walls or something?"

DOWN AT THE UNIVERSITY at Laramie, before school got underway, a crew was digging up the sewer line in front of one of the sorority houses. At the same time the Sigma Chis were having a national convention of their fraternity on the Wyoming campus. A couple of Sigma Chis walked by the big hole and one of them told the guys digging: "You know it's a lot easier going through the window."

September 8, 1976

EVERY COMMUNITY has its own idiosyncrasies about where it sits in relation to where everyone else is. I got in a tiff once with one of my "imported" reporters who insisted on going by "downriver" and "upriver." You go "down" to Worland from Greybull, I told him. "But that's upriver," he said. But I told him: "No, you go up to Billings." "No, that's downriver," he insisted.

Listen, I finally said, you gotta believe. Don't ask me to justify why it is; just put this down someplace so you'll write it right and not stir up the natives.

From Greybull:

"It's down to Worland, Thermop, Casper, Lander, Laramie and Denver.

"It's up to Lovell, Byron, Billings and Montana.

"It's over to Cody, Gillette and Sheridan. And you go over to Basin, don't ask me why.

"You go UP the mountain and To the Park and OUT to Shell and OUT to Otto and if you're not properly confused by now, just remember I don't make the rules. I just live here!"

OX ZELLNER, who coached football at Greybull and Billings before going into business in Casper, still referees and officiates at Wyoming sports events. One of my favorite stories about Ox was when he was coaching during a Greybull-Worland game and a play by Greybull went no where.

"Who called that dumb play," Ox boomed out in his loud voice.

Then he stopped, a stricken look crossed his face, he turned around to no one in particular and said just as loudly, "My God, I did!"

September 22, 1976

A SALESMAN who lives in Billings told me Monday on the phone, I saw you on Grand Avenue at 5 p.m. Saturday and honked but you didn't wave. "Are you crazy," I told him. "Five thousand cars during the rush hour and I'm supposed to be looking for you?"

WELL, SOMEONE ELSE saw me, too, that night and that was a patrolman between Bridger and Rockvale who stopped me because I didn't have both headlights going. No ticket, a friendly guy, just wanted me to get two lights instead of one.

He walked around to write down my license plate. "How did the game go?" he asked.

Okay, I said. And then wondered: "How did you know about the game?"

"Well, I've been sitting off the road there, out of sight and on the CB I've been picking up all the Wyoming cars as they go back home. A lot of them were talking about the game. And I talk to them, myself, once in awhile over mine here. They ask eventually, 'What do you do, farm around Fromberg?' 'No', I say, 'I'm that Smokey you just passed, hidden off the road here.'

"And you know something, there's just nothing but silence then. Not a word! Not a word!"

October 6, 1976

A FOOTBALL PLAYER who doubled as a Powder Puff football "coach" recently said he immediately noticed one great difference between girls and boys football. The huddles are filled with the mingled aromas of Strawberry and Charley and Raspberry perfume!

ONE OF MY ACQUAINTANCES in my town was very jealous of her cooking. If you asked her for one of her recipes she would give it to you – but she would always leave out one ingredient. So something always happened to your try! Never the same as hers, never as good. Took a lot of comparing and a lot of years for the women in town to finally figure that one out.

MILLIE BUCHANAN, who is an attractive dental assistant in Greybull, was getting the next patient ready. He was a very solemn five-year-old who kept staring and staring at Millie. He didn't say anything, but he never took his eyes off Millie. Suddenly he brightened up. "Oh, I know who you are," he told Millie. "You're the Tooth Fairy!"

October 13, 1976
THE BEST DESCRIPTION of how I feel on some of those Monday mornings is like Charlie Brown said he felt the other day, "Just like the two of clubs!"

RIGHT AFTER the first debate it struck me that Jimmy Carter can say the dumbest things and make them sound intelligent; while Gerald Ford can say intelligent things and make them sound dumb. However, after last week's second debate I think both of them can say DUMB things and make them sound DUMB. I don't mean to sound disillusioned, but is this the first "deck of cards" with two two of clubs?

OVERHEARD IN A mechanic's telephone conversation: "Is the ignition key on your car the same as the one that opens the door? (Pause) The ignition key? (Pause) Lady, that's the one that runs the car."

YOU GOTTA BELIEVE that this swine flu is bad. Anything that would have a name like that has gotta be bad.

October 20, 1976
WE WERE TALKING about lonely stretches of road and someone remarked "That would be a bad place to have car trouble."
And someone else answered: "There isn't any place that's good to have car trouble."
Which is right, of course. A car's a marvelous creature until it turns up lame, in the front yard or out between Casper and Shoshoni.
But I have to believe that the frustration quotient rises in direct proportion to the number of miles from home, how dark the night is, how many hours before or after midnight or if it's stormy or not. Wyoming is a big, wide state and it's bigger and wider and lonelier than ever when your car's conked out on the side of the road.
Having been on the other end too many frustrating times myself, I've always stopped to see if I could help. When you're on the road a lot you seem to run on to a continuous number of stranded people. I've carried guys to get gas and others back out with gas. I've pulled people out of ditches, snowbanks,

changed tires, loaned jacks, jumped cars, hauled people to town. Once last year after stopping beside a stalled car outside of Lovell, I drove on in and made a call to his wife: "Gloria, you don't know me, but your husband said to bring a crescent wrench and a screwdriver out to him 10 miles south of town."

The CB radios are improving things. You're not quite so alone if you know someone is listening. And help is on the way quicker with CB's. CB people take pride in giving such help. I guess I do, too.

I've had close calls, though; this Good Samaritan bit can backfire. In the 1960's I was helping a truck driver put on some chains on Togwotee Pass after it had turned slippery. And some tourist gal ran into the front of the truck while we were behind. Luckily her car was small and the truck was big. The exact same thing happened last summer on another stretch of road when I stopped late at night to jump a guy's pickup with mine. While we were working between the two pickups, a car hit the back of the downhill pickup and scrunched me between them. I was sore for a week, but lucky at that. It was another small car.

I suppose someday a person is bound to stop at the wrong time. The world is changing and as much as we don't want it, Wyoming is changing, too. The time may be closer than I'd like it to be when you won't dare stop along these lonely Wyoming roads with a helping hand. A lot of people don't stop even now.

Still, "Need any help?" can be the nicest thing you can say (or hear!) along some of these Wyoming roads.

October 27, 1976

THEY SAY THAT flying is 95 percent boredom and five percent sheer terror. I think my early flying was exactly the opposite: five percent boredom and 95 percent sheer terror!

WE HAVE A CARTOON hanging up on our kitchen wall where the gal of the house — an obvious lover of plants and flowers — has just dropped her watering can in fright. The husband over in his chair and almost buried among the greenery, is saying: "Well, if you're going to live in a jungle, you've got to expect snakes."

November 10, 1976

THE IDEA WAS, that as long as I was going all the way to Nova Scotia to make a speech, that we might as well get away from it awhile . . . not read a newspaper . . . or watch the campaign anymore. Instead, to shake cobwebs and stale thoughts, to wander through the beauty of Nova Scotia, to catch the fading fall of New England on the way home, and maybe — if we didn't get mugged and shot at and scruffed up in the process, maybe to see a little of the bright lights of New York City.

And we got to do it all eventually except, of course, we didn't get mugged in New York City and we found we didn't want to stay away from the campaign and the election news.

Actually, you're never very far away from home, no matter how far away you seem. You pick up a TWA magazine, someplace over Ohio and there is Slim Warren of Cody inside, one of the featured pictures in a fine article on Cody artist James Bama. And you get to Halifax, Nova Scotia and a big Scotchman named Jim MacNeil comes up to you and says he reads your column each week. Jim newspapers on Prince Edward Island and he is a subscriber to the Wyoming State Journal at Lander. I find it astonishing that you can go thousands of miles to another country, and find a subscriber who says, "You know, I read your column."

I HAD ANOTHER TIE in Nova Scotia but I didn't know where to go to search for it. My mother's McKenzie people were Tories and fled to Nova Scotia during the Revolutionary War. But all the ties were eventually lost or forgotten in these 200 years. So I could only do, as my sister suggested, smile and say hello to every McKenzie I met, because "we're probably related somehow."

NOVA SCOTIANS thought Ford would win the election. They hoped he would. And they wanted to talk about it. So we didn't "get away" after all. And by the time we got down to New England to walk the streets of Boston on a beautiful November election day, it was all very much around us. And very much all right. You don't escape – nor do you want to – the historical significance of being in Boston, Mass. on election day. But I found it ironic that I was probably the only Republican Kennedy in Boston on Election Day, 1976!

November 17, 1976

LEONARD COWAN of Basin got the old arched windows out of the remodeled Big Horn County courthouse and incorporated them into his new kitchen. They're real antiques. But the glass is so old that now, Leonard says, when you watch the dog run across the backyard, "First he's long – and then he gets real short – and then long again."

November 24, 1976

THE FUNNIEST STORY of the week was the one where the bunch of cowboys turned the steer loose in the bar. I'm sure the bar owner doesn't share the hilarity, but that's a classic. The historical experts say the West died years ago, but they don't live in the West. As long as there are cowboys, so will there be a West.

December 8, 1976

WHY RESTAURANT OWNERS get gray . . . when basketball teams arrive . . . In the wake of one team's departure from the cafe several weeks back, the waitresses discovered a spoonful of green beans under every clean, upside-down coffee cup.

December 22, 1976

DON'T KNOW WHERE you go to find out what is happening, but I am partial to the barbershop. That's where the action is in my town. If you listen long enough, most everything that has happened or that is going to happen or that SHOULD happen is brought up in the barbershop. The female has long been maligned as being the gossiper of the human species. This is in error, of course, because women never gossip as much as men. Men call it by a different, more earthy name. But it is the same. You can spend a half hour at the barbershop or the coffee counter or the salesbarn or on the street corner and find out just about whatever you want to know!

December 29, 1976

GAMES KIDS PLAY . . . at one department store they had about five "PONG" games all on and going. While I watched, a kid came over and one by one fiddled with each set so the "ball" was being hit by both paddles back and forth, pong, pong, pong, all five sets, programmed to go on like that until the store closed. And then the kid stood back with his arms folded and a silly grin on his face, just pleased as punch. He was about 25 years old!

THERE'S A CERTAIN camaraderie among those of us who are still shopping on Christmas Eve. We all wear the same look, hurry around in the same way. I imagine you saw very much the same expressions on those people aboard the Titanic when it was going down.

AMONG THE SEVERAL posters that appeared under our family's Christmas tree this year was this one, entitled:
WHY WORRY?
There are only two things to worry about.
Either you are well or you are sick.
If you are well, then there is nothing to worry about.
But if you are sick, there are two things to worry about;
Either you will get well or you will die.
If you get well, there is nothing to worry about.
If you die, there are only two things to worry about.
Either you will go to Heaven or Hell.
If you go to Heaven, there is nothing to worry about.
But if you go to Hell, you'll be so damn busy shaking hands with friends, you won't have time to worry.

1977

January 5, 1977

Irv Davis who lives up on Shell creek pulled me out of the ditch by his house again the other night.

That's twice now I've needed his chain and his four-wheel drive not to mention his good humor to get me out of a fix.

"By golly, Irv, it's me again," I told him as he came out of his house. He'd heard the wheels spinning and the engine racing and he'd recognized the sounds. When you live "by the side of the road" you hear what's happening before you see it.

"Well, I've pulled a few out over the years," he told me.

"But I bet not many twice like me," I said.

So we hooked up his four-wheel drive to the Buick down off the side of the road and it came out just about as quick as it went in. A few minutes before, I had run out of percentages. A light snow on a slick road, the wrong twist, however slight to the wheel, and I was spinning around before I could do anything. The fact that it didn't turn over, that it missed those big old trees by Irv's place and wound up without a scratch, was also beyond my control.

Now, back on the road the car was like a horse who has been bad and pretends nothing is wrong. Just sitting there waiting. Except for going the wrong direction everything was normal.

We gathered up the chain and stood in the middle of the road for awhile.

"I'm in debt to you twice now," I said to Irv.

"Yeah, that other time was something wasn't it?" he chuckled. And then we both laughed, remembering it. A one in a million deal, too, that time was. Must have been 15 years ago, in the middle of deer hunting and a hunting buddy and I were on Irv's land in back of his house. We were in my old pickup, inching along, looking for a buck in a big herd of does that had come down out of White creek to Irv's alfalfa field.

Suddenly the whole front end of the pickup dropped out from under us. Both wheels. Stopped like we'd hit a wall. When we got out, we found we'd run both wheels into a deep, narrow irrigation ditch. And just buried them. But then here was Irv again, coming across the field in his outfit, a big chain and a bigger grin. After much jockeying and digging and a little winching and we were out.

A couple of days later in the mail I got an envelope from Irv. Inside was an Ace Reid Cowpoke cartoon. It showed two old guys hunting deer in a pickup. One guy is driving and the other is sitting on the fender. The truck is headed for the biggest ditch you ever saw. But neither guy is looking. They're both watching some deer. The guy on the fender has his gun out and he is saying: "Go a little slower, Knute. I think I got a bead on one!"

On the cartoon, Irv had scribbled my name over one guy and my buddy's name over the other.

When you live in a house by the side of the road, as poet Edgar Guest would have us do, sometimes you gotta help as well as "watch the rest of the world go by."

And some of us you gotta help twice!

January 12, 1977

OUR HOUSE CANNOT DO without a dog any longer. We've had all kinds of mutts and strays, one beautiful big Boxer who died of old age finally, and saddened us all; and the last one, a giant of a yellow Lab who definitely should NOT have been a house dog. He had a tail capable of wiping out three African violets with a single swipe. And four paws that could hold more mud and water than our irrigation ditch, all of which ended up daily on the kitchen floor.

When he disappeared one night, we said, no more. We get too attached. (How many times have you heard that one!) The house is finally staying clean, the food bill has been reduced by 20 percent, and I haven't had to get up to let anything out for months. Besides two cats are enough.

But we're not kidding anyone. We miss a dog. All of us. We miss something that will keep us company, show some concern for our feelings, be a friend when no one else will.

Did you ever see a cat wag his tail, just because you walked into a room?

January 19, 1977

A MEMBER OF Claus Heppner's architecture firm from Denver, working at the Basin bank, lost her cigarette case on the Basin street one night last week. Someone found it and left it at the grocery store for her the next day. "It's unbelievable," she said. "I didn't know people and places were still left like this."

February 2, 1977

SEEMS STRANGE TO BE having the state basketball tournament this time of year . . . Reminds me of the Big Horn Basin coach who finally got his team to the Wyoming 1970 tournament. None of them had been there before, and the coach was a little apprehensive how they would react to the pressure. "I didn't have to wonder long," he recalled. "The first player out of the dressing room had his jersey on backwards!"

February 9, 1977

A LARAMIE NEWSPAPERMAN was telling about the St. Patrick's Day when the editor invited an old Irish printer to write the editorial for the day in

Gaelic . . . which he did . . . and when it came out it was a great success. No one could read it, of course, since no one could read Gaelic. If they could have, it would have been an even bigger smash. Because the old printer had spent the whole editorial describing what a dumbbell the editor was!

February 16, 1977

I WALKED TO THE EDGE of a very fancy indoor pool in a Wyoming motel last week and there in the bottom was an empty swimming suit!

A FATHER WAS telling me about his son in college. "He is one of those DECADE students," he said. "He's going to be going to school for ten years."

THIS SEEMS TO BE A week of memory time. I was laughing with a young married girl of 25 over the weekend. She had just run across a picture I had taken of her 18 years ago when she was in the first grade. Now that in itself is not so startling. I've been in the newspaper business for 30 years – more than that if you count the times I spent as a young kid in the print shop – and in that time you take a lot of pictures and write a lot of stories.

What made this one so hilarious was my memory of taking the picture and her memory of having it taken those 18 years ago. I had gone to the first grade teacher with the biggest stuffed rabbit I could find and asked her for a cute little girl with big eyes to pose for a picture. The teacher said she knew just the right little girl, but she was out at recess. She'd have her come to the office. But from the little girl's point of view (as she told me the other night) "I had been out on the playground pounding heck out of some little boy. When I got back to the room, Mrs.____ said 'Go to the office.' I was scared to death. I thought, I shouldn't have beat up that little boy. When I got to the office, someone stuffed this big rabbit in my arms and said sit down here. I was so glad. No one ever said a thing about that little boy!"

February 23, 1977

WOKE UP JUST AT DAWN to the strangest sound the other morning . . . Looked out to see a bunch of chukars just outside the window . . . Heard a lot of sounds in 20 years on this same Wyoming hill, but was never serenaded by 20 or 30 chukars before.

March 2, 1977

IT SEEMS GROSS discrimination for a barber to charge as much for a guy with hardly any hair at all as one with bunches and bunches of it. But my barber – when I insisted the other day on some sort of logical explanation – said the charge in my case was not so much in cutting it as in FINDING it! . . . which got me thinking back to the time when my youngest son was only a little fellow – three or four – and after studying the old man very hard for several days, asked me "where did you put all your hair?" like it was in a drawer someplace, all in one piece!

HAD TO DRIVE the old truck this week for several days because I couldn't get time to fix the flat tire on the pickup. Thought maybe if I waited long enough the wife would change it, but after I came home the third day and asked, "How come the pickup tire is still flat?" she said "I guess 'cause there's no air in it!"

March 9, 1977
IT WAS CONRAD FIORELLO who said: "As long as there are final exams, there will always be prayers in the public schools."

A FRIEND SAID HE overheard a couple of old Wyoming ranchers in the bar. They'd been watching a couple of young guys sparking a couple of girls. "Oh," said one, "if I could be that young again and know what I know." "Not me," said the other one, "not me. If I could be young again, I'd want to be just as dumb as I was!"

March 16, 1977
You probably didn't know Reuben Reifschneider.
But then again, maybe you did, because there were an astonishing number of people all over Wyoming he knew or who knew him. If you ever ran into Reuben, you never forgot him. There was only one Reuben. His mold was most surely thrown away, shattered after the cast into a thousand pieces so that no one else anywhere could ever be like him. He was a blacksmith who barely weighed 140 pounds. He was thin and little – you would probably have to say scrawny – and you wondered how in the world he could spend 40 years of that tough, sweaty kind of work and still keep going. He was a longtime Wyomingite, out of the Lingle area, and a Legionnaire, a Mason, a hunter, a bowler. He was also the good-natured title holder of "Wyoming's Ugliest Man" which now will surely retire with him. He was a constant story teller, a constant talker. Above all, a talker. He had a story for every conversation subject. I always told him, "Reuben, I never come down to talk to you, I come down to listen." When you first came in the shop door at Greybull, he would take over the conversation and keep it going through all your instructions for the job; then right out the door with you, right up to the pickup, even after you'd started it and rolled down the window, almost right out into the street with you.
But he never bored you. His stories were too good, his knowledge of what was going on too interesting, his humor catching. Good nature is contagious. When he held court, it was a lot of fun.
I've lost track of how many things he built or fixed for me. For 20 years he kept my place going. Pumps, tractor attachments, garden cultivators, welded pipe. Some of it, piddling little things that he shouldn't have messed with;

some, big things he got some satisfaction out of.

There was no chestnut tree outside his shop and he would have looked ridiculous standing under it if there had been. This was no "mighty smithy stood." Longfellow's smithy was not 140 pounds. But that rippling muscled guy in the poem couldn't have fixed anything any better than Reuben did. He had learned his profession in the old school and he knew it well. He took great pride in that knowledge as he should have.

His delivery, though, was notorious. It was the ultimate in exasperation. An emergency he treated like an emergency. You got it right then. The average job took a little longer, like a week maybe. The job you didn't need in a hurry got done only when it moved into the emergency status. Somewhere down on the floor of his shop, in the pile over to the left of the door are jobs yet. There's three sets of unbuilt gate latches of mine down there. They've been there for years. When I asked about them the last time, Reuben pointed out with a grin: "Well, if they're not out in the wet, at least they won't be rusting away."

Reuben achieved notoriety, too, in the early 1960's when he went on the Art Linkletter show to win that second "Wyoming's Ugliest Man" title. Doc Chambers, formerly of Cody, won the first one. The contest was a brainstorm of Frank Norris, the present director of the Wyoming Travel Commission, who was then in Greybull. It was a typical Norris promotional idea. It worked! The contest went into a second – and last – year and Reuben's reign started. Reuben's 15-year hold on the title was truly a reign. He got a tremendous kick out of being known as the state's ugliest man. Tourists who had seen him on the show continued to stop by the shop just to see if it was all true. When the Cody Enterprise published a story about him in its tourist publication, Big Wyoming, he had buses of people stopping by. They weren't disappointed. He didn't bore them either.

But all this is gone now. Reuben's death last week at 60 closes many chapters, shuts off the new laughs that would have been there, the new stories that won't be told.

When you live in a town, you get to know a lot of people. You make new friends as the years go by. But some day you have to say goodbye to many of your old ones. That's the hardest part of living in a community. All the goodbyes you have to say.

March 23, 1977

ENJOYED THIS old Mark Twain quote: "Reader, suppose you are an idiot. And suppose you were a member of the legislature. But must I repeat myself."

SOLD A ROAN HORSE I raised at the horse auction the other day, and now she belongs to someone else. Or does she? I'm not so sure. It may always be "my horse that someone else has." You don't always let go of it. When there were still Herefords on my place, I bought a cow from Adam Preis of Emblem

Bench. The next spring when she calved out, I thought it might make a good feature picture. So I took a picture of her walking with her day-old calf out in the pasture. When the paper came out Thursday, Adam saw the picture, turned to his wife (she told me this) and cried: "Hey, there's my cow!"

April 6, 1977

I WAS GOING TO "wax eloquent" over all swelling leaf buds on the lilacs, the dogwood looking springish, the pussy willows out . . . But this morning all those weekend signs of spring are buried under blowing snow. But that's Wyoming. "How do you people out here get used to Wyoming winters?" the out-of-stater asked me? It's not the winters, lady, it's these springs you have to worry about!

April 13, 1977

YOU OTHER PARENTS out there, with more experience, and with kids going back to school or off to a new job or going back somewhere after being home for Easter, do you ever get used to sending them away again?

I LIKE TO WATCH A duck fly. A hawk is always looking, looking. The magpie barely gets there and the goose flies like you'd expect a goose to do, pushing through the air, talking and yapping about it all the while. The eagle soars and the songbird flits about from post to post and branch to branch. But the duck wants to get there. And it goes about it just as fast as it can. Neck out, wings pounding the air, wind-sleek, the duck goes at only one speed, fast. There's no slow speed. It's all downhill and it looks magnificent to me cutting across the sky.

April 20, 1977

ONE CHANGE that President Carter could make is in the post of FAA deputy administrator . . . and his old pilot friend, Tom Peterson is rumored in line for it. Remember, Peterson was the one who flew Carter around in a single-engine Cessna, much to the dismay of everyone but Carter and Peterson. Flying magazine tells the story of the time the Secret Service demanded the "first seven seats" of Peterson's four-place Cessna 172. "They refused to accept the idea that a presidential nominee was riding around in a single engine four-place airplane," the magazine pointed out. "Legend has it that Tom lined up three brand new 172's, put cardboard signs on them reading Section A, Section B and Section C, and told the Feds they were to sit, please, in Sections A and B."

May 18, 1977

AMIDST THE MANY feelings that go through your mind as you watch one of your kids go through a University of Wyoming commencement is how much all of us parents and kids want to see each other. As the graduates file in, people start waving all over that big fieldhouse. And you can see all the graduates doing the same thing, searching the crowd for those they want there on this big day. The difference is the restraint. The graduates do it with studied nonchalance while their folks are all but doing handstands on the seats. A guy behind me, in exasperation, hollered out, "Hey Jack, look up here!"

I would be very surprised if everyone in the place didn't, finally, find each other among all that crowd.

And you can't keep the people from saying what they want to say, either, at a UW commencement. They want to say what they're feeling.

For awhile everyone was going along with the announced instructions to withhold any individual applause until all the college graduates had been recognized. The crowd was polite and quiet, until one cowboy stood up with the announcement of a name, stood right up and raised his big black hat in the air and shouted: "Way to go, Terry!"

That, as the show business saying goes, loosened up the crowd!

And from that moment on, if you wanted to say it out loud, you did.

"All right, Cindy," cried one guy as she got her diploma. And there were a lot more "way to goes" and some just plain "Yeas" and whistles and handclaps. And one great one some young guy hollered out: "That's my mamma!" And sure enough, she was a mamma among a lot of kids, getting her degree years later than the others.

That's my boy and that's my mamma. It's all the same thrill.

May 25, 1977

IF THE OWNERS OF Seattle Slew had known how far he was going, they might have named him better. That's a horrid name. It's hardly Man of War, Bold Ruler, Citation or Secretariat. But as the man said, it ain't the name that makes him go.

I HAVEN'T SEEN THIS kind of flower yet but I want a flower that comes up in March, is hardy through the tough Wyoming spring, blooms three months, takes no water, destroys all the weeds in a three-foot radius around it, is free of all bugs, and then disappears in the fall, leaving no leaves, no old withered stalks, no trace . . . until the next March.

I FOUND IT AMUSING at the Greybull awards night that two out of the three people awarded perfect attendance pins for not missing a day of school weren't there to get them!

AND IT WAS THE same night that Mrs. John Anderson of Shell (who said she had been branding calves all day) leaned over after an hour of sitting, and whispered: "And I thought that saddle was hard today."

June 1, 1977

THERE ARE TIMES when the song, "Happy Birthday" is mercifully short. And other times when the Star Spangled Banner is unmercifully long!

AND I NOTICED AT the UW commencement no one knew the words or the tune of the official University of Wyoming song. I was astonished to learn it wasn't Cowboy Joe.

BITS AND PIECES . . . CAN'T REMEMBER where I saw it, but some guy at a convention won the door prize . . . and was given, appropriately, a door! . . . HAVE ALWAYS THOUGHT the flagpole companies should paint a mark halfway up. Half mast flags, like there were again Monday on Memorial day are only "halfway up" according to the guy down below, and that means anywhere from one-quarter to three quarter . . . RAN INTO SOME termites up in the Big Horn mountains at about 8,000-feet elevation which I found hard to believe. Shouldn't have, I guess. Termites are everywhere.

June 8, 1977

THE TOWN WATER LINE has finally reached out to our place.

That means, borrowing national calamity, we'll be able to put the lid on the cistern for good. It's time of joyous occasion. Not unless you have suffered with a cistern can you appreciate the significance of saying goodbye to it. On the eve of this happy day, I find myself thinking:

– That I'm not sorry in the least the hauling water days are over. After 20 years of living with it, I know of no job worse.

– That you haul water only to a nearly empty cistern, not to a nearly full one. If you wish to refine the phenomenon even more, you can say you haul much of the time only after you're out!

– You're seldom ahead of a cistern, always behind it, so actually the availability of water is a factor in many decisions, the washing, the company coming, something you never thought about at all when before you just turned the faucet on.

– That it will be years before I will stop listening unconsciously for the pressure pump to go off (thus assuring there's still water out there.)

– I suppose the habit of not wasting water is engrained forever. A running faucet is intolerable. I turn them off even in hotel rooms and other people's houses.

Why can't I conserve gasoline and electricity and heating energy like I do water? Obviously I've never been without the others. I learned water's value by living without it.

Yet I have this unsettling feeling that as time goes on I, too, will tend to forget how precious water once was. It will be easier to "turn on the faucet." I've caught myself thinking about Art Collingwood of Shell. Some years back the ranchers up there were meeting to talk about the Town water line. They'd been hooked on to the line for years. But now there were complaints of water rates, lack of pressure, gripes about the line and the service.

Then Art stood up and asked: "But have you forgotten how we used to take the sleds and horses in the winter and fill a barrel from the creek?"

June 22, 1977

I TRIED TO HEAD off a hard-headed cow by throwing a big rock at her through the fence the other day. And in my perfect, off-the-mound follow through, perfectly threw my hand right into the gate pole. It was the cow's fault, of course. But I can't remember what I said exactly. Probably something like, "Oh, gracious, I've hit the fence with my hand." Can't remember if I said anything to the cow or not.

I KEEP THINKING of that guy in Thermopolis who threw a rock at his bull . . . hit it in the head . . . and promptly killed it!

MY WIFE, BETTY, and I were discussing something from opposite ends and she came up with this wifely logic: "Listen, if your information conflicts with my preconceived notions, it's just too bad for your facts!"

THINGS A FATHER is reminded of on Father's Day, No. 22, just past:

That from the very beginning the kids knew you better than you knew yourself. How did they find out so soon that I would, predictably, act exactly the same way to the same situation regardless of how often it happens.

That if you're going to teach the kids tennis, you're going to eventually LOSE at tennis.

That you have to get new stories every year and forget all the ones about the old days you thought were so good.

That it is much easier to be a Father than a Mother.

That you never listened enough. If I were to go back and do it all over again, I would still talk like an adult but I'd listen like a child.

That the song is right. In the early years I never "had enough" time. Now when I have the time, they don't.

That turning the porch lights on and off, on and off, is really a very dumb way of signalling your daughter that it's time to come in.

That those Little League games did not matter after all.

That I wasn't always a Father. I was also a Son and when I was a Son I DID NOT act like a Father!

That the kids know their generation better than you. They are not asking you to join it, only to understand it.

That no mistake they will make will be any greater than the ones you made or could have made.

That lying awake waiting for everyone to finally get home doesn't hurry them along any faster.

That it helps to be able, without flinching, to drive cars with dents in the fenders and scrapes along the sides.

That no amount of time will erase those memories of field and floor, of stage and podium, of pickup trucks and mountain trails and splashing in lake water, of belly laughs and tears, of hunting camps and dance recitals, of hot bread specially made, of funny birthday cards, of shared work, shared triumphs, shared years with some kids who will say, every so often, "Hey, way to go, Dad."

July 6, 1977

ONLY BY CHANCE DID I hear on the noon radio broadcast that Bjorn Borg had won Wimbledon. So I figured I had a lock on the bets around the television set since the tennis match there was "yet to come." But I loused it up, 1) by being too eager (I couldn't believe my good fortune); and 2) by not being able to disguise my joy that Jimmy Connors had lost. As my "pigeon" said later, "I knew Borg had won by how happy you were."

THIS IS THE WEEK you can write it 7-7-77.

July 13, 1977

MY FRIEND, Frank Casey, said we are having some GOP weather. Okay, what's that, Frank? "Awfully windy."

LIKE A LOT OF LITTLE towns in Wyoming, Greybull has a town whistle which sounds a curfew. It is the same whistle that blows for a fire, only it keeps blowing over and over for a fire and only one blast for the curfew. It is safe to say no one pays the least bit of attention to the curfew but everyone jumps when the fire whistle goes on.

All this town whistle procedure can be lost on strangers passing through. The other morning at 6 a.m., a fire broke out and the whistle dutifully went off. A local CB listener heard a traveling CB'er talking to another right afterwards. "This is the darndest town," the out-of-town CB'er was saying. "They blew a whistle for you to go to bed last night and this morning they blew another one for you to get up."

July 20, 1977

THERE'S A LOT of grasshoppers that sound like a rattlesnake, but a rattlesnake NEVER sounds like a grasshopper.

July 27, 1977

THE SIXTEEN CENT postage for first class mail the post office department is talking about is more understandable if you realize that only six cents is going for actual mailing costs. The other 10 cents is for storage!

DON'T KNOW WHAT we would do without the postal service to talk about. It's the same up in Canada. Went there for a press convention last week and that's what those Canadian publishers were talking about. In fact, they did more than that. They held a pony express ride of 202 miles to show the post office you could mail papers quicker by horse than by the post office.

The horses took off with the papers at the same time they were mailed in the post office. Riding in relays they made the 202 miles from that town to Winnipeg in 15 hours and 48 minutes. And they beat the post office by a couple of hours!

THEY INTRODUCED one Canadian publisher from the podium who was in his 90's and had been a member of the Canadian Press actively for over 50 years. That got a big hand. But what really brought the crowd to its feet was the next announcement that he had also been a silver medal winner in swimming in the 1908 Olympics.

August 3, 1977

FOR SOME TIME I'VE been going to mention the American habit of saying "Bye bye" to say goodbye. It's difficult to imagine a sophisticated, world leader country like United States resorting to something like "Bye Bye" to conduct their daily dialogue. The phrase started out in baby talk, and at times sounds ridiculous; other times it seems to fit, sort of. It's widespread, that's for sure. I thought I would find that only housewives and salesmen used "Bye bye" very much, those who are used to the chic and the quick. But when you're looking for it, you find many using it.

What do you use instead?

Well, "Goodbye" is too final. Just plain "Bye" is too short, apparently, for these gimmicky times.

Nobody uses "So long" anymore except Lowell Thomas.

"See you later" always reminds me of the Fifties Jive Talk and not many date themselves with that.

The kids have abused "See ya" for two generations and probably will continue to do so.

Cowboys and farmers say a lot of things in parting, but they never say "Bye bye!"

You don't usually say "Bye for now" unless you're writing a letter.

And there're some pets like "Cheers" and "Be good" and "Come and see us" which doesn't mean come and see us at all; it means "Goodbye." All of these sometimes fit on a person and sometimes don't.

Are we down to "Bye bye?"

In the last week or so I kept track of some conversations and I heard "Bye bye" from a press salesman, one lawyer, several housewives, a National Park Service Ranger, innumerable secretaries and receptionists, at least six salesmen, a newspaperman in Canada and I myself said it 11 times.

So, with that, bye bye!

August 17, 1977

THEY TELL THE STORY in my area of the two old ranchers years ago who had to bury one of the members of the community. They were digging his grave, just the two of them, when they hit sandstone and the going got awful tough. After struggling an inch at a time they got down about four feet.

"Don't you think that's deep enough, Otto?" his friend asked.

"Listen," Otto said, "here's one guy I don't want crawling back out again."

So they went down another foot and a half!

August 24, 1977

I was already in the Establishment by the time Elvis Presley arrived. I was into it even deeper by the Beatles time. So I never looked at either one in proper perspective in their debuting years. And was, if the truth were known, even more fuddy-duddy in those days than I am now.

I cannot, therefore, ever be accused of knowing what was going on in the American musical world and what Elvis and the Beatles contributed to it. The papers are full of how it was and what it was since Elvis' death, and talking to me as if I should have known it, too. Well, I didn't! In typical Establishment fashion I thought it all just a fad that would go away as soon as short hair came back!

Once not too many years back, I was listening to a song played by Henry Mancini or someone of like mellowness.

"Now there's music," I informed my son.

"Ah, ha, Dad," he chortled. "Do you know who wrote that song and played it first."

I can't imagine, I said.

"It was the Beatles," he cried with glee, "those great Beatles."

So, like I say now – 20 years later – that's music.

August 31, 1977

THERE'S NOTHING QUIETER than a house after the kids have all gone to school. Our house is shuddering through such a time now. No one at home but the old folks. A friend of mine, Jack Williams, solved it when it happened to him. He bought a dog – the family's first one – the week after his last youngster, Son John, left home. Jack's neighbor came over that night, looked at the new dog and exclaimed, "Well, I see it didn't take you long to replace John."

THE WYOMING HIGHWAY PATROL had a booth set up at the Wyoming State Fair at Douglas this year. Right next to them was the Swine Booth. "Is someone trying to tell you guys something," one woman asked the patrolman.

September 21, 1977

DOWN IN LARAMIE if you have a dog in the car and drive up to a certain liquor store, they give you your booze, then a lollipop to the kids – and get this – a dog biscuit to your dog!

AND ALSO IN LARAMIE at the UTEP game last week a couple of policemen sat on the student side and after a while confiscated a bottle of booze. The reaction by the students was silent, but swift. They started passing their empty bottles through the crowd and up to the policemen. The pile grew!

I REMAIN CONVINCED that a tornado touched down briefly in our backyard a couple of weeks ago although officially no one has said so. The damage was too much for a gusty wind. The uprooted big cottonwoods, the carport flipped away, a big water tank lifted off its stand. But the other day I found what I thought would be the clincher. A strange 1973 Wyo trailer license plate lying right by the uprooted trees. Number 9-95 trailer, Wyo 1973. It was lying in the grass and it wasn't there before the wind. It could have been picked up at the airport across the river, I reasoned and although it seemed a little too much Wizard of Oz and Dorothy's house-in-the-air, still if it was a plate from the airport my tornado claim would be vindicated. So I put in a call to my old friend, George Hoffman, county treasurer of Big Horn county, and asked him: "George, could you tell me who license plate 9-95 trailer was issued to in 1973? I think I'm on to a hot story." Sure, George says, and in a few minutes comes back to the phone. "That plate," he says, "was issued in 1973 to one Bruce M. Kennedy."
Oh.
So much for that idea.

September 28, 1977

BITS AND PIECES . . . YOU CAN SAY WHAT you want about those Wyoming cottonwoods; it's this time of year when you can appreciate them the most. Rivers and creeks all over Wyoming are filled with their yellow and gold colors . . . AS MUCH AS I'VE IRRIGATED the road you'd think something would have grown there . . . WHICH REMINDS ME of things you learn about irrigating when your wife does it. Did you know, for instance, that an overripe zucchini squash works fine to block off a row of water? That was a new one on me, too!

October 5, 1977

PRINTERS WILL TELL you that the easiest to read combination is black ink on yellow paper. Nature does this every October when she fills a yellow cottonwood with a bunch of blackbirds.

VIC BOELENS told me the other day why he left the farm on the Greybull river and moved to town: "I just had more work than the wife could do."

October 12, 1977
PUTTING THINGS AWAY for fall is not half as much fun as getting everything ready for spring.

IF YOU DON'T THINK the country is going to hell, just remember that out of all the problems we have, all the troubles we face, all the great decisions that need to be made, the one problem that caused the most flap in recent Ann Landers' columns was how to put the toilet paper on the roll. (So it rolls off the front or off the back) Jeez!

October 19, 1977
OVERHEARD CONVERSATION, one guy talking about another: "Oh, he's just a scrub bull."

October 26, 1977
I WALKED DOWN through what we call the "lower pasture" on our place the other day. Just five acres or so of pasture that's seen better days. It needs plowed up and I was trying to decide whether I wanted to go through all the hassles of "farming" again or just let it be a newspaperman's pasture and look like hell.

It used to be Northrup King's No. 5 pasture mix when I put it in 20 years ago. It wouldn't be any Northrup King ad now, though. Things are growing in it Northrup King never heard of. But it wasn't always this way. For years it was lush and thick and you could cut hay off from it all season long and still pasture it during the winter. I never could get over how it grew. Twenty years ago I got my first ulcer trying to make that pasture take. That was the same year they turned the water out of the ditch for three weeks to kill moss. And a little bit of me died each week with the pasture. There's something devastating about watching something you plant, die from lack of water. Bugs are bad, poor soil a trial, but no water, nothing stuns like that.

So after weeks of worrying and stewing, I gave up on that patch of ground. I kept watering it just because I didn't know what else to do and kept the stock off it, but it was a goner I knew. And with it, all the money for that seed. But the next year there was green showing. And the next even more. It took, but I still don't know why.

Now it's time to start over with it. I'm not sure I'm man enough, not sure I'm farmer enough. And you know what they're saying about the water next year. I couldn't take that no water again. That's why a part-time "farmer" is never a farmer. When they tell you maybe the water will be short next year, a part time "farmer" has a choice. A farmer doesn't!

November 9, 1977

THE HUNTER'S WIFE has a special place reserved for her Someplace. A friend of ours, whose husband had been up on the mountain for half the week, was in the grocery store. And lo, there was her husband! Well, hi, they both said. She thought to herself, I'd better hurry home and get supper for him. So she did. But he didn't show. She waited. He still didn't show. Finally it dawned. He'd just come down for some groceries and had gone right back up.

November 30, 1977

ONE OF THOSE MISS WORLD girls said she was 5 foot 12 inches tall which means she prefers men who are 5 foot 15 inches tall instead of those who are 4 feet 18 inches tall.

THE ROAD I TRAVEL a lot runs along the bluff above the river and there're trees growing up out of the bottom so when you drive along you're even with the tops sometimes. And so when a hawk perches in those topmost branches, he's actually just car window height, and this places a different perspective on it all.

The other day one big old boy was there in his usual perch as I drove slowly by. When we were eyeball to eyeball, he gave a little hop – just a slight movement – set his wings straight without a flap and soared off towards the river side. It was done with such grace you just marveled at it. No wasted motion, no wings flapping. Just a graceful step off into space.

Animal movement is often like this. It can be in such harmony with everything.

Our dog runs and runs and when she hits the ditch she glides over it. A perfect movement. Not a muscle out of place. And she does it that way every time.

A rodeo horse strides out, front hooves reaching for the next grasp of air, over and over, down the arena, and the muscles ripple and the sound of the gallop comes back in constant rhythm. It's always a beautiful sight.

In that Sunday night Gunther Gebel-Williams show, three tigers jumped over each other, over and over with such fluid movement, you couldn't tell one from another.

We humans aren't this way. We spend years making a ballet step perfect, a pole vault smooth. The grace of a swimmer, the pure motion of the jump shooter, the poise of the walk, we have to learn all of this, some of us never.

The animal is blessed with it. It may have been a tradeout. We get the brains, but they the style.

December 7, 1977

Who was the first jump shooter in Big Horn Basin basketball?

Before we start arguing about it, let me set the rules. It has to be as close to today's pure jump shot as possible. The perpendicular leap, the ball released at the top of the jump with a one-handed shot. You can name a lot of them after the 1950's in the old BHB conference. But wade back through those earlier years of two-handed set shots, the one-handed pushes and the underhanded free throws.

Anyone come to mind?

I tried the question on several long time (mark now, I didn't say "old time") coaches and players from those years after a Sports Illustrated article about the jump shot piqued my interest. The SI story also tried to pin down who invented it and failed. No one is sure. But a Joe Fulks from Murray State in 1943 popularized it. And SI mentioned Kenny Sailors, the Wyoming great who "used a shot somewhat like a jumper when Wyoming won the NCAA in 1943."

So who was first back in the Big Horn Basin?

How about Raymond Beaver of Manderson in 1939 and '40? That's who Bill Bush of Lander remembers it was.

"Beaver would jump up and turn loose, from anywhere, even the center of the court," recalls Bush who played at Thermop in some great years and later coached at Lander in the 1940's.

"He shot a little more over the shoulder, but it was a jump shot and he could hit with it anywhere," Bush says.

Beaver played on those Manderson teams when there wasn't any A, B, C classification. He was the oldest of several basketball playing brothers – Billie, also of Manderson, and Cecil, who played his last year at Basin in 1947. Neither shot a jump but both were consistent high scorers.

Billie, who lives in Worland now (and whose son, Mickey, was a Worland great), agrees that brother Raymond was first. "It was a jump shot and he shot it from all over," he remembers. Beaver was only 5-11 - 6', smaller than his brothers that followed. He has lived in California for years.

But if Beaver figured out what the future trend of basketball shooting was going to be, no one else did until the early 1950's. Then Terry Eckhardt of Worland came along to devastate everybody. And the switch was made en masse.

As Jack King, who coached Lander in those years, described it: "By the mid 1950's you had to shoot jump shots to survive." His first player to use the jump was Bert St. John in 1954.

In those 10 or 15 years before the big changeover, though, there were some great BHB shooters. But apparently they weren't the pure jumper. Many remembered Elwood Smith of Cody, "a tremendous shot," Keith Bloom of Powell recalls, but not that his shot was the pure jumper. Smith was killed in the Pacific in World War II.

And the name of Benny Earl Henan (I hope I'm spelling some of these names right) of Lander kept popping up as one of the conference's greatest shots. But still not quite the pure jumper.

Bush coached a turnaround jumper for his post man. Jock Bosnic was one at Lander during his great career. But the guards and forwards didn't shoot jumpers.

Bill Sharp of Cody was just starting his eventual great jump shot when he played in 1947 and 1948 at Cody high. It was later at UW when his jump shot was so sensational. It didn't matter in high school, as his coach, Bill Waller, pointed out. "Sharp could shoot any way," Waller recalls.

Charley Roberts of Worland, who has been in BHB teaching and coaching for over 35 years, was coaching at Lovell in the early 1940's. He doesn't recall any pure jump shooters then but Lovell in those days, as now, shot the eyes out of everyone, regardless. His most consistent shooter from those Lovell teams?

"It was Bob Doerr," Roberts remembers.

During the 1940's the two-handed set shot was going and the one hander was used more and more. But the feet didn't leave the floor. Not both at once, very often anyway. There were "a lot of stride shots," Jack King called them, and much experimenting as all kids who shoot baskets will do. "We were in a transition period over several years," Bloom says. Shots began to resemble a jump shot and then Terry Eckhardt came along to convince everybody.

"Eckhardt was the first real good jump shooter," Charley Roberts believes. King agrees: "Eckhardt was the one who hurt us the most."

They said the same thing about Raymond Beaver back in 1939!

December 14, 1977

AT THIS POINT IN TIME, I think the most overworked phrase in America is: "At this point in time . . . " You hear it all the time. A Washington department head on the Today show Monday used it three times in three minutes. So if Washington is using it you know it's got to be overworked. At one point in time it was a good phrase. At this point in time we need to think up another one.

AMAZING HOW FAST a phrase or word will pop into everyday language. It sounds so good the first time you hear it, you have to try it out right away. Besides, it makes you "with it". (How can you fall out of the mainstream if you use all the words and phrases of the mainstream?) So we all end up talking like each other for awhile, until another catchy one arrives. And then we spin the new one along until that one wears out.

It would be nice if we could exchange the King's English as fluently. Alas, we are a nation of phrase-talkers and cliche-lovers and our speech is full of current idioms or cuss words or both. Although we greatly admire good English and good speech in others, we never sustain it very long in ourselves.

Johnny may not be able to read or write, but not many of us are showing him how to talk either.

A COUPLE I KNOW HAVE CB tags of St. Peter and St. Peter's Angel. On a trip up Sylvan Pass, climbing up into Yellowstone Park in two vehicles, they got to talking back and forth on their CB's. At the first call ("St. Peter's

Angel calling St. Peter") they had an astonished audience. One guy cut in immediately. "I didn't know we were up that high," he exclaimed.

December 21, 1977

AT THE NURSING HOME Christmas party last week, I couldn't recognize who was playing Santa Claus. I whispered too loud, I guess, when I asked my wife who Santa was because the little boy in front of us turned around and said:

"It's Pat Sanders. I can tell by the way he walks."

THAT'S OCCUPATIONAL hazard, I suppose, for all Santa Clauses. Your cover gets blown. Especially if you do it too many years in a row. George (Conoco) Scott did it for years up at the Shell schoolhouse. He was always the Christmas party Santa there (and a lot of other places, too.) So the kids got on to him and he and Johnny Haley figured it was time for a switch. That one year, then, John got into the suit and hid out in the back room. George arrived in his usual clothes to visit with the kids. They thought that was great, George out there and not dressed yet.

"When are you getting ready," they teased.

"Isn't it about time for you to go outside and come back in," they poked at him. "You're late, you know," they laughed. He wasn't fooling them. THEY knew who he was.

And then Johnny walked in from the back all dressed up in George's Santa Claus suit.

There was this immense quiet over the entire schoolroom.

Eyes would turn to look at Santa. And then back at George. No one said a word.

It turned out to be the best Christmas party the Shell school ever had.

SANTA CLAUS AT OUR house is a Girl!

SHE is the one who decorates the house and makes pine cone wreaths and hangs mistletoe and pine boughs and strings of popcorn and turns the house into red and green.

SHE is the writer of Christmas cards and the keeper of addresses and last year's list and the one who always writes more than just "Merry Christmas" on the cards.

SHE is the one who remembers the out of town family, who makes all the Christmas lists and does the shopping and who always finds just what the kids want (and the man of the house, too.)

SHE wraps the gifts, decorates the tree, makes the candy, cooks Christmas dinner and makes Christmas what it is supposed to be.

No question about it. Santa is a SHE!

1978

January 4, 1978

The people of the Fair Sex and the People of the Stronger Sex had lived joyously together in the World for many centuries. And the two nations had become very compatible and very happy together and they still called each other Women and Men in the habit of their forefathers.

And it came to pass that many things happened to the Peoples and many things changed except one time each year and it was always the same. This was the Long Weekend of The Games.

These were the Games of the Old Men Who Had Been Doing It Longer. And the Younger Men Who Weren't Quite So Good and the Games of the Younger Men Who Thought They Were Very Good. And you could even watch the Games of the Alsorans and Mighthavebeens and many other numbing contests.

Now everyone could see the games through the Big Screen in their homes. But it was the men who watched most and it became known as the time the Men Went Away From the House without ever leaving it.

For many years, this had bothered the Peoples of the Fair Sex. They became Widows Before Their Time and were lonely and their gloom deepened and not a few became irritable and some even jealous of the great enjoyment their men were having. They could have joined in, too, but the Fair Sex correctly saw there were much more important things to do.

So it came to pass the Plan From Houston, conceived many years before, was put into effect. The woman, simply, would cut the Big Cable. And thus, there would be no picture for The Long Weekend of the Games.

And so it happened and though the Games went on No One in the World saw them except for the few who had been picked by The Computer to be there and throughout the rest of the land there was a Silence.

There were no yellings and screamings from the Rooms of the Big Screens.

You could not hear those famous words like: "This is the biggest play of the game." "The clock is against them." "The offensive line is blowing them out of there." "He heard footsteps." "He has a great pair of hands." And other such things.

And no one could care what the Greek Named Jimmy gave for Odds and Point Spread and it was different trying to think of something else besides the Games.

And the oldest announcer among them was not heard telling how it used to be in other Rose Bowl games and how he had seen all the big plays and thus, nothing could remind him of nothing.

For awhile the women feared that the men would not know what to do. But the men of the houses began to actually stand up for long periods of time and to walk around and to act alive.

Some even asked if there was anything the Fair Sex wanted them to do. And a few of the very brave volunteered to help with the Dinner of the New Year. In the Lands of Warm Weather many people left their houses and even where the Minuses showed on the Special Scales and it was cold on the Outside, some of the men went to look at the Sun and to feel the Fresh Air in their lungs. And not a few mentioned how different it felt once again.

The Bottles of Special Hops made from the many spring waters of the country went unopened. And everyone felt better for this. The women began to cook real food, and to speak words back to their men, and to smile again.

And Families were reunited and the People played in the snow and went to see other Peoples and they talked with their kids and took books down from the shelves. And there was rejoicing throughout the land.

And the women came to their men and took their hands and consoled them in soft, pleasing voices and reminded them: "Honey, it's only a game."

February 1, 1978

DID THAT WYOMING LICENSE plate that popped up in the movie, "Close Encounters of the Third Kind" say county "44"? And it wasn't four over four (like the double digit plates are) but forty-four, two fours right along side each other. Hollywood wanted to make sure we had enough counties and people out here.

ONE THING I HAVE always noticed about contest judges (no matter what kind of contest) is how perceptive and intelligent judges are when you win . . . and how out-of-touch, one-sided and just a little stupid they are when you lose.

SENATOR CLIFF HANSEN tells the story about the time an English exchange student named Peter was at the Hansen ranch in Jackson working for awhile. Peter had been fixing fence and he woke up one morning to find it raining. The old foreman asked him, "Do you want to use my heavy raincoat?" "Oh no," Peter answered, "I have my umbrella."

February 8, 1978

You aren't supposed to write editorials for just one person, the thought being that if your scope is that narrow you might as well shake your fist at him across the table.

But when someone asked me if there had been such a time for me, I had to admit there was once I wrote one editorial for just one person. Rather it was one I DIDN'T write. Because actually I said nothing, I wrote nothing, which has to put the piece among the very best I ever did!

It was very partisan politically back at that time and when Charlotte, a Democrat, stopped me on the street, I could tell she was very irritated.

"I just hate those editorials of yours," she jumped right at me.

They were very Republican editorials in those days, very Republican, and Charlotte, being very Democratic, the two of us were miles apart.

"Well then, just don't read them. Just pass over Page 2 and read something else," I suggested.

"Oh, if they're there, I have to read them. But I hate 'em," she said. And we parted, one in each direction, properly still 180 degrees apart.

Now back in those letterpress times, each line of type was moveable. We could do all sorts of unpredictable things with one person's paper, often with hilarious results. We changed locals so the preacher would say things he shouldn't and husbands would do things they shouldn't. There were things put in that the censor would not pass on normal days, and some things even bad proofreaders would usually have caught. But all of this was just in one paper. 2,999 papers would be right – the one paper with the "victims" changes would be wrong. And only the outraged victim and the gleeful printers would know.

Our pleasures, simpler in those days, were easier to accomplish. As we got more modern it got harder to do. One line of type now in offset printing is far easier to set, astonishingly faster to produce and to run. But once set up and ready to go, it is almost impossible to change just one line in today's newspaper without doing the whole process over again.

Not so in the old days. We were one-line-at-a-time publishers. Oh, you had to go to a great deal of trouble to personalize a paper. You had to stop the press, unlock the forms, pull out the line or lines you were changing. Go to the Linotype, set the new line, put it in the form, lock it up again, run one paper, stop the press. Then take the one paper, get it folded, search out the victim's stencil, stamp just that one paper with the right name so it would go to the right person. A lot of effort, but the anticipation of the outrage the next day sped the work along.

So now you know how that editorial to Charlotte was written.

After all the press run was done, except for one last paper, I stopped the press, went to the editorial column and took out that column of editorial type. In its place went what printers call "furniture" or blank spacing so that when we ran the press again for Charlotte's one paper, the long two editorial columns came out completely blank. Just white space. Two long columns of nothing where the editorial normally was.

Among the phones that rang the next morning, I knew one would be Charlotte.

"Okay," she said, "very funny, very funny. I know what you're going to say. This way I won't have to read your editorials. But just send me a regular paper. I can't stand what you write, but I can't stand not knowing if I should be mad or not either!"

February 15, 1978

COLUMNIST MIKE ROYKO of the Chicago Daily News writes with a double-bladed sword and he uses it with great glee to cut and hack away at everyone in sight. He causes as many people to bleed as any columnist in America. When he stabs, you feel it. And it's such a long sword. You can be hidden away in self-imposed exile in San Clemente and still feel the pain.

Royko was mentioning Richard Nixon the other day and in a pointed sarcastic lunge at the ex-President, Royko called him "Our National Wart."

Oh, that's cold.

You can bleed in several places from that one.

Being called "scheming" or "devious" or "arrogant", all those are just words. A Wart is a state of being.

Erasing tapes, staying out of the courts, ducking an impeachment, all these are sly schemes of life. But once it's said you can't escape being a National Wart. That could be a life sentence!

February 22, 1978

IT HAPPENS EVERY YEAR. Some taxpayers who've cheated on their tax returns try to make up for it later by sending anonymous payments to the IRS. (The IRS calls it "the conscience fund.") One taxpayer sent $300 recently and a note explaining that he could not sleep at night for worrying about his tax evasion. His letter ended: "P.S. If I still can't sleep, I will send more later."

THE TRAVEL commission is hearing continual comments from people who think that Devil's Tower was a prop in "Close Encounters of the Third Kind." Yes, and we tacked up the Tetons for "Shane", too.

IF EVER A DOG lived up to that "faithful dog" routine it has to be our neighbor's old pooch who every noon accompanies the kindergartner up the lane. They walk together to the bus, very slowly. They're always early to start, but they dawdle so much along the way, they always have to run the last 100 yards because the bus is already there. But the dog always walks slow when the boy does, and runs when the boy does. He sits and waits patiently until the boy gets on the bus. Then he watches it as it drives away, up the hill and finally out of sight. He always waits to make sure it isn't going to come back. This takes an extra minute or so. Then he goes over and sniffs around where the boy got on. Only then, when the boy is gone for good, does the old dog head back to the house, running pellmell down the long quarter-mile lane. Anxious to get back home. Duty's done.

MY DIET/CONDITIONING deal isn't working all that great. I ran two miles the other day, but I ate four miles.

March 1, 1978

IT WAS SNOWING AND THE wind had come up a little on the ski slope. Behind me I heard this little kid hollering to his same age friend, "Hey this snow hurts your eyes when you're coming down." He thought a minute and then said outloud to himself, "Well, I close my eyes part of the time anyway."

Young man, I know the feeling.

OUT OF A FLYING magazine comes the story from last year in Arizona when two government jets were trying to track a light plane suspected of smuggling drugs. As the Feds wondered aloud why they couldn't spot the aircraft to the south, a voice broke into the Customs frequency. "That's because I'm not going south. You guys are dumb, dumb, dumb." Surprised the Feds asked for a repeat. "Dumb," was the response. "D-U-M-B."

THE MOST PERFECTLY-shaped cottonwood I've run across in Wyoming is a big patriarch on the old Jim Moberly place on Shell creek, right alongside the borrowpit on the road that takes you to Sheridan.

Probably 50 or 60 years old, it's grown very evenly and the crown is just what you'd think a cottonwood ought to look like. Every branch has been in place all these years. It's the kind of tree you pick out to photograph over and over, in all kinds of light, summer green and fall gold. And because the Big Horn mountains offer a perfect backdrop, no picture ever really fails.

But lately I've noticed she's getting a little unkempt in these declining years. One bottom branch is growing at an odd angle, straying down from all the rest, like an unruly strand of hair.

I just itch, when I see it anymore, to stop and whack at it with a chain saw, and comb it back into place.

March 22, 1978

ONE THING ABOUT LIVING ON a country road in the springtime is how quickly your car takes on the perpetual color of unwashed mud. You can't afford to wash it. The mud always wins anyway. You can always tell the "countryfolks" in a small town this time of year. They're the ones with the mud-colored cars!

I HAD TO DRIVE the pickup through all the mud in our lane to get to a dry spot down the road where I could run! Somehow that doesn't make sense. This running's okay, I guess, but sometimes I wonder if Mark Twain didn't have a point. He hated exercise, "I see no advantage in being tired," he always said.

March 29, 1978

I'VE JUST FINISHED five days of batching . . . wandering around this house all by myself . . . watering a bunch of flowers I don't know the names of, feeding a bunch of cats and a dog whose names I should know, feeding myself after a fashion, all the while trying to keep the house looking like I HAVEN'T lived in it . . . and I'm here to tell all you gals that anything you want to say about Women's Lib, I'll agree, I'll agree, I'll agree.

WHAT UNSEEN FORCE propels kids to all do the same thing at the same time? In our town the past week it's been kites. And I drove to a couple of other towns over the weekend and all along the way it was kites. It wasn't all that windy, but what there was was being all used up! Next week it will be something else, marbles maybe, and every kid in town will be doing it. Then that fades and the marbles and the kites end up in the same forgotten place and youngsters are running off to do something else.

It's the same with us older folks. First it's snowmobiling, then it's cycles and then it's just plain bikes and then it's CB'ing and then it's drag racing and then it's something else. The dedicated ones stay with it all the time, but most of the rest of us drift from flying one kite to flying another and another, using up all the "wind" we can.

WE HAVE A FRIEND whose kids are growing up or gone and there are no "little ones" around the house. "I miss them," she says, "the little grade school size who are so much fun and talk so cute and who are so honest with you. So I've made it a rule when they come around the house to sell something, I ask them in, for just a minute or two and give them a cookie and talk to them and ask them questions and we have a great time. And I have "little kids" around again.

We tried it at our house the very next week. And she's right!

April 12, 1978

THE BUFFALO AT THERMOPOLIS are pretty to watch this time of year when the grass greens up . It's always a thrill to drive right down through them on the roads that wander through the state park. I once hired an editor from back east right in the middle of that herd. I was trying to convince him to come West (this was before the natural push this way was on). But he was sold on coming, right there, with buffalo out each window. The fact that he never made a good editor and eventually moved on wasn't the buffalo's fault. They'd done their job.

THERE'S A GUY IN our town who just bought one of those little riding tractors.

"I'm going to plow a few gardens and push a little dirt around," he told me, "as soon as I can get some attachments for it."

"When will you get those," I wondered.

"Soon as I save up enough coupons," he said.

Coupons, I thought, what kind of a deal do they have now to save coupons to buy garden tractors. He saw my puzzled look and before I could say "what coupons are those" he slyly said, "You know, those coupons with George Washington's picture on the front."

April 26, 1978

PEOPLE SELDOM UNDERSTAND that how long it takes to paint a picture (or write a story) is not the criteria of talent. One artist friend, when someone asks her, "How long did it take you to paint that?" always replies, "Twenty years" which is how long she has been painting.

THOSE OLD WOOD TYPE letters are really popular. That's been obvious for some time now. But I didn't realize how popular and how expensive they are. In one shop I noticed the letters had been arranged in six or seven letter groups, spelling such things as TENNIS and KITCHEN and things like that. Each set cost $50 or $60 bucks. Being an old letterpress printer in earlier days, I couldn't resist asking the owner about them. "What you see there," he said, "is all that's left out of 4,000 letters I bought from a shop in England. I put them together in my spare time. Now what are there, six or seven sets. I made a good deal on that."

I guess he did. If you put a calculator to that transaction he had 4,000 letters he probably bought for a song, put them together and sold them for about $7 for each letter which comes out to about $28,000.

I don't know what we were doing putting out a newspaper in the old days. We should have been selling the type.

Bruce Kennedy's Sage Publishing Co. acquired the Greybull Standard in 1978 and his "Getting the Bull by the Tail" column began appearing again in the Greybull newspaper.

May 4, 1978

When I thought I had let go of the tail, here I am grabbing on again. But it's always been a good ride!

IF YOU WANT TO BEAT all the neighbors with the first leaves of the season, plant a willow. If you want to have the last leaves in the neighborhood, get a black walnut.

One thing I have never understood about a black walnut is, if it has the last leaves on, why does it also have the first leaves off in the fall? But it compensates for this contrariness by having beautiful lacy leaves, well-shaped trees and an abundance of walnuts. That's not a bad trade-off.

It takes a long life to enjoy them, though. They grow by the half inch, not the foot. A cottonwood will be a big tree by the time the black walnut is just a kid.

The two in our lawn are still "young" trees but they must be 35 or 40 years old. Randa (Harvey) Krueger, who lived here before us, planted them. She got them from the Smith place, the first place that Trapper creek flows through on its way out of the high country. No, it's not a native Wyoming tree. Those black walnuts up there were planted by a pioneer family from Missouri who brought along a bunch of seedlings to Wyoming 75 years ago.

Now when Trapper creek comes tumbling down out of the mountains, it flows quietly through a grove of Missouri black walnuts for a couple hundred yards. Not many mountain creeks in Wyoming do that.

So, from Missouri to Trapper creek to my place . . . and that's a long ways from Gurney's catalog.

May 11, 1978

MY FRIEND, Turk Lassiter, who is hobbling around with "football" knee surgery, says he doesn't understand it. He only watched one game on TV last fall.

SOMEONE HAS asked that this bit of Ben Franklin wisdom be repeated so she "can get it down right" which I suspect means someone will hear it repeated again! So, as Poor Richard says, "The good or ill hap of a good or ill life, is the good or ill choice of a good or ill wife."

AFTER YEARS OF WAITING I am absolutely pessimistic that the government will ever voluntarily reform itself. Indeed, the opposite is true. It is growing, costing more, becoming more inefficient. And with it, so are taxes, inflation, wasted money. It isn't even holding its own anymore. Or making any attempt to do so. Instead there are more ratholes for more of our money, more government for us to cuss, more loss of freedoms.

Neither Congress nor a half dozen Administrations have made a serious or sustained attempt to reduce government in 30 or 40 years. Nor have the states or cities. But unfortunately, neither have you or I. That is the crux of what has happened to us. We demand more services, more protection, more governmental favors. We have never asked for less. We ask for less for our neighbors. But not for ourselves. We want "his" program cut back but we want "our" services to remain. We want our wages increased and protected, but we want his cut. We want his crops on the free market and ours subsidized. Our town needs this street project or dike or airport and sewer system, but the town down the road should pay for its own.

As long as all this government, broken down into its infinitesimal pieces, is demanded by the American people it will continue to grow. If the people want it stopped, they will have to stop it, at their level. At the governmental level, city, state or national, it will not stop.

If there ever was a time, it seems to me, when the smallest component of democracy, the individual, has a say, it is this time. The louder he or she speaks, the deeper they feel, the more they will be heard. It is a two-part commitment. First to ask for only the essentials. Second, to demand outloud – to anyone who will listen – that it stop.

May 18, 1978

OUR DOG'S BITE IS nowhere near as ferocious as her bark but when you're a stranger on the place she makes you think it is!

Set foot around here and the dog does her best to run you back off. It's all bluff, I'm convinced. I don't think she'd know how to bite, but you never know. And I haven't picked out anyone yet for her to try out.

With the winter of very exasperated and impatient teaching behind us she's getting better about holding back, and sometimes now she doesn't go past the end of my voice. I think we're making progress – she's barking less and I'm screaming less. And she has yet to run anyone off.

But tomorrow the Internal Revenue Service guy is coming for an audit and I've told the dog that the day is a "day off" from all this "training." "Tomorrow," I've said to her, "tomorrow, you can do anything you like!"

FEW FLOWERS LAST long enough for me. If I had my druthers, I'd find a way to make a flowering crab hold on right up to the Fourth of July! And surely an iris deserves more than a week. And those big gorgeous peonies? A sunflower will bloom along the roadside most of the summer, but a tulip fades away before school's out. A plum tree sets on and then gives way to a cherry tree which then lets the apples take over. One morning it is breathtaking. A few mornings later it's fading.

Life goes too fast. Even the flowers are in a hurry.

May 25, 1978

GURNEY SEED COMPANY exchanged some of my dollars for some of their plants, but as usual what I ordered didn't come. Among the mimeographed apologies was a "free gift" from Gurney's, a six-inch Russian Olive tree.

Mr. Gurney, you gotta be kidding.

A Russian Olive is not something I cherish between one friend and another. It's like exchanging ragweed plants. I hate to be picky about the gift, horse's mouth and all. But if you think Russian Olives grow so good for you back in Yankton that you have a surplus, come to this part of Wyoming. In the past 20 years they're grown in epidemic proportions along creeks and rivers, along fences and ditchbanks, wherever water flows and robins fly. Sometimes when I look around it seems that's all I see. Another one I don't need.

Why don't we do this? Why don't we send you all the extra Russian Olive trees I have and you send me all your extra six-inch Scotch Pines.

June 1, 1978

ON THE IRRIGATION DITCH, "highority" is always better than "priority," a friend reminded me the other day.

June 6, 1978

AT THE MEMORIAL DAY services at the cemetery there was one veteran in the firing squad who had remembered his Army days well. A couple of unmistakable signs of old spit and polish, a little more precision, a straighter back maybe, something there that had lingered on through the years. And the salute. Especially the salute. If you want to pick out a soldier, look for his salute.

That simple act of bringing the hand to the head should be so basically easy, but in truth a whole lot of us never saluted right. There's a soldier's art to it. It has to do with the way the hand is brought up, an arc that swings the hand to the head so the wrist is cocked just right and the palm lays where it should. It's a smooth yet snappy motion and when it's all done, the elbow is in exactly the right angle, the fingers touch where they should and most of all it FEELS like it's right.

Some salutes look like a bandage over one eye.

Others seem to count if they touch any part of the head. Old generals never salute right. Neither do new recruits. In between, thousands try to get it right.

Wars, of course, are not won or lost on whether an Army can salute. Yet in a way they are. It is part of that military tradition that holds armies together the way the nail holds the horseshoe. If enough nails catch, the shoe will stay on.

Military tradition is centuries old, a thousand nails old. A salute is the part you see. The rest you feel. The military has so many things I don't like, it is no place for me. But there were some parts of the tradition I found irresistible. That compatriot in the firing squad had found them that way, too. And if he wasn't Regular Army, he had learned Regular Army ways. That's all it takes from generation to generation to keep an Army going. And that is why in these post-Vietnam days of no draft and changing lifestyles the Volunteer Army is struggling. The tradition has been short circuited. Right now the chiefs don't run the Navy anymore.

BOB HOPE SAID he went around with Billy Carter in Washington (in the best line out of his special the other night) and they went to see the Lincoln Memorial. Hope said Billy looked at the statue and said, "He sure was a big guy, wasn't he?"

June 12, 1978

IF YOU HAVEN'T bought groceries much lately, it's educational to stand there with a small sack of groceries in one hand and $25 in the other and know you can't keep both.

THE ANNUAL TOWNWIDE celebration for Greybull, the Days of '49 is over. It's a good thing. Three days and three nights establishes some sort of limit on human endurance. But amidst all of the activities and celebrations and everything else, the one striking thing about it is how many people come back to it. It's become a truth in the last 30 years that if you stand on one corner of town long enough you would see everyone you ever knew!

DON'T KNOW WHETHER inflation has hit the hardboiled egg value out of proportion or not but this sign was in a Bishop, Calif. delicatessen:
HARD BOILED EGGS
Wear and tear on the hen	03 cents
Rent on hen house	03 cents
Chicken feed	03 cents
Rooster Tax	05 cents
Boiling water	01 cents
Total	15 cents

COUNTY TREASURER George Hoffman, who completed the mini marathon, has been running for years, way back when no one else did it. In fact, he's been running longer than half the contestants were old!

AND YOU'VE BEEN AROUND a long time in Greybull if you can remember when it wasn't a Rock Concert they held on the Greybull football field but the 49er rodeo itself . . . BUT AT THE ROCK CONCERT Sunday there were all sorts of strange faces, too. And for the record book, let it be said that before they lifted the ban at the gate on taking booze inside, some of the largest sleeping bags in the world went through those portals.

June 19, 1978
GOING THROUGH YELLOWSTONE Park the other day I noticed how many patches of snow were covered with pink "snow mold" until in some places the snow looked more pink than it did white. I assume that's what it is, snow mold; someone who knew a lot more about things than I do, told me a long time ago that's what it was. So if I'm saying it wrong, I'm saying I'm sorry ahead of time. Anyway it's pink and it's out of place and it's an unexpected bright color.

Seeing it again always reminds me of the time I was on the operating table, nervous and scared, all "prepped" and waiting for the doctor to come in. But when he finally came in and over to the table, instead of saying, "Well, what have we here?" like they do in the movies, he said to all the nurses standing around, "I was up in the mountains yesterday and there was this pink stuff all over the snow. Do you know what that is?"

No one did. So from my prone position at the bottom of the circle, I informed everyone "That was snow mold." I can remember all those eyes turning down to me – that's all you see from an operating table anyway are the eyes above the masks – and there's this pause in the conversation, so I tried to explain again. But that's the last thing I remember before that operation, saying "snow mold" – funny words together anyway – and out of a very dry mouth, and all those eyes and knowing they were probably saying, "Gosh, we're just getting ready to give him the anesthetic and he's delirious already."

June 26, 1978
    WHEN I WAS GOING ALONG the road the other day, a meadowlark flew up ahead of me, taking off in that usual flutter of wings and I didn't pay much attention as it got altitude and circled back across.

    Suddenly it just fell out of the sky in front of me and dive bombed headfirst into the road. If there'd been a noise, I'd sworn someone shot it. And all that was left was a pile of feathers. It was still 30 yards down the road and hadn't moved. But when I ran up to it, it righted itself, got airborne enough to clear the fence and landed out of sight in the field. It obviously preferred flying with a headache to my clumsy attempts at bird first aid.

    The bouncing telephone wire above was the story I guess. Flying at full speed and hitting a telephone wire can put you on the ground pretty fast. And this looked like a young bird who may not have seen all that many telephone poles. Even birds share our problems. Will either of us ever teach our teenagers how to drive!

    FIRST CUTTING OF HAY is up and if there is any smell as good as freshly mowed hay, I don't know what it is.
    Oh, well how about wet sagebrush?
    Well, that, too . . .
    Or walking in a saddleshop where they still handmake the saddles.
    Or smelling freshly baked bread.
    Of course, but . . .
    I know but . . .
    Haven't you just walked by one of those yellow rose bushes in bloom?
    Yes . . .
    Or been outside in the morning after a rain?
    Or smelled bacon over an open flame?
    Stop, stop. You're confusing me with facts.

July 3, 1978
    THAT BIRD I ASKED you about, the one that dives down and makes the odd sound, is a Common Snipe. Dr. Howard Willson knew that one right off. I didn't think there were any snipes in the world. At least none ever came in my empty sack, way back when. But that's what it is, a Common Snipe. And I was curious how old Roger Tory Peterson would describe that in his Western Guide. If you're interested, he says it sounds like "hollow winnowing huhuhuhuhuhuhuhuhuhuhuh." And I'll let you say that out loud.

    So there are really snipes after all. The one time I sat waiting for them, they never came my way. They say the human mind forgets all the bad things in life. Ah, that's not true. I can remember that snipe hunting night almost 40 years ago explicitly. I can even tell you right where I sat, back of Jim Zaring's house, up on the canal with an old gunny sack, open and waiting, and this vague feeling that something wasn't all that right. Where for instance, were all the rest of the kids. And if they did roust out a snipe, how in the world would it ever come my way, hit my open sack out of all the sacks open in northwestern Wyoming. And why was it so quiet? Where were all the beating sticks among the bushes? And the other kids' voices? And hers particularly. The one who talked me into this, the one I'd jump off the mountain for? What is a snipe anyway? A snipe? How can a nine-year-old be so dumb and smart all in the same instant?

How long is a snipe hunting night? Long enough to last 40 years, that I know.

And now Doc Willson says there is such a thing after all. Amazing. I would never have believed it.

July 24, 1978

WENT THROUGH A TOWN in Montana the other day that had the cemetery on one side of the road. Directly across from it is the doctor's office!

IT'S THE CHECKERBOARD that makes Life interesting.

It's the loud and soft, the bright and the dull that keeps everything alive. The squares have to be different. You have to have non-emphasis to appreciate the emphasis. When you shout all the time no one hears. When you're forever whispering, no one listens.

If you pull and slack, you ride a horse better and get along with people easier. All praise is no praise. All criticism is no criticism.

Life has to be more than just one color. You need a dash of red on that gray dress!

OVERHEARD CONVERSATIONS . . . In a group talking about beards and shaving off beards: "God, old Joe should grow his beard back. He shaved it off and he looks like an old prune."

August 8, 1978

AT THE CARNIVAL at the end of Greybull's main street recently, ex-GHS quarterback Dave Williamson unlimbered a hot arm at the football throw and hit 15 out of 16. But he was topped by the next guy. He got the ball, turned around and punted it down main street!

August 14, 1978

YOUR TOWN STILL has a small town heart if it collectively stops for a beat or two every time the fire whistle goes off.

I ONLY WOKE UP once early the other morning when Cal Lawton of Greybull was aerial spraying for mosquitoes. That was the pass he made in one of our bedroom windows and out the other!

August 22, 1978

NOW THAT THE KIDS have all left home, we're faced with the terrible realization no one's left to take the blame for everything! All the tools not in place, all the lights left on, the car out of gas, the water not hot, the stove on, everything that goes wrong now is OUR fault. After 25 years, I'm not sure I can handle that kind of lonely pressure.

WYOMING FALL sometimes begins on the first day of August, just a hint of autumn in the way the air feels. By the twenty-first day it can be unmistakable. Of course there aren't many Monday mornings that look all that great anyway. But stretch a big blue cloudless sky above me, soften the morning with a little chillier air and the summer is over. No matter that it may heat up in the afternoon. The morning has already crept into fall.

August 28, 1978

THERE'RE PLACES all over this state you can be alone, for miles in any direction, for hours on end. We're pushed by population increases and energy booms, and some open spaces bulge in new directions. But Wyoming and solitude are still synonymous. And even the President can't trade for that!

BITS AND PIECES . . . WHY DOES A PERSON talk to their pets? Or am I the only one that does that? Sometimes I'm grateful that the only people who can hear me talk to my dog or cat are my dog or cat! . . . THE PRETTIEST SIGHT from the air for me continues to be sunlight sparkling on water. Sometimes it takes the breath away it is so startling.

September 6, 1978

EVERYONE HAS THEIR own horror stories about flying Frontier Airlines so you don't need to hear mine. Suffice to say, I didn't get where I wanted to go when I wanted to be there! And it was on the "going home leg" which magnifies a traveler's outrage several hundred times. The statistics whether you're stranded or bumped going or coming may be exactly the same as far as I know. But the anguish has to be higher if you're hung up heading home. There's something about the last leg being the longest, knowing home and bed are waiting, when you can't take another hotel room, anymore cigarette smoke, another fast food meal . . . and then someone's saying "Flight 604 has just been cancelled."

This whole business of flying has spoiled us. As a nation we're flying all over – more so now than ever – and going an amazing number of places. We send sons and daughters, mothers and fathers, friends, business associates, customers off in a hundred different directions day after day, with outstanding success. And all with an astonishing low anguish quotient.

But somehow Frontier has changed the odds. Or so people think, which sometimes amounts to the same thing. For all the good Frontier has provided us for all these years, for all the air travel it has brought Wyoming when there was no other, it has a terrible reputation. If suddenly Frontier eliminated all the mistakes and never committed another one, it would be 20 years before its present reputation was lived down.

I was astonished at the number and the fervor of the stories floating around the waiting area. Everyone had two! Or more! "One time I was. . ." triggered a dozen conversations.

And it is not just passengers. Said the driver of the hotel limousine: "Oh you're from Frontier. I hear a lot about Frontier. I could tell them a few things." And the hotel clerk: "Yeah, sometimes we reserve 50 rooms at a block for them."

A newspaper friend in Montana calls it the "Peanut Airline." ("All they ever give you are those roasted almonds.") And someone asked if I knew what a Frontier breakfast was. I didn't. (It is a Granola bar and coffee.)

The stories went on and on. Apparently so does the lousy reputation. Maybe that comes with the territory, of being the only game in town, although it has always seemed to me a monopoly has the greater obligation to do good. I suspect Frontier is not as good as it should be but not as bad as it's said to be. And, as part of its captive audience, I'll be back!

IDELL SCHUTTE certainly did a much better job landscaping and displaying the buffalo statue than either Lovell or Bridger did with all their metal sculptures.

September 11, 1978

A WAITRESS in Lincoln, Nebr. very embarrassingly asked me if I wasn't Jerry Ford! Imagine a Kennedy being taken for a Ford. Well, we do have one thing in common besides being Republicans. We both have wives named Betty. Beyond that . . . well, come to think of it, I did stumble a little coming in to the place.

YOU DON'T NEED TO say things right when you're driving along and holler out the car window at someone. They can't hear you anyhow, past the first word or two. We never think about that when we do it. We have some bright thing to say to someone running or standing on the curb. So we roll down the window and holler out something as we speed by. The person on the road, going at a different speed than you, sees your mouth open, hears the first word and then wonders what else you were saying. You, on the other hand, have gotten the whole sentence out, it sounded great, you're very pleased with yourself, and you don't know you weren't heard.

When you think about it, standing still conversation is often times like that, too. One person doesn't need to be moving not to be heard or not to listen. Two people can accomplish the same "not hearing" standing side by side!

September 18, 1978

A NEPHEW OF MINE, a Montana cowboy, shared a delightful story about growing up in the Big Sky country before television.

"We were just little kids, always lived in the country, and we found this ball at school. Gee, it could bounce good, better than anything we ever had before. We played Annie Annie Over the schoolhouse with it for days until we lost it down the chimney. The next time we got to town we got another ball. But it didn't bounce anywhere near like the first one. We kept going back and asking for the 'other kind of ball' but we never again found one that bounced like that first one. We talked about that ball for years.

"It wasn't until a long time later we found out about it. We didn't know any better. We were just farm kids who didn't know it had been an old tennis ball!"

September 28, 1978
ONE OF THE ASTONISHING things to "oldtimers" in Greybull (and I use the term loosely to mean anyone here five years ago) is how many "new" people have moved in. In a town where everyone used to know everyone – or thought they did – the number of new faces and new names is startling.

A town is always changing. One quarter of the population is supposed to shift every five years. Greybull's increase in the past few years is higher and more noticeable, and many people know what F.L. Hamilton meant when he told me, "I see more Greybull people I know in Billings than Greybull people I know in Greybull."

TALKING ABOUT THOSE trips to Billings reminds me of how Doc and Olive Walker of Basin never had to keep telling their kids "what town was next." The Walker kids were like everyone else's little kids on a trip to Billings. They couldn't wait for the next town but they never knew the name of it. Before each town was the inevitable, "What town is next, Daddy?" Olive, being a teacher and practical, solved that one. She made them learn the name of every town up the line and at a very tender age they could rattle off Lovell, Cowley, Deaver, Frannie, Warren, Bridger and on up to the Big City.

October 2, 1978
IN MY FLOWER BOOK nothing shines like a marigold.

If you only let me have one kind of flower, that's the one I would choose. This is not the choice of the other person who plants flowers around our place. She has a dozen other ones that go in the ground ahead of marigolds. But for me the marigold is the one that turns my head.

This time of year I always wish I'd planted more of them. In the spring I visualize this blaze of glorious orange and it's never as much as I want. I saw a formal type garden in Montana that was marigold heaven, with tall ones and short ones, yellow ones and orange ones, big and little, some delicate, some fluffy. And they just went on and on in perfect harmony. That's the way I'd like mine to look but they never do. What's left, though, gets my undivided attention and affection. It's just what I think a flower ought to be.

Marigolds haven't always been so "perfect." There was a time when you grew them outside, but never brought them inside. The odor was just too much. That all changed with David Burpee of the seed company. Jode Beck sent me an article from the Christian Science Monitor about marigolds that described how Burpee tried for years to take the odor out of marigolds. After years of disappointments Burpee received, in the late 1930's, some seeds from China which were said to produce odorless marigolds. The seeds yielded thousands of seedlings, most of which grew into scrawny plants with tiny, stiff flowers. But one plant, just one, produced magnificent golden blossoms – and no odor. That one plant reproduced these same qualities in its offspring and in the offspring of crosses, some of which I will again poke into the ground next spring.

THAT METAL SCULPTURE of the wild mustang horse at Lovell early Sunday morning had an empty Coors beer can stuck in its open mouth.

October 10, 1978

That Howard Cosell!

I wish he had worn better through the years. I was going to put down that I wished he could be retired, but I caught him last night again and, to be fair, he wasn't as bad as I wanted him to be.

Most of the time I'm fed up to here with his smugness. I guess I object to being a captive audience. The printed media, most especially newspapers, offer the reader more of a choice. You can "turn me off" right here – and still go on and read the newspaper. But to turn off Howard in the middle of one of his long sentences means also turning off the entire game.

I had been thinking of making a point about "industry responsibilities," of not saddling all of us with someone so disagreeable. After what I thought was dismal performance during the baseball playoffs, it seemed time. But then last night he was not such a bore, even charming a time or two, which is an odd word to use about someone who has made a career of being a loudmouth. I had to admit, he isn't all bad.

When he's hot, he carries you along. (His halftime show highlights can be fast paced and interesting.) He's a very poor third to Gifford and Meredith but he contributes.

Someone said Howard Cosell was an American institution. Please don't call him that. An American phenomenon, possibly; a phenomenon because he is a sports fan who made good on national TV. Mostly, still, he's a fan. He sees the game like a fan, not a professional. He reacts from the bleachers, like I do. In the baseball playoffs he'd make some observation that seemed very sage, until Jim Palmer, would make his. Then you knew immediately that Cosell, the fan, was talking and Palmer, the pro pitcher, was knowing. Howard by himself may seem like he knows, but he lags far behind the professional. There is a saying often used and it can be used for Howard, too, "He doesn't know what he doesn't know."

And he's always trying to make trouble. Something is always wrong between a player and a coach, between two players, between management and the coach, between the fans and management. This is a typical weakness of the fan. A player does not perform because he is human and cannot always be perfect. No, the fan implies he does not perform because something or someone is causing problems. Howard Cosell carries this fan thirst for a fight to even higher levels – he himself gets involved in as much of the controversy as he can. When it isn't there, he stirs it up. When it is there, he boils it over. The fan's shouts are lost in the crowd's roar; Cosell's are embellished with big words and a singsong voice and channeled into the microphone he's sticking in front of your face.

"Telling it like it is" is not that at all. It is telling it like Howard thinks it is!

He likes to show off his memory and it is a marvelous memory. But in these days of free agents and quick trades, expanded leagues and more players, his memory is getting cluttered with meaningless travels back and forth.

And oh he likes to talk. Americans as a nation do not like talky people. The guy in the bar in the Ali-Spinks fight who kept hollering to Spinks to "hit him in the mouth" was giving universal instructions. But Cosell, though he invokes similar outrage, has been able to jump out of the way for years now.

So, after 10 paragraphs of trying to outtalk Howard Cosell, I find I, too, have lost. Howard, as usual, has the last word!

October 31, 1978

THERE OUGHT TO BE SOME place to run in a city the size of Rome, I told myself, and so when I was packing I threw in my Adidas and warm ups and sure enough, there were plenty of places an American jogger could jog. The streets were either crowded or speedways but you could take your time and make it down them. And there was a long, long run down either side of the Tiber River that was quiet and beautiful and very long. In the large park area of the Borghese Gardens was a regular track and lots of paths. But the one I couldn't resist running around was the Circus Maximus. Shades of old Ben Hur . . . on foot!

There's something about running around the same track 2,000 years after the chariots raced around it that lengthens the stride. It's a long track, more U-shaped than oval like a race track and much longer. A wall was down the center dividing it and you could see where the seats along the sides had been although all the marble was long gone. 150,000 people used to sit there. On one side up against the Palantine hill were the ruins of Augustus Palace, still three stories high, where even more people used to watch.

But the mornings I ran, it was almost deserted. A couple of people walking their dogs, another person cutting across it to go to work. Only one other runner was there, an American in a pair of bright blue warm ups. His wife ran with him a while, and then waited at the end while he finished. I was going to stop to talk to him, but he finished ahead of me and moved off with his wife. He had not run hard and I wondered if he was quitting, but as I watched he moved off with his wife and she reached up and patted him on the back. I figured he, too, was going home with a notch in his Adidas!

A friend told me he thought running around the Circus Maximus had to be a good conversation "dropper." You know, something like: "My knee has hurt ever since I ran around the Circus Maximus." It's different anyway. You'd have to have an awful dull imagination not to be awed by it a little. Running past old chunks of marble and over little pieces. The longness of it, so different than a regular track. Going along the old seats. The Temple of Augustus in ruins yet still three or four stories up in the air. Rome itself, a Rome of 2,000 years ago, chariots and horses and crowds.

I tell you, it's pretty hard to keep stride with your fist clenched high above your head!

November 13, 1978

AL SIMPSON IS GOING to have an outstanding career in American politics.

We are sending back to Washington a senator elect who has the youth and vigor for years of contribution, who has the knowledge and dedication for a productive and formative career in helping guide America.

He will be heard and understood. I have liked his common sense, his grasp of essentials, his pleasure in Wyoming life. The great independence this Wyoming life stamps on us is deeply engrained in Al Simpson. He'll bring this asset to the Senate. He's a native son to be proud of and it's a pleasure and joy to send him off to Washington.

SOMEONE WAS kidding Red Michaelis about how bad his coffee was at his Greybull barbershop. "Where did you get this stuff," they said. "It should be all right," Red claimed, "I brought it down from hunting camp."

November 20, 1978

I HATE TO BE PESSIMISTIC but if this is what I feel like after two weeks of winter in November, what will I be feeling like after two weeks in February?

I DON'T UNDERSTAND why everyone connected with my diet objects to my having a piece of apple pie for breakfast. I need my fruit, don't I?

I WISH SOMEONE would find a snow tire that will start beeping in the garage five days before the first snow storm hits.

November 27, 1978

This year the sun decided to shine on Thanksgiving Day and when I slogged through the snow around the place, the shadows filled all the holes back up again. It wasn't all that warm, but then it wasn't so cold either. The bright sun for a change made it seem warmer. A good day to be out – all Thanksgivings are – a chance to reflect and think and put things together. To remember what Thanksgivings are for.

I thought I'd be alone, leaning up against the fence there, but a young man came up behind me. I didn't recognize him though I thought I should. He was quiet, just nodded hello and let me talk. "It's a sign of our 20 years difference," I told him, "to let me start rambling like this and not letting you talk. But I've been coming out here on Thanksgiving Day for a lot of years to see what the day is like on the outside. Somehow all the things I'm thankful for are much sharper and clearer out here, They're easier to see. So I've tried to spend part of every Thanksgiving Day in this sun or the snow or the cold or whatever the day has been.

"That's why you're here, too, I suppose," I said to my new companion.

He nodded again and looked like he'd speak. But I was carried along now; there seemed to be things to say.

"We're probably not thinking the same thoughts today, you and I. That's those 20 years. Now I'm not trying to play the old man-young boy role here, and I don't know you at all. But still I know how you look at Thanksgiving and what it holds for you. It was the same with me. Those first things, the chance to be on your own, to start life, to see a family begin. That's what was in your thoughts. You took it for granted you were supposed to be here. When you gave thanks it was because you were finally starting.

"If we'd know how little we knew, would we have ever started? Oh, I'm sure. Life assumes we'll be blissfully ignorant of such things. The quest is reward enough. You don't care how much work or frustration or despair there'll be. Just give me that chance. Try me. Let me show you.

"And if I don't know how to write this year, by next year I will. That was an early Thanksgiving thought, too. But that next year is always the next year and the next and the next. To get the right word at the right time every time you want it is a lifetime's work. And the last word you ever write you should be saying, 'Was that really the best one I could have put down?' That's a lesson of years, not of youth. At your age you are never troubled about keeping the mind sharp. Or holding the discipline. You take that for granted, too. But you can't let the pen rust.

"You can't let anything give in to rust. I used to think only the old ways were the best. My way, the way I grew up, that was the way the world should go. That's what you think, too, now, but that will change. You may even be astonished at how mellow you've become. Whatever happened to that intense young man who believed so strongly in his side that he could see no other? Now he sees four sides to every question, can allow others to make mistakes, can understand much more of that strange process we call human behavior, and refuses to argue about everything that comes up. Can you become mellow without becoming soft? I don't yet know the answer to that.

"In those early years, you're so wrapped up in your kids, you see little else. You could never imagine a time when your kids wouldn't need you, but it comes all too soon. As it should. Now you need them as much or more than they need you. And that, too, Thanksgiving after Thanksgiving, is the way it is supposed to be.

"And your feelings for Wyoming, now that won't change. We're blessed with that, you and me, blessed with the openness in land as well as in people. It's a state as broad and as big as that sky and gives us a life as independent as you could ever find. Be thankful it's still that way; be aware it always needs protecting.

"There's another thing you'll forget to think about when you're starting out. That's your health and the health of those around you. Probably the most precious of gifts. But this too takes years to understand.

"And people, the hundreds of people you will know and get to know. The long parade of faces of neighbors and friends and acquaintances, all touching your life. That's truly a blessing. You'll see that, too.

"Things don't really change. You come out here, full of turkey and good feelings, with thoughts of life and forks in the road. You see life clearer, your Faith is renewed, and your Thanks are deep. That's Thanksgiving outside."

We were both quiet then. I was a little abashed I had said so much, monopolizing the day's talk. I felt close to him, though, even if he hadn't been able to say much. I reached around, to put my hand friendly like on his shoulder. I was astonished to find he was gone. I don't think he had said a word, and now he disappeared. It was as if he had never been there.

Then I understood. Today was not his walk. That had been 20 years ago.

December 11, 1978

WONDER HOW MUCH in building costs and high interest rates we would have saved if we'd gone ahead with some kind of a high school building program years ago. Especially the high school gym. That's a national shrine to "Use it up, wear it out, make it do." . . . AT THE FFA FROZEN FISH sale Saturday I couldn't tell who was the most frozen, the fish or Kent Judy. It seemed like a perfect day to sell frozen fish – you might lose the salesmen but you'd never lose the fish.

BACK ON THE FOOD AGAIN . . . That big Chinese dinner we had out the other night reminded me of the time my daughter, Ann, Pat Shelledy, Sandy Michaelis and a Worland girlfriend went to Billings, ordered four different kinds of Chinese dinners . . . and then every 10 minutes got up and rotated chairs! That way, in typical young girl fashion, they got four dinners for the price of one.

1979

January 4, 1979

I always knew that someday I would do this. That as a newspaperman in this small Wyoming town I would sit down and write words of my father's death.

Yet, when you say you are prepared for something, you are only prepared in small mechanical ways. The pen will write because it is mechanically supposed to write, but it never writes by itself. Though you are ready to take it in hand, as the years go on you are lulled into thinking they will always go on and tough words to write, hard thoughts to put down may never need be written. Inevitably, though, they are, no matter how hard you have wished otherwise. Only the reverse of life's logical progression would have prevented it.

Gib Kennedy

Many sons, given this space, could write as much or more about their fathers. I recognize the advantage of newspapering. This is not an attempt to glorify. My father of all people never sought glory or chose the spotlight. But there are things I wish to say about Gib Kennedy.

People have talked to me about my dad for many years and invariably they always say one of three things:

His word was always good.

He was the most honest guy I ever knew.

He helped when I needed help.

That was Gib Kennedy's astonishingly simple code of ethics and he made it work to his satisfaction for 83 long years.

Though he was an "eastern" Omahan when he came to work one summer in 1910 on Chuck Brome's ranch at Worland, the West branded him quickly. He was as independent as it was. It colored his speech and thoughts so that in later years when he described someone as a "scrub bull" you knew exactly what he meant. He liked its "pretty country" and its people. From that time on Wyoming was the only place he wanted to be.

He probably should have stayed in the Army. He was a perfect cadre. His voice never lost its first sergeant quality. He epitomized what a first sergeant should be. Patriotism to him was breathing. He was the guy who you would expect to be in some forgotten Philippines Army post saluting the American flag every evening.

He could have been in law because he loved the way law works, he understood its logical sequences, the theory behind it, the records it required. He liked to read and study and use good words. Above all he knew the simple principle of recognizing right from wrong. Justice to him was just that.

I never knew anyone who was so quick to see right or wrong. He instinctively knew it. I envied that in him all his life.

He joined Basin when it was just a young town, opened an old-fashioned personalized business of service that retired when he did 45 years later.

He had friends everywhere he didn't know he had, he was respected and trusted and "his word was good" and that makes a very solid bottom line.

He had enough go wrong in his years to have complained. But he never did.

He lost his hearing in 1929 and suffered through the old Sonotone headpieces and recharged batteries for over 35 years. Then in the 1960's, a couple of operations restored his hearing. In my old age when I should be losing it, he said, I got my hearing back.

My mother died in 1949 and Dad chose to be a widower for 29 years. I was shocked to discover one day that Betty and I had been married longer and had more years together than Dad and Mom did.

There was never a more honest man than Gib Kennedy. Diogenes' search could have ended, I often thought, right in Basin, Wyoming. Honesty was easy for him because he never thought anything about it. It was never a question with him.

He loved the Legion, thought for many years the Canal was his; believed in manners, old school manners and used them; had a finely honed sense of humor, an intimate knowledge of local Basin history; he could bawl you out until you were limp, and for years was as erect and straight-backed as the young second lieutenant who mustered out in 1918.

He made mistakes as a father. So have I. So will all fathers. That, too, is inevitable. He misjudged some people terribly, he fiddled too much with time-consuming details. He was hopelessly unmechanical, he was afraid of "muddy" roads even after they were paved, spent too much time at the office, he was too much the loner, he panicked over bad weather, he never understood women but was utterly charmed by a pretty girl.

He grew old gracefully and without regrets. He told me one time he thought he would "outgrow this senility." He could look back all those 83 years and be proud, as he said, that "I've come all the way on my own steam." In the end he had too many years and too many complications.

He had lived in Basin 55 years. It was more a part of him than any other one place. He had given it much; it had returned it to him. Yet at least one generation – maybe two – have probably never heard of Gib Kennedy. That's not surprising. The longer you stay, the less who stay with you. But in the crisscross patterns of small town life, everyone can eventually touch each other. At the airport to help load him into the plane for Billings Sunday were Del Atwood, a longtime friend, and Bill Cowan – he'd watched Bill and me grow up together. And Randy Sullivan, who taught me to fly, would be the pilot; Pat Yeager, who treated him so nice at the hospital, would go along; and helping on the ground were Randy Baugh and Bob Hawkins who didn't know him but knew me. And as they got ready to go, Dr. Willson came over and put his arm across my shoulders and said, "We'll get him right up there." I appreciated all of them. So did Dad. That is the way small towns will always be. You care and they care and a man can live a long and fruitful life "under his own steam" and when he leaves it, he leaves much good behind.

January 11, 1979

EVER NOTICE HOW MUCH more you suffer when you find out someone living 30 miles away has 20 degrees warmer temperatures?

I've about decided it's much better if you never look at a thermometer or try to figure out chill factors. I've been cold ever since they've started to talk about chill factors. I know I was a lot warmer not knowing.

THAT'S WHAT Ned Kost Jr. in Basin figured out with his thermometer. He asked on the phone the other day how cold my thermometer read and I told him 40 below. "Mine says 45 above." But how can that be, Ned, we're only eight miles apart, I asked. "Oh, I put a heat tape on my thermometer," he said. "Now it reads 45 above. It's all in your head anyway."

IT'S AMAZING how much you look forward to 10 below when you've been in 40 below.

SOUNDS TRAVEL SO MUCH further, something about bending the sound waves downward. The other night when it was so cold, a train whistled through town and I thought it was coming right into the bedroom. Even the dog jumped out of the way.

AND I GOT TO WORRYING about the birds, too, in all this winter misery. So I rigged up a bird feeder that wasn't quite ready – no post to put it on and no good place to put it. I filled it up and the birds came and then I wondered whether I should worry about the cat getting the birds. I should have worried! I looked out the next day and the cat was not only around the bird feeder, she was sitting right inside it!

January 22, 1979

FROM UP ABOVE, it must have looked like 40,000 shovels were at work Monday.

In many places if you didn't shovel, you didn't get out. In many others no matter how much you shoveled you still didn't get out! The wind spent part of Sunday night and Monday morning pushing the snow one way and here it is Tuesday and many are still trying to push it back the other. In truth the wind always wins. It's only that it gives up. And then back to shovel.

Many have mentioned how hard it was, packed solid like it was tamped. No light and fluffy stuff that. Once you think of snowflakes you don't think of them as being a foot square. Herman Mayland told me, "If you'd been shoveling with me today you wouldn't have had to jog for a month!"

I tried our lane without the shovel first. You can bust through, I said. Not that stuff. After I'd hit it I thought maybe Bob Walton had poured it. Back to the shovel.

EVERYONE IS ALWAYS saying, Think what you'll be able to tell your grandchildren about this winter. But I don't want my grandchildren to hear that kind of language.

February 15, 1979

WHEN I GO down to feed the horses, I always have to put old Cocoa's hay on a special "plate". That means it's way over to one side, away from the other horses, particularly that black one who can't stand Cocoa, and I've always got to fill her "plate" up last so the other horses are already eating and can't see her. Otherwise she never gets to eat until everyone else is done and the choice stuff picked over. Because she's last on the pecking order, she's last to eat, unless the soft-hearted guy feeding her takes special pains and doesn't just dump it over the fence.

Cocoa has always been last at whatever she does. And all the rest of the horses let her know it. In the peculiar way of animals, they always choose to put her down, to kick her around, and to leave her out of the scheme of things. I can remember the time my neighbor, Metz Smith, turned a bunch of his horses into the pasture with mine and everyone got along okay except Cocoa who was promptly ostracized. She spent several days by herself, off to one side, while the rest cavorted around the place. She was last again. She'll always be. She's over 20 years old and should be the matriarch of the place. Instead she's clearly at the bottom.

Pecking orders fascinate. All animals have them. Our old tom cat bossed our place for years, howling and yowling about everything. The little cat never uttered a peep. When the old cat went, the little cat was boss and become the howlingest, yowlingest cat we ever had. It was her turn, I guess.

You can raise chickens and among the roosters one will dominate. Remove him Monday morning and by Tuesday another rooster has become the top one. It is he who comes at you when you open the door, raising his neck feathers and looking ferocious. Remove him and Wednesday you'll have another cocky one.

Even the birds in the bird feeder chase each other down the ladder. Cows, dogs, everything has its own special hierarchy that all the rest know, recognize and understand.

Animals are just like people. Or is it people who are just like the animals? A Shell rancher told me one time that he could look in his herd and see a personality trait that fit just about every person on Shell creek. I knew exactly what he meant, the aggressive ones, the whiners, the playful ones, the workers, the gentle, the hot tempered. They were all there. And all in their "order."

But I told this to Ted Anderson when he was still around and Ted, a little startled by the thought, blurted out, "By gosh, I think he's been out there among those cows just a little too long!"

February 22, 1979

THE HUSBAND WAS DOWNHILL from me, already through the hard part of the hill and his wife was still up above, working up her courage to ski down it. Apparently the courage building had taken some time because she was stalling, doing more looking than moving. The man hollered up in a loud exasperated voice, "Come on, just force yourself to go through that stuff."

"Why don't you just shut up!" the woman hollered back, whereupon a half dozen other women on various parts of the hill started clapping.

March 8, 1979

HAROLD LOCKARD who has been keeping track this winter said Greybull has had 70 days when it went zero or below! No wonder you were cold.

Lynn Severance, who was owner of this Greybull Standard from 1946 to 1959 and a part of the Standard for many years afterward, died in Sheridan last week.

He was one of that last generation of country editors who were also country printers, a generation that chose printing as much as newspapering, and who worked and produced weekly newspapers as much by their technical skills as by their pens. That's not necessary in these times. But it was then and it was for them, and with them as they go now passes a part of newspapering that will never come back.

Lynn Severance spent nearly 50 years in the business. He worked in the old Billings Polytechnic (now Rocky Mountain) print shop as a student and eventually managed the shop while still in school. He went on to the University of Missouri and then back to Montana where he owned the Lodgegrass newspaper. He ran it nearly all by himself for several years (and in his typical shrewd business way ran a dance hall on weekends!) until he was asked to run the Sheridan Star. So he closed up the Lodgegrass paper, put out its final issue – the final issue of the last paper Lodgegrass would ever have! – and went to Sheridan.

After several years he came to Basin in the early Forties to work for Press Anderson at the Basin Republican Rustler. In 1946 he purchased the Greybull Standard from Axel Lilja. It was then where Gary Hartman's office is. In the early 1950's he moved the paper to its present location, dismantling and reassembling all the equipment himself to get it into the basement. And all between press days.

It was typical Lynn Severance to take on a job of that proportion, to be smart enough to know how to do it, to work out the mechanics of it, to work night after night to finish it, and to do it himself instead of hiring it done.

In 1956, in a search to find someone to work the front office for him, he found us working in Lander. He made us one promise. He would sell the paper to us. He did, three years later, on such ridiculous low terms that even two young kids with no money could make it. So we worked for Lynn Severance for three years and then he turned around and worked for us for nearly 12. From the beginning the relationship was not as much buyer-seller as it was a three-way partnership. It was our learning period. We sought his advice hundreds of times. Lynn gave advice without our asking a hundred times! We still worked the front shop and he took care of the back shop. For years. He never did agree with all of our ways, nor us with his. But we agreed enough and it worked. In those old days of hot type, we always knew – the three of us – that if it really came down to it, we three could get the Standard out.

By the time we got here Lynn had served his time on all the committees and 49er jobs and Chamber of Commerce hours a small town insists you do. He had been instrumental in getting the Greybull River road paved. And he had traveled hundreds of miles with E.T. Foe on tourist and road and Greybull projects.

He spent 30 years in Greybull And if you remembered one thing about Lynn Severance it would be his quick wit. He was blessed with an Irish sense of humor. My God, he was quick. He had a way with words, too, picking out a word to describe something that was so incongruous it was right. He didn't care for the putting down of words on paper. He always preferred the printer's ink of the back shop. But he should have been forced to write a column. It would have been a hilarious success. Because if Lynn wanted hilarity, there was hilarity.

He was always in a hurry. He abused his stomach by always pushing too hard. He never had anything but a definite idea. And if there can be Irish wit, then there may also be Irish moods. He was a very good printer, a very fast one. He really knew human nature and with his alert, sharp mind had a wealth of information to pass on.

We've quoted him a thousand times, retold so many Lynn Severance jokes in our family they're a part of the Kennedy family jokes. There are still things we do the "Severance way." What he taught still sticks. What we enjoyed together still remembered.

He gave a shove to two young kids and pushed them out into the newspaper world . . . and then stayed around for many years afterward to watch over us.

We've always owed him more than the price of the paper.

March 22, 1979

IN GOING THROUGH some family papers, I came across a letter from my grandfather who ranched near Powderville, Mont. to my mother who was in college at Missoula. The letter was written in January, 1921 and it had this paragraph: "There was a wedding up the river at Charlie Johnstones. Chester Dalin was the man but the lady's name has got away from me. They celebrated Friday night with a dance. Another masquerade ball is the order for Powderville on the 21st of Jan. I wish you were to attend. I do not know what I shall do for a costume this year, but you bet I will have something. I certainly got more fun out of that spotted suit of yours last year. Why the whole thing was just one long scream of joy."

March 29, 1979

IF YOU HAVE HOPED Wyoming's new senator, Alan Simpson, would remember in Washington what he said in the campaign about cutting government waste and excessive spending you would have enjoyed watching him in action a couple of weeks ago.

I did. The committee hearing, heading for a noon adjournment, was almost over when I slipped into a back row seat. But Simpson's thrust to talk about cutting spending postponed lunch for everybody.

It may have been a small place to do battle – a hearing of the Environment and Public Works committee meeting on the Corps of Engineers budget. But it gave Simpson the chance to say some things he's apparently been wanting to say about politicians' fiscal responsibility. And he also got a lesson from old veteran Sen. Ed Muskie that when you rock the boat you're gonna get a little wet.

Simpson, the freshman, and Muskie, the old timer, ended up the two antagonists. Muskie, smooth and knowledgeable, and righteously indignant at times, verbally bloodied Simpson around the head a little after Simpson had told the committee the senate seemed to be "paralyzed to vote" for reducing spending. But Simpson made his point and he also gave notice he would try to make it as often as he could.

It was enough of a breath of fresh air that the hearing ran two hours overtime.

Simpson said he didn't feel the politicians were listening to the people. They wanted spending cut, he pointed out, and cited the 29 states which had asked for a constitutional convention on balancing the budget.

"The politicians talk about it (cutting spending) but nothing is done about it," Simpson declared.

He asked for a 10 percent cut across the board of the Corps of Engineers proposed budget.

That brought Muskie out of his chair. He chose the time to give a long dissertation on his philosophy of budgeting. He knows the subject. He's chairman of the budget committee and he can talk. He can also be very sarcastic. And he turned the point so it sounded like only newcomers make such statements, that freshman senators should wait a little before speaking out, that only the Senate – the old Senate, that is – knew how to run things.

I was amazed how successfully he turned the eyes in the room towards Simpson and his 10 percent proposal even though Dem. Sen. Pat Moynihan from New York had earlier proposed a 20 percent cut!

Once when Simpson said something more about politicians, Muskie shot back quickly (and loudly): "You're a politician now, too, you know."

"I will not subscribe to the meat-ax approach to budgeting," Muskie declared. "You must be selective. To cut high priority items with the same 10 percent you cut the low priority items is not right."

He had nothing but ridicule for those who want to balance the budget. He cited all sorts of economists who said don't balance the budget. He scoffed at the 29 states who had felt "compelled between lunch and dinner to ask for a constitutional convention" on balancing the budget. He talked on a wide variety of budgeting problems. He said his committee would cut the budget below President Carter's recommendation. He was very smooth and believable. He had the entire attention of the room, but he seemed to be talking just to Alan Simpson.

It was so evident that Sen. Pete Domenici of New Mexico interjected that he felt "my good friend from Maine" should not be indicating that this was just the fault of "my friend from Wyoming." (Whereupon Simpson said, "I can take care of myself!")

Muskie assured everyone this is not the case. "The Senator from Wyoming is learning the ropes, and from what we have seen here today, he is certainly going to learn them," Muskie said.

"You should say these things," Muskie told Simpson.

The hearing was winding down to the vote. The vote was inconsequential. The philosophy was what was hanging in the air. Simpson, crouching down so his long, lanky frame could get behind the microphone, and peering out above his half glasses, had been both very articulate and very "down home" as he often is. He wanted to say one more thing.

"Perhaps my tenor will change in six years. Right now I am a freshman, and I believe in this."

Damn, it was fun to watch.

Simpson's vote went down 10 or 12 to 2. Only Republican Sen. Mike Gravel of Alaska went with him. It is not easy to tell the Senate what to do.

But afterward – the hearing had quickly adjourned – Muskie drew Simpson aside. They walked out together and down to the Senate Chamber. Muskie was talking very earnestly. I heard him in the elevator saying to Simpson, "The first person I debated in the Senate was Wayne Morse." He had some advice for Simpson and some encouragement. The old hand was helping the new one. The new one was a comer.

April 5, 1979

THE RIGHT SIDE (instructor's side) upholstery in my airplane is worn out, holes and tears and threads showing. But the left side seat (pilot side) is not. It's in good shape. I asked John Elgin (I wonder) if that shouldn't be telling me something.

April 12, 1979

ONE OF THE IRONIES of America is that the government publishes (and you and I can get free) any number of pamphlets and publications on how to successfully run a business!!

THAT WAS WRONG in last week's Standard about the river bridge being built back in the 1930's . . . It was put in there in 1949.

ISN'T IT SOMETHING that all those old garages we built years ago for the Model A type cars (and which grew way too small for the modern automobiles) are now just the right size again for the compacts.

April 19, 1979

AFTER SITTING THROUGH hundreds and hundreds of meetings, large and small, in all kinds of places with all kinds of people, I've come to the conclusion that no one knows or understands "Roberts Rules of Order."

Only a handful pay any attention to it, and those of us who sometimes try to pay some mind, don't know them at all.

Meetings flounder along, take longer than they should, are disorderly, back up and start over, probably most aren't even legitimate at all. Yet every one is supposed to be governed and controlled by Roberts Rules for assisting the democratic process. They're easy enough to learn – we just haven't learned them.

I have a solution. It won't help us now. But it should years down the road. We should make it compulsory in the grade schools. We should require each student to learn Robert's Rules, early. Then we should insist that every junior high class meeting, every party committee, every youth activity where a meeting is held be thus conducted with Roberts Rules. And on up through the grades, the high schools and into the outside world.

We would immerse Roberts Rules of order everywhere.

And I make that a motion.

"I HAVE LEARNED," a friend of mine in Laramie said, "never to lead the applause. The last time I was first I had daydreamed off somewhere else. The speaker finished. I applauded. But no one else did. He had just said Grace."

May 5, 1979

DURING APRIL I ESTABLISHED some sort of record at our local

Post Office.

For three straight Monday evenings I made the closing mail only by a whisker. After knowing all day long (nay, all week long!) that the mail closed at 5:30 p.m., I was there give or take thirty seconds or so either way, just at 5:30 p.m. In fact it was so late, I had to poke open the paper and package slot and holler in at Marge Hankins to be sure it would still go out. For a newspaperman who has lived with deadlines all of his adult life, you would think I could make this deadline, too.

But making the deadline is not the point of all of this. What I am trying to say is how can I write with such a forked pen? How can I lambaste the postal department on a regular basis and still ask them for a little extra consideration when I let the clock beat me. Three Mondays in a row yet! And all those times I forgot my key, had an important package looked for again, mistakes caught.

The only explanation I can come up with is that our post office in our town does not belong to the other Postal System. They know how to run a post office. It's those guys back in Washington who keep fouling up things!

YOU'RE GOING TO TELL me this could not have happened. But cross my heart . . .

The telephone company told members of the striking Local 2-656 of the Chemical and Atomic Workers Union they could get a phone to their trailer on the picket line outside the Dresser plant north of Greybull.

The problem was they would have to get it across the road. There's a culvert there, but it's nearly filled with standing water and you can't push a line through. Now what could swim underwater for that distance and bring a line up the other side?

Well, how about a carp? Paul Hartsock went out Sunday and fished for two hours hoping to get a carp. Instead he wound up with a sucker which he took out Monday morning, tied a fish line to it and dumped it in one end of the culvert. The idea was brilliant but the fish would only go two thirds of the way down the culvert and then back out again.

Someone said that George Greene has a duck that ought to work. So they got the duck, retrieved the fish, tied the line to the duck and put it in the end of the culvert. Well, there was some question for awhile in the duck's mind. But I gotta tell you it worked, and the duck came sailing out of the other end eventually, with the line trailing after. And eventually the phone line pulled through after that.

See, I told you you wouldn't believe me.

May 17, 1979

DO YOU, TOO, SIT IN restaurants and public places and try to figure out what the guy next to you does for a living? The guy at the adjoining table at Trader Vic's was a big guy, but well turned out. Spoke in a deep, halfway modulated voice. His companion was thirtyish and what you would have to say was

VERY well turned out. They were companions, but not very close. It looked like they might like to be but they weren't. It was obvious he was trying to help her with a problem. There was mention of a third party. They had two Mai Tai's apiece, a big dinner and were still talking earnestly when they left.

Okay, I said it's obvious. He's a lawyer with a client. You could tell by the way he talked. He's confident, knowledgeable. She's asking him for advice. This was an easy one.

The waiter come over to the table. "Say," he said. "did you recognize that guy?"

No, I said, who was it?

"That was Ralph Kiner," he said, "the old baseball player. He's with the Mets now and they play the Giants this week and he's in a day ahead of the team. Big guy, isn't he? Big like a ballplayer."

So much for my powers of observation. But I know some big lawyers, too.

May 24, 1979

I SEE A STORY WHERE they claim that more suicides occur on Mondays than on any other day of the week . . . which explains a lot of my Mondays.

I STILL THINK THE best place to get a feel of how "small town" the state of Wyoming really is is to attend the University of Wyoming graduation ceremonies. It's amazing how, in the whole stream of young people crossing the stage, you can pick out kids you know. And not just kids from your own community, either, but from others nearby. And graduates, too, who once lived in your town or whose Dad you know or whose name you recognize. There's a lot of "family" there.

Noticed where one candidate for a Masters Degree had written his thesis on: "The Buckhorn: A Study in Bar Sociability." I'll bet that was an education!

Mercifully, the University of Wyoming does not have any speakers at Commencement except for the governor who always, no matter who he is, feels obligated to say the same thing: Now that you've graduated, stay in Wyoming.

And at the conclusion, everyone is always supposed to sing the Alma Mater. They print the words in the front of the program. It's always a surprise to find out it's not "Cowboy Joe!"

AT THE DENVER AIRPORT I was standing by the window when a mother brought her very young son over to the window to show him the planes. "See that one there," she said, "the propellers are going so fast you can't see them."

Which was all very fine, but the one she was pointing to was a jet!

June 14, 1979

IT WILL SEEM STRANGE to have a Greybull without a George (Conoco) Scott. George had been a part of the town for a long, long time, going clear back to those days of the 1929 flood when he was the guy who dropped the dynamite out of the plane to bomb the ice jam. He'd been with the fire department for so long, had hunted all over this country, delivered gas up and down the area for years and years. He was bus driver to generations of kids on Shell creek and Santa Claus to a whole bunch more year after year. He knew everybody, was always friendly, always had a smile, always on the go, always something going on.

YOU CAN ALWAYS TELL the strangers. In one bar Friday night, amidst the loud talk, near fights, arms over shoulders, many laughs that only a Western bar can have, someone said: "Hey, look, there's some people who have never been to a 49er celebration before." How can you tell, someone asked? "That's easy. Look at their eyes." Sure enough. When you looked over at them, their eyes were as wide as saucers.

FOR ONE WHO HAS NEVER done it before, the 10.5-mile run over 49ers was something else! I see by the reports that I finished third in my division. Well, that's not quite right really, because out of three finished places open for 36 years and older there were only three of us running! So if you say I finished third, you are correct. But it is much more accurate to say that in the 36 years and older division, some guy finished first, Big Horn County Treasurer George Hoffman finished second and somewhere way, way back down the road, I finished last!

July 19, 1979

AS THE SUMMER GOES along it becomes more and more evident those elm trees that winterkilled last winter won't be coming out of it. They're gone for good, the vast majority of them, and even the ones that looked for awhile like they might snap out of it, would probably be better off cut down.

That deep, long-standing cold weather just wiped them out. And not just the elm trees, either, but weeping willow and locust and other of the less hardy kinds. And a lot of apple trees. Driving down Wyoming you can go through town after town with bare trees all over. Windbreaks down in the Riverton area have big gaps of dead trees in them. If you pay close attention to the houses as you go along there's seldom one without one bare tree or bush or a browned out evergreen.

I suppose that's one of the best indicators of how much colder it really was last winter. Because those trees have been growing a long time – a couple of generations, some of them – and it wasn't until last year they didn't make it through the winter. You can tell the grandkids all about this, but it won't bring back the trees.

People are starting to cut them down now. After a decent interval for optimism, late starts and wishful thinking, now the chain saws are out. By next spring new trees will be growing. It won't be elm trees, that's obvious. And it won't be cottonwoods either. As a people we've decided we don't want the old cottonwood although in fairness to that venerable Wyoming pioneer it didn't winter kill last year!

July 26, 1979
I USUALLY DON'T let the gnats and bugs and mosquitos beat me but by golly this year I've already conceded. They've chased me in the house for good. What a weather cycle. Colder than we've ever seen. Drier than we've ever seen. Too hot. Too buggy. It would be of some comfort if we could blame this all on the Arabs.

THE LAND-LOCKED BILLINGS sailor/boat-builder/chiropractor who put together his own oceangoing boat (which he launches in the Pacific soon) was quick with a word when he said it "sleeps four, eats six and drinks eight."

August 9, 1979
IF YOU DON'T THINK a lot of people are interested and fascinated about packing horses up into the high country, would you consider this statistic. That "Horses, Hitches and Rocky Trails," Joe Back's outstanding book on packing has sold 40,000 copies, according to last week's Dubois paper. And if you're one who hasn't read it, you've missed a great one! My copy is dogeared and worn and rain-soaked and, Joe Back, I've blessed you many times!

THE PAPER SAYS that Wyoming still holds the record for per capita consumption of beer. We're supposed to have consumed 52 gallons of beer per year which works out to be about 520 cans or bottles of beer in a year's time. Have you hit your quota yet?

August 16, 1979
SOMEONE WHO really didn't know what they were talking about wrote us in a press release the other day that "The course will include both black and white photography." Which means, I guess, that you print those white pictures and I'll print the black ones!

THAT MOTORCYCLING couple who breezed by Dale Wright's Standard Station in Greybull last week wasn't letting traveling get them down. While he drove the cycle, his wife was sitting behind him . . . knitting an afghan! Honest. Carolyn Wright saw it.

August 23, 1979

I KNEW THE MIDDLE-AGED COUPLE were tourists. It's an age-old giveaway. Two people go to a strange area. They hold hands walking down the street. They never hold hands at home. Not even in the backyard where the neighbors might see. Especially not walking down the old hometown street. What would people say? But come to a strange town, a strange country, unknown, "alone." Hold hands. Who cares? Who knows?

But this hand-holding couple had a double whammy on them. They not only were holding hands walking down the streets in this little Wyoming town. A sure tourist giveaway. They were walking under an umbrella!

WELL, IT WAS TIME this week to send the youngest off to school for another year. And this morning old dad offered to take all the pile of stuff heaped up by the back door and fit all of it into the old Buick. He asked for the job actually, and he got it easy enough!

That loading up the car is not a chore. It's a pleasure. It's the sort of job a Type A personality just relishes in. You have all this stuff, boxes and cans, breakable and unbreakable, squares and cylinders; and you make them all fit together so it all will travel a couple of hundred miles in one piece. What a way to get the adrenalin flowing! It was the same way on pack trips. Sometimes you couldn't hardly get old dad out of camp because he spent so much time packing up everything. But the packin' up was always as good as the ridin'.

And now it was another packin' up job. And by gosh it all fit. Some of it that could have stayed home even got in. Everything tight. No rattles. No rubs. No problems. And at the end, someone always has to say, I sure hope you don't have a flat tire!

No, the loading isn't what's difficult about going off to school for those of us who stay at home. The loading gets done. All the stuff gets in. No, the hardest part isn't here.

The hardest part is watching him drive off.

September 13, 1979

RAN INTO OLD FRIEND Bill Michaelis in the Irma Hotel dining room the other day.

He takes me back a few years. We grew up at the same time in Basin, went to school and ran the streets and did all the things that kids in a very small town do.

But the story we really share is the time we both got involved with a live Thanksgiving turkey that turned from black to white overnight.

We'd both wound up in Greybull in the 1950's. The week before Thanksgiving I got a call from Bill at the Standard. He said he had the damnedest story he'd ever seen. He still couldn't believe it. He bought this turkey to fatten up for Thanksgiving. It was a regular looking old black turkey. He'd taken it out to his in-laws, the John Schmers, to fatten it up. It had been there several days. Yesterday he'd gone out and the damned thing had turned completely white. Instead of the black turkey it was a white turkey. Same size. Same small cage. "It even had the same markings around the head," he told me.

Now I'd known Bill Michaelis a long time. He is not a practical joker. If he tells you something, it's gospel. Besides, I sensed a great story. So Bill picked me up and we went out to the Schmers. Sure enough, that was the whitest turkey I'd ever seen. There were black feathers all over the bottom of the cage. It looked like the moult of the decade. Besides Bill was absolutely convinced. And he convinced me.

So I got him to get the turkey out and I got my old Speed Graphic and took a bunch of pictures of him holding the turkey this way and that. Boy, it was a white one. And I took all the notes I had to get, we put the old white bird back in the cage and we took off.

The next day I got this call from Bill. He was mortified. We'd both been had. His family had pulled the joke on him. Picked up a white turkey and spirited away his old black one. They were all peeking out the windows while I was documenting this epic transformation with Bill holding the turkey first up and then sideways and then this way. We must have looked pretty foolish!

"Gosh, I'm sorry about all this," Bill kept saying. "I just wish I'd never called you."

"Bill," I said, "don't be sorry. It will always be a better story this way."

September 20, 1979
WAS SURPRISED HOW many people got up to watch the lunar eclipse the other morning early. Monte Lewis south of Basin even got up and plowed through it!

September 27, 1979
WE ARE SOFTIES, we human beings. We grow sunflower seeds for the birds to eat in the winter so they'll come back in the summer and eat all the cherries and plums and strawberries.

ODDS AND ENDS . . . SPRING IS FULL of green and new life and bright sun and early summer has its share of fun and longer days. But nothing quite equals this soft light and stillness of fall . . . WHICH REMINDS ME, that I should ask you if you have started on your list of Things I Didn't Do Last Year Before Winter Got Here and I Should Have.

CAME DOWN FROM THE mountain with a load of pine logs and met Heinie Meier who said he was going to go up to his cabin in the mountain pretty soon with a load of wood.

Now, wait a minute, I said, I'm coming down with pine wood – in fact I came right by your cabin. How come you're "going up" with some wood.

"Oh, I take up Chinese elm," Heinie said, "Burns slower and a lot better."

October 11, 1979

THERE ARE TWO SONGS in this old country that no one can sing. One is the Star Spangled Banner. The other is Happy Birthday to You.

Every hour of every day, somewhere in the world, someone is butchering Happy Birthday. I was reminded of this recently when I heard an announcer trying to sing it on the radio. Gee it was bad. I turned with the rest of the crowd to watch a bunch of happy people singing it loudly but awfully in a restaurant last week. Terrible. I tried to join in another time not long ago and sang just as badly as everyone else. Often, out of tune, a half note behind.

But even knowing how terrible it sounded, I didn't care. I was just like everyone else. I WANTED to sing it. It matters not how old you are, whether you're in the park or at the bar, male or female, in groups of five or fifty, we want to sing Happy Birthday. It's a happy, fun time, with someone you like. And to heck with how it sounds.

If it's your birthday we'll sing for you. You're supposed to know that no matter how awful it may sound, we mean every word of it!

THE UW STUDENT was not a bettor. But his friends persisted. Finally he agreed. He'd put a dollar on Wyoming against Colorado State. His friends thought that was great. Roger had finally made a bet. Later on, though, they found out he'd made a second bet. This time he put a dollar on Colorado State! A real gambler, that Roger!

October 18, 1979

THE SHAPE LOOKED LIKE something I should recognize. But I'm still not used to this new riding lawn mower all that much. And this was the first time I'd tried out the lights and night mowing and I was very anxious to get on with it. So I decided, without stopping, whatever it is I'll just go on over it.

On the next round I saw what it was. My wallet! Very chewed up. So were most of the credit cards, all the papers, pictures, non-important things you think you have to carry. In pieces all over the lawn. It took two full handfuls to get it all to the kitchen table. Not much left when you looked at it in the light.

What pieces there were, we sent off to the credit card companies and other places for replacements. They've been coming back now, over the last month, one by one. I'm trying not to think what the VISA and Texaco and Phillips people said when they held up a corner of one of my shredded cards. Look what this dummy out in Wyoming did!

Losing your wallet is one of Life's dreaded moments. But that's respectable. That's God's will. Having it stolen? You can shake your fist at that dirty trick. But running over your own wallet with your own lawn mower? Line up over there with those guys with hammers who just hit their own thumbs.

THE PAPERS HAVE carried the story this week about the last surviving

Marine, Rene Gagnon, who was in the famous picture of the flag-raising on Iwo Jima. He died in New Hampshire. Six men participated in the fateful moment, captured on film by AP's Joe Rosenthal. Gagnon was the last survivor. A footnote to that historic time involves Wyoming and a Marine named Donald Ruhl, who gave his life near that flag raising a short time before. Ruhl fell on a Japanese grenade in a foxhole and saved the lives of several of the men who would a short time later raise the flag on Iwo Jima. He was awarded the Congressional Medal of Honor posthumously. Ruhl was from Montana, and inducted from Columbus, but his family moved to Greybull during the war and he is buried in the Greybull cemetery.

SLIM BREWER has sold that old Army Dodge of his. What was almost a Greybull institution is now parked at Rice's Body Shop after Larry Rice bought it. Slim drove the old army-colored vehicle, a 1941 half-ton weapons carrier, for 31 years. (He bought it from Ernie Rice back then.) Now to recognize Slim you have to look for a new Jeep pickup.

October 25, 1979
THE TREES WERE THE ONES who really suffered in last year's tough winter. All summer long I kept looking over Greybull at all the dead limbs among the green trees. And then this fall when the trees turned, it seemed like you could even see it more. So the other day – before the leaves fell off Betty and I got in the car and drove up and down the streets, clipboard in hand, from one end of town to the other, counting all the dead ones.

I wouldn't have believed it!

It always has looked like a lot of dead trees. But who would have thought it would go to 750 by actual count? Seven hundred and fifty dead trees, all victims of last year's cold weather.

And I didn't count:

a) any trees which had been obviously dead the year before and not cut down yet.

b) And no trees with still a little life left, those with some leaves. But they're set back so far I probably should have counted them.

c) No trees in hedges, those rows of small elm saplings that spring up some times and you just let go.

d) No trees less than one inch thick were counted although this probably, too, was a mistake because they were started as trees and now they'll have to be replanted.

e) No trees on the alleys which were obviously a "sprout" left unattended and now grown to tree size.

f) No apple trees or other small fruit trees although again these probably should have been added. But it's hard to see some of them in backyards.

g) Same for any evergreens. Didn't count these either. Should have but I keep hoping they'll come back somehow.

So if the count had included all the cripples, all the possibles, all the little ones, the fruit trees in the back yard, the evergreen ones, it would have easily gone over 800, maybe even 900.

I didn't think there were that many trees in the whole town.

Some homes had 10 to 12 trees dead. The park had 20! Few places escaped. And I counted ones Larry Probst has already cut down; and those at Bill Bruce's, too.

Are there any left, you're asking? A lot. All the old cottonwoods (which seldom die. They just blow over. And a lot of other species, very good trees, weren't hurt. Some of those exotic ones got it, though. And those old silver leaf maples took it hard. Many killed back and it was hard to tell if they would pull out of it. I didn't count them either, actually. But I was surprised they were susceptible to the cold. They've always looked big and strong-limbed to me.

It was the elm varieties that took the beating. Many were weak anyway. But they'd grown up easily in these Wyoming towns, and fast. And pretty soon you had a town full of them.

Not any more. They're gone. Most of us waited the whole summer to see if they'd pull out of it. They didn't. Hundreds of them will be coming down.

By spring, it'll be the darndest pile of firewood you've ever seen!

November 15, 1979

I THINK WE HUMAN BEINGS fail to realize that the high of this very moment is only of this moment. It will never carry over in the intensity and magic that it will right now. It is of this time, of this moment. And to go back and recapture it another time is nearly impossible.

How could that have been so great, you ask in later years? But it was. It was fantastically great. It was for that time, that one marvelous time.

Let's go back and see the rain on the streets. Let's see that old buddy of mine. Let's go back to that restaurant. Let's ride up and see the wild flowers or see the sun set on the water. All great trips, all great memories that never seem to be again just what it was then.

That is not so bad, though. Where we make it impossible is wanting to duplicate the old days, the old times, the time before, the last time.

I once grew (quite by accident) what to me was a perfect yellow rose. I never saw a flower like it. I even carried it down to the old Standard's editor's desk and looked at it and looked at it. I can see it yet today. A perfect shape. A perfect color. No matter which angle you looked at it. Perfect. I was enthralled with it. How could one rose be so perfect to me? I don't know. But yes maybe I do. It was only perfect right at that time. No flower I ever grew since ever was as good.

But we need to live now for now, not now for then. It is today which is most important. What are the streets like dry, not wet? It is this new cafe, not the old one. It is the sunset this evening, the flowers I picked this afternoon, these are the glorious ones. These are right now. I cannot forever chase after yellow roses that cannot grow again.

December 13, 1979

WHITEFISH, MONT. has a big National Guard Sherman tank at the football games and when touchdowns are made the tank fires off its cannon. So during the Whitefish-Deer Lodge championship game when Whitefish put across its first touchdown, the cannon dutifully fired. Deer Lodge then came back and scored a touchdown of its own. But the cannon remained silent. This outraged one Deer Lodge fan who stormed over to the National Guardsman and demanded that the cannon fire for the Deer Lodge touchdown, too. The tank, he reasoned in a loud voice, belonged to the taxpayers, not Whitefish. "And it should fire for our touchdowns, too." When the National Guardsman ignored him, the fan tried to fire the cannon himself and in the ensuing melee was taken off to the pokey. It would seem, if you're going to have a tank at the football game, you've got to take your own!

AND ON THIS SUBJECT of football, if Pat Dye is any good as the new University of Wyoming football coach, he'll be here only two years. If he's bad, he'll be here five.

January 31, 1980

WE IN THE WEST pride ourselves on our western hospitality but we can't match that Southern hospitality. A couple of Wyoming strangers can be made to feel immediately at home and not just by one or two, but by everyone you meet. We have been in the South at conventions before and it has always been the same. They are gracious and considerate and friendly. And their manners are exemplary. If you stand back and observe them you'll notice another remarkable thing about Southerners. They not only display good manners to strangers but they display good manners to each other. They treat each other politely and with consideration. We in the West cannot match them on that. Our problem is that we sometimes treat strangers better than we do each other.

February 21, 1980

WISH WE ALL could get together on the spelling of Big Horn. It's a pet peeve of mine to see the river Big Horn; the sheep Bighorn; the county Big Horn; the national forest, Bighorn; and the mountains, Big Horn. The Billings Gazette consistently spells it the Bighorn Basin, which sends me into a frenzy. I'm getting so I can't stand the sight of the little "h"!

VALENTINE'S DAY found me at the last minute standing around the flower shop looking at all the flowers that weren't there! George Greene said he was over at the Drug Store just before closing time and was among four guys looking at three Valentine cards left!

February 28, 1980

IT TOOK A BUNCH OF kids no one knew, coming along at just the right time and in just the right place, to show America how really great it is, how much we can be unified, how strong and magnificent we as people can be.

All the grain embargoes, all the boycotts and the clenched fists did not say it as well as the U.S. hockey team in the 1980 Olympics did. No message was as clear as that one, not for what those youngsters won, which is remarkable achievement in itself. But for how the rest of us reacted to it all. It instantly brought us together in one prolonged shout, one long waving of the flag. Once savored, the country could not get enough of it, and as one TV commentator described it correctly, he just wished it could go on and on. Even Eric Heiden, whose Olympic accomplishments were just as triumphant, kept saying he couldn't get enough of that hockey team.

How it could fall on the shoulders of 20 young men to show the world will remain one of life's improbables. Their youth is undoubtedly what makes it so great. That was the country's exhilaration in Charles Lindbergh's flight. That a young man would do what no one said could be done, and would do it all by himself made the feat even more extraordinary.

And thus it was, too, in Lake Placid. Watching the U.S. Olympic hockey team these past two weeks fighting this battle of theirs, alone and unknown, has been rare experience.

March 6, 1980
I GOTTA TELL YOU, Red, I miss the meeting place!

NOTHING IS MORE FUN to watch than a little calf who has just hit this Wyoming country this early spring. But then I say this about every colt I see . . . every puppy . . . each new kitten . . . the lambs, the chicks, the little ducks. They all win my heart.

March 27, 1980
THE PERSON WHO uses the brooms in our house bought a new one the other day and the label on the outside claims it has a sweeping distance of 97 (ninety-seven!) miles. A man had to figure that one out. Only a man would sit around and try to measure how many miles someone else could go with one broom.

THAT NEW WYOMING law that extends your driver's license for four years instead of the old three will mean one definite thing to me. Now I will forget to renew it in four years instead of three!

WHEN YOU LIVE IN THE country every place, large or small, has to have its own names for its various parts. This is something a family does so everyone grows up knowing what everyone else is talking about. You just can't say the pasture or field when there's three or four. It has to be the lower pasture or the hill pasture or some such. Otherwise no one knows where to go or where you are or what gate to open.

But by golly a Sheridan rancher has this figured out better than that. He paints his gates different colors. It's a lot better, he claims. When you say, "go open the green gate" there's no mistake.

April 3, 1980
RICHARD BANGS, the Billings Gazette's Wyoming editor, has written about my phobia against seeing Big Horn written Bighorn. Explains Rich: "I noticed you are upset about the Bighorn Basin. If you watch our style carefully, you will note we are consistent in our use of Bighorn and Big Horn.

"Natural entities such as rivers, mountains, BASINS and forests are written as one word with the little h, in agreement with state and federal maps. Man-created entities such as counties, companies and school districts are written as two words.

"I'm sorry you don't like the little h. Just thought you would like to know our reason for giving the little h fair play."

April 10, 1980

THIS WINTER WEATHER in April is what we get for having spring in January. But spring will be along one of these days. The trick in Wyoming is to recognize it when it comes. Some years it will last as long as a couple of days.

Everybody waits for spring. Few people wait for winter. We tolerate summer and look forward in varying degrees to fall. But spring. Everyone can find a reason for spring.

It always seems a long time coming. One year, after a long winter, my brother-in-law who farms back in Nebraska went to the doctor. He'd been feeling lousy for weeks and thought maybe he'd better check on it. The doctor looked him all over, had him get dressed again, and said, "Been a long winter, hasn't it?" My brother-in-law allowed it had. "I've seen a lot of you guys this week," the doctor went on. "You all have the same thing. It'll clear up. You'll be all right as soon as you can get into the fields."

And he was!

SLIM NIELSEN and his son, Roger Nielsen who was up from Green River for Easter, and I tramped around our place Saturday looking for all those Russian Olive trees I keep moaning about. We found some that would make even Mr. Gurney envious, and they took back several good 3 or 4 foot ones. I still have several thousand!

April 17, 1980

A FRIEND OF BERT HARRIS' was taking him through the oil company's fancy new office out in the woods back East, and as they passed one room, a wave of laughter came out of it. "What's going on in there?" Bert wondered. "Oh, they just raised prices," his friend replied.

THIS PRICE OF GAS is changing our lifestyle in the smallest ways. Like that fire the other day out north of town. Cub Collingwood said he got all ready to wander out and look at it, and then figured out it would take him $5.00 worth of gas just to go.

IT SHOULDN'T MAKE any difference at all where you sit or which stall you're supposed to go into or on which side of the harness you work the best. But in this scheme of life, somehow where you are put means being happy or sad. We were talking about this the other day and everyone had an example of an old cow who wouldn't let down her milk if you put her in any stall but her own. We had an old cat that used to stand in front of "his" chair and flick his tail back and forth waiting for you to get out. I have a very dark memory of working my first team of horses, a young "city" kid, as Shelby Gibler called me, and getting things in an awful mess because the horse that was supposed to go on the right ended up on the left. But it's not just animals. It's people, too. Herman Mayland said he could remember someone on a shearing crew quitting because he didn't get the same seat at the table he had before. A family files in to eat and never gets in the wrong chair, twenty years later. Why is it that we function better (or think we do) if we never get out of the same old rut? When one of Betty's relatives came to visit he always wanted to sit in my chair by the window. He'd make a beeline for it every time. I discovered that if I wanted that chair of mine, I had to come to the dinner table at three o'clock in the afternoon!

April 24, 1980
HEARING ALL THE FLIES buzzing around these days reminds me of that story about the sleepy guy who was bothered in the middle of the night with the incessant buzzing of dozens of bugs. So he grabbed the insecticide can and sprayed heck out of the room. When he woke up the next morning he was flabbergasted to discover he had just sprayed his entire bedroom with red enamel paint.

May 22, 1980
THERE'VE BEEN A LOT of tough Monday mornings to wake up to over the years, but you never had to face one with volcanic ash before!

SOMEDAY WE WILL LOOK back and realize the Tough Winter of 1979 did us all a favor. In one mighty swing it got rid of most of those messy elm trees.

WHICH REMINDS ME that if you want to get tested, tackle a stump. Any kind of stump. Elm tree or otherwise. You can cut a morning's worth of wood, shovel a ditch, hoe a garden, run six miles, do dozens of other different things, but none will test your mettle like a stubborn stump. The hole you dig first is never big enough. The root holding it the tightest is somewhere way out of reach. You need a short-handled shovel, a long-handled ax and a pick that doesn't weigh a ton. If stumps didn't want to fight, you could get them out easier. But I never saw one yet, that didn't punch it out to the end.

THINGS THAT ONLY happen in small towns department: I was out of town when the fruit trees came in on the weekend. So the girls at the post office asked Jim Horn if he couldn't keep the trees for me so they wouldn't dry out. When I picked them up several days later, the trees were sitting in a pail of water all wrapped up in burlap. Stark Brothers couldn't have done a better job themselves!

May 29, 1980

IN CALIFORNIA THERE are ordinances against the keeping of roosters. Too noisy in the morning! You can keep hens but you can't keep those crowing roosters. This only happens in America where you buy noisy power mowers, screeching motorcycles, rattling air conditioners, whiny chain saws, ear-splitting electric guitars and thunderous stereos. Your mistake, Mr. Rooster, is that you should be doing your crowing at high noon, not four a.m. At high noon, you'd be drowned out.

A MEADOWLARK HAS BEEN out on the town two straight nights running at our house. But I don't want an ordinance against him. Even in the middle of the night, a meadowlark sounds good. Friday night, he let loose at 2:42 a.m. The next night, right in the middle of the rain, he let out again at 1:44 a.m. Just out howling, I guess.

I WISH THE TV GUIDES would tell us when the Miller Lite commercials would come on so I could watch only them and turn the rest of the programs off.

IT WOULD NOT RANK as a spectacular archeological find. But it was spectacular enough. For it's not every day you find a very red rock stashed way among some old lilac roots.

It was not just any red. It was PAINTED red! Not a bit of the original rock showed. It was about the size a very small fist could handle and some little hands a long time ago had carefully painted it a bright red all over. It looked suspiciously like it may have come from the bottom of the can of International Harvester red paint Bob Foe sold me 20 years ago. That kind of bright, bright red.

And it had weathered well. It was as bright a red now as an IH tractor. But then it should be in mint condition, very gently placed like that in the old leaves and dirt of the lilac bush south of the house. It would still be there if the old lilac's time hadn't come. Chopping and hacking it out uncovered an old truck and a piece of a plastic gun. But the red, red rock was the real find.

Red rocks just don't happen often. Those don't wash down from the Big Horns. Or show up in the bottom of post holes. Or at the top of Mount St. Helens. Not there. Not anywhere. No, red rocks are very carefully made by little hands and expanding minds. By a discovery of bright colors and private things. A rock like this you paint for yourself, to keep and hide away. It was a part of you, once. A long time ago.

Later when you grow older you'll play jokes with paint and spray cans and repaint bikes and pails and one quarter of the north wall of the garage. And if you're real devilish you'll find a perfect cow pie and spray it all silver from a spray can and then gleefully watch your dad as he walks down the lane and sees this phenomenon lying there. I know this, because for a minute I thought my whole herd of six had some horrible intestinal disease.

But no, these are older kids experiences with paint. A carefully dabbed red on a small fist of a rock is the work of the very young. Still young enough for new thoughts and new experiences and hopes for all the "somedays" ahead.

But the joy of the making of it and admiring it and putting it away – no matter how bright and wonderful that might have been then to the "creator" – did not equal the feelings many years later of a very sentimental old "discoverer."

June 19, 1980

WILL ROGERS, is supposed to have said (I never heard this one before): "The mildest winter that I have ever experienced was the summer I spent in Wyoming."

July 3, 1980

THERE'S A MAN UP near Glacier Park in northwestern Montana who is so fed up with litterers that he put up five signs, Burma Shave style. They read: "Inconsiderate" . . . "Sons-a-bitches" . . . "Throw their beer cans" . . . "In the ditches" . . . "Burma Shave."

YOU GET THE FEELING the lady wasn't in Dubois very long when you hear her tell someone else, "DEW BWAH is such a pretty little place."

July 17, 1980

IT MAY BE THE SIGN of the times that America is looking forward more to finding out who shot J.R. than who is to be the next president of the United States.

I WISH WE DIDN'T have to go around digging up graves of other generations. The papers are carrying the story of the unknown Civil War veterans whose graves are being moved and put into a common grave to make room for present-day veterans. I think the old guys have got a right to stay.

July 24, 1980

WHOEVER IS RESPONSIBLE in Wyoming's state government for the fine job in preserving Fort Fetterman outside of Douglas should have the thanks of all of us. Very informative, very interesting. It's not hard to think about the Old West when you're standing in the middle of the old parade ground, surrounded by a beautiful Wyoming sky and the grass country spreading out before you for miles. The Army said it was bleak and lonely duty though. A hardship fort. The main reason: There were no women around!

DO ANY OF YOU OLD TIMERS remember a cowboy named McGrath who once when he was young rode his horse into a Greybull saloon in the early 1910's or 1920's and roped all the mounted deer heads off the wall? That story showed up in Ivan Doig's fine book, "This House of Sky." McGrath ended up a sheep rancher in the White Sulphur Springs country in Montana.

August 28, 1980

A RETIRED COUPLE FROM North Carolina stopped at the head of our lane in the middle of all the wet weather a couple of weeks ago. They were wondering if they should go out the bentonite road to see Devil's Kitchen. I turned them back. It had rained all night, even the gravel roads were mushy, and that road is no place to be in a camper and a conventional pickup with North Carolina plates.

Besides, it's hardly worth the trip in dry weather, if you'll pardon a native's impression of it. It's just an eroded hole in the badlands. There're dozens of them. This one though, has a very catchy name. I've never found out who it was who coined it, but it must have been the same guy who came up with "Hells Half Acre." Same kind of a deal. A much better name on the sign than the hole in the ground behind it.

But back to the North Carolina guy in his seventies who was venturesome enough to want to try it any way. Give him an "8" for that. But give him a "2" for Wyoming weather. Because he told me:

"One thing I like about Wyoming," he told me, "is that you can always predict the weather." When he saw my startled look, he said, "No, really. That's what I've found out. You know what is going to happen to the weather. Back home in North Carolina that's never the case. We have 55 inches of rain a year and you never know when it is going to rain. Here you know what the weather is going to be. I like Wyoming for that."

I was trying to think afterward. I believe he is the only person in my 50 years of living in Wyoming that I ever heard say that!

IN THE EARLY DAYS (1930's) of Sun Valley there were two dormitories, one for the young men and one for the young girls working there. Averill Harriman had them named, Boise and Idaho. That was an old man's name for them. The kids promptly dubbed them "Boise" and "Girlsie." . . . AND ANOTHER what's-in-a-name, that snake plant is also called "Mother-in-Law's tongue".

VIVID DESCRIPTIONS: From Hugh Maller talking about a horse in the salesring: "He'll paste the brim of your hat up against your forehead for the first 200 yards."

September 4, 1980

ONE OF THE FASCINATING parts about a cottonwood's make-up is its quirk of yellowing only one small branch in late summer. Just one branch. The rest of the tree will stay green for another month. But that small splash of yellow, already changed to its fall color, is a reminder the summer is going fast . . . or gone forever.

WHICH REMINDS ME I could have made a list in 1960 of all the things I was going to do that summer and I still wouldn't have it all crossed off by the end of this 1980 one. But not everyone is sorry to see the summer go. Answering the roving reporter's question: "How so you feel about going back to school?" one Bobby Smith answered: "I'm ready. My mom wants me out of the house so bad."

GOING BY THE OLD refinery the other day and looking at those silent old smokestacks reminded me of the first two weeks I was on the job as a reporter for Lynn Severance at the Standard. I took a picture of Bill Unterzuber's moving rig taking an old steam still out of the refinery yards and up the viaduct in September, 1956. I put a headline on the story and picture which read: "Old Steam Still Leaves Refinery." And the next day some old timer came in – I can't remember now who – and said with a smile, "Young man, there hasn't been any steam leaving the refinery for seven years now."

AND WERE WE SPEAKING of gardens? When I asked Betty how come we were having another BLT for lunch, she said: "That's because we've got an awful lot of T's."

September 11, 1980
THE MILEAGE BLACK TYPE sometimes gets always amazes me.
Remember the guy up in Montana who painted his own Burma Shave signs? And blistered the litterbugs with: "Inconsiderate . . . sonsabitches . . . throw their beer cans . . . in the ditches."
The same week I reprinted that in this column several months back, a traveling South Carolina couple stopped in Gillette and picked up the News-Record on the newsstand.
They carried the column – about those "sonsabitches" – back home with them and took them down to the local newspaper columnist, Ashley Cooper. He writes for the News and Courier in Charleston, S.C. And in his column on Aug. 5 he put down: "Tommy and Patty Farrow of 179 Rutledge Ave. recently drove many miles through Wyoming. Granted that the population there is much smaller than in Eastern states, but they were still amazed at how clean the roadside was.
"Then, writes Tommy, they got an indication of how some of the Western citizens feel about littering. The indication was in a column by Bruce Kennedy in the Gillette News-Record. Bruce reported that up near Glacier Park in northwestern Montana there's a guy who has put up Burma Shave-style signs which read: "Inconsiderate . . . sonsabitches. . . throw their beer cans. . . . in the ditches."
Now, that's a pretty good circle. But it's still got a way to go yet! Another Kennedy, a Hugh Maclean Kennedy who lives in Charleston, too, wrote me a letter enclosing the Cooper column. And he wrote:
"I'm enclosing a clipping from Ashley Cooper's column in the Aug. 5,

1980 News and Courier.

"I like your straight-forward approach towards 'sonsabitches.'

"I would like you to know that my wife and I live in the old section of Charleston, which is known as South of Broad (street) and is locally abbreviated as S.O.B. – which is no disgrace here. Of course, Tommy and Patty Farrow live Slightly North of Broad, and are known as S.N.O.B.'s."

So that's what Hugh Kennedy of Charleston added to it.

But wait a minute. I'm not done yet. I want to tell you some more about Hugh. He's chief of the Kennedy Society of America. And he wants me to join up with the rest of the Scots and Scots-Irish who form the society. "Our interests are social, familial and historical," he writes. "We have nothing for sale. We publish a newsletter and gather the history and genealogical information available from our members."

Of course I'm going to join! Old Hugh is undoubtedly part of my Roots. A long lost cousin of a cousin of a cousin. A "Scotch" Kennedy yet. Maybe even a Republican. Hugh said he even had a son in Florida named Bruce. We're all Kennedys.

Just think it all started with some guy talking about "sonsabitches" up in Montana.

October 9, 1980

WHEN LEE KUNKLE came out to our place he had to first pass muster with our belligerent dog. Lee had pretty well made friends with him when he lit up a cigarette. The dog started growling and barking all over again. "Well, that's the first time that ever happened," Lee remarked, "the first time a dog ever told me I couldn't smoke!"

MRS. FLOSS LAWSON, who is in the Greybull Nursing Home, was 90 years old Tuesday. She was telling her daughter, Mrs. Dorothy Gruden, how alone she feels sometimes when she thinks of her friends and family who are gone. "I miss all of them," she said to Dorothy, "and I miss . . ." and she named her brother and sister and others close to her.

"I know, Mom," Dorothy said, "I miss them, too. But you know, one of these days, there'll be a Grand Reunion and we'll all be together again."

Floss didn't say anything and sat there awhile in silence. Dorothy wasn't sure she understood.

"You agree with that, don't you, Mom."

"Oh yes," Floss replied, "and I think I will take a potato salad."

October 16, 1980

Jim Quigg had been retired 13 years when he died this past week.

But I wish he could have been superintendent of schools forever.

Life does not grant us such wishes. It won't hold only the best years or stop age or keep all our health. But we won't see again what J.C. Quigg did for

Greybull schools and the thousands and thousands of kids who went through them. He dedicated his life to this one school system and this one community and his contributions to it should not be forgotten.

Jim Quigg was one of those old school educators who believed in teaching and in kids and though he was a natural administrator, he had one instinctive priority: the education must be good. He wanted kids taught. Of all the things we should remember about Jim Quigg was not how much money he saved the taxpayers or how tight the ship was run, but how much he gave to our kids.

He did not have any money to run the school. This county was and still is one of the poorest counties in the state. It has had no increase in population base for 30 years. It has no mineral wealth. It has not participated in the natural boom and growth the state has enjoyed.

Despite this lack of financing, he still tried to keep expenses down and taxes as low as he could. He did not believe in taxing the people. For years he kept the school mill levy BELOW the maximum. That saved taxes. That's what he believed in. The very next year after he retired the mill levy went to the maximum and it has been there ever since.

He never even paid himself enough money. The community never knew this. But he cheated himself on his own wages. When I asked him once why his wages weren't as high as other superintendents, he said: "That's enough for me." Those wages, too, went up when he left.

He didn't believe in debt and felt the rest of the town shouldn't either. So out of operating funds he built band rooms and added vocational buildings and still kept the school going.

In retrospect he probably ran too tight a ship. The battle of the penny overlooked the war of the dollar. Buildings old in his time are even older today. A long-term building program initiated then would have been marvelous money in the bank now. But the community gave him little indication of this. The school boards didn't. This newspaper didn't. There were no petitions, no community action. In fact, a few years later, the town was embroiled in a swimming pool fight, and a few years after that, the community turned down a bond issue that cost us heavily in inflated dollars and loss of time.

But it was not the tax money he saved that is Jim Quigg's contribution. It was the school he ran. Going through those years with him I don't think we fully understood how much he gave to that. It wasn't just sports which he loved and understood, although they were something. Remember Unterzuber and the early 1940's. Remember the John Kosich years of the 1950's? And ten years later the Buck Eckroth teams of 1959, 60-62?

But think back on the band program. With a school exactly the same size, Chuck Rutherford had a 125-piece band that was the pride of the town. And a music program that kids never forgot. And Nellie Fletcher's contributions through all those years.

We didn't know how good a school it was.

Jim was not as effective in his later years as he had been. He let himself be pushed around more by the school boards and the community. In long public life it is difficult not to make public mistakes. His health was not good. The changing times were catching him. So was age itself.

But he never stopped appreciating young people. He knew them all. He had known many of their parents as kids. He kept track of where they were, what they were doing, and what they had accomplished. He considered a lot of teachers he'd had under him as his "kids." He kept track of them, too. He was always a teacher with a teacher's great pride in his contribution, however slight, in shaping a youngster into an adult.

My memories of Jim Quigg go back 40 years when I was a kid on the sidelines watching him referee basketball games. One vivid picture I keep which showed the esteem and respect this Big Horn Basin held for him was the 1959 presentation ceremonies at the Thermop BHB basketball tournament. The description in the Greybull Standard the next week read: "Quigg, who was asked to present the first place trophy to Greybull's team, received a standing ovation from the capacity crowd. As he walked to the middle of the floor, the crowd rose and stood in respect through the presentation. The ovation was spontaneous, packed with emotion. No one sat down."

I started missing Jim Quigg 13 years ago. And I'll never forget him.

November 6, 1980

WHAT'S ALL this stuff about LEEVERS instead of levers? That's what the news commentators kept telling us to do? Go in the booth and pull the LEEVER. Sorry, I went in and pulled a lever. It's always been hick to say crick and now it's not clever to say lever. Walter Cronkite may have pulled a LEEVER but I distinctly recall pulling a lever.

November 13, 1980

I FOUND THIS "RECIPE" in an old print shop:

RECIPE FOR PRESERVING CHILDREN
1 large grass field
1/2 dozen children
2 or 3 small dogs
a pinch of brook
& some pebbles

Mix the children and dogs well together. Put them in the field, stirring constantly. Pour brook over the pebbles and sprinkle the field with flowers. Bake in hot sunshine and when browned remove to the bathtub.

November 20, 1980

I WAS STARING at the TV set and the Canadian stations had several football games going. When I flipped to one, lo, there was old Tom Wilkinson still throwing the football! It looked like the good old days again.

Just 20 years ago last Saturday, Tom Wilkinson and the rest of that fine 1960 football squad beat Evanston 13 to 7 at Greybull to win the State Class A football title.

And if you'll pardon an old fan's nostalgia, that was a memorable November afternoon:

Greybull was to go on to another two good seasons, sharing the state Class AA-A title with Laramie in a non-play-off in 1962.

But 1960 was the first for a long time. The low-scoring game broke in Greybull's favor when Wilkinson faked a fourth down punt and passed to Butch Sommerville. It was Greybull's game after that. The play wasn't called from the bench. The punt had been. But Wilkinson decided to go for the pass and whispered to Sommerville only when the huddle broke. Such stuff football is made of!

And so was Buck Williams' great afternoon. Coach Buck Eckroth called it the "best physical effort by any player I have seen." Betty was a great Buck Williams fan. She yelled so much every time he did anything that Belle Sanders who was sitting in front of Betty and didn't know her then, turned after the game and said, "You must be Buck Williams' relative."

What a bright sunny November day it was. Temperature in the mid-forties, the whole town on the sidelines. And incidentally, it was Oscar Shoemaker who announced the game.

The Buffs had not had an easy time getting there. Greybull's powerhouse of 1962 rolled over everyone undefeated, some by terribly lopsided scores. But the 1960 squad lost to Worland, then barely squeaked by Thermop, regrouping when the lights went out for a half hour; played Lander in a play-off 33-7 on election day when JFK was elected; then survived a scare with Buffalo 23-14 in a playoff after the regulation game ended.

At the Buffalo game, Greybull had played three games in eight days.

Mike Oliver asked who else was on that team. Well, I looked it up to be sure and here's who the Standard listed on the roster.

Wilkinson at quarterback; Sommerville at fullback; Skip Anderson and Buck Williams at the halfbacks; Bill Werbelow and Larry Krusee at ends; Homer Small and Paul Sanders, Leland Cathcart, Jake Strohman and Albert Twomey at the guards and tackles; Steve Rogers, linebacker; John Madsen at center. Also lettering were Bill MacAdams, Milton McAdams; Rick Minter, Larry Dockery, Clyde Douglass, Dick Thorley, Pat Schmidt, Doug Snell, Ron Sawyer, and Wilbur Powers, as manager.

Those names take you back any?

December 4, 1980

WITH THE COLD WEATHER coming on, someone down at the University got one of those anti-freeze testers to see how their car would stand the winter. The car tested out fine. Then they decided to test the Screwdriver

Punch left over from last night's party. It tested out at 10 below!

IT GIVES YOU SOME idea of the size of our town when the only time you're held up in traffic is when they're moving sheep across the Big Horn river bridge.

BUT THERE'S ANOTHER small town that has licked its traffic problems. That's Bridger, Mont. I don't think they're running their speed trap any more up there. They don't have to. Bridger's reputation for nabbing Wyoming speeders going through the town has had everyone apprehensive for years now. Traffic goes down main street at a snail's pace. It must be four of the slowest blocks of traffic in the Rocky Mountains. So what if they're bluffing now. I'll let you call 'em!!

December 25, 1980

It's time to say Merry Christmas . . . that time of year when you send your special hellos and thank yous to all those who have been a part of your year and a part of your life since the last Merry Christmas.

So it's Merry Christmas to all those who smile when you say Good Morning . . . who recognize and wave at the pickup as it goes by . . . who say something nice about those words you write . . . who ask about your kids and how they're doing . . . who say you look thinner (when you're actually not!)

And special Yuletide thanks to all those who watered the main street flowers and keep them growing and blooming . . . and to Idell Schutte once again for the idea . . . you brightened our summer. And to Art Ernst who endures our very bad, bad jokes about the post office with astonishingly good humor . . . to the gym construction crew for putting up that "tallest tree" in town . . . to Marie Hart for the very good idea for the flag on the library lawn . . . and thanks from all of us tennis players to those who finally got the town some courts . . . they're really a fine addition.

And a personal Merry Christmas to Charlene Collingwood who always gives 150 percent service at the First Greybull Insurance . . . to Carolyn Wright for always remembering the Greybull Standard . . . to Morris Stoddard for remembering the last guy on the ditch this summer . . . to Bill Murphy who always waves when you meet his school bus.

Merry Christmas to Earl Jensen for his work with young athletes and the extra hours he spends every year. And for his free advice to those "older" runners.

Merry Christmas to Father Ron Stolcis for decorating the big, big tree in front of the Catholic parish. It's beautiful.

And Merry Christmas to Coach Tom Harrington for your continuing inspiration to young wrestlers. You and I shared a great friend named Jim.

And a very special Merry Christmas to Doc Rogers whose long years of service and work in this community can never be acknowledged enough.

To those whom I meet at the post office morning after morning... Bonnie Kelly, Harold Lockard, Slim Brewer, Plet Avery, Ben Minter, Bill Murdoch, Arlene Van Gelder, Heinie Meier, Judi Roice, Bill Shelledy, Chot Smith, Bill Wilkinson, Dwight Winsor and many others. I won't see you on Dec. 25th so Merry Christmas from another "Boxholder".

And to Frank Hinckley, too, of the Post Office regulars, Merry Christmas. Just think what fun you're going to have for four years watching the Conservatives floundering back in Washington.

Merry Christmas to all those subscribers in other towns and states, far-off and next door who keep track of Greybull through the pages of the Greybull Standard.

And I have to say another Merry Christmas to Jack Williams for all his laughs he shares... though not always when I want him to!

And the Best of Yuletide to Red Lindsey for many, many past favors and considerations. I owe you several, Red... and to Paul Clark for his constant wit and good humor... to Billie Nielsen at the Safeway checkstand for her bright smile... and to Ron Wright and welcome back to Greybull... to all those at Hawkins and Powers who answer back on 122.8... to Ray Heinzen for adding to those good times at the end of the canyon...

Merry Christmas to Earl Reilly who agrees with me... sometimes... but who always is a lot of fun to see and spar with.

And Merry Christmas to Pat Shelledy for running with me last May though we didn't know until we were done it would turn out to be Ash Monday!

Merry Christmas, too, to Rev. Floyd Ellison for his dedicated and devoted service to both the Greybull and Basin communities for all these years. You have made many, many friends.

And to all the "neighbors" along the road home... the Dave Graunkes (whose great yard makes me feel bad), the Fred Powers, the Guy Wilkinsons, the Jim Cliftons, the Gary Goods, the Del Edelers, the Art Baughs... and especially to Metz and Thelma Smith for a quarter of a century of neighborliness along this same stretch of Shell creek.

And to all you new people we'll meet this next year and all the little kids who grew up so much during 1980, to all those who live in this fine Wyoming community, the best of holidays and the merriest of Christmases.

1981

January 8, 1981

THAT RAINBOW ON CHRISTMAS day was a real stunner. Up on Shell Creek it was a full one – from one beautiful side to the other. When Frank Hinckley looked out and saw that Christmas rainbow he immediately thought back to another one 60 years ago in Cowley. So he called up his brother, Devere, and asked him if he didn't remember such a rainbow then, too. "Of course we got into an argument about what the cow's name was," Frank says, "but we both remembered that rainbow."

WE ARE MAKING TOO much of this Pat Dye thing. Wyoming is never going to be able to keep a first class coach any longer than it takes him to find a bigger and better job. And out there in the football world are one heck of a lot of bigger and better jobs. Bigger towns, bigger player draws, bigger alumni associations (and richer!) bigger conferences, bigger perks, bigger prestige and most of all HOME. Coaches go back home. They want to go back to their roots, to the home country. More important, so do coaches' wives. They want to go home, too. There is no blandishment in this Wyoming that some other school couldn't top. We are a way station and will always be in the competition for top coaches. Frankly, I prefer to be such a stepping stone. The alternative to the Wyatts and Devaneys, the Akers and the Dyes is a lot of average names.

People have been crossing Wyoming for years to get to some place else. Football coaches do, too.

January 15, 1981

I SUPPOSE YOU'VE heard about the Wyoming rancher who went to Washington to complain about the coyotes wrecking his sheep herd, and how ineffective current predator control measures were. The rancher was assured by the Interior under-secretary that effective means were immediately forthcoming. In fact, the department had recently funded the manufacture of a pill to rend the male coyote impotent. In reply, the rancher gave him a contemptuous look and said, "Now I know you have no concept of Western ranch life. In Wyoming coyotes E-A-T sheep."

January 22, 1981

WHEN DR. A. S. ROGERS saw how great his cake looked at his special reception Sunday (he's retiring after 33 years in the community) he remarked that "it looked so nice I think I'll embalm it and save it."

January 29, 1981

THE MOMENT ALWAYS decides the perspective. This has been a grand week while America welcomes home its hostages. But how short memory is. I can't remember what we did for the members of the USS Pueblo 15 years ago after the North Koreans released them. But I hope we did something.

OF ALL THE DRAMATIC parts of the 14-month hostage crisis, none was more pure American than the yellow ribbon touch. It caught on with typical American speed, was instantly a symbol which Americans love to have, was easy enough to be faddish and faddish enough to be acceptable. And then it burst with a frenzy when they all came home again. I'm not necessarily talking about the big yellow bow on the Super Bowl! But that was also typical American. If it is good, it must be better bigger. That was a bit too much.

But all the little ribbons on thousands of lapels and car aerials and flagpoles, now that was a national sight.

I still think about the Casper high school editor who decided several months ago to put a yellow ribbon in every copy of that week's issue and ask her readers to attach them to the car aerial. God bless her for her thought and her initiative. She left a lot of her elder editors far behind.

DO I HAVE THIS all wrong or doesn't the yellow ribbon go clear back to Custer and the Seventh Regiment and its regimental tune of Garryowen, the old She Wore A Yellow Ribbon? You don't have to be an old cavalryman for that tune to stir the blood. Troops riding across Montana grass, blue uniforms with yellow stripes, bugles, horses and leather, pick the symbolism you want.

Over in Japan during the Korean War the Seventh Cavalry Division was stationed in northern Japan. And they would come down to Tokyo for R&R and eventually end up with other GI's from all over, drinking beer and telling stories and singing ribald songs at the Rocker Four Club. But always, before the night was out – and sometimes several times in between – the 7th Cav GI's would start singing, She Wore A Yellow Ribbon. They sang it and sang it, a bunch of young Americans who didn't want to be in the Army singing an old Army song.

BUT THE YELLOW RIBBON that keeps me choked up was the one tied around that old oak tree. That's a true story, you know, a tear-jerker if there ever was one, about when the ex-convict was welcomed home. The first time I heard the song I recognized it from the story and I was telling a very, very good friend about it over lunch right afterward. I got so choked up and he got so choked up I couldn't talk and he couldn't listen. What an emotional tug at the old heart that one was.

And so also with the safe return of the 52!

February 12, 1981
RAN ACROSS THIS IN a story I was reading: "I was running on a narrow, curving trail in the rural south when an approaching female runner took one look at me and screamed, 'Pig!'. I was stunned, but not too stunned to retaliate. 'Fat old cow!' I turned and yelled at her, just as I tripped over the biggest pig I had ever seen."

February 26, 1981
WE WERE TALKING ABOUT a young man in town and someone said "How old is he anyway?" and my friend answered: "He's 85." "He can't be that old!" "He has to be," my friend replied, "to have done all the things he's said he's done."

ONE THING I HAVE NOTICED as the years go along is that legs of chairs stick out further. I used to be able to approach a chair barefoot without it attacking me. But lately I have lost several toes by walking too close. Life deals many stings as it goes along, but none quite like toe against chair leg.

March 5, 1981
WE GOT THE KIDS' "baby pictures" out the other night, a slide show for the family home together for the weekend.

There were all the baby pictures of the kids, from three months on up to 13 years. How could they have been so little? And grown up so fast?

Then there were all the "baby" pictures of Betty and I, ages 23 up to early 30's.

I hadn't realized we'd married so young.

The girls recognized and remembered every dress or outfit they wore . . . which has always been a family joke. (I don't remember what we did, but I can remember what dress I had on.")

For my part, I managed to get at least one picture of every car or pickup we've ever owned.

I mean, after all, you've got to know what's important.

March 12, 1981
THE NAME JACK WADDELL popped out of a newspaper story the other day. That wasn't the same Jack Waddell I used to know around Greybull – he's been gone for years. But it triggered a face, a time, a memory or two.

I can distinctly remember the time Jack lost his driving privileges. In those days the Elks hadn't built their convention hall addition and from the old building to the corner was a parking lot. Usually full. Well, Jack drove in it once from the main street and hit the first car he came to. Then he bounced over and hit another on the other side, got it straightened out and bashed into a third one; careened off that one and managed to hit another. That made four.

He was in the clear now but he headed right straight for the brick wall of the DeSomber apartments. He didn't stop. He kept going until he ran the nose of the car against the wall and there he floorboarded it and spun his tires, baffled that it wouldn't get out of the way.

When the police came and moved his car away from the wall, they asked the first most logical question:

"Have you had anything to drink, Mr. Waddell?"

To which Jack replied: "Only a little dinner wine, sir."

April 9, 1981

THOSE PAINTED NAMES and initials on the south entrance to Wind River Canyon are a disgrace. I said that here several years ago when there were only three or four names. Now there must be a hundred! Way up the rock face of the first tunnel. They look awful. We should never have let this get started. One set of initials by one dodo "inspires" some other dodo. That first bunch should have been sand blasted off. It still isn't too late.

The part that worries me about this is the license it seems to give to do it anywhere else in Wyoming. We have gone for years and years with thousands and thousands of people traveling through, and no one has painted up the rocks or scrawled their initials. Look how long the Wind River canyon has been left alone. We have millions of square feet of vulnerable blackboards, absolutely unprotected, absolutely unpatrollable. It is your personal code that protects Wyoming. It is also "what the other guy does." If he puts up a painted name, another seems to follow. And another and another until you have a Wind River canyon. The abnormal becomes "normal." And if you have the Wind River canyon defaced that way, what prevents North Fork from being next? Or Shell Creek. Or Jackson Hole?

A mountain canyon is many things to many people. But we can't let it become a blank wall for graffiti.

THOSE BIG, EX-AIR FORCE KC-97 cargo planes Hawkins and Powers have purchased have a payload of 80,000 pounds. Bert Harris says he puts that into perspective by realizing the plane could carry four hundred 200-pound fat people! Gene Powers says he figures it out differently. It takes 15,000 (fifteen thousand!) gallons of gas to fill the plane up.

April 16, 1981

THAT BRAND NEW, long-legged adorable colt which is running around our pasture has to be the prettiest and cutest one to ever arrive. All things little are cute. But a colt is always a special gift. From those long, long legs right down to the whiskers on its chin. It'll melt your heart right out. As my neighbor, Metz Smith, says, "We ought to raise them just to look at them."

THIS HAS BEEN A GOOD spring . . . I've already fought and licked two stumps and I'm still on my feet.

April 23, 1981

MY FRIEND WHO IS trying to quit smoking came over to the table and announced: "Well, I reached for my last cigarette today" . . . pause . . . "A car almost ran over my hand."

BITS & PIECES . . . THOSE "BEWARE OF DOG" signs you see more and more are more impressive than the old No Trespassing signs. It somehow . . . well . . . has more teeth in it . . . AND A SIGN ON THE wall said: "Hug your printer. He's your type."

AFTER 15 YEARS OF beards and longer hair, it is hard to imagine when beards were rarity enough to cause heads to turn. But back in the Fifties Jack Stockwell had to fly his son, Jim, back to Missouri. So he rented a plane from Mel Christler, put on a big hat and headed eastward. At the time he was growing a beard for the Days of '49 celebration in Greybull and it had grown to a good proper length. When he landed at Missouri and taxied up to the stopping place to get out, the first person he saw was another bearded guy running towards him. This guy really had a beard. He came running up to Jack, stuck out his hand and announced ceremoniously: "Brother Alderman."

Well, Jack got that straightened out and he told the guy he'd be right at home among the beards back in Greybull this month. Jack asked him to come out. Besides, Jack told him, you'd win the beard contest hands down.

May 7, 1981

DO THEY MAKE A PLACE where the flowering crabs bloom all summer . . . and the tulips last into July just before the daffodils and hyacinths would begin to fade. And peonies go for months and so would lilacs. And iris – oh, those iris – they'd go all the way to the first freeze.

I WAS WONDERING OUT LOUD why a person would continue to grow more flowers, put in more grass, add more trees, plow up more ground and just make more and more work for himself. "That's like going out," Paul Barnett said, "and stealing a shovel."

AROUND THE TOWN . . . EVERY TIME I LOOK at the new gym I still marvel, after all these years, that it's actually going up . . . AND SPEAKING OF YEARS, the story on Rick Minter's promotion at Husky Oil reminded me that it has been nearly 20 years since he graduated from high school. Impossible! I can remember when he came up to me at a summer baseball program, a very young boy growing "old" in junior high, and solemnly told me: "Mr. Kennedy, would you please put it in the paper that it is Rick and not Ricky anymore."

June 4, 1981

IF YOUR TRIFOCALS decide not to let you see what you should; and the hammer decides not to go where it should; and your finger to be in a place where it shouldn't, by golly you can create a numbing experience. I mean it can make an indelible impression on you. I've got a big white bandage from over the weekend to show you what I mean. You may have already seen it. Seems like everyone else has. I keep answering a lot of questions. There's something comical about a bandaged finger, I've figured out. It's a common experience for one thing. What finger hasn't seen better times. We've all been there.

And it's so big for another. And impossible to hide. It's too big to go in your pockets, too sore to hide under your coat, too stiff to tuck out of the way someplace. It just sticks out like a – well, I was going to say – a sore thumb!

June 11, 1981

BITS & PIECES . . . DIDN'T YOU LIKE that item about the policeman, 34, who went back to high school to break a drug ring. He had a terrible time keeping up with his studies, which his kids found hilarious. And the guy said: "It was tough learning how to go back to a society I left 13 years ago. You have to learn how to shuffle your feet again." . . . I NEVER KNEW so many people knew how to swing a hammer until I hit my thumb with one and now I'm getting all sorts of advice.

SAW OLD FAITHFUL go off last month . . . Haven't been over that way for awhile; it's still a sight. It's the first time we ever drove up five minutes BEFORE it went off. Usually the Kennedy family luck is to drive up five minutes AFTER it went off. This time, though, we parked the car, walked up to front row seats, and there she went! She's a grand one.

Standing there among the rest of the spectators, all of us looking the same way at the same thing, always reminds me of the Reader's Digest story about Old Faithful. That was the young guy wearing the official looking uniform who walked out in front of everyone several minutes before it was due to go off. He was carrying what looked like an old steering wheel. He walked right up to within 20 feet of the geyser and then stuck the wheel in the ground. And sat down behind it. Everyone was looking at him. He turned the wheel just a little. Old Faithful spewed out a little steam. Then he waited. Then he turned it a little more. Old Faithful put out some more. He turned it a very hard turn. Old Faithful shot up about three feet. Another turn; another foot or so. More wait. Then a couple of hard turns. More steam and water. Suddenly he was very busy. He turned and turned, faster and faster; he was frantic now. Old Faithful shot way up in the air. More and more steam and hot water high in the sky. Then it was over. The young man turned the wheel in the opposite direction and stood up. Everyone cheered!

June 25, 1981

I WAS RIDING WITH SOMEONE who stopped at the Probst-Stockhouse corner where the old four-way stop signs used to be. When I looked at him he said: "I'm stopping just this one time . . . to make up for all the other times I didn't stop."

RAN ACROSS THIS piece of advice to a high school graduating senior who was on his way to college:

"Congratulations on your good record in graduating. Don't lose ambition but at the same time don't cultivate it inordinately for some time you will realize that life has many disappointments and that many objects of human pursuit and desire are not worth following. I hope hazing is a good deal modified. As much as possible avoid sports, trickeries and larks that theoretically are innocent college pastimes and wool pullings over the professor's eyes, but practically may be far otherwise; such as cigar smoking, card playing, beer swilling, etc. all on the sly. Don't get out too often with the girls sleighing, etc. Time enough hereafter when you need not devote so much time to study. I wish that you may find your college life pleasant." This was written from Mount Joy, Penn., Aug. 6, 1885, to my great uncle from his uncle. We found it in some old family papers.

July 9, 1981

IT'S AN ABANDONED homestead in a pretty place, like hundreds of others throughout the West. The old cabin, the old barn or shed, some currant bushes that look out of place, a tree that's bigger than the rest. And always the apple trees. They stay behind waiting for years and years. On this particular place – and it's not too far from here – there was something different. Four big spruce trees. All in a row, equally spaced apart. The daughter had the explanation: "Those are Dad's trees. One for each of his daughters. Every time he had a new daughter, he'd go out and plant another spruce tree. He had four and there's four trees. One of them was for me."

Oh, I wish I had done that.

THE FIRST SWITCHBACK of the Shell canyon "new switchbacks" gives us the most magnificent view looking up Shell canyon we've ever had from the road. That will soon become the most photographed view of Shell canyon. In one great shot you can see the creek, the canyon walls, the climbing road, Copeman's Tomb and the country on either side, the country way on up above. The view has always been there. The Big Horns haven't manufactured any new sights for several hundred million years. But to see it you had to park your car at the parking lot at the bottom and walk over the hill to the other side. No one but a few fishermen ever did. Now you can drive right by it.

July 30, 1981

THE DOGS IN THE KENNEL had been barking and barking and I went down early to let them out. It was barely light. Just before I opened the gate, I felt that odd sensation of someone looking at you. I turned around. On the telephone pole, peering out from behind it, were three small raccoons, stacked one above the other, all on the same side, all looking at me. My gosh, they were cute. I went over and shooed them off the pole and kept the dogs penned up a little longer. I couldn't get over how cute they were. But, of course, they always look cute when they have yet to eat your sweet corn.

August 6, 1981

"I'M PRETTY GOOD," someone said to me the other day. And so I said to her what Kenny Cyrus said to me some 40 years ago: "What do you mean just 'pretty good?'"

I was just a very young boy, running around with Kenny (who now lives in Green River) in our hometown of Basin. And he invited me over to eat dinner with his folks for the first time. Which I did. And I wasn't all that comfortable being company, scared to say the wrong thing or afraid I'd drop something on the tablecloth. It was all great food as it always is in someone else's house. I can't remember what we had but we did have rice pudding for dessert because Mr. Cyrus wouldn't eat any. Said he'd gotten his fill of rice pudding in the Army in World War I. That's all they fed him. Funny that I'd remember that, but I do.

Well, anyway, the meal was over and I knew I was supposed to say something. And I really didn't know what to say or how to say it. Finally I blurted out, "That was a pretty good meal."

"What do you mean 'pretty good'?" Kenny said. "Is that all the better it was? I thought it was very good."

"Well, that's what Bruce meant," his mother tried to cover up for me.

"He should say it's very good, then," Kenny insisted.

"Okay," I said, red-faced and mortified, "it's very good." Which it had been.

But from then on, "pretty good" never meant what I thought it meant and for years I never used it at all.

August 20, 1981

HAD A BAT IN THE HOUSE the other night . . . Hope everyone who has a bat in the house acts with more bravery than I did. I discovered a bat in the house is a lot different than a bat outside. It is forced to fly lower, about head high. No, make that jugular high! And the effect on me was startling. It was hard to see it finally fly out the open back door while I was cowering in the corner.

THE CAR AHEAD OF US was Bud and Connie Collingwood. We followed them up to the stop sign on the Heights road leading out on Highway 14. Bud stopped. He looked up the road. Connie looked up the road. No one was coming. They drove on out on the highway. I pulled up to the stop sign. I looked up the road. Betty looked up the road. With four pairs of eyes, how can we husbands ever go wrong!

August 27, 1981

FROM SPORTS ILLUSTRATED comes this: "Norm Van Brocklin, former NFL quarterback and coach, describing the brain surgery he underwent two years ago. 'It was a brain transplant. I got a sportswriter's brain so I could be sure I had one that hadn't been used.'"

September 3, 1981

MY MEMORY IS IN that stage when it keeps crunching up the computer cards. Otherwise why can't I put the right name with the right face? Or remember what someone told me just last week? Or if I've told the same story to the same person, put down the check, mailed the mail, turned the coffee water off, let the horses out.

I punch all the usual buttons and pull the normal levers, but the screen sometimes comes up blank. Or worse yet, I FORGET to punch all the usual buttons and pull the normal levers. Either way there's zilch on the screen.

I'm amazed, though, at all the old, old computer cards. Someone really made them. They never fail. Ask me what Billy Zane said to me on the Basin courthouse steps in 1939 and I'll tell you word for word. What's more, I can probably tell you the color shirt he had on. And if it was sunny or raining. In other words, I can tell you about your grandfather. But I have absolutely lost track of your grandson.

What was a perfectly good system before is now in a state of folding, stapling and mutilating.

I've come to expect that at least one-third of all statement envelopes won't have the right address showing through the little window once I've sealed them up . . . that I'll call someone Joe who should be John . . . that I'll remember today something I was supposed to do yesterday.

And don't let me tell you one of my stories. I've probably already told you. Maybe a half dozen times. I can't seem to remember who has suffered through those old stories and who hasn't. I've decided to start over with my stories anyway, a clean slate. Nothing but new ones, untold ones, from now on. The old ones never were all that great!

It's these present times I'm having trouble with. The other day my son and I went to play tennis. I went upstairs to change clothes. I came down and we walked towards the car. He looked down at me. "Don't you think you ought to put on something?" I looked down at me. There I was in my jockey shorts. I had my racket and my sunglasses. But I'd forgotten to pull on my tennis shorts.

A guy like that should not be on the courts.

And just last week, coming home in late afternoon, I glanced over at the hangar. The door was open. "Who was the dumb ninny who left the hangar door open," I thought to myself. I taxied on a little further and looked again. "I know who it was," I said outloud. "The dumb ninny was you."

You know, the dumb ninny who forgets to close the hangar door is also the dumb ninny who forgets to put down his landing gear!

So that's the way it goes. And one of these days if you hear of an airplane that came in without the gear down and the guy steps out clad only in his jockey shorts, you'll know I'm having just another normal day.

September 24, 1981

YOU'D THINK THAT WITH all the blue sky we have above us in Wyoming nothing else blue could compete with that. But this morning I saw a pair of bluebirds on the roadside fence and what a brilliant splash of blue they were. You forgot all about the blue sky.

BUT IT IS ALWAYS those little things that affect us. You walk into a supermarket with shelves stocked to the ceiling, thousands of items at your fingertips, air-conditioned, spotlessly clean . . . and the check out girl says a cross word to you. You're down on the store for a week. You can get along with a big crack in the windshield, but absolutely can't abide a little squeak in the door. You can tolerate a bad bruise on your arm but nothing hurts like a sliver under your fingernail. You've lost the whole morning, but you fret and stew over the light that just changed to red. One flower on your desk is prettier than the whole row outside. One kind word is of more value than 100 plain ones. We place a lot in those little things. We'll never change. That's the way we're put together.

October 1, 1981

I HEARD THIS A LONG ways away from Casper, Wyo. but the cab driver who asked where I was from said she (yes it was a "she") had friends in Casper who had always tried to grow tomatoes up there. But they'd never ripened. Great frustration just to get one red tomato. One late summer they left Casper on a trip with still no red tomatoes and the neighbor sneaked over and spray painted all the tomatoes on the bush. Two weeks later the couple came home, wild with joy at seeing the red tomatoes out in the backyard. But alas, up close it was the same old story. Under that red paint, a lot of green tomatoes.

October 27, 1981

Every time I leave for a little while, Wyoming sure looks good when I get back. There seems to be a direct proportion to how often I think about blue sky and dry air and how many days we're away. I guess it's the fickleness of human beings that we want to be away when we're home, and home when we're away. Anxious to be gone – and after awhile, anxious to get back. You can see a few of the world's sights, savor surf and snow, travel miles, see new things. But once again, when it's over, there are few sights in the world as comforting, as relaxing, as downright heartwarming as seeing your own bed with the covers turned back.

OVERHEARD CONVERSATIONS . . . "What do I want to travel for," he said. "It's all I can do to get back and forth to Shell creek."

November 12, 1981
ARE YOU READY for another bum rattlesnake story?

Those Nebraskans around Lincoln aren't. They're up in arms because they think Wyoming rattlesnakes are bumming rides to Nebraska on the coal trains. Regular hobos, they feel, riding the rails via the coal cars and then swinging off as the trains slow into the Waverly-Greenwood-Ashland area.

Hey, that's not true say the railroad bulls along the tracks. Both Union Pacific and the Burlington Northern are disclaiming such an invasion. There's no Wyoming rattlesnakes in our trains, they claim. The railroads have even sent men out to check all the reported sightings. No confirmation. "As nearly as we can determine after diligent checking with numerous persons in both Nebraska and Wyoming, there have been NO confirmed reports of sightings of rattlesnakes," wrote Joe McCartney of the UP.

But the Nebraskans aren't convinced. One safety memo, for instance, out of Telex-Hy-Gain company, warned its employees to watch for the rattlesnakes because the BN track goes within 100 yards of the firm's plant near Waverly. Apparently one rumor started a flood of them and now many Nebraskans are positive Wyoming is shipping out more than just coal on those long, black trains. They're sure that riding along on top of the lumps are some Wyoming hobos with forked tongues.

And no bum story the railroad comes up with is going to change their minds.

BITS & PIECES . . . YOU KNOW YOU'RE getting old when there are four of you sitting around the table looking at each other through 12 different lenses . . . ANOTHER FORMER GREYBULL football coach has won a state football championship. Ed Rohloff took his Miles City team to the top of the Class A title in Montana last week, winning the game with a fourth down and goal, three-yard run and trailing 6-7. There were only 22 seconds left.

IT IS ONLY EIGHT miles between Basin and Greybull but for all the weeks and months – and sometime years – between seeing old friends, it might as well be eight thousand miles.

November 19, 1981

THE NEW GHS GYM is going to knock your eyes out! I'm not sure we'll know how to act in it. Not after all those years in the old one.

A young boy and I were standing in that old gym once and he asked me how old it was. Well, it's been here awhile, I told him. "In fact," I said, "I played in this gym myself when I was a kid." And his eyes got wide and he looked at me and then around at the gym and I suddenly had the feeling that maybe the Romans had built it.

OVERHEARD CONVERSATIONS: The young couple was watching a middle-aged couple dance very smoothly together out on the floor and when the young girl said something about how well they danced together, the young man said petulantly, "They ought to be able to dance smoothly, they've been dancing together for 25 years." Whereupon someone else leaned over and said, "Yes, but they were doing that 25 years ago too!"

I TURNED OUT ONTO Rimrock Road and then drove slowly down Lane 33 1/2 until it melded into Road 29. I poked along up to Highway 14 and then wandered off to Horseshoe Lane after a half mile or so. Went on down Horseshoe Lane for a ways and then cut over on the Spur Road until it hit Shady Lane. Turned down Shady Lane and went as far as I could before it ran into Rimrock Road again.

Translation (before all the new road signs went up): I turned left out of our lane and went on down the hill towards Metz Smiths. Drove on over to Butch Denzins and then up the road past Garnett Lake to the Shell Highway. Turned back towards town, drove on until I hit that new patch of paved county road coming up out of the Heights. Went on down it past Hector Goods and Gary Shottons and Peewee Huffmans, by the Collingwoods and the Houses. Turned off at the cutoff road that runs by Ed Rechs. On up the road and instead of turning towards Ivy Maxons went to the right past Bill Cliftons and Pappy Boyds. Then on down past Earl Cliftons until I ran back into the road along the river. And then on home again.

My we're getting uptown!

December 3, 1981

DIDN'T REALIZE HOW MUCH I watched other people at the GHS basketball games until you put us all at one side of the new gym. I don't for one minute miss the old gym, but I think I do miss looking across and seeing the other half of the crowd. But I'll get just as used to this as I did to looking across from "my spot" in the southwest corner of the old gym to all the "regulars" in their usual spots.

Those who watched GHS games regularly through the years had long ago determined their various places to sit. It might as well have been reserved seats. Scott Smiths and Metz Smiths over on the north side, the Doc Kellys on the end in the NE corner, Doc Rogers on the SE corner on the end; Slim Brewer and the Gernants in the middle on the south side. And over in our spot, the Larry Bullingers, the Darwin Yates, the Bill Shelledys, Scotty Hinman and Bob Bentley.

If we sat anywhere else to watch a basketball game, it was in another town and another gym!

December 10, 1981
WHY IS IT A QUIRK of the mind that you always remember the very cold days and the very hot days much more vividly than you remember the very nice days.

THAT MILLER'S HIGH Life ad with the horse and sleigh is still the best Christmas ad on television. It doesn't matter that it has been running for several years now. It's still perfect for Christmas. There's nostalgia, good times, a horse's breath on a cold day, warm lights in snow covered houses, sleigh bells, white, cold snow, a trotting horse and a trip that goes from daytime to nighttime you feel you've made many times before. Aw, heck, I'm just a softie for it and my world just stops until it finishes.

THAT BIG OLD cow and her calf were right in the lobby of the Sheraton last week and the young man who had been hired to watch over things asked the rancher, "Should I give them any hay?"

"No, young man, you shouldn't," he said. "The less in, the less out."

I THOUGHT the Greybull police car hiding behind the Town Christmas tree was a little much Thursday morning. Ho, Ho, Ho, everyone.

December 17, 1981
GOT A LITTLE BIT more to add to those hitchhiking rattlesnakes that were supposed to be leaving Wyoming on the coal cars and winding up in Nebraska . . . The original article claimed the UP said there couldn't be any snakes in the coal because the coal was mined at too high altitudes for rattlesnakes . . . I wrote to UP and pointed out that was certainly news to the Powder River Basin! And all the rest of Wyoming! Joe T. McCartney, director of public relations for the UP, in a letter he wrote back said: "Our operating people assured me that there were no rattlesnakes near our loading facilities because of the altitude. Later on, they called back and said, 'Well, maybe not a lot up that high.' Then someone called and said, 'There could be a few, but they're tame.'" . . . So now you know . . . There are only tame rattlesnakes riding the rails.

December 24, 1981

MERRY CHRISTMAS!

It's Merry Christmas time of year again, time to send your holiday greetings to the many people who share this life and who helped make 1981 a good year.

So it's Merry Christmas to all those who put up flags that fly . . . those who keep the streets clean . . . and grow flowers . . . and put up Christmas lights . . . and pour our coffee and fill our mailboxes and teach our kids.

And Merry Christmas to all those who smile when you say "Good Morning" . . . and to the PP&L crew for all community favors, past and present . . . to John Haley and his red suit . . . To Mayor Bob Nielsen on completing his first year in office . . . and to another Nielsen named Slim who is kind enough to remember words I write and laughs we've had together.

And special greetings to Art Sylvester for thinking of us and the paper several times last year. You're a good friend to a lot of people, Art . . . And to Claire Carey for encouragement and help to the Standard Staff . . . and to Cecil Yates and Guy Wilkinson and Ron Wright for kind words during 1981 . . . and a special Happy Holiday to Mrs. Jack Core from this writer of newspaper columns.

And to Frank Casey, a very Republican Merry Christmas. I know the load of suffering you're carrying, Frank, what with this Reagan guy and all. And, honest, I don't mind that you keep reminding me how you feel!

Merry Christmas to Ray Heinzen of Shell. We don't blame you for what you had to do, but we want you to know we miss you and what you had and all those good hours we spent at the end of the canyon.

Merry Christmas to Dr. Ron McLean for the tennis last summer, even in the rain! I'm practicing, I'm practicing . . .

Merry Christmas from all of us skiers to Jim Collopy for taking on the ski area . . . and to Mark Bentley, too, for his good work as always up there.

And this may not reach you in time for Christmas, Renee, but a Merry Christmas to Renee Collingwood who will be in Maraloma Hospital in Lancaster, Calif. for another month and a half after a cycle-car accident. Here's to your speedy recovery in '82.

Merry Christmas to Dr. Tim Graham – an alumnus of the Greybull Standard high school photographer corps (who helped me take pictures years ago) and who has now hung up his veterinary shingle in Basin.

Happy Holidays to Ned Kost, Jr. whose phone at Basin often rings mine at Greybull with some astonishing information and sometimes quotable stories!

Merry Christmas to Sharon and Jim and Alan at the airport for getting me out and back.

Merry Christmas to always cheerful and helpful Dixie Cummings in Big Horn Federal . . . to Axel Stockhouse and his many extra hours he devotes helping the kids on the Paintbrush staff . . . to Dick Karhu for the always friendly wave from the post office jeep . . . to Harold Lockard and Betty Leavitt and their 90th birthdays just a couple of weeks ago . . . to all those in the 49er run, hopefully I'll see you at the finish line again next year . . . and Merry Christmas to Roland Smith for always waving to his "neighbors" . . . to Harold Darr for extra service to us at the Basin post office this fall . . . To Betty Nelson (or whoever did the window in Western Floral this Christmas). What a lift that window gives . . . and a special thanks from all of us to people like Alma Bruce and Gerry Winsor . . . and all the others who donate time and thought to those in the Nursing Home.

Merry Christmas to newcomers Steve Kapas and Randy Becker, both new policeman, and to Bill Braden, Doyal Waterworth, John Siekierski and Roger Clapper who have just moved to Greybull this past month. And to all the rest of you who arrived in 1981 to make this your home, a very Merry Christmas from all of us.

And for far-off Tom Wilkinson who hung up his football cleats this year in Edmonton, Canada, a Merry Christmas from all of your loyal and long-standing fans in Greybull. We've always been so very proud of you.

And to old friends Jess Black and Scott Smith of J & S on their new venture . . . And another Merry Christmas and welcome back to the Mel Christlers who have moved back to Greybull from Thermopolis.

To all those people who live in other places and keep track of Greybull through the pages of the Greybull Standard, including Barry Olson of Wilmington, Del.; Russell Simpson of Belmont, Mass,: Alice Whaley in Hardin, Mont.; Dr. and Mrs. Jack Lester of Devil's Lake, N.D., Lt. Duane Powers, Ted Anderson, Jr. of Roseburg, Ore.; the Bruce Campbells of Glasgow, Mont.; Frank Linn of Albany, Ore.; Robert Turner, Charles Wood, and Richard Gormley, all in Denver; Jerry Crawford in Petaluma, Calif. and 74 other Californians who subscribe to the Standard, here's a very special Merry Christmas to you across all those miles.

And to all you new people we'll meet this next year and all the little kids who grew up so much in 1981, to all those who live in this fine Wyoming community, the best of holidays and the merriest of Christmases.

1982

January 4, 1982

THIS IS THE FIRST year I never made one New Year's Resolution. Which only means I waited all these years to get older and wiser and much more practical.

January 11, 1982

THE ONLY "REAL" MEDICINE I ever prescribed was Blackberry Brandy. Which I consider a great stopper for the flu bug. I once prescribed it to Bob Foe, who took a small bottle home, poured out a little jigger at the kitchen table and downed it. His wife, Wanda, a registered nurse, asked "What's that?" "It's Blackberry Brandy." "What's it for?" "It's for the flu and it's not half bad." "Who prescribed that?" Wanda wanted to know. "Dr. Kennedy." And Wanda, incredulously, "DOCTOR WHO?"

My credibility in the medical field was very short-lived.

NEARLY TWENTY YEARS AGO I bought a book written by Edwin A. Peeples. It was about the craft of writing and using words and his philosophy of putting things down on paper. It was a book that touched you very quickly and made a tremendous amount of sense. And since he was a writer who could write; and not only write but explain how to write, the book soon became well-thumbed and constantly referred to. I was always going to send a letter to him telling him what a great job he had done. And how much the book meant to me. But all these years I never did.

A couple of months ago I decided to buy some copies of the book for gifts. But the bookstore lady said she didn't have it in stock.

"Apparently it's still in print. I can get you the number to call," she said. "And you can order it yourself."

So I put in the call back east. It was a Pennsylvania number. I explained to the guy who answered the phone what I wanted. The Edwin A. Peeples book. A couple of copies.

"Well, this is Edwin A. Peeples," he said. "I'm still answering my own phone."

Imagine, just like that. Pick up the phone and in less than 20 seconds, talking to someone you've admired and "listened" to and thought about for so long.

And so, I got to say to him personally — and say it over and over — what I've always wanted to tell him all these nearly 20 years.

January 26, 1982

THE YOUNG MAN, obviously in high spirits, looked around at the crowd and exclaimed: "You can never have TOO much fun."

Boy, I thought to myself, if that isn't true. You can have too much of a lot of things: Too much work, too much pressure, too much waste, too much of everything. But fun. You can never have too much of that!

IN THE PHOTOGRAPHY judging at the Wyoming Press convention Photo Judge Dick George of Douglas was commenting on the picture. It was a full figure shot of a good-sized man, most of him hanging out over his belt.

"Here's a picture with too much belly and not enough face," George commented. And then added: "Which is true of a lot of us."

February 9, 1982

WEATHER EXTREMES DON'T bring out the best in me. I get grouchy and pessimistic and feel abused whenever it gets below zero cold. It's just too cold. And I get grouchy and pessimistic and feel abused whenever it gets in the 90's and 100's. Too hot then. Those extremes just get to me. However, some close members of my family say that even in perfectly good weather, I am sometimes grouchy and pessimistic and feel abused!

February 22, 1982

OF ALL THE COMEDIANS who've come and gone on television, I think I miss Artie Johnson and his Laugh-In antics most of all . . . IF YOU HAVE A YOUNGSTER who is going away from Wyoming for a few years and is afraid he or she will miss Wyoming too much, send along a copy of A.B. Guthrie, Jr.'s "The Big Sky" . . . or "The Way West" . . . or both . . . They'll breathe sagebrush into any room. Thirty years ago in a far off place I read my copies until they were in tatters.

COULDN'T RESIST THE "Apples For Sale" sign alongside the road last fall. When the man in his eighties came out of the house, we talked for some time about the crops and the weather and the world in general. I loaded the bushel in the trunk. We were still talking. Pretty soon he said, "Well, you young folks have a good time today." Young at 50? Old at 80?

"These have got to be good apples," I said to Betty. "They are grown by a man of exceptional perception!"

March 2, 1982

OVERHEARD CONVERSATIONS: "My daughter and her husband want to build their own house, just like we did. I told her you can do it all right, but remember one thing: A marriage can only stand one such house building."

ONE OF LIFE'S LESSONS – and it takes a long time to learn this sometimes — is that there is always someone who will be faster or smarter or bigger or stronger or better at all the things you strive to be. And when you're young, when it matters so much, it seems so wrong and so unfair to have Life be this way. But the lesson learned, finally, is that you have had only one real competitor all this time. And that's been yourself. You have always been able to be faster or smarter or stronger or better.

The question in the end, is, have you?

March 16, 1982

BITS & PIECES . . . I KNOW YOU'VE heard before that a Wyoming 10 is a 4 with a 6-pak . . . WE CAN SAVE WHOLE forests and whole rivers full of fish, but we can't save our most exhaustible resource, ourselves, from self-destruction. And so last week, we lost John Belushi.

I DON'T KNOW HOW you rate the past session of the Wyoming Legislature but the Friday following adjournment the wind was still hitting 120 mph across southern Wyoming.

HARRY BARNETT AND Joe Carey (who are cleaning out the old bar on the corner) carted out the old neon sign that said "BOB'S BAR" Monday. It used to hang outside in Greybull's "old days" but it's been stored in the building for years. You've been here a while if you ever saw Bob Avery turn it on. Harry says he's taking the sign home.

March 23, 1982

NOTE TO THE GUY in the pickup loaded with hay pellets Sunday afternoon who lets his big dog ride in back. I heard you coming up behind me while I was running south down US 16-20 by the Greybull river bridge. But I didn't know you had a big, furry dog along until he barked right in my ear. I could tell by your big grin that you've never seen a grown man jump 20 feet straight up and 15 feet sideways all in one motion.

JERRY HENDERSON, president of the Wyoming Gas company in Basin, just ended a year's chairmanship of the 14-state Midwest Gas association. The chairman's dinner was held a couple of weeks ago at Kansas City's Arrowhead Stadium Club. It looks out over the stadium where the Kansas City Chiefs reign during season. The association gave all the usual speeches and presented Jerry with a big gavel. But what really made an impression, Jerry said, was that they flashed his picture on the stadium scoreboard for an hour and a half!

WANDERED INTO A ski shop in Steamboat Springs a couple of weeks ago and there sitting on one of the display shelves was Doak Walker's Heisman Trophy. It was absolutely stunning. Obviously I never saw one before and probably won't again, although someone told me on the USC campus three of them are on display, starting with O.J. Simpson's. But Doak Walker's was right there in front of you, out in the open, just a part of the place. He won it in 1948, playing for Southern Methodist. How did it get in Steamboat? Well, he's married to Skeeter Werner, who owns the ski shop. She's a Steamboat native, a sister of the great Buddy Werner, the USA Olympic medalist who was killed in an avalanche.

I was surprised how big the figure is on the trophy. I guess I expected it would be smaller. And the color is an unforgettable bronze. The figure is in that classic runner's pose. The one thing that catches the eye immediately is that old style helmet.

Funny how that old flat helmet adds the class to the trophy. The helmets themselves never had any. Wearing them was next to nothing. Basin High School still had a bunch when I went through. You could bend mine quite a bit when it was off your head. And sometimes you could bend it when it was still on your head! But it was Reynolds Kost, I think, who had the limber one. He could take his, fold it up, and tuck it in his pants when he didn't need it on his head!

March 29, 1982

IF YOU'VE EVER packed in the mountains on horses (or ever wanted to) that book, "Packin' In on Mules and Horse," by Smoke Elser and Bill Brown has a lot in it. One story they told was of Smoke taking on a job packing in a 400-pound piano seven miles to a Montana mountain cabin.

First, he found the stoutest horse he could, a great big old mare. Then he built a platform and put this up on top of her. He found three sturdy pine poles and rigged up a block and tackle. He hoisted up the piano with the block and tackle and then walked the horse and platform underneath. He lowered the piano onto the platform, lashed it down on all sides until it was balanced. And off they went!

One horse went on up ahead with the three poles and the block and tackle. Smoke came along behind leading the horse and piano. Every half mile or so, depending on the terrain, they'd stop, set up the poles and block and tackle, and let the old horse rest or drink. She got so she recognized what the poles were for and really lit out for them for her rest stop!

They made the trip okay. And the piano is still up there.

April 13, 1982

THE GREAT GAPS in any logic I may have presented to you today can be directly attributed to the 70-degree weather outside Monday.

April 27, 1982

THE ARGENTINA-BRITAIN conflict brings that old World War II story to mind about the first orientation program American soldiers went to before joining up with the British. The American intelligence officer conducting the orientation stood in front of a large map of the world. All the old, pre-war British Empire was in red. Canada, Australia, India, Burma; and red in Africa, the British West Indies, on and on. The sun truly never did set on the British Empire. The officer let this all sink in for a moment and then he took his pointer and tapped the world with all Union Jacks flying on it.

"This was not," he said, tapping his pointer once again. "This was not settled by a bunch of sissies."

May 12, 1982

IF YOU GAVE ME ONLY six things I could look at outside in May in Wyoming, I'd take:

1) Any big flowering crab in full bloom, just before the first petals fall and the pink fades. That big mass of beautiful color takes over a whole yard.

2) Any new colt, say about a week old, that has figured out how much fun it is to put his head down and kick up his hind legs. Just for a second that perfect bucking horse in miniature. The head cocked just right, the back arched, the four legs stiff; and then a race around in a circle like a kid turned loose. I wish you could get paid for watching new colts in the pasture.

3) A tossup: Between any Nanking (or Chinese) cherry blossom with the sun behind it, that frail pink that a breath would blow away. Or a stunningly yellow daffodil just after it first comes out.

4) A flight of Canada geese low on the river . . . and if you won't let me have a whole flight, give me just one, at the tree tops who doesn't see me and comes right over the top of me.

5) Any field of grain up about two inches. That soft light shade of green can't be found in any paint can. If you really want to catch a breath, make it rain on it for a day and let me look at it again after the sun's been out an hour.

6) A calf running away from you at full speed with its tail straight out. If that sight doesn't bring a smile on a Wyoming spring day, you're just an old grouch.

May 24, 1982

IF ANN LANDERS is in trouble from recycling her letters, then I suppose I'm in the same sort of hot water with those Poor Richard quotes (which begin each of these columns.)

Cross my heart I haven't rerun any columns in the 25 years since this column has been going. Other than a lapse of memory or a rehash of an old joke or favorite out of the past. But I have to confess to recycling some of the better Poor Richard sayings off and on over the years. Poor Richard aka Richard Saunders aka Benjamin Franklin was prolific enough with those quotations. But when you use one each week (or most weeks) of a year, year after year, you're bound to use them up.

And so, like good old Ann, I've laid a couple of these on you more than once!

Actually there's a bunch which haven't been used at all. For there are Poor Richards, and then there are Poorer Richards; and then again there are some Poorest Richards. I've hated to use the Poorer and Poorest when the good ones are so good.

Also, there's some which give a pen some pause. I've hesitated for obvious reasons to use the one which says: "Beware of the young doctor and the old barber." (1733) Or the one: "After three days men grow weary of a wench, a guest and weather rainy." (1733). Or his (1734) admonishment: "Be temperate in wine, in eating, girls and sloth or the gout will seize you and plague you both."

And I've had mixed feelings about using: "Fish and visitors stink in three days." Or "Never praise your cider, horse or bedfellow." (1736). Or "Dally not with other folks women or money."

And I've felt all my doctor friends would land all over me if I used: "There are more old drunkards than old doctors." Or "God heals and the doctor takes the fees." Or the lawyers with: "A countryman between two lawyers is like a fish between two cats." (1737). Or "A good lawyer, a bad neighbor."

And I was sure that some would accuse finger-pointing if I used: "Sound and sound doctrine may pass through a ram's horn and a preacher without straightening the one or amending the other."

And there's Poor Richard's counsel about "light heeled mothers making leaden-heeled daughters" and more on unmarried daughters and men without wives and a whole bunch of other pithy and earthy advice that still lay untouched.

What I'm trying to say is the Poor Richards are about used up. And with this confessional, what's left will all be "first timers." No more repeats! When the Poorer Richards are gone; and then the Poorest Richards are sifted through; and all the too earthy ones and the ones I don't understand, I won't be starting over.

Maybe I'll send them to Ann Landers!

June 22, 1982

A YOUNG BLACKBIRD not too long out of the nest, barely feathered and all head, was perched on the fence as I went by, and I couldn't help but think that it was the ugliest damned thing I'd ever seen. Only a mother blackbird could love that.

AND ANOTHER BIRD – this one a full-grown flicker – is attacking all the knot holes in our cedar siding. Apparently it's trying to nest. At least it will peck out a hole big enough to crawl into, then it pulls out all the insulation until there's a good-sized cavity. We've tacked up pieces of board over each new one, but the dumb bird will go right to the next knothole and start over. We're beginning to feel like the only hollow tree covered with Olympic stain in northern Wyoming.

BITS & PIECES ... THAT WAS AN INTERESTING Wyoming spring we had ... Started one morning and it was over by that evening ... SOMEONE WONDERED if our string of Lombardy poplars were a short-lived tree. Can't answer that but we planted ours in 1957 ... that's 25 years ago, and even after a setback in the winter of 1979, they're still growing.

July 13, 1982

I WAS GETTING READY to tell someone how to tell time by the sun – something I had picked up when I was a little boy – and I told him when it was an hour before sunset, the sun was just about an inch off the horizon.

And then I thought, now where did I get an "inch." It didn't make much sense to him and not much more to me. Thinking about it later, I knew that "inch" came way out of the past someplace. It just popped out of the subconscious. An inch from the horizon. That has to be little boy talk. Way back. Just for the heck of it, I took a ruler out, faced the sun and held it out at what would be little boy arm's length. Sure, enough, it measures an inch all right, an inch from the sun to the horizon with just about an hour left.

THE DARNDEST TIME-TELLING deal I ever got into was one summer in high school out at Burlington. I went to work for Owen and Bessie Dill when they were farming the Con Meloney place. The first time I was going out on the tractor for the day, I wondered how I would know it was noon and lunch time. I didn't own a watch. "Oh, when lunch is ready," Bessie said, "I'll just wave the blanket." I was incredulous. But how will I see that, I asked, but no one else seemed to question it. I went to the tractor, convinced I would never eat again.

That morning I worked in a way-off field and from ten o'clock on, never took my eyes off the house. Sure enough, eventually I caught sight of Bessie waving the blanket. I came joyously in!

The next day it was the same, but as the week went on, it began to work for me just as it has for many, many others. Rural ESP I guess you'd have to say. You'd be riding along and suddenly it was like someone was looking at you. You'd look toward the house, and sure enough, there was Bessie waving the blanket. You'd wave back and head for home. Dinner was on.

When you've got rulers and blankets, who needs a watch!

July 27, 1982

DR. JEFF BALISON was probing around on the top of my head, up there where there is more " bare" than "hair." "Does that hurt?" he wondered. Nope. "Does that hurt?" Again. No not yet. "Does that hurt?" Nope. "I got a little bit of hair that time," he said. Now that, Doc, I told him. THAT hurts!

HOW DID THE RUSSIAN Olive trees ever get started in this country? They couldn't be a native. In windbreak plantings maybe? Birds will spread them until they're just everywhere now. River bottoms, canal banks, along ditches, gray patches here and there in all directions. You see more and more heaps of dead Russian Olive trees piled up around the country where exasperated people have grubbed them out. In two years, the trees are kind of pretty; in five years they're very noticeable; in ten years they're taking over the place.

MY SISTER HAS taught first grade for many years and should write a book on all the things first graders say. This year a little boy wondered how long she had been teaching. She told him she'd taught first grade for 19 years. "Gee," he said, solemnly taking her literally, "you must be tired."

AND ANOTHER DAY one of the little kids took a bad knock on the head at recess and instead of going back to class just went on home! In the search for him teacher asked another little boy where Johnny was. "Oh, he got hit on the head. I think he is suffering from Milk of Magnesia."

August 2, 1982
Willard Scott is an instant friend.

It takes about as long as his big handshake and you've known him forever. That's become his trademark on the NBC Today show every weekday morning and that's the way you find him when you shake hands with him in Greybull, Wyo. He's the same old Willard, the same good old boy who established immediate rapport with the country as part-time weatherman, full-time entertainer, long-time friend.

His trip to this part of Wyoming – to Shell Creek and the Big Horns for a few days and then on to the Parks – was not his usual ambassador role of parade marshall, master of ceremonies, public speaker. He makes dozens and dozens of those. Instead, his daughter, Mary, majoring in animal science at the University of Arizona, has been spending some days this summer at the Flitner ranch on Shell creek. So Willard and his wife shed their celebrity status for this trip and as guests of Dave and Sue Flitner, joined their daughter to see some of Wyoming.

When I talked to them, they'd just come "down off the mountain" ("I got to get these local phrases right," Willard said) after spending the day in the Big Horns, lunch at the cow camp cabin, the long pull up Black Mountain road, the cool temperatures on top.

"When I tell people in New York that I just spent five hours driving and never saw a person, they won't believe me," Mrs. Scott said.

She is very personable like her husband. Quick and articulate and gracious without trying, like a lot of those who live in the south. She's obviously been a big part of his life and success.

They're seeing much of the U.S. What Willard Scott has become in two very short years is the goodwill ambassador for NBC. His down home style, sometimes corny, always believable and the best ad libs at 7 a.m. of anyone in the business have made him a traveling advance man for the network. He's immensely popular wherever he goes. That's an amazing accomplishment but Willard appeals to people. He is one of us. TV producers and directors and many stars don't always understand this. But then they are not "one of us" either.

He is big like you'd think, but bigger, taller, mostly; he is funny like you'd expect, but funnier. A never-stop patter of good humor and laughs and stories; lord, the stories, one after another. Yes, he talks in superlatives and, yes, he doesn't wear his hairpiece except on the show. Strange how vain TV is as if it mattered with Willard Scott.

As Cleo McKinney said, who talked with him on Greybull's main street, "I would have known him anywhere."

The one thing the TV Willard Scott doesn't show is how serious his eyes can become. They are very brown and very direct and sometimes very serious. Not always the eyes of the clown. But this is serious, tough business, this role of the clown.

No, I didn't ask him if Jane Pauley is as beautiful in person as she is on the show (I assume that). And no, I didn't wonder if they missed Tom Brokaw (I assumed the world knew that, too.) I did mention Bryant Gumble seems to be catching on and Willard's guarded "he is getting better all the time" made me wonder if the transition had been shakier in private than on TV.

Many of Willard's jokes and ad libs convulse the crew behind the cameras – you can hear them laughing on set which is as high a compliment as you can get. When I mentioned this he knew it, too. "Hey, those are the guys that count."

And I wondered how his stand-in, Cliff Morrison (who's leaving for a big job on the West Coast with ABC) was coming along with his nervousness. It was far more obvious a year ago. "You get the butterflies sometimes facing the cameras and thinking about the millions of people out there watching you." Willard with butterflies? They don't show, Willard.

And he told about standing up there going through his routine and right there in front of him out of camera range is the producer with his hand going round and round. Hurry it up, Willard. Faster, Willard.

Not much pressure up there at the top.

We talked, too, about hurrying through the weather presentation and thus cutting Willard's air time.

Back to the serious eyes again. Back to the producer with the circling hand.

"I'm not a weatherman. I am an entertainer. We talked this week in New York about the time slot. It needs enlarged."

Willard's appeal is directly to the people. A great asset. A great asset for the network, too. More and more people are seeing this as he continues to wear very well with the country. When he first came up to New York from his Washington station, they panned him in the sophisticated city. But within the past month some sophisticated New York writer has written a sophisticated piece praising Willard Scott and so, as Willard says, "I have arrived. When they do that in New York, you've arrived."

And we talked about his 100th birthday feature which has become his private territory on television. It's been a great success.

"It just sort of happened. Someone sent in a letter and we read it and it grew and grew. Now we have more than we can get in."

I hadn't realized anyone missed. I thought everyone who had a 100th or more birthday was Happy Birthday'd on the Today show. Not so. Time runs out.

"Do you realize there are 18,000 people in the U.S. who are over 100 years old? They are forming an organization. It's one of the fastest growing segments of the population," he pointed out.

I mentioned Uncle Sim Cockins who died in Basin the night before his 100th birthday. "It happens all the time," Willard said. "We have to keep a file on everyone right up to broadcast."

One thing they've found in all these centenarians, Willard says, the one common thread running through all of them is their ability "to roll with the punch." The positive attitude. It's not "the whiskey and cigar every morning routine." But their inner calm and peace that add the years.

And there's over 18,000 of them. Let's see, five shows a week, 52 weeks less two weeks off, less three weeks on the road. That's about 260 shows. If everyone 100 or over had a happy birthday said by Willard Scott on the Today Show that would be seventy-seven (77) each day. That would take five Willard Scotts! And there's only one. But Willard, what would we do with five of you!

August 16, 1982

IF YOU PLAYED FOOTBALL or basketball in the Big Horn Basin in the late thirties and forties, O.J. "Red" Deveraux had to be one of your referees. That's just the way it was back then. He reffed everything and everywhere and he was part of your growing up process. Red says he still runs into people who remind him of those games. One guy up in Montana, the other day – he's a business executive up there – told Red he always remembers the time Red exploded and nearly threw him out of the game for using a four letter word on the field. How times change. Now even the referees must color the air.

THE STORIES GOT AROUND to snakes and I said the snake fright I remember most was the time I opened the corral gate and went to do something for an hour or so. I went back to close it. When the gate swung open it stopped right under one of those old low hanging black willow trees. Some of the branches in the summertime actually touched the gate in fact. I was thinking about something else and wasn't paying much attention when I reached up to grab the gate. My hand and the big old bull snake's head arrived on the top pole of the gate at the same time. He was coming right down out of the tree by one of the limbs to the gate and on down. He looked about 20 feet long and four inches thick. I thought it was a boa for sure. I don't remember exactly what I said in my fright but Red Deveraux probably should have thrown me out of the game.

August 24, 1982
DON'T KNOW IF YOU'LL ever use this bit of household information, but should black hornets ever build a nest way up on the side of your house (like they did ours) here's how to get them down. Take one of those plastic sprayers you hook on the hose. Fill it full of Malathion. Set it on the long stream. Stand back a cowardly 25 feet and let them have it. The porous nest soaks up the Malathion, traps all the hornets inside, kills them, collapses the nest and voila! They're gone! I thought it was pure genius born out of pure cowardice.

August 31, 1982
IF BETTY HAD her druthers, all the flowers would be red. If I had mine, they'd all be yellow. The compromise makes a pretty sight!

FIXING FENCE THE other day (all by myself) reminded me of other times when I had help, reluctant help to be sure, but help nevertheless. However, as a father I had certain pressures I could bring to the working force! And I must say I got a lot more fencing done in those days than I have since. It's still a chore, alone or with a bunch. Once when our youngest was very young, we were fencing away and he said in his very little boy voice, "When I think of being a cowboy, I don't think of building fence."

September 7, 1982
LIFE HAS ALWAYS been a balancing act: One way over here but not too far over there. Do this, but not that. Be tough, but not belligerent; firm but not stubborn; knowledgeable but not opinionated. From the beginning we're asked to lean this way but not too far that way. And for the rest of our lives, we work that high wire from this side and then that side, treading the fine difference of rights and wrongs.

"Be confident of yourself," we're told. "But . . . don't be so cocky."

"Speak up," they tell us, "say what you think." But . . . don't be such a loud-mouth.

"Think of yourself first," but . . . be compassionate of others. Look at the other guy's side of it, but don't compromise your principles.

"Smile and be happy with the world," but . . . don't be so silly and giddy.

"Be firm and steadfast in your convictions," but . . . don't be so stubborn.

Work hard, but . . . don't forget to play. Play hard, but don't forget to work.

"Take care of your business and it will take care of you," Poor Richard says. But (they say) . . . don't bring the office home with you.

Be independent, but don't . . . ask for your own way all the time.

Everything is NOT good in this world. But . . . everything is NOT all bad either!

Tell the truth, but . . . don't hurt people's feelings.

Turn the other cheek, but . . . don't let anyone walk over you.

Don't be ruthless in business, but . . . don't be a sucker.

Lead that horse, don't drag him. Give advice, but don't preach. Save your money, but don't be stingy. Don't be a coward, but no fighting. Be serious, but why so solemn.

Push hard to get there, but don't overdo. Set your standards high, but don't wish so much. Get exercise, but don't strain your heart. Don't look back, but remember the past. Live for the present, but look to the future.

Life's waiting . . . the wire's out there . . . why do we hesitate so?

September 22, 1982

Severance, where are you when I need you?

Here I am, with pieces of this ancient Babcock press scattered all over the Cody Museum, and you can't be around to help.

Lynn Severance. I've been thinking of him all week. How he would have loved this job of putting together an old Cody press for a museum. He's been gone several years now, but he'd left printing and this side of the mountain even before that. This week was one of many when I'd wished he could be back.

He was one of Montana and the Big Horn Basin's early printers, the last of the breed of guys who ran weekly newspapers with ink on their hands from morning to night. He was at Lodge Grass and Sheridan and Basin for awhile and then bought the Greybull Standard in 1946. After working for him for three years, Betty and I bought the Standard from him in 1959. He stayed on at the Standard for another 12 years with us. And I learned much from him.

But Lynn always despaired of my mechanical ability. He was very impatient with it. I don't know how we ever worked it out between us. He was as quick and clever with machinery as he was with wit and words. I went by the book. If it was written down, I could figure it out. But to look at gears and cams and levers was a Rubik cube in cast iron for me. Once when an old Greybull Standard machine broke down and we were both deep into the grease and dirt, I decided to look at the book. I found what I thought was the answer. I'll never know if it was or not. Because when I handed the book with the opened page to Severance, he just glanced at it, took the book, put it down on the floor and put his knee on it! At least it kept his knee off the floor.

Now I have a press apart, crying to be put back together this week, and I don't have any book to look at! Severance would get a kick out of that. I qualify in part for the job because it's the old Cody Enterprise press from the earliest days. It left Cody when bigger presses came in – the Double Ought Miehle that Jack Pierce remembers was there. And it wound up in Lodi, Calif. where it just kept on running. It didn't know any better. Someone took good care of it. It didn't realize it was a museum piece and a part of Cody's past that the Cody museum people felt should be kept around. The Enterprise staff agreed.

So it's back in Cody, a donated piece of the old Enterprise showing off to the general public.

But it arrived torn down for shipping. When we opened the back of the U-Haul truck (Paul Fees drove out to Lodi to get it), it was a hodgepodge of iron and steel. "It was all in one piece when Paul left California," one of the staff deadpanned.

There's another Babcock press just about like it here at Greybull. That's the one Severance and I had so much to do with. It's ancient, too, just about the same age as this Cody Babcock. But there's no Buffalo Bill in its past and no claim to museum fame. So it sits in the Standard basement, waiting for I don't know what, a dusty cousin of this spanking clean little lady at Cody.

Neither Severance or I would have ever pegged the old Standard press for a museum piece. Severance had it apart back in the early Fifties. He moved from one end of main street to the other between press days, Wednesday to Wednesday. Tore it all apart, piece by piece, and moved it with just one high school kid and the flat bed winch truck from E.T. Foe's. And it still sits in that same place 30 years later.

The old press ran week after week until 1966 when we went offset and began printing on Mike Vukelich's new web press at the Enterprise. (That web press, brand new in '66, burned in the Enterprise fire of 1974.)

The Basin Republican-Rustler also still has an old Babcock, the same size as Greybull's. So there were three Babcocks operating at the same time in the 1920's in this area. That Babcock salesman must have been a pistol!

The first press ever in Greybull arrived in the back of Editor Ralph Woodward's wagon. He'd brought it from Meeteetse where he'd published the Wyoming Standard for a couple of years. He loaded his whole newspaper in that wagon and drove to Greybull in 1907. The section crew helped him unload it, over in the building where the Rock Shop is now, by Aldrich Lumber. Whether it is the same Babcock that's down in the basement now, we'll never know. It's old enough to be. The same vintage. But I always thought it was too big. Anyone who would know, Press Anderson, Axel Lilja, Lynn Severance, they're all gone.

The Cody press is only half the size of the Standard's Babcock, a buggy not a wagon. Two pages up instead of four. A cute little trick!

Presses in pieces. I never think of a press torn down without remembering when Thermop Editor Bill Black donated a press to the state pen. They sent an inmate from the prison print shop up to bring it back. He promptly took it all apart like a clock. It littered the back shop floor. "How are you ever going to get that all back together," Bill asked? "Mr. Black," he replied, "I got all the time in the world."

Well, this dainty little lady in Cody won't wait that long. She's "back home", cleaner than she's ever been, primped and polished, ready to show off to the world.

It's enough to make an old printer smile for days!

September 28, 1982

EVERYONE, IT SEEMS, READS the Readers Digest. So anything you quote from there, you do so at extreme risk of having been read already. But these are worth the risk: One was about the guy in the 10-kilometer race who had filled out his entry application and turned it in. Under the question "Previous Best Time", he answered: "Kay Nash, high school homecoming dance – 1972."

October 5, 1982

BITS & PIECES . . . I'M NEVER SORRY when they turn the water out of the ditch this time of year. It's the best excuse I know of for not irrigating for another six months . . . BUT GETTING READY for winter is another thing. I'm like my neighbor. Gary Good says it's sometimes spring before he gets everything ready for winter.

GOT ANOTHER CONVENTION joke . . . this one from Bil Keane, the delightful author of "The Family Circus" comic strip who lives in Phoenix. He said his neighbor, Erma Bombeck was a bad cook. "The last time her husband had a hot meal was when the candle fell over on his sandwich," he quipped!

MY DAD BELIEVED in waving.

He believed that if you were traveling down the road and saw a guy out irrigating or fencing or standing by his back door, you waved at him. Whether you knew him or not. You don't have to know someone to say hello. That was his philosophy. And a wave, that unspoken hello, was how you went down the road and how you went through life.

"That's the way we do it in Wyoming," he would say.

Once a niece asked the obvious little-girl question: Why did you wave at him, if you didn't know him? Dad looked at her very sternly and admonished her for forgetting. "This is Wyoming," he told her.

The Wyoming he first knew in 1910 as a 15-year-old boy wasn't all that much older than he was, and when he came back in the 1920's to stay for good, Wyoming already had made its impression.

Here was a place that had more cows than people, more empty space, more lonely time, fewer bonds. And when you saw someone else along the road you always waved.

What made it work so well for Dad (and all of us who tried it afterward) was that the other understood the philosophy, too. For he always waved back!

October 25, 1982

SOMEONE ASKED IF Hawaii is full of people. Of course it's full of people. But half of them wear bikinis.

ON THE HAWAIIAN STAND there was a bunch of Hawaiian Passion Fruit for sale. The sign read:
>Passion Fruit
>Men: Limit One
>Women: No Limit

November 2, 1982

It's going to be strange not reading Adrian Reynolds column in the Green River Star. It's been appearing on this editorial page for over 25 years and Adrian was still writing it in these last months before his death two weeks ago. No one else in Wyoming newspapering has written a column so long.

I have been one of its long time readers, going back to the Fifties with him and I always thought Adrian Reynolds put as much into a column as any one could. He wrote with quick thoughts and sometimes short, staccato sentences. If you knew Adrian, you know how much he liked to talk and ramble and spend hours on a subject. But his column thoughts were shortened and varied as if he knew he didn't have all that much time to tell you all he wanted to. He used the three dots (. . .) that Walter Winchell perfected and so many of us adopted, and with his three dots, Adrian could lead you along from one thing to another without stopping for breath.

He had four main themes: history, politics, water and desert. And he knew them better than most of us ever will. What fascinated me particularly was his absolute devotion to the desert or semi-arid land of Sweetwater county. He wrote of fauna and flowers, places and pictures that none of the rest of us saw. I still marvel at both his ability to see it and his ability to write it. It was home and he rejoiced in it.

Column writing for a newspaperman truly is "the best of times and the worst of times." It's the one place, the one corner which is yours to do and write as you please. Whatever else you do in the newspaper business, this is your space for your private thoughts.

But it can be your demon, too. Since you have the corner to fill, fill it you must. Once you start, no one else is going to take over. What is your strength – to have your own corner – becomes also the problem. That Adrian Reynolds' Chewin' the Fat kept going, week after week, year after year, for this quarter of a century was high newspaper accomplishment.

Adrian and I talked about his column at a press convention some 20 years ago. I was making a start at Greybull, a young newspaperman who also had a column. And I was already experiencing the "worst of times." I marveled at how consistent he was. And that he kept going. We talked of this at some length and I can remember he told me that sometimes "when things got tough" on time and deadline, he would just sit at the Linotype and set it directly, not bothering with typewriter and paper, but going directly to hot lead, one slug line at a time. Maybe you have to be a printer from the old days to appreciate that, but the message was never lost on me.

He always called his column "Fatty" in conversation and print. I could never get used to that name, a bad mental picture, I guess. But it was affection for him. And "Fatty" it always was.

Adrian Reynolds never forgot how to get news. He was forever the reporter. Not all newspapermen keep that as they go through life. We get soft and out of touch and lose the spark. But if you ever read Adrian's column, you knew he was never out of touch.

Pens won't write forever. We all know that. But many a newspaperman hopes to do like Adrian Reynolds, to go right to the very end of his career, keeping on writing and writing, sharing thoughts, filling your one part of the paper. And that's what Adrian did so well for all those years.

November 3, 1982

A MONTANA OUTFITTER says once he was taking a couple of aspirins and his hunting companion wondered what he was doing. He said he had a slight headache.

Replies his buddy: "I knowed you was goin' to have trouble with that head the first time I saw it."

November 16, 1982

SELLING IS A great game. The entire business world, from the biggest company down to the small little shop vitally depends on it. But you've got to keep at it. And you've got to care. That Reader's Digest story was very true . . . about the woman coming out of the men's store loaded with packages. She stopped by the front door where a young, well-dressed salesman stood, obviously someone of importance. "I just wanted to tell you," the woman began, "that your salesman over there (and she pointed to an older man back in the store) was extremely helpful to me. He made suggestions, he helped me with colors, made sure everything was right. It was a pleasure to have him wait on me. And I bought more because of him. I just thought you ought to know that," she finished.

"Thank you, ma'am. I'll be sure to tell him. He'll appreciate what you said." The young man sighed. "You see, he's the boss."

SLIM BREWER thinks we ought to take the old buffalo bull off the front page of the Greybull Standard and put it with the metal buffalo down by the library-museum. He thinks we'll get a better cross.

December 14, 1982

I HEAR LOUIS BIRNBAUM is in ill health out in California.

He's the legend of 1930's Big Horn Basin football when he coached Basin to its 1938 football championship and then went to Greybull the next year to coach eventual BHB champs there, too.

He's been out in California for years – he coached a Hollywood high school for a long string of seasons before he retired. With more success.

I never think of Birnbaum without thinking of a bunch of Swedes in Copenhagen. He had this short yardage pass play, designed for the goalline, which he timed with a jingle you had to say to yourself. When you'd finished saying the jingle, you were supposed to turn around and where you turned around, there was the ball!

You hear much about timing these days in the pros. The receiver goes out, the quarterback goes back, both execute and there the ball is, right where one threw it and the other turned to it. But the pros don't time it now like Birnbaum did. His play was about the same. But his jingle was different. He used help from a bunch of Swedes. On Birnbaum's teams you learned to say: "Ten thousand Swedes, laid in the weeds, in the Battle of Copenhagen." Bang. There was a ball!

"Ten thousand Swedes, laid in the weeds . . ." That's what they did in Basin. Then he went to Greybull and they learned it there. He told me even out in Hollywood, after the War, with all those free-spirited Southern Californians, he taught them the same thing. "Ten thousand Swedes . . ."

Somehow, ten thousand Swedes seems a long, long way from Monday night football.

SOME DAYS EVEN the Post Office can't win . . . At the Greybull PO a woman brought in a big package and asked to have it weighed. She needed to know because she was sending it UPS.

THAT FROSTY MORNING last week there were seven pheasants roosting high up in one tree on the road home. Five trees down the road was a bald eagle sitting in another. And still further down the road about 30 robins were congregating on the top branches of a couple of trees. Maybe it was warmer up there.

December 22, 1982

It's time to say Merry Christmas . . . that time of year when you send your special hellos and thank yous to all those who have been a part of your year and a part of your life since the last Merry Christmas.

So it's Merry Christmas to all those who grade our roads . . . who refill our coffee cups . . . and pack our mail . . . and put the flags up on main street each holiday. Merry Christmas to everyone who waves as you go by . . . who say nice things about words you write . . . who ask how the kids are doing.

And special Yuletide thanks to Lon Stadtfeld for help with water and hay during the year . . . and to Vernon Henderson for the extra help in getting me back into the mowing business . . . and to John Tarter who always takes time to stop and say hello and ask about a mutual "friend" of ours.

Merry Christmas to Gary Hartman and Lee Kunkle and the Althoff Construction Co. for the assistance with a patch of asphalt 30' by 40' at the airport just when I'd given up hope . . . and a Merry Christmas and Good Luck to the new mayor of the town, F.L. Hamilton, on this beginning of your new term.

Merry Christmas to Mr. and Mrs. Guy Wilkinson who left that place by the side of our road and moved to town. I'll miss seeing you on the way back and forth to home.

And especially Merry Christmas to those who put up outside Christmas lights this year for all the rest of us to enjoy. There seems to be more lights each year, more ingenuity, more new wrinkles and they all look nice.

Merry Christmas to all the railroaders who had to leave us during 1982 and move across the mountain . . . Nicky Markos, Doug Scotts, Terry Earleys, Steven Hansons, all now in Gillette, and the Randy Booths and Alan Bentleys in Sheridan to name a few. This old place is not the same without you.

And special greetings of the season to Red Michaelis for your good humor and good stories . . . you always brighten the day . . . and to Sam Good for all the help this fall with a bunch of youngsters . . . and to Jim and Connie Porter of Buffalo for stopping by and talking "old times."

And a Merry Christmas to the Stan Grahams, Al Doornbos, Scott Kents, Butch Denzins, the Del Edelers and Art Baughs and of course, Metz and Thelma Smith, all who let me have the right of way down the "track" in front of their houses.

And to other runners like young Bo Bergstrom, and Doug Vickerman who continues to run so very well out in California, and Dan Close, especially for the inspiration to move the 49er run to the highway, and to everyone else who puts one foot in front of another, Merry Christmas from another one who does.

Merry Christmas to Dave and Sue Flitner for the chance to meet an "old" friend for the first time. It may be my imagination, but hasn't our weather improved since he was in Wyoming!

Merry Christmas to all the cooks at the Senior Citizens Center: Betty Lipp, head cook: Judy Thorp, assistant; Mabel Jean LeDuc and Vera Good, green thumb workers; and Anna Perry, volunteer. You sure feed a bunch every day.

Merry Christmas to Bill and Pat Hayes in far-off Netherlands. It was great to see you in Big Horn county . . . hope you'll come back to Wyoming to stay when the time comes.

And Merry Christmas to Newcomers Joyce Porter, Ralf Hutt and Mary Flon who've moved to Greybull in the past couple of months . . . and a brand new Merry Christmas to Herb and Diana Kulow of the First National Bank who'll be spending their first Greybull Christmas this year.

A very special Merry Christmas to Mrs. Daphne Hartman who reminded me on GHS Graduation Day this May of another time we'd spent together . . . when she was my first grade teacher in Basin some 46 years ago.

Merry Christmas to a couple of old Greybull friends I keep running into in other places, the Earl Madsens in Billings, Wilbur Powers in Sheridan and Kent Hanson in Billings.

And Merry Christmas to a whole streetful of other people who make life a lot easier and more pleasant, Donna Dalin at the Bank, Melanie Edeler at Probst, John French at Bluejackets, Joe Castro at the Big Horn Co-op, all the crew at Coast to Coast, Brad Wright, and of course, old friend Jack Williams whose sense of humor is boundless.

Merry Christmas to Fred and Pam Jolley (we hope to share the tennis court again with you this spring) . . . and to all the Safeway bunch for all past favors . . . to Bob Hallcroft for his work with the recreation program . . . and Merry Christmas to Herman Mayland for many enjoyable hours spent together.

To all those people who live in other places and keep track of Greybull through the pages of the Greybull Standard, including the Bud Clines at Powell, Charla Barkell of Hereford, Tex., Elsie Berger in Chicago, Lester Blank in Milton Freewater, Ore., the Henry Bonds in Durango, Colo., David Carne in Pass Christian, Minn., the Paul Claviers in Casper, the J.J. Coynes in Lakewood, Colo., the Stan Davis family in Haywood, Wisc., Frank Dieners in Billings, Bernadene Horton in Brea, Calif., and Anthony DeSomber in Santee, Calif. and to 74 other Californians who subscribe to the Standard, here's a very special Merry Christmas to you across all these miles.

And to all you new people we'll meet this next year and all the little kids who grew up so much during 1982, to all those who live in this fine Wyoming community, the best of holidays and the merriest of Christmases.

1983

January 17, 1983

WE WENT for quite a while before we managed to chip the first dish in our set of "new" everyday dishes. I thought maybe we were going to set a family record with this bunch. It went for several years unblemished. But now the chip is there, as big as it can be, and the pressure's off.

One thing I've noticed about a chipped dish. Once you chip a dish, it gets more use than any of the others. Every time you sit down, it'll be the one dish on the table for sure. The logic is: If it is already chipped and something happens to it, so it's gone. It's been gone already anyway. Use the chipped one and save the others. It never goes to the bottom of the stack. It's dispensable. And always on top.

But I've discovered one other thing. Once a dish is chipped, it becomes indestructible. You not only can't chip it again, but it never breaks. Another dish will break and a cup will go. But not the chipped one. It's going to be around a long time.

SOMEONE ASKED ME a couple of weeks ago what I did for New Year's Eve. Well, I told him, I did what I do just about every New Year's Eve. I fell asleep in front of the fire and about 11 o'clock I went to bed.

"I do the same thing," he said, "except it's two or three o'clock in the morning and I'm in front of someone else's house."

February 8, 1983

THERE'S A LOT of pretty sights in this old country but few match the American flag standing out in a breeze.

WHEN FLORENCE COLEMAN found out I wanted some iris plants some years ago, she waited until she'd thinned out her fine garden and then brought over a basketful of separated bulbs. I planted them just like she said to do. And they flourished. In a dozen different beautiful colors. When it came time for my thinning, I dug them all up, separated them and put them in every bare spot I had. On impulse I counted all the individual "Coleman" iris I had growing on the place. It came to just over four hundred plants!

Florence died in Basin last week. She was 82. My memories of "Coleman," as we kids called her, go back to grade school days when she and Roy lived in the old Basin grade school basement. She would spend hours and hours of recesses playing jacks or checkers or holding jump ropes or just talking to us kids. She was a lot of fun. And now I have 400 more memories of her.

I ALWAYS LIKE TO remember the story of the time Richard Whaley and I were sitting in Doctor Roger's office. They were tearing out the wall between the old office of Attorney S.W. Davis' office and the doctor's office. It was a perfect sound proof wall, double built, offset studs and all. After we'd watched the work for a while Richard, quick-witted as always, said: "I can't figure out if that sound proof wall was for the screams in there (pointing at the lawyer's office) or in here" (the doctor's office).

February 15, 1983

I DECIDED TO GO run a couple of miles yesterday.

It was either that or go out and have a couple of beers.

That's what Saturday's paper said I could do. Either run. Or have three beers a day. The old ticker would end up with the same HDL cholesterol level either way.

So saith a couple of Baylor College of Medicine researchers. Their study showed runners don't end up with any more HDL protection against heart disease than the guy who sits down to a half-six pack of Miller's Lite every night.

WhooEEE! Won't that raise a lot of glasses.

And after all the insufferable ways joggers have been acting!

I have never heard all the beer drinkers in the world howling with glee at the same time. But it must make a thunderous roar.

HAPPINESS IS looking at the speedometer just as 9999.9 turns over.

HAPPINESS IS also digging a big spoon into a bowl of vegetables and coming up with NOT ONE cooked carrot!

February 22, 1983

CHARLOTTE ADAMY had the solution for my "cooked carrots." She says she takes out all the carrots from her soup, puts them in a blender and dumps them back into the soup. "Now that really makes great soup," she says. And NO visible signs, no big spoonfuls of cooked carrots.

BUT EVEN WITHOUT the cooked carrots, I've been out of sync lately, off feed a little, which is probably a touch of the twelve-month flu again. That's what we all have: the year-around flu. Tell me a month when either you or I or someone else we know doesn't have the flu. It's a year-round medical certainty someone will be down with it. It appears to be the only disease that laymen can accurately diagnose! But even when we're right only half of the time, I wish we could do something about the other half when it really is the flu. It would have been nice, in the Original Scheme of Things, if the flu could have been like measles and chicken pox. Have it once when you're in the fourth grade and be done with it.

March 1, 1983

FEW TV SHOWS ever have the chance to create such a natural "goodbye" as M*A*S*H was able to do. Not only was the show closing down because the actors and actresses wanted it to end (and thus no advertising pressure). But it was "goodbye" to go home. That double goodbye – where the characters got to say goodbye to each other and the audience to say goodbye to all of them may never be engineered again.

THERE ISN'T AN ex-serviceman alive who can't remember how glorious it was to finally be going home for good. It is an indescribable feeling of elation and freedom that lasts a lifetime. Which is a good thing. Because once is enough.

March 7, 1983

I KNOW SOMEONE who is spending some time in the obstetrician's office. She reports all 50 of the waiting room magazines are dog-eared and well-thumbed. Except two issues: The Life magazine with Brooke Shields in a bikini on the cover, and the Sports Illustrated swimsuit issue with Cheryl Tiegs on the cover. The patients aren't relating to those right now!

THE EVOLUTION of refrigerator language has been interesting. It took the kids growing up in the late Twenties and early Thirties a long time not to instinctively call it The Icebox. Then 10 years later it became The Frigidaire. After that, The Refrigerator said it for 30 years until someone who liked chic, quick words shortened it to just The Fridge. I can't imagine my dad calling it "The Fridge."

MEMORIES DEPARTMENT: I had several things on my list to talk to Doc Rogers about (Boy, this has been a few years back.): Two football players had been injured and a guy was in the hospital with a knife wound from a family argument. I needed to know their condition before the paper came out. So when I got Doc on the other end, I started down the list.

"How about Tom, Doc. What's his injury? Will you recommend he play?"

"He can't play."

"Well, then, what about Skip? What's his condition now. Will he suit up?"

"He can't play."

"Well, this guy, D._____ A._____, you know the one who was stabbed? How's he this week?"

There was this long pause. Then Doc said very slowly, "He can't play."

March 31, 1983

THOSE MARLBORO ADS always stop me . . . I keep looking at the scenery to see if any of it is a piece of Wyoming. Most of the time it ALL looks like Wyoming. But I wish they'd advertise something besides cigarettes.

FOUND THIS PIECE in an eastern paper which had reprinted it a couple of times. It was originally attributed to an 85-year-old Kentucky woman who entitled it, "If I Had My Life To Live Over." She writes:

"I'd like to make more mistakes next time. I'd relax. I would limber up. I would be sillier than I have been this trip. I would take fewer things seriously. I would take more chances. I would take more trips. I would climb more mountains and swim more rivers. I would eat more ice cream and less beans. I would, perhaps, have more actual troubles, but I'd have fewer imaginary ones.

"If I had my life to live over, I would start barefoot earlier in the spring and stay that way later in the fall. I would go to more dances. I would ride more merry-go-rounds. I would pick more daisies."

OF ALL THINGS that fly over us nothing will turn heads as much as a long line of geese, honking and squawking along. Going one way it means fall – going back the other, spring. It's a true call of the wild: Wherever you're going, take me with you.

April 4, 1983

WHAT DID YOU think of Richard Chamberlain's comment about his cats. He doesn't have cats anymore. Now he's got dogs. The COYOTES got his cats! Jeez. The wilds of Los Angeles. Cat-eating coyotes. Out here in good old Wyoming all the coyotes eat are sheep.

GETTING THOSE PRIORITIES straight: Went by a farm yard Friday where a bunch of kids were playing touch football . . . in the roping arena!

THE ONLY THING YOU really need for a Wyoming Easter outfit is a good, warm coat.

April 12, 1983

AT FREEPORT, ILL. the name of the school team is the "Pretzels." Years ago when the school wanted to honor the local brewery, Pretzels was the only non-alcoholic twist they could come up with . . . BUT I STILL LIKE the Belfry (Mont.) Bats.

NOTHING LIKE AN April day when you wish it were January again.

JAMES WATT SHOULD have lived in our house that one year. If he had, he would never have mistaken the Beach Boys for decadent rock culture.

The Beach Boys were our wake up call for one whole semester. You'd hear the alarm go off downstairs and then there'd be a pause, waiting for the surf to come up, and then bam! The Beach Boys tape would start. I've laid on as many California beaches at 6:30 a.m. as anyone in town!

What James Watt needed was a teenager around the place to tell him what was going on. But even with a teenager around to show the way, you have to listen. That's Watt's biggest problem. He doesn't listen. Or maybe it is that he WON'T listen. He has always seemed above dialogue, a little out of touch, with tunnel vision going in other directions than anyone else's.

But this has all been hashed over many times. Repeating it is unnecessary. You get the feeling, though, that not recognizing something as apple pie as America's Beach Boys has cut into Watt's credibility. Who would have thought the environmentalists should have been talking about the Beach Boys instead of redwood trees. Wouldn't it be ironic that something as innocuous as Beach Boys music would be Watt's unraveling.

He didn't need to have ever heard a single mellow sound from the Beach Boys to understand what they are to America. Nor is it a requirement for the Secretary of the Interior that he whistle Beach Boys tunes. But he does have to use judgment and discretion in imposing his stern will and personal prejudices over the rest of us and over that great part of America under his supervision.

Yes, our household could have helped James Watt avoid this cultural shock. It's too late now. Our house has been quiet for years in the mornings. Gone are all the California Girls and the warm sun and the sunny beaches. Everyone's grown up – even the Beach Boys themselves – grown up and gone away. And I mean it's really quiet at 6:30 a.m. at our place. But I gotta tell you, there are some mornings when I still hear the surf pounding.

April 19, 1983

SOMEONE SAID, "What's the noise at the other end of town?"
"They're having a track meet," I said.
"They can't be. This is too nice a day for a track meet in Wyoming."

WHEN GOD MADE horses, he never figured on barbed wire.

YOU CAN TELL YOU have a very good neighbor when she slows down on the dusty road as she goes by and gives her running neighbor a space of clean air. I appreciated that, neighbor.

WE WERE TALKING about New York City and 42nd street and living out here in small town Wyoming and I told them Greybull had a 42nd street, too, but it was somewhere out near Otto.

April 26, 1983

PART OF EVERY work day you have to stop and pick up all the tools and put them away, if not in their right place, at least somewhere in the vicinity of the right place. It's always precious time, postponing quitting time like it does.

If you took, though, all the time you spent putting away tools and added it up for the year, it doesn't total the time you spend looking for a tool that never got put away, that was left out when you quit and eventually "disappeared."

Bruce Kennedy's favorite photos

Bruce Kennedy used a bulky Crown Graphic press camera early in his newspaper career. He loved photography and was a leader among Wyoming publishers in using good pictures. On the following pages are some of his best photos from the Greybull Standard – most were prizewinners.

March 9, 1961
Is this the March lamb that brought in the month? Big, soft ears, lopsided face and stiff little legs — is it the official herald of spring with a fresh Easter look? Or it might be any one of hundreds of lambs that arrive in late winter in Big Horn County. This photo of Thelma Smith's lamb was the most popular of Bruce Kennedy's pictures. It was taken on the Smith lane on lower Shell Creek.

August 3, 1967
Congratulations, Grandpa! Three of Ted Anderson Sr.'s grandchildren give him a big welcome when the Greybull engineer made his last run Saturday. The royal welcomers were Nancy Anderson, Russ and Kay Dillon.

August 30, 1962
When a boy's got his writin' book and a box of colors, a pencil and, above all, a smile as big as life, you don't need many guesses to know where he's headed. And like Mike Dean Christianson, hundreds of boys and girls were making that trip on the first day of school Monday.

March 22, 1962
This is not exactly first class travel accommodations, but a runaway hog can't be choosy. The hog jumped out of a pickup last Wednesday near the town hall and the town crew caught it in Core's used car lot. The hog belonged to Amos Howe. He left it in a pickup while he ran some errands. He got back in time to help Clair Stearns, John Boyd and Jim House get the hog back into the pickup.

May 9, 1963
"Can I come up," asks First Grader Paul Johnson to Engineer Percy Beach. If you were one of those down at the station Sunday when the steam engine made its memorable appearance, you know what the answer was.

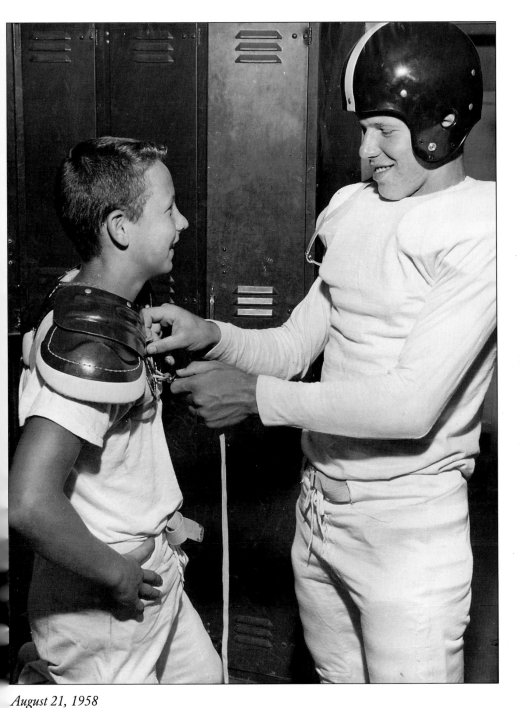

August 21, 1958
About ready for the opening of rugged football practice and the 1958 Buff season is last year's letterman, Jim Schuyler, and a newcomer this year to the Greybull squad, Punky Twomey.

June 6, 1957
Chuck Peterson was mounted on Poco, the horse atop Probst Western Store. Peterson and Johnny Caffeen were in the midst of changing Poco from a palomino to a pinto!

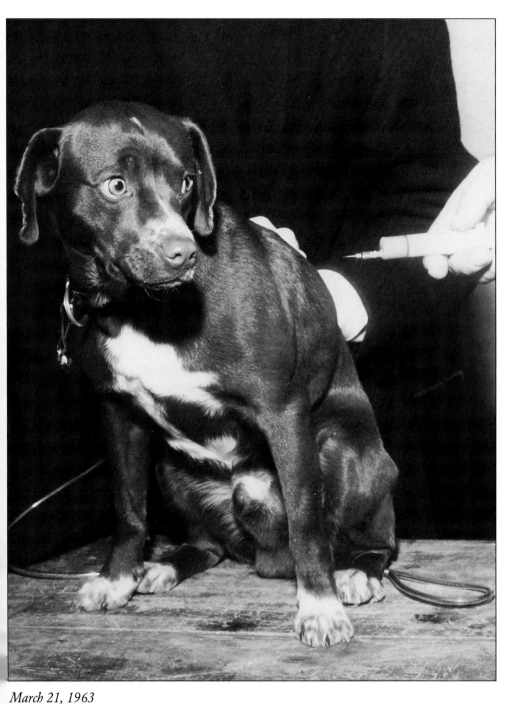

March 21, 1963
The Hank Maser's dog Coco isn't too sure about the needle Doc Lester is getting ready for him. Coco was among 33 dogs who went through the agonies of getting a shot for rabies Saturday. And the dogs, as you can tell from the look Coco is giving that lethal instrument at right, didn't like getting shots any better than humans do.

March 19, 1964

A game of marbles can draw a crowd of kids, like the bunch of smiling-faced kids who were watching Jimmy Porter try to hit Bruce Burkhart's marble out there in the foreground. Some of the others on hand were Pat Hubbard, Jay Burkhart, Billy Hunt, Jock Rech, Jerry Groseclose, Johnny Porter, Gary Groseclose and Alvin Castro.

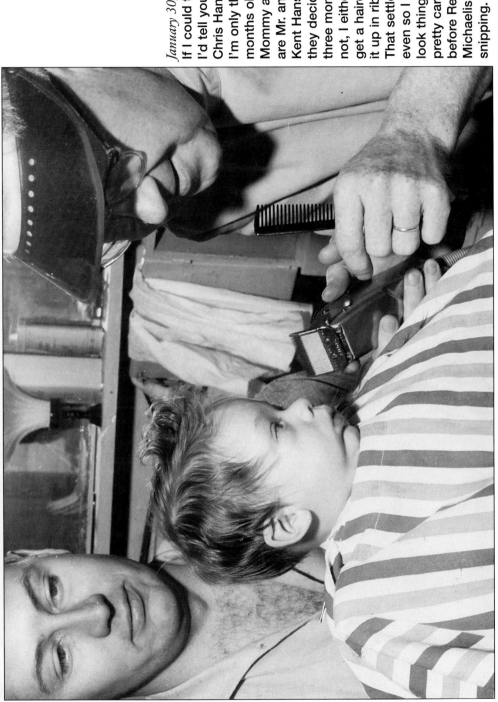

January 30, 1964
If I could talk . . . . I'd tell you that I'm Chris Hanson and I'm only three months old. My Mommy and Daddy are Mr. and Mrs. Kent Hanson and they decided that three months old or not, I either had to get a haircut or tie it up in ribbons. That settled it. But even so I wanted to look things over pretty carefully before Red Michaelis started snipping.

September 1, 1960
The first day of school is a lonely one for a dog at the Greybull Elementary School

August 31, 1961
For about half of the Greybull school kids, schooltime means bustime as well. And morning and night, for the nine-month school year, kids like the Scott Smith family watch down the road for the first sight of the bus.

July 23, 1959

Greybull's shopping district attracts them all, we suppose, even the woman shoppers among the chickens. At least Mrs. Leghorn is unperturbed about joining the many Friday morning shoppers. How the chicken made the trip to Greybull no one seems to know. But she walked the streets until Steven Hanson outran her and took her home with him.

February 17, 1966

When you're a bum lamb, you have to take your meals where you find them. This little tyke out at Bob Harvey's place on the Greybull River isn't minding a bit that there's no wool on this old cow and she says "moo" instead of "baa." When you're on the bum, a meal's a meal. The lamb was born crippled. Before it was discovered, its original mother had dried up. The Harveys were just about to make a bum lamb out of it when the lamb found old Bossy and her calf . . . and a free meal ticket.

July 13, 1961 On the way to the hospital after falling nearly 100 feet off the sheer wall of the rimrocks Thursday morning, is 12-year-old Ken Stockwell. The Greybull boy suffered bruises, a concussion and shock, but no bones were broken. The accident occurred when crawling across a ledge to Daredevil cave.

Ice jamming the Big Horn River channel from one end to the other threatened to flood Greybull Tuesday afternoon. But dynamite blasts like this one set by Morris Avery and the helicopter (upper middle of photo) shook loose the large mass of ice just before the Basin ice came floating down. The dike, a long narrow five-foot strip of dirt in the background, kept the water out until the ice could flow down. Just after this charge was set off the big chunks of ice in the middle moved out downstream farther. There they clogged again. But a final blast around 4 p.m. jarred the mass loose and it went out.

June 20, 1963 Water spills over Highway 20 south of Greybull. The W.F. Unterzuber house is in the background. Muddy, silt-laden water was pushed out of creek and river bed by four days of heavy rains.

October 21, 1965 A weakened bridge sent these CB&Q cars of sugar beets to the bottom of the gully, stacking them up one after another. The bridge across the gully gave way after the engine and two cars passed over, dumping all the rest into this mess. The train, loaded with beets for the Lovell factory, was traveling between Deaver and Cowley.

Bruce and Betty Kennedy

THINGS YOU REMEMBER on your son's birthday . . . ABOUT THE TIME when he was just a little boy and someone had told him your tongue would stick to a cold pump handle. Not having a cold pump handle he tried the next best thing: he climbed up to the freezer compartment in the refrigerator. Sure enough, it stuck! In fact, it REALLY stuck. We found him hanging on to the refrigerator insides and gurgling as loud as he could for help. For the record, water poured on a tongue and a freezer compartment parts the two. But the memory is there forever.

May 2, 1983

IN THE PAST 30 YEARS I've run into any number of businessmen who will argue the merits of newspaper advertising with me. But I have yet to find one who will let me put in a simple little 2 column by 5 inch ad for him, advertising that he will give away a $20 bill to the first 500 people showing up in his store.

NOTHING IS AS DESOLATE as the sight of papers and trash blown up against a fence. Trash laying around is one sight. But trash sticking to the sides of a fence means the wind's been blowing from a long ways off and nothing is around to stop it. It also means that if it blew there yesterday it'll probably blow there again this afternoon.

AND THIS FROM AN unknown author: "Ran into an old classmate the other day. She's aged so much that she didn't recognize me. I got to thinking about the poor thing while I was combing my hair this morning. They don't make good mirrors any more."

May 17, 1983

MY IDEA OF A FEAST is to put gravy on the table first and then anything else you want to go under it. Everything tastes good with gravy. Well, peas don't, of course. Nothing makes peas taste good. And I've never tried gravy on Jello. But gravy does wonders for most everything else for me.

Much of its culinary attraction is that it's full of cholesterol and calories and everything else sinful. Sin always tantalizes. And the sin of gravy is that it not only tastes good, but everything under it does, too. If I'm going to sin, I'd just as soon do it with gravy.

I worked for a farmer in Burlington once who said the same thing about real cream. He loved cream and it was always on the table. "I'd eat alfalfa if I could have cream on it," he would say.

Well, don't pass me the alfalfa, but I would take another helping of gravy!

OVERHEARD CONVERSATIONS: Standing behind a couple of young men looking over the road race results, and one runner said to the other: "Doesn't it just kill you when a girl goes by and you can't catch her."

Move over, young man. Your race has only begun.

May 23, 1983

OUR OLD PINTO mare is 26 years old this spring. We've had her for all but one of those springs. She was just a yearling when we traded Allen Goodwin a ton of last year's hay for her. I always figured the hay was worth about $14 at that time. The horse, in all these years, worked out considerably more than that. But gee, 26 years is a long time to be a pinto.

HOW COME THE DEER eating YOUR pasture look so much more graceful and wild and pretty than the ones eating MY pasture?

May 31, 1983

DARBY HAND AND I made a deal.

He was running a Basin pool hall with a single pool table in it. I was a young junior high kid with a passionate desire to learn to shoot pool.

I had tried teaching myself. But at the time pool was a dime a game, and a lesson however painfully self-taught, was also painfully expensive. If I played with the other kids it still cost me a dime a game. Loser paid. I didn't win many.

So Darby made this offer. He would let me use the table for free. If someone else wanted to play, I would give up the table. I could come in any time I wished. We would keep the deal for as long as it took me to learn the game. Then I would become a "paying" customer again.

That was our deal. And it went on all one summer. Just the two of us down in Darby's dingy, dark pool hall. If there were more than two lights in it, I can't remember them. A little kid who wanted to learn to play pool and a stooped old man who was letting him.

I don't think youth ever realizes how much the older generation wants to help the younger. The desire of one generation to teach all it knows to another is a strong urge. Left to our own, we eventually learn the basics, and if we are particularly adept and talented, we may even get pretty good at things.

But our parents, our teachers, older people we work for or know or neighbor with, they want to spare us the heartaches and long apprenticeships of self-teaching. They know the answers. They want us to have them without waiting. All through life there are Darby Hands to help you. And with things much more important than playing pool. Shooting pool is not one of life's prerequisites. You can truly live without ever lifting a cue off the rack.

But at the same time it was desperately important to me. If I had asked Darby how to irrigate out of the ditch, he would have been just as generous with his time and patience. Then, though, it was pool.

I have been reminded of this twice in the past five days. Once with a man whose abilities in his field have always impressed me. We are not that much different in ages, but he is light years ahead of me in what he knows. He is generously passing along this personally-collected knowledge and I am sometimes despairing of learning it all in time.

"Do you think I'll ever learn this?" I asked him last week. And it reminded me of Darby Hand and his deal with me all those years ago. It took me all summer to learn my pool lessons. I had a terrible time with it. Pool is a straight line and angle game. Everything is a true line. The cue must be straight, the eye must "see" the straight line, correct for the angle which then becomes another straight line. If you chalked lines on the table after every shot, the table would be covered with all sorts of lines and angles. But they would be all straight lines. This I couldn't understand in the beginning. Eventually Darby's deal paid off for me. I did learn how. Pool was not the monster it had been. I was close to public acceptance with my young peers again. I would not go through life shelling out dimes after every pool game I played.

On my "graduation" day, Darby and I sat down and went over the deal again. I would become a paying customer once more. No more practice for free. That was okay. It meant I'd learned. And then Darby said in his very serious way, something I've always laughed about.

"Bruce, I didn't think you'd ever learn to shoot pool."

Then this Memorial Day weekend, wandering through the Basin cemetery, I came across Darby's headstone. He's been gone for over 35 years, a part of those young years of mine. And I thought what a fine life this is that we share with each other. We never know how good it is when it's going by. Had I been able to look ahead these 40 years I would have worried less then about pool, and a whole lot more about some other things. But life has always been for right now. The best is never what was before or even what is ahead. It is right now, today.

And that summer Darby and I had some pool to shoot before other things could get done.

June 6, 1983

MEMORIAL DAY TAPS reminded me that no Army custom can stir the emotions like the playing of Taps. My most unforgettable Taps was hearing it played at the Custer Battlefield the last week of June, 1951. Seventy-five years ago that day Custer and the Seventh Cavalry had ridden the last time and the Park Service was commemorating the anniversary. Gen. Jonathan Wainwright, who had fought his own losing battle at Bataan, was the main speaker. And sharing the platform with him were several very old Indians who actually had been at the battle as youngsters. That was an incredible bridge with the past for me. Somehow Custer's Battle had always seemed back in antiquity. But that day there were those alive who had actually seen it happen.

But it was the Taps I remember the most. They played it from all four corners, the first one close by and then each successive one further away, until the last notes came rolling over those green Montana hills from a long ways off. It had been a wet June and the grass was headed out and high and in that deep quiet, the wind kept catching those long stems and that was the only sound you heard. The wind in the grass and the sound of a very far-off Taps. That day, you rode with Custer, whether you wanted to or not.

BITS & PIECES... THIS HAS BEEN one of those years when you're not as much thankful all the outside trees and plants made it through the winter as you are that they made it through the spring... SOMEONE ONCE said: "A small town is where everyone knows whose check is good and whose husband isn't."

STEPHANIE AND TOM Wamhoff found a big propeller off a boat on the north side of the highway just past Balo's (across the river from our house). It has "Kennedy" written on it. She called to tell us they had it and that Tom said they wanted the rest of the boat!

June 13, 1983

IT IS THE perversity of human nature that we watch weather for its abnormalities instead of watching it for its normal pattern.

Because weather can change so much in such a short time, we have become convinced that it is always changing, always whirling around us out of control. Actually it is working on a pretty consistent pattern, month after month, year after year. It is cold usually at the same time, hot usually at the same time. It is wet and dry, freezing first and freezing last, on a loose sort of schedule. It can be all of these at any given time or NONE of these. And because it is not always consistent, we have come to believe it is never consistent.

Last week it rained on the Days of '49 weekend, that second weekend in June celebration in Greybull. It usually does. There have been more wet 49ers than dry ones (and I mean here the collection of outside moisture!). The Greybull river flooded this weekend. It often does this time of year. This is our wet season.

I hate to travel the second or third week in March. Around the spring equinox time. Around state basketball tournament week, if you will. That's a stormy time in Wyoming.

Six months later it's the same pattern, the fall equinox and you can plan on the second or third week in September being wet or snowy or cold or all three.

The ice in the Big Horn normally goes out Mar. 10, there is usually a snowfall just before Christmas to make it white, the growing season is pretty well established, the lilacs are about gone by Memorial Day, the flowering crabs are out the two weeks before. Patterns and percentages. Chances are it will be this way. It might not be this year, but the percentages say it probably will be.

The State Agriculture Department does this now with frost figures. It has worked out all the probable fall frost dates by past patterns for all the different areas of the state. It's interesting. And consistent.

We don't remember weather like this, though. We live in today's chilliness, this afternoon's thunderstorm. Weather is perverse enough to try anything on us at any time. And as soon as some fool says there is a pattern to Wyoming weather, a good wind will come along to blow him and his logic into the next county.

THE BIG FIRM IN California was trying to send some papers back for me to sign and send on to the Wyoming Secretary of State and they told me they were sending it "by courier."

"What courier?" I asked.

"A regular courier service," he said.

"Out to Greybull?" I wondered. "Do you realize how far apart people and airplanes are here? The last couriers we had rode horses and fought off Indians. And besides we live two miles out of town."

"No, we're going to send it by courier. They guaranteed two-day delivery. But we need an address."

"Okay," I said, "officially it's 3370 Rimrock Road."

"Is that all I'll need?" he wondered.

"Put down, 3370 Rimrock Road, first house past the old Winkler place," I said. I suddenly found that hysterical and started laughing wildly into the phone. People who don't live in small towns never understand small towns.

"I don't get it," he said. "What are you saying?"

"In-house joke," I said. "Sorry. Forget it. Just send it."

So he did.

But now it's six days later and nothing's showed up yet. They probably still can't find the old Winkler place.

June 21, 1983

NOTHING LOOKS bigger than a horse in a bar. How do I know that? I saw one ridden into a bar a couple of weeks ago. It sure filled the place up. You could tell the natives. They all stayed in their seats.

June 27, 1983

THE WOMAN HAD to be a tourist. She and her husband were strolling up on the Big Horn river bridge one evening last week. She was carrying a rolled up umbrella. The only time you need an umbrella in this part of Wyoming is if your daughter gets the part of Mary Poppins.

THERE'S A SEVERAL-MILE stretch of Cody-to-Greybull highway going east that lines directly up with Cloud's Peak, all 13,165 feet of it. You couldn't find a better pointer if you tried to aim the hood ornament yourself. Someone ought to put up a sign.

IF THEY'D GIVE me another sign on that road, I'd put it on Eagle Pass going west on 14-16-20 and make everyone stop and look at that great expanse of Wyoming sky and mountains. It's a breathtaking look at Wyoming and the West. Especially in morning and evening. A great half-circle from north to south.

YOU'RE AN OLDTIMER if you still think Miller Time has something to do with these darn things flying around the house this week.

AND SPEAKING OF MILLERS, I have to tell you again about my brother-in-law who never thinks of our house without remembering the time the miller flew in his ear.

Five of us were standing in the middle of the room (it was just this time of year and the millers were out) when someone suddenly turned out the lights. Whatever the miller was doing before the lights went out, he now made a straight line dive for Glenn's ear. And disappeared completely.

Since none of us could see it, we thought he was kidding about the miller in his ear. He was indignant that we thought he was faking it. He was also in pain and discomfort which didn't contribute to his good humor. In other words he did not laugh at all our jokes about it. We wound up in the hospital emergency room where Dr. Howard Willson took out – sure enough – a full-grown miller.

"It must have felt like a B-17 in there," said Dr. Willson.

"It did," said my brother-in-law.

"We're sorry we laughed," said all the rest of us.

July 3, 1983

SHE HAS ONE OF everything she's supposed to and two of everything she's supposed to and it's all put together in the most engaging and enchanting way. A first-time grandfather should be automatically pardoned for being wildly prejudiced about a few days old little girl. Little babies can never know how much joy they bring until they, too, have little babies. You spend all week thinking about the day her mother was born, a generation ago. And then, last week, Ashley arrives and you're blessed all over again.

Right now she's just three pounds less than a 10-pound bag of flour and not much longer. And she has a crooked little finger on each hand, just like her mother and her granddad have. Her great-grandmother lay in the hospital bed trying to straighten my little finger. As if by sheer will she could. It has a curve in it, not a kink, but a curve nevertheless. What a present to give a little girl! Hopefully Ashley got some of the good with some of the bad. We're all that mix. And the little fingers will never show!

She creates another "granddad" in our family again, however timid and tentative he may be now. I expect him to be more aggressive as the years pass. After all there's ball games to play and mountain trips to make and things to talk over with this young sprite.

What will she be? The whole world is there waiting for her. What will she do in it? Run fast? Stand up first? Smile best? Will she ride a horse full out up the lane like her mother did, pony tails flying. Will she really have pony tails for awhile? And white dresses and jeans a half size too tight?

Will she study law? Or be a doctor? Or a journalist like her mother? She may even be president of the United States someday although when I mentioned this to her slightly chauvinistic brand-new "uncle", he said he wasn't certain sure whether the country was ready for that or not!

Oh, I don't know. I won't see it in my lifetime probably. But Ashley might. She will see a whole lot of things none of us are seeing now. She will do a lot none of us expect, be part of things none of us predict. That is the way of generations.

And your thoughts – once you're past the littleness of her and the 10-pound bag of flour bit and the curved finger – your thoughts go to those years ahead. You want her blessed always with the best of life. Only the sunshine and the laughing times. You want her shielded from all the heartaches, all those disappointments. No eyes clouded with tears, no teenage slights, no bruised hearts. Only happy smiles and tanned legs and dreams that always come true.

Life makes a marvelous march through generations. You give a part to each, and however diminished your contribution becomes as the generations go by, still in each, you have a say. She is a part of you, yet not you at all, but Ashley, a new person, an original spirit. The gift we gave – the gift we ourselves got – is to be someone like no one else. That is really her inheritance.

Life without her was brimming full. Amazing that the cup can hold more.

July 10, 1983

HE AND I WERE both at the same airport at the same time and the talk got around pretty quickly to airplanes.

"The sweetest one I ever had was a little Bellanco," he told me. "That was quite a while ago, but boy she was fine. Here look," he said. And he reached in for his billfold and started flipping through the card pullout.

"This is her," and sure enough he had a picture of the yellow Bellanco.

"That's me standing alongside," he pointed out. It was the same tone of voice you use when you're sharing pictures of the wife and kids ("And this is when we were in Yellowstone Park.").

We both looked at the picture for a moment.

I thought how different it was to be clucking over a wallet picture of an airplane. I've looked at my share of wives and kids and girlfriends and maybe even a horse or two. But never an airplane.

"You know, though," he said softly, "I got a chance to sit in another Bellanco the other day, and by gosh it wasn't as I remembered it."

It wasn't as I remember it. It never is. Airplanes, girlfriends, the old house, the hometown. They're all different when you go back. Life is trying to be kind when she lets us remember only the good life. She lets us spoil ourselves with nostalgia and shining memories. She never scolds for embellishments or exaggerations.

But she never intends for us to go back either. For as my pilot friend found out, "It wasn't as I remembered it."

UP ON THE CREEK they say you can tell who's been watching the Playboy Channel by the way the satellite TV dish is turned the next morning.

July 19, 1983
ONLY IN A SMALL TOWN Dept.: Rev. and Mrs. Michael McMillan have a little boy, Jacob, who likes to mail letters. So when Mrs. McMillan went to the post office with a letter the other day, she promised Jacob all the way down he could "mail" it in the letter slot. But in the rush of things she forgot and before she could think she'd dropped the letter by habit into the slot. Jacob was devastated. But in this small town, she could go to the window, ask for the letter back, give it to Jacob who dropped it back in the letter slot again. Just like he wanted to do in the first place.

DON'T KNOW WHAT made me think of this – it's hardly the season for it – but I was at a Gillette basketball tournament in 1963 (up in the old gym) and they had the usual line-up of pretty girls in formal dresses handing out the trophies. There were plenty of trophies – all three classes, A, B and C, were there. It was the usual procedure. The announcer would call out the school, the team captain would come out on the floor, the girl would step forward, the player would solemnly take the trophy. All except one lad. Before the girl could get out of reach, he had leaned over and kissed her. Which brought a big roar from the crowd and as the whistles and stomping died down, one big voice from among the players hollered out: "Get ready, you in the white!"

August 9, 1983
QUOTE OF THE WEEK: "They (two people who had jumped up on the bar and started dancing) didn't even order a drink before they jumped on the bar. I just reached over and got my baseball bat and shinned them a couple of times. You've got to educate them once in a while." – From the reminiscences of a woman bartender in Montana.

BITS & PIECES . . . I SUBMIT that getting "shinned" with a baseball bat would have instant educational success . . . DOES A BUILDING ever last longer than the circus poster plastered on it? . . . AFTER THE KIDS left home we were amazed to find all the vehicles would still run with the radio off.

I WAS SITTING outside Pahaska last week watching all the tourists when a tall, slender guy came out. He didn't have much hair left and what was there was combed straight back on the sides. But his forehead was absolutely tanned, like he'd been golfing every day forever. He was smoking a pipe and laughing with someone. And watching him standing there, tall like I said, but with a very slight bent to his shoulders, tanned, and with that pipe, I thought for a minute I was seeing Clint Core again. Gosh, I miss that guy.

August 16, 1983

DID YOU CATCH WHERE Andy Rooney, the columnist, broke two ribs when the top rung of a ladder broke under him. His wife told him he was too heavy to be standing on the top rung of a ladder at his age thereby "stabbing me twice in the same sentence," Rooney said.

August 30, 1983

THE COMPUTER AGE is upon us. And with it "old" problems and "new" problems. Consider what happened to the Hungry Horse News at Columbia Falls, Mont. Editor Brian Kennedy writes in his column:

"If you ever thought your name was just another number in this computer age, then your name can't be Mr. Old or Mr. New.

"Our computer at the Hungry Horse News made that mistake not long ago with Donald Old of Bigfork and Wendel New of Columbia Falls. Both are subscribers whose names thoroughly confused our computer.

"Our machine has been working nicely since it was installed last fall. Each week it prints about 4,000 subscriber address labels in four hours.

"But Mr. Old and Mr. New crossed its wires.

"Two of the key words in our machine's memory are 'old' and 'new' which we use to describe subscribers. 'Old' subscribers are currently on our subscription list, while 'new' subscribers are just that, new.

"Mr. Old was a new subscriber so when we typed his name into the computer, the machine presented a list of current subscribers just as it was programmed to do.

"And when we wanted to update Mr. New's current subscription, we typed his name and the computer was ready to enter a new subscription.

"We never imagined subscribers would have the same last name as our entry words. It was enough to make us laugh . . . and cry. What are the odds against something like that happening?

"After soothing the smoking computer, we solved the problem by simply adding a blank space before each name so they have four 'letters' in their names now instead of three.

"So everything is fine for the moment until we get a subscriber named Erase, or Enter, or Error, or (heaven forbid) Mr. Off."

September 6, 1983

HAPPINESS IS WINNING your first football game of the season.
Happiness, Happiness is winning your second.
But it's Happiness, Happiness, Happiness if the second is Lovell.
And Happiness, Happiness, Happiness, Happiness if it is Lovell at home!

September 12, 1983

IF WORLD WAR II seems a long ways back – and it is – consider how many years have gone by since World War I? Jim Robertson, who is 88 and who was a doughboy in that war, remarked the other day that, "Hardly anyone remembers that war anymore or us who were in it." Jim was three years old when the Spanish American War was on, served in World War I in his twenties, was 46 when Pearl Harbor was bombed, was in his fifties in the Korean War and nearly 70 when Vietnam was going on.

September 27, 1983

HAVE BEEN MEANING TO report on our own personal PIC (Pick It before the Coons) program for our sweet corn. We got there twice before the coons did. They got there twice before we did. So we each got mad twice but then we each got half, too.

THEY WERE TALKING about Frank Hinckley's hay crop at his retirement dinner Friday night and Esther Lindsey reminded everyone that when lightning struck at the Hinckleys last month starting a brush fire, Frank met the fire truck from town with: "Forget the fire. Put the water on the alfalfa."

October 4, 1983

IN NEARLY 30 YEARS of planting trees I never planted one I didn't haul dirt to. I've wheelbarrowed good topsoil, manure and peat moss from a quarter mile away just to give those new roots in this new hole a good start. So you can imagine what green thumb shock I'm in to have a Carl Whitcomb, nursery researcher at Oklahoma State University, tell me I shouldn't have done it this way. The best way, he has proved, is to use the same dirt you took out. Don't use the new, good stuff. Roots will stay in the good soil and not reach out. Planted in the same soil in which they're going to grow, trees will send roots out faster and further.

Trees, like kids, grow in spite of us!

And come to think of it, aren't kids that way, too. They can get too much too quick. They can be protected and coddled more than they should. They can be discouraged from leaving home and striking out on their own. And it's not what they need. What they need is a little push, a little shove.

A nudge from the nest is a fresh start.

November 1, 1983

I KNEW IT WAS BACK there somewhere in the tangle of choke cherries and lilac bushes. And sure enough when we cut away all the brush and dragged away all the undergrowth, there was Kiki, the cat's grave of 20 years.

I can't hardly remember that cat. The whole rest of the family can, especially the kids. My job isn't to remember the cats. I'm supposed to remember all the cows we had and the bulls' names we raised and what each one of all the horses looked like.

But I do remember that cat's funeral. That was a very solemn and sad time. It was our first real cat and she made her home with us from then on, on her terms, as cats do. And she was a mother and a grandmother, too, probably. The inevitable happened, though, and now it was time to say goodbye. The boys must have built the cross (it's still there strong as ever) and we all trooped out to the site. It was our first funeral which only deepened the sorrow in a lot of little hearts.

The little girl waited until the rest of us had turned away and were leaving. And when no one could see her, she went to the grave by herself. I looked back just as she pulled the flowers out from behind her and put them down on top of that old cat for the last, last time. Gosh, those little hearts break so many times.

When I was looking at the grave and remembering all of this, I wished again I could have done more than put my arm around her shoulder and say some trite words. You never do enough. Little kids feel so deeply. When I looked closer at that old cross I noticed hooked around it, with its leather all twisted and shriveled up, was Kiki's old collar, little bells and all, just where the kids had put it 20 years ago.

December 6, 1983

STOP ME IF you've heard this story about the pig before. But a retired executive settled in at his country estate and before long had purchased a young sow from his farmer neighbor.

Everything went along fine for several weeks until the young pig began acting restless and unhappy. He called his farmer neighbor for advice. The farmer had a prize boar named Oscar and he suggested a tete-a-tete between Oscar and the sow be arranged.

So the executive put his pig in a wheelbarrow and took her next door for a day with Oscar. This seemed to work wonders and every time the sow acted up, the executive carted her off to Oscar.

Several weeks later the executive had to make a trip to the city. When he got home two days later, he asked his wife if everything had gone all right.

"No, I don't know what's wrong with your pig," she told him. "That sow climbed in the wheelbarrow yesterday and won't get out!"

December 12, 1983

BITS & PIECES . . . IT ISN'T Christmas season anymore until the Budweiser TV commercial arrives (the one with those beautiful horses trotting through the snow) . . . Same for the Miller's High Life ad with the horse and sleigh . . . AND SPEAKING OF Christmas ads, will anyone ever top the Marlboro Christmas magazine ads.

I MAY HAVE THE Christmas spirit, but someone else, as usual, is doing all the work. And I'm not alone this season. I don't see any men mailing packages, buying Christmas wrap or making holiday cookies or decorating things up. Our house is like many others. We have two Santa Clauses in it. One does the Ho Ho Ho's . . . and the other does all the work.

December 20, 1983

It's time to say Merry Christmas . . . that time of year when you send your special hellos and thank yous to all those who have been part of your year and part of your life since the last Merry Christmas.

So it's Merry Christmas to all those who cheerfully carry our groceries to the car . . . who keep the streets cleaned up . . . and the flags flying when they're supposed to . . . who smile back and wave hello . . . who "warm up" our coffee and put out our mail . . . who remember words you write . . . and ask about the kids.

And a special Yuletide thanks to Doris Judy for a "sunflower stop" . . . to Dale Hill in Coos Bay, Ore. for a treasured letter . . . to LeRoy Kingery for some very much appreciated words . . .

Merry Christmas to Mel Christler for many past favors and for always moving things around for me out at the hangar.

Merry Christmas to the Bryants . . . it's good to see you back at the lumber yard . . . And a Merry Christmas to Rod Smith for all his good summer help . . . and to Bill Murphy and Ed Huddleston and all the rest of the school bus drivers . . .

And special greetings to Judge Gary Hartman on his appointment to the bench, although we're still not used to saying "Judge."

Merry Christmas to all those ex-Greybull area people who live in far-off places . . . the Billy Cliftons in Alaska . . . Eloise Cortez Kaneshiro in Hilo, Hawaii . . . Bill and Pat Hayes in the Netherlands.

Merry Christmas to the new retiree, that Hinckley on Horse Creek. But how do we argue now, Frank, when we both agree they're all rascals.

Special holiday cheer to a long list of people who make this life so much more fun . . . Ron Wright and Dorothy Bernard at the bank . . . Ina Collingwood . . . Helen Saban and Dick Karhu at the post office . . . Dixie Cummings at Big Horn Federal . . . Dean Douglas . . . and Paul Collingwood . . . and Butch Rimer.

Last year it was Merry Christmas to all those railroaders who left us to head over the mountain . . . how about a special Merry Christmas this year to all those who are still here! The railroad has been in Greybull a long time and many second generation names are on the old call board.

Merry Christmas to Tom Black of Basin for the laughs we had this year about the old days and Troop 34 . . . and to Mary Sackett who reminds me how much we both miss a photographer we know . . . and to Ivy Maxon who always waves when we meet on the Heights road.

Merry Christmas to coach Tim Nolan and his GHS football team for its successful season, and Lonnie Koch and his fine girls' swimming team. You all brought great credit to yourselves and to ALL of us.

Merry Christmas to Joe and Laura Little up on Shell creek, and you're right, Joe, that "Man From Snowy River" is worth seeing twice.

And a special Merry Christmas to Jerry Groseclose, Class of '73, whose enthusiasm for seeing the old high school bunch even made us oldsters feel a little younger once again.

Merry Christmas to Art Sylvester for all you've done for us now and years ago and for being such an unforgettable person.

And Merry Christmases to our neighbor down the hill, Marcel Smith . . . and to Carrie Cheatham at the Elevator who helped so much to send Christmas "out of town" . . . and Jim Ingalls of Basin for helping us out of a tough spot . . . to Barbara Miller for the "extra hands."

Merry Christmas to Lee Crawford for the fun and excitement of watching you play football and the memories of another Crawford from back in those Old Fifties.

Merry Christmas to Wayne Paris and Mike Green for coming over when something's wrong. Someday I will call and just say "hello" . . . Merry Christmas to Betty Nelson and those Western Floral holiday decorations. What a knack for bright windows at Christmas time.

And Merry Christmas to Mrs. George Haddenhorst, Leonard Leveraus and Mrs. Edythe Sherard, all in the Thermopolis Pioneer Home and Mrs. Florence Selvidge.

And to all those people who live in other places and keep track of Greybull through the pages of the Greybull Standard, including Rachel Hogue in Bryan, Tex.; Bob Jackins in Northy Weymouth, Mass.; Aaron Krueger in Danube, Minn.; Bob Lundbert in Lincoln, Nebr.; the Lewis Normans in Riverton; Mrs. Charles Ondracek in Roundup, Mont.; Joe Pavlus in Westminster, Colo.; Roy Preator in Soda Springs, Ida.; Dick Reeds in Pine Bluffs; Bill Grant in LaMirada, Calif.; Lynn Williamson in Norwalk, Calif.; and 52 other Californians who subscribe to the Standard, here's a very special Merry Christmas to you across all those miles.

And to all you new people we'll be meeting this next year and all the little kids who grew up so much during 1983, to all those who live in this fine Wyoming community, the best of holidays and the merriest of Christmases.

1984

January 3, 1984

BE IT RESOLVED:

That in this great new year ahead of us, I will not take thirds and fourths and only seconds for a little while longer . . . that I will not watch Nebraska football teams on TV anymore . . . or talk about the weather all the time . . . or yell back at the TV set . . . I will stop thinking about Howard Cosell and Ted Kennedy . . . or having dark thoughts about the Dallas Cowboys . . . that I won't retell any stories I told you in 1983 . . . and I'll cut down the number of times I'll ask you, "What's new?" . . . that I'll floss my teeth . . . and won't finish your sentences for you.

But seriously, that I will try to stop saying and writing "got" and "get" so much.

Ditto for strings of prepositional phrases.

Ditto for "there is."

Ditto for "marvelous" and "fantastic."

That I will not say the current cutesies like "bottom line" and "that's what it's all about" longer than one month.

That I will look up . . . look around . . . look longer . . . at more things . . . not wait till dark to see if the sky was blue.

And resolved to see what I'm looking at. Is it the flowers I see or the broken fence behind? Is it WHO is saying it or WHAT is he saying? Is it the IDEA I'm against or just because it's CHANGE?

And resolved that the pen will not gather another year's rust.

Be resolved that the sun can shine without being out . . . that more miles can be run . . . that more smiles and waves come back if more smiles and waves go forth.

Resolve, too, not to be agreeably mellow. Seeing all sides of every question banks the fire too much. It needs stoked up more. To say what you think, to believe in a cause, to stand up and be counted is part of life's obligation. The number of years you spend at it should not diminish the will.

Resolved, to take pictures I want to frame . . . feel a horse underneath me . . . sit for an hour and watch a mountain creek flow . . . write letters to people I don't know.

Resolved, that I replace the loss of old friends who lived here many years with the pleasures of new ones who have just arrived, that I do not live in this town without discovering who else does, too.

Above all, not to squander 1984. Not let it slip by. It is going to be a precious year, quite possibly one of momentous changes in thought and direction, and not one hour should be wasted.

January 9, 1984
I'M BEGINNING TO think this having grandchildren is just a whale of a lot of fun!

That new resident of Columbia Falls, Mont., a little Kennedy named James McKenzie, has made his appearance, slightly late by almost a month, but apparently ready to charm us to death.

He was a pokey little thing, though.

When the stork hadn't arrived yet by the time the holidays were over, his father wrote that maybe they'd better put out some cookies and milk! I wish I had thought of that one.

And, of course, when December went by, there went the 1983 deduction. And when January was less than a day old, there went the First Baby of the Year, too.

But James' timing as a newspaperman was impeccable. He arrived on Thursday, the day after his father's paper was out. I can tell you already he's got printer's ink in his blood someplace!

January 17, 1984
I HAVE NOT often resisted trying to hit a wastebasket across the room with a wadded up piece of paper.

I have not often hit either. But an engaging article in Sports Illustrated by another "thrower," Johnathan Walters, has convinced me that missing doesn't matter. No amount of misses can ever take away the thrill of hitting one great toss, a throw of unbelievable proportions and magnitude that will last you all your life.

As Author Walters says, "You want to make it and you do" and "you feel a surge of power and confidence" that can turn your whole week around.

I've only had one great toss in a lifetime of trying.

Through the years I have made some "impossible" hook shots into wastebaskets, and I've had my share of paper clips and ice cubes that went to the mark. Once down at Ed's Phillips 66, Ed Huddleston and the boys were engaged in tossing empty oil cans at a trash barrel 60 feet away. They asked me if I wanted to try. Of course I did. My first shot rattled right into the barrel. No one could believe it. Me either. So I tried again. Another one rattled into the barrel. And I tried again and another one went in! Unbelievable. Three in a row before I missed forever. No one remembers this but me. None of the boys will remember. That's what happens to throwers. Only you remember your own throw.

But all the oil cans and wadded paper and snowballs I can think of were nothing to the one back in our old kitchen.

I had been helping my mother put dinner on. She handed me a big spoon and said, "Put this in the mayonnaise jar on the table."

We were standing in the middle of the kitchen and the table was a good 15 feet away. All the rest of the table was set, plates, cups, food. The jar of mayonnaise sat right in the middle, top off. It was a temptation my teenage impulsiveness couldn't resist. I turned and without hesitation (had I hesitated, surely reason would have taken over) sent the spoon flying, like a knife thrower, end over end for the jar.

There wasn't time to see the odds against it. Only in retrospect could I appreciate the impending disaster. A heavy tablespoon on a 15-foot trajectory becomes a lethal weapon on top of a set table. The spoon was turning over and over and had to be turning just right to land in the jar. Even a close miss would be catastrophic. Spilled food. Broken plates. Glass everywhere. After all, this was not a light ball of wadded-up paper I had sent through the air.

But at the time of the toss I was supremely confident. All great throws are supremely confident. It is what makes you throw in the first place. You just feel it's right. It's that one Supreme Moment.

And mine was that spoon. It headed right for the jar, on a perfect line, tumbling over and over, and just at the right instant the spoon part turned up and then down through the top of the jar and landed plop in the soft mayonnaise.

An unbelievable shot. My mother let out her breath. For an instant that was the only sound in the room. Neither of us could believe I had hit it. Or that I had TRIED it.

But it had gone in! And I danced in the street for days.

January 31, 1984

I CONDUCTED MY annual seminar on good manners in the ski line to a bunch of kids the other day. As usual, it failed spectacularly.

You'd think by this time I would have learned to close my eyes and clench my teeth and quit embarrassing everyone around me. Instead I did all but wave my ski pole at a couple of line-crowding kids. And in the real light I looked as ill-mannered and foolish as the kids did. Maybe someday I'll grow up, too!

But I continue to worry about bad manners. It seems a national blight and every year in the ski line (or on the road or in the store or the classroom or home) it's just as bad as ever.

Bad manners are not the root of our national trouble. They may only be a symptom of deeper problems. An indifference to others, maybe. A lack of understanding and compassion. Selfishness. Surely a lack of the education you don't read from books.

You don't teach someone else's kids good manners in public. In reasonable times, I understand that. But let a youngster crowd in ahead of me or jump into my turn instead of waiting, or worst of all, play the amoeba game (one pair divides into two) and I'm suddenly an old crab.

Bad manners seem so unreasonable to me. To be reasonable and fair, I take my turn, you take yours. I have to wait; so do you. We are not talking how LITTLE time is involved between the time you step ahead of me, what 30 seconds?

We are talking about your taking that 30 seconds FROM me. It is theft, an intrusion of good nature and peace of mind; it is an unwanted crossing of our territory. I can choose to give you that 30 seconds and let you go ahead. But it is my choosing. And good manners are just that. Your choice to see the world from the other guy's side.

At present it is not the ancient "do unto others" it should be. And were we to teach more of good manners and respect for the other guy, many other lessons would be easier taught as well.

February 6, 1984

DON'T KNOW WHETHER spring is here or not, but I watched four robins ALL skinny dipping together in one of our mud puddles. Had to be just a February frolic and not an end-of-the-year bath. You get wet enough in a mud puddle, but I don't see how you can get clean.

AND WHILE WE'RE on the subject of mud in February, this is that time of year when everyone wears a stripe of mud on your pant leg, the same height up on your pant leg as the muddy bottom edge of the pickup door.

TREES THIS TIME of year always amaze me. It's time to walk around and see how they wintered and what branches must come off. Every February when I do this I marvel how much they've grown. Like kids, they're little one year and all grown up the next. One thing about trees, though. They never leave home!

February 14, 1984

WOOD SMOKE SMELLS so good . . . anytime . . . but especially on cold winter evenings. All those wood burning stoves in use now are making our towns smell like mountain camps and ski trips to happy places.

THE OLD DELANE'S Cafe is coming down. John and Leota Paris sent a lot of hamburgers out of that kitchen. They named it after their daughter, DeLane. John said he could always tell when someone was new in the Chamber of Commerce. They'd call up for memberships or ticket sales and ask for "Mr. DeLane."

A SMALL TOWN never lets you leave. No matter how many times you physically go, there's someone who never forgets you, who remembers your folks or how you played ball or how you looked when you were a kid or something funny you said. Someone always keeps track. You always "belong."

I love a small town for that. No matter how many miles away you go, you never leave.

You don't even have to be born there, just live there a time and you're part of the town's life. A town will always adopt as many sons as it raises. And it keeps doing it year after year, generation after generation. The family always keeps growing.

This is a small town anywhere. Tommy Lasorda (of Los Angeles Dodger fame) went to Italy once to see his father's home. His father had come to America as a young man and stayed. Lasorda recalls: ". . . I went over to Italy to visit my father's home in the Abruzzi region, where they were honoring me for helping them with the amateur baseball movement. There was a little parade in my father's hometown, Tollo. And there right in the middle of town, was a banner that read, in Italian, WELCOME TOM, SON OF SABATINO LASORDA . . ."

You're always a "son" or a "daughter" to someone in a small town and they never forget you.

February 21, 1984

ABOUT HALF THE country must listen to Paul Harvey's radio broadcasts.

That's what it seemed like from those who said they heard Shell creek resident Joe Little's item about the tailless cow. Harvey used it on last Wednesday's broadcast and the phones began ringing about it the same day.

Joe and Laura Little had been at the Greybull livestock auction a couple of Fridays before. A pen of heifers had gone through and one of them was born without a tail. The auction crew cut that cow out of the bunch and there she stood tailless and alone. A person behind the Littles said: "They ought to buy her wholesale and then RETAIL her."

The Littles thought Paul Harvey might like that one. So the next week they wrote it up and sent it to: "Paul Harvey, Chicago, Ill." Linda Scharen at the Shell Post Office put the Chicago general zip code on it. Just a few days later, Harvey had it on his show. (Who says the Post Office can't deliver mail.)

"The way he had it wasn't exactly the way it happened," Joe pointed out. "He had me hollering it out. But it was the guy behind me who said it."

Despite Harvey's use of poetic license to change things around a bit, the item was picked up by any listener who had ever heard of Greybull, Wyo. or Joe Little.

A Little tale of a tailless cow. Harvey couldn't resist it.

OVER 307,000 RABBITS were killed in the 1982 hunting season in Wyoming. That's astonishing enough. But think how many there'd be if we had NO SEASON at all.

IF THERE IS a Plymouth Rock Society or an Order of the Mayflower Bunch, I'm sure they will be astonished to learn that my sister has traced our roots back to three of the 100 people who rode the Mayflower to the Colonies in 1620.

She found it on our Grandmother Hart's side, whose ancestors married into the Tabers, who'd been Warrens and Cookes before that. Thirteen generations back and the hundreds and hundreds of offshoots of those old Mayflower family trees must number thousands of similar descendants.

Those prim ladies in Boston who thought they had exclusive rights won't want to hear that!

Had someone told Grandmother Hart back in the 1890's she had some Mayflower blood coursing through her veins, I'm sure she would have said, "I've got enough pilgrim right here – I don't need any more."

She was still in her late teens in eastern Montana when she agreed to marry my grandfather, a widower with two young sons. Agreed on one condition: that he would let her finish school. "I'll ride in with the boys and we'll go to school together," she said. And she did, up early in the morning to do the ranchwoman's chores, then the three of them riding off to school during the day and back home that night. And it went on until her first baby came and she never went back to finish.

Pilgrim enough, indeed. Who needs the Mayflower when you've already got Montana!

February 29, 1984

EVER SINCE THE snow has gone I've found a half-dozen things lying around I thought I'd lost forever. And now I won't have to put the pump away after all. It's still laying out there in the yard, waiting for me to take it to the garage before winter hits.

BACK TO THOSE rabbit statistics, there's more than you realize out there. Walt Preis of Emblem said he noticed quite a few killed on the road last summer going to Cody. So he kept track on the way home. From Sage Creek to the Emblem post office (about 30 miles) he counted 118 dead rabbits along the road.

March 6, 1984

IF SOMEONE IS going to run into you, it's your new car, not your old battered pickup. If something is going to happen to a horse, it will be to the best horse you have. If a vase or cup is dropped, it's the expensive one or the family heirloom, never the old ones. If you crack a plate, it's your good china, never the mismatched one you should have already thrown away. If you snag a dress or a coat, it's your favorite one. The equation is simple enough: If it's good it will break. If it's old it'll keep.

March 10, 1984

DOES YOUR FAMILY have marks on the kitchen wall so you can watch the kids grow?

We did for years. And then we covered them up with new wallpaper. A mistake, I think. I wish now we hadn't. There's some things progress and passage of time should not erase. Especially when you want to remember. We at least could have "cheated" and moved the old marks to the new paper.

I always liked those marks. It was a kick to see them take off up that wall. The beanstalk surge in the early high school years when they go from little junior high kids to adults in a couple of summers. The girl falling behind a little. The boys surging ahead. I remember being surprised how each one always looked so big the day the new mark went up. The old mark always looked so much smaller.

One month we must have made three separate marks because he was sure he was growing.

And then the time they first passed Mom's mark. And wonders of all, then they passed up the Old Man himself. A red mark day on the wall, that one.

The ritual of marking was always the best part of the game. The ruler on the head, "now duck down," the pen mark, the essential date alongside. Look at you! Look at me! "Then" and "Now." Always, how do they grow so fast.

A family's march up the wall. All of it's there, underneath this fancier wallpaper. We should have left it be . . . for the old folks' sake.

March 20, 1984

WYOMING'S REPUTATION for bad weather will linger in people's minds forever. I'm resigned to being unable to change that. I try. Every time I talk with someone who shakes his head over our "bad winters," I try. But I convince no one. They don't want to be convinced for one thing. A woman from the east coast asked me Sunday: "How long is your summer out here, one hour?" Would it have done any good if I told her yesterday was a marvelous soft March day, in the fifties, with the flickers calling and no snow left for miles? Would it have done any good to tell her how blue the sky can be, how dry the air is, about chinooks, or how bright the sun will shine for hours and hours of most every day? Would it have done any good? "You wouldn't kid me," she said when I tried. No, I wouldn't kid you, but I'll never convince you either.

March 27, 1984

THERE WERE SEVERAL times in the last 10 days when I was very glad my woman from back East didn't come around here and see my "warm, balmy" Wyoming winter.

I honestly do know better than to write about Wyoming weather.

Someone called from another state after reading last week's paper and wondered how the weather was. I knew immediately what he meant. If you're very brave (or maybe very foolish) in the newspaper business, you make predictions and positive statements about Wyoming weather. None of which the next day prove out!

If you're very smart and very safe, you leave talk about what the weather will be and should be up to Willard Scott.

THE GREYBULL VFW post received a notice from the IRS addressed to: "Vetrans o Fareign Wars." I thought you had to be older than a fifth grader before you could work for the IRS.

April 3, 1984

IN THE BEGINNING they should have pronounced it CRICK, not CREEEEK. That would have made our Western slang legitimate. Real men don't eat quiche and they don't say Creeeek. My tongue just balks at Dry Creeeek or Cow Creeeek. I'll say Shell Crick to the very last day. Somehow saying he's a Shell Creaker does not mean the same as a Shell Cricker.

ONE OF THOSE COLD DAYS last week I saw a very little boy going home from school with his coat unbuttoned. It was too cold for that. It was a warm enough coat, but there wasn't a button in a buttonhole.

Should I worry? Not me. Not any more. I've stopped worrying about little boys who walk along streets on cold days with their coats unbuttoned. For nearly 30 years I've worried about one little boy after another who didn't want to button up his coat. And for over 30 years now little boys have been growing up to be big boys without any ill effects that I can see. This community has been full of little boys who've come and gone, who've grown from little to big in spite of unbuttoned coats. And in spite of my concern. Why should I worry? There are 25-year-old men running around these streets right now with big beards and broad shoulders and at least six inches taller than I am who once spent eight weeks out of every year walking around with unbuttoned coats.

They don't need me anymore.

WERE WE TALKING about little boys? The little boy behind me had the hiccups. Now unbuttoned coats I can ignore. But not hiccups. Because I can cure your hiccups . . . any hiccups . . . in about two minutes. But when I started to turn around I caught The Look from Betty. "DON'T" The Look has said for three decades. So I didn't. Too bad. I could have stopped those little boy hiccups.

My family has learned never to have the hiccups in my presence. Or I go into a paroxysm of efficiency and intrusions that drives everyone wild. But it works. It's simply just swallowing several times without taking any other air in. You can drink small repeated sips of water or you can try to swallow several times without water, it's the same principle. You don't need a sack or to put your head between your knees. But you can't take in any more air while you're swallowing and you can't take any deep breaths afterwards. Breathing carefully after the hiccups stop is a big part of the trick. If you don't you'll trigger them all over again.

You think I'm kidding you. Hey, I wouldn't kid you. Ask my harassed family. I learned it way back in the summer of '49, working for the highway department on the Shell canyon road. I had a classic case of repeating hiccups and I tried every remedy offered. The simplest one really did work. Now I've given up saving the world from unbuttoned coats. But I still hold hope for saving it from hiccups.

April 17, 1984

TOM GOTON had it right when he said you need two guys burning ditches on a windy day, one to do the burning and one ready to call the fire department.

THAT DEAD CAT had been out on Highway 14 a couple of miles east of Greybull for several weeks. Right in the middle of the road. The highway striping crew came through and . . . you guessed it. Went right over the cat!

April 24, 1984

AMAZING TO WATCH a newborn colt struggle up on all fours so soon after birth. I'm glad he can't watch me struggle out of bed each morning trying to land on all twos.

THE CHECK FOR MY income tax last week was numbered 1040 but I'm sure the irony will be lost on the IRS. This is the time of year they don't want any of us to smile.

May 1, 1984

YOU'RE AN OLDTIMER in Greybull if you remember the Daylight Saving Time weekend when Father McBride told his parishes in Greybull and Basin to be sure to "come an hour later" next Sunday. He never mentioned setting the clocks ahead, just kept repeating to "come an hour later." So that next Sunday morning, sure enough everyone came an hour later. Except that everyone set their clocks ahead and THEN came an hour later. Father McBride just set his clock ahead. When he went to church at Greybull no one was there. So he went to Basin. No one was there either. But an hour later, with all the clocks set ahead and another hour tacked on, wouldn't you know, everyone showed up.

May 8, 1984

I ONLY SAW FOUR other runners I knew in the race Sunday.

Our Brian and Carol, Clint Preston and Clint's friend, Jim, from Seattle.

The rest of the 30,446 people in Spokane's Bloomsday Race were friendly enough and happy enough and had common bond enough to all be friends. But unless they wear their green Bloomsday '84 T-shirts, I'll never recognize them again.

If you asked all the people in the Big Horn Basin to gather in one place Sunday morning and then run down the road, all together, for 7 1/2 miles, you have some idea of what it was like to run in the Spokane race.

I'm used to races in slightly smaller proportions. To put 30,450 people in one place all with the intent of running in the same direction for 7 1/2 miles boggles the imagination. It boggled reality, too. For miles it was a steady highway-full of bobbing heads. At the start it was just a shuffle, even a walk at times. I didn't think it would ever stream out. But eventually, when the hills were there and the five-mile sign had been passed, the crowd thinned a little and you could find some room.

It was not a run as much as an experience. If you would have tried for time and pushed and jostled your way to your expected speed, I think the crowd would have cheerfully clubbed you to death. All the elite runners, the invited notables, had a special front place start so they could run a race. But the rest of us just went with the crowd.

What a crowd. Miles of it, snaking around the countryside. I looked down the road when it dipped once at all the people ahead of me and just laughed out loud. The guy next to me said, "But look over there, too." And on the next hill, a mile or so away, the same long snake of people.

They'd started the race on three different parallel streets. Eventually these melded into one highway that circled out from Spokane and then came back again. They'd color-coded your expected finish time so the faster runners went ahead and the slower (even many walkers) could be in the rear.

But it didn't matter. For the first miles you just went along with the pack, hoped you didn't fall or drop your glasses or lose a shoe. The horde would have marked your back with a thousand Nike treadmarks if you'd ever laid flat.

In last year's race a girl stumbled and fell into the guy ahead of her. In her frantic, clutching efforts to stay upright, she grabbed at the guy, got his shorts, continued on falling and pulled those shorts right to the guy's ankles. I ran for a mile and a half with one hand holding on to my shorts. But the danger passed.

It was an amazingly well-run race. There had to be thousands of city volunteers. The National Guard was out, our cab driver said he was helping at a first aid station, people checking times, registering runners, handing out T-shirts, even giving post-race massages. Even the Spokane newspaper prints EVERY single name and time of the finishers.

At two hours and a half people were still crossing the finish line.

One man stood out in front of his house clapping and saying, "You're all winners." As I went by I wondered if he was going to say that for all 30,000!

Miller's Lite handed out white painter-type hats, an instant advertising gimmick, and for a time half the heads were white-hatted. Someone in a Cola can ran, and another guy had a big model boat on his head. One group of five ran in abbreviated tuxes and there was a squad of Marines running in cadence, with flag and all. But the rest looked like runners any place, except that there were so gosh-awful many of them.

They started the race by an aerial bomb from a helicopter. I thought that a nice gigantic touch for such a gigantic race. Crowd psychology is astonishing, either in it or out of it. The excitement is catching, the reaction really contagious. Up on the building at our starting point was a bank digital clock. The crowd could hardly contain itself as 8:56-8:57-8:58 counted down. When it reached 8:59 everything was just a roar. And then that big reverberating boom from above. We were off at a walk!

But miles down the road, bobbing heads stretched out in front of you, the highway still full, even some on the sidewalks, you had a taste of the size of it all, the fun of it all and the wonder that you could put that many people in one place and pull it off.

The paper Monday said 30,450 people had finished the race. I was number 6,728.

May 22, 1984

THIS WEEK I'M looking at all this spring work still to do, all the things still to put in the ground, all the hours that aren't there. Remind me next winter when the seed catalogs come to staple each one shut immediately upon arrival.

MOST OF US who think we're overworked should go shoe a couple of horses.

I REALLY DON'T know quite how to take this, but the nurse after my medical exam said, "You're in pretty good shape for the shape you're in!"

May 29, 1984

IF IT HADN'T BEEN for some struggling lilacs around our house we'd had precious few flowers to take to the Basin cemetery this Memorial Day.

We counted up and found that in 27 consecutive years of picking Memorial Day flowers this was the first year we didn't have enough of our own. Too late, too cold, too dry for all but lilacs, which bless them, carried the day. Other "neighbors" at the cemetery had similar luck. Many yards were apparently like ours this year.

Always marvel at how pretty and green that old hometown cemetery has become. It's been lush green and full of trees for so many years now it's hard to remember when it was once a gravel hill with a cemetery perched on it. No trees, no grass, just a dry old Wyoming hill straight out of "Shane." Now, you'd never recognize it.

People really do care about the past and those we miss. It shows every Memorial Day. And for those who take care of cemeteries, it's a year-around Memorial Day.

Can't help but walk around and remember. One thing about it, the town I knew as a boy has moved up on that hill.

June 12, 1984

CODY ENTERPRISE editor Carl Bechtold, who ran in the nine-mile 49er run in Greybull Saturday, came over to the house for a bite to eat afterward.

When we'd finished and Carl had pushed his chair away from the table, he deadpanned: "Well, I hate to run and eat, but . . ."

THE AMERICAN OBSERVANCE of 40 years since D-Day was history itself. I thought it an exceptional several days. Particularly fascinating was watching the replay of the 20-year-old interview with Walter Cronkite and Dwight Eisenhower, retracing the invasion through Ike's memories. I had the same thought afterwards I've had many times: America was very fortunate to have produced a Dwight Eisenhower when it did.

June 22, 1984
TRIED SHOOTING a gun with my trifocals for the first time the other morning. Rest easy all you things that move. You're in NO danger from me.

I'm blaming the same trifocals for either raising up too quick or not ducking soon enough . . . can't figure out which . . . but the 2x6 rafter took a big divot out of the top of my head, right where there isn't any grass to lose.

SHELL CREEK IS as high as many can remember. If you can't drive up to see it, you can tell by just holding a glass of Greybull water to the light.

June 26, 1984
THAT OLD PICTURE Rev. Floyd Ellison has of some of the Basin Troop 34 Boy Scouts at the old Greybull swimming pool brings back memories. I was running through the names and faces and came to Fishy Trout. "There's Fishy Trout," I said. Wait a minute. Fishy Trout? How could anyone be named "Fishy." So I called up Bill Cowan. I knew he'd remember. Sure enough, there was a "Fishy" Trout in our youth. His name was John Trout, Bill remembers, and his dad ran the Standard station across from the courthouse. We kids slapped "Fishy" on him as soon as he hit town. He left before high school days and he's somewhere out there in the world, probably hoping no one remembers he was once called "Fishy."

It was strictly reflex recognition for me. If I'd stopped and thought about it for a minute, I couldn't have told you who he was.

TRIED TO WRITE that last paragraph and keep the "olds" to a minimum. That's hard. The old Boy Scout Troop 34. The old swimming pool. The old Standard station. Somehow I can keep remembering the "old" and can't remember the "new."

"OLD" IS A FUNNY word. We use it affectionately more than we realize. I've often wondered where that constant phrase "old boy" ever came from. It goes back a ways. And remember that classic Cary Grant story when someone wired him about his age? "How old Cary Grant," read the telegram. Grant, who never liked to tell his age anyway, wired back, "Fine, how old you?"

TRIVIAL PURSUIT is a game which tests your knowledge against someone else's knowledge on a variety of subjects. It's a game of advancing around the board on a combination of dice rolls and answered questions until you have scored the most and win.

The key is if you can answer the questions, some of which are extremely easy (those being the ones the other side draws) and the ones which are extremely hard which, of course are the ones you draw. The questions are on a grouping of subjects: sports & leisure, science & nature, history, entertainment, geography, and art & literature.

Our family, who all came home this past weekend, came up with the great idea to chuck the patented questions for one night and add our own family history and thus we played Kennedy Family Trivial Pursuit for one hilarious evening.

Everyone contributed questions which the Keeper of Everything Else gathered together on 3x5 cards. I didn't think there were that many questions to ask. But the card pile was a handful and more than a laugh-full. We went through all the cars we ever had, all the horses' names, all the dogs and dogs' litters, a whole crazy bunch of memories of high school days, grade school parties, sports, family milestones.

But there was family history, too. "When did your granddad first come to Wyoming?" (1910.) "Where is your other granddad buried?" (McCool Junction, Nebr.) "What is the significance of Jan. 5?" (A wedding, a recent birth and two other birthdays.)

Some tricky ones, too. "What doctor did the family ski with?" (Dr. Patricia Shelledy Lye who just graduated from medical school.) "Who chalked up the most rebounds?" (Not either of the boys, but Ann, who "chalked" up ALL the rebounds as manager/statistician one year.)

"How many of the same teachers did all three kids have?" (The answer was written down as five, but the kids came up with another half-dozen.) Many names from those days. Elvin Saul. Dan Martin, the bus driver. Old Tick. I seemed to hear Jerry Groseclose's name a lot!

I didn't remember I remembered so much. But on the other hand, maybe I should say I'd forgotten how much I've forgotten!

But the years come back to be forever fixed again and in a game that was supposed to have winners and losers, this was one that had only winners.

July 2, 1984

SEE BY LAST WEEK'S Greybull Standard (in the "Old Days Headlines") that I "won" the prize for growing the worst beard during the town's 50th anniversary celebration 25 years ago. That's a true story. It was the worst! Even after 25 years I can remember how awful it was. Someone told me at the time it looked like it had been hailed out. Really a scraggly-looking thing . . . so bad it apparently rated headlines twice.

That's a small town for you. Only in a small town can you be embarrassed for the same thing twice in 25 years.

July 9, 1984

I WAS ONLY IN the third grade the summer I visited the old family ranch in Montana. Every morning when you woke up the doves in the cottonwood trees along the Powder River would be calling to each other. It sounded like the whole river bottom was full of doves. I was many years an adult before I discovered they were called Mourning Doves, not Morning Doves. But to me, it still should be the other way around. They were early morning sounds, happy, not sad, of a Montana summer.

July 17, 1984

A TOURIST IN THE Park from southern California told us he and his wife have been coming to Yellowstone Lake "every year since 1952."

"We missed last year and took a cruise," he said. "Didn't like it. Wished we were here. So we're back again."

Thirty-one summers on the lake. Not many northern Wyoming people have been to the lake that many times in their lives.

THAT'S REALLY ONE of the problems living in Wyoming. You live your life in southern California dreaming about a mountain lake so that's where you go for your vacation, year after year. You live in Wyoming and have a dozen mountain lakes within your reach, a hundred trails to cross, creeks to fish, mountain flowers to see, aspens to turn, elk to chase. To pick out Yellowstone Lake for two weeks for 31 years is to slight hundreds of other places all within a half day's drive.

I WAS IN THE BIG HORNS the same weekend the five Michaelis boys – Red, Jim, Dick, Bill and Mike – had their reunion at Arrowhead lodge. Forty-two Michaelis' showed up, between kids and spouses and brothers. It was quiet where I was, but then I was 20 miles away!

July 24, 1984

I'VE BEEN THE last guy on the ditch for 28 years now. One thing about it, when you're the last guy on the ditch, you can never be accused of stealing water.

THE FARTHER NORTH you go the longer it takes the sun to set. So if you're nervous about these days of less and less sunshine, you could always keep moving north . . . the only problem being that eventually you'd have sunlight at midnight but you'd be looking at it out of an igloo window.

THE YOUNG GIRL went to the jukebox and said, "I'm taking requests."
"Oh, anything you play is okay," we said.
The first selection came on while she was still punching away. It was Bobby Darin's great old classic, "Mack, the Knife." Oh, the feet just start tapping to

that one.

I felt really good about that. That song goes back a few years. She was perceptive in knowing "the beat" would reach us.

"That was just perfect," we said.

The girl looked a little embarrassed. "Oh, that was a mistake," she said. "I punched the wrong button."

July 31, 1984

WALLY MAYLAND SAID he saw my comment about being the last guy on the ditch and never being accused of stealing water. Wally says on Bear Creek "you can be the first guy on the ditch and never be accused of stealing water!"

EARLY THE OTHER MORNING when the fire whistle went off, it started a couple of coyotes over in the foothills howling. I don't know what that says about civilization. Either the coyotes are moving in too close or the fire whistle has suddenly been turned up louder.

August 21, 1984

NED KOST, JR. of Basin says he waits until his weeds are three feet high before he chops them. He thinks they suffer more that way.

IF YOU'VE EVER doubted that Greybull wasn't built on a sandbar, walk downtown and look at the middle of what was once the street . . . It's pure sand.

September 4, 1984

THERE SURE ARE a lot of good cooks living around the Greybull tennis courts . . . or am I only playing around dinnertime?

SPEAKING OF COOKING smells, I've lived long enough to know that bacon frying has to be the best smell that ever comes out of a kitchen. Bread baking is a second, but nothing tops the smell of frying bacon.

FOR YEARS NOW . . . after learning it the hard way . . . we've had a tacit agreement with the coons.

We'd plant twice as much sweet corn as we could ever eat. The Kennedys could have half. And the coons could have half. That way, we'd both get corn. In other words, enough corn to go around. We tried to be selfish for years and just plant what we could eat. The coons didn't understand this arrangement and thought we'd planted it for them. So they took it all. Now, though, with half for them and half for us, there's usually been enough to go around.

You gotta be quick, though. Coons can't count. They remind me of some businessmen I've known. They take their half first. Sometimes they try to take our half, too. If we're still smiling, they try a cantaloupe or two. They like the bottom line and the bottom line to them is when the last ear of corn is gone.

So going halvers has worked after a sort. We had some outrage and some clenched teeth but we did have some corn. But this year we got smart. Several people said an electric fence makes good businessmen out of bad coons. So after the first coon visit this summer, we put one up. It worked! The raids stopped. And the corn kept producing. This was the first year we had our half and the coon's half, too. We had corn every night. In fact, we never had so much corn. In fact, I'm sick to death of sweet corn. We froze it, ate it, froze some more and ate some more. Talk about greedy businessmen.

When we were down to the last two dozen ears, we quit. Let the coons have the rest, we said, and switched off the electric fence. Sure enough, two days later the coons came back and took what was left.

Bon appetite, fellows.

September 11, 1984

FLOATED THE RIVER the other day. That was on our summer list. A lazy afternoon in a canoe, seeing how many bends the Big Horn makes between Basin and Greybull.

Amazing how still the river is. With noise all around it, the river remains whisper quiet. No white water in this stream, just a slow-moving old girl who doesn't say much.

A lot to see along the way, surprisingly, but what caught my eye was the rope hanging from the old cottonwood growing along the bank. Someone had shinnied up and tied the rope over one high limb so the rope dangled out over the water a couple of feet from the bank. By crawling up the bank they could swing out Tarzan style clear out into the river before they let go. Gee, that looked like it could be fun. No one was around when we floated past, but the bank was worn with tracks of a thousand little feet. It was a hallowed spot, no doubt about that.

FRANK HINCKLEY, as a candidate for the state senate, had to make a little speech at the Democratic Rally the other night. Afterward, Red Michaelis came up and told him: "Frank, I enjoyed that speech the second time just as much as I did the first time I heard it in the barber shop."

WHY DO THE YOUNG see things so much more clearly than the old? Everything is black and white, no grays at all. There's only one side and one solution. Only one passion and one ideal. And there's no time. It has to be saved right now or it will be catastrophe right now. God bless them. The world could not do without them. There's plenty of us old guys and gals around to look at eight sides of every question, to worry about consequences and ramifications, to weigh feelings and bruised egos in equal parts to political faiths and cherished opinions.

But never enough youth, never enough strong voices, never enough raised banners.

September 18, 1984

I LIKED JOHN MADDEN'S comment about Chicago Bear Walter Payton . . . "Someone said that when Walter went through the assembly line, he got all the top parts . . . the best engine, the best wheels, the best air conditioner, the best of everything."

Now you know what happened to you and me . . . Some of our parts aren't so hot!

THIS IS APPARENTLY the time of year that broken bones and horses go together. In the past six weeks in our little town, all in horse-related accidents, Jolene Whaley broke her pelvis, Mary Flitner broke her arm, D'Arcy Hart broke a leg, Tom VanGelder broke his ankle, and Mike Hinckley's brother, Tom Tisdale of Kaycee, broke several ribs on their pack trip into Lake Solitude.

September 25, 1984

WAKING UP SUNDAY MORNING to over a foot of snow in the yard, the first thing I heard was a robin singing. I assume he was singing, but then I don't know robin cusswords. I assume the first thing he heard was my "singing." But then he doesn't know people cusswords.

October 3, 1984

A COUPLE OF OLD cabins were built in the Big Horns along the old mail route from Hyattville to Sheridan in the early days. One of them was built where Mail creek flows into Shell creek a couple of miles above the Shell Ranger station. It's been gone for years now. But Clair Stearns says he can remember it. In fact, he said he took a picture of it. Or rather he took a picture of a porcupine climbing up it.

"I was more interested in the porcupine than I was the cabin, though," Clair says. So he got a little of the cabin and a lot of the porcupine, he says. "I had a camera right there, but I didn't get the cabin."

That's the way of life. The present never sees much of the future. What's happening now is infinitely more important than what will be going on 60 years later. A porcupine climbing up a cabin wall is an event. The cabin won't be noteworthy for 30 or 40 or 60 years yet.

THIS HAS BEEN A strange year. One thing that happened was the magpies discovering they like the dog's Purina Hi-Pro. It sits outside by the side door in a little white bucket, sort of a dog self-feeder. You know, fill the bucket and let her eat when she wants. We've been doing this for years. This is the first time the magpies found out about it. Now they line up for their share. Day or night, it doesn't matter. The dog's a nervous wreck fighting off the scoundrels.

But they really like the stuff. I think we may be feeding the entire northern Wyoming magpie population. If you have a magpie on your place that barks and wags its tail, you'll know where it's been.

October 8, 1984

ONE THING ABOUT a pole fence, you can lean over it, lean back on it, straddle it, vault over it, sit on it, none of which works very well with barbed wire.

IF YOU ARE SHIVERING just a little these cool fall mornings, don't complain. When Don Presgrove of Greybull got off the Navy plane at Antarctica (where he'll be for six months on a civilian job) it was ninety-five BELOW!

November 6, 1984

THE GOOD LORD knew what He was doing when He let us go through only one set of teenagers in a lifetime.

SOMEONE ASKED ME the other day who was Greybull's first streaker. Well, I know who should be called officially the "first one" but I ain't a-gonna tell ya her name. Unofficially there was one 25 years ago who streaked all the way from south of the depot to the main street on a busy Tuesday night.

But I never got that one's name!

He was a bum traveling through and his companions had rolled him down on the tracks someplace, took everything he had, including all his clothes, and turned him loose. He took off for the lights of town and came hollering and hallucinating right down the sidewalk that summer night. It was a warm Tuesday and tourists were walking the streets and several places were open. And here was this bum suddenly right in the middle of all of us playing like a streaker.

Only one person in that whole crowd of us showed any presence of mind. As the bum came hollering and stumbling down the sidewalk, this guy ran over, grabbed the bum by the arm, hustling him over to Charlie Shirran's pool hall, opened the door and before you could holler "Don't look, Ethel," the "streaker" was inside that all-male bastion and out of sight.

The first unofficial Greybull streak was over.

November 20, 1984

DALE HILL OF Coos Bay, Ore. supplied the name of the guy who herded that old Greybull streaker into the pool hall in the 1960's. It was Charlie Smith who had the presence to haze the bum out of sight. Dale writes that he had come out of a Shell canal board meeting with Smith and they were just coming up to the cafe. "All of us except Charles Smith were so surprised that we just gawked at him. Smith grabbed him and hustled him into the pool hall where someone found a coat to cover him with."

Dale continues: "Charles Smith was farming the place I always referred to as the Braden place. He was from Montana. Others in the group were Lyle Halstead, Truman Durfey, Bob Chapman and maybe Don Gould."

"And that's The Rest Of The Story."

November 27, 1984
THOSE OLDTIMER STORIES that Wyoming didn't have nearly as much sagebrush as there is now have some truth. Naturalists who claim to have studied it say the sagebrush was all over the state in the old days but not nearly so dense as it is now. It didn't expand so much as it did grow thicker . . . or so say the scientists.

BUT THICK OR THIN, sagebrush is still unmistakably the smell of the West. Once, when I was pining away my freshman year at Nebraska, my mother sent me a couple of sagebrush candles. (I think she got them at Frannie – someone was making them there in those days.) And that was literally packaging Wyoming for a lonely kid. Just to open the box was enough. You could smell Wyoming clear down the hall.

OFTEN THOUGHT OF those sagebrush candles and a mother who would know what her son missed. No one ever tells us how to be good parents. We are into it before we really know what to do. And we're out of it before we learn all the lessons. So no one ever "teaches" it. My mother's gift was to know how someone else felt. Not necessarily the way SHE felt but the way HE felt. She knew I missed her and home and friends and town, but she also knew I missed the sky and the mountains and all of what is loosely called "the West." So she sent a piece of it in a sagebrush candle and every time I opened the box I was "home" again.

December 4, 1984
WE SENT A BRIGHT red wagon off to someone special the other day. And we didn't bother to wrap it up. She's not old enough to read, of course, and not quite quick enough yet to see the picture on the outside.

But the UPS man didn't know all this and when he came to the door with it, he didn't want to be giving away Santa secrets.

So he knocked on the door and when the Lady of the House answered, he said in a soft whisper, "I have a red wagon for someone here." That's known as UPS Santa Service. No extra charge. Gratefully appreciated.

BITS & PIECES . . . SEE MANY CHRISTMAS lights up around town. The reason ours are always late is that I keep waiting for the coldest, bitterest day to put them up . . . DID ANYONE ELSE order lily bulbs which were then back-ordered and didn't arrive until late November? It isn't every year you plant lilies Nov. 29 with an ice pick.

YOU'D THINK IF you moved on to a place, it would be your "place." But usually it isn't. It's the place of the people who lived on it before you did.

If you're Brown and you move on to Smith's place, you are not living on Brown's place but on "the old Smith place." It won't be the Brown place until you move off it. Then it becomes "the old Brown place."

But you have to stay awhile to have a "place" in your name. You don't get any distinction if you move off too soon. Many people can live on "the old Garnett place," but for years, through all sorts of tenants and short-term owners, it is still "the old Garnett place."

You can also have a "place" if you're the first one on it. If you're an oldtimer, you tend to remember it from the first one on it. So it's "the old Braden place" to you. The trouble with this, of course, is you have to be talking to oldtimers all the time because only the oldtimers remember the oldtimers. Everyone else is up to the present, say the last 40 years, and now know it as someone else's place.

A "place," of course, has ground around it, not street lights. You can have a place in town, but it's not really a "place." A place is in the country. And it's not your "place" while you're on it, only when you leave it. It's one last gasp of ownership really. You may sell the land, but your neighbors will still keep your name on it for years afterward.

December 18, 1984

It's time to say Merry Christmas . . . that time of year when you send your special hellos and thank yous to all those who have been part of your year and part of your life since the last Merry Christmas.

So it's Merry Christmas to all those who put up flags to fly . . . who "warm up" our coffee and put out our mail . . . who smile back from the teller windows and check out stands . . . who remember words you write . . . and ask about the kids.

And a special Yuletide thanks to several who wrote very nice letters during the year . . . Tim Cummings in Hamilton, Mont. . . . Mary Lee Haddenhorst in Littleton, Colo. . . . George and Dailiah (Basinger) Smith in Pleasanton, Kans.

Merry Christmas to Bill Peters for the help with a Christmas present that really can ring in the new year.

Merry Christmas to Herman Mayland for a good ride together up to the Pitchfork Ranch horse sale this fall . . . and for helping me sit on my pocketbook.

Merry Christmas to Earl Reilly for our talks at the Post Office and for all the "right" mail you keep sending on to me . . . Now it's my wastebasket that looks full and not yours!

Holiday Greetings to Mark Bentley and the rest of the Town Council for those fine new tennis courts . . . what a joy they are . . . and a big Greybull welcome and Merry Christmas to all those new Burlington Northern employees who moved here and helped "bring back" the railroad.

Merry Christmas to "Supt." Dean Douglas . . . that turned out to be a great street you supervised . . . We may be "hiring you back" to tell the boys how to put down some of those first block main street sidewalks that are frost heaving.

Special Holiday Cheer to my old coffee partner, Jack Williams (will you ever run out of stories and memories of old Greybull?) . . . Amos Small for your always cheerful hello . . . Walt Preis for several good letters and good thoughts during the year . . . Mildred Warfel for your kind comments . . . and the neighbors down the road, the Al Doornbos, or should I say down the "graveled" road, Al . . . to Doug Miller for making that old garage disappear . . . to John Hesco for always helping out the weekend carpenter . . . to Linda Presgrove for putting up with my forgetfulness.

And to all you snowbirds who are southbound this time of year . . . every time we think of you down there in the sun, it seems to get 10 degrees colder up here.

Merry Christmas to Bob Wallin and the rest of the airport board for the new lighted windsock at the airport. Even MY trifocals can pick that one up.

And Clair Stearns, Merry Christmas this 1984 and a New Year's resolution for 1985: We'll take those trips to the mountain together we kept talking about in '84.

And a Happy Yuletide to the 1984-85 boys freshman basketball team for already lighting up the scoreboard so . . . and maybe lighting up future GHS basketball as well.

Merry Christmas to Charleen Collingwood and good luck on your recovery and your return to main street.

And special Holiday Greetings and special thanks for favors this past year for Steve Olson . . . and Rick and Ken Bryant . . . Liz Patterson . . . Roland Smith . . . and Willie Stout . . . and Greg Stockwell . . . thanks for the helping hands.

Merry Christmas to Lois Johnson of Basin . . . the next election night, we watch together I promise not to stew around so! . . . And to Tom Clucas who stopped by from Missoula for a good visit this summer . . . And to Art and Rose Brown of Basin for remembering things we wrote . . . And Merry Christmas to Harold Lockard in Casper . . . we miss our daily meetings at the Post Office, Harold.

And I wish we could light up this Merry Christmas to the Dolan Scharens of Shell as brightly as they have lit up Shell town with their many Christmas lights . . . They say the kids of the area are enthralled with that marvelous "gingerbread house" . . . and so are the old folks.

And a very special Merry Christmas to Mike Hinckley who walked, drove, and rode the campaign trail this fall . . . and now you have coming up (just as Doc Rogers said you would) those 40 days and 40 nights away from the old guy.

And Merry Christmas to all those of the Campaign of '84 who worked so hard and did so much . . . Esther Lindsey, Gary Good and many, many others . . . and to those who put down their voting thoughts and feelings in black type: Derb Linse, Bruce Bergstrom, Lorna Patterson, George Michaels, Jim Whaley, Bob Wallin, Mary Raffl, Red Michaelis, Otto Gernant, Dr. A.S. Rogers, Bob Nielsen, Bill Shelledy, Mary Flitner, Eleanor O'Neill, Hector Good, Marvin Hankins, Ron Wright, Jim Core and Bill Murdoch.

And a very, very special Merry Christmas to The Senator himself . . . Good luck on your trip to Cheyenne next month, Frank . . . You have the confidence and support of a large chunk of this county.

And to all those people who live in other places and keep track of Greybull through the pages of the Greybull Standard, including Bertha Grisham in Oologah, Okla.; Frank Cortez in Yuma, Ariz.; Pat Sills in Metter, Ga.; Lucille Crain in Casper; Almira Brown in Sarasota, Fla.; Leigh Sherman in Billings; Don Browne in Denver; George Bickford in Bradenton, Fla.; Frank Linn in Albany, Ore.; J.J. Coyne in Lakewood, Colo.; Harry Good in Medford, Ore.; Zeva Smith in San Francisco; Barry Hunter in Grass Valley, Calif. and 41 other Californians who subscribe to the Standard, here's a very special Merry Christmas to you across all those miles.

And to all you new people we'll be meeting this next year and all the little kids who grew up so much during 1984, to all those who live in this fine Wyoming community, the best of holidays and the merriest of Christmases.

1985

January 2, 1985

THE MOST FORLORN sight this time of year is the old stripped Christmas tree out the back door.

IF IT'S A NUTTY driver ahead of me, I usually assume the worst and say, "What does she think she's doing?" But then on the other hand Betty assumes the worst and always says: "What does he think he's doing?"

WE WERE TALKING about New Year's Eve celebrations . . . My sister's most memorable was spent in Hyattville at Hap Crain's bar listening to Hap's stories (no one had stories like Hap.) At the stroke of midnight, Hap ran out into the deserted Hyattville street and fired his shotgun in the air. With a start like that, my sister always claimed, the year had to be a good one.

January 15, 1985

STORIES YOU HEAR years later . . . Once when Scotty Hinman and Stan Flitner, who grew up together on Shell creek, were on the mountain, they decided to see what a piece of baling twine tied across the Granite creek cattle guard would do to tourist traffic. It was that old yellow twine in those days and they tied together a bunch of pieces so it stretched from one side of the cattle guard to the other. Then they hunkered down out of sight on each side of it and waited for the tourists.

The first guy blazed right through it without hesitation.

They tied it back up again. And down in the borrowpit again.

The second guy stopped in a hurry, got out cussing, took out his knife and cut the damned thing!

More retying and restringing. Back in the borrowpit again.

The third guy comes along. Now this is a different type of folk. He gets out of the car, goes over to the twine, unties one of the knots, gets back in his car, drives through. Then he gets back out again, walks back to the twine, picks it up, pulls it tight and reties the knot!

Someone told him always to close gates out West.

February 4, 1985

NO ONE RANCHER is like another. That's one of his marks on the world. To do things his way. Not the other guy's. As many ranchers do their own thing as any other group.

Look at pole gates. No one gate is like another. They don't always even swing . . . some of them slide. A lot of them drag. Most are single. Some are doubles. No standard width. Or height. Metal. Rough lumber. Poles. Finished lumber. I even saw an old bedstead on hinges once.

They're hinged through the gate post, around the post, on top of the post. They'll spin on the ground or on the cross piece above. Some open out. Some in.

A gate is a gate is a gate. Except when it's mine.

Feeding cows in the winter is another individual mark. Flying over a white Wyoming this time of year you cross field after field where stock has strung out behind a hay wagon. No two fields seem the same. One place will start out at one end and throw it willy-nilly clear to the other. The next one will be carefully parallel, up and back, up and back. One guy had even made lanes. Down one side, over a couple of "rows", a careful turn, down the other, another careful turn. Another place spread it out in a gigantic fan with the spokes running out from one corner.

The best one was a spiraling circle. Someone had started in the middle of the field and worked around and around maybe ten times, each new circle bigger than the one before. It looked like a huge curly-cue on the snow.

A guy or a gal or both out there in ten below weather just doing their thing.

February 12, 1985

WE WERE TALKING about turn signals the other day. And how strange the old arm signals look when you see them now. Just the other day the driver coming at me appeared in some kind of trouble. Actually he only had his arm out the window trying to turn right.

But arms have been out and lights have been in for over 30 years now.

And it's a good thing. We could never have negotiated the freeway system with our arms out the windows. Now the only time you have an arm out is to shake a fist.

A turn signal in our little town once helped capture two hoods holding a town cop hostage. The California couple had spent the afternoon in the old Norris Hotel bar. After enough liquid refreshment they apparently decided to knock off this sleepy burg. Which they later tried that night, were surprised by Cop Glenn Coxen, took him hostage at gunpoint and started driving around and around in the squad car.

It was never clear why they wanted to drive around town in a police car or what they were eventually going to do. But they held a gun on Coxen and he just kept driving. The police chief, Ted Olson who was off duty, spotted them. He began following them in his own car. Coxen came to the main street by the old Big Horn Federal office, hit his left turn signal and proceeded to turn slowly into the street.

Olson, following behind, saw the turn signal, sped around the police car and turned back around to ram it into the curb. The turn signal, Olson always said, gave him the time to hit the car.

The story didn't end there, of course. (It never does. Nothing's THAT easy.)

The man actually shot Coxen, who later recovered. The couple ran off into the night, held two other families hostage for awhile, ran a road block and were eventually rousted out of a haystack the next morning by Cash Boylan and his pitchfork.

That was 20 years ago but turn signals were already old stuff. Actually another footnote to modern driving was why Coxen was driving. He had to. The other two couldn't work a straight stick.

February 19, 1985

YOU KNOW YOUR parents thought a great deal of you and a great deal about you but you never know how very, very much they did until you yourself have been a parent a long time.

ONLY the Post Office could put on a two-cent first class mail increase one day and then take a holiday the next.

February 26, 1985

WE HAVE ANOTHER car now. The old one left with 92,000 miles on it. And I have been reminded by those others who also drove our family cars through the years that this is the first car the family ever traded in without a dent in it. No fenders pounded out. No scratches smoothed over. No doors caved in and redone. No touch up paint. Not mint condition, mind you. But an unblemished life on the road. That definitely establishes a new family first.

It was also the first car, the family gleefully points out, ever driven almost exclusively by people over 50 years old!

March 12, 1985

I FEAR MY REPUTATION is at stake on this river ice business. I'm writing this on the 12th and the ice in the Big Horn river is soggy, caving-in, broken up in spots, with water standing over it in many places. But it's still there. You keep reminding me I tell you every year the ice will go out between the 10th and the 15th of March. And while I still have three more days to go, I'd hate to think it would turn stubborn and wait on me. That's doubtful, though. The Old Girl wants to shed her ice this time of year and by the time you read your paper this week, the ice should be on downstream someplace.

ON A T-SHIRT in Ketchum, Idaho: "Ketchum? Hell, I Can't Even Find 'Em."

March 19, 1985

FOR THE RECORD, the Big Horn river ice went out Saturday, Mar. 16 . . . a little late to be normal but not late enough to break the cycle. River ice is part of the basic weather pattern like the two weeks of rain in June and the Christmas snowfall. Those seldom change. But swirling around these are all the abnormalities: cold when it's supposed to be hot, hot when it should be cold, winds, droughts, freezes. And that's "the weather" as we know it.

SPRING IS such a fine time.

All the things wanting to grow, just waiting their time, asking for nothing more than a longer day and a little more sun. I can see already winter has asked a price. Wyoming is not for the delicate. You gotta have heart to see a March in Wyoming.

That little golden willow I've been babying is back to ground level again. Cold weather didn't do it in. Some yearling horses feasted on it sometime this winter, chewing it all around so no amount of doctoring will save it.

It should be used to starting over. This must be the eighth time it's tried again. Its sister trees all around it are big trees now. But this little guy just can't seem to put it together.

Funny how life is that way. One takes hold and the other doesn't. One is coddled and struggles. Another shouldn't make it but flourishes. I looked at my little old willow and thought back on all the times we've fought survival together. First, I burned it; then some bug set it back. It never did grow as fast as it should. It was always young and must have tasted better. At least the deer preferred it to the others around. Now it's the horses' turn. So it's back to the ground again. I don't mind if it doesn't. Maybe it's trying as hard as it can, although I suspect it sometimes.

You don't have to tell some trees to try hard. They just do it. Over on the other side of the place we finally burned up the stump of an old tree that just wouldn't give up. It was only a pencil big cottonwood shoot the first time I saw it. It had sprouted alongside a turn on the concrete ditch. When the water rushed down the hill and hit that turn, it slopped out a bit, just enough to water that little tree. I remember thinking at the time, by golly, anyone who wants to grow that desperately deserves a break.

So I let it go. First it caused a problem with the ditch. Then it grew into the way of the fence. When it grew on up, we discovered it was right under the power line. As the years went on, the Pacific Power and Light crew had to come out and trim it back. Not once, but a couple of times. Finally, it had to go. Between the wires, the ditch and the fence, it was quite a production. For three more years, I fought the stump. It never really did give up. It's still in the ground someplace. Undaunted, but out of sight.

I never did break that tree's spirit. That was a tree that wanted to grow. It relished its place. It was bold and free and full of confidence. You got the impression, watching it march through life, that if a yearling horse had taken a bite out of that tree, the tree would have bitten right back.

March 26, 1985

BEN JOHNSON, the movie actor, sure had it right when he advised his friend, Kenny Call, about going into the movies. Acting pays better than rodeoing, Johnson is reported to have said. "And besides, it's easier to act like a cowboy than to be one," Johnson said.

April 2, 1985

WE WERE TALKING about March in Wyoming. A couple of weeks ago Jack Williams was washing down the sidewalk in front of Williams Department store. It's on the north side of Greybull's main street and the snow had left the usual accumulation of last fall's dust and the past winter's debris. The hose cleans that off better than anything. Besides the sun hits the north side of the street and it was bright and warm that day.

Over on the south side of main street, though, where the winter sun never hits, sidewalks still had snow and ice on them. So merchants on that side of the street had the snow shovels out, chipping away at the remains of winter.

A garden hose on one side and snow shovels on the other. A Wyoming spring arrives.

FOR YEARS AND YEARS the Department of Agriculture and the state ag departments throughout the West have spent thousands and thousands of dollars experimenting and studying overgrazing of grasslands. For as many years they have been admonishing farmers and ranchers not to overgraze, not to put too many animals on too small a piece of ground. Now the Park Service comes along years later to spend a lot of dollars and time trying to prove that Nature can take care of the buffalo in Yellowstone Park.

April 16, 1985

THE CEDAR WAXWINGS bombed our satellite dish the other day. I suppose now we're in for a bunch of crappy reception.

April 23, 1985

WYOMING SPRING is when you have to put your heavy, warm coat and hat on to go admire the Nanking Cherry bushes in bloom.

I JUST LEARNED that "decimate" literally means to kill every tenth person (if you're old enough to remember your Latin). The closest I ever came to that was lining up with a bunch of other draftees in 1951 at the Denver Induction Center. That day they were drafting Marines along with the Army. So every fourth man was a Marine. The sergeant walked down the row of us counting: "One, two, three, Marine. One, two, three, Marine." Chilling. I assume that was "quartimate."

THE SAME PLACES ON your fingers that tie shoes, type words, button shirts, hold a pen, turn a key, use a knife, hold a nail, guide a string, tighten a nut, are the same places that get cut, burned, nicked, scratched, pinched, blistered and slivered.

April 30, 1985

AH, THIS SUN feels nice. As the years go by I understand better the direct correlation between being colder and being older.

HOW CAN YOU NOT like a Golden Willow when it stays a pretty color all winter, leafs out first in the spring and then lingers last with its leaves in the fall?

THIS IS THAT BEAUTIFUL time of year when the sun has found us but the bugs have not.

May 14, 1985

OUT OF CURIOSITY, I always price Russian Olive trees when I wander through nurseries. I'm always a little shocked at what the price tag says.

How can someone charge money for something that grows like weeds at home. Maybe I'm more amazed that someone would actually pay hard cash for something I keep chopping down. One of us is not looking at this quite right!

But I suspect it is the beholder's eye again. A single, pretty yellow-blossomed Russian Olive in your front yard looks much different than the dozens growing along my irrigation ditch.

Russian Olives grow so well in this country we should raise them for a cash crop. We could become the Russian Olive Capitol of the world. Maybe we already are.

WE WERE TALKING about old dogs that live their lives in small towns, and someone mentioned the old, shaggy guy who'd follow Clarence Ortman down to the drug store and then lie outside in various stages of simulated rigor mortis.

Every day for months that dog looked like he died right there on the street. You never saw a dog who could get into more odd positions. His head would be one way and his legs another. Sometimes he lay half in the gutter and half out of it. Sometimes all four legs would be in four directions. He'd sleep that way for hours. He never looked real. He never looked alive. At least twice a day someone with a long face would approach Clarence in the drug store and say, "I hate to tell you this but your old dog outside is gone." But it was always the same. He was still alive at 5 o'clock. That was the only dog I ever knew who practiced leaving us. When he did finally go, he knew just what to do.

May 28, 1985

WE WERE TALKING ABOUT our favorite colors and I immediately started to say it was blue. But then I remembered a certain shade of brown I have a weakness for and I can't be so positive. It depends on what it is and where it is. I can't imagine a blue marigold or a purple cottonwood leaf. Life does not put just one color up on the screen.

As much as I still like most shades of blue, a gold October sun shining on gold cottonwood leaves is unforgettable. So is the flash of a gold bullock's oriole or the happy face of an Orange Lady marigold.

And red as in a blazer or the deep splash of a red geranium or the red, red stripes of the American flag.

I would guess pink turns me off the most, and chartreuse. And green never did do much for me. We're not counting black and white are we?

A purple shirt you won't see on me, but a lavender iris is a marvel. Yellow can be awful, bilious is the word. But some yellow is stunning. You see it in roses and some sports cars and occasionally summer dresses. A Senator Dirksen marigold is that yellow.

We were so charmed once with an aquamarine blue and a coral red paint combination we painted several kitchens with it. We had it so long even the food began to look that way.

That's a color's power. You want it around; you want it to stay around, and forever might not be long enough.

Once when I was a growing teenager I had a very dark blue shirt which I wore to shreds. It was one of those gabardine material shirts we wore in the '40's. A pair of tan gabardine pants and a gabardine shirt, that was the uniform. Every Saturday night for one whole summer I wore that blue shirt to the community hall dance at Greybull. Freddy Gould and Gene Dobbins music and me and my dark blue shirt. Week after week, Saturday night after Saturday night. Somebody else might have wearied of seeing me in it, but I never did. When I finally had to throw it away, neither I nor the dances were quite the same again.

June 4, 1985

OVERHEARD CONVERSATIONS: "If the smoke alarm goes off in our kitchen then dinner's ready."

SOMEONE ASKS: "Do I talk and write too much in clichés and worn out phrases?" If you have to ask, you probably do.

Sometimes you can find out how much you do by putting a couple of paragraphs of an imagined speech on paper. Go through it and underline or capitalize those words or phrases you want to emphasize or the ones you felt were the strongest or made a good point. Read it again with the underlines. You'll probably be disappointed to find your intended strong points are really clichés and tired phrases.

The English are not always the American's favorite people. But one admirable trait surely is the Englishman's ability to express himself. He is articulate, he uses common words in an exceptional way, he has his thoughts in order.

We Americans have had the same language, the same exciting choice. But as a people we believe more in "doing" than in "saying." Our impatience and our love affair with material things has led us away from words and writing. We chatter more than we talk. We watch more than we read. We neglect the English language.

Not so the Englishman. Most of all he has mastered the English language and once that noble creature is with you, you do not need clichés and profanity and trendy expressions. There's no room for them.

June 11, 1985

GALE LARCHICK and I were talking about what was good for the flies and bugs and after going through all the sprays and wipe-ons we came to the conclusion that the best one of all is October.

NOTE TO MRS. CHAPMAN who called the Greybull police about the skunk eating her dog's food last week: He didn't get enough at your place. He was at ours a couple of nights later, nose buried in the Purina Hi-Pro. This is one time the dog and I agreed on something. We didn't interrupt! Old Man Skunk ate all he wanted.

THE CANOE RACE from Basin to Greybull is NOT on for the Days of '49 which is probably a good thing. Betty had thought we ought to enter us and our canoe. "What day did you want to finish?" I wondered.

THE HIGHWAY DEPARTMENT should take a bow for the fine new road on Emblem Bench. That's going to be a smooth place to drive. It was a long time coming. The 10-mile stretch of old road was of 1930's vintage, believe it or not. Yet it is the most traveled tourist road in northern Wyoming in the summertime. But it's brand new now, all redone in time for this year's tourist season, although the tourists will never appreciate it as much as the rest of us will.

THE REASON THE PAST is so comfortable to think about is what we DON'T remember about it.

June 18, 1985

YOU NEVER KNOW how fast your car can go until the light turns yellow.

EVEN IN THIS COMPUTER age, the best piece of office equipment you can have is a yellow pencil. The trick is not having it, but USING it.

IF I HAD BEEN a trooper with Custer's Seventh and fell on that Montana hillside 89 years ago, I would have wanted you to leave me be forever.

Don't dig me up and move me somewhere else.
Don't try to figure out how old my leg bone is.
Don't take my wedding ring off my finger.
Don't worry about what shells I was shooting or what shells the Indians

were shooting.

Don't sift through all the sand around me.

You won't prove anything by where I was. Ten thousand Indians and you're trying to figure out why one bunch was here. It couldn't possibly matter 90 years later.

Just let it all lay where it fell.

I took my one last look at Montana sky right here, on a June day probably much like today is, no clouds, a blue sky, a little wind. The grass would have been headed out and tall by then if I would have thought to look. But that's where I was that day at that time and that's where I'd like you to let me stay.

This is no treasure hunt. It's a battlefield. And it's only a battlefield because I was here. It's a cemetery, my cemetery and only mine because I'm buried here.

Just leave it be.

Just leave me be.

June 25, 1985

WHEN DOES AN OLD TREE finally quit?

My old Haralson apple may be close to it. The wind helped it along this past week when it broke it off about four feet up and just left a forlorn-looking old stump.

It was recovering from another wind storm from eight years ago when it suffered this last indignity. Before that I'd burned it once, a brush fire that got out of hand. (Don't they all!) Now it has to start all over again and I'm not sure how much courage it has to go on.

It's been one of those fighters we talked about before. A tree that just doesn't want to give up yet. It takes the raps and keeps on going. I'm always inspired by that determination. In 30 years of growing things you know how fragile life is, how easy it is to lose to the drought, the heat, the deer, the bugs, to the grower himself! Now we're back to a stump, that old tree and I, 30 years of growing and just a stump. If it isn't going to give up just yet, neither am I.

July 9, 1985

WE USED TO POKE good-natured fun at my dad's little cards he carried around in his later years. He always put everything he wanted to tell us on them. All the news of the family, the news of home, the news of people we knew, the news itself sometimes or something he wanted to talk to us about. Reaching his hand inside his shirt pocket for his little cards meant it was his turn to talk. We used to smile at each other and the kids would look at us and it became part of the family. But those were the days when we could remember things. We never said, like we do often now, "I had something I wanted to tell you, but I forgot what it was." We never got clear home and said, "I forgot to tell them about . . ." Back then we were still remembering what happened the day before. Now it's time (Dad would be amused!) for my own set of cards.

July 16, 1985

I HAVE LONG complained about how discourteous a telephone can be. A telephone call interrupts everything. It has preference over conversation, sleep, a business transaction, dinner, yard work. Nothing waits for it. There are some calls you would stop time itself to take. But you can't choose which ones. And that's the rub.

All this is to prepare you for a telephone story with a happy ending. I'd just bought something and Cub Collingwood was taking my ten dollar bill. The phone rang. Oh, oh, I said to myself. It'll be a while before the change comes back. The phone rang again. Cub reached for it, said "Hang on a minute" and put it right back down. Didn't even say hello or ask who it was. Just "hang on a minute." I got my change, my thank you and was headed out the door before he picked it back up again.

Say, I like that idea. When you call in the middle of something and I say "hang on a minute" you'll know I've adopted a new policy. No offense, but I'll be right with you. In just a minute. And I promise not to finish lunch first.

July 23, 1985

FIVE YEARS FROM now will that little girl ever remember when she said "chokecherries" for the first time?

Or that she saw a big, big rainbow (a ". . . bow") or heard a peacock or played with Puppy or said Hi to the horses 20 times a day?

You old hand grandparents ought to be able to tell me. When you baby-sit your two-year-old granddaughter for 10 whole days for the first time can she ever remember as much as you hope she will? Does she take a piece of this old Wyoming back with her forever?

Will she remember that "Black" is a blackbird but "Bird" is a robin?

And that Robin Smith's peacock says ". . . eow, . . . eow" which sounds almost like a cat when it come out. But if you're two years old there's a definite difference between the ". . . eow" and the "meow." Old People can't hear it but Little People can.

Or that the color book of her mother's she looked at had all the dwarfs beards each colored a different color. Two generations in the same color book. She can't possibly remember how great her grandparents thought that was.

And will she remember that "Just one more" (make that "jus one mo . . .") with one little finger up came from Wyoming?

Will she remember hollering "hi' and "bye" every time someone left the house? It's been a while on this place since that happened. You forget how much you looked forward to that in those old days past.

Will she see a horse trailer in Santa Fe and call it "Dude" thereby confounding everybody? But the horse inside going up the mountain was old Dude and so the trailer was "Dude" and the horse was "Dude" and why is that so confusing?

And horses, oh, the horses! Hi Horse and Bye Horse and Hi Baby Horse and Bye Baby Horse. There have to be hoofprints galloping across that little memory this week.

Will she remember how she tried to deepen her voice the way her granddad talked? Or that Shell creek was a "Bath". So was the Big Horn river. So was the ditch by the house.

Will she remember all the flowers she kept smelling, the raspberries she helped pick (and spilled over!), the riding lawn mower that made too much noise, the Wyoming mosquitoes that tried to carry her off?

And that glorious rainbow that started at Wayne Barnett's and stretched clear to Hyattville. Now that was a ". . . bow!" She can point right to where it was if you ask her.

As the years go by you forget the World of the Little People. As all grandparents find out, the reason this seems so new once again is that our kids were never this small. When we were raising kids, they went from babies to junior high in 18 months.

And so this new little one with her big eyes and her engaging ways comes to visit and you want to send her home with all these pieces of you and home and Wyoming summertime.

She can't possibly remember them all. She's too preciously little yet. But that's all right. Her grandparents will remember enough for all three of us.

August 6, 1985

A MONTANA WOMAN who worked in a check out stand for a long time told the Hungry Horse News one of the funniest experiences she ever had was the elderly lady who bought the Rainier beer. "One day an elderly lady, frail and hunched, wandered to the beer coolers at the rear of the store. She returned to the check stand with two cold packs of Rainier and plopped them on the counter. As she dug in her pocketbook for money, I noticed that her hands looked remarkably young and strong. I looked more intently at the woman, and then realized that the old woman was actually a teenage boy with the best make-up job I had ever seen."

August 12, 1985

WE WERE TALKING about killing flies . . . When things are slow in one small Montana town, the police dispatchers sit around swatting at flies and keeping track of the kills. But it isn't as easy as it sounds. To make sport of it, they cut a big square out of the middle of the fly swatter!

I'VE HAD DAYS when everything I touched seemed to have a big square hole cut out of the middle.

CLIPPED THIS OUT of another paper last week: "There's only two kinds of pie I like – hot pie and cold pie."

August 20, 1985

THE TROUBLE WITH the beef industry is that it is raising something good for you. If it were raising something bad for you, like tobacco, it would have all sorts of government protection and subsidy.

WHAT DID YOU think of that great Satchel Paige quote in the news last week: "How old would you be," Satchel asked, "if you didn't know how old you were?"

August 27, 1985

SOMETIMES I'M CONVINCED that I only raise three crops a year: Milkweed, Foxtail and Gumweed.

YOU KNOW THAT pesky gumweed is in Peterson's Rocky Mountain Wildflower book. It's also in my State of Wyoming noxious weed books. We're back to the "eye of the beholder" again. On your place it's a wildflower. On my place it's a weed.

PETERSON'S BOOK said the Indians used gumweed as a medicine. And I've noticed there haven't been any sick Indians on our place in years. It may be powerful stuff.

FOR MORE THAN 30 years now I've been very grateful I didn't have to do two-a-day football practices this time of year. Believe me, boys, I've never found anything in life that two-a-days prepared me for.

WHEN THE TWO young men from Massachusetts on bicycles flagged me down, I thought they had trouble. The only trouble they had was that they were TIRED! They wondered if I'd take them to Shell "so we wouldn't have to ride it?"

"But I thought that was the idea," I told them but that came out sounding old and grouchy so I loaded bikes in the back and boys in the front and we rode for 15 miles in a pickup. It was the first time I'd ever been on a bicycle trip from Seattle to Boston.

September 10, 1985

THE ROBINS HAVE been bombarding our windows the last couple of days. They keep thinking they can fly through them. They've also been in the grapes gorging themselves. Which may be their problem. Taking of the grape and flying don't mix.

September 24, 1985

IF I EVER WROTE a book on Coaching Younger Kids, I'd have 12 chapters and 11 of them would be about giving encouragement instead of criticism, of finding something good kids did instead of forever finding something bad.

I knew this 45 years ago. And nothing in all these years since of watching or participating in grade school and high school sports has changed my mind.

All any youngster ever lacks is confidence. His or her mental attitude is far more important than physical skills. The youngster can work on his physical skills. But confidence has to be supplied by adults. Or at least it shouldn't be taken away by adults.

Few youngsters find confidence by themselves. They need to be told they are becoming capable, that they "have it", that what they are doing right then is succeeding. But that always they should be searching for the ability to do more, to accomplish better things, to enlarge and expand. This is the essence of teaching.

But an adult never seems satisfied with a youngster. An adult is never able to take the youngster just as he is right then. The adult is forever looking at the child at what he "could be" or "should be." And thus the criticism or "motivation" as it's often called.

And so, my 11 chapters would be filled with examples of kids you and I both know, of times lost and times won, of adults who prodded and pushed when they should have smiled and pulled.

What would be in the 12th? That despite all the mistakes we make, what marvelous fun it is to watch kids growing up and playing games along the way.

October 15, 1985

IT OCCURRED TO ME the other day that it had been exactly 40 years since I'd heard anyone use the word "jollify" so I wasn't even sure there was such a word. Maybe old Will Robb just made it up that day. "It's time to jollify," he'd hollered. He was standing on the hill waving me up to the house. "It's time to jollify." I liked Will. He was in his mid-sixties then and he had a fun way of talking. For all I knew he'd made the word up himself. I'd never heard anyone else ever use it. I tried it myself a few times, just because it sounded good and seemed to fit. But I always gave Will credit for it. I figured it was his word. I got curious the other day. Maybe there was such a word. So I looked it up. Sure enough, Webster's says it's colloquial "to make or be jolly."

That's a Will Robb word for me.

We'd just heard the news that Japan had surrendered. It was V-J Day 10 miles east of Burlington and I was a sophomore kid working on Owen Dill's farm. Will had come to help out for a couple of weeks. V-J Day had arrived in the middle of a bunch of post holes and after we'd gathered around the radio and heard it all, I went back on out to my shovel. Will came to the top of the hill, hollering about quitting working today. "This is a time to jollify," he cried.

So we went back up to the house and sat around the day. That evening Owen went to town and bought some ice cream and we had fresh strawberries and ice cream and went to bed.

I heard later that all over the United States strange girls were kissing men in the streets that day. Mercifully, my sophomore imagination was spared knowing this. I settled for the day off and ice cream and strawberries.

October 22, 1985

THERE IS SOMETHING so very final about a leaf falling to the ground. It took several weeks in the spring to grow. It endured summer's buffeting of heat and wind and wet. It made it through the first storm of September and then lazed away the changing color days of fall. But when it cuts loose and starts down, in only a few seconds it is gone.

YESTERDAY THE WIND was from the south and all the leaves blew across the yard and ended up on the north side. This morning the wind is from the north and now all the leaves are blowing back to the other side. This is a game the wind and leaves play all fall. They have so much fun with it I try never to spoil it with a rake.

October 29, 1985

SOMEONE PULLED UP to a stop sign ahead of me, stopped, and just when I thought he was going to stay stopped, he screeched on across the road ahead of me. I hit the brakes and then looked twice to make sure old J.B. Suiter wasn't appearing out of the past. That's what he used to do. He'd come to a stop sign very properly. Complete stop. But then he'd just gun it on across whether anything was coming or not. He never looked one way or another, only straight ahead. Guess he figured he'd made the stop okay. The rest of the burden was on you. He wasn't trying to miss you as much as you ended up trying to miss him.

He sat way back in his seat when he drove. He looked like he was holding the steering wheel at arm's length. And his eyes never strayed from straight ahead.

He could cross an intersection faster than anyone I ever saw. You only had a quick glimpse of him. Which was probably a good thing. Your heart can start again if it hasn't been stopped too long.

BETTY SAID SHE wouldn't have a year that didn't have an October in it.

SUNDAY AT THE HORSE sale Nowles Mitchell and I were sitting high up on the top row talking about shooting a basketball. And I was reminding him of the theory of flicking your wrist. "You have to flick your wrist, really pop it," I told him, "to put the proper spin on a ball." I popped my wrist down to show him a couple of times. Pop. Pop. "All great shooters have it and anyone can learn it. But you will never have a real dependable shot until you do this," and I flicked my wrist a couple more times.

I suddenly had that feeling of people looking at you.

"Nowles," I said, "I can't look. Am I bidding on this horse?"

He looked down at Hugo and Bob. "I think you are."

I'd popped that wrist down two times too many. I've heard of people pulling their ear and buying an old chair, but I never heard of anyone shooting a basketball and buying a horse. Someone made the next bid and took me out. I looked down at Hugo. He was looking right at me. I made a savage cut across my throat. Gale Larchick said later he saw my wrist going down and he wondered, What's Kennedy doing buying that trashy horse?

But I didn't buy him, thankfully, and I learned something: Don't shoot basketballs at a horse sale.

November 5, 1985

MY SISTER, WHO IS keeping track of all the family history, unearthed some old pictures of the McKenzie clan's ranch on the Powder River in Montana and sent them along. No one is sure of the year but it had to be a bad one! That's the sorriest, skinniest looking bunch of old cows you ever saw. All colors and all horns, only one shape and that was thin. One little calf wasn't as big as a big cat. And all of them standing in an old cottonwood pole corral that looked as scraggly as they did. Right behind the corral were a couple of old limbless cottonwood trees that had apparently taken turns being hit by lightning. It wasn't a time to be in the cattle business. Or at least not take pictures of it. They looked like some of those pictures the Democrats keep using to show how bad things were under Hoover.

JUST GOT BACK FROM an Aunt Jemima run.

You hear of planes coming in from the south loaded with stuff you're not supposed to have. And up in Montana the Canadians ferry Coors beer by air across the border. Well, I made it back from the Southwest (where it's on the shelves) with half a case of Aunt Jemima pancake flour. And I'm assured now of a pancake high of several years running.

This is "The Original" Aunt Jemima pancake flour. Not the buttermilk variety or those other kinds. This is the old fashioned blend you don't see on shelves here anymore. Which is a shame because pancakes will never be pancakes without the Old Aunt Jemima. Nothing makes pancakes like the original old blend.

I said this same thing some years ago, too, when I ran out. And several people took issue. It's not easy to explain that pancake flour is not all alike and some things in this world should never change. My old grade school buddy, Ross Crosby, even sent me a package of HIS kind of pancake flour then all the way from California to show me how wrong I was. But I remain convinced you haven't tasted pancakes until you've tasted Aunt Jemima, the Old Aunt Jemima. They'll just melt in your mouth!

November 12, 1985

WE WERE ALL IN the same art studio looking at pottery and vases and the young man ahead of us was telling about the guy just leaving who'd been looking for something for his mother-in-law.

"I said, 'Now here is a vase that is very narrow at the top and wide at the bottom.'"

"The guy looked at it for a minute and said: 'That's my mother-in-law.'"

THE LATE BARTIE BENTLEY'S NAME came up the other day. He was on a place south of Basin for years and he once gave marvelous advice on irrigating a pasture to Jack Kinghorn who passed it on to me: "Water it often and get over it quick."

MARY SACKETT CALLED on Armistice Day Monday to remind me that it was Gib Kennedy who had the Civil War cannons cemented in the Basin library lawn so they would always be there. "And we should always remember that," she told me.

I woke up Monday thinking about Nov. 11 and Dad. Mary's ESP was working well. Armistice Day was one of Dad's big days. Memorial Day was the other. These weren't Holidays these were Special Days. Holidays were like Christmas and Thanksgiving. But the days that were for veterans had special circles on the calendar.

The pair of cannons were special, too. They had belonged to the old GAR post in Basin and when the last of those old Civil War veterans died, the cannons came to the Basin American Legion. The pair guarded the Basin library for years, just sort of pulled on the lawn. Every Halloween the Basin kids would drag the cannons around town and leave them in the middle of the main street. Others thought they shouldn't be in Basin but somewhere else, like Cheyenne.

Dad's solution was to put them in immovable concrete. And, right or wrong, they've been there ever since. They've seen three more big wars and innumerable battles and skirmishes, both international and local. They're on their second library. That was a fine battle. Old cannons in front of new libraries could split the Union. But they've stayed, as Mary reminded me, hunkered down for almost 50 years in Dad's concrete.

November 19, 1985
THE ONLY THING constant is change. That's been said a thousand times and it will be as true the last time it was said as it was the first time.

NOTHING WORKS in cold weather . . . but mostly me.

A SUN THAT SHINES on a wintry November day is worth 10 or 20 degrees higher temperature and 50 degrees higher spirits.

November 25, 1985
THOSE NOTES I WRITE to myself in the middle of the night are interesting. They would be even more interesting if I could read them. Most of the time they look like I either didn't turn the light on or I had my eyes closed or both of the above. My handwriting, which suffers in broad daylight, is worse in the middle of the night although someone once told me that my writing often looks likes it's done in the dark anyway.

When I can read them, I don't often understand them. I keep remembering that often-repeated story of the guy who woke up in the morning and looked at his pad by the bed. It read: "Banana skins are very tough." I've written my share of banana skin notes. But inspiration is an elusive creature and you have to be quick when she hovers by the bed.

WE WERE ALL AT THE water meeting and they were telling us there was so much "shrink" by evaporation from the dam to headgate and then more loss from shrink from headgate down the canal and I kept waiting for someone to ask about "Neighbor Shrink" and no one did. But then we were in a room full of neighbors!

December 2, 1985
LAURA LITTLE IS right when she says the one saving grace of winter days is that they are short. What would they be like if it was still light at nine at night!

LAST WEEK'S STORY ABOUT the newsstand triggered some memories. Ellen Whipps was reminded of the time her husband, Fritz, rescued Harry Gillett from the newsstand at Basin.

Harry had paid for his paper all right and the thing opened as it should. But it grabbed a piece of Harry's coat when it closed up and he couldn't get it out.

He didn't have any more change to open it up again and as much as he pulled and tugged, the newsstand wouldn't let go.

It was one of those cold winter mornings, too, when the last thing you wanted was to be in the clutches of a mad newsstand.

Someone else came along and they didn't have any money either. Finally

Fritz showed up with ransom enough to free Harry.

Moral of the story: Don't turn your back on a hungry newsstand.

December 30, 1985

WE WERE ALL SITTING in the boat heading for the beach. It was warm, even sticky just a little, and everyone was either in a bathing suit or a pair of shorts. Most were barefoot. A guy in his sixties with a good, deep tan was up front. Without his shoes on you could see something was wrong with his foot. It looked like part of the instep missing and it sat on the deck at a slight angle. It wasn't deformed, but then it didn't look quite right either. It was one of those things you noticed right away and then looked someplace else so you wouldn't be staring.

He was a friendly guy. Been around a lot, seen a lot. He must have known people were looking. He shifted his weight a little and said, "The old foot's acting up some today."

Someone who had made friends with him early grabbed the opening. "What did you do to the foot, Skip?"

He turned it slightly and then back again. He hesitated just a little until everyone was looking. Then he said: "A shark took it."

You could hear several people draw in their breath. Everyone WAS looking at him now. Was he kidding? He wasn't. A shark had taken it years ago, when he was a nine-year-old kid in San Diego. A beach abutment had given way underneath him. He fell and broke his hip and then tumbled into the water. A shark had made one pass and hit his foot before they could get him out. He had two long years in the hospital, but he went on to a fruitful and successful life. And when anyone asked, he had the perfect, unforgettable explanation: "A shark took it." You could have buggered up your foot in all kinds of ways, an industrial accident, a car wreck or even something exotic like a rodeo or a pro football game. But nothing stops the conversation like, "A shark took it."

It's especially unforgettable sitting in a boat in the middle of the ocean.

1986

January 7, 1986

WHEN ART SYLVESTER put out his hand and our little Jimmy reached out and slapped it, I should have known a two-year-old grandson's education starts earlier than you realize.

And the first time he said, "All Right!" in his little boy voice, I knew it for sure.

The babysitter's daughter in Montana is a cheerleader, I find out. And she has found an eager student.

"All Right!"

You take him over to the window so he can see the Christmas lights go on.

"All Right!" he cries.

He tears ribbon and paper off and brings up something that makes a bunch of noise.

"All Right!" he shouts.

He can give you a good cheerleader imitation with both hands up, fists clenched and he's got the "high five" move down real good.

But it's the "All Right" that's melded into the vocabulary.

We watched The Karate Kid over the holidays. If you're into kids, you're into The Karate Kid. I think big people like it as much as the little people do. It's a story about the good guys beating the bad guys and has an old man in it who knows everything. All of us were engrossed in the final match scene. The Karate Kid against the world. He goes up on one leg, the bad guy comes at him and POW! We all explode in claps and cheers. And behind me I hear this little voice saying, "All Right! All Right!"

January 14, 1986

I AM NOW THE proud owner of a bright Nebraska Big Red cap. Boy, it's a beaut. Marie Hart brought it back to this old Nebraska alum from the Fiesta Bowl. Hey, but this isn't just any old hat. If you press the hidden spot on the bill, it plays "There Is No Place Like Nebraska, Good Old Nebraska U!" I'm telling you, that's a hat. If you see me with it on and I have both hands up in the air, you know the band's aplaying.

AN ANNIVERSARY of sorts slipped by me last month. If I would have remembered to light the candles Dec. 6, I could have marked the beginning of my 30th year of writing a Wyoming newspaper column.

Instead I "celebrated" by promptly missing two columns in a row, a sin columnists aren't supposed to commit. If you're going to shout about continuity and longevity and anniversaries, you shouldn't sneak two weeks off.

But that first column effort of mine — a five-paragraph output the old Greybull Standard files show — came out in the Dec. 6th Standard and has been going week by week ever since.

At one week at a time a column doesn't add up very fast. But 29 years can be a spell.

You don't start writing a newspaper column to see how long you can go. In the newspaper business you're never writing past today anyway. A newspaper column is only a part of yourself, that corner of the paper that's yours for this week. The next week is another one. In 1956 I didn't know where it would all lead. Frankly, in 1986 I don't know either. It's still a column at a time, who knows, maybe another 30 years.

I was startled, though, reading through that first effort of 1956, to realize again how there is nothing new under the sun. Last week you indulged me and let me write about my two-year-old grandson. Twenty-nine years ago I was writing about another two-year-old, one who stood back from the Christmas tree and threw the tinsel on with gusto. That two-year-old in 1956 was last week's two-year-old's dad!

January 21, 1986

FOR THE RECORD I'm not winning my continual battle with the Lovell stoplight. The light, which is the ONLY light in town, I might add, will stay green for 20 minutes until I drive up. Then it promptly turns red. Apparently it senses my feelings for it. The other night after a very late plane connection in Billings, we drove through Lovell at 2 a.m. There was only one other car on the street, the other cop. The light was green until we were a block away. Then it turned red! I never saw such a sadistic thing.

THE NEXT TIME someone kids you about having snow in Wyoming on July Fourth, you can remind them that we also had, on January 17, 1986, rain and a rainbow!

January 28, 1986

TRITZ JUROVICH, who died recently in California, was another in a long list of Thermopolis high school graduates to become coaches.

In proportion, no other Wyoming town has produced as many coaches. The list reads like a Wyoming Who's Who. Bill Bush, Jack King, Jack Aggers, Joe McKethen, Moe Radovich, Spike Vannoy, Hank Cabre, Jurovich, Eddie Bunch, Phil Crouch, George Johnstone, and I know there are ones I'm missing. Jack King believes it started back with Joe Bush, a longtime coach and superintendent at Thermopolis. It was his inspiration as a coach and teacher which encouraged his early students to follow, King believes.

"He was the first role model. And it just kept going," King says.

Some of those first students started coaching in the 40's. And every decade since there have been Thermopolis graduates coaching somewhere.

February 4, 1986

MONTANA'S SUPREME COURT has ruled that tavern owners can be declared negligent if a drunken patron is involved in a car accident after being served alcohol.

This is wondrous logic.

There are only two culprits in this, the booze and the drinker. Not the tavern owner or the bartender or the bottle-maker or the car manufacturer. If the law does not choose to prohibit alcohol entirely, it should not ask anyone else to be liable except the drinker himself.

I assume the court ruling applies to the State of Montana's retail liquor outlets as well. It would be hypocritical if it didn't. It is only legal semantics to wonder whether an unopened bottle sold at retail is a different weapon than a poured one in a bar. The State of Montana itself should be just as liable as the bar owners.

Alcohol consumption creates tragic problems. But it is a problem of, first, the alcohol and, second, the drinker. Montana's court decision places an unfair proportion of blame on the bartender.

MY SISTER SAID it's official now. She has been accepted as a bona fide member of The Society of Mayflower Descendants. She and a cousin of ours traced back mother's family to John and Francis Cooke who made the voyage on the Mayflower. Which makes me officially a Mayflower descendant, too, I guess. But, gee, it may have come too late. Think what it would have meant to know this in the third grade. And all those Thanksgiving programs. I could have carried a gun and worn ruffles and a big hat instead of being one of the cornstalks.

February 18, 1986

THIS IS BOB LONG, the former Green Bay Packer talking: "I remember once in Green Bay we'd won a ballgame on Sunday and came the Tuesday films, Lombardi was hopping mad. We got to the meeting and he slammed his fists at the table and he said, 'Gentlemen, there's something wrong with this team.' Christ, we'd just won seven in a row, I think. He said, "I know what's wrong with this team. It's a lack of basic fundamentals. We're going to start all over again, we're going back to the basics. Blocking and tackling.' The room was tense, puzzled. These are guys up to 35 years old, hiding behind each other, not looking directly at him. He reached out and picked up a football on the table, and said, 'Gentlemen, this is a football.' And here comes the voice of Max McGee from the back of the room. 'Hold it, Coach,' he says. 'You're going too fast.'" – from Tom Dowling's book, "Coach, A Season With Lombardi".

February 25, 1986

JUST AS I WAS passing the small car, I noticed the book. It was riding cheerfully along on top of the car, right over the driver's side. He'd put it there, forgot it, got in and drove off. The book, like a faithful old dog, just sat where it was put and for miles now, face to the wind, it had been heading to town. I waved the guy down. When he turned toward me, I could tell he expected the worst, like a wheel was coming off or something. He was relieved to find it was just an old book. His wife thought it was hilarious. I had the feeling they would talk about it again.

IN DEAVER, your morning Billings Gazette is delivered horseback by a young cowboy wearing paperbags front and back. In 10 years he'll be riding a motorcycle to herd cows.

SEVERAL OF YOU have asked what that black mark on top of my head was from. I suffered it tracing a crack across the concrete floor under the press. I put my trifocals down closer to the floor to see it better and charged along with lowered head (I really shouldn't tell this) until I ran right smack into the press. It was a scene right out of the Three Stooges. My head will heal eventually but my dignity has suffered irreparable harm.

March 11, 1986
AMERICA IS THAT place that sends out millions of dollars in foreign aid to strange countries and then has to have Willie Nelson put on Farm Aid concerts back home.

WYOMING PEOPLE always speak of "country" with special reverence. It's "good country" or "big country." It is the Cody country or the Hyattville country. It's "high country" or "good country" or sometimes just plain "a lot of country."

SOMETHING HAS reminded me of the old man who was in the same room Dad was in the hospital. He was asleep when I came in but my talking woke him up and immediately he wanted to know who I was. I tried to tell him, but he couldn't hear. I raised my voice but he was still befuddled.
"Oh, you're the guy who cleaned out the wells," he finally said.
"No, that's not right." I went over to his bed. "No, I'm Gib Kennedy's son. That's Gib over there in the bed. I'm his son."
"Oh," the old man said, and closed his eyes. I went back over to Dad's bed.
In a minute I heard the old man say out loud. "Well, those wells needed cleaning out anyway."

March 18, 1986
I HOPE WYOMING can find another Jim Griffith out there someplace.
We were very fortunate to have him as a public official all these years and now that he is retiring, we could use many more like him.
He's been a very intelligent, selfless public servant, doing more than the

job required, forever cheerful, always personally courageous. The newspaper profession lost a talented member when Jim moved from Lusk and the Lusk Herald to Cheyenne. But the entire state was the gainer.

March 26, 1986

THE PAINT THEY sold in Basin, Wyoming, in 1935 was really good stuff. When they put that on, it just stayed there forever. You didn't even have to be a good painter to spread it on. Any old brush would do and it would still stick. I can show you a place on the side of the Greybull Oddfellows brick building that's been painted with the stuff now for 50 years. And though it's faded and wearing, you can't mistake what it says: "BH '35."

Those painters in the Basin high school Class of 1935 were 18-year-old seniors in 1935, which would make them nearly 70-year-old grandmothers and grandfathers and probably even great-grandmothers and great-grandfathers. And that old paint's still there.

FROM AN ASSOCIATED PRESS news report: "People are most likely to suffer strokes between 8 and 9 a.m. – the time already known to be most dangerous for heart attacks – and experts believe these crises may be triggered by the stress of getting up in the morning."

Boy, isn't that the truth!

If ever there was scientific reason for staying in bed and not getting up at all, there you have it. Why should we endanger our health and the happiness of all those around us by getting up. Stay in bed, I say, and you'll last as long as that 1935 Basin paint.

April 1, 1986

AMOS SMALL AND I were talking about a mutual friend from the "old days." We agreed he was a little wild, maybe even a little touched. I said he'd never been the same since he was hit in the head by that horse. "Well," said Amos, "it's always nice to have an excuse."

YOU KNOW HOW QUIET a ski chair lift is. Especially the newer ones when the pulleys are tight and things haven't started to squeak yet. You're drifting up above other skiers coming down underneath you and you can hear the sounds of their skis on the snow and catch parts of conversations as you pass over. The young man coming down lost it and went into the classic fall, rolling down towards us. His hat came off and one ski pole landed 10 feet up the slope. He was snow all over. He immediately started cussing and cussing, unhappy with the snow and the hill and himself. We glided over him and on up. He was still cussing. The young lady in the chair behind us leaned out and called down to him: "Are we having fun yet?"

April 14, 1986

MY DAD HAD STRONG feelings about waving to people in the fields. He never drove by an irrigator or a person on horseback without waving to him. As a boy I always marveled how many of them would wave back. "Do you know him?" I asked once. "I don't need to," Dad replied.

When Dad's niece, Betty Lynn, was a young girl, she wondered about it, too, driving along with him. She remembers, "I asked him, 'Why are we waving to everyone?' He looked at me very sternly and said, 'This is Wyoming.'"

I still wave to people. Well, most of the time, I do. Sometimes I don't see you quick enough. Or you're driving a new car. Or I'm thinking about something else which seems to take a lot of energy anymore.

In the old days truck drivers used to flash their headlights at each other. Just a quick on and off when they were approaching each other down the road. But that highway camaraderie faded away when trucks multiplied so fast.

The late Paul Schubert, when he lived up Shell, solved the numbers problem. He would wave at every pickup regardless, figuring that if you drove a pickup you either lived on Shell creek or were heading to or from the mountain. And that earned a wave from him.

We all have our "automatics." I try never to miss waving at all snowplows, schoolbuses, UPS trucks, and those kindred spirit strangers with ski racks or horse trailers.

It's always better to wave too much than too little, it seems to me. And one thing I've learned. It costs nothing to wave.

Besides, "This is Wyoming."

April 29, 1986

I'M SURE YOU'VE noticed that "old" papers have old names. Papers that have been around for 80 to 100 years or more are Leaders or the News or the Bulletin or the Press. And nearly always with the town's name. If we started over again with newspapers, no editor would use such names. In the 1950's Bob and Roy Peck were in a merger of two Riverton papers and the new name was The Ranger. I don't think there's another Ranger any place.

In Canada a newspaperman started a paper ten years ago and called it "The Scratching River Post." Mel Ruder started a newspaper near Glacier Park after World War II and called it an unforgettable, "The Hungry Horse News."

That name, while immediately recognizable, can cause problems. Last week an Oriental gentleman called publisher Brian Kennedy long distance to place an ad in the paper. The connection was lousy; his English not much better. It was a tough conversation. He couldn't understand how a hungry horse related to the newspaper. "All I want is to place ad," he said again and again. Finally, though he never understood the name history, the ad deal was made.

There was one requirement. Payment had to be sent in advance.

"Oh," he beamed over the phone. "To feed the horse."

May 6, 1986

THE TALK WANDERED to Russian Olive trees and Merl Gipson said the Russian Olive tree story he liked best was when the Montanan stopped and asked the late John Neiman if he could pick some Russian Olive seeds out of the trees. (I never did find out what for.) The Neimans were living on the old Unterzuber place on the Greybull River then and Russian Olives were everywhere. The guy came back after awhile and asked if he could climb up in the top of the trees "where the seeds were better."

"Yes, you can," John said with a straight face, "but don't break any of the branches."

The guy solemnly promised he wouldn't.

May 27, 1986

WHEN GOD MADE little colts, He should have added about two more inches to their tails. The flies and bugs are happy about it, though. A little colt's tail is not much of a weapon. It does a lot of wagging and waving, but it doesn't hit much.

THEY SAY THAT Frederick Remington was one of the few early artists to show horses with all four feet off the ground. No one believed it was true for a long time. I once took a picture of a polka dancer with both feet in the air at the same time. I didn't know that was possible. But I had the picture to prove it. I snapped it at a town celebration dance just as he and his wife were taking off on a wild polka. She was still on the ground, but Jim was in the air a good ten inches. Both feet. It just proved to me that you don't have to stay on the ground when you polka. And it may also explain why polka dancers have so much fun.

WYOMING SUNRISES and sunsets are treasures. If you have time for nothing else in the day, you should take time to see one or the other. People all over America who are surrounded by trees or concrete or other people never see sunrises and sunsets. In Wyoming we're blessed with one after another after another. Not many days go by in a Wyoming year when the sun doesn't shine and not many when a sunset won't grab you for a few moments.

June 3, 1986

SOMEONE BROUGHT UP working on Sunday and that was the argument Frank Pearce once got into with a young woman at the dinner table. She was on the side of not working and Frank was for it. For every argument the woman put up, Frank had an answer, a typical, quick Frank Pearce answer. It appeared to me the table was siding with Frank and his humor. It appeared that way to the woman, too, because she grew increasingly irritated.

At one point Frank said: "I may go to you-know-where for it, but I worked a lot of Sundays."

"Well, you'll have a lot of company," she snapped.
"Oh, I don't aim to run the place," Frank said.

HAVE BEEN WATCHING a nest of robins grow up. I don't see how that many feathers can all fit in that one small nest. Feathers and beady little eyes, that's all you could see.

Then one day we looked in and they were gone. Just like that. That's what happens to kids. They always leave home on you. One minute they're growing up. The next they're on their own.

June 17, 1986
REPRINTING THIS bumper sticker so close to Father's Day is dangerous, but have you seen the one floating around Montana that says:
"Did you wake up grouchy today?
Or did you let her sleep!"

THE MORE THINGS change, the more they stay the same. Phyllis Deveraux Friesz who lives in Billings reads the Greybull Standard on Sunday after her folks, Red and Ruth Deveraux, bring it over. A couple of weeks ago her eye caught the "Looking Back" column of the "good old days." One of the items mentioned that "Phyllis Deveraux had left for Girls State." That same Sunday, Phyllis had sent her daughter, Ruth Spencer, off to Montana Girls State! Just 30 years apart.

June 24, 1986
WHEN THE FOUR daughters of George and Ida McKenzie brought their husbands and children back to the ranch on the Powder River in Montana for a reunion in 1936, I'm sure they thought it would be one of many they'd hold. It was the first time they had been together since their father's funeral a couple of years earlier. And in the pictures we have, everyone is young and laughing and all wearing Alf Landon for President buttons. As a reunion it was a great success. As families go, it was tragic. Because that reunion was the last time the family was ever together again.

It was not a close family like some. The father had been the strong tie. Some of the sisters got along, but not all four. Two half-brothers had already been kicked off the ranch by the stepmother in a bitter fight. In a year or so she would do the same to the eldest sister's husband, and the ranch, split up, and out of the family, would go to other owners.

It was still Depression, still dry years. The war would be coming and the sisters scattered to California, Michigan, Washington and Wyoming. Without the ranch and a place to go home, the families found "home" in other places. Two of the sisters died early and the families lost even more touch with each other. That 1936 reunion, in a rush it seemed, was 50 years ago. The family was not together again.

Last week in Nevada, my sister, bless her, decided to do something about that and for the first time in the 50 years she managed to bring all but two of the first cousins together in one place.

You can't catch up everything in 50 years but you can sure hear some family stories you never heard before.

The first winter Grandad spent in eastern Montana in the mid-1880's he used up all his money on his grubstake and didn't have enough money to buy a coat. So he spent the winter with his band of sheep with a blanket wrapped around him Indian-like. That would give you an appreciation of what a Montana winter would be like.

One of his grandsons remembers him putting him on the horse buckrake and saying, "Whatever you do, don't let go of the reins." A half a day later in the hot sun and too full of soft artesian well water, the youngster fainted and fell out of the seat. "When I came to," he remembers, "I was lying on the ground, but I still had both hands tight around the reins."

And why didn't someone tell me before that my grandmother liked snuff and then graduated to honest-to-goodness chewing tobacco!

And do you remember the time, someone said, when Ella came home from Bozeman with college ideas about boiling potatoes. "You don't use any salt. It is better for you." Her dad took one bite of "Ella's new way" and "his mustache just stood straight out." He grabbed the salt shaker. Ella was crushed. Her sister-in-law, predicting the outcome, had heavily salted the gravy. So it was a double disaster. Her advice to Ella was sound: "Don't try to change what a man likes to eat."

"Your mother taught me how to whistle," one of my cousins said. "She could whistle beautifully." I thought, did she teach me? I couldn't remember.

Another cousin remarked that I looked a lot like he remembered my dad looked. He couldn't remember that, I thought to myself. That 1936 reunion was 50 years ago. But then I looked at his older brother and he sure looked like Uncle Jim Graeber to me. And that was 50 years ago for me, too. The mind has tremendous capacity.

But it wasn't just the old days. One of the in-laws owns a landscape business in Salt Lake. He did the landscaping for a Utah prison. "One thing about doing prisons is you can drive by anytime, day or night, and see your work. The lights are always on!"

Another great-grandson specializes in vegetable plant diseases for a big seed company. He has been very successful. But it ruins his own garden. "All I see when I look at my garden are all the diseases. My neighbor has a garden, too, and he's perfectly happy with it. It's full of diseases, too. But he doesn't know it. I see his plant diseases. But all he sees are the red tomatoes!"

One cousin retired after spending over 30 years on tugboats around Los Angeles. In 1936 he was haying in Montana. He found he loved the sea and tugboats. He loved their status in the harbor, the power, the "guts they have." He was headed, after the reunion, to visit another tugboat friend in Seattle.

We'd talked much this day. He was my age, my favorite of those days I visited on the ranch. He was the third child, the "sunny disposition one" as Dr. Spock says. I told him that. He pooh-poohed it. I could see he didn't believe in Dr. Spock. It was time to say goodbye. It had been a tremendous idea, this reunion. Dick and I shook hands. I started to say the banal goodbyes. But he beat me to the first words. "We probably won't see each other again," he said. I looked at him closer. The sunny one was very serious. "I know you're right," I said. We grabbed each by the shoulders. It didn't feel like it had been 50 years.

What makes blood flow so wonderfully thick?

July 1, 1986

THEY'VE FINALLY TAKEN OUT the concrete median strip that ran the 12-block length of Greybull's North Sixth street.

I never thought I would last longer than it did.

That darned thing was there for over 25 years, a mistake from the very beginning, a monument to the concrete lobby. It held the ice in the winter and the dust in the summer. You could not make a left hand turn into a single business along those 12 blocks unless you turned at the corner and backtracked. Instead of preventing accidents it caused several. Everyone seemed to hit it. At times it had more tire rubber on it than the street itself. But it wouldn't go away.

Several other towns around had the same problem. But they solved it easily by just ripping it up. At that time the concrete median strip was an integral part of highway planning. They later found paint stripes and painted islands would do just as good. So other towns gladly took out their median strips. Not Greybull.

I wrote my first editorials against the median strip in the 1960's. So much for the power of the press. When it takes over 20 years for anything to happen, "it ain't you who done it!"

But I'm happy to see it gone nevertheless.

July 8, 1986

ALL POLITICIANS IN western parades ought to have to ride a horse.

That's not without its hazards, though. I can remember Jim Patterson telling about the Basin parade when they put the mayor horseback. Jim was one of Wyoming's earliest cowboys – in those wild times before the century – and he never understood why everyone couldn't ride a horse. But this particular mayor was quite a bit overweight. He hadn't been on a horse since he was a kid. He sort of just teetered up there in the saddle. Jim said they solved it by having "two of the boys ride alongside of him, propping him up so he wouldn't fall off." It didn't look all that authentic, but he made it down main street.

July 22, 1986

THE OLD GUY FROM Florida in the big white Cadillac pulled in just ahead of me at the unleaded pump. So I waited my turn while he got out and started fumbling with the gas tank door. The switch for it was apparently inside. He hollered into his wife in the front seat, "Open it up." Nothing happened. He hollered again, this time sticking his head inside the window. She was opening the glove compartment door and pushing things but nothing was happening. Lawrence Hanson came out to help. But everything to push was inside. The guy was getting very exasperated. His voice raised a half-octave. Finally he got in and pushed it himself. He got back out. The tank door released and he took the cap off. He looked at Lawrence and me standing there. In a very deadpan voice he said, "New car. Old woman."

AT THE SHELL CENTENNIAL . . . THE IOWA STATE geology students "band" of clacking rocks drew laughs all the way down the street in Saturday's parade. That's the first true rock band I ever saw . . . THAT PARADE, incidentally, was quite a parade for a little town. And they say 1,200 people were there to see it . . . RUTH MEIER'S picture she painted for the Pony Express was perfect. It made a fine belt buckle for the riders and a fine first cover for the letters . . . AND THOSE PHOTOGRAPHS in the school house were a Family Album in the truest sense. Jade Smith rephotographed and mounted 195 pictures for the display in addition to the others there . . . WILLIAMS DEPARTMENT Store had a window display on the Shell celebration and it read: "Congratulations on your 100th and Best Wishes from your biggest suburb."

July 29, 1986

WHEN THEY ABBREVIATE "Wyoming" down to "WY" something goes right out of it for me. That isn't Wyoming. That's a "W" and a "Y." WYO is Wyoming. WYO looks like Wyoming. It's solid and feels right. I don't know what WY looks like. It might as well be WG. Or WM. Whatever it is, it's not Wyoming.

You need some character in an abbreviation. It must say something, not just be a bunch of letters. Dropping the "O" off WYO is like stopping talking in mid-sentence.

But we're trapped in computereze and our friendly, comfortable WYO is lopped off to fit a two keystroke rule. We've become a land where you shorten the states' abbreviations and add on to the zip code numbers.

I LIKED THE WAY Dwight Tracy, publisher of the Mission Valley (Mont.) News at Ronan, makes the right names work. No shortened abbreviations for his family of baby owls he rescued from the hay swather. He published a family portrait last week. With names of all four. They were: Big. Second from Big. Third from Big. And finally, Fourth from Big.

August 19, 1986

SUMMERS ARE all the same.

I've spent a number of them now and as I see this one end, I've decided no summer was meant to be complete. All summers will be unfinished. They all end before their time. They're not meant to be long enough. If a summer ran six months long, I'd still be saying "Where did it go?"

If I had this summer to do over, I would probably goof off just as much as I have, get just as little accomplished, throw away the same unfinished list. And say to you the next time I saw you, "Where did it go?"

I've also noticed how much longer a summer is at the beginning than it is at the end. For those whose summer is the push, push, push of summer work and not tennis whites and laying by the pool, it's the other way around. It's the end of the summer that drags. But the rest of us are a culture of ex-students who can't wait for school to be out and the sun to shine day after day. We start the summer thinking it will last forever and squander it from the very first day.

August 26, 1986

WHEN YOU COUNT all the casualties of Frontier Airlines' closing, you have to mention the peanut farmers of the country. Frontier must have bought more peanuts — and handed out more peanuts — than any airline flying.

September 2, 1986

EVERY THURSDAY my old mentor at the Greybull Standard, Lynn Severance, used to get what he called "cardiac exhaustion." It was his theory that three days of getting the paper out left the old heart plumb tuckered out. I think he thought of it like a runner at the end of the race. You just need time to "cool down," walk it out and give the heart time to catch its breath. Hence was born the Thursday "holiday" when you could never find the editor in the office where he was supposed to be. He was out somewhere "resting" his heart. All of us took those Thursday holidays in the weekly newspapering business, but Lynn Severance was the only newspaperman I ever knew who gave it medical status.

September 10, 1986

OVER 25 YEARS AGO Irv Wilkinson and I walked down to his old homestead below the rock bluff east of Greybull so he could show me where the gas well, Miner's Delight, burned for 18 months. Irv's place was in that big bend of the Big Horn, about east of where the Greybull river runs in. We spent most of that Sunday afternoon wandering around there and Irv told one great story after another.

One was about a music peddler who wandered on to his place by mistake and had to ford the river during high water to get out. The other day I was looking down from an airplane on that spot in the river and couldn't help think of that story.

In Irv's words:

"One time a music peddler turned down the wrong road and ended up down in my place," Wilkinson remembered. "And we thought he'd be with us until the mud dried up. But he made a ford across the river that I thought wasn't possible, and went on his way.

"This fellow was trying to get to Linn's place over on the mouth of Shell creek, but he took the turn into our place instead. They told him down at Basin Gardens – he was coming this way – to take the first road to the left. So down he came into my place and the road was too muddy to get out. This was in the early 1900's.

"He said, 'How am I going to get out?' I told him I didn't know. You can't go back up; it's too muddy.' 'Well,' he said, 'I guess I'll ford the river.'

"I told him he couldn't make it. The river was high then and I would have never tried it. But he whipped up his horses and started across, standing up in that old buggy he had and his horses swimming for all they could.

"I never thought I'd see him again. I was sure we would have to fish him out. But he pulled up on the other bank. Then he turned around and waved to me and was gone."

I always liked that story, especially when the peddler turned and waved. I'm a complete softy about a wave. Wave down from a ridge at me or out a car window driving away or from a long ways down the road and I'll remember it forever. It is at once forever final and yet one last bit of closeness. You can be blocks away or across a muddy river and it means the same.

You see a lot of waves in the movies although Shane never waved back at the end and neither did the girl in The Third Man. But Shane was shot up some and it was right that the girl never turned back to Joseph Cotton but kept walking down that long, tree-lined street.

But most of us wave, at one time or another, clinging to that one last second. It had been 50 years since Irv watched that guy and his wet buggy but he never forgot the wave right at the end.

September 23, 1986

IT WAS Ade Prindle, the Basin gravedigger, who showed me how to shovel.

Several of us little kids were watching him dig a ditch for a water line. Ade who spelled it with a "d" not a "b" and was always talking, always starved for conversation, climbed clear out of the hole to show us how. I don't know if the others ever thought about it again, but for me it stuck forever. Leverage, he had said, leverage saves your back, the fulcrum of the shovel handle over the thigh, the push with the legs. And the dirt will fly.

And fly it always has. Moving dirt. By golly, that's been a lot of fun. People think you're crazy when you tell them you like to shovel. Even before backhoes, they thought you were slightly touched to love to grab hold of a shovel handle.

But there's something about digging that fascinates. I'd sit on piles of dirt and watch for hours as the Basin town crew dug ditches. It was all by hand in those times. Long narrow deep ditches, with shovels of dirt flying up out of them. The carefully-planned stairstepped levels, like an archeology dig, so you could climb out. And always talk, a lot of talk. One thing about the mechanized age, you don't enjoy half the conversation.

I don't know if Ade Prindle liked to shovel or not. But he sure got a lot of practice. In his younger years he had run things you don't talk about in a family newspaper. But when I knew him he was old and destitute and he dug ditches and graves to get by. My mother's favorite story about him was the time he slept through the funeral. The Basin cemetery sits on top of a gravel hill but today's beautiful grass and trees hide the tough digging. Going down through all that gravel that hot morning wore Ade out. He leaned up against another headstone after he'd finished and took a nap. He was still asleep when everyone showed up and kept on sleeping through the graveside services. He was still asleep when everyone left.

Old gravediggers, I learned, are always accorded special status.

Obviously, I did not become a gravedigger. But I look back on shoveling just about everything else. Dirt, sand, mud, grain, sugar beets, gravel, ditches, postholes. One summer on the highway crew on U.S. 14 Al Denny and I had to load dump trucks by hand out of a sandpile near Granite Pass. We used scoop shovels because it went faster. That was the fun, trying to beat the clock on how long it took us. For a kid under 20 it was great. It's amazing how fast a truckbox can fill when you're trying to beat both the clock and each other. I never beat Al — he was not about to let a kid do that — but enough sand flew to satisfy me. A tourist car stopped once and a guy got out to tell us we were nuts. We were, of course, but that's what happens if you like a shovel in your hands.

Hector Good always makes fun of my irrigating shovel which is not an irrigating shovel at all, but a digging shovel. I keep telling him, give me a shovel I can dig with. I don't want one of those little teaspoon types.

So I confess to my love of digging. For several years now I've been wondering if that paper up north that keeps trying to personalize obituaries by putting in things the person liked to do — crocheting, rock hunting and so forth — would somehow find out about my shoveling. And you'd pick up the paper someday and find out my big accomplishment in life was moving dirt with a shovel.

"Heck," you'd say as you picked up the paper, "Heck, I didn't know old Kennedy liked to shovel."

Now you know.

October 7, 1986

CLYDE DOUGLASS of the Wyoming Travel Commission wishes me "lots of luck trying to get folks to write Big Horn Basin."

"Some time back," he writes, "we had a woman in this office who was an expert in getting the two spellings exactly backward. To help her, I put together this paragraph, and eventually it ended up in one of our brochures:

"'Traveling in northcentral Wyoming, you'll encounter a number of natural features bearing the same name – Big Horn. For example, west of the town of Big Horn lie the Big Horn Mountains and Bighorn National Forest, out of which flows the Little Big Horn River of Custer fame. The Big Horn River, on the west side of the Big Horns, runs through the Big Horn Basin and Big Horn County into Big Horn Lake. The lake is within Bighorn Canyon National Recreation Area. All of these features owe their name to the bighorn sheep (one word, without capitals).'

"It didn't help. Finally I told her to remember it this way – if it has four legs or is administered by the feds, it's one word."

I HAVE NEVER BEEN able to tell who is the most nervous before high school football games: The kids down on the field or the parents up in the stands.

October 14, 1986

THE OTHER DAY at the Irma Hotel in Cody I got to do what I've been wanting to do for a long time: to shake Richard Farnsworth's hand and tell him how much pleasure he's given me in his many recent films. It was also a chance to tell him how good he looks on a horse. Because he can really ride. I even got carried away in the glow of celebrity-talking and used "beautiful" which prompted him to say right away, "Well, I didn't look so beautiful coming down off the mountain after elk hunting yesterday."

GREYBULL HAS had a long succession of mayors and to pick out "the best one" would be unfair, if not impossible. But at the top of any list would have to be the late Earl Madsen. His term came at a tough time for Greybull city government. It was just recovering from a series of past mistakes and it needed a strong hand. Earl Madsen saw his role as mayor to move the city to solid footing. He would do that, he said, and then step down. That's exactly what he did. He was an excellent administrator and a skillful handler of people. To watch him in action was a lesson in management. I was at every meeting he ever conducted and I still marvel at his sense of what to do. He was one of the few mayors who believed the Council, not the mayor, should make the decisions. He would do all the work, if necessary, but then he would come to the Council with the proposition, lay it on the table and then say, "Gentlemen, what is your pleasure?"

Democracy works by being dedicated to the present. Whatever has gone before is never as important as solving what is on the table before you. So countless public servants serve their terms, "spend their present" so to speak, and then step down. And democracy is not good about remembering. Old faces and other times are rapidly forgotten. But if you should think about those days behind us, remember that Earl Madsen served you very well.

October 21, 1986

MY MOTHER-IN-LAW is 84 years old this year. She told us she realizes she's slipping a little, especially when it comes to remembering things. "Anymore," she told us very seriously, "I just can't remember any of my Latin."

October 28, 1986

THE TWO CALIFORNIANS had finished up their business with us in Cody on that beautiful Wednesday last week. And one of them wondered about Yellowstone Park. How far was that from here? Not far at all, we said. You should go. It would be a marvelous day for it. Good weather. Clear skies. No traffic.

"Is Old Faithful still going?" the younger one asked.

"Gosh, I'm sorry," I said, "but they shut it off Oct. 1. Tourists all gone, you know."

He looked at my face quickly. He sensed he'd been had.

"Look," I said, to make amends, "I'll call ahead and see if they won't turn it back on for you."

Now he knew he had.

But they went anyway!

November 4, 1986

WHEN MANY OLDTIMERS got together for a Big Horn County historical society meeting last year, they were talking about building the old cabins out of cottonwood logs. That reminded Clair Stearns of the shed Al Kershner said he built out of cottonwood logs. They shrunk an inch a year for 13 years, Al claimed.

November 18, 1986

"YOU NEVER really own land. You're just renting it. Oh, you may have the deed to it and pay money for it and you may live on it a long time. And if you're lucky, your family can be on it through some generations. But it's only yours for as long as you're on it. Then it becomes someone else's."

Bob Harvey died this past week at his home on the Greybull river. We had been friends a long, long time. But when he first told me this about owning land, I was a very young man and I'd just been living a few years on the first chunk of real ground I'd ever owned. And I wasn't real sure I believed him. A house is one thing, but land is another. And here I owned ground now and it was mine and I didn't think he quite understood how much I loved this piece of land that was ours. To walk over it and dig in it and make things grow on it. Just to be on it when the sun was coming up or going down. To see it change with the seasons, the green and the brown and the white. To set the root down as deep as it would go and never want to pull it up. I wasn't really sure Bob understood how I felt about all of this.

But he understood. He was passing on a truth and he knew I didn't know it yet. I had to learn it for myself. And I would later, that land is only yours as long as you're there. That's why the love affair – if you have one with a particular patch of land – should be intense as it can be. It's yours for just now.

November 24, 1986

THE GREYBULL swimming pool was all paid off this summer. The last mill assessment made the final payment this past June. If we would try to build that today, 1.) we'd never build it for what it cost then. But that's academic, because 2.) you could never get a bond issue to pass in these times no matter what the cost. We were either very foresighted or very lucky. I choose to think how smart we were!

MOST OF US keep talking about the slow mail these days and how long it takes a letter to go from one place to another. I spent time walking the Old Mail Road in the Big Horns this summer and I couldn't help but think how long it took a letter in those days to make a trip.

The route ran from Hyattville to Sheridan and then back again before there were any other roads or ways to get into the Basin. I know very little about it, how often it ran, when mail stopped in the winter, when it picked back up again in the spring. But the road – it's not a trail but a two track wagon road – is still visible and in many parts usable up over the Big Horns. It's become part of other roads in many places, but it can disappear completely on you.

Fred Conners was a driver on the trail. When I first came to Greybull he would come in the Standard office to talk about those trips and those days. But I was too young to know what I had and I let him slip away without writing down what would have been a fascinating story.

I remember him saying he drove a horse and buggy over the road. But when you walk the road now, soft with this kind of living we have, you marvel at how he ever did it.

Clair Stearns was told the Army built the road sometime in the 1880's. That would make sense because it had to take a lot of men and equipment to hack a road up over a mountain in those times.

On the section of it we walked this year (from the ford of Shell creek up the south side of Shell canyon to the bottom of Crooked Creek hill) there were still bridges and log corrugates visible. They had a U.S. Army look to them. I'll see if I can look that up someplace.

We weren't the only ones who walked where Fred Conners had been many times. In the register at the top of the grade are many old-time Greybull names. How about "Ed Shoemaker" on Sept. 14, 1956. Or "S.A. Doctor," and "W.H. Jones" who apparently made the trip together on the same day, "7-6-57." And "Clyde Forbes, Oct. 57." And a bunch more: Bob Chapman, Nov. 4, 1976; Greg Goodwin, July 12, 1969; LeRoy and Earl Klitzke; Buck Knowlton, Oct. 1970; Francis Dean of Winchester, Ind., Oct. 15, 1956; and a couple of newcomers, Lorree Carroll, Oct. 19, 1981; and Walt Jenkins, Oct. 30, 1980.

You can't walk that road without thinking about Fred Conners. His name won't ever be on any register up there, but he made those tracks you and I see. And he made them a long, long time ago.

December 16, 1986

PATRICK MURPHY was questioning the Greybull-Basin rivalry. Yes, it's been going on for awhile. Actually started around 1907 when the CB&Q wanted to build a roundhouse and division point at Basin and the townfathers there objected to such a rough bunch. The railroad moved on to Greybull and started a town. It's been a friendly and sometimes unfriendly rivalry ever since.

December 24, 1986

It's time to say Merry Christmas . . . that time of year when you send your special hellos and thank yous to all those who have been part of your year and part of your life since the last Merry Christmas.

So it's Merry Christmas to all those who smile back from teller windows and checkout stands . . . who bring iced tea in large pitchers . . . who put out our mail . . . who mention words you write . . . and ask about the kids.

And a special Yuletide thanks to Clyde Douglass at the Wyoming Travel Commission for advice with "Bighorn" and "Big Horn." And Andy Leavitt for help with the Old Mail road over the mountain. And Jack and Derb Linse for corralling a stray.

Merry Christmas to Barbara Ellison Green and LaRae Kinghorn Smith and all the other Basin High School alumni who are working on an all-school reunion in '88. Count all of us in.

And speaking of fellow BHS grads, Merry Christmas to Jerry Henderson . . . I will miss our conversations on those second Tuesdays of the month, Jerry.

And Holiday Cheer to Slim Brewer and Amos Small and Dean Douglas and Paul Clark and the rest of the boys at the Parker Cafe counter who dispense conversation and conviviality in equal proportions. Next time I'll buy.

Merry Christmas to Bill Peters for letting me "store" my old side delivery rake for a couple of years before I picked it up . . . and to Frank and Grace Cortez for that muy bien box of Aunt Jemima from way down south . . . and to Linn Cropsey for filling in those details of Greybull and Shell history we asked about this year . . . and Holiday congratulations to Vera Saban for her book in 1986 with illustrations by Sonja Bernard.

Merry Christmas to Bill Murdoch and his fire department crew who were able to keep Greybull free and clear of any fire hazard signs again this year. I never go by those stumps on South 6th without sending a good-for-Greybull fist in the air. It's not often you can defend a town's honor with a chainsaw.

Special Merry Christmases to Dixie Cummings who is always helpful and always cheerful . . . and to Dick Karhu who keeps the post office in flowers and green, green grass . . . and to Ann Hanson for those beautiful lines you draw . . . to Tim Flitner for your good advice and assistance that Saturday in August.

Merry Christmas to Randy Sullivan for some right seat help so I could keep an appointment "up north," clouds and all.

A very Merry Christmas to Bill Shelledy because you're a great friend and confidant, and a special holiday greeting on your recent retirement this past year after a long, successful career with Big Horn Federal Savings and Loan. Your steady guidance at Big Horn Federal established it as a true Big Horn Basin institution and allowed it to grow and expand far beyond its early Greybull hopes.

Merry Christmas to Steve Cannady for always invaluable advice for four-legged creatures. And who knows, if our forefathers had spelled differently it might now be Steve Kennedy and Bruce Cannady.

Merry Christmas and thank you to Terry Kunkle who knows what should go on a pickup and how to make it look right.

Merry Christmas to Dee Clifton for helping a neighbor's foal with some late-at-night horse medicine . . . And Merry Christmas to all our other neighbors and friends we pass on this same road morning and night and many times in between. Hope we see you down this same road all through '87.

And to Art Sylvester, a Merry Christmas for those won't-fit-in-a-pan trout from "Dry Creek" and a treeful of thank yous for all past favors and kind comments.

Merry Christmas to all those who wave back . . . who say hello with a honk of the horn . . . who reach out a hand . . . who laugh at old stories.

Merry Christmas to Frank Houk for sharing a Trapper Creek road this July.

And a heartfelt Holiday Greeting to the Shell Centennial committee and all those who helped this special Wyoming community mark its unique 100 years. What a grand time, from beginning to end. And to all those who've called Shell creek home one time or another, all the best for 1987, the beginning of Year 101.

Merry Christmas to Mike Schutte for his generosity to his hometown. You remembered your hometown, Mike, but it remembers you, too, and all those times you delighted us on these ballfields and basketball floors.

Special Yuletide Greetings to Herb Kulow for a thoughtful gesture . . . to Wes Herman for watching over the place this year . . . to Herman Mayland for some grand visits . . . to Jim Robertson, it's nice to see you "downtown" again, Jim . . . to Brenton Leavitt for your many good stories and good conversations and good counsel.

Merry Christmas to Gretel Erlich for sharing some perceptive writing and deep thoughts with the rest of her "neighbors."

Merry Christmas to Karen Foe for all the comfort and help you give others. Your Christmas Spirit is 12 months long.

And a very, very Merry Christmas to Chuck Williamson although really it's the winner of Saturday night footraces who should say "Merry Christmas," not the loser. But Happy Holidays anyway. I didn't know I could learn so much humility in the first 10 yards of a 40-yard sprint up the Big Horn river bridge highway.

And Merry Christmas to Alberta Storeim who should have warned me about Chuck!

All those Christmas lights say "Merry Christmas" better than any of us could. This is Greybull's toughest year, yet more people have more bright, cheerful, fun Christmas lights than ever before. To all of you in Greybull and Shell who put up lights, Happy Holidays from all of us.

And to all of those people who live in other places and keep track of Greybull through the pages of the Greybull Standard, including James McHugh of Magna, Utah, Connie Michelena in Greeley, Colo.; Orin Oleson in Yuma, Ariz.; Richard Gormley in Denver, "Sam" Jones, with her Army husband in Germany; Myrtle Prugh in Eureka and Don Schuyler in Rona, and 43 other Californians who subscribe to the Standard, here's a very special Merry Christmas to you across all those miles.

And to all you new people we'll be meeting this next year and all the little kids who grew up so much during 1986, to all those who live in this fine Wyoming community, the best of holidays and the merriest of Christmases.

December 30, 1986

A RUMOR FLOATING around one Montana town was that it would soon be getting a new football coach, a Chinese football coach, named Win Won Soon.

THIS IS THE SEASON when corks pop a lot. The most spectacular cork-popping I ever saw was at a Cody Enterprise Christmas office party in the early 1970's. Someone shook the champagne bottle a little too much and when the cork went, so did a big fluorescent light fixture overhead. A perfect launch.

1987

January 6, 1987

Don't know whether newspaper people are supposed to have worse desk tops than the rest of you. But it seems we are bad offenders. The Publisher's Auxiliary trade magazine once ran a contest to find the worst editor's desk. The winner was a guy with a bowl of strawberries on top of everything else. I'm sure I've mentioned this before. It made a very lasting impression on me. But I've always considered that my desk could not be the worst as long as I kept the strawberries off the top of it.

January 20, 1987

I THOUGHT WE HAD a cat again. Would have been the first one in a long time. It was my fault. The cat was hiding out down in the haystack, burrowing back between bales, and every time I fed horses it thought it ought to have something, too. I must be mellowing. My rule against any more cats suddenly seemed pretty harsh on these chilly mid-January mornings. So I bought a box of Purina Cat Chow – the first in years – and now the cat really sets up a howl when I show up. It knows a soft touch.

We had a bunch of cats once. Ran out of names eventually and went with Kiki I and then Kiki II and III and so forth. If we'd kept on that way, I think this present one would have been about Kiki 88.

Now I notice the old yellow boy is gone again. Wasn't there this morning. That's the trouble with drifters. Get a good meal under their belt and they'll wander on down the road again.

THE THREE-POINT SHOT should not have been added to high school basketball. It wrongly shifts the emphasis. Basketball is a game of finesse and ball handling, passing and tough defense, not just bombs from outside. College is suffering from three-point-itis, too, with a line that's too close. From that distance it's hardly extra skill. The other day I saw a four-point play – a three-point shot and a made foul shot. Four points in a basketball play? You have to be kidding.

January 27, 1987

SOMEONE WHO IS very close to me is having his 30th birthday and the big Three Zero is on his mind. Funny how your perspective changes. Down the road that big 3 0 Birthday is lost among the others. I told him I couldn't even remember mine. He won't either. But this is the kind of unsolicited advice that the older generation finds so easy to give and the younger so hard to accept.

Life is generous to us with its perspective, though. Remember the joke about the two old gentlemen slowly walking down the street together. A very pretty girl passed them and the two old guys stopped and turned around to look after her. One of them sighed: "Ah, to be seventy again."

February 10, 1987

IF YOU WERE around in 1936 you will appreciate some of the thoughts in this essay about those good old days. It's only reprinted in part here, but you get the idea of its theme:

"We were before television, penicillin, polio shots, antibiotics and frisbees. Before frozen food, nylon, dacron, Xerox and Kinsey. We were before radar, fluorescent lights, credit cards and ballpoint pens. For us, time-sharing meant togetherness, not computers; a chip meant a piece of wood; hardware meant hardware; and software wasn't even a word.

"In our time, closets were for clothes – not coming out of, and a book about two women living together in Europe could be called 'Our Hearts Were Young and Gay'. In those days, bunnies were small rabbits and rabbits were not Volkswagens . . .

"When we were in school, Cheerios, frozen orange juice, instant coffee and McDonalds were unheard of. We thought fast food was what you ate during Lent. We were before FM radio, tape recorders, electric typewriters, word processors, Muzak, electronic music and disco dancing . . .

"In our day cigarette smoking was fashionable, grass was mowed, coke was something you drank and pot was something you cooked in. We were before coin vending machines, jet planes, helicopters and interstate highways . . . You could buy a Chevy coupe for $659 but who could afford it in 1936? Nobody. A pity, too, because gas was only eleven cents a gallon . . ."

Art Brown of Basin shared his copy with us. We thought we'd seen it before. So we dug it out. Sure enough, it was the same. Small World Department: It was written by Betty's aunt, Avalon Hart in Lincoln and given to an AAUW luncheon last summer.

WITHIN ONE month I had one vehicle turn over 333333 and another one hit 123456. Ah, life's little pleasures!

February 17, 1987

IT IS A HAPPY coincidence that the February Reader's Digest quoted Angie Papadakis on this marvelous thought about Americans: "You may go to France, but you will never become a Frenchman. You may go to Greece, but you will never become a Greek. You may go to China, but you will never become a Chinese, to Japan and never become a Japanese, but anyone can come to America and become an American. That is the greatness of this country we call the United States of America."

FRIDAY, THE 13TH has come and gone this month. But there'll be another one in March. That occurred back in 1942, also. I was 13 that day, 13 on Friday, the 13th! I went around v e r r y c a r e f u l l y.

March 3, 1987

THERE ARE kindred spirits out there. Walt Preis of Emblem, another speedometer watcher, writes: "It is interesting to note that others are number conscious also. I am usually nine miles early or two miles late. I did catch 44,444.4 in front of Chopping Motors in Riverton last summer. Also, a 77,777.7 at the Grabbert Ranch lane another time."

MARCH 2ND was my dad's birthday. He would have been 92. And as usual whenever that day comes around, the thoughts go back to him and his life and his influence on our lives.

By coincidence — and maybe it wasn't — over the weekend Nina Horton of Basin ran across an old six-inch ruler with Dad's name on it. He used it for a business advertisement. Nina had found it among some things she saved and she kindly sent it on to me. And within a day Mary Hoffman of Worland told us she could remember Dad's cramped, backhand signature coming across all the Big Horn Canal checks at the bank through the years.

We are a part of all that has gone before us, more so than we realize. I shake my head in disbelief sometimes. I'm either saying or thinking or doing something exactly like I remember my dad doing. Oh, it's not always the good and the positive. Because it's not just the good and the positive that are passed along in life. But hopefully the right mix is there, both for what you got from the past generation and for what you in turn give to the next.

A very good friend of mine who read some of the words I wrote when Dad died said he did not think he was old enough yet to know his dad. That's true of all friendships, I suppose. It takes time to know others. But it is especially true of your parents because you spend many years being kids around them and not adults.

It took me a long time to know my parents and every anniversary that passes I'm aware I know them — and myself — a little better.

March 10, 1987

IF YOU CAME UPON a big rectangular stone inscribed with Daniel Boone's name on it and with additional instructions that there was more on the other side, would you turn the stone over?

Apparently old Daniel knew you would because he is said to have perpetrated a long-running practical joke back in the early 1800's involving just such a rock.

The American West magazine (which, incidentally is a well done job and a welcome part of the monthly mail) brings the story back through the recollections of one Billy Dixon who wrote about it in his autobiography.

Dixon ran across the stone some 50 years after Boone had chiseled on it. It was between Plum Creek and Julesburg in southeastern Nebraska, he claimed. Boone had pounded out an inscription along with his name, and then added that further information could be found on the other side. The rock was too big just to casually flip it over. In fact, Dixon and his friends had to hook a team of oxen to roll it over. You could see marks and tracks around the rock where others had done the same thing over the years.

So the rock was rolled and the dirt brushed away from the inscribed words. But the joke was on you. Because what the one side of the rock said so did the other. Both sides said exactly the same thing. And that was the genius of the joke and of Daniel Boone. Once the joke was played on you, it was ready to play on the next. And the next. And old Dan is still laughing.

AROUND GREYBULL . . . Today (Mar. 10) would have been the "regular" day for the ice to go out of the Big Horn river. But it's three-week-old news this year. The ice couldn't resist these nice days anymore than we could and it went out Feb. 19 . . . And speaking of things that go . . . with the moving of the Big Horn Co-op station to its new location, the two blocks of main Street are without a corner service station for the first time in a long time. For years the town had Fletcher's Standard (where the Silver Spur is); Patterson's Garage and Texaco (the abandoned building south of the post office); the old Conoco station (where Scott McColloch's office is); and the Co-op station which outlasted them all.

April 7, 1987
IT IS A LAW of Spring that the wind velocity will increase by 20 knots from the time you strike the match to burn the weeds and the time they start burning. Ditto for the wind direction. If it is from the south when the match is struck, it will be from the north before the fire is over.

WHICH REMINDS ME that one of the sure signs of spring in our country is how many fire calls you have on the first warm weekend.

April 16, 1987
THAT YELLOW "Drifter" came back for another meal. "He's" been gone for weeks now and the other day "he" was back in the haystack. Only now "He" is a "She" and "She" had Three and now we are Four. Moral of the story: Never feed a traveling "Man".

April 24, 1987
TREES ALWAYS grow faster than you think they will. One day they're just a sprout. And the next, they're grown up. A lot like kids. The secret to growing trees is not the water or the coddling or the pruning. The secret is to get them in the ground. Just get them in the ground. Give them a couple of years and they'll be there forever.

THE WEATHER always seems to be sorry after a storm and apologizes with an especially beautiful day.

WATER IN THE DITCH this morning. That spooked all the horses. They couldn't remember what it was, I guess. When you're at the end of the ditch, it sometimes helps to have a good memory.

THAT LAVENDER or purple color on Paul Murdoch's little Volkswagen makes it look like a very bright Easter Egg running around. Actually it is not purple, they tell me. That color is "Inventory." Inventory is when you go around Mike Clifton's Paint Shop and pour all the half-used cans into one batch, mix it up and spray it on. Voila! Inventory!

April 28, 1987
TOM SHALES, the caustic critic of "The Washington Post", describes PBS television as "English people talking and animals mating, occasionally interrupted by English people mating and animals talking."

MORRIS AVERY had an old Aircoupe he flew around in the Forties and once he and Hap Crain went to Jackson. While they were there, they bought 30 pounds of Star Valley cheese and then went on to West Yellowstone. In the hottest part of the afternoon, they decided to fly on back home again. That plane didn't have all that much soup anyway and Hap wasn't exactly a dainty little thing. Besides they had 30 pounds of cheese aboard.

But Morris started on down the runway anyhow. They cleared the ground but the heat and the altitude and the weight was working against everything. The old plane kept wanting to settle back down again. Morris struggled with it and it would gain a little altitude and then sink back down towards the ground.

Finally, Morris hollered at Hap, "Throw out that damned cheese."

Hap was horrified. "We can't throw it out, we just bought it. Let's eat it."

May 12, 1987
ONE OF LIFE'S GREAT pleasures has to be reading the Boston Globe in Boston the day after anything but the day after a Celtics game is especially marvelous. For me, to see it as a newspaperman is to be grateful that great newspapers like that exist. That is what journalism is supposed to be. That's what we all want it to be.

For a Celtics fan, you have to be ecstatic over three full pages of coverage, no fewer than five big stories on the game or the individuals and two full columns of "trivia" and quotes and incidentals.

Besides, the Celtics WON!

AND TO MAKE IT even more astounding, in the airport the next morning, there was Red Auerbach, cigar, green shirt, raspy voice and all, holding court with a half dozen people at one of the loading gates.

Being in Boston, the Celtics winning, old Red Auerbach, The Boston Globe, all in one morning. I thought maybe they were going to have to carry me feet first onto the plane.

May 21, 1987

SHORTY COLEMAN was janitor in the Basin school when I was growing up and one day the study hall clock stopped. Shorty had to bring his long stepladder over to start the thing going again. The whole study hall was watching him. It was one of those old clocks with a big glass door and it hung high up on the wall. Shorty got the clock going, climbed down off the ladder and started out the door. He stopped at one girl's desk and in a loud voice said: "I'd stop, too, if I had to look at you kids all day."

I NEVER SAW an old couple drive fast or a kid drive slow, although one time Lon Stadtfeld and I had a drag race down 27th Street in Billings in the middle of the afternoon. Lon was in his seventies then and I, well, I should have known better.

But we both pulled up in adjoining lanes just as the light turned red. The traffic had thinned out there by the Gazette and we were first in line going south. It seemed natural to lean out and holler over, "Want to drag, Lon?" He thought I was kidding but I busted out in good shape and left him behind.

The next red light stopped us. I looked over at Lon. By God, he was serious about this. He was looking straight ahead, gripping the wheel very tightly. I got ready, too. Betty and Louise were beginning to be horrified at these old coots. The light turned. Lon took a good jump and we were rollicking down 27th at much too fast a clip. We lasted another block before giving up such childish impulses

I still don't know why we didn't get picked up. We should have. And I've often wondered how silly two sober, upright Greybull citizens would have looked standing up in front of a Billings judge on charges of drag racing in broad daylight down Billings' 27th.

June 1, 1987

BETTY COULDN'T figure out how come the pancake flour was so lumpy this time. She fished around and pulled out two big radishes. When you have a 14-month-old grandson visiting, and he's been carrying around two big radishes all one morning, and the cupboard with the pancake flour is just floor level, and there's a big, dark hole in the top of the box – just radish size – with all this, you're just bound to have radishes in your pancake mix.

June 9, 1987

I WAS HANGING AROUND outside a big airport the other day. What a noisy place. No wonder all the ground crews wear ear plugs and protectors. No noise is pleasant stuff but airport noise seems even more high-pitched and whiny. You never had to wear ear muffs in a train station. But then you never left for a hundred different places on a hundred different planes in a couple of hours like you do at an airport. It's a trade-off, one of those modern put-up-with-it to get-more-out, that we live under nowadays.

Funny how times change, though. A lonely train whistle to a dreamy young boy (and I know this from firsthand!) was a ticket away. Some far-off place was beckoning. Just get on it and ride to adventure. Now planes leave airports every minute and far-off places are not far-off at all. As for the noise and frenzy, young people live with noise and frenzy all the time. What's so special about airports? It's the way we live now.

To put this in perspective I suppose you'd have to imagine standing around some old Western train when the train first clattered and whistled in and all the old people held their hands over their ears. What a noisy contraption. But then some young boy or girl turned around to the old man and said: "Gee, Pa, this looks like a lot more fun than a horse."

June 25, 1987

CALIFORNIA HEADLINE: "Roadkill Recipes: Food That Wasn't Fast Enough."

A PARKING in front of a house is about as useless an idea that Americans ever had. Wonder who started it? You have to say the idea sure caught on. All across America we had to put up with a four-foot wide patch of grass that was not big enough to be lawn and too pretty to be a sidewalk. It's somewhere in between and in the end, nothing.

You can't water a parking right. It's too narrow for the big sprinklers and little sprinklers never reach. For a while back in the Forties, there was a parking sprinkler which consisted of four small sprinkler heads strung out on a section of hose. It was good for nothing else but sprinkling parkings and didn't even do much of a job of that.

So it usually doesn't grow very good grass. Many parkings wound up in concrete or gravel or sometimes just dirt. Anything but that cussed dinky plot of grass to take care of.

For years now modern cities have built sidewalks right to the curb. That's what they used to do with boardwalks. Built 'em right to the dirt road. We should have left it that way.

THIS STORY about Tom Dewey came out of the National Press Club. Seems Dewey and his wife were eating dinner Election Night 1948 and the papers had all predicted Dewey would beat Truman. The candidate said to his wife, "You know, Mrs. Dewey, tomorrow you will be sleeping with the President of the United States."

And Mrs. Dewey said, yes, she guessed that was right. In the morning at breakfast, someone brought in a newspaper with the big headlines that Truman had won, not Dewey. It was Truman who was the winner.

The Deweys looked at the paper.

And Mrs. Dewey said: "Should I call Mr. Truman or should I wait for him to call me?"

June 30, 1987

THAT TRIP ACROSS the new Big Horn river bridge at Greybull puts you right alongside the old bridge with a view of it you couldn't see before.

Up until Saturday's first opening, you had to be in the river to get that close to it. Now you cruise along beside it and it's right out the window. I don't mean to be unkind, but seeing it up close doesn't make it look any younger. The wrinkles show. It's old-fashioned and tired and not at all as smooth and sleek as the new one.

You see the bridge up pretty close when you float the river. Floating the river is always quiet, and when you get to a bridge after miles of willows and cottonwood trees, a bridge always looks bigger and more imposing.

It's a prop, though, and it just sort of slides by like everything else as you drift along

One quiet September we were floating about 500 yards from the bridge when a couple came across on a cycle. They had coasted down the hill with the throttle cut back so they, too, were just drifting along.

There's an absolute stillness to some moments. It's as if time goes by frame by frame. One by one. A pause. And then a frame. This was one of those moments. We heard the guy say, "Look, there's a canoe in the river." We could see their faces turned towards us. The voice just floated down to us. We both waved from the canoe. Their faces were still turned to us as they kept crossing the bridge. They waved back. Life just seemed to stop on that frame. It was quiet and nothing seemed to move. Then the frame advanced and both the canoe and the cycle went on.

That's what the old bridge is, and all of life, I guess. In the stillness of the moment it's there. And then it's gone.

July 7, 1987

IN HELENA, THERE'S a local pub called "The Windbag Saloon." That fits. It's the bar where the politicians love to hang out.

I'M REMINDED AGAIN WHAT I'VE ALREADY learned about high school class reunions (this summer we're going through our third one at our house). And that is:

a) You're better off if you don't listen to all the stories of what happened 10 years ago.

b) If you do listen, you'll have a tendency not to believe them. Believe them!

c) I didn't think there were enough hours in any one day; or days in any one week; or weeks in any one year for all that to have happened! Again, believe.

d) After listening carefully, I can only assume we were not in the country then, which is the same conclusion my own parents apparently came to.

e) I've further concluded life with teenagers is actually really blissful for parents. If you don't think they're blissful, think of what they'd been like if you'd known what you know now!

July 21, 1987

TEN-YEAR-OLD Christopher Lee Marshall is trying to be the youngest pilot to fly across the country. He's being accompanied by his flight instructor, Rowe Yates, the paper says. That has to be the same Rowe Yates who soloed me at Greybull. But I wasn't 10 years old and I certainly wasn't planning to fly across the country!

August 4, 1987

PASSED Yellowstone Lake the other day, and I'm always reminded of the guy who couldn't get his car started that afternoon along the "beach." We'd been picnicking and he and his girlfriend had been necking and there were only the two cars along the whole stretch. After awhile they decided to move on to another pounding surf. But his car wouldn't go. It sounded to me like it was flooded. He just kept grinding away. And no fire. Pretty soon he decided he should ask for some help. We were the only other car. I knew he didn't want to come over. In the first place, you should be able to start your own car, most of the time anyway, and in front of your girlfriend, especially. Then, too, they'd been purposefully oblivious to us, creating their own solitude when there wasn't any. Now he'd have to enter back into the world of picnicking parents and a bunch of little kids who'd been watching most of the time anyway.

He was flustered. It was written all over his face when he came up. He really didn't want to do this. "Say," he said to me, "I can't get my sar carted."

Boy, I almost lost it. I had this crazy hope that I could come up with something in inverted answer in the next few seconds. Something like, "Gon't wo, huh?" Or "I'll lo gook." But I blanked out. Right then it was not to be. If someone ever does that to me again, I'll be ready. But I wasn't then.

And honest, I didn't laugh outloud. And I did get the thing started. It was just flooded.

August 18, 1987

I HAVE A LETTER composed to Mark Van Every, the Bridger-Teton National Forest spokesman about that tornado in Jackson. Van Every quotes a Chicago professor as saying the tornado that blew down those 15,000 acres of timber was the only recorded tornado at that 8,500-foot altitude.

The tornado was "not only extremely rare but may have been the only one of its kind that has occurred at this elevation anywhere in the world," Van Every said.

I'm trying to point out to him that there have been numerous tornadoes in the Big Horn mountains at that elevation or higher. In 1959 a tornado roared over the south rim of Shell canyon which is between 8,800 and 9,000 feet. It blew down a swath of timber that is just now coming back, hit Granite creek campground, and then hopped and skipped on up the mountain, touching down at various spots above 8,500 feet.

Other tornadoes have hit through the years. On July 4, 1978, a tornado devastated the timber around Ranger Creek Ranch which is 8,200 feet and then went on up the hill for at least several hundred more feet. The tornado had already hit the Flitner cabin and buildings near Battle Creek further south at almost 8,600 feet.

I think the good professor should know this.

WE WERE SITTING around talking with the Bill Shelledys and I had a story of the old days I wanted to tell and when I'd finished, Betty exclaimed: "I've never heard that story before!"

By golly, that's the first time that's ever happened to me. That I could come up with a story she hasn't heard three dozen times already. Thirty-six years of married life and three years of college courtship, all the time listening to the same old stories, over and over, and she hears a brand new one. An honest-to-goodness brand new tale of the old days.

I tell you, it's been a good summer!

August 25, 1987

MEMORABLE QUOTES: From a Bob Marshall wilderness outfitter: "I didn't even know I was in trouble until I looked back and saw all them spur marks on my saddle."

GIL AND JADE Smith woke up on the Oregon Coast earlier this month to find Shell, Wyo. on their doorstep.

The Sunday paper had been delivered to their cabin door and one of the main feature articles was on the Big Horns and Shell.

"Wonder what the odds would be of finding such an article on any given day 1,000 miles from home?" she asks.

The article, written by Portland Oregonian staff writer Jack Hart, is one of the best on the Big Horns that's been done. As young college kids twenty years ago, he and his bride were headed back to the West Coast. They bumped up against the Big Horns at Sheridan and decided to sidetrack. They eventually wound up at the Bluejacket Guest Ranch.

"At the bottom, in the dark and cottonwoods," Hart wrote, "we turned off the highway, crossed a plank bridge and rented a pine-paneled cabin on the creek. We built a fire in the riverstone fireplace, and listened as the creek burbled and a chilly wind hissed down through the canyon. The whole scene, my introduction to the Big Horn Mountains and Shell Canyon, still lingers, 20 years later, vivid as last night's movie.

"The memory lasted far longer than the marriage."

(He came back this summer, found the Kedish Ranch and rejoiced in the fishing and mountain life one more time.)

September 2, 1987

ONCE, A LONG TIME back, Slim Brewer, Bob Johnson, Frank Hammond and Joe Preator were packing down out of the high country around Emerald Lake in the Big Horns and they came to a sign that read, "Cookstove Basin." Frank's horse stopped right by the sign and just stood there. The rest of them moved on down the trail a little, but Frank's horse kept standing by the sign.

"What's he waiting for," Slim said he hollered back at Frank. "He's reading the sign and trying to put it in horse language," Frank said.

THAT'S A VERY fine Hallmark commercial about a very considerate father, a daughter with a new driver's license, and a bashed up garage wall. I'm just a terrible softie for those kind of commercials. But I thought, too, how true it is that kids may need all sorts of punishments for little misdeeds and problems, but never for the big crisis. My dad acted with first sergeant toughness all my growing up. I thought he was terribly unfair and very picky. But the first crisis that came along in my life, he acted completely different. I was astonished. Here I had really fouled up. On the ten scale, my third grade foul-up was about a 14. But he was calm, helpful and very considerate. That was just one of several such times before I left the nest. And Dad was the same each time. I promised myself as a young man that if I could ever be a father, I would do the same. Only my kids know if I succeeded.

PATHS AND TRAILS never run straight. They always wander. They seem to be made by people and animals who can't concentrate. It isn't that the trail doesn't go from point A to point B. You arrive all right, but not by the shortest distance. There are a lot of wiggles and curves along the way.

It isn't all that easy to make a straight line across the earth. Thousands of people trudged along the Oregon Trail from east to west and that's one of the biggest squiggles of all. From the air you can follow it to the horizon and see it still wandering from side to side off into the distance. Always heading west but always crooked.

The only straight road you see out in the hills are the pipeline roads and these don't follow a track, they follow a pipe.

It's hard to make a path run straight. When I started to grade school from the north side of Basin, the walk to school was an angle across what is now the baseball field complex. It was a hay field then, one of the many the Wyoming

Gas company owned around town. Jack Twomey would put up hay on them and then in the late fall and winter time the kids would cross it going to school.

The path was always crooked. It went from the northeast corner to the southwest corner, but never in a straight line. One morning when I got to the field, it had just been plowed and worked down. There wasn't a mark on it. I was the first one there. And I can remember thinking this is one path that is going to be in a straight line.

I started very carefully keeping my eyes up and to where I wanted to go. I walked slowly and carefully. At the end I turned to look. It was a very twisty path. Just like all the others had been. In my mind I was making a straight line, but my feet didn't make it come out that way.

When I came back home from school that night, all the other kids had walked along in the very same places I had, keeping all the wiggles intact, all the crooks the same. The first guy gets to make the first crooked tracks. And everyone else follows. That's the way roads are made. And no one ever made a very straight one.

September 8, 1987

SEE WHERE Alf Landon is 100 years old. Cub Smith called to say he'd seen that, too, and that Landon was the first president he'd voted for. "He got beat so bad," Cub pointed out, "I'm not sure voting for him the first time is anything to brag about!" Cub remembered as a teenager on Trapper Creek talking to old George Jenks, an early homesteader up there, who said he'd voted for Lincoln.

"He had lived in Kansas then. I worked it out, his age and all, and he could have," Cub said.

And a vote for Lincoln WAS something to brag about.

GARRISON KEILLOR says it's just as true everywhere else as it is in Lake Wobegon: That most of us have better children than we deserve.

BLAMING THE KIDS for everything is easy exercise. I had a 70-year-old friend who lived in California and while he was buying groceries, the stacked island of canned peaches tumbled over. My friend thought to himself, some kid must have knocked it over. He went out to the car and his wife started complaining immediately how some kids were rocking the car. It turned out they'd just been through a California earthquake!

October 13, 1987

WE'RE STILL wondering whether our string of lombardy poplars will turn golden this year. Some years they do, some they don't. They seem to be more sensitive to temperature and moisture than the other trees around them. Everything else will be picture-perfect gold and yellow and those lombardies will stand over there, pouting, brown and ugly. They're fickle trees anyway, fickle about growing and staying healthy and just as fickle about joining a pretty fall. I should have kept track, but not more than a half dozen years out of their 30 have they bothered with fall. I should go out and talk with them. All the kids will be home at the end of this month. It would be nice if those trees could put on a show. After all, the kids and the trees all grew up together.

November 3, 1987

SAW A PINK HALTER (the horse kind) hanging on a rack with all the usual blue and red and brown ones. "Who would buy a pink halter?" I wondered. Turns out they're a hot item. Many are sold. For various reasons. One Cody young woman buys everything pink she can find. Halters, blankets, etc. There's a very good reason for all the pink for her. It keeps her cowboy brothers from latching on to her stuff.

November 10, 1987

THIS WANT AD was in the lost and found section of the Hungry Horse News: "Lost, blue sleeping bag between Kalispell & Hungry Horse Reservoir. Part of matched set. Wife cold."

November 17, 1987

SOMEDAY, WHEN THEY publish a book with all the known one-liners of UW Basketball Coach Benny Dees, I hope they include that one in this week's Sports Illustrated about the Alabama player he once coached. "If his IQ was any lower," Dees says, "we'd have to water him."

OUR FURNACE runs just fine until the first cold snap. Then it goes on the blink and someone's got to come to tell us that it will be a week before the part arrives. Naturally this week is the first touch of day-to-day cold weather we've had. By Saturday it should be warmer again, whether the furnace is working or not.

The furnace took its cue from the septic tank which quit working when all the company arrived two weeks ago. Septic tanks always work when no one else is around. Ours likes to fail when the house is full.

It probably also failed this time because it noticed the tractor wheel had collapsed under the loader weight. That usually only happens when the loader is full (like this time). As long as the tractor sits, everything seems to work A-Okay.

You can say the same thing for the VCR decoder which suddenly isn't decoding and the faulty alternator in the car which just as quickly ran the battery down for a couple of nights.

Country living is sometimes sitting around waiting for the next thing to break down, wear out, plug up, go off, quit cold, freeze up, fall apart, burn out.

December 1, 1987

IT IS ONLY my imagination that I am more thankful on a bright sunny Thanksgiving Day than on a dreary, cold, windy, wet one. The things I am thankful for have no relation to sunshine and wonderfully blue Wyoming sky. Love, family, friends, laughter, a place on Life's path, these aren't just for fair weather. They're comfort for all seasons, for all the days that aren't so cheerfully warm.

Yet I cannot help but think on this annual Thanksgiving walk around the place, on one of the brightest of all Thanksgivings, that the fine sunshine of this November day is a special blessing.

I feel blessed, too, by Wyoming. I will be forever thankful that Wyoming was where the root went down. I could have lived many places, I'm sure. After all, millions of people do and they are happy and thankful and at peace, too. But Wyoming was for me and I chose not to test myself in other places. And when I walk around on Wyoming ground and look off to Wyoming mountains and cottonwoods along Shell creek, I don't need other choices.

People see different Wyomings. I wish everyone could have seen it on this Thanksgiving Day, 1987. Our Nebraska guest goes home before the weather changes and I have made her promise to tell every Nebraskan she meets that she basked in six weeks of beautiful sunshine and clear Wyoming skies. "Back home" they've had some Nebraska snow and cold and a very bad-tasting dose of Barry Switzer's Oklahoma.

James Michener once wrote, "Wyoming is a state I cherish, one of the truly distinctive areas of the United States." And so it is. The root stays.

Walking around all the trees, I'm not sure they've grown much. It's hard to tell, year by year. Like kids, they're small for awhile and then big forever. One huge old cottonwood had to be trimmed back. It looks awful and the mess underneath looks worse. The tree trimmer was leaving Wyoming for warmer days. I caught him at the start of his off season. He scuba dives then, for months. Right now he's in the Cayman Islands. He probably spent his Thanksgiving diving off the big Wall. I don't blame him if he's forgotten my tree. But I think of him as I look at it.

I ignore all the fences that sag and the weeds that needed cleaned up. This is not a day for chores. The new flagpole is different. That demands attention. After all these years of thinking about putting up a flag, I finally did it. Today it looks especially fine, but then, when the breeze hits the flag, every day is a Thanksgiving.

Thanksgiving is a day when you don't think about materialistic possessions Instead it's a sun on your face, a family that remembers, friends that are close, trees that age, another generation that's beginning. The list is long.

I want to add a piece of Wyoming land to the list, but maybe an acre of ground is as materialistic as a VCR. When ground is not your livelihood, it is a luxury. But I have a little chunk of hillside that I've piddled along all year on, a "new" pasture of just barely an acre, and I want to put that on the

Thanksgiving list. I wind up this day down there looking at it. It's all planted now, marked out and ready to grow next spring. It never had a plow before, never grew anything but weeds and one old cottonwood that lightning eventually felled. I spent hours on this little place. Grubbed off the sagebrush and greasewood, burned the rest of the tree, moved fence, hauled off all the junk, enlisted Floyd Collingwood's dozer for a couple of hours, picked up rocks for a couple of months.

Now I'm done, in time for this November day and in time for next spring. You have to wonder how it will do. But if it doesn't make it, I still haven't lost. I've planted all sorts of trees and bushes that never grew. But many have and still are. I've written thousands of words that have been forgotten. But some have stuck and stayed around. You get many chances on the things that count. A man would be a fool if he didn't give thanks for that.

It's been a good day for a walk around, for flags that fly and land that gives pleasure. The sun's still shining. It does that often in Wyoming.

December 22, 1987

It's time to say Merry Christmas . . . that time of year when you send your special hellos and thank yous to all those who have been part of your year and part of your life since the last Merry Christmas.

So it's Merry Christmas to all those who smile back from checkout stands . . . who bring "seconds" for our coffee cup . . . who fly flags . . . and grade roads . . . and bring iced tea in large pitchers.

Merry Christmas to those who say kind words about columns just written, who ask how the kids are doing, who wave at the pickup as it goes by.

And a special Merry Christmas to Dale Hill in Coos Bay, Ore. who so often sends back warm thoughts to his old hometown country and especially that great letter this summer.

Holiday Cheer to Dean Douglas whose daily walks around Greybull keep him in touch with many people. Those one hundred and thirteen blocks each day are a marvel, Dean.

Merry Christmas to John McGough and his new project with the old stone schoolhouse. We wish you luck on your new venture, and this time the toast is ON US!

Special Yuletide Greetings to Bob Nielsen for his help on our flagpole project. If you hadn't been able "to get up in the air," Bob, that old flag would never be flying now.

And we want to say Merry Christmas to Ron Wright and the rest of the "alumni"; to Vern Henderson for the use of his trailer for a very long and heavy pole; and to Bill Peters who made it that way; to Mart Hinckley for help with some hay; to Shirley Presgrove for all the trims; to Randy Sullivan for a ride over the mountains; to Wayne Paris for literally "baling me out" this fall.

Merry Christmas to those who dance on patios on warm spring nights, who make Christmas wreaths out of pine cones and ribbon, who remember

Frankie Norris stories, and who come back for Greybull high school reunions.

Merry Christmas to all those who gave us the new bridge. Funny, how the mental picture of the old one is fading so fast. And Merry Christmas to those young ladies who flagged us down and smiled and waved even though they did the same thing every day to 3,000 other people, too.

Merry Christmas to Tammy Greene and Brenda Hunt for their fine pinch-hitting at the Standard this fall.

And special greetings to George "Pat" Brown of Basin, who retired this 1987 from the Wyoming Highway Department, after a long and fruitful career. Pat's contribution to Wyoming roads, and particularly to those you and I drive on in the Big Horn Basin, should be remembered for a long time. Always helpful, always knowledgeable, he gave us miles and miles of good roads.

And Happy Holidays to Marjorie Good in Slidell, La., for sharing a Montana license plate; and to Mary Lee Haddenhorst of Littleton, Colo., for some very kind words.

Merry Christmas to all the walkers who walk out our way for their exercise and to all the other walkers, too, who make that trek down the road a ritual. Pardon the pun, but you're on the right track.

And hopes for a very white, white Christmas to Emerson Scott and his Big Horn mountain ski area. We wish you many, many such white days in this forthcoming ski season. Your enthusiasm and good sense have given us new hope that we will once again have a ski area here.

Merry Christmas to a bunch of old friends we used to see on Greybull's main street so often in those "other" Christmases, the Skip Schuylers, the Lee Kunkles, Ruth Meier, the Willie and Ben Minters, the Ed Huddlestons, Bill Shelledy, Ells Stott, Doc Rogers, Bill Simpson, all business and professional men and women who've retired now. And Chris Paustian, Lee Grenier and Frank Hinckley from the bentonite plants.

Merry Christmas to all those "boxholders" who get their mail at the post office every day and stay around long enough to say hello and to tell me "what's new."

And speaking of the post office, special Holiday cheer to the ladies there, Helen, Kathy and Donna for all their good-natured assistance. When you hear someone criticizing the Post Office Department for lousy service, they are not talking about Greybull's.

Merry Christmas to Wee Collingwood . . . we have a mutual friend in Alexander Valley who now knows TWO people from Wyoming!

And Merry Christmas to the Gary Goods and the Sellars and Del and Marilyn Edeler and all the rest of the neighbors and friends we pass on this "neighborhood" road of ours day after day.

And a heartfelt Merry Christmas and the sincerest of best wishes to the Metz Smith family and the tragedy of this 1987. Our thoughts have been with you many, many times this year.

Merry Christmas to Doug Meier and welcome back; to State Senator Jim

Whaley who stepped in to pinch-hit for another good friend; to J.L. North in the Nursing Home; to Brad Wright who's spending his first season in a really White Christmas place, Antarctica; to Charlene Collingwood for all her good service and her good nature.

Merry Christmas to Stan and Mary Flitner who let me tag along up in the Big Horns on a sorrel horse.

And to all of you who said Merry Christmas to us with your Christmas lights, Merry Christmas back again, from all of us who enjoy them so much.

And to all of those people who live in other places and keep track of Greybull through the pages of the Greybull Standard, including Jean Morris in Nikiski, Ark., Joe Pavlus in Naperville, Ill., Don Ressler in Holly, Minn., Mrs. A. L. Thayer in Florissant, Mo., Warren Turner in Tulsa, Okla., Bill Wilkinson in Sidney, Mont., Paul Menzel in Los Angeles and 39 other Californians who subscribe to the Standard, here's a very special Merry Christmas to you across all those miles.

And to all you new people we'll be meeting this next year and all the little kids who grew up so much during 1987, to all those who live in this fine Wyoming community, the best of holidays and the merriest of Christmases.

December 29, 1987

UNDER THE headline, "PLASTERED 'POKE PEEPS THEN PLOPS" the Hungry Horse News had this story a couple of weeks ago:

"Flathead County Sheriff's deputies solved a peeping tom incident at Rogers Lake Friday evening by following the hoofprints of the man's horse, and a few other signs.

"The man was cited for criminal trespass for allegedly riding his horse to a window where a woman was sleeping on a couch in the nude. He claimed to be looking for cows, and she didn't appreciate his attempts to get friendly, the sheriff's report said. He rode off when she went to get a gun and call authorities.

"When deputies came to investigate, they learned several other residents had seen the rider, who appeared drunk. They tracked him for three-eighths of a mile to the home of two elderly ladies with whom he was having coffee (although they reportedly didn't know who he was.)

"The deputies said he was easy to follow because he appeared to have fallen off his horse five times."

1988

January 5, 1988

SOMEONE CALLED to point out that John Wayne died in a couple of other movies, not just "The Cowboys." One was the old war movie, "The Sands of Iwo Jima." I saw that show in a Tokyo theater in 1952 with about a half-dozen other GI's. The rest of the place was filled with a thousand local Japanese. The unnerving part of the experience was listening to the Japanese in the theatre yelling for the Japanese on the screen. When the Americans were ahead, it was dead silence. When the Japanese were ahead, it was pandemonium. John Wayne and the Marines may have won the battle on the screen, but the Japanese won the theatre. If John Wayne died, I didn't know it. I was too busy worrying that World War III was about to start.

January 12, 1988

J.T. MALMBERG'S pickup in Cody turned over 200,000 miles last week and if you're an odometer watcher, too, you will appreciate the ecstasy of seeing all those figures rolling over. Wrote J.T. in the Cody Enterprise: "Oh, it's great. You can get straight fours or straight sixes, but to get straight nines and then straight zeroes all within a tenth of a mile is wonderful."

January 26, 1988

BITS & PIECES . . . THE NBC-TV camera crew following Vice President George Bush around unloaded a dozen big metal containers at the Billings airport Monday night. "Just a change of clothes," one of the crew told me, which is a double put-on because TV camera crews never look like they change clothes . . . ON THE OTHER HAND, the Vice President looked dapper by the time he'd made it to Greybull Tuesday afternoon. You would never know he'd been up all night fighting with TV commentators.

THE CROWD AT THE Greybull Elks was big for Bush. The place was packed. Band and all. Gale Larchick, who was waiting around with the rest of us, said he "thought everyone had moved out of Greybull. But they haven't."

February 9, 1988

IT WAS ONE of those glorious hours at the end of a day of skiing when you sit around outside with other skiers and let the last of the sun hit you. If you're lucky the alpenglow will be just starting up on the hill and everyone sits around and thinks about the day and talks about other times. The conversation from other tables is loud and friendly and very fraternal. You're tired and exhilarated and it's been a very good day.

But not everyone always feels this way, I guess. At least the guy with the boots in his hand had other thoughts. He walked by the table and went right to the trash can and threw his ski boots into it. Slam. Bang. As if to say, "I'll never have to wear those damn things again." Then he turned around and walked away.

So much for the alpenglow.

March 1, 1988

REMEMBER WHEN the girls who worked at the Big Horn theatre in the 1940's all wore gabardine and satin uniforms? If you do, then chances are you bought popcorn and candy from Jill McIntosh.

"I got a high-paying job then at the theatre selling popcorn and candy (with) a salary and commission and often made $12 to $15 a week. But I had to clean and stock that cubbyhole and it was a messy job. The ticket seller, ticket taker and usherette all had gabardine and satin uniforms, remember? Ray DeSomber was my boss and most of us who worked for him were just a little bit afraid of him," Jill writes from Temucula, Calif. where she and her husband, Red, are "on the road."

"In our Christmas box from home we found Gretel Ehrlich's new book and the Shell Valley one. What good memories both had in them. They made me think of old time things I now miss," she says.

"Do you remember the old viaduct that came into Greybull from Basin and ended at Williamson's little grocery store? One time my cousin, Bert Leonard, and I pulled his little wagon to the top, got in it and sailed down to the bottom, crashing in Mr. Bellamy's yard. We were bruised and later spanked for that thrilling trip."

"Those were the "10 and 11" years when "we were taking hikes up on the bluff and lowering ourselves down into some old cave, climbing down to the old 'island' we called it. We would also get under the old bridge that covered the Big Horn – not the one they just tore down – but the one previous to that. It had planks you could see through and it rattled and made scary noises when cars and trucks went over," she writes.

And before that "we kids would pull a wagon around a few blocks and gather up empty beer bottles, take them to the back door of the Smokehouse Bar and sell them for a penny each. Our goal was a dime apiece which bought us a ticket to the Saturday afternoon movie," she remembers.

"And do you remember Jim Kelly's little gray coupe? He was the only lawman the town had and he worked from late afternoon until midnight. And if it was a cold winter night, he could be counted on to take a bunch of us home when we had to work 'till 10.

"And the ice skating pond with the old warming shack . . . the band concerts in the park . . . the dances at the Community hall . . . playing near the river and the railroad tracks, both no-no's if our folks found out," she says.

"I feel sad thinking most of the people I baby sat for or worked for are gone now," she says. "Ray DeSomber, Clyde Francisco, Lewis Hankins, Clifford Holm."

The McIntoshs have been traveling most of each year for the past four years, going from one part of America to another. They wind up the winter months in southern Arizona. They're always seeing people from home. They've been traveling with Pat and Sheila Tomlinson and this year Art and Gladys Baugh were "camped across the river from us." Over Christmas they saw the Larry Bullingers and their son and daughter, Matt and Nan. In January she "ran into Betty (Vaught) Stabler in our RV Camp near Sun City, Calif."

"We have been on the road seven to nine months out of the year for four years now and still one of my happiest moments is for the mail to catch up with us and find letters from friends and news from the Standard about the old hometown."

March 8, 1988

THE ICE IN the Big Horn river at Greybull decided not to wait for my prediction of the usual Mar. 10 date and went out exactly a week earlier. It also rained that same Mar. 3 evening which explains in part why the ice went out early and why those who predict ice going out shouldn't!

March 17, 1988

THERE HAS BEEN apparently only one mild winter in Greybull's brief history when the Big Horn river did not freeze over. That was the winter of 1957-58. Many of us remember that time and my authority for all the winters before that is the late John Loveland who told me then he had never seen the river open all winter before. John kept track of those things and he'd lived here since before 1900. Well, that's not exactly the way he said it. His exact quote was: "I've lived here since the Big Dipper was a tin cup."

March 22, 1988

WHEN THE STEWARDESS on the United flight taxiing into the Denver terminal told us the Browning, Mont., boys' basketball team was on the plane, too, heading for the All-American Indian tournament and added, "we wish them the best of luck," the whole plane broke out in applause.

I thought afterwards how you can get caught up in applause. It just comes out of nowhere, instantly. It can be absolutely irresistible and happily contagious. It is especially easy if it deals with youth and games and winning. Athletes represent our hopes and our dreams, either ours or our kids or our town or our country. And from the beginning of all time we have cheered them on. And so we did the Browning Indians.

And lest you think I am an absolute romantic, I know we were down and on the ground. The cheering and clapping on landing is always greater than the cheering and clapping on takeoff.

March 29, 1988

YES, THAT WAS John Tarter who was volunteering to put up the flag at the Post Office each morning the past couple of weeks. John's philosophy on the flag: If the American flag is flying on flagpoles all across America, then no other flag can.

FROM ALL THE comments on Jill McIntosh's memories of Greybull's Thirties and Forties, I think Ray DeSomber may well be the most remembered man of the time.

BRINGING NEW HORSES into the world for the purposes of raising and selling them has not been the best of businesses these past years. Recession set in some time ago. But each spring is a new crop. At the post office the other day, Sheriff Gary Anders rolled down his window and wanted to know if I'd "had" any colts yet.

Not yet, but close, I said.

"How many colts are you going to have this year?" he wondered.

I told him it looked like I'd be up to 10 this year.

"Boy," he said, "you're really a slow learner."

May 3, 1988

THE DOG WAS only a mite of a thing, not more than 10 inches long and six inches high.

But I didn't know that.

It had been following me along the Rimrock Road by the river for several dozen yards without making a sound.

But I didn't know that either.

It wasn't really going to bite me.

And I didn't know that.

What I did figure out was that I was airborne the instant he started barking. I could have landed in the river if the wind had been just right. Back on the ground I turned to see the little bugger scooting off for home, immensely pleased with himself.

I had hoped no one saw me. Murphy's Law of Running says you are never alone when you look your worst. And I wasn't. When the guy in the pickup coming towards me passed by, his big grin filled the cab.

THAT LONG, FASCINATING article in Sports Illustrated about the seven-mile cave in the Big Horns is the one in Trapper Canyon. Don Smith who played around the entrance as a kid, remembers before World War II when the water ran into the cliff. That was before the cliff sloughed off and covered things up more. Now the water just sort of sinks out of sight and doesn't reappear for miles on down below.

The Sports Illustrated article shows the route of the cave, the Great Hall cavern, all the tough climbing and crawling along the passageways. The article calls it the deepest known cave in the United States.

At one point there's one narrow passage only 12 inches wide. If you aren't already claustrophobic or don't like mountain climbing UNDER mountains or being wet and cold or in the dark, that 12-inch passage, as Don points out, will eliminate a lot of us.

May 10, 1988

JUST THIS MORNING on the traveling Today Show Leslie Caron shows up and I understand you have to be several generations old to remember "Gigi" and that wonderful time in cinematic Paris. But it is an omen of the week of very successful ladies. Thank Heaven, as Maurice Chevalier sang in that classic musical, "Thank Heaven For Little Girls."

ACROSS THE GOLDEN Gate bridge and a few miles further north is a little, almost-five-year-old girl with potential problems with some very purple tennis shoes. I kept telling her I thought they would turn blue as soon as she washed them. She insisted they wouldn't. But she wasn't really all THAT sure. I thought for a while I would be in dutch with her parents since it appeared those shoes might never see water. But several months ago she flew to the closet and produced a pair of still very purple tennis shoes. They'd survived the "wash." And they were still purple. You can't fool those California girls.

UP NORTH OF US if a couple of boys get a little sister next month, they're going to find out you can't fool Montana girls either!

May 17, 1988

WE DROVE DOWN the streets of Neligh, Nebr. last week. We were looking for the little house we used to live in 34 years ago. Funny how people do that. Go back in time to see where they lived, the old house, the town's streets, the still familiar names on businesses. The houses, if they're still there at all, invariably look smaller and older than you remembered. The trees are bigger and the house smaller. One goes up, the other seems to go down. Life's teeter totter.

And that was the way of the old house in Neligh, too. Far older, a lot smaller than I thought it would be. The big tree in front, much bigger. We've been back before through the town, but I can't remember what the house looked like in between times. I remember what it looked like way back when and what it looked like last week. And there's been a few years in between, for both of us.

It's true that "home" is a part of all the homes you ever lived in. So it was with this little aging clapboard house with the high-peaked roof and the still red-painted windows. First newspaper job out in the world. Just home from overseas. A "non-Wyoming" state to try out. Life's start. A career to learn.

Down at the newspaper office the day after we moved into it, the boys in the backshop dug out the old files to show me a picture of "my house." Someone had moved it in from the country a few years before and in the process the house had split in two, right in the middle of the road. Hence the picture in the Neligh News. I was mortified. So much for the smart, young businessman with the "new" house to live in. But we had great fun in that little Nebraska place, patched seam and all, for a year until Wyoming pulled us back. And the splice never did show.

May 31, 1988
I'VE ALWAYS LAUGHED about the Ace Reid cartoon where the city guy is talking to the rancher and the city guy is saying, "I'm here to buy cattle and you hicks can't fool me. I want 20 cows and 20 bulls."

June 9, 1988
THAT WAS A BLUE MOON we watched Tuesday night, May 31. Someone had to tell me that's what it was. It looks like any other moon except it was the second full moon in the same month and it happens only once every 2.72 years. Hence, "once in a blue moon," which everyone has said at least once in their lifetime whether they've seen a blue moon or not.

Remember that oldie, "Blue Moon", which Vaughn Monroe used to sing. I just thought he was sad and lonely. I never really knew there was such a thing as a blue moon. Up in Northwestern Montana there's a bar with a long reputation called "The Blue Moon". The sign out front says "Free Champagne to the Ladies" which gives you some idea of how many ladies normally go in. And a lot of stories up there start with, "Once, in The Blue Moon . . ." giving another twist to the old phrase.

Our Blue Moon down here came up at the end of our lane and poured light the length of it. A beautiful sight. "White in the moon the long road lies," Poet A.E. Housman once wrote. And so did ours.

June 14, 1988
A TOWN CELEBRATION (like Greybull's Days of '49 last weekend) eventually becomes just like the school seems to be. Those who go and those who have fun seem to be getting younger and younger every year . . . THE YEAR BEFORE we moved onto this place, some old boy ended up in the draw off the hill east of the house late one 49er night. Randa Harvey said she and Oral didn't know it until the next afternoon. The guy wasn't hurt and he just slept in!

June 21, 1988
THE BASIN ALL SCHOOL reunion is only a few weeks away. I already got an inkling of what might be in store for those rekindled memories when Delbert Crandell stopped by the house. He and his wife are visiting here for

several weeks from Camas, Wash. Delbert wanted to know if I remembered the old '41 two-toned green Chevrolet MY dad had! Of course, I remembered that but how did DELBERT? I suspect all our memories are clearer of those old school days than any of the decades since.

DELBERT ALSO reminded me of how I used to unhook the speedometer on that old Chevy and drive the heck out of it. Not as many kids had their own cars in those days and if you didn't have wheels, you had to rely on the old man's. And if the old man had to keep track of mileage for business, you were suddenly faced with terrible dilemma. When you got the car, should you drive to and from and no more. Or should you incur parental wrath by driving the heck out of it and risk not getting it again. The third alternative was immoral and unethical. Unhook the speedometer and chip in for the gas. The Devil put all sorts of laughs and girls and good times in front of me and then pushed me hard from behind. The speedometer never turned over for hundreds, maybe thousands for all I know. And that little old car ran forever.

July 5, 1988

A REUNION OF A class is one experience. The reunion of a time is another. And so when one thousand of us descended on Basin this last weekend, it was not so much that we were there to sing the old school song, but to savor those great memories of life as kids.

Growing up is such a precious time. You're young but you're old. You're smart but you're dumb. You know a lot but you don't know anything. You work but you play more. You're sad but you laugh a lot. The bad times are there. But you remember the good times more. It's the beginning, the time for the mold to set, for the stamp to put its mark.

This happens in all sizes of towns, but ours was a little town and this weekend confirmed what we always have known. It was quite a place to grow up.

Basin is still small by surrounding standards. We old alums nearly doubled its size for the three days. Officially we were the classes of 1923 through 1968. Forty-five years of graduates. But we brought along the faces and memories of everyone who ever lived there in those times, young and old alike.

My dad and mom "were there." A lot of people mentioned them to my sister, Elizabeth, and me. So were many other parents. Those are strong memories. You'd shake hands with an old friend and remember their mom or dad. Small town people always help raise you. And you really never forget the influence. That's always been a small town's strength.

It's a feat when a town of 1,200-1,300 has almost that many arrive to shake hands. But it was expertly done, and smoothly arranged. And we stood in the old grandstand and applauded the committee's efforts.

It looked for awhile Sunday morning as if we might have to applaud ourselves during the parade. After all if everyone is in the parade, who watches it! Freddie Clements, before we started, said we might be like the scene in Lake

Wobegon when it took all the people in town to be in the "living flag" on the street. There wasn't anyone to see it! But a parade is a draw and people were actually there to watch the flatbed trucks and buses filled up with old Basin graduates. My sister's class of 1949 rode in the garbage truck which she was assured was no reflection on the class!

My old grade school buddy, Ross Crosby, came "home" from California. The Crosbys left when he was 13 – 46 years ago. But Basin has always been hometown for Ross. I don't think he forgot anything that ever happened in those years. He asked if I could remember the circus we kids put on. Only vaguely, I said. A couple of hours later, my sister was going through the family trunk downstairs and came across a letter from Ross' mother to our mother in the hospital telling her about "the circus the kids are putting together. (Your) heir is the man on the flying trapeze." Such is the stuff reunions are made of.

You learn that a name tag can never save you. If you don't know the face in front of you, you can't sneak a look at the name tag unless the printing is one foot high.

Few were much taller when they came back. A little wider, maybe. "You've fleshed up," one classmate was told by someone downtown.

You see everybody. You miss everybody. For many there were miles and miles between the present hometown and the old one as well as years and years. Some of us never got too far away from each other but never crossed paths. Bill Wesnitzer and Ralph Small wound up in Cody and I in Greybull and we shook hands again 40 years later.

Arlene Jackson of Moorcroft told me that joke about the reluctant bull I had in last week's column was an old, old clunker. And it wasn't peppermint, Arlene said. It was licorice!

At reunions the older classes hear a lot of talk about retiring, going to be, just am, have been. And about hair, gray, gone, going to be there a long time yet. I noticed one of my old friends had kept his hair. Beautiful, wavy blond stuff. He was older than I and still had this marvelous thatch growing up there. You notice things like that after being reminded for three days that I'd left my hair at home. I tell you this guy really did have a beautiful head of hair. On the very last day someone said "hair" again and I mentioned to him that it was okay for him to laugh, he had hair. He had a big grin on his face when he leaned that thick head of hair down to me, and said: "I'd only do this in a reunion." He pulled up the wavy forelock for me to see. He was wearing a toupee!

July 19, 1988

ONE STATISTIC that will apparently stay on the books despite our hot, dry weather of the past weeks is the warmest temperature ever recorded in Wyoming. That was at Basin, 114 degrees, on July 12, 1900. Yes, those were the good old days.

August 9, 1988

WHEN YOU WALKED down the street with my dad, you walked in step. Oh, I don't mean to a cadence or that you had to march. I mean when your left foot hit the sidewalk, so did his. When your right one went down, so did his. If you began out of step, Dad would take that little half-step shuffle and get in step with you. He never said to you in his first sergeant's voice, "Get in step." He got in step for you. He did it every time we ever walked. That's the way Dad thought men should walk down the street, in step, not "out of kilter". It was an old Army habit that never left him.

When I was smaller and realized here was something adult that never changed, I tried to change it myself. So I would take my half-shuffle and get out of step. Dad would take his and get back in. I would go out, he would be back in. But I wearied of a game that I could never win and we'd go on down the street like a couple of corporals walking back to the barracks.

I liked the way my dad's generation did things their own way come hell or high water. You couldn't change them. In the end you didn't want to. They went on that way the whole distance, independent, most of the time predictable, loyal to a town, a job, a life. They believed in tradition and manners and hard work. They followed "what was right" which in today's standards would be an argument in itself. But to them it was either right or it was wrong. And they followed that code – my dad would have been in step – for as long as they walked down the road.

I TRIED MY BEST to write 8-8-88 as many times as I could Monday. Have to wait 11 more years to get to 9-9-99. And if you're a numbers watcher, you're going to delight in 10-10-10 in 2010.

August 23, 1988

THE PAPERS ARE saying now that the Yellowstone Park fire is "worse than expected" and "at times out of our control." I thought it was bad and out of control the first day.

Every fire has the potential for going out of control. That's mostly what fires are about, whether it's a lowly bunch of backyard weeds or a city block in Buffalo, Wyo. All fires can go bad. The tragedy of fire is that usually it cannot be stopped. To see a fire left to intentionally burn, for whatever magnificent ecological reason, makes it even worse for me.

It should have been no surprise in July that this summer was going to be a scorcher. From the beginning the Weather Service had been predicting a summer with less than normal rainfall and hotter than normal temperatures. You don't need someone else to predict winds in Wyoming. They are always with us. You don't boat on Yellowstone Lake on summer afternoons. The wind and waves are nearly always up. This high plain that's Wyoming is wind country. It's only the degree that varies, a breeze or a gust, and either one makes a fire potentially dangerous.

In retrospect, it was a bad decision. In face of continued dry conditions and predicted hot weather, many thought it was a bad decision from the beginning. We will be lucky if it doesn't become much worse before we can be saved by the September equinox storm.

I CAN ENDURE many things about this Yellowstone fire, but I wish people would stop telling us how wonderful it's all going to be afterwards. I'm tired of smoke and heat and red sun and stories about the rebirth of the forest 100 years from now.

August 30, 1988
IF I HAD ONE wish for a change in these Wyoming towns of ours, I would wish all the House For Sale signs would disappear and everyone could sell a home for the price they asked and everyone could buy the home for the price they wanted. And each house that came on the market thereafter would be sold before the month's end, so that you would never have to drive through forests of FOR SALE signs anymore.

And when all the homes were sold and everyone was settled and contented, then I would condemn all the abandoned buildings and the old sheds and garages. And if no one wanted them or would not fix them up, I would move them off the property and find some energetic souls to plant flowers and evergreens in their places. So that instead of weeds and ugly and awful-looking places, you would have green and pretty, and only a FOR SALE sign once in awhile.

September 6, 1988
OVER THE WEEKEND I drove over 250 miles up and down Yellowstone Park and I was miserable much of the time. I am still miserable today, writing about it. This old friend of ours, as you and I knew her, is gone. She just won't be the same. There will always be magnificence, unless that, too, is burned up in the end. There will still be long stretches of green and marvelous wildlife and many stupendous sights. But you and I will never see it again in that wild, primitive, untouched state of yesterday.

I kept thinking Saturday as the miles went by about what the Associated Press writer wrote from the Park several weeks ago. "No one who is alive today will ever again see Yellowstone Park as it was." I might have dismissed that as too gloomy a forecast if I hadn't driven those same Yellowstone highways Saturday that he had.

I thought it was an awful sight. I wasn't prepared for the expanse of the burned areas. The length of them. The breadth of them. The ones burned alongside the road. The ones on the horizon. Some areas are obliterated, trees uprooted from the intensity of the fire storm. In other places, the dying trees still stand and will be standing that way for decades to come.

The Park Service is busy defending the let-it-burn policy with leaflets and stories and taped radio broadcasts. "Marketing" is the stupid word Superintendent of the Parks Mott said the other day of the efforts to convince people the Park forests will be better. In the same interview Mott is quoted as saying that it is not all economic gloom since much money is being spent to fight the fire. That is an incredibly flippant statement from a high government official when a million acres are afire, tourist business is wrecked, hunting is cancelled, air polluted and Cooke City, Mont. might burn up. You wonder what kind of hands we're in.

I wouldn't know if the burn policy is right or wrong. What is at issue is not the righteousness of letting forests burn, of trying to play God with millions of acres of trees, it is the misapplication of such a policy. The judgment in Yellowstone this summer of when to use the policy and when not to was atrocious. The difference between a bulldozer fire line scar at the start of the fire and one at the end is 500,000 acres of burned trees.

After every paragraph, after every statement the Park Service makes about how fine the forest will eventually be, someone else should always add: The fires remain out of control and could have been stopped.

I knew I would be too gloomy with this today. But I hate goodbyes to things old and familiar. It's heart-breaking to see waste because of poor judgment. But great chunks of the Park remain, or did anyway Saturday night, and enough majesty to make the heart sing and bring the laughs back. Don't know whether you saw it or not, but one angry Montana columnist said he didn't think Yellowstone Superintendent Bob Barbee should do anything but sell tickets at the front gate.

And when I walked over to the Big Horn county car parked by the burned trees, the guy from Frannie leaning against it looked at me and just shook his head. First he said something I can't reprint and then he said: "I'd like to take Barbee and sit him up there on top of that." And he pointed to a 30-foot tall old snag, pointed and sharp at the top. In our misery, we both laughed and tried to visualize Barbee sitting up on that old snag. Still selling tickets, maybe.

Not many tour buses these days in the Park. But I heard of one going north in Canada that said: "NORTHPOLE".

The wildlife is incomparable with or without the fires . . . two buffalo bulls chasing a coyote, right on his heels until he jumped aside . . . a bull moose so perfect in the river people sat right down on the high bank above to watch . . . buffalo strung out along the winding river in a scene Charlie Russell painted a dozen times . . . a monstrous bull elk guarding a patch of sunlight in the timber.

The red sun was coasting down through the smoke when we turned for home, throwing one long streak of red on the Lake. Just as we went by, six trumpeter swans took off in formation and wheeled back towards the red color. That great old Yellowstone Park had one last thing to say before we left. And I won't forget: I may not be the same, she was saying, but I can still be magnificent.

October 25, 1988

IT'S A LONG ways yet to ice in the river, but I came across this historical aside about the Big Horn. I know you must think I dwell on the ice going out around March 10 to 12 year after year. But consider, in "Souls and Saddlebags," an early-day minister described being stranded on the west side of the Big Horn while the ice went out. Date of the ice break-up: Mar. 15, 1897.

November 8, 1988

AFTER FOUR DAYS of catch-up visiting, when most everything had been said at least once, my alert and quick 86-year-old mother-in-law decided it was time to relate what had happened to each family in the old town of Niobrara, Nebr.

So down each street she went, house by house, bringing up names from those 50 years ago, and telling what had happened to all the Lutts and the Eberlys and the Skokans in the half century since.

If you know Niobrara, Nebr., you know it isn't a big town. In fact, the old town was completely abandoned and everything moved up on the hill to escape the rising Missouri River waters. So the houses have been gone for a number of years, just like many of the families. She, herself, has not lived there for nearly 50 years. But she can always go back to it in her memories and often does. And she has never lost track of the neighbors.

There's a solid comfort in all those small town ties. I can remember being overseas and "delivering groceries" to stave off the homesickness. I did the same house-to-house ritual, going down each Basin street, trying to see if I could remember every house where I'd delivered groceries out of Luke Ridley's old pickup. I wasn't good enough to get them all, but I got a lot of them and I can bring up a lot of them right now. Old friends, familiar faces, all ordering groceries from the Palace Market.

That was a good job for a restless teenager. The pay was peanuts, but Luke was crazy and fun and you got to drive a pickup all over town. In those days all you had to do to have the day's groceries on your kitchen table was to call the grocery store before a certain time and the restless boy would bring it out that afternoon. Years later he would lay on his Army bunk and try to remember your name.

November 15, 1988

MY SUPPLY OF paper clips has finally run out. For the first time in 15 years I'm going to have to go to the store for some more. For sometime now I thought I might have an inexhaustible supply. But, by golly, the top came off the last box this week and that great hoard of Scoville No. 1 paper clips is gone.

At one time I had a dozen gross. That's what the young lady in our old office supply department had ordered. I said, order us some paper clips. She did. She ordered a dozen. Except that she put down a dozen GROSS. Now that's a pile of paper clips. They arrived in big boxes. Little boxes of paper clips inside larger boxes inside great big boxes. It was a definite corner on the paper clip market.

Oh, I said bravely, I'll use them up. Instead of sending them back, just let me have them.

We sold the usual amount, but I carted most of them home. That's been a while ago. Now they're gone. Thousands and thousands of paper clips. A dozen gross of boxes of 100.

I have not been in the newspaper business. I have been in the paper clip business.

I SOMETIMES WONDER if time goes fast or if time goes slow. You look around and it seems like you've been here a long, long time. But wasn't it just yesterday that the kids were around? It can't be six months since we moved the gated pipe out to the fields. And now here we're just picking it back up for winter. I can remember perfectly what happened last Halloween. Surely 12 months didn't already go by. But the other day I missed lunch and it was 3 o'clock before I was near food. Those three hours seemed like a day and a half. You fly home from California in five hours, but gee, San Francisco seems a long ways back. I can remember what went on 30 years ago, but you have to remind me of last month.

The logical part of your mind knows that a second is a second and an hour, an hour. Their march across the days and the years never varies. Each frame goes by, click, click, click. But the other part of you, the part that dreams and looks back and peers ahead, it forgets the ticking clock. It can't measure in seconds and hours, but only in old times and other places and past happenings. And there's no hands on the clock for those times.

November 24, 1988

THE WOMAN CALLING the Dale Wright's home after supper was obviously a saleslady. She told Carolyn she had a call for "B. Wright." Carolyn said she must mean Brad Wright. The lady said she guessed she did. When would he be back?

It just happens that "B. Wright" is working on a six-month stint in Antarctica. This is Brad's second tour. He'll be there another three and a half months.

Well, Carolyn said, he'll be back in February. The saleslady was incredulous. February! Yes, Carolyn said, February.

Well, where is he, the lady wanted to know.

"Antarctica," Carolyn said.

The woman hung up. She must be used to put-offs but she must have said to herself, I've never heard the Antarctica one before.

SOME CHRISTMAS TOYS arrived the other day, in those boxes with the pictures on the outside of what's inside. If grandkids lived here, they'd figure out Santa pretty quickly. When I got home, the boxes were in a small pile with this note on top from the UPS man, Rick Werbelow:

"Betty, I sure hope Bruce likes his Sit 'n Spin and GI Joe set. It looks like he is going to have a fun Christmas Day."

December 13, 1988

SOMEONE HAS listed the ten top jukebox singles of all time. Do any bells and whistles go off when you remember:

Elvis' "Hound Dog" and "Don't Be Cruel" (both on the same record); Bill Haley's "Rock Around the Clock"; Fats Domino's "Blueberry Hill"; Patsy Cline's "Crazy"; Otis Redding's "Dock of the Bay"; Marvin Gaye's "Heard It Through the Grapevine"; The Doors' "Light My Fire"; Bob Seger's "Old Time Rock & Roll"; The Temptations' "My Girl"; and Bobby Darin's "Mack the Knife" which absolutely HAD to be on this list!

If you counted, you know that makes 11 not 10 but Elvis got two on the same record.

If Big Brother appeared and said, Okay, forever more, you can hear only five of these 11 songs, which five would you pick?

If he became very agitated and told you that no, you could have only ONE to hear again, how would you choose?

I'd sit back and fold my hands behind my head and say, Hey, Big Guy, just keep playing "Mack the Knife" over and over.

Bobby Darin would sometimes announce the song, saying, "I now want to sing an old Hungarian folk song" which would bring hoots and hollers from the crowd who knew what was coming. It is an old song, actually, 1928, I believe which proves that something good did happen in Hoover's time. But it took Darin to make it go around and around on the jukeboxes. It was his song in the end and his forever.

Like all songs that appeal, you hear it played in many places. Even from a fast food chain TV commercial which has been corrupting it to sell hamburgers and I have to boo and hiss and throw things until it fades away. Alas, nothing is sacred in the World of Greed. Mack the Knife pushing hamburgers. "Casablanca" in Ted Turner's new colors. Awful.

But the old, good song is still around. You hear it all the time. Old Mack is still in town. Which will always be great news.

December 20, 1988

It's time to say Merry Christmas . . . that time of year when you send your special hellos and thank yous to all those who have been part of your year and part of your life since the last Merry Christmas.

So it's Merry Christmas to all those who pack out our groceries . . . and fill iced tea glasses . . . who bring the papers and the mail . . . who wave back . . . and remember words written . . . and ask about the kids.

And Merry Christmas to all those people in the world who want Greybull bentonite and ship by Burlington trains and ask for Hawkins & Powers airplanes. Cheers to you all.

And Holiday Cheers, too, to all the Greybull area kids who excelled in music and math and athletics and brought honor back on the rest of us. And a special Merry Christmas to Jamie Crawford for all her state honors and awards in basketball and volleyball. And to Beth Nolan and Dan Close for their coaching talents and abilities and their contributions to those championship cups in the trophy case.

Merry Christmas to all the Legionnaires who put up the flags on the main street and to everyone else who flies the American flag from their lawn or porch. And a special mention to John Tarter who believes flags should fly.

Special Yuletide thanks to Press Stephens and Gretel Erhlich for the little puppy who is now a big puppy and who is turning out to be much smarter than we are. But it was the same when we raised our kids. They learned in spite of us and so will this little gal. I have the feeling, though, we may be too old for this "child-rearing" business. You forget what 24 hours of kids are like.

Holiday Greetings to Mike Boson for the generous sharing of time with us, to cheerful Rick Werbelow for his help and good humor, to Carrie Cheatham at the Greybull Elevator and Lawrence Hanson at the Co-op for past favors and extra help, and to Slim Brewer for all those coffee-time stories of the old times.

Merry Christmas to Robb Dalin for those days this summer and the stack of hay down at the barn. They don't eat it as fast as you can stack it, Robb. It just seems like it.

Merry Christmas to the excellent school administration of Frank Houk and the high standards he has set and maintains. This is a good school and the community should be proud of it.

Special Holiday greetings to old friend, Slim Nielsen. You're right, Slim, those Russian Olive trees we dug together off my place years ago have really grown on your place. It was a good swap: off of mine and on to yours!

And an Extra Special Merry Christmas to all those Greybullites who live in far off places, Paul Valasek in Zurich, Switzerland, and Pat Gilmore with the Navy in Waianae, Hawaii.

And back in the States, a Greybull Merry Christmas to Sam Michaelis Jones in Manhattan, Kans. (Your phone call was great, Sam.) Jeff Tolman who is having an outstanding law career in Poulsbo, Wash.; Bob Turner in Denver, who has never forgotten the old town of Greybull, and Bob, we haven't forgotten you.

And Holiday Greetings to the Glen Dalrymples in Lancaster, Pa. for a special visit this summer.

Merry Christmas to all of us who ever remembered Ray DeSomber in the Big Horn theatre, who watched Greybull-Basin play football on the gravel, smelled the old refinery smoke, tasted that god-awful water before the Shell water line, who drank coffee in the Griffin Inn, swam in the old pool at the park, remember a coach named Birnbaum. If those weren't the good old days, there never were any.

And a Special Holiday thanks and greetings to Butch Denzin for helping out a neighbor several times this year, to Jill McIntosh for sharing some old Greybull memories, to Mel Christler for a helpful summer check ride, to John French who always knows which song to punch on the old jukebox, to Bob Hunt and Hank Letellier for keeping a couple of old tractors going.

Merry Christmas to Beryl Lesser who's in Salt Lake this winter for helping us "clean up" a couple of sacks of black walnuts. Merry Christmas to all those who migrated back to Basin for an unforgettable reunion of 40 classes and to Lois Johnson who had much to do with its great success.

Merry Christmas and best wishes to Jay Wilkinson at the salesbarn; and to Greybull's new mayor, Mike Mayville.

And to all of you who said Merry Christmas to us with your Christmas lights, Merry Christmas back again from all of us who enjoy them so much. And a special holiday thank you to the Dolan Scharens and John Haleys in Shell and the John Coynes and Victor Strubes on the corner at North 3rd street for some truly marvelous lights.

Merry Christmas to Judge Gary Hartman and Bob Wallin for their efforts and initial work on the gravel project at Hawkins and Powers this fall.

Holiday Cheer to all those who walk or run out country roads . . . who gather together after "horse sales" . . . who call back on 122.8 Unicom . . . who say hello with a honk of the horn . . . who reach out a hand . . . who laugh at old stories.

Merry Christmas to those who get their mail in the morning at the post office and stop to talk, Jim Horn, Russ and Dorothy Kimbro, Earl Reilly, Bonnie Kelly to name just a few.

And to all those people who live in other places and keep track of Greybull through the pages of the Greybull Standard, including O.J. "Red" Deveraux in Billings; Patty Crumrine in Macon, Ga.; R.W. Carrell in Town Creek, Ala.; Lois Blakesley in Soldotna, Ark.; M.J. Brown in Clackamas, Ore.; Tom Foe in Vancouver, Wash.; Renea Gernant in Seward, Nebr.; Earl Jensen, Sr. in LaCrosse, Wis.; E.F. Lockard in Greensburg, Pa.; Doris Parker in Castlerock, Wash.; Marc Miller in San Pedro, Calif. and 41 other Californians who subscribe to the Standard, here's a very special Merry Christmas to you across all those miles.

And to all you new people we'll be meeting this next year, and all the little kids who grew up so much during 1988, to all those who live in this fine Wyoming community, the best of holidays and the merriest of Christmases.

December 27, 1988

WHILE YOU'RE SITTING around these next weeks watching football games, ponder this unponderable: That no matter how many records continue to fall, no matter how bigger, faster, stronger players get, no one can punt like they could in the old days. The National Football League punting record is 51.4-yard average and it was set by Sammy Baugh 48 years ago.

So for nearly 50 years thousands of footballs have been kicked by equally thousands of feet and no one yet has bested 51.4 yards per kick.

If you want your son to go into the record books someday, start teaching him to kick a football.

One little boy who may have a prize foot sat behind me on the plane last night and kicked the back of my seat for a couple of hours. Now that kid's got a leg on him. He could have put that seat of mine 51.4 yards in the air if it hadn't been bolted down.

His mother had just had a long talk with him about hostility as we taxied out. "You are always hostile to everyone," she said to him. She was a teacher (she later told her other seatmate) and now she was practicing on her vacation as some teachers do now and then. This time it was on her own kid.

"You're too hostile," she told him several times. Each time the back of my seat went forward about three inches. When you're a little boy in an airplane and your mother tells you you're too hostile, you don't kick your mother. You kick the seat in front of you. That's another law of Murphy. Murphy also insists that if the planeload of 100 people has only one hostile, little boy, he will sit behind you.

Back in the Sixties when Greybull had a couple of state championship teams, the 1962 team only punted twice all year. It was the only fault in a dominant team. But then that's why it was a fault: they dominated. So when it did come time to punt, Larry Dockery had little or no practice. His first punt was like Bradshaw's. It didn't travel 10 feet off the ground and never touched a player on either team in 50 yards. His second punt was even more sensational. This one went straight up in the air 50 yards. When it came down, Dockery himself caught it behind the line of scrimmage, and as big as he was, ran it far enough for a first down.

When you can catch your own punt, you don't have to practice on airplane seats.

1989

January 10, 1989

PRESS STEPHENS gave Stan Flitner the perfect gift for Christmas. It was a jigsaw puzzle of Yellowstone Park. Except Press had dumped out all the pieces and substituted charcoal!

ONE OF GREYBULL'S early-day teachers was Mrs. Myrtle Hunsaker, a woman of spirit and gumption, and so she was understandably excited about the 50-year-reunion some years ago of one of the old, old GHS classes she had taught. Chuck Peterson said he was delivering mail to her house that summer weekend of the reunion and Mrs. Hunsaker, then in her eighties, met him at the door.

"Have you seen any of the kids yet?" she asked excitedly.

January 24, 1989

WHENEVER I SEE someone taking inventory around this first-of-the-year time I remember Dale Foe telling about inventory at the Foe-Saunders Lumber company in Greybull when he was a kid. After the physical count was taken out in the yard, his father would sit Dale and his brother down in the office to convert everything to board feet. Sorry, no pencil and paper. The boys had to do it in their heads. It was a game. The old man would call out the number of 2x4's and whichever boy got the right answer first WON! They'd go all through the pile of lumber that way, the old man calling out the boards and the kids mentally racing against each other to come up with the board feet.

That was over 50 years ago. I asked John Hesco how they figure inventory at Aldrich's now. The computer does it automatically. It keeps the running inventory as each day goes by. January 1 is not much different than May 23. No one has to sit around a pot-bellied wood stove on a cold January day trying to make your mind run faster than your brother's.

Times change. We call it progress. Right now I've progressed so far I can hardly add up a column of figures with a pencil and trust them. The same figures in a calculator somehow come up with a different answer. I have no pride anymore – I go with the calculator.

But I'm missing the point here. It's not what method you use to arrive at the figures, but what you do with the figures. That's the incalculable worth of the calculator and the computer.

Still, you have to wonder about the lazy mind. They say you can improve your memory anytime you want by just using it and exercising it. There was a craze for awhile when I was a kid to memorize a deck of cards. Shuffle the deck, memorize the order and then call each card out as you turn them over one by one. This was much easier than you think since you could memorize in blocks of 13 or 10 or whatever. And no one ever asked you how many board feet there were.

Names are another one. All our lives experts have been telling us the secret of success among fellow men is to remember names. It has done little good actually. The most common name in America today is "Hi There." You'll see someone coming towards you and you know you should but you don't remember and neither does he or she and pretty soon you're too close and so you both say, "Hi There." You'll bump into someone coming out the post office door and catch him off guard and you say hello and he calls you by name, "Hi There."

The nation's colleges are embroiled now in the simplest kind of mental exercise. Whether a freshman athlete can pass a test or not to play athletics. The NCAA has passed Proposition 48 which simply says a freshman athlete receiving an athletic scholarship must post a score of at least 700 on a standardized test called the SAT. Passing the rule caused such an uproar among blacks, who said it contains cultural bias, that the 48 rule probably will be rescinded. But a 700 SAT score is 204 points below the average student score. Tennis great Arthur Ashe is quoted as saying a "700 on the SAT exams – that's like a D average – is so low that cultural bias . . . probably won't even play a part in it." One Los Angeles sportswriter gave the test to his sixth grade daughter who passed above the 700 score.

We're not talking about mental gymnastics with board feet here or memorizing a deck of cards. We're not even worried whether you can remember someone's first name. This is just a ridiculously low basic standard to enter college. It shouldn't have anything to do whether you can play ball or not. It has everything to do with how much you worked to get an education.

What seems so wrong about the Proposition 48 fight is that its opponents are not asking certain athletes to make a 700 or D grade score. They're asking them to MAKE LESS THAN 700. Even the old yellow pencil can come up with better figures than that.

January 31, 1989

AROUND GREYBULL: WHAT WILL this old town do with no Friday nights at Blue's? . . . I'M THE OWNER of a Bill Wilkinson baseball card (courtesy of Jeff Tolman in Washington). Bill's the son of Jim Wilkinson and a great-grandson of Jim Bluejacket, the old pro baseball player in the 1910's. Sorry, no trades.

February 7, 1989

WHEN THE BARN is bigger than the house, my mother always used to say, the man rules the place. When the house is bigger, it's the woman who does. I say, if you've got a garage in this kind of weather, no matter how big your barn or your house, that means you're both smart.

February 14, 1989

ONE MONTANAN suggests the state change its state bird to the magpie which goes a long ways to show how addled the brain can get in bitter cold weather.

PLAYING AROUND WITH some numbers . . . The oldtimers who were in World War I are really up in years now. Unless you lied about your age to go to war, you have to be a minimum of 89 to have been serving on Nov. 11, 1918. That would make you 18 in 1918.

World War II has the same age boundaries. Unless you put down your age wrong when you went in, you have to be at least 62 to have been in that war. That's 18 in 1945.

There've always been wars and veterans.

In those Memorial Days of my youth, various Civil War veterans put up the wreaths for their comrades, Mr. Kimbro did it for the Spanish-American War dead, and the firing squad was all World War I veterans. If I were to go back now to the same cemetery, members of four wars could still be present in that little town, WWI and II, the Korean War and Vietnam.

The fact that so many people marched to war throughout our history says more of the individual people who went than it does of our collective ability to keep peace.

February 21, 1989

ONE WAY TO KEEP warm in Wyoming is to call all your friends who are living in warmer places, like Phoenix and southern California. I talked to Wee Collingwood in Ramona, Calif. Tuesday morning who said he "was just standing here with the doors and windows open, wondering who's going to mow the lawn, Ina or me and I think it'll be me!"

SAN FRANCISCO Columnist Herb Caen says 81-year-old Walt Stack broke his collarbone in a tumble off his bike. He "has to cut down his daily regimen (bike to Aquatic Park, run across Gate Bridge and back, swim in Bay) to a mere 10-mile run and a dip off the Dolphin Club. His neighbor asked him the other morning, 'How do you keep your teeth from chattering in that icy water?' Walt: 'I leave 'em in the locker.'"

February 28, 1989

NEARLY 25 YEARS ago I wrote down the things I liked and I was thinking about that list the other day, wondering how many I would still like and what I might like better now. So I dug out the November 25, 1965, Greybull Standard to see if the years changed anything.

They haven't. I still like . . . "a Cole Porter song . . . a wave of a hand from a friend . . . rustling satin . . . a long thin-necked bottle . . . memories from hearing Jo Stafford sing . . . clear water in a mountain creek . . . a pretty girl's smile

... the first strings on a guitar, vibrating in their low voices ... the smell of someone else's first puff of cigarette smoke ... the gray and white ruggedness of the Tetons ..."

And I also put down ... "a flicker's springtime chant ... Sentimental Journey ... saddle leather ... a bass voice ... pottery blue ... a boy's sunny face ... a gymnasium floor's freshly varnished smell ... a dog's wagging tail ... purple tulips ... a football afternoon ... laid Roman brick ... band music ... a little girl's brushed hair ... sunlight on water ..."

Back those 25 years ago I was right in listing ... "any sunset ... horse's hooves on a paved street ... October's stillness ... a happy ending ... the Flag out before the wind ... the thought of the far-off sea ... a strong handclasp ... a son's pride in you ... sagebrush after a rain ... red, Shell country dirt ... a street light flowing in falling snow ... a friend's approval ... everyone saying the Pledge of Allegiance together ... a job done ... contrails in the sky ... soft fur of an Angora cat ... a free Saturday afternoon ... praying together ... light-face sans serif type ... finding an arrowhead ... the smooth touch of a Formica counter top ... a good laugh ... a flock of wheeling blackbirds ... a mournful harmonica ... old people's common sense."

If you asked me now, 25 years later, if I had forgotten anything, I think I would add in this 1989 ... any iris, especially yellow ones ... fresh asparagus ... Yellowstone Lake ... long lunches ... a convertible top down ... cashmere's touch ... alpenglow ... a good Chardonnay ... a black horse running ... back lighting ... digging ... good jazz and good big band and a good beat to dance to ...

And maybe put down ... eating outside ... late afternoon sun on a pole fence ... Western names like Misty Moon Lake and Teepee Pole Flats ... mountain flowers ... quick wit ... a colt playing ... Western roots ... grandkids ... a tennis ball well hit ... blue anything ... a whisper landing ... a beautiful rider on back of a horse ... young people's promise ... good verbs ... laughs from other years ... holding a listener ... praise of tall sons ... the afterglow of a long run ... thoughts of parents ... marigolds ... other heads turning to watch your grown-up daughter ... friends who go "way back" ... a word that's right ... old trees you've planted ... memories that make you smile ... and this great, old Wyoming, where all this happens.

March 7, 1989

YOU HAVE TO THINK spring is not too far behind the magpie flying north down the river yesterday with a big stick in its mouth. It was headed for a new nest somewhere, one of those big ugly things that magpies call home. I've always thought it was typical of the magpie to throw together such a mess for a nest. It's just a big pile of sticks stuck up in some tree. It's always four or five times bigger than it needs to be and it'll be there for years, inhabited or not.

It's just like a magpie, loud and obtrusive, no class and no consideration. The magpie doesn't care what anyone thinks of him or how he looks or what he does. His pile of sticks is just a place to crash.

For all I know that one I saw was heading north to Montana where someone has wanted to make Magpie Heaven. I've lost track of that story about the legislator wanting to make the magpie the state bird. I never knew whether the guy was joking or not. But Montana politics are never easy to understand.

March 23, 1989

I WILL ALWAYS wonder if the Big Horn river ice would have gone out on time if I had just stayed home and not said anything about it.

As many of you are reminding me, I did say the ice would be gone again this year on time, that good old Mar. 10th date when the channel at Greybull clears out. Bold words for someone who was leaving the day before to see if Hawaii's March sun is any hotter than Wyoming's. If you're brash enough to try to publicly outguess Mother Nature, you should at least stay home to agonize a little.

The ice was still laughing at us two weeks later when we got back and then fiddled around for another day or two before taking its own sweet time to move out over the 23rd and 24th. That may have set a record for being late. As it turned out, the old Big Horn could have used more of that Hawaiian sun than I found.

April 11, 1989

THAT OLD BALD EAGLE was sitting on the same old limb in the same old cottonwood tree on the way to town the other day. He's been up there many times, a comforting, stable, familiar sight. I am saying "he" when it could be a "she" and "same old" when it could be any number of bald eagles for all I know. But whoever it is, it's been up there over and over again in these past years.

What I find the most fascinating about this particular limb and tree is that it is not only the bald eagle(s) who perch up in that same place. But a half-dozen or so other birds, too. Mostly hawks, big and small. And always a magpie at some time. It seems to be a limb a bird would like, a streetcorner up in the air where things hang around.

But it's always the same spot in the tree. Different birds, but the same perch. Several other trees are near, growing up out of the side of the hill like that. But the birds choose this one where they can look up and down the Big Horn river running below and watch whatever birds do when they hang around on the corner.

I like this repetition of order. In the midst of what seems like endless disorder, you can make some sense out of birds who like to sit in the same place day after day.

Animals are often like that, thankfully. They'll make a trail and use it for years. They come back to the same place to nest or raise their young or stop over on a migration. Our first roads came from paths animals made. The

Indians followed the same twists and turns, the settlers made them deeper and finally roads came. We have one such road right on our place, a game trail once, an Indian path later and finally a road that crossed Shell Creek to early settlers on the east side of the river. Only pieces of it are left now, the rest wiped out by barns and fields and other modern things. Probably the most famous "trail" is New York's Broadway which cuts an incongruous diagonal across Manhattan. But it was a path first and then an old road long before surveyors came along to make streets run at right angles to each other.

Birds fly to the same branches and animals pace the same paths and some things never change.

May 2, 1989

READ SOMEPLACE that a robin isn't listening for the worm. Since they only see straight ahead, he's trying to turn his head so he can see where he's going. I know that feeling. But I thought it was these trifocals.

JOHN WOODEN'S basketball philosophy (he was the great UCLA coach who has no modern peer for winning) is really a philosophy of life: Teach them all you can about the game and then let them play it.

Wooden's in the news much these days. He's up in years and the Final Four is just over which reminds everyone of those incomparable UCLA days. People talk and write about Wooden because they keep trying to figure out why he won so much. I think that's easy to see. Wooden was a teacher, a great teacher, and only coaches who are teachers really succeed. No teacher like Wooden ever tried to be the student. Those great teachers you had exalted in what you did, not what they taught. They inspired you to do what you could do, not what the teacher could do. They didn't play the game for you, or worse, get in the game with you.

I feel the same about being parents and employers and even friends. Teach them all you can and then let them play the game.

May 9, 1989

THERE'S MUCH more to the story of how and why I got there, but I found myself in the back of a four-horse trailer Thursday night, holding a newborn colt and heading for Del Snyder's place.

The noise was terrible. How do horses stand it? I've never been in such a noisy, clattering outfit in my life. Every bump seemed to bring more din.

But it wasn't the godawful noise that was so disconcerting. I couldn't help but think how goofy I must look, standing there all alone in an empty horse trailer. You couldn't see the colt. He was tall all right, but only I was showing. I briefly considered holding his head up so at least his ears would show. But even vanity has its limits. So I just stood there feeling foolish as we went by cars and people.

I can tell you exactly how I felt. It was just like I'd been caught for not growing a beard and I was on my way to the horse tank.

June 7, 1989

THIS MEMO WENT up in a San Francisco store (or so Herb Caen of the Chronicle tells us). Store Manager Sue Tabor put it up. She calls it one of her "inspirational" messages to fire up the troops. It points out:

"Every morning in Africa, a gazelle wakes up. It knows it must run faster than the fastest lion or it knows it will be killed. Every morning then a lion wakes up. It knows it must outrun the slowest gazelle or it will starve to death. It doesn't matter whether you are a lion or a gazelle, when the sun comes up, you'd better be running."

TOMORROW we can write June 7, 1989 as 6-7-8-9. And that won't happen again until Jan. 2, 2034, according to L.M. Boyd who keeps track of things like that for America. Didn't I read he once called Casper home? The way people are moving out of Casper, that may become a trivia note itself.

June 12, 1989

OVERHEARD CONVERSATIONS . . . Between a little boy and his grandpa, underneath the stands in the middle of the dust storm at the Days of '49 rodeo Saturday afternoon . . .

"Why don't they just call it off for a while until the wind quits blowing, Grandpa."

"No, they won't do that. Cowboys are tough. Spectators aren't."

IF YOU WONDERED if anyone was downtown on the Days of '49 Saturday night, at one time around 10 p.m. the cars were bumper to bumper from the stoplight back to the A & W!

I'M AN ABSOLUTE softie for young colts at anytime but especially at that magic moment when they're turned into the pasture in the morning. All the energy of the new day is used up in that first long run away from mother's side. And then it's a kick or a jump or some improvisation of both. They'll run away at each other or away from each other. They're both very awkward and very graceful, both a little kid and already a grownup adult. Life's just a game, they're saying, and if you don't believe that, catch me if you can.

You never know what they'll be worth in the years ahead, but right then they're priceless.

June 30, 1989

TWENTY-FIVE years ago in Greybull we had a store with this sign on the wall. It fits reunions and grandkids being home and any part of life when kids grow up. It read:

Boys today have . . .

3 steady girl friends
6 meals per day
18 best friends
7 things to do right away
254 things to do before homework
23 schemes for making money
1001 ways to drive teachers wild
2 awestruck parents.

July 6, 1989

IF YOU BURN my flag, you're going to have to shinny up the pole to do it, and I want to tell you ahead of time, when you come back down, I'm going to bash you over the head with a ball bat.

I'll just be registering a protest. Isn't that okay? So don't call the cops or your lawyer or the civil rights union. It's just you and me, expressing ourselves. My flag's burned but you have a crease on the forehead. That still doesn't make us even, but it's a start.

The privilege of Free Speech does not give you the right to holler, "Fire," in a crowded theatre, as Justice Oliver Wendell Holmes wrote many years ago. And the right of protest should not extend, it seems to me, to the desecration of the American Flag. The Supreme Court ALMOST agreed with that and the resulting 5-4 decision is heating up the summer.

My new flag arrived in the days that followed the Supreme Court's decision and I pulled down the old one the wind had beat up and hoisted this beautiful new one. The timing was coincidental but it suited my mood. This flag flying now is a size larger than the old one, and its colors are crisper and it's nylon, too, which is smoother than the cotton was. That makes it more eager to pick up the breeze and it's moving a lot now. More often I'm saying, "What a grand sight that is."

And it is, too, always a thrill, always a reminder of where we live and what a great gift that is.

July 13, 1989

THE CBS MORNING weather news always scrolls down some forecasted temperatures for a bunch of cities and towns across the United States and Tuesday morning they added "Otto, Wyoming, 82 degrees."

It's not every day you can see Otto, Wyo. on the television screen. In fact, it's not every day you can even see Otto! Just a spot, not a very wide one at that, on a Wyoming country road but CBS wanted you to know it was going to be 82 degrees there Tuesday.

Otto, Wyoming. "Don't spell it backwards," Press Anderson always used to say when you mailed the papers with him at the Basin Republican-Rustler. Newspapers all going to the same town were wrapped in one bundle and the name of the town written on them. In some shops in those days one person would gather a town's papers together and roll them up in a wrapper. That person then would pass the bundle to someone else who would write the name of the town on it. The first person always had to call out the name of the town.

Press always added a little extra to each one.

"Indianola, the holy city."

"Otto, don't spell it backwards."

And on down through the list until all the bundles were wrapped and written on.

"Otto, don't spell it backwards."

For the record, Tuesday morning, CBS didn't.

July 18, 1989

WAY BACK WHEN, those early town fathers thought of calling the town "Alamo" but settled on "Greybull" in the end. That could have caused all of us problems down these years. No one would ever believe you were from the Alamo. And "Alamo, Wyoming" never would have sounded as right as "Alamo, Texas" does.

The Alamo hotel was stubborn about the name, though, and it was The Alamo for a very long time even if it was in Wyoming.

It sat across the street from the newspaper office and gradually grew older and older until eventually it was torn down. In later times it might have been saved and restored but it went without a murmur then. Now another empty building stands where it once did. That's what is called progress.

But for a awhile in those old days it had a run at it. And except for a couple of "nay" votes, it could have been "the Alamo hotel in Alamo, Wyoming."

August 8, 1989

THEY NEVER MADE a summer long enough for me. You could add a couple more Junes and maybe the first half of another July and I'd dance at your wedding.

I LIKE THE way "Pryor Fire" rolls off the tongue. I don't mean to make light of burning trees, but there is a lilt to Pryor Fire.

MORE RANDOM thoughts on the dying summer . . . IF YOU have tried everything else to keep the bugs off, you might try Snuggle (the fabric softener). That's what the firefighters in Colorado were using this summer. I gave it an afternoon's worth and while I don't know if it kept off the bugs any better, I sure did smell purty . . . SOME marauding beast has been tearing off blooming marigolds and littering the ground with them. After blaming rabbits and deer, we've discovered it is a badger. That's our first badger around the place in all these years and it happens to be one who likes picking flowers.

August 15, 1989

BILL GREER'S HORSE went flying at the grand entry of the Big Horn County Fair Saturday night.

"He hadn't been there before," says Bill, who is treasurer of the Fair Board. "And he didn't like the carnival and he didn't like the noise and he didn't like the people. He just didn't like anything."

Just inside the gate, the horse said to heck with this, and he bucked and bucked and bucked around the arena, finally ending up over at the chutes. With Bill still aboard.

"It sure got the rodeo off to a good start," Bill says.

NO MOMENT plays longer than that. Just a moment. It happens and then it's gone. You'd like to hold on to some more than others. And some very special ones, you always wish you could keep punching the replay.

I have a moment like that for you. It was at the VIII World Veterans Championships in Eugene, Ore. recently where 4,950 athletes from all over the world competed in various track and field events. Men's competition began at 40 years, the women at 35. Twelve age brackets separated the competitors and there were those in the nineties competing.

The oldest raced first. And in the 200-meter dash, 94-year-old Wang Chingchang of Taiwan raced against 90-year-old Herbert Kirk of Bozeman. Sports Illustrated describes the action of this venerable pair:

"Wang bolted to a five-meter lead off the turn. But Kirk charged with 80 meters to go and passed Wang with 40 left as the crowd stood roaring. Wang, amazingly, dug down and repassed Kirk, winning by a foot, 52.21 and 52.33. But this race wasn't over."

And now for the moment. I'm glad you're reading this yourself. I tried reading it aloud to someone and I couldn't make it. The voice wouldn't hold. I had to pass the paragraph across the table.

"Kirk, who had given up tennis at 86 because he could no longer see the ball, didn't see the finish line either. He kept right on sprinting. Wang, fiercely competitive, went with him, and they dueled for another 70 meters before they were stopped. As they trotted back, it was in front of a delirious, tearful throng."

August 29, 1989

I LIVE ON a road that gets longer and longer.

You'd think modern roads would grow shorter and shorter. Not ours. It keeps adding on and making more turns and, the newest wrinkle, adding more stop signs. So when I drive to town now, in the late 1980s it is just over a half-mile longer than it was the first time I drove it in 1956.

Then the "Greybull Heights Road" turned off at the river bridge and you went north along the river until our lane showed up. It had been that way for years. It replaced an old road that came up out of Shell creek and went along the ridge of hills east of town. Eventually, a "new" bridge went in and the "new" Heights road was cut along the river's edge. It was to last for decades.

But you forget how progressive progress can be. The highway department announced in the late fifties it was dangerous for the road to turn on the highway at the bottom of the hill. It had been doing it for years. But now it was "dangerous."

So the county came in, tore out the big culvert across Tin Can Alley and tore up the road. (The culvert eventually went out to a county commissioner's place in the north end). The road was rebuilt up a hill to the east which meant now you had to turn up a long hill, drive to the top, and drive another 400 yards to the highway. Then you had to drive back down the hill to hit the river bridge. I've measured it many times: it's about a half-mile round trip.

Thirty years later, the highway department put in a new bridge and built a new boat ramp road not too far away from where the old Heights Road used to turn on the highway. I guess it's not "dangerous" anymore.

Now, just last week, the city crew had to square up the old "new" road at the top of the hill and they built a nice sharp, right angle turn to what was for 20 years an oddball curve across someone's private property. It adds about 75 yards to the trip.

Then to make it look real pretty, the city added three stop signs, one on each corner of the new turn, to regulate us same old people who've been on the road for years, all going the same place, to and from town.

But wait, more progress. The county saw all those purty red city signs, so further down the road, where it becomes the county again, they put up their own stop sign. It stops traffic at the "Y" but they put it on the thru traffic road and not the feeder road.

So we had an old road 30 years ago to carry people to town and it never went up a hill or stopped or had a square corner. Now it goes up one long hill and down another, has four stop signs and one very square corner. Ah, progress, how do we get along without thee.

September 7, 1989

WHEN THEY TALKED about the Montana Centennial Cattle Drive this summer, I always had this vision of Civil War bivouacs in large open fields, the endless tents and campfires, groups here and there or sitting by countless little fires. Of large black hanging kettles, of horses tied to ropes. And somewhere a harmonica playing or a soft song in the night air. Sheer size and numbers, people and horses en masse.

I was not disappointed to see the real thing.

By now, The Drive is almost over. But Saturday and Sunday, in that gigantic field west of Roundup, there was army enough for a Montana Potomac. Tents, people, wagons, horses, trailers, and one huge Budweiser circus tent in red and white and flying flags. It was an army spreading out over 50 acres of alfalfa field and in a couple of days, it would move, like all armies do, down some road and make history.

The wagons were all circled up in various parts of the field. That was the plan: To put several counties together into one "circle." They'd stay in the same circle for The Drive. In a weakness of modern usage, they were all color coded. None of this Company B stuff. It was the Blue Circle or the Red Circle or black or white or whatever. I asked someone where the Magenta Bunch was, but I was only half-joking. There probably was one.

But the circles were the key. They became the army companies, the control unit. So you went to the blue circle to camp, your duffel on the wagon was loaded in the blue circle wagon. And on through the day. And besides, all the wagons drawn up in one circle after another, my that's a sight.

Thousands of people. And more to come. As the weekend wore on, more army would arrive. This staging area would look even more like it was waiting for U.S. Grant to ride in to give approval.

In all of this, one horse hauler was hardly noticed. But when I wished Brian and Carol "good luck" and "a good ride" and headed on down the busy road back to Billings Sunday, I already knew it was a success.

You had to wonder if Montana could ever pull this off. It was a great idea on paper, but the logistics of that many people and cows and horses appeared horrendous.

But city folk forgot two things. One, that armies before even the Roman days won wars by moving thousands of people and horses across hundreds of miles. The army system of having the general's orders finally seeping down to the private still works. Using the same army logic in 1989 Montana works, too.

Second, it was to be ranch people who made this thing work. This is what their lifetime has been, making things like this work. Not on this scale but with the same odds. And outdoors. And with horses. And with neighbors. It is their contribution that should be remembered.

Ranch families were everywhere. It was like a big stockgrowers convention at times. Especially in the Budweiser tent.

Everyone was friendly. This was a special occasion. You could feel that. People stuck out their hand and said their name everywhere you went. There were a lot of smiles. People weren't complaining about the rain that doused everyone Saturday night. Or anything else. It was the rancher's approach again. Many of the wagon people had just come off the Helena trip. One man said this was his third wagon ride of the summer. He'd been more than a month on the road.

It wasn't all that rustic and roughing it. Some enterprising people had a shower outfit set up. The water was probably okay, but the lines weren't. Lines were deep at the telephones. AT & T had a bank of six phones at the area. They had a busy time, too. You can't put 4,000 modern people without a phone for too long!

And the BUD WEI SER girls were there. They were in white mini skirts, a double knit kind of material and across the top in front were the three letters.

BUD or WEI or SER. So when they stood alongside each other, it spelled out the beer. But it was not the letters that the crowd was looking at.

Live music in the Budweiser tent . . . They had two of those tents, one set up already at the first night's camp and one at the staging area . . . They will hopscotch them apparently so there'll always be the big tent waiting . . . biscuits and gravy for breakfast if you wanted . . . One tent was set up on a flatbed truck after the big rain . . . that's dry bedground . . . Beautiful wagons . . . much care and affection there . . . no dogs, very few kids . . . Horse trailers on the road, bumper to bumper . . . for days. It 'll be the same thing when it's all over.

They took your horse after the health and brand inspections, put a sticky number on him, same number stuck on the halter and led him off to the pen. In the morning the idea was to get your halter off the fence with your number on it and hand it to the guy on horseback. He'd get your mount. That's as close to valet parking as a cowboy will ever get.

The Billings Gazette had a tent set up. And selling papers, of course. I couldn't resist a Sunday paper. I pulled the tent flap back and handed in two cups of coffee and the Sunday paper. "You don't want to rough it completely," I said.

One woman in breakfast line was telling another one that she'd had to ride her horse "a couple of hours" to "settle him down." "He gets that way if he can't do what he wants," she said. I told Carol, "Remember what she looks like and ride on the other side!"

The official "uniform" of The Drive has to be the canvas duster with the brown color. Hundreds. Saturday night after the big rain, it was the yellow slicker.

But down the road between Billings and Roundup – where The Drive would go the next day – not everyone was as excited over all of this as I was. When we drove up the day before, along the route where the cattle and horses would go, some old boy and his wife, both in their sixties, were out on the highway. They had a crowbar and they were taking down their mailbox. Guess they figured if they were going to save the thing, they had to take it down before it was trampled to death.

September 12, 1989
ON VISITOR'S NIGHT at the Great Cattle Drive, I was introduced to the man who was in the outhouse when the wind blew it over Tuesday night. He was a celebrity, of course, because his mark on the trail was to have been in exactly the wrong place at the wrong time, a fate all the other 2,399 people would manage to escape.

"It was quite an experience," he told me with a straight face.

When I tried to keep my face that way, straight and sober and understanding, he said, "That's all right. Go ahead and laugh. Everyone else is."

And I couldn't help it but I did. Sorry, Britt.

The wind had been fierce that night when they set up camp. No rain, but just a lot of wind. No one thought to tie down the portable potties. (They would on later days.) And the wind grabbed that one and pushed it right over. Worse, it fell over on the door. So that Britt couldn't get out. He just had to wait there for help.

Naturally a lot of people gathered around. He could hear them outside. Someone said, "I wonder what he looks like?" Then they got ropes and pulled it up and he could open the door to cheers and whoops and hollers. It's not every day you're trapped in an outhouse in middle of a Montana prairie with 2,399 people looking on.

Later he went to the concert with us and we were standing there listening to Hoyt Acton's deep voice. I started laughing. Britt turned around.

"I know what you're laughing about," he said.

And I was.

AND THEY TOLD ME about the cowboy at the breakfast circle another morning, complaining about his poor condition from the night before.

"I'm not sure what happened," he said. "But I remember someone asking me if I was dancing. I thought I was until someone stepped on my hand."

ONE OF THE DROVERS said: "That morning that old longhorn had its calf, all the cowboys made a big fuss and gathered around it to look at the little heifer. She was quite a celebrity."

AND LATER, on Friday someone didn't get the outhouses around to all the circles very fast. And one cowboy who couldn't wait any longer, roped a couple, hitched them to a team and dragged them over to where he wanted them. Fortunately for my new friend, Britt, he was not in one!

September 20, 1989

MAN CANNOT live by bread alone, of course, but he can get by with one old favorite coat forever. An old coat always fits. It never fights you or binds you up or feels too bulky. It's always comfortable and friendly and sits right. A coat has to sit right. And the old coats always know how to do this. You get used to each other. I guess that's the main thing. And you wind up spending a lot of time together like old friends should, many miles down many roads. Inevitably, all this shows and your old down buddy begins to look beat up and dirty and badly in need of a bath. Mine hit that plateau here not so long ago and I handed it over.

Betty was going through the pockets and pulled out a rock. "What's this?"

"It's a pretty rock," I said.

Now you don't need an old coat with deep pockets to bring home a pretty rock. Little boys have been bringing home pretty rocks in pants pockets for a long time. Mothers get used to this. But it just happened that I found this pretty rock when I had the old coat on.

"I think it's agate without any moss in it, but I thought it was worth keeping," I said by way of explaining.

"Shall I put it up in the windowsill with the last one," she asked me.

I looked over at the kitchen windowsill. I'd forgotten about that one. That was another pretty rock. This was a different kind. It was yellow and it had odd streak in it. I found that one down by the barn. I can't remember whether I had my old coat on or not.

I picked up the yellow one from the windowsill. It was prettier than I remembered. Strange how rocks turn out. You find a brilliant colored one among a whole bunch of dull ones. They can be green or red or yellow, streaked and spotted. They have no history like a fossil or an arrowhead. Just a rock. Someone with a better eye and talent to cut and polish can make rings and tie clips. They know the kind of rock and how it was formed. To me it's a just a rock. It has to be pretty, mind you. But like Gertrude's rose, a rock is a rock is a rock in the end.

"Maybe they could both go to the garage with the others," she said.

That's true. From the windowsill after awhile the rocks end up in the big can in the garage. Only the real good ones, of course. I think the yellow one is worthy. I'd have to think about the almost-agate one. You can only cache the very best ones.

Our grandchildren come to visit and bring in pieces of Dave Walton's crushed gravel. These rocks are only real pretty when water is on them. So the jars get filled with water. Mason jars of wet crushed gravel are harder to put on windowsills.

"I don't think I'll keep the agate one," I say out loud.

The old rock can in the garage is too full really. From now on it will have to be a real gem to be saved. There are some dandies out there though. Many memories. Bob's red-painted rock is there still, probably the most brilliant of all. He wasn't very big when he painted that with Bob Foe's International red and buried it in the lilacs. I found it years later and knew instantly what had happened. You couldn't throw that one away even if Mother Nature had a helper with a red paint brush. Rocks are memories after all. Like everything else as you go along.

I didn't realize that can is so full out there. I carried home more than I realized. But by golly, some of them are really pretty. A guy's just got to be more choosey.

"I think I'll keep the yellow one and toss that agate-looking one," I said.

You can't keep them all.

September 26, 1989

THE BIG HORN RIVER looks so calm and peaceful these days. Hard to remember back when it was a dirty, roily river and Boysen Dam hadn't been built yet. Kids all along its length swam in it and never told their anxious parents they did. Seeing it now, moving quietly along and only changing colors after a storm someplace, it's hard to bring back pictures of that swift current and changing sandbars and most of all, that silty, dirty color of a truly old west river.

Jerry Porter remembers jumping off the old Basin bridge to Basin Gardens.

"One day it would be three feet deep where we jumped and the next it would be eight feet," he recalls. "It was changing all the time. You never knew what it was going to be."

Our parents would have been horrified. But if you found a garden hose afterward, you could wash all the silt and muddy water off and no one would ever know.

WHEN BOB CAROTHERS picked up one of those old-fashioned wood stirrups, he figured he could make a matching one out of cottonwood. It was one of those big, heavy things, about five to six inches wide and one piece of wood bent and shaped to make the stirrup.

So Bob found the right piece of cottonwood and spent the next year painstakingly bending and forming it into shape. It was one-quarter of an inch at a time. It took a long time, but he finished it, attached the leather and it really looks fine. Then he found out that you could take hickory, steam it and put it into shape in a day.

He's sure now he has the only cottonwood stirrup in the world.

October 3, 1989

MY BAD DREAMS usually run the same old tapes.

I'm either walking into class for the first time in weeks and the professor says we're having a test today which I know nothing about. Or I'm trying to take a picture and only a few minutes of sunlight are left. I can't get the film loaded or the camera to work or the people to stand right and all the time the light is running out.

Or sometimes the plane is leaving and I'm not walking fast enough or packing fast enough or something is slowing me up. The faster I try to go, the slower my feet move and down the street I can see the plane or the boat or the train pulling out.

I have several tapes on Running, either away from something or towards something. But my feet either don't move at all or so slowly I'm getting nowhere.

For a long time I kept playing the High Place Tape where I was perched way up in the air, on a very small space. Like the top of a flagpole. Or a high mountain peak that comes to a 2x2 pinnacle. And I'm on top of that, paralyzed, afraid of falling and unable to figure out how to get down.

And I haven't muddled red-faced through the No Clothes one for a awhile either where I am in a crowd and everyone has their clothes on but me.

The other night I stumbled on to the Storytellers Tape for the first time. A bunch of you are standing around and I am telling you a story. But right in the middle of it, I realize it is the wrong story.

I start a new story.

A couple of you drift off.

I keep telling the story. It goes on and on. Slowly, like the running.

A few more of you walk away. A couple of others start talking about something else. I keep on with my story. It's getting longer and longer with no point. I can't remember the punch line exactly. But I desperately keep on talking.

Several more people leave.

I'm trying harder to tell the story better. But more people walk away. Pretty soon I look around and no one's there. No one. I'm telling a story and no one is around the fire anymore.

And I never do finish the story.

YEARS AGO, when Frank Hinckley was working on a construction job around Glendo, one of his workers took off down the road early one morning with just a little bit too much to drink. Frank went after him and finally caught him on the road to Cheyenne. The guy was barely creeping along, about 15 miles an hour.

"Where are you going?" Frank asked when he got him stopped.

"To Cheyenne," the guy said.

"At this rate, you'll be on the road a week."

"I'm driving just as fast as I can see," he told Frank.

October 11, 1989

IT SEEMS LIKE many months ago when I told you about riding along in a horse trailer with a 12-hour-old colt. Well, we came back again, the two of us, a Sunday ago, but this time he was old enough to ride by himself back there while I herded the pickup along. It was a much different ride than the last time we were together on the road.

He's five months old now, tall and black and healthy as can be. He's more Del Snyder's baby than mine. She was the one who spent the nights up with him, who fed him his bottle and then his bucket, who coddled him and encouraged him for all that time. She did a wonderful job with him. He's really quite a kid now. Not spoiled or any bad habits. Easy to be around. No problems with the other boys and girls his age. She calls him "Lucky" because he was that in so many ways and we call him "Little Gib" because someone else we knew had the same tragedy when he was born.

If he comes to either name, it will be all right. The real joy is that he's around, the last colt of a grand old mare, and he looks like he's going to be a dandy young man.

But does he have a love affair with a bucket. Show up with a bucket and he's back to the good old days. What a fuss he makes over an old bucket. That's his blue blanket, I guess, the one strong memory of an orphan childhood.

So in about four or five years, if you see me riding a black horse down the road, hide the bucket. Or I'll lose him right there.

October 19, 1989

"YOUR LITTLE SON just learned a new trick," I told Ann when he and I came back into the house.

"What was that?" she asked.

"To spit," I said a little mortified because everyone knew immediately that on the way back up the hill from the horses Granddad had set a very bad example.

Little boys two years old don't miss anything. They may not know how to spit, but if granddads spit, they spit. If granddads cuss, they cuss. It's one of the dangers of life. You have to keep remembering that.

Actually, I've been thinking about this quite a bit lately, because I can tell you exactly when I learned how to spit. It was in our bathtub at home and I must have been about ten years old. I had never been able to spit right. That bothers some ten-year-olds. So I set a pitcher of water next to the bathtub and practiced and practiced. It must have stretched over several days. I can't remember learning anything quickly. But, finally, one day, it was perfect. It was long and accurate and made just the right sound. Some things matter, you know.

In those days I was running around with Kenny Cyrus who was a couple of years older than I. But he couldn't spit at all. I knew this. Now I could. It was hard to wait until the right time. But it finally came.

"Where did you learn to spit like that," I can remember him saying. He was amazed. I knew he would be. So was I, of course. It was a time for a shrug of the shoulders and some offhanded reply. I don't remember what I did. I probably blew that part. After all it's a little much to expect a ten-year-old to have both studied nonchalance and be able to spit right.

November 7, 1989

"THE REAL POWER is in the clicker," Jack Williams pointed out to me today.

Hey, don't laugh, it happens. Whoever aims it at the TV set instantly establishes the balance of power. Try it yourself at home tonight.

ONE THING I've noticed about some Clicker People is their nervous trigger. They can never watch any show very long for fear of missing something else, somewhere else. The Clicker will punch one show, watch it just long enough to know what's happening, and then – CLICK – on to another channel. Sometimes they can get off five clicks in less than two minutes. So it seems like a very fast and blurry slide show. The slower Clicker People let you watch long enough to become interested and then – CLICK – on to the next channel. Either way, Jack's right, the power stays with the Clicker.

November 14, 1989

FOR ONCE, even television is having a hard time keeping up with what is happening in Europe. The incredible sight of people going through the Berlin Wall for a visit is followed the next day with the Wall starting to come down. On the CBS morning show an author of a book on the Wall cautioned "not to expect today's events to mean the Wall will come down." The next day, the Wall WAS coming down. This morning the early news was less than an hour old when the Czechoslovakian government voted to open its borders. Networks had to break in with a "Special Report" just to keep up.

A week or so ago President Bush was talking about the "remarkable turn of events." By the week's end whatever was "remarkable" wasn't nearly as startling as what was happening this week.

I thought the pictures sent back a few weeks ago (it seems like forever now) of the people walking to freedom through the Hungarian fields was one of the most incredible sights I had seen. In days it was hundreds of thousands walking and driving and queuing up to go. In less than days, it was the Berlin Wall itself that provided the gates to freedom.

It can be successfully argued, I'm sure, that all times are historic. Any special moment in the sun's path has its own place, its own significance. But make no mistake about these moments in Europe. These truly are unforgettable.

I KEEP THINKING about all the graffiti on the west side of the Berlin Wall. I had not realized it was so profuse and so colorful. It is only on one side of the wall, of course, the freedom side. It was still cold concrete on the other. That was one of the fascinations for East Berliners to see when they came across this past week. To look at all the painting and expressions of color and thoughts on the wall that looked so foreboding on the other side. Freedom means many, many more things than the unfettered license to put up graffiti. But for the Wall it was a perfect expression.

November 21, 1989

HORSES AND LLAMAS on the same mountain trail continue to draw interest in horse magazines. The llama is becoming more popular and the horse more wide-eyed. A subheadline in Western Horseman magazine puts it this way: "If you and your horse haven't met one of these critters on a narrow trail yet, you still have time to prepare."

I still like Joe Little's comment about the horse that spooked in the Big Horns when he ran into one of the forest service llamas. "All his life," Joe describes it, "he had been looking for a llama and he finally found one."

November 27, 1989

MY MOTHER'S father ran away to sea when he was only 14 years old, stowing away on his brother-in-law's clipper ship in 1870. The ship didn't get back to home port in New Brunswick until 18 months later. Then, in another 10 or 12 years he "ran away" again, but this time to Montana where he went into the sheep and cattle business and eventually wound up building a ranch across the Powder River from Powderville.

I often wondered if he missed the sea. This week my cousin sent me a letter he'd written to her mother on Feb. 26, 1922. He was 67 and helping his sons through a cold winter at the ranch. He thanks her for the valentine she'd sent and was assuring her he was in good health. He wrote:

"I have been able to go to the cattle every morning to help feed and that is no small chore as we had to get everything in. Your guess that everything was under a heavy snow blanket is about right and the temperatures would make an average of zero for the last 50 days. Some mornings the Powderville thermometer has recorded 40 to 45 below. However, we are bringing the cattle through in good shape and when this long cold spell comes to an end, as all things do, we will forget the discomfort and look with a sense of satisfaction that we have conquered the adverse conditions and won . . . Of course, we have our usual talks about the south and the best place to move to, but that is just the normal condition of Montana folks when the weather bites and the water freezes in the wash dish.

"Kenneth has picked upon Honduras. Harry's choice is Arizona. Louie has no choice but the kids must go to school, while I turn my eyes towards Pensacola Bay with a longing for the best it offers, yet knowing that every place has its unpleasant fixtures and that it is impossible to run away from yourself, and that yourself is just a bundle of habits, plus natural inherited instincts. There is so much cross pull between these that no one can be perfectly happy in any place under the sun. However, I would like to sit for a while out on the end of the L & N Pier and catch fish and watch the ships come and go. There is a lot of romance left in me about ships. They always have a story all their own, of their visits to foreign ports, of the close calls they have had with the Typhoons, Monsoons, Western Gales and Hurricanes.

"Yes, I like to be where the ships come in and maybe yet it will be so if I live long enough and Ella and Agnes, Leila and Alyce (his four daughters) get settled down to something steady. Then I have a dream of spreading my wings for the southland by the sea. Perhaps my dream may come true. In the meantime I must get the cattle back to a paying basis and when the U.S.A. recovers from its knock out and its people crowd toward the West as they will in a very few years. Then someone will get the Crescent Ranch and a stranger will dip his cup in the tank by the door and call it good. Better have a drink, Agnes, while we own it. There is none better."

The tank by the door proved stronger. He was to see eight more Montana winters and he never did get to the L & N Pier.

December 19, 1989

It's time to say Merry Christmas . . . that time of year when you send your special hellos and thank yous to all those who have been part of your year and part of your life since the last Merry Christmas.

So it's Merry Christmas to all those who bring more ice tea . . . who put out the mail . . . and put up the flags . . . who wave hello . . . and smile back . . . and ask about the kids . . . and check out the groceries . . . and plow streets in snowy times.

And Merry Christmas to all those who come out our way to walk and run and ride horses on this road of many STOP signs.

A very Special Merry Christmas to Del Snyder for all the hours and tender care spent with our mutual four-legged friend. He is "Lucky" to be around and very lucky to have come to your place that lonely night. He's growing great and you can be sure, neither of us will forget you.

Happy Holidays to Jerry Porter for sharing dinner that September night and here's another toast to all those growing up years in Basin.

Merry Christmas again to Butch Denzin for all the hay we move between our two places. And to Kane Morris who put it all in the right place.

And Merry Christmas to those who ride horses in mountain places and across red Wyoming dirt; and to all the regulars who stop in at Red Michaelis' barber shop to see what's going on.

Merry Christmas to all those who remember when the hollyhocks grew alongside the south side of the gym . . . who ever climbed the fence at night to swim in the old pool and never got caught . . . who remember the Daley Drug Store . . . and when cars were sold at Beale and Carey . . . and the Bird Grocery and when everyone danced at the Dreamland in Basin. If those weren't the good old days, there never were any.

And Merry Christmas to Rick Minter out in California for sharing a seat at a Greybull football game this fall except we spent as much time talking about other "old football" games as watching the one in front of us. Hey, those WERE the good old days.

Merry Christmas to all those who gather to celebrate 50th birthdays in old school houses . . . to all those who sent me Bill Wilkinson baseball cards . . . to Irma Schmoldt and LaRae Smith and Daisy and Bob Chapman and Ruth Whaley for sharing laughs and conversations this past year . . . to Claudine Murdoch who makes the Chamber office such a happy, cheerful place . . . and to the Dolan Scharens at Shell and everyone else who put up Christmas lights for the rest of us to enjoy.

Merry Christmas to the County Crew who spent some time below our place this summer but I can't decide if we've improved things or not yet.

Special Yuletide thanks to Louise Powers and Ora Probst who took some old grape vines of mine and made wondrous Christmas finery out of them. And for all the other bits of P.E.O. bows and pine cones and special touches of yours that became so many wreaths in so many homes.

To Lew Dunning, Manager of Maintenance Operations for United Airlines in far off Taiwan, a Special Merry Christmas from an old friend who wants you to know your letter was great and made a good point and just two weeks ago I took your advice and went United! Taiwan seems a long ways away from the days when you were in GHS and feeding the old press for us after school, Lew.

Merry Christmas to all those who pick up their mail at the post office each morning and stop to say hello, including Bob Garland and Bill Murdoch and Johnny Hoff and Sheriff Gary Anders and Buzz Winsor to name just a few.

A special Merry Christmas to John Anderson for extra help and advice to this part-time farmer; to Ron Fiene for his willingness to boost this town of ours in so many ways; to Joe Little for all the posts and poles and holes in the ground; to UPS's Rick Werbelow who brings all sorts of things to our house including a lost purse in the road this fall; to John Moberly for letting me know about the fence; to cheerful Tina Spragg who always asks about a mutual "friend" we have in Montana.

And an extra special Holiday Cheer to Lisa and Brad Dalin for giving us LISA's. You put new life back into an old institution and we toast you.

Merry Christmas to the old stone schoolhouse and its "schoolmaster", John McGough, for his hard work and determination to create a haven for books and art and traveling people. You have saved a tie with the past and made something for the future, John.

And special thanks and Merry Christmas to Russell Simpson in Massachusetts, and Harriett Nau and Dorothy Welton in Arizona and Ned Kost, Jr. for remembering words I wrote in '89. And Merry Christmas, too, to Bill Clifton for remembering a story about a car hopelessly stuck in the sand years ago. I'd almost forgotten it, Bill, until you brought it back.

Merry Christmas to Afton Evans who keeps asking her mother, Kathy, where the little horses are when they drive by our pasture. And to another little five-year-old down the road, Brandy Wilkinson, who scolded her barking dog when I ran by: "Don't bark at him, he's my neighbor."

And Yuletide Cheer to Gale Larchick for many past kindnesses . . . and Gary Good for sharing a new garage this summer, the water this fall and all the Christmas lights along our "neighborhood" this Christmas . . . and to another neighbor, Elaine Sellars, hope you're feeling better now . . . and thanks to Lane Keisel for help with a piece of ground this spring.

And Merry Christmas to old Spooky Shows, wherever he is. Remember him, Marion and Brenton, he was the one with the tattoo on his arm.

And to all those people who live in other places and keep track of Greybull through the pages of the Greybull Standard, including David Carrico in Charleston, S.C., Roy Buchmeier in Lander, Bill Collingwood in Vancouver, Wash., Tom Clucas in Missoula, Mrs. Billie Emert in Auburn, Ala., Mrs. Pete Fowler in Phoenix, Roger Huffman in Medford, Ore., Susan Valasek in Sugar Hill, N.H., Mrs. Frank Linn in Albany, Ore., Gerald E. Lewis in Belmont, Calif. and 47 other Californians who subscribe to the Standard, here's a very special Merry Christmas to you across all those miles.

And to all of you new people we'll be meeting this year, and all the little kids who grew up so much during 1989, to all those who live in this fine Wyoming community, the best of holidays and the merriest of Christmases.

1990

January 25, 1990

"It was the computer that saved us," the out-of-town speaker told me that last night at the Wyoming Press convention. "I don't know what we'd have done without them."

Oh, golly, I thought to myself. Does anything ever change in this old world?

More than 30 years ago we went to our first press convention, two very young and wide-eyed youngsters who had decided to spend the rest of their lives in newspapering and we were sitting clear in the back row so no one would see us and we wanted this bunch of successful and prominent newspaper people to send us back home full of inspiration and grand newspaper thoughts.

The discussion was on improvements in newspapering. "I'll tell you the thing that's helped us the most," the Wheatland publisher said, "was our new posting machine."

My God, I thought, what does he mean? A posting machine. We're supposed to be talking about journalism, about words that describe and ads that sell and editorials that improve. A posting machine? That was incredible. Even a barely-started young man in his twenties knew that was incredible.

Now just as incredibly, we're talking about computers in exactly the same tone of voice. The mechanical occupies us too much. Of course, computers are wonderfully important to all of us now. The point is, though, that is not what makes a newspaper. A yellow pencil can make a newspaper. The crudest of cameras have taken some marvelous pictures. No computer ever sold an ad. It is not mechanical that produces newspapers but heads and hands.

I keep thinking how awful it was that Will Shakespeare never had a word processor.

But enough. Not all conventions are talk of posting machines. It is a gathering, like all others, where people who do the same thing can talk about it over and over. The room was full of young people. Not much gray hair in this bunch. It is startling to be reminded how much of journalism is done by young people. Newspapering always has been a game for the young. And they have been eager and very willing and very dedicated and that is always inspiring.

A "young" newspaper was there, too. A USA Today executive was a Friday speaker. He mentioned that USA Today only had 2,800 subscribers in Wyoming. One lady wanted to know what "we could do to help" raise that subscription figure up. Another incredible. Lady, we have met the enemy and he is that guy standing at the podium!

The biggest hit of the convention was Gov. Mike Sullivan. He got raves for being eloquent, coming down hard when he had to, expressing himself, talking of Wyoming and just plain being around. Someone from Kansas who was there was astonished that "the governor could be so accessible." She pointed out, "We never see our governor."

But then she asked me if we had movie theaters in Wyoming which I thought equally astonishing.

I also discovered that this column is the longest-running column in Wyoming newspapers now, 33 years of it, starting back in December 1956. Some years were a whole lot better than others, but they were there. Margaret Peck at Riverton told me she burned out and just had to stop writing hers. She and I were the last two columnists left who started in the 1950's.

You can't escape those thoughts of the past at a happening like a convention. Sons and daughters of people you knew for a long time are there. People you work with are taking more responsibility for Wyoming journalism. The batons keep being passed, everywhere.

Driving back through a January Wyoming was like a clock never changing the hour. Same old snow in the gullies. Shoshoni without any trees. The windy places bare and the rest still with the white stuff. A few new calves on the ground. Earlier every year. Pretty soon these Big Horn Basin ranchers will have to decide if they're going to go visit the kids for Christmas or stay home and calve. Wyoming and Life just keep going on. You can mark the years in many ways, from one press convention to the other if you want. That's as good as any. Check off another year. And another convention. Nothing – and everything – has changed. It's still a great place to newspaper.

February 1, 1990

THAT BIG cottonwood contest to find the biggest Wyoming cottonwood this Centennial year is intriguing. We all should measure ours. It would be interesting to know the biggest one in the town or county. The Society of American Foresters said to measure the circumference at 4.5 feet above the ground. Then measure on the ground the crownspread (or the dripline) which is the distance from longest branch on one side to the furthest on the other side. And finally, the height. That might take a transit. (If you can reach to the top of the tree to measure, you probably shouldn't enter.)

You can measure the height by using a stick and marking off twelve times the stick's length from the tree base. Put the stick on the ground, (says my old Boy Scout book) and sight to the top of the tree. Measure where that line intersects on your stick. Every inch equals one foot on the tree. It's those two triangles of the same shape. The small one at the stick and the large one at the tree. One is 12 times the other.

Believe me, if yours is big enough to compete, someone will be out there with a transit to pinpoint its height.

NEVER CAN be around the Wyoming Travel Commission without thinking of Frankie Norris who was the first long-term travel director. He never changed with the governors as his predecessors did and it gave the commission some continuity. Frankie knew about continuity. He was Frank Norris to all the state except his hometown of Greybull. "I can always tell when I am home," he said to me once. "Everyone starts calling me Frankie."

WE HAVE A grandson who was involved in an indoor head-on collision and came out with, as he described it, a very "flat lip."

February 6, 1990
I'VE BEEN WANDERING around looking at old cottonwood trees this past week, trying to see if there was a winner among the old patriarchs of the area.

Some are truly big, especially out in the country. Most of those old timers in the towns were chopped away from houses and power lines a long time ago. Urban progress does not leave much space for a cottonwood tree that wants to grow too much. Along the ditchbank it's different and some of those old carefree ones have grown pretty tall.

Greybull hardly has an old cottonwood left. Slim Nielsen has a dandy right by his front door. There's another big old one down by the old pump house in the south end. But most of those cottonwoods you remember from other years are gone now. They grew too old or too big or too close or all of the above.

They all came from the river. Either there already or dug up and planted in those early first lawns. Many of the ones in the country came by the same route. We still have several in our lower yard, brought up from the river by the Joe Clucas family 60 or 70 years ago. I didn't realize they were so big until I put a tape around them.

We played around with this big cottonwood tree stuff once before and the late Jim Whaley called to say I caused him a lot of work that afternoon. He'd been measuring all the cottonwoods along the Whaley road. Fifty or sixty years earlier, his grandmother had dug them up from the Big Horn river bank and took them home in a wagon. She planted them in a long row by the road. Some are gone now, I noticed, but still at least one huge one is left.

There're many big ones like it around. What will win that centennial tree contest won't necessarily be the biggest or the tallest. It'll have to be the balance, the combination of the three. There're just too many old cottonwoods that can qualify. But I don't think I saw a winner yet in the ones I picked out.

February 15, 1990
I'M MELLOWING, I'm sure, because I'm beginning to develop a soft spot for the old magpie. I spent much of my life in that foreign country, The Past, hating and vilifying those old magpies. There was a time when their incessant noise was unbearable. All that carrying on and the pilfering of dog food, and the suspected raids on other bird nests made me furious with them.

But I don't know. They've put up with me for a long time. They still come around the place. Maybe they like the dog food still. One pair has an old nest they've been sneaking back to this week. They mate for life, you know, which is not all that bad a trait in the animal kingdom. Or anywhere else. And this one pair is back again, maybe the same pair from a year ago. They don't care if more winter weather jumped on us this week. They're still making a fuss over house-hunting.

You know, we tried to eradicate the magpie in this country. We even had contests for little kids to bring in magpie legs and paid them 10 cents a pair. Thousands of legs would come in. They were eating the pheasant eggs, we said. We shot at them, chased them away, did everything we could to eliminate them. It was a grand failure.

I may call a truce. Stick around, old birds, if you want. At least until the dog food runs out.

February 27, 1990
ONE OVERWHELMING difference between these days now and those elusive "old days" is the number of family snapshots taken. In the trunk downstairs, when we go through the photo albums of my growing up or the precious few photographs we have of our parents' early lives, you could pile them in one corner.

Today, one color picture after another spills out of our automatic cameras. Of kids and dogs and trips and occasions and relatives and more kids and birthdays and casual visits and more kids. In the old days it was all black and white and now its Kodak color. It may not be necessarily discriminate now or not always very selective. But it's still a vivid, wonderful trip through our present lives.

Sometimes I wonder if there aren't more pictures pasted to the refrigerator door nowadays than all the pictures we have of those good old days.

I watched that fine scene in the Seventies film, "Going In Style" when Willie has died and George Burns pulls the old box out of the closet with Willie's things. He sifts through the cards and mementos and the very few pictures. There's one of Willie holding his two-year-old son. And another when he was married. And one in his Army uniform. And one of a trip to the beach they'd taken. That's the way life used to be. A small bunch of pictures in an old box. Each one was meaningful beyond description. Each one described a time more than an instant. "That's when I was in the Army." "That was when Johnny was two years old." Nowadays there can be a picture for every week that Johnny is two. Or every trip you ever take.

No one need ever wonder what life was like in these times. We will have thousands of frames from 35mm cameras and video camcorders to show you.

ONE OF THE BEST photographers I ever met was George Strickland of Greybull who took most of his pictures of the old days during 1910's. He was just a little kid then. But he'd been bitten by the photography bug and he was determined to learn to take pictures. And did he ever. He not only took them, he taught himself the darkroom and did all his own developing and printing. It was amazing to me, 40 years later, to take these negatives he'd saved, put them in my "modern" enlarger and discover Greybull, circa 1910.

He took pictures like we take them today. Of everything. As often as he could. Of everyone he knew. He had a photographer's eye and a little boy's enthusiasm. That's a great combination. The Greybull Standard used a dozen or so in the 50th edition in 1959 which delighted George and everyone else who saw them. You had to keep reminding yourself that these were taken by a 12-year-old boy with an old box camera. The refrigerator door in the Strickland house may have been the only one in town with pictures pasted to it.

THURMAN HURST came to Greybull on Apr. 1, 1907, and he and Eddie Mead were the first two boys in the new town. He was just 11 years old. One of the next boys to move to town was Jess Perkins. Fifty years later Thurm recalled:

"The first time I ever saw Jess Perkins was right out here on main street. They were holding an auction sale and old Colonel Cropsey was crying the sale. Jess walked up to me and said, 'Who in the hell are you, kid?'"

THAT MUST HAVE been a recurring story among young boys in those early Wyoming years. The late Paul Peterson told me of growing up in Cody's first days and seeing a new boy, Milward Simpson, in town. Paul was with several boys in the street and Milward walked up to them. Milward was chewing tobacco which made a real impression on the Cody boys. "What the hell is going on around here?" Paul remembers Milward saying.

March 6, 1990

OUT THERE IN this old world isn't there someone like UPS who wants to run a post office? Someone who won't charge us 30 cents every time we want to send a letter somewhere?

UPS has taken over our package business in America. Federal Express and others deliver overnight service. Surely there is someone else who would like a private enterprise crack at moving letters, newspapers and mail.

If we ended the post office monopoly, we would probably see it happen.

I thought two-bits for a stamp to mail a letter was pretty high-priced. I hate to say it, but many of my letters probably aren't worth two-bits. I know they are going to have to improve to be worth 30 cents.

The Post Office system has been trying to make the customer pay for its mistakes for a long time now. It can't seem to run in the black. Eighty-three percent of its expense is labor. It lost the package business to a better operator, UPS. It must be losing more fast service to Federal Express. It has eliminated the old subsidies newspapers and magazines used to enjoy. But it has to be subsidizing the huge amount of junk mail at third-class rates.

The real problem is not raising first class to 30 cents. The ink will hardly be dry on the new 30-cent stamps before they'll ask to raise it another nickel or dime. In 1963 you mailed first class for a nickel. It is the system at fault, not the user who is now being asked to stick five more cents up in the corner. Raising rates haven't cured the ills before. It won't now either.

OUR SECTION of ice in the Big Horn river jumped the gun a little and went out Mar. 2. It only missed the Mar. 10th normal time by a week. That's not bad considering the warm winter we've had. There always have been extremes with the ice. Normal is this second week in March. But back in the shivering winter of 1917 the ice stayed in the channel until Mar. 29.

March 13, 1990

IT'S THAT annual time when I am reminded I was 13 on Friday, the 13th. I can't remember what I did on that day in Basin, Wyo. except I gingerly went through it so nothing would tip the balance between bad luck and good luck. It was a very quiet day. It wasn't until later years that I did wild and reckless things on my birthdays to prove I still could.

HAVE YOU noticed when you were young and were always wanting to be older, your birthday came around every 18 months. Later on, it's only six months between another candle on the cake.

WHEN THAT abandoned City of Worland water tower fell on the Murdoch house in Worland, that wasn't the first time Bill has had experience with things falling the wrong way.

The one last week was the more spectacular. Instead of taking it down in pieces, the City decided to drop it all at once onto a large pile of sand in the street. That's where the City wanted it to fall, but one of the legs buckled at the last instant and the tank fell right on top – SMASH – of the Murdoch house. The picture looked like a big satellite had fallen out of the sky and just squashed it.

A tree limb did almost the same thing once before to Bill at his home in Greybull. But it took out the deck instead. Bill had decided to lop off the big hanging limb. He notched and planned the cut and put the chain saw to it. His wife, Dawn, and the family cat were on the deck watching. The heavy limb twisted at the last moment and headed for the deck. Dawn and the cat dived safely back in the house. The deck wasn't that fast. The limb came down – SMASH – right on the deck.

"The cat didn't come out of the house for a week," Bill said. "He'd go to the window and look up at the sky, but he wouldn't go out."

March 20, 1990

A PARTNERSHIP to me always should be treated like a 60-40 partnership regardless of the actual numbers of shares owned. And, further, each partner should act like he or she had the 40 percent. If you are the minority partner, you will always treat the partnership differently. You will want to make it work without the clout of owning the majority share. When both partners approach the partnership this way, with a sensitivity of the minority partner, and forgetting for the moment who owns what, a partnership has a better chance of long life.

April 3, 1990

I WILL ALWAYS think something went out of small town journalism when we all became educated. What was news then is probably still news today. But we don't say it in the same way the old boys did. The 1916 Greybull Standard, for example, ran this item:

"Last week Dan O'Brien 28, made his tenth unsuccessful attempt at suicide. Unless Dan is careful, he will some day die a violent death."

And in June of the same year: "Jim McKay, a sheep herder who has oratorical abilities that will put W. J. Bryan to shame, entertained a large crowd on Greybull Avenue Sunday afternoon until Marshal Latham arrived and escorted him to the city bastille where he remained until Monday when he contributed $7.50 toward the fund to defray the expense of maintaining the town of Greybull."

April 10, 1990

WHEN I WOKE up to a 20-degree morning Tuesday and the wind blowing in from the northwest and then a light snow starting to fall, I thought to myself, "What a perfect day for a Wyoming track meet."

ONE YEAR in the Sixties the Greybull Standard received this letter from Slim Nielsen:

"Dear Editor:

"At the campground last night, three of Greybull's oversize mosquitoes cornered a rather plump tourist lady in her tent! She was mortified with fear and proceeded to evacuate by crawling under the bottom. Being rather slow she didn't make the grade and this one mosquito hit her with his motivation! The resulting injury required the services of a doctor and 12 stitches! And it only takes three in a potato sack!

"Then it happened again. This skinny fellow was standing by his automobile when two of these pesky mosquitoes made a dive for him. He ducked – they hit his car. The best estimate we could get to repair the damages was $416.32.

"We were too late to help these people, but I wanted you to know that being a good editor you helped me by printing the city mosquito program.

I rolled up the program and killed eighty-seven in twelve minutes so I know it works."

Slim Nielsen

April 24, 1990

ONCE I ASKED Riley Wilson what Greybull looked like in 1909 when he came to town. Riley was an old-time railroader and there wasn't much more than those two steel rails going across a sagebrush flat. The town had begun in 1907 and was to be incorporated in that year of 1909. But Riley saw it when it was just making a beginning.

I wondered what it looked like to him when he first saw it.

"Well, I'll tell you," Riley said. "It was just like the fellow said to the girl: 'Honey, you look like a million!' She said, 'huh! Brother, you never saw a million.'

"'That's right,' said the fellow. 'You look like something I never saw.'"

WHEN YOU'RE young, you think that only old people can be characters like Riley Wilson was. This is not true, of course. Each generation brings its own crop. You and I see our contemporaries as quick-witted and individualistic and fun to be around. The younger person will look upon them as a little bit eccentric, a whole lot funny and really quite special. It is said, the older the actor the more he plays the role. Which is also true of all "old" characters.

Riley relished those moments on stage. I was an enthusiastic audience. It made for sparks.

I WORRY about America's continuity of life, the passing of one generation's knowledge on to the one coming up. I'm sure it has always been the older generation's lament that the younger does not appreciate what went on before, is not learning what it should, has neglected old values. I'm arriving at that stage when I can look at the past and not necessarily see the future. I don't care about what the cars and computers will look like. Science and materialistic achievements will forever exceed the previous years. But we really haven't improved on the humanities very much, the way we talk and speak, what we read, what we believe our culture is, how to appreciate the arts, to feel the passion of music and writing and inspiring brush strokes.

Riley Wilson was a passionate believer and student of Roberts Rules of Order. It is a magnificently structured way to provide order and procedure out of the chaotic tendencies of people in the mass. I fear for old things like Roberts Rules of Order in these days. Our society does not seem especially attuned now to doing things in orderly fashion. Or for establishing traditions and long-standing associations which make families such a permanent force.

In my business of newspapering we violate enough of the "old rules" of ethics and honesty and obligation, not to mention grammar and spelling, that our newspaper ancestors must be groaning in agony and embarrassment.

The Census Lady (as one of my friends called her) asked if I spoke another language. No, I told her, I do not. I speak only English. I try to speak it very well. I try to write it well. I am still learning this after 50 years of trying. I do not hope to succeed as well as I want. I know I will always wonder if the last word I write will be the best one I could have used.

I love the English language. It is the most powerful and descriptive language ever spoken. It has given the world one common language bond above all the other languages and dialects and symbols man has used. Its library of books on every conceivable theme is too awesome to describe. It is one of America's greatest assets.

How strange it seems to know our "old enemies," the Russians, want to learn to speak English and our "new enemies," the Japanese, already do and yet some Americans want to speak something else.

I am not against learning a second or third language. I have my foreign language credits. I could and have managed in non-English environments. The intellect should be expanded. The education broadened. I believe in that passionately. But even more passionately I believe English can be our only official language. And further, I wish we spoke it better and wrote it better and believed in its power more.

I'm not pulling for going back to the old days. We don't need a sagebrush flat with a single railroad track through it "that looks like nothing else I ever saw." But we do need to remember what made us so proud of our fathers and mothers and their forefathers before them.

May 7, 1990

THANK HEAVEN, for little girls who grow up to be mothers and then have days named after them.

I've been thinking this week about all the mothers of all the kids I grew up with. I can remember every one of them. I can see their faces and hear their voices and remember old stories of my youth and my friends' youth. In small towns and rural areas, you grow up with everyone else. Everyone helps raise you whether either you or they are aware of it. What they say to their kids, you hear. What they tell their kids, you share. You're at their house, around their table, in their yard. They rear their kids and you tag along. Your mother raises you and your friend listens in. It's always been that way in very small towns.

Leila Kennedy

My mother replanted some iris one summer day when I was very little, about third grade size. There were just the two of us that day. Mother took a picture of me hoeing up the dirt. My hands were far down the handle since it was almost too big to manage. My hair is standing right straight up and if you'd seen that mop of hair you'd said to yourself, now there's a kid who'll have hair the rest of his life. Which tells you something about predictions. We were talking about old snapshots a couple of months ago, how in those days we took few pictures and they represented a time. That picture of me hoeing in the iris bed would have had written on the back, "This is Bruce in the third grade."

The iris were those old-fashioned, small purple ones. Not fancy and not big. Not by today's standards. Mother liked them. In another couple of years she would take them over to the "new" house and replant them there. We went over 20 years ago and dug them up and brought them back to our place. By now they're over 60 years old. I need to redo them this summer and put them in another bed. A little boy with a hoe and shovel again. Strange that it doesn't seem all that long ago.

May 22, 1990

SOME DIABOLICAL person sent me one of those "Equationanalysis Test" which has a bunch of numbers and a bunch of letters and you're supposed to solve the equation. For instance, 26 = L. of the A. They give you that one: "26 = Letters of the Alphabet." Why is it that the question always seems so absurdly hard and the answer so absurdly easy. And this being so, then, what is:

a) 7 = W. of the W.

or

b) 12 = S. of the Z.

Tests like these always seem to bruise my ego a little. All around me, people are putting down the answers and I'm still chewing on the end of my pencil. In the end, when you add the scores all up, I not only started slow, I ended slow. As usual, I had the lowest score in the household.

I read about a national figure the other day who became so frustrated on not being able to do crossword puzzles, he just set aside the time and learned how. Now he breezes through them and for all I know is one of those hateful people you read about who do the New York Times puzzle in 15 minutes.

c) 88 = P.K.

d) 13 = S. on the A.F.

e) 90 = D. in a R.A.

When you do silly tests which show how quick you are, you can't help but think about all the information you must have forgotten through the years. People are forever saying how much more the kids know these days than they did "in our time" and people have been saying that same thing for 150 years. And if it were really true, we would have nothing but Einsteins graduating this week all over Wyoming by the mere progression of education alone.

The brain is never as lazy as the person carrying it around and you stumble around with some silly test and you wonder if you have remembered anything. I loved my mother-in-law the day she told us that she sure was failing now that she was in her Eighties. She just couldn't remember her Latin anymore.

f) 24 = H. in a D.
g) 57 = H.V.
h) 4 = Q. in a G.
i) 29 = D. in F. in a L.Y.

YOU WERE right if your answers included, a world, a zodiak, a piano, a flag, an angle, a day, a sauce, a game, and a month.

May 28, 1990

ON THE PAST few Memorial Days, we've taken some extra flowers along and left them with an old friend who was very kind to us for many years. Her immediate family is gone and hers became one of those headstones that was bare on Memorial Day.

So we've been leaving a few iris she liked so well. This morning on the headstone was a carefully-wrapped bouquet of Indian Paintbrush. Another friend had stopped by.

There is a special touch to Indian Paintbrush. Only a poet could have named it. So it is blessed with its name and blessed with its color and it is making broad strokes across our green and wet Wyoming this year.

How can such a small handful look so perfect on a white headstone? Or a bowlfull thoughtfully placed in front of the out-of-state guest so dominate the table?

I do not know if I stop and smell the roses enough, but a little dab of pink and red in a Wyoming prairie will set the brakes. I am so partial to things Western. It is a disease of long years spent in the same place. The same good place, I should add. In the spring, Indian Paintbrush is one of the reminders of how vulnerable I am.

Our very small patch of Indian Paintbrush on the hill has relished this wet spring. It is tucked away among the sagebrush and you must stumble over it almost to see it. I always thought that was for protection, but the wildflower book says it is a semiparasite and feeds off the roots of other plants.

"This plant is a semiparasite, making only a portion of the food it requires. Its roots grow into the soil until they touch roots of other plants such as the sagebrush. They then penetrate the tissues of the host plant to steal part of their food. Throughout the ages, the paintbrushes have so developed this habit that they can now scarcely live without the aid of other plants."

So it's hard to domesticate and that part of the Master Plan is okay with me. It belongs to the Wyoming that's wild and free.

June 5, 1990

LAST WEEK, I was climbing over the pole fence and just fell off. By gosh, that ground came up fast. Don't know yet what I did. But I missed something and down I went.

You'd think a guy would be able to ride a pole fence.

Then, the very next day, I walked out of the horse trailer, put my foot down for the last step inside and missed it completely. Stepped right out into the air and down I went again. Another big thud. Twice in two days. This one hurt worse than the first time. You don't get used to throwing yourself on the ground willy-nilly. I was a little slower picking myself up off the ground the second time. That first dive off the fence, I bounded right back up again to make sure no one saw me.

That's a conditioned response in modern humans. It's not so bad if you fall. Just make sure no one sees you. When you're a little kid and spill off your bike, you jump right back up as fast as you can and then look around to see if anyone saw you. For good measure, you pretend to carefully look over your bike as if something mechanical had gone wrong.

You see skiers do the same thing. Someone will take a terrible fall, pick themselves up and then look up hill to see if they can spot the rock that dumped them.

It wasn't a rock that caused one of my most spectacular ski cartwheels, but my ego. And this time everyone was watching. In those early years of Antelope Butte skiing, Kent Holcomb of Sheridan taught a ski class. Down below me, I could see the class lined out and I thought, I'll just flash past. And right in front of them, I caught an edge and plowed snow with my head for 30 feet. When I stopped, I was right in front of Kent. He said, "Care to join us?"

But horses can't talk and they can't laugh at you either, laying there on the ground. With luck, they didn't see me either.

June 12, 1990

THE BARBARA BUSH Wellesley speech quote Time magazine liked was: "At the end of your life, you will never regret not having passed one more test, (not) winning one more verdict, or not closing one more deal. You will regret time not spent with a husband, a child, a friend or a parent."

LITTLE Eric Gifford had the right technique in the sheep riding contest Saturday. He came out of the chute with his face buried deep in the wool and his arms wrapped around as far as they would go. He went all the way across the arena and looked headed for Cody before he finally let go. That's the way you win those rides. Hold on for your life. One little boy told Charlotte Hinckley he had been practicing all week on his granddad!

June 19, 1990

A COUPLE OF DAYS after Father's Day I was holding a very little boy and drying the tears over a broken water pistol. He was just devastated because this brand new red "shooter" would not work at all. He'd picked it out himself just an hour before and now it was worthless. It didn't help that his older brother's new cap pistol worked just fine. And he doesn't yet understand El Cheapo plastic products that shouldn't be on the market. It all added up to major catastrophe.

So an old guy's arms were around a very little tyke and we walked away from the scene of all the problems to commiserate together. His father and I had done the same thing more than once in other years. I truly suffer when they are disappointed. I am just as angry as they when they are angry. I ache when they ache. I am exasperated when they are exasperating. But I am helpless when disappointment sets in. I am an old softie when they hurt so inside.

Oh, little boy, I thought, you are going to have other times like this, many water pistols that sputter, many slights and passing overs and near misses. Life keeps insisting on repeating that. And parents will continue to share the hurt just as I did with your father in another generation and my father with me in still another. You won't always be such a little a guy, though. Now we can pick you up and hold you and carry you off to some private little place until the tears go away.

June 26, 1990

YOU CAN ALWAYS tell newcomers to a wagon train. They are the ones with clothes still clean. It doesn't take long to change that. Wyoming dust and camp life soon put age on a pilgrim. And the sight of a long line of wagons and riders raising far-off dust will forever put a stamp on your soul.

After two days last weekend, my wagon train clothes were presentable enough to belong, my horse was moving and my heart properly captured. And I rode it two fine, fine days through the Burlington and Emblem country with the Centennial Wagon Train.

Romantics are easy to please. Surround us with horses and the sound of rolling wagon wheels and the world seems such a better place. Throw in old covered wagons and a big chunk of Wyoming sky and the hook is set. You can smother us with dust and send the temperatures in the high 90's and we'll groan about it but never change places. What you are doing overwhelms all else. People watching from the sidelines say how hot it looks and how dusty it must be and how dirty everyone is. But their perspective is different than the one you have when you twist around in your saddle and look back at all the wagons behind you, still coming a 100 years behind you.

Monday's crossing of the benchland west of Emblem and south of the Highway 14-16-20 Cody road was a magnificent sight. There was a road across there I never knew was there and the traveling orders were to "stay in the tracks." So you weren't riding out to the side which was not as much fun or as independent as it had been the day before. But it served to keep everyone in the same line and bunched together. The head wagons made a wrong turn, too, (even those in the old days made wrong turns) so the line had to wait for some to backtrack. It all contributed to a wonderful long line of riders and wagons against the still white mountains to the west and the Big Horns to the east. In the train you'd hear people saying, "Look back, look back," and when you did, nothing but wagons and horses and mountains and sagebrush and blue sky would be in sight. Wyoming, still the same after 100 years.

And if you wanted more authenticity that day, we made the Dry Creek crossing, white wagons going down the grade and up the other side and then stringing back out again.

The wagon driver behind us was a little concerned about whether he had any brakes. His outrider rode back to see him. They talked a minute and the guy ahorseback said, "Well, if you don't have any brakes, you'll know it soon enough." It was the sort of wagon you wished you were in back of on a hill, not in front.

The conversations you heard were great. One pack outfit had come apart in camp the night before. "You sure gave us a lot of laughs last night," someone who'd seen it said.

I rode up along side a guy in a buggy pulled by a pretty fine-looking horse. I told the guy that. "Everyone should have a horse like this," he said. But he spoke too soon. Five hundred yards down the trail, the horse balked and wouldn't move. Other wagons waited and then moved around him. When I looked back the last time, he was still trying to get the horse to go.

Three antelope came out of the sagebrush and ran alongside this strange sight of wagons blocking the way. "If this had been for real," someone said, "we'd be having antelope for supper tonight."

It was real in every other way. You don't travel by horseback and wagon wheel without being for real. Sunday morning the rodeoing was amazing. Two days of rest and a bunch of new pilgrims in camp made that morning's start memorable. For about twenty minutes horses were blowing up everywhere. One guy's packhorse blew up and bucked in a big circle until everything was off his back. Another packhorse ran right down the line of outriders scattering horses ahead right and left. In front of us one guy's horse spooked and sent him flying. Another horse and rider to the left did a complete cartwheel and both got back up on their feet.

Horses jigged and snorted and ran away and everywhere you looked was a brand new scene. Horses were charged up from each other and wanting to go. They were hearing new sounds. It's obvious that a wagon wheel rolling on a hard dirt road does not sound the same to a horse as it does to a romantic.

"How are you doing?" I said to another guy on a little black horse.

"Okay, now," he said. "This is our first morning and right away he bucks me off. I got back on and he drags me through camp. I finally had to take him over the hill out of sight before I could get on him."

I don't know that this happened every morning. It didn't on Monday. But it made for a memorable start for us.

Rode for awhile with Spud Jones of Cody. He was there for the same two days. A busy square dance caller, he had to be back this week. "I have four squares to call," he said. But for right now he was pulling a pack horse and "helping out with the wagon ahead."

One wrinkle the old wagon trains didn't have were friends waving at you from the roadside and recognizing you under the dust. In Burlington, Russell Horton and Richard Gormley gave me a bad time about my dirty chaps. "I'll bet he spent the night rubbing rosin on them to make them look authentic," Russell insisted.

Camp was part authentic and part not. Rules are relaxing as the end nears. The train will more than double in riders this last week into Powell and Cody. With good roads near, pickups and trailers and campers are showing up. Out on the trail it's 100 years ago. In camp, we're part 1890's and part 1990's.

The water truck parks and people come with their bottles and pails and their shampoo. That was a revelation to me. Modern generations do not want dirty hair. They want it clean. And so they stoop under the water truck hose and someone holds water on them so they can shampoo. Person after person, men and women. "I've washed my hair every day in camp," one woman told me. Hair means more to us in these modern days. I suppose it meant much way back then, too, but if the Indians took it off of you, it really didn't matter whether you'd just shampooed it or not.

Randy Blackburn, who broke his arm and had it pinned during the wagon train's first week, walked by his portable electric fence around his horses and just touched the wire to see if it was hot. The charge went straight to the metal pins in his arm and sent him to his knees. Something else the oldtimers wouldn't know about.

The sounds of camp start fading after dark. People settle more and the shampooing is over. Horses don't talk to each other clear across camp so much, although only for an hour or two will they ever be completely quiet. Somewhere someone is playing a harmonica. All the old tunes. A harmonica at night always reminds me of either a Civil War bivouac or the Old West. Tonight it was definitely a cowboy. For an hour or two we had acid rock. Someone opened their pickup door and turned the radio on. Later it went to country western and still later it went out completely. I wondered where in the world would acid rock come from on a night like this. In the morning I looked over at the pickup and it was the young lads who pull the portable potties from camp to camp. Workers not travelers. No harmonica times for them.

It's too hot for a tent. I scratch out a place around the cactus and figure I'll never sleep. I'm wrong. I do. The stars are magnificent. If you're the type who does not stop and smell the roses enough, you are also the type who does not look at the stars enough. About three in the morning, the nighthawks go over with that funny coughing sound they make. The horses are stamping around more. A little breeze starts at one end of camp and comes over my way, going from sagebrush to sagebrush until it's where I am and then it just brushes over me, cool and little restless. And it leaves and goes on to the east, towards the new day, towards where the sun will start to shine soon on another day on the wagon trail.

July 10, 1990

"HAVE YOU SEEN the kids yet?" Dorothy Rath asked me in the middle of last weekend's big Greybull all-class reunion. And we had a good laugh over it.

"Have you seen the kids yet?" That should be the byword on all class reunions. That's what Mrs. Myrtle Hunsaker asked Chuck Peterson years ago when one of her classes had come back for a reunion. But it was their FIFTIETH reunion! If you were one of Mrs. Hunsaker's kids in old Greybull, you were a kid a long, long time!

"Have you seen the kids yet?" If you didn't, you weren't looking very hard. They were everywhere. This little town had about 1,100 more "kids" in it Friday night than it will this Friday night. That's a committee estimate of the kids who were here over the three days. Mrs. Hunsaker would have had a wonderful time.

SOME NICE little person gave me a card which read:
"Grandpas are storytellers, big word spellers, ballgame yellers.
"They're silly-songers, take-alongers, big-and-strongers.
"Grandpas are kiss-and-huggers, pigtail tuggers, dolly snugglers . . .
"They're funny teasers, bounce-on-kneesers, and super-duper grandkid pleasers."
Hey, I'm guilty.

THAT SAME LITTLE person told her mother that she thought I ought to come over to the Gillette Air Show "today" (this was a week ago) "and do some of his tricks."

The biggest trick I have is the landing which is sometimes a knee-knocker, knuckle-buster, high-bouncer, slip-shodder, too-faster, stomach-twister, crowd-pleaser.

July 17, 1990

I HAVE TWO of those orange canvas irrigating dams but one has a good-sized hole in it and I've relegated it to the spare status. The other day I grabbed the wrong one and I was way up on the ditch, in the water before I saw I had the one with the hole. I set it anyway. It was late and I didn't want to go all the way back to the house. Of course, the water just poured out the hole. Water usually does what it wants to do. It looked like I was going to have to go find the other dam. Then I saw an old Budweiser can someone had thrown out along the road and I said outloud, "You don't suppose . . ." Sure enough, it fit the hole and best of all, fit it snug enough to stay in. So if you go by our place and see a dam in the ditch with a Budweiser beer can sticking out, you'll know why.

JAMES MICHENER made Wyoming headlines in the past month suggesting that someone buy a Wyoming ranch so youngsters 50 years from now will know what ranchlife was like. He didn't say so, but it would also be nice if calves could stay up above ninety cents.

Michener said, too, he'd mentioned a fence around Wyoming some years ago "to keep the goons out" and he guessed he "still thinks that."

The first person who ever came to Wyoming probably said that. So have most of us who've ever lived here for very long: "Now that I'm here, you can close the gate."

What we really mean to say is that we don't want anyone to wreck our Wyoming. But we'd take more business and more jobs, a broader and bigger tax base which translates to better schools and more plentiful government services. We'd take more oil wells and more tourists, more water and more irrigated land, and more opportunities for our young people.

And you don't do any of this without opening gates to people, those of us who have been here a long time, and those of us who came last month. We were all out-of-towners at one time or another. Or our parents were.

This is the way it has always been. We have sought the Wyoming balance of an unspoiled country with a chance to make a good living. It's worked for a very long time now. We ought to keep that guy on who's been running the gate.

August 14, 1990

THEY CALLED Locksmith Willie Stout to Shell to open a locked car for a group of traveling Germans Saturday night. They had locked the keys inside. Willie was in bed at the time. He's "saved" many such lives. In the summer, the Shell Falls rest area in the Big Horns is a popular place to lock yourself out of the car. Everyone piles out and no one remembers the keys.

Willie opened one locked car door up there but no keys were inside. The family had called down to Greybull, waited for Willie to come up and then found out the keys weren't where they were supposed to be.

The wife had been driving.

"Where did you go when you got out of the car?" Willie asked, trying to help.

"Over to the lookout there, by that ledge," the woman pointed. Everyone trooped over to the ledge. The keys were right where she'd put them, hours before. Just another one of those happy vacations.

August 24, 1990

MY FRIEND, Darwin Yates, bored with TV one night, wandered through the Greybull area telephone book and found many names that went together. Like "the Bushes, Berrys and Thornberrys". And "the Roses, Trees, Sage and Douglas". Or how about "the Bakers, Cooks, Farmers, Millers and Brewers?"

Or "the Shores, Bass, Netts, Frey and Brooks."

It makes you realize there were berries a long time before there were Berrys. And bakers before Bakers.

In Old England what you were or what you did made a difference to your name. Those old timers further complicated things when they tried to tack on where you lived, too, so they added the name of the town you lived in to your name as well, and then changed it for each of your kids where ever they moved. It soon became catastrophic. Finally, they settled on one surname and that stuck.

And that was no "Small" or "Little" thing, going on with Darwin's list.

It was, in fact, "Good, Noble and Wright."

And it made sense out of all the "Blacks, Whites, Browns, and Greens." Or it did, "Moore or Lessers."

It became "Clear" not "Rainey." "Close" not "Farr." And a whole lot more of "McIntoshs and Cores,
"Bonds and Whipps,
"Norths and Wests,
"Hills, Peaks and Dells,
"Horns and Noyes,
"Ruddys, Riles and Claypools,
"Tarters, Perkins and Watkins,
"Hawkins, Hendrys, Blanks and Mace,
"Asps and Leaches,
"Finks and Foes,
"Jacksons, Jeffersons, Kennedys and Johnsons,
"Frenchs and Scotts,
"Porters and Shepards,
"Armstrongs and Powers,
"Fosters and Parents,
"Lewis and Clark,
"Raths and Storeim,
"Houses and Wards,
"Castros, Cortezs and Coronados,
"Beavers, Herrens, Swans and Cranes,
"Wades, Pools, Moss and Reeds,
"Kings, Harts, Royals and Bishops,
"And last but not least, the Amends."

August 28, 1990

YESTERDAY Joe Scharen stopped me at the post office to tell me that he was glad Darwin Yates and I were "Scharen" those names with everyone last week.

September 18, 1990

A MITSUBISHI executive says one of the reasons for his Japanese company's success is that "we can speak better English than we did 20 years ago and we are more confident." That's the way it goes in America, the Japanese learn better English and our kids' reading scores decline.

So how do you put a trade embargo on the English language?

It is foolish to suggest that if we learn better English in America we can keep the Japanese out. Rather it shows what is important to the Japanese modern culture is not so important to us. We do not believe it is necessary to learn to write well or speak well in order for us or for our children to succeed. That language is the very basis of education and thus the very soul of a democracy has been ignored. And now America finds itself with all kinds of problems we cannot solve, lack of family life, decaying cities, drugs, increasing crime, illiteracy, violence, lack of respect, racism, stupid bureaucracy, a general decline in our basic freedoms. It is a long and disheartening list.

We let the standards slip. We did not pass down one generation's strength in what was right and wrong. This is what education gives a country, an inner core of beliefs and values to cherish and follow.

The immigrant family who came to America in these past 100 years knew the answer to this. Unable to speak English themselves, they struggled to learn it and to be a part of America, and, most of all, to make sure their children "got an education." Their passion for America has been one of this country's most marvelous assets.

We need to rekindle that fire.

October 2, 1990

IT TOOK AWHILE for the guy I heard about at the airport to find the rattle in his new Cadillac. It seemed to be in the door. It just rattled and rattled. It went on for months and they couldn't find out what was wrong. Finally, the dealer tore the door apart. Inside they discovered an empty beer can and a message that read: "You finally found it, you rich SOB."

October 9, 1990

POLICE in the Flathead Valley were alerted by concerned citizens that a man was chasing his wife with a bow and arrow. Officers apprehended the man who turned out to be chasing a bear instead. Oh, well, the old gal doesn't always look so good in the morning.

WAYNE RANDOLPH peeked in my office and started laughing. "This place looks as bad as my shop!"

A FISHERMAN walking along the Wind River canyon highway had a good-sized fish in one hand. I honked a couple of times as I went by and he raised the fish way up for me to see. Fishermen are just crazy about showing you what they caught. I don't blame them.

Our son took the train back to a friend's wedding once and as Amtrak rattled through the Midwest, it passed a small creek. A fisherman was standing alongside the track and as the train went by, in a memorable moment, he held up his catch for the passengers to see.

October 16, 1990

THE HUNTERS the other morning made a long string of red taillights past our lane, heading for the hills where all the deer were. The early morning traffic is always like this on these first days of the season, a rush "for the good seats" somewhere up there in the dark. We watched them go by, the seven of us, me by the kitchen window and the six deer eating in the marigold patch. All summer long I've chased them out of the flowers, hollering and cussing at them, waving my arms and making a big fuss. But they must know I'm all bluster and show. Two days into hunting season and they're hiding among the marigolds.

I keep remembering an old movie with a little Fido terrier type dog in it and somehow the scene was on a shooting range and the kid in it started firing wildly in all directions. Everyone was ducking and running for cover and the little dog trotted up and sat in front of the target. He knew where safe was!

The deer in our part of the world head for the marigold patch. It's the same principle.

WHEN I WAS on the road to Cody last week, I knew I was near a momentous time because the speedometer was about to hit 88888. Somewhere on the streets of Cody, it would be turning over and I immediately knew exactly what I would do. I'd look up J.T. Malmberg at the Cody Enterprise, who also appreciated numbers coming up on speedometers, and together we would watch it go to all eights.

Sure enough, I had ten miles to spare. So I ran some errands and drove out on the Powell highway to use up the numbers. But when I turned around, I knew I had gone too far. By the time I would reach the Enterprise office, it would have turned over too many miles. I came on into town, hoping I'd misfigured, but by the Y-Tex building, I knew I was in trouble. I would be two or three-tenths of a mile over. I'd miss the all-eight rendezvous with J.T.

I did the only thing I could do. I took a side street, turned around and slowly backed my way to the Enterprise back door. It still read 88887. As someone said, these things are important!

When I triumphantly went in to find J.T., he was gone! All that anguish for naught. He was out on a call. And I had to go on down the road, forward this time, and all the 88888's came up as I headed for home.

October 30, 1990

WE'VE REACHED that delicate balance of fall when more leaves are on the ground than on the trees. And that means what's left of our golden fall will go by very fast indeed. Late turning trees never last as long as the early ones. As my neighbor says, some are "still firing" but most of them are gone.

This year is our one in ten that our lombardy poplars will turn gold instead of some icky brown color. I've never figured out what makes a lombardy one of the worst fall trees there is. Boy, they're finicky. They want a fall that's just perfect before they will perform. As always, though, it's worth the wait. When they do turn right, that big splash of yellow and gold makes up for all the other dull years.

I never walk through leaves without thinking of very long ago days. That's a very little boy feeling, walking along in a layer of noisy leaves, kicking them up ahead of you. I try not to do it now when anyone is looking.

YOU HAVE TO wonder what the Wyoming Centennial Tree in Albany county looked like this fall. Being the biggest in Wyoming should have made it the biggest show. If you didn't see the measurements, it was 31 feet around, 64 feet high and a crown spread averaging over 100 feet. That beat anything I measured around Greybull this year by several feet. That was a good centennial gimmick. The Wyoming foresters deserve a hand. Someone should make a postcard of it.

November 27, 1990
THAT OLD SUN sure wants to quit sooner than I do these November days.

WE PUT a plastic wood type of filler in all the flicker holes in the house siding this summer. And I think the flickers really like it. They managed to peck it all out in no time at all.

LEFTOVER TURKEY remains one of the great by-products of American Life.

December 4, 1990
YOU KNOW I am hopelessly old-fashioned when I tell you how awful I feel reading about mothers going off to Desert Shield and leaving three-month-old babies at home.

The Montana National Guard unit from the Flathead Valley left for the Mideast last week and among all the pictures taken was one of a young mother saying goodbye to her very tiny, three-month-old baby.

For me, it was a dreadful sight. I have a difficult time understanding the logic of this. I don't think it has anything to do with women's rights or equality. It has to do with motherhood and caring for a baby. All of life tries to protect its young and care for its mothers. Society, courts, the workplace all recognize the importance of a mother and her baby. My gosh, even our pets and the stock we raise are afforded the special status of motherhood. But not in the U.S. Army.

It is ironic that men could be exempt easier in the Vietnam War or the Korean War or even World War II than new mothers can now in these "modern" times.

Women should be allowed to do whatever they want to do without any "male" restrictions. I fervently believe this. But I'm having a terrible, old-fashioned time watching a very young mother in battle fatigues kiss her baby goodbye and march off down the street.

December 11, 1990

I HAVE discovered something from the old days that is far superior to anything we have like it today. In the summer of 1916 a young man named Bobby Farrington of Norfolk, Va. wandered into Greybull. He was looking for a wrestling match and after some talk around town, Red Wiley of Greybull said he would be glad to oblige. So they set up a "catch-as-catch-can" match, the paper described it, with the best of two falls. The match was set for a week away and each man spent the time training. A ring was set up in the Bijou theatre and at the weigh in, Wiley hit 135 pounds and Farrington, 145. Not big guys, you're saying, but look how long they went at it!

The first fall came after 38 minutes and 35 seconds without a stop until Wiley put both of Farrington's shoulders on the mat. They rested for 15 minutes and went at it again for another 14 minutes before Wiley once more got the pin. Thirty-eight minutes in one stretch and 14 in another. Take that, Hulk Hogan, you wimp!

December 18, 1990

It's time to say Merry Christmas . . . that time of year when you send your special hellos and thank yous to all those who have been part of your year and part of your life since the last Merry Christmas.

So it's Merry Christmas to all those who fill up our iced tea glasses . . . and carry the mail . . . and put up the flags . . . and decorate the town . . . and plow streets in snowy weather. And to all those who wave hello as the pickup goes by . . . and ask about the kids . . . and laugh at old stories . . . and remember words written.

And a very special Merry Christmas to those great people who brought the west end of Main Street alive in flowers and lights this year. That "Lasting Legacy" made a lasting impression on all of us. A splendid idea by Randy Waddell and to all those other Centennial Committee members who made 3,000 flowers and 5,000 lights brighten our town: Ron and Patricia Wright, Linda Meyer, Nan Probst, Annette Dillon, Axel Stockhouse, Andy and Kathy Smith and Vera Hesco, thank you and Merry Christmas from all of us.

Holiday greetings to Bob Carothers for helping us remember a story of old Greybull and for the very fine visit this year to "talk it over" . . . and to Kathy Evans for trading some iris with us . . . and to Willie Stout who keeps you either locked in or not locked out . . . I don't know what we'd do without you, Willie . . . to Del Snyder who once again answered my call for help and headed me in the right direction . . . and to Earl Reilly who straightened me out on several old roads coming into Greybull as well as those rascals "back east!"

And more Yuletide Wishes to Art Brown of Basin, wagon train photographer extraordinaire, who takes flattering pictures of part-time cowboys. And to Russell Horton, Dick Gormley, Jonathan Davis and many others along the trail who waved and said hello.

Merry Christmas to Doc Rogers who is our conscience on our hospital and who always seems to be there when we need him just like he always was for so many years as a doctor in this community.

Merry Christmas to Darwin Yates for his Hunt both North and West, Farr and Close, through Hills and Peaks and Dells, to find names that would go together like Black and White. And as Joe pointed out, thanks for Scharen that with us, Darwin.

And Holiday Cheers to Mayor Mike Mayville for putting a STOP to the Stops on that intersection out this way. And to Gale Larchick, too, for his help. The ride to town isn't five seconds faster but it's a whole lot smoother.

Merry Christmas to old friends Reynolds and Thelma Kost of Basin who have moved on Shell Creek . . . to John Koller, new president of the First Interstate Bank and Welcome to Greybull, John . . . to Emerson Scott at the "new" Antelope Butte for adding the extra runs and opening up the trails at this fine ski area. This should be the best year yet to ski Antelope Butte. No, the best year was the year Emerson took over!

A warm Merry Christmas to Frankie and Lee Good for taking over the raising of a pretty bay filly after her mother left us. She's grown into a fine young lady, thanks to you two.

Merry Christmas to all of us who remember Clarence Ortman's dog who used to sleep on main street in the oddest, rigor mortis positions; who played games when Red Deveraux refereed; who remember the Medford Jewelry store; who danced to Freddie Gould and Gene Dobbins; who went to parties at Trapper Lodge; who ate Tournament Queens; who drank coffee at the horseshoe counter of Birdie's Cafe; who watched Chuck Unterzuber run the football. If those weren't the good old days, there never were any.

And speaking of those wonderful old days, Merry Christmas to Roberta Bullinger and Charlene Collingwood and everyone who helped with the Buffalo Roundup and to everyone who came back to the old hometown this summer.

One hundred Merry Christmases to Mrs. Pauline Tatlock who is celebrating her 100th birthday this week. Happy Birthday and a very, very Merry Christmas to you, Pauline, and "happy" and "merry" are two words I always think of when I think of you.

And another Merry Christmas goes to Frank Murray and his crew at the Wagon Wheel who had to suffer through a long, torn-up road summer. In hindsight, Frank, what we should have done is let them run the cafe and you should have been building the road.

Holiday Greetings to Jack Clucas and Marvin Hankins and others who have worked so hard on the Shell Watershed project and the Lake Adelaide dam improvement. Several generations will use the water you have saved but no one will appreciate it more than those of us who will use it now.

And another Merry Christmas to Marvin Hankins for his time and knowledge on a long, interesting trip to the Northwest to find a mutual friend with a blaze face.

Merry Christmas to Slim Brewer and Clair Stearns and Jim Horn and those who pick up their mail in the mornings at the post office and always say hello. And to Helen Saban at the post office who rescues forgetful patrons who leave their key at home.

Merry Christmas to Mel Christler for his dedication and perseverance in bringing Columbine II to the blue skies over Dwight Eisenhower's hometown this fall. It is often a single thought and dream that changes things and Mel's desire to see the once proud presidential plane of Ike's back in the air was a reality in the Kansas skies in October.

Merry Christmas to Rev. and Mrs. Ralph Temme in Billings. I never go by the Emblem Lutheran church without thinking of you. And to Gene Powers who got me off the ground one summer day. And Merry Christmas to Harry Allen for a Mar. 13 afternoon in Meeteetse; to Josh Staudt for some advice this fall; and Frank Hinckley for continuing conversations; Press Stephens for the lessons on hockey; to Russell Bond for his help with a horse trailer; to Dwayne Gernant for some good talk on the "old" days of the Seventies; and to Skip Schuyler for being such a fine guy.

Merry Christmas to all those who put up Christmas lights this season – more than ever before, I'm sure – and especially to Maurice Carney way west of town that we can see so well from our side of the river.

And to all those people who live in other places and keep track of Greybull through the pages of the Greybull Standard, including Bruce Maxon of Jameston, N.D.; Jim McHugh of Manchester, N.H.; the Bill Michaelises of Fort Collins, Colo.; Tim Miller of Farmington, N.M.; Hervey Moores of Killingworth, Conn.; the Tony Nittingers of Sayre, Penn.; Jeanine Rice of Seattle; PVC Dean Stockert, APO, New York; Gerald Christ, FPO, San Francisco; Mabel Webb of Brownsburg, Ind.; Shirley Young of San Jose, Calif. and 55 other Californians who subscribe to the Standard, here's a very special Merry Christmas to you across all those miles.

And to all of you new people we'll be meeting this year, and all the little kids who grew up so much during 1990, to all those who live in this fine Wyoming community, the best of holidays and the merriest of Christmases.

1991

January 1, 1991

BITS & PIECES . . . THE INDIANS knew what they were talking about when they measured years by the winters. This past week or so proves that lasting through the winter is the trick of stringing the years together . . . I MAY HAVE seen too many Lassie movies in my youth but no dog is prettier than a collie dog running along a road.

MANY OF THE world's truest statements are embroidered on white cloth and put in little frames and hung on walls. And maybe the truest of all of them is the one that says: "When Mama ain't happy, ain't nobody happy."

January 22, 1991

JACK WILLIAMS is always toasting with the standard "Here's mud in your eye" and the other day one of his little grandkids was trying it but couldn't remember it exactly. "What is that about dirt in your face, Grandpa?"

JACK'S GRANDKIDS are just like all yours and my grandkids. Jack told them once, "If I had known grandchildren would be so much fun, I would have had them before we had kids."

And one of his grandkids said right back: "Grandpa, if we had known how much fun grandparents would be, we would have you before we had our parents."

EVERY CHRISTMAS the Lonnie Kochs in Greybull have a display of Christmas lights that spell P E A C E. It faces U.S. Highway 14 coming down in town so the road traffic can see it from the highway. Since the war in the Gulf started, they've turned it back on. It fits!

January 29, 1991

I SPENT THE WEEKEND with someone who ended many of his breathless sentences with "I will" as in "I'm going outside, I will." And it reminded me of several other people through the years who put their own twist to their talk.

A Chicago Army buddy always added "ain't it?" to everything he said. It didn't matter whether it was a nice day or whether he was going downtown, every sentence had "ain't it?" at the end. It was weird conversation. When someone says to you, "Let's go eat, ain't it?" what are you supposed to say? Even in south side Chicago that has to be strange.

With Ralph Senift, who has been gone for years now, he answered himself. He repeated the verb at the end of the sentence, as in, "I put this right here, I did." Or, "It is in the wrong place, it is."

When I first came to Greybull, Oscar Shoemaker told me about Cliff Lenninger, a longtime town employee, who invariably prefaced his thoughts with the same phrase. Always the same phrase. I thought Oscar was kidding me. He wasn't. Several months later Cliff was at the Council meeting. It was the first time I'd seen him. Someone asked him his opinion about the discussion. Cliff, never in a hurry, turned sideways in his chair and put an arm over the back. Oscar wouldn't look at me. Cliff said in his slow way, "Well, fellows, when you come right down to it, there's just this much about it." Just like Oscar said he would.

But in all those idiosyncrasies of those old days, you never once heard the incessant "you know" of modern times. I'm bothered by that one. I still think we should find some way to bleep "you know" out of all spoken language. Easterners have been saying this for a long time. It perfectly suited jittery, fast talk. It was verbal punctuation, a jab, a question mark in an odd place. It was brittle and impersonal. The blight spread with increased television and now it's like a nervous tic, you know?

February 28, 1991

THAT PIECE of ground we've been fighting over in the Persian Gulf, the province of Kuwait, is about 100 miles across one way and 100 miles across the other. That's no bigger than the Big Horn Basin. Or in Wyoming terms, a line from the East entrance of Yellowstone to the Big Horns and south from the Montana line to Thermopolis. Not very much real estate to bring so many armies together.

OVER CHRISTMAS when I couldn't make a toy go together or some computer thing work, I'd holler, "Jimmy, come over here and make this thing go." And my seven-year-old grandson would fix it in a jiffy or punch the right keys and we'd be off again.

How do those little buggers know so much that us old guys don't?

Back home I turned on the TV – I can do that pretty good – and some ad was showing an old geezer trying to make a VCR work. He, too, hollered, this time for a pretty little granddaughter who comes over and punches the proper buttons. I can relate to that commercial!

Funny, how life changes. We used to have commercials about old grandfathers showing youngsters how to put the worm on the hook. Now we have commercials about very young children showing old people how to work a VCR.

Youngsters are fascinated with video and computers and electronics. Because it fascinates, they want to learn it. That is the key to education, of course. If it can be fascinating and interesting, it can be teachable.

Almost everything you learn you have to teach yourself, one way or another. A good teacher makes it go much faster. But you have to listen and learn and make sense of it in your own terms, which in itself is a form of self-teaching.

I do not think I will teach myself all these new things. I will leave it to the youngsters. I'm still trying to learn the old stuff. If I get into a bind or something won't go, I can always holler: "Jimmy, I need you again!"

March 5, 1991

ON THIS TUESDAY morning, Mar. 5 the Big Horn river ice at Greybull is making its way out of the channel, a couple of days earlier than its "normal" breakup but close enough to remind us that many things don't really change. Most years it's this week when the ice will go, give a few days on either side of Mar. 10 or 12. This has always intrigued me, as you know from all the other years I've been writing about it. I like to find something solid, something very organized in an otherwise very fast-spinning world. That the river ice will wait until the first two weeks in March to leave means that there is, after all, order amidst the chaos.

Last year it was Mar. 2 when the ice went out. This year it was Mar. 5. Our warm winter threw it off by a couple of days.

This is not to say you can predict Wyoming weather. You learn not to try! But weather has a certain predictable nature. It will do certain things at certain times. One of those is this week in March when the warm days are longer than the cool nights and the ice just gives up.

YOU NEVER KNOW it at the time, but the years your kids are growing up are the best timetable you will ever use. You remember things by how old your kids were. Or what grade they were in. Or when they had the measles. Or broke their arm.

It's the way you remember everyone else's kids, too. By where they were with your kids. Which kids were in which grade at which time.

This may be another way of saying how much we cherish those years we spend with our growing children. Our lives revolve around their lives, our lives ARE their lives. They are never very far from our thoughts, long after they have left home.

FOR AS LONG as I can remember I have worn ties with stripes. Ties that don't have stripes don't seem like ties. Polka dots and small squares and little circles, they're passable. But it's the stripes I prefer.

Nowadays stripes are out. Fancy patterns are in, the swirls and paisley shapes and all that stuff. If you want to date yourself, wear a striped tie.

So I wandered over to the tie counter at a fancy men's store and had the guy drag out all the chic and smart and uptown stuff. Wasn't a stripe in the lot. I picked up one dude-looking thing and was holding it up to the light.

"How much is this one," I asked him?

"Sixty-five dollars," he said.

"You're kidding me," I said. "You're not saying $65."

He was.

I held it up again, and let it twist around so the light could catch it.

"This is a ton of hay," I said. "A whole ton of hay. 35 bales. Does this look like a ton of hay to you?"

He said it looked like a tie to him.

No, I told him, I don't see a tie. I see a ton of hay, all stacked neat and square, green on the end where you're taking off the bales and a bunch of hungry horses standing around looking at it.

"Besides," I said, "if it were a tie, it'd have stripes on it."

April 2, 1991

APRIL FIRST in our family is always a day to toast the past. It was another April 1 in 1959 – 32 years ago this year – when Betty and I bought the Greybull Standard.

I do not remember if that first day of April in 1959 was as bright and sunlit as the one a couple of days ago was. But all the years since certainly have been.

I do remember Lynn Severance was afraid we would be scooped with our own story, April 1 not being on a Thursday that year. So he drove Betty and I down to Byron McHale's house where Claudus had all the paperwork done. We signed in the McHale living room instead of the downtown lawyer's office where someone might see us. And we were able to put our own story into type before anyone else did.

In the newspaper game, you have to take whatever little victories you can!

Lynn Severance had promised us he would sell us the paper and he did, on such ridiculous terms that we couldn't possibly mess up. Then he turned around and worked for us for 12 more helpful years.

That we chose April First to become newspaper publishers was by pure chance. The books just came out that way. Though it would cause some merriment that it was also April Fool's Day, nothing could dampen our glow. Not even after 32 years.

This year April 1 came after a very fine Easter Sunday when the grandkids chased down the Easter eggs and we sat around letting the Wyoming sun bless us. We even flew a kite that we bought years before and never took out of the box. It seemed like the right time to do it. It flew, too, a big long-tailed dragon one straight from a long afternoon at Fisherman's Wharf in San Francisco where you're always a kid, thinking about the future and dreaming pleasant thoughts of the past.

It is fun to look back 32 years ago. We thought we were very adult at the time, "old enough" anyway to own a newspaper and make it go. I doubt that we looked quite old enough to the community. But do you ever?

Art Sylvester asked me one time how many words I had written. But then he answered his own question: "How many nails have I pounded?"

Nails and words. You can't keep track. You measure them by years, I guess. From one April 1 to the next.

This year our April 1 anniversary wasn't quite over when one of our favorite mares gave us a bright new sorrel colt. It wasn't due yet and the three of us stumbled around in the dark for awhile before things were settled. But it was a grand thing for her to do! She's lived too long with us in this family.

No, I promised her, I will NOT name it the Greybull Standard! But I will think of something special, something very special, for a special kind of a day.

April 9, 1991

WYOMING'S DIRT must come in 57 different varieties. The mountain soil, the good river bottom land, the gravel, the gumbo, the deep color of the meadows, the grasslands, all the miles and miles of the sagebrush country, the sandy soil of old rivers, the dry powder of the badlands, the red Chugwater, the white alkali, gray bentonite, the black coal. Take your pick. Some of it is more sacred than others! But it is all Wyoming.

MY CHOICE of Wyoming dirt to admire forever is the red Chugwater streaks like those around Shell and Tensleep and the west face of the Big Horns. A footprint in that red dirt is there forever, even if you rub it out.

April 16, 1991

IN THE ANIMAL kingdom all very young creatures are cute and cuddly and fun to watch. But nothing is as precious and heart-warming as a new colt.

The colts this year aren't any cuter than those were last year. But this is this year and last year is ancient times and all those precious little things running around last year are gangly teenagers now who go off in all directions, all legs and tails and hair flying. There is no resemblance to little brothers and sisters of this year.

One infinite wisdom of creation is that no creature should ever be like another. This is to be a world of individuals forever, in horses and people and all other things. So the colt comes and you're sure it will be like its mother. But it not only doesn't favor its mother, it doesn't its father, either. Or its brother of last year. I'm me, she says, when she looks at you with those little ears forward. And aren't we all, each one of us from a different mold and a different time and a different place.

In one of her early morning walks last summer, Brenda Walton went by three little owls sitting on the same barbed wire. What a special treat that must have been to see! I envy the moment.

I suspect three very young owls, unlike three young colts, do look very much alike. It makes you wonder if little owl molds are used over and over and not thrown away.

But if little owls are the same, all the rest of us are not. We may run in the same pastures, you and I, but we never bump into another just like us.

WYOMING has twice as many horses as Kentucky does, but don't jump to any "out West" conclusions. Iowa, Missouri and Illinois all have MORE than Wyoming.

We have 53,042 horses in our state, a total which is dwarfed by Texas' 477,028.

I see there are 123 horses in the District of Columbia. And some place there must be 123 front ends, too.

April 23, 1991

THEIR GRANDMOTHER says that the time to see grandchildren is just before they go to sleep at night and just after they wake up in the morning. That's when you will know them the best. That's when they, without realizing it, will feel closest to you. Little kids are very soft and vulnerable then. And defenseless. They are full of cuddly animals and special blankets and they look so very small in all the pillows and covers and bears.

Night brings very confidential talk. Kids can suddenly discover a brand new thought. They become conspirators. The talk just pours out. They want you to sit on the bed. Sleep seems a long ways away. Their eyes sparkle and they laugh a lot and they can be very happy. Even when it is one of those times when they are just too sleepy to talk, they still don't leave you until the very last second. They want you there when they drift away. They make you feel that you are the last thing they are thinking about before they go to sleep.

In the morning they want to sit on your lap and not talk and be held. They need someone to wake up with. They do not want to start their day without being with you first. You are something special because you slept in the same house with them. It is a bonding of sorts. The soft vulnerability lasts through the night. Ahead is the tumultuous day. For just this quiet time before it starts, the two of you share the quiet.

WHY DO WE PUT so much store in snow surveys and predictions of water supplies. When April started, all the surveys showed below normal water supplies for the summer. One week later, we had the biggest, wettest, longest spring snow storm in years. So much for a shortage of snow.

Water is timing, not depth of snow. It's when the stuff comes that makes grass grow and streams run. You can have short snowfall and a March or April storm can save you. You can have a mountain-full of snow and a hot spring will cause too quick a run off. Spring grass can start out green and lush and then never keep going if extremely dry weeks follow.

Water runs off too soon or too fast. It rains at the wrong time. It snows at the right time. Rains drag out just right one year. They happen all at once in another. But whatever happens, it is all beyond our control. Or our predictions.

What are we predicting, anyway? We take today's snow depth and predict next spring's weather. We laugh and laugh at everyone who tries to predict Wyoming weather. Yet we solemnly absorb all these predictions of future Wyoming water supplies.

Even armed with these very fallible predictions, agriculture continues to go on with usual planting and crop management. In face of even the direst reports of what the water supply will be, agriculture takes each year as it comes, trusting the weather will turn right. And if it turns wrong, that maybe it won't be as bad as it could be.

BAD WEATHER always makes me think of what Herman Mayland always said: "You don't know whether you have a sheepherder until he goes through a snowstorm."

April 30, 1991

FOR A LONG TIME I was always homesick whenever I read A.B. Guthrie, Jr.'s "The Big Sky" and "The Way West." I had certain passages picked out that I would read over and over, clinging to the thoughts of Wyoming and the West, of sagebrush and the mountains and those great expanses of land and sky and western life. I was never homesick for "home." My folks were wise enough to make me independent and self-reliant very early. Maybe it was the times, the war years and being on your own so soon. I always have thought earning so much quick money so soon in life as we kids did in those years made a great difference in our lives.

So it was not that home in Basin that kept me awake at night with lonely thoughts. It was Wyoming and that life among western people in western country. It always seemed odd to talk about it. Others made fun of me in both college and the Army over it. You don't pine for Omaha. But I did for Wyoming, with a lonely passion and a dedicated promise that I would come back to it someday.

Guthrie's words and thoughts were marvelous companions. I still cherish them. He really did know the West. That was his great success. He, too, had been homesick for the West and Montana and he spent years away from it. When he finally got back home, he never left it again.

Montana very soon became the Big Sky Country even though both that book and "The Way West" were set as much in Wyoming as Montana. The Wind Rivers, the Popo Agie, the Oregon Trail, South Pass. The sky is big enough and grand enough to cover both states. But Montana claimed it and Guthrie both.

This week Guthrie died at 90 years old. It seems unbelievable that his most famous books were written over 40 years ago. It may be time to read them again. Even if you're not homesick anymore!

When the Army finally said they didn't want me any longer, we wound up in Denver, in civilian clothes and heading home. That night we went to a movie. It was "Shane." And I was ready for the West and ready for "Shane" and it was wonderful. The Tetons on that big screen were the most magnificent sight I'd ever seen. The color, the quiet, Shane riding down the Snake river valley. It was a magnificent homecoming, a magnificent show, surely one of the five best westerns ever filmed. And at the end of the credits, "Screenplay by A.B. Guthrie, Jr." It fit. Who else? I was home.

May 7, 1991

YOU AND I and three other people have one square mile of Wyoming between us. That's what the population density surveys show. If you divided up Wyoming's population into its square miles, 4.8 people would have a square mile together. I choose that patch of timber and rock west of Jenny Lake for ours. Any objection? Now don't tell me you're holding out for the square mile lying south of Shoshoni!

May 14, 1991

THE EBB AND flow of patriotism is a fascinating American story. A year ago the nation was burning the flag. Now it flies proudly everywhere. After Vietnam, war movies were lifted off the screen, we cussed the country and the military and forgot our pride. But years passed and Ronald Reagan's patriotism was his badge and his scepter and no one was more successful or popular with it.

These thoughts came to mind when I ran across an incident in Greybull in April, 1918. It was at the height of World War I. The town was in the midst of the second Liberty Bond drive. The unions had erected a flag pole at the intersection where the town's lone stop light is now. And the flag flew there every day. People were rolling bandages and cutting gauze for the troops overseas. Cigarettes were gathered and shipped. Every week someone gave a patriotic speech. It was wartime and the town was at war.

People were serious about the Liberty Bond drive. The town, determined to make its quota again, had organized committees to cover every house in town. One of the committees working on the south end asked an American of German descent to buy a bond.

He refused.

They then asked him to sign a loyalty card as requested by the government.

He refused to do that, too, and said he would "do nothing for the government."

The committee was outraged. They went back uptown to main street. It was evening and the committees were gathered around the streets reporting in on the drive. The more they thought of the insult to America, they hotter they got. A crowd formed and went back to the southend house.

The guy was in bed. They rousted him out and made him put on his clothes. There were many loud voices but no violence. They took him outside and put him at the head of the crowd. Someone handed him an American flag on a pole and he was made to carry it, marching up the street towards town, a long string of people behind him.

When the crowd reached the flag staff at the intersection, they stopped him and gathered around. He was asked if he had any statement to make. He did. He said he apologized for his action and "claimed he did not mean anything in his remarks." He showed a little defiance when he said he did not believe the committee had any authority to question his loyalty. But he was immediately meek and subdued again. It was not a time for argument. Someone in the crowd lectured him about America and the war. He stood there, still holding on to the flag, wondering what would come next. Someone took the flag from him and several voices told him to go back home.

He walked through the crowd. A person hollered at him to remember "what we've told you." It was seven or eight blocks back to his home. It must have been a very, very long walk.

May 28, 1991

THAT THOUGHTFUL, quiet time spent at the cemetery on Memorial Day has passed by once again. You remember family and friends so many, many times during the year, but never all at once like you do on Memorial Day. To walk down those rows on a bright May morning is to walk again the streets of youth and growing up and all the years that have come between then and now. I am always humbled by seeing so many names that I remember. I can tell you stories about each one, several stories of each if you have time. It is forever astonishing that so many people I know have flowers and flags flying on these Memorial Days. It is even more astonishing to read the dates when they left and how long, long ago some of those goodbyes have been.

The cemetery this year looked beautiful. We've learned the lessons of putting down irrigating pipe and growing grass on these gravel hillsides of Wyoming. A true Wyoming cemetery still looks as Wyoming did at the turn of the century. The one at Shell is such a cemetery. There's another along the Interstate north of Sheridan, some graves and crosses up on the hillside. But our others now have watchful trees and blooming shrubs and they look very, very green on Memorial Day.

It depends on where you live in Wyoming what flowers appear on Memorial Day. This was a lilac time for our cemetery. Some Wyoming springs use up our lilacs before May 30. Not this year. It was a very purple day. And I saw some beautiful tulips – a very nice touch – near one old friend's headstone.

When you bring your flowers to the cemetery, you always leave some of yourself.

That moving letter from the Civil War officer to his "Sarah" which was one of the closing segments of the PBS Civil War series was around this Memorial Day. I would imagine it may well become a Memorial Day tradition to hear it on the air or see it in print. It is both joyous in spirit and so sad in reality. He was killed the week after he wrote his truly eloquent words.

His sons would have lived into the 20th century and their great grandsons or daughters would now be middle-aged, and they, too, may have carried flowers, maybe even lilacs, to his grave on this Monday past.

Out on lower Shell, in another cemetery a couple of Saturdays ago, we said goodbye to Vonnie Harnden. It was another bright morning, and another green cemetery and more names of people you remember from the Odessa community.

She was a grand spirit, that Vonnie. She touched many people in this community. She certainly touched Betty and me during those years we shared the workload on the Greybull Standard.

I loved her column. She wrote it every week for the Standard for a long time. People still remind us about it. She had a talent for the preposterous. She seemed to be able to make even the funny, funnier. There were many laughs in her words, many crazy situations. Things seemed to happen to Vonnie that happened to no one else. Her humor was the strength of her column, as it was of her life. It was a professional column by someone who would have hooted at being called a professional. But it was great reading.

So you say goodbye to a co-worker of long years ago, who helped you over the rough spots and made you laugh when you didn't think you could; who threw together floats for the 49er parade without you knowing it; and the day we left the Standard in 1974, wrote a column we knew nothing about and sneaked it into print. Great times, though. Great lady, that Vonnie.

June 4, 1991

WHEN THE BULL SNAKE ran across the road and headed for the culvert, Butch Denzin got out of the pickup and went over to look for it. He couldn't see it and figured it must have gone in the culvert. He took off his hat and kneeled down to look in the culvert. He was clear in the ditch and rested his head against the bank. He suddenly realized his head was resting on the snake which had stretched out along the bank. Butch went straight up in the air!

June 11, 1991

THAT WOMAN who chastised Casper columnist Paul Krza for writing "one-sided editorials" gave me the best laugh I've had in a long time. In 40 years of newspapering, I never heard that one before. If you don't write editorials that are one-sided, lady, you ought to throw them away.

IT WAS A grand touch to include the old Jaycee crew as Grand Marshals of the 49er parade.

That was a long 46 years ago and now another generation of young people has come along to make sure the old 49er celebration keeps going.

We should have insisted that all these new generation of 49er workers and chairmen be in a big wagon of their own in Saturday's parade so we could have applauded them all the way down main street.

June 18, 1991

GRACE LAKE in the Big Horns is a beautiful waypoint on the south way in and out of Lake Solitude. The trail is steep and you just sort of come on the lake when you're going up or down. It doesn't take long to go by it and then you're back into the trees again. It was also the home of one of the biggest brook trout I'll ever see. It is also the place where a black and white Daredevil lure works perfectly.

A father does not have to be a fisherman to have a fisherman for a son. The Good Lord is understanding about such things. And He blessed our Brian with all the instincts of a fisherman. I do not know what He had to do with a black and white Daredevil lure. But that, too, helped immensely.

It was such a black and white Daredevil that enticed an old granddaddy of a brook trout to leave the deep water of Grace Lake. He'd been there a long time and he'd grown very thick through the middle like old brookies do. He was quite a fish. He made us all happy, particularly the little fisherman who'd landed him.

It also made the reputation of that black and white lure. It's been a favorite for Brian ever since. Once in the Mission Mountains of Montana, he went fishing with some new friends and was the only one catching many fish. Early the next morning he woke up to see someone already fishing. The guy was using Brian's black and white Daredevil. He'd gotten up very early and stole it out of Brian's fishing bag.

Not too many years ago, Brian decided he wanted to go back to Solitude and fish again those lakes and places of younger years. Those golden trout above Solitude, the west end of the lake where the fish are so eager to see you. And especially, Grace Lake, the favorite place where the brook trout grow old.

So we went back again, just he and I, and we went to all those places and made one last stop on the way out at Grace Lake. It was early evening, enough time. An Eastern couple were camped there. They hadn't had much luck fishing yet, they said. Brian went on to fish the old place again and I messed with the horses. He came back with fish, but none to match the old boy of the 1970's. It was a special time, a special fish.

Then in a gesture that overwhelmed his old man, Brian walked over to the young people and handed them that old black and white Daredevil.

"It's worked wonderfully for me here on this lake," he told them. "I know it will work for you."

I'll tell you his dad rode tall in the saddle out of the place that day.

I like to think that those two kids tried the lure right after we left and within minutes, caught a fine brook trout – not as big as "ours", mind you – but one big enough to make an unforgettable Wyoming memory.

Life revels in repeating itself. Put the years on fast forward and now you're blessed with your own son. And he's casting a hook and worm into the Whitefish fishing derby pond along with a couple dozen others his age. There are so many little fishermen with their dads that you fish in one-hour shifts.

The pond is stocked with several thousand two-pound rainbow so you know they are in there. But no one is catching anything. And the hour is running out.

So you help the little guy put on the black and white Daredevil and, of course, you know what's going to happen. With five minutes to go, Jimmy drags in a fish and people are clapping because it is a big fish and a little boy's face is shining. And Dad's, too.

Good things just seem to happen when you put on a black and white Daredevil.

July 2, 1991

THAT MONSTROUS WIND in the Big Horns June 25 that knocked down all those trees came within a day and 32 years of the tornado which flattened a big swath down Shell canyon in 1959. Same direction of wind – the southwest – and not too many miles apart.

ANOTHER SUMMER and the Big Horn Canyon isn't going to attract any more visitors than it has all the other summers. Ironically, it is too close to Yellowstone and the Tetons and too far away from population centers. Tourists want to either get to Yellowstone Park or want to get home. And they're in a hurry both directions.

People who love the water and boating aren't going to haul a boat 2,000 miles when they can dump it in the water an hour from home. A large manmade lake in the middle of Missouri or Minnesota will attract more people in a couple of weeks than Yellowtail reservoir will all summer. It never reached any of the potential we all hoped it would, and all the federal money you want to throw at it now won't make it take off. It's beautiful and it's Wyoming and it's ours. But it's doomed to a minor role in the Wyoming tourist picture.

July 9, 1991

I WAS AMONG the tourists wandering around through the Kings Saddlery museum this week. You never saw so many saddles all in one place, but I found only one E.C. Burroughs saddle in the whole bunch. I'd be interested in knowing if anyone around the country is still using a Burroughs saddle.

He was still making saddles in Basin when I was a very little boy. The one thing I remember about that shop more than anything else was how good it smelled.

July 16, 1991

I HAVE been astonished at the number of people who still ride a Burroughs saddle. The "newest" saddle has to be at least 44-45 years old and the oldest saddle may be almost 60 years. All still in use. Are there any more out there? I'm going to need more time on this one.

July 23, 1991

ONE OF MY "life projects" as a young man in my twenties was to reconstruct and preserve old Fort Stambaugh near Atlantic City. I decided I would use my spare time from my Lander newspaper job to identify the buildings and mark out the foundations of that old fort so people could see at least what the old outlines were. I had this idea about plaques and signs and even plotted a pathway approach so a person could visualize what it had been like on that sagebrush hill.

I was fascinated that you could stumble onto a fort like that, untouched and unmolested, and be able to look at old foundations and see square nails on the ground. You could walk across the parade ground — as little as it was — or stand in front of the officers quarters or go over to the blacksmith shop. Even the old cut pieces of logs that shored up the officers porch lay in a long row, untouched for all those years. Nothing remained but the foundations but your imagination, as in most history, could supply the rest.

The National Archives sent me a map of the fort and I identified every building and structure except the flagpole hole which I never found.

I must tell you it was a wonderful time. No one else went out there except for the very casual wanderer. I worked weekends for months at that fort and no one was ever there but me. In those early 1950's, people weren't paying much attention to old forts and historic things. The average person was not into metal detectors yet or digging up historic sites which is why Fort Stambaugh, after only eight years of activity in the 1870's, could lay undisturbed and almost forgotten 80 years later.

I made a vow that I would only pick up what was on the ground. I didn't think you should be digging and poking at it. I hoped it would be there for years and years so you could walk over to it and imagine life there. It lays in the middle of a long, flat plain. The Wind Rivers are to the northwest. You look south to where the Oregon Trail goes and west to the gold mining of South Pass City and Atlantic City. It is true West and older days, Indian wars and U.S. Cavalry, high plains sagebrush and Wyoming skies. On some days it could make the heart beat faster. I wanted it to stay that way forever.

How naive the young soul burns! Newspapers called stronger than forts. Life went a different direction. You cannot take forts along when you move to a new town. Or a "life project" either. The times changed, too. In a half dozen years people would come flocking to that place and see it as a dig site. I went back a bare 10 years later and a big hole was dug near the barracks. A shovel was stuck in a big pile of dirt nearby. It was trampled and beat up. I never had the heart to go back.

A friend of mine is going to the fort this weekend. He and I share its fascination. I envy him for going back. It is a wonderful place. Once it was even more spectacular.

July 30, 1991
    HAVE NEVER known whether you saved time by going around the back of a vehicle to get to the other side or by going around the front.

    It looks like a natural shortcut to open the door and bail out around the back. When you go around the front, you have to go around the open door. That always has seemed like extra steps. So I've headed toward the back of the outfit to get to the other side. Now I've discovered I've wasted untold amounts of energy. I should have been going around the front all these years.

    It's 11 steps around to the other side when you go around the back of my pickup. It's only 10 steps – even with the pesky open door – when you go around the front. It took me several Chinese firedrills to figure this all out. The steps worked out that it's longer around the back than around the front. No wonder I'm tired all the time.

August 6, 1991
    "I SEE YOU like spaghetti squash," Lawana Rainey said when I handed her my honeydew melon to check out.

    "What do you mean spaghetti squash? This is supposed to be a honeydew melon."

    "It looks like a spaghetti squash to me," she said, still with a straight face.

    "What have I done?" I said. "This is a guy who has brought home a head of cabbage instead of a head of lettuce. Have I goofed again and picked out squash for honeydew?"

    "No, this must be a honeydew," she said, wearying of toying with such a gullible grocery shopper. "I'll go ahead and ring it up as a honeydew."

    When I got home, to my great relief, it WAS a honeydew, but I'm afraid my confidence may have been dented a little.

    I DON'T KNOW why I go down to the grocery store anyway for all the mistakes I make, except that I see so many people I know.

    I WATCHED a big Hawkins & Powers slurry plane come home yesterday. They often fly the downwind leg over our house and it's a splendid sight to watch this huge plane glide so gracefully across the sky. It's long ago been proven that huge planes can fly, but I marvel at it anyway. The bigger the plane, the more graceful it seems. I have never seen my plane flying overhead, but I know it just flies across the space. It's too little, by comparison, to be overwhelming. It cannot look so effortlessly flown which may be the pilot! But mine is a little outfit with only one engine and while it scoots along fine, by golly, it doesn't catch the breath like those big boys do.

    On the ground, looking up as the sound and sight floats over you, I've always had this urge to wave at it and the pilots who fly it. I've resisted because it's a foolish thought, a giving in to emotion of the moment and the magnificence in a Wyoming sky. Besides, who would ever see a wave from so far above, with only seconds to pass over an old guy on the ground. It's only sensible to just look and not give into that urge to lift a hand to the sky.

But it was a wonderful sight, that big plane, and I thought maybe someone was coming home for awhile and that always makes me emotional. And I said to that little dog who's always with me, "Puppy, just look at that? Isn't that something?"

And my hand went in the air and I waved to them until they cleared the other end of the field.

August 13, 1991

AMERICA'S favorite general formally retired this past week and he never dressed up for it. Gen. Norman Schwarzkopf apparently was afraid his image would be tarnished if he showed up in anything but those old Gulf War camouflage fatigues. No disrespect, sir, but frankly I thought you might have been just a little out of uniform.

It was time for spit and polish, good old Army shiny brass buttons, all that protocol the Army loves so much. Put me down for an old fogey for wanting you to show up with all the braid and gingerbread.

Clothing experts say uniforms are the best outfit a man can wear. They say that's why the tuxedo is so impressive. Everyone looks alike but everyone looks good, they claim. If a man wants to look his best, a uniform is the ticket. It may also mean we men can't dress ourselves. Left to our own choice of fabric and color, we don't look so great. Put us all in "uniform" and we shine.

It's also been said that a uniform is one way to a woman's heart although I have no supporting data whatsoever on this. But one friend of mine, with a sigh, did say she sure liked a uniform. "It's a good thing I never lived near an air base," she told me.

The services have spent thousands and thousands of dollars and man hours designing uniforms so the military looks wonderful when it dresses up. The World War I Marine "dress whites" were "magnificent." A very good authority, my mother, told me this when I was just a youngster. "Your dad looks great in his Army uniform but Frank Ramsey looks magnificent," she once told me.

By golly, John Tarter looked okay in his Army parade uniform in the Cody Stampede parade. And you couldn't miss his 30 years of yellow hash marks on his sleeve.

"You didn't hardly have enough arm left for any more," I said to him.

"That's why I retired," he said. "I ran out of arm."

John had two tours in Germany, two in Korea and two in Vietnam before retiring in 1971. Three wars are a plenty.

And J.D. Perkins was home the other day on Navy leave. He went to boot camp out of high school and now he's a commander. That's a great accomplishment. He is close to retirement with years of underwater time in submarines, a great education from the Navy and another career ahead of him. He was one of the high-ranking officers who advised and assisted with the making of "The Hunt For Red October." ("That did for the submarine service what 'Top Gun' did for the Air Force," he says.)

After once watching him grow into a football uniform, it's a little overwhelming to put him in Navy white. Our town's kids grow up and go away, become adults and live their lives, but we always remember them in those years when they were kids.

AROUND GREYBULL . . . YOU'RE AN oldtimer if you remember when Post Creek had a pipe in it and you stopped there for a drink or water for the radiator or both.

August 21, 1991

I DIDN'T KNOW you'd spend so much of your life thinking about youngsters. But you do. It doesn't matter what age you are, a youngster is somewhere in your thoughts. Your own kids, the neighbor's kids, the young person you're trying to help, the kid on the field or on the court, the ones who work for you, the ones who wait on you or who make friends with you. And of course, your incomparable grandkids.

We're really softies for what young people do. This is not to say they always do or act as we'd like them to act. Or that we'd want to spend all of our lives raising kids again. But don't they make the old world a different place?

September 3, 1991

I WAS PLODDING along the field with my head down and my thoughts on the office and the day ahead and I almost stepped on the Monarch butterfly struggling on the ground. It was late and I was pushed and I was three steps past it before I stopped. Surely, I thought, nothing is so pressing that the office clock can't be held up a few minutes while I see what's wrong with that butterfly.

So I turned back and found the spot of orange again. The butterfly was caught in a weed with some spider web in it. It's fluttering wings weren't strong enough to break loose. I reached down underneath it and brought it up in my hands, pulling away all the weed and web and opening my hands so it could fly. And fly it did, making wonderfully happy zigs and zags, up and up until it was gone.

It's not every day you can set a butterfly free to dance off in the sky.

September 10, 1991

PEOPLE HAVE been giving me a bad time about being "Post Creek old timers." Apparently, I should not have mentioned old timers and the old Post Creek pipe in the same breath. Terry Overgaag Busch said it for many when she wrote: "I sure didn't expect to be called an old timer at age 45! But we always stopped at the pipe at Post Creek going up and down the mountain when we were little." To make sure I got her point, she wrote this on the back of a postcard with a picture of the old switchbacks on the front!

IN THE 1920'S, Earl Reilly was to play for the big dance the John Linns were having on their lower Shell ranch. But no one could get across the flooding Shell creek. In those days, you never cancelled a dance. They hooked up a hay wagon, loaded it with rocks and drove it into the high water. They put a plank from one side to the wagon and another plank from the other side of the wagon. Earl says you walked up one plank, across the hayrack, down the other plank and danced the night away.

September 24, 1991

I HAVE A single Sen. Dirksen marigold on my desk to remind me how all marigolds should look. It's the last one of the season — the rest of the few "Dirksens" have been put away to try to save the seeds. Anymore, if you want to grow this "best of all" marigolds, you have to struggle from your own seed. It's hybrid and it's facing extinction at our house.

I don't know why they do that to us. Ten years ago you could buy Sen. Dirksen marigolds from the seed catalogs. It's a multi-petaled flower that's a perfect color of yellow. But they don't sell it anymore. It's like many other things these days, if it's a good thing, they stop making it.

I have a passion for yellow flowers. I enjoy the reds and the blues and the purples. But it's the yellow that makes me weak. I have often wished that the Organizer of the Big Scheme of Things hadn't been so generous with yellow flowers because I think He gave away too much yellow to the weeds of the world. Gumweed and dandelions and sunflowers, even greasewood put yellow out into the air. I try to ignore this digression and concentrate on endangered marigolds like the Dirksen.

October 1, 1991

THE FLY BUZZED around our outdoor lunch and landed smack on top of my lemon meringue pie.

"There's a fly on your pie," my lunch companion said.

And that, we both laughed, sounds exactly like something Dr. Seuss would say.

A fly on your pie.

The cat in the hat.

Sneetches from the beeches.

Fax from Prax

Green eggs and ham.

It was a wonderful crazy world he created. Six of the ten best-selling children's books are his, the paper said in his obituary last week. Those other four must have really been something. I don't know how you compete with a cat in the hat and a Grinch who stole Christmas.

Dr. Seuss, knowing the child's love of fantasy and absurd, or rhyme and rhythm, turned nonsense into fun. He could enter the child's world easily and comfortably, treating them as equals and companions. He had an edge on all us parents, of course. There is a difference in "entertaining" kids and "raising" them. Little kids don't read books when they're misbehaving and coughing in the night or being horrid. Reading a book is a fun time, a soothing time and a quiet time to be together.

But you're not a parent for very long before you know Dr. Seuss' value to little kids who like to hear stories read aloud.

We are in our second batch of kids now with our Dr. Seuss reading. I often wonder what these grandchildren's parents think when they read aloud again about Green Eggs and Ham. One thing I do know: When you turn Seuss loose on your kids, only good things happen.

OLD in the COLD . . . Twenty million of us — including Jay Leno — had the same thought when the paper came out last week: If you find a 4,000-year-old mummy in the Alps, clad in leather and wearing tattoos, did you find the Harley, too?

SCARS from CARS . . . One of these days we are going to look around at the scars on our hillsides and wonder why we never stopped the cars and cycles and four-wheel outfits from driving up them. What a legacy to leave the future generations. And believe me, those trails will still show for years and years to come.

A KNOCK on the ROCKS . . . I feel the same way about graffiti on our rocks and roadside cliffs. The last time I drove through Wind River canyon I was shocked at how much the graffiti had grown from just a few words sprayed on. Several of us pleaded and pleaded with the Highway Department to keep the first ones off so others would not be encouraged to add to it. And that's exactly what happened. No money, the highway department said. I think we should have found it someplace. That canyon had gone for years and years without defacing. Wyoming has miles and miles of rock cliffs. I worry that spraying names on rocks, a contagious disease, will spread.

HOLLER if you're a CALLER . . . The receptionist was filling out the entrance form and we said, yes, we were from Wyoming. The town was Greybull and she stumbled a bit over this one, so we spelled it out and then she asked:

"Do you have a telephone?" in the same kind of voice that would say, "Do you have indoor plumbing?"

Yes, we said, and gave her the number.

"Actually, this is the neighbor's number," I said. "When we get a call, they ride over to get us."

That seemed to be okay with her. You know how these Wyoming people are.

October 8, 1991

SOMETHING that tasted good to the pack rats up on Beaver creek were the dinosaur bones of "Big Al." One of the Montana State paleontologists told me they woke up one morning to find the bones had been chewed on overnight. The excavation crew had left the bones exposed so the 2,500 school kids could see them. The pack rats spotted them first. The crew painted some bad tasting stuff on them – shellac, I think she said – and the midnight dinosaur snacks stopped.

AMAZING bit of news, that big dinosaur. What seems to be more amazing is why someone waited nearly 60 years to dig again in that rich area of the old Barker Howe homestead.

In the 1930's, Dr. Barnum Brown's exciting find of dozens of dinosaurs made headlines everywhere. Complete dinosaurs were stacked one on top of another and many eventually made their way back East. That old find isn't 300 yards away from this new discovery of the allosaurus. With all the stir now, it is puzzling why someone hasn't deeply searched in that same hillside many times.

"We intend to do more digging," the University of Wyoming person in charge at the dig told a group of us. I would think so. I hope it doesn't take another 60 years.

THE FIRST TIME I saw the headline "Big Al", I thought they were talking about Wyoming's other Al who makes his own headlines. Wyoming has to be the only state in the union who had two "Big Al's" in it at the same time.

IT MAY be sinful how much I love October.

October 15, 1991

A COTTONWOOD is a tough old tree, perfect for Wyoming, strong enough to fight back at the wind and poor moisture and cold Januaries. Most aren't all that pretty. Most seem out of proportion. Limbs grow on their own, one way and another. The crowns can be haphazard and unkempt. No one tree looks like another. It puts its energy into surviving not into being tall and stately and symmetrical and pleasing to the eye. It grows leaves and gives shade and is hell for stout, as the saying goes.

But they have one glorious moment in the October sun. Nothing is as golden against a blue sky as a Wyoming cottonwood when the leaves turn. I've been driving around looking at some handsome specimens, marveling that such a nondescript tree in green leaves can turn into such a Cinderella in the fall. Some have absolutely every leaf the same color. They've all turned together so this one, bright perfectly gold tree is all one magnificent color.

Wyoming is blessed by its cottonwoods. They grew when no other tree would. They are being pushed out of the riverbeds now by the pesky Russian

Olive and we are planting more sophisticated and prettier trees around our homes. But isn't the old cottonwood a sight in the fall!

SOMEDAY I hope to write a story about memorable times a rope was thrown and when I do, I have to include the time George Warfel and three of his buddies rode into Deer Lodge. That was a long time ago and George was 17 and working on a ranch over there. The boys hit town and discovered a big revival tent up and the sinners and saints inside were in full voice. One of the boys took his rope out and threw it over the main tent pole, dallied up and rode off. They caught the four boys, threw them in jail, fined them $15 bucks apiece and banished them from town for 30 days!

THAT MAGICAL MOMENT when you hold a new life in your arms has graced our house again. Seven pounds and ten ounces seem so fragile when someone hands it to you, but all life starts preciously small like this. I tried to look down and see whether this new Kevin looked like Jeanna or Bob, certainly not me with all that hair. But the longer I studied, the more I could see he would always look like Kevin! That is the beauty of birth. We are all originals. There may be a dash of you and a pinch of me but there's a whole lot of just good old Kevin.

I remember being a very proud father. There isn't a greater thrill. But I am happily a grandfather. This is progeny you are holding, after all, another generation to carry on for other generations you've been a part of. It has always been this way and always will be, but each time it happens it is just as great.

So welcome, Kevin, this very newest of the next generation. I've had some experience now and I can't tell you how much fun it's going to be watching you growing up.

October 22, 1991

IF YOU LIVE along a dusty road, you will appreciate what Montana Columnist Larry Wilson wrote when he said: "A long Indian summer does have a few drawbacks – the road is still so dusty that folks who live within a couple of hundred yards of the main road tend to have gray complexions, live in a gray house with gray yards and have a gray dog."

October 30, 1991

IF IT IS TRUE that the brain only remembers the pleasant good things of the past, how come I can remember what a lousy hunter I used to be?

Why is it such a vivid memory of being cold or wet or both? Of tents that caved in with snow, of horses running off in the night, of being too far away, or too close. Or it was too light or too dark, too wet or dry. Of driving and driving or walking and walking or riding and riding.

How come I can remember so clearly running up a steep hill in heavy snow with pacs and coveralls and a big coat and not lasting 40 steps before my glasses fogged over and I had to carry them the rest of the way, out of breath and blind as a bat?

How come every dark early morning for years reminded me of hunting?

Memories of dragging and carrying, harder work to get it out of there than to get there in the first place.

And what keeps the mental picture so sharp of the boys' faces, coming down off the mountain in an empty pickup and meeting someone in another pickup with nothing but horns and legs sticking out of the back end?

Days long gone now. It's just as well. The elk were never in any danger. I was on their side most of the time.

November 12, 1991

JUDY GARLAND and Gene Kelly were crooning in each other's ear in "For Me and My Gal" the other night when I was flipping dials. The old late, late movie from those good old days. They were barnstorming the country on the train when I broke in on them and the rails were clacking and the towns were flitting by. In those days to show time passing on a train, names of towns would flash on the screen as if you were clattering past them. Well, they did this time, too, and the town names came whizzing by: "Sauk City, Minn." and "Broken Bow, Nebr." and then "GREYBULL, WYO". Honest, Greybull, Wyo. right up there on the screen, in the movies, the big time, sharing the marquee with Broken Bow, Nebr. I tell you, those were heady times!

SOMEONE ELSE who remembers other days in Greybull is Diana Schutte Dowling of Helena who also likes chocolate sundaes. She wrote she "has never found any sundae anywhere to beat the hot fudge sundaes I used to make at the Big Horn Drug in the '50's. I still dream about 'em. Just as Earl Madsen used to come in daily for his chocolate malt with a raw egg in it (I couldn't believe it – but I saw it before ROCKY) I used to rush to work after school to have some of that hot fudge and real vanilla ice cream. 37 years later my derriere still is proof of this."

HELEN REYNOLDS died this month. She was a former co-publisher of the Green River Star with her husband, Adrian. The wire service story on her death said she had "published the Green River Star for several years."

"Several years" indeed. Adrian and Helen published the Green River Star for over 20 years, from 1955 until 1975. Twenty years is a long time. "Several years" was just last week. You just can't capsule two decades into "several years." Twenty years of paying bills and meeting payrolls, of collating job work and taking ads. Helen did the bookwork and kept track of the jobs and kept the business end going. Adrian was absorbed with the news with a reporter's love for the story, the story, the story. Helen made sure the place was running. For over 20 years.

But how is The Present to know all of this? Life is today, not last year, not

40 years ago. Today is full of people doing their thing, working their job, raising their family. Yesterday someone did this, someone else met the payroll and took the ads and made the books balance. We lose track, while living in the present, of what our neighbors and our old friends did in their lives. I was saddened in my dad's later life to see him wish people would remember what he had done, the projects he had completed. It was inevitable that at least one generation would grow up in that town in Basin and never know him except as an old man. It happens to everyone, the same way. That, too, is inevitable. Hundreds of people that you and I know have done grand things, made great impressions on others, helped build their town and their business, put marks on the wall that won't ever be erased, for decade after decade.

The Present condenses all of this into The Past. Into "several years" if you will. Today is what The Present sees most clearly. Someone else makes a mark on the wall. Someone else starts a run of 20 years. Someone else comes along. The circle never stops.

November 26, 1991

NATURE isn't supposed to like straight lines. It's how you tell whether man has been messing around outdoors with his squares and plumb lines. The straight line bit isn't always true. Rock strata and dirt formations laid one on top of another can be very even and true. Some look like they had been drawn with a straight edge. There are very tall, straight pine trees and graceful upright grass stems. But basically the outdoors is filled with bumps and curves, uneven patches, and lines that make no sense.

I would have done a terrible job with such designing. It would have been all straight lines and correct angles if I had been given a free hand. I like fences that march in order, one post after another, in solemn file and straight as far as the eye can see. I like irrigation pipe stacked up neat, ends lined up. And hay stacks that are square. And long rows of corn, all the same height and color. I like to drive by crops just rowed out, long and straight rows, walking by the window, line by line. I like grass to end sharply before the concrete begins, the even edge of redwood between flowers and walk.

Oh, I am smitten with curves and bends and all of nature's marvelous uneven creations. But I have a weakness for seeing things in order, row by row, straight and true. They would have kicked me out of the forest long ago.

A LETTER WRITER to the Missoula daily newspaper has the perfect answer for all of us who keep writing about limiting Congressional terms. Her solution: Limit all column writers to 12 years!

December 10, 1991

THE MORE WINTERS I spend the more I like the south side of the house. I'm getting like our old dogs used to be. Every old dog we ever had would follow the sun around the house on these Wyoming winter days. That warm spot where the sun poured in would soon be covered with some old dog, sleeping the day away. When the sun moved, so did the dog. No sunny spot was ever lonely for long. It always had a dog on it.

Our present little dog is too young to feel the pull of the winter sun. She still thinks keeping company is fun. One of these days when the bones creak and ache and the chill sets in, she'll undoubtedly seek the sun and those warm spots on that south side. She may have to fight me for them.

OTHER WARS . . . As I watched the aging veterans of Dec. 7, 1941 sit in those stands at Pearl Harbor – and I say "aging" kindly because they are not much older than I – I could not help but think how many veterans of wars I have seen in these years.

The "oldest" people I ever saw were the Civil War veterans around Basin when I was a kid. Bearded and bent, slow of step and speech, they were ancient indeed in a young boy's eyes.

Once I heard Indians at a Big Horn/Custer battlefield podium speak of their part in that one-sided battle. I've known Spanish-American War veterans, those of World War I, Pearl Harbor, World War II, the Korean War, the Vietnam War. It makes you wonder if we have ever been at peace.

IN 1951 I was in basic training with a German Jewish young man who was in the Army to obtain his U.S. citizenship. He spoke with an accent but then he never talked much to any of us. He spent a lot of time by himself. One day, trying to make conversation, I asked him "where he was 10 years ago?" He looked at me for a moment and said, "Buchenwald." I thought he was joking. He wasn't. Another war, of the worst kind.

December 17, 1991

IT WAS IN December of 1956 that I started writing this column in the Greybull Standard. It was our first Christmas here, the second tree for a little 18-month-old son who was delighted to help "throw" tinsel on the tree. I never knew until then whether tinsel looked better hung carefully on the tree or just thrown helter-skelter. Frankly, I couldn't tell the difference between his wild throw and my careful hang. And he had a heckuva lot more fun at it.

I wrote about that tinsel throwing in one of those first columns way back then. I just looked it up. And I am a little dismayed that I wrote it so poorly. But then I am looking at it from 35 years away and though I thought I knew it all then, obviously, I didn't.

Thirty-five years is a long time, I guess, to put out a weekly column, not every week, of course, for all those years, but enough of the 52 chances to be creditable. Several of us in Wyoming journalism wrote columns in those years. This one is the only one still going.

I thought of these 35 years a couple of weeks ago when that Missoula person thought we column writers should be held to 12 years of column writing.

That was to be our punishment for editorializing about limiting congressional terms. If we wanted those old pols to be turned out after a couple of terms, then we black ink people should cover up the old typewriter ourselves.

But that wouldn't have been any fun for me. That would have meant quitting 24 years ago and I was just getting a head of steam up.

It has been a bunch of black ink. Some of it's been okay, a few met some self standards, quite a lot is parochial and timely and doesn't mean much read today. That is one thing about columns and black ink. They're all in the files. You can say you worked a good day or raised good beans or rode a fine horse and I'll take your word for it. If you want to see my mistakes and mediocrity, it's still in black type in a newspaper file someplace.

So it's an anniversary of sorts, this month. I kid people who ask and I tell them I am going to write a Wyoming newspaper column for 50 consecutive years. That's only 15 more years, I say. I'm already two-thirds of the way. They always laugh and go along.

But I'm only half joking. I really do intend to!

December 23, 1991

IT'S TIME TO say Merry Christmas . . . that time of year when you send your special hellos and thank yous to all those who have been part of your year and part of your life since the last Merry Christmas.

So it's Merry Christmas to all those who bring pitchers of iced tea . . . who fly flags . . . and clean the sidewalks . . . and check out our groceries . . . and make the coffee . . . who fix things you break . . . and find things you lost . . . and make sure your morning paper is there every day. And to those in snowplows and delivery trucks and street sweepers and county graders for making life easier. And to all those who recognize the pickup and wave or honk as you go by . . . and laugh at old stories . . . and ask about the kids . . . and mention words you write.

And a special Merry Christmas to Earl Reilly for letting me travel back in Greybull time one Wednesday afternoon, over those old roads to Shell 70 years ago and all the memories that went with them. And once again, Happy 90th, Earl, and for all the years you gave to this community.

Holiday Greetings to That Main Street Crew for another bright year of lights and flags and growing colors on the west end. What a great idea that was . . . And Merry Christmas to the town crew for the work on the rest area east of the bridge and especially the trees planted on the hill. We'll look up one of these Christmases not so far away and they'll be grown up and tall and very impressive indeed.

Merry Christmas to the boys downtown who admitted a newcomer to the gatherings in the morning where old stories are told and the world's ills expounded and strong opinions given and all done in such hushed tones.

A special greeting to Harry Kimbell who moved to Billings this year and yes, Harry, we DO miss you! . . . and to Jerry Porter for a fun night . . . and to

Pat Harrison and Thad Harper for assistance this summer . . . to Ben Menzel who raced the snow and won! . . . to Jerry Storeim for all those laughs and a promise in this aging '91 for that special sign of ours to be done in '92 . . . and Merry Christmas to Cora Grant for a special call one Thursday morning . . . To Terry and Amy and Frank for pleasant times alongside a running creek . . . for "neighbors" Dave and Brenda Walton for help, past and present . . . to Paul and Norman Collingwood for good advice to an initiate . . . to Linda Noyes for taking care of my "bookwork" and especially for the good laugh one day last summer . . . and to Dr. Benjamin Mills for staying with us.

Merry Christmas to all the people who walk or run out our way and especially Debbie Urbach who stopped by our house on the way to her Montana reunion.

A Happy Holiday to Dolan Scharen for seeing that the water made the long trip from Adelaide to our place this summer, a wonderful sight at this far end of the ditch.

And a special Holiday wish to Dave Van Gelder for adding Greybull's biggest mural to Greybull's tallest building. And the lights are great, Dave.

And Happy Holidays and Thanks To All Those who are giving us this balmy December weather. It looks like the Big Horn may not be frozen over on Christmas Day and you won't see that very often.

And MERRY CHRISTMAS to Betty Stoffer and her MESSAGES on the Shortstop SIGN. If I don't wreck first trying to read both sides, I remain a faithful reader.

Merry Christmas to those who remember Harley's Grocery; when Don Bailey took care of the high school; when the southend viaduct went down the hill to the east by U-Smile; the old Beale & Carey auto dealership; the booth in back of Carroll Durkee's Big Horn Drug; when Josie ran that little all-night cafe; to those who played football on a gravel field; who danced on Saturday nights in the Community hall . . . who remember when the junior high teams were the "Dinosaurs"; who heard summer band music in the old bandshell in the park. If those weren't the good old days, there never were any.

And those days not so long ago when you listened to Iver Love's stories . . . heard Charlie Rutherford's GHS band . . . laughed at Doc Chambers' antics at the Norris Hotel . . . cheered for John Kosich's teams . . . made way for Slim Brewer's old Army truck with the big shaggy dog in the back . . . Those were good times.

And Holiday Greetings to Elaine Sellars who shares that Apr. 1 opening business date with us . . . and to other new arrivals on main street, Brad Wright at the Smokehouse, Ron Wendling at Big Horn Drug, Dave and Kelly Williamson at Casa Grande; Jeanne NiCastro at The Hen's Nest; Glenn Loran at Glenn's Boot Repair; and Scott Good at Big Horn Co-op's new lumber yard.

Merry Christmas to Andy Leavitt, Mid Rannells, Brenton Leavitt and all the others who still ride a Burroughs saddle. Old E.C. made them to last!

A Greybull Merry Christmas to Bud and Opal Spence in Douglas; Allie

Minnis in Colorado Springs; Tom and Del Black in Sells, Ariz.

Holiday Congratulations to Sandra Michaelis Jones who graduated from college this month and Merry Christmas from all your fans and friends.

Merry Christmas to old friends, Ellen Whipps and George Hoffman, who have answered so many courthouse questions and helped with so much information all of these years. Again in 1991 I had to call on you both for help. You have been a great service to this community in your many years in county government.

Special Holiday Cheer to all those who put up outdoor Christmas lights this year, more than ever it seems, particularly up on the Heights . . . to all those who ride old "Bob's" horses . . . who spent a summer evening watching geese land on a special pond . . . to those who drive by and stop to look at the colts in the pasture each spring . . . and all the fellow boxholders who say hello to and from our daily stop at the post office, Bill Murdoch, Christine McMillan, Wayne Randolph, Janet Stockhouse to name just a few.

And to all those people who live in other places and keep track of Greybull through the pages of the Greybull Standard, including David Kost of Casper; Jean Hiser of LaCrosse, Wisc.; PFC Jerry Hughes, FPO, San Francisco; Debbie Isbell of Key West, Fla.; Tim Miller of Farrington, Minn.; Orpha Nichols of Rich Hill, Mo.; Peg Sanders of Longmont, Colo.; Asa Stout of Tucson, Ariz.; Myrtle Prugh of Eureka, Calif. and 42 other Californians who subscribe to the Standard, here's a very special Merry Christmas to you across all these miles.

And to all of you new people we'll be meeting this year, and all the little kids who grew up so much during 1991, to all those who live in this fine Wyoming community, the best of holidays and the merriest of Christmases.

1992

January 7, 1992

THE GOVERNMENT never could count. Associated Press reported this week that "The FDA had previously estimated that 2 million women were affected (by the halt in silicone gel breast implants) based on the number of reported implants, but it halved that estimate Monday because most women receive two implants instead of one, agency spokeswoman Betsy Adams said.

THERE MAY be some mental deficiency in a pair of grandparents who would buy a five-year-old grandson a set of drums (little boy size) for Christmas (that's what he asked for!) and then have Christmas at their house!

January 21, 1992

MY PARTNER on the Antelope Butte ski area chair lift said he was from Red Lodge and he was a ski racer and he was 10 years old and he was having a lot of fun at the races the past two days.

One of those great kids you like right away. A few freckles across his nose, a good honest face and very talkative. Adults didn't bother him.

I was curious where he had stayed during this race weekend.

"We're down at the Clucas' Bed and Breakfast," he told me. "Oh, the food is so wonderful. Yesterday morning we had pancakes and eggs and this morning we had French toast and an omelet thing. It was good. Mrs. Clucas is really a good cook. We just ate and ate."

You can put a little boy up on a good ski hill, challenge him with a race course ("I think I'm in first," he'd offered), make the days bright sunny ones, fill the hill with racers and skiers and what does a little boy remember most? Mary Clucas' pancakes and French toast and that "omelet thing."

THAT LITTLE BOY'S drum set we mentioned after Christmas eventually went back in the box and was shipped to its "permanent" home in Montana. His father wrote last week:

"The drum set Santa Claus brought our five-year-old son is still in the box. Hey, I can't find my screwdriver.

What IS a screwdriver?"

CHUCK PETERSON shares the joke of the three worn-out bills waiting to be burned at the Federal Reserve. One was a $100 bill, a $20 and a $1.

"I've spent a good life," the $100 bill said, "vacation spots, fancy dinners, the works."

"For me," the $20 bill said, "it's been groceries and gas bills."
"How about you?" they asked the $1 bill.
"Oh, you know," the $1 bill said, "go to church, go to church."

January 28, 1992

ARE LITTLE KIDS with red hair ever called "Red" any more? When I was growing up, there were all sorts of "Reds" around. I spoke to a couple of them just this week. But the "Reds" you talk to these days aren't little boys anymore!

I can count eight "Reds" I've known, at least one "Sandy" (Jackson), a "Pinky" (Alexander) and a "Speck" (another Alexander) in these two towns of Basin and Greybull. But they all have had their red hair-inspired names a long, long time. (Michaelis, Leavitt, Dunn, Deveraux, Lindsey, McIntosh, O'Neill, Greene.) I know I've missed some.

Nicknames somewhere along the line must have died out. If you're short these days, you're not a "Shorty" for the rest of your life. If you're tall and lanky, you won't be a "Slim".

And if you have red hair in these times, you may be called Sean or Shane or Josh or Chris, but chances are you won't be "Red."

February 4, 1992

I MUST BE missing something but I don't recall that Japan came to the United States and started our drug problem. They didn't grow marijuana or coca plants; they didn't sell the drugs; they didn't encourage our young people to experiment; they didn't seduce our culture to allow drugs to become so much of our national disgrace.

Japan didn't come to America and become the Mafia 80 years ago in the 1920's. They didn't contribute to the growth of organized crime or its influence or its abuses in the years that followed. It did not export a philosophy of crime. There is nothing Japan ever sold or ever practiced that has any parallel to the crime in America in this last century.

It wasn't Japan who came into our school systems and changed educational standards. The Japanese did not tell American parents that school was too hard or that homework didn't matter or that sports counted more in life. It wasn't the Japanese who turned on our TV sets.

It wasn't the Japanese who started deficit spending and then kept at it and kept at it until each president who is last, spends the most, has the highest debt. Japan does not vote for our politicians, did not create pork barrel spending, or pass laws to re-elect itself. Japan did not invent graft and influence peddling and political double talk and send them to the United States. It didn't spend the Social Security Trust Fund for something else.

Japan didn't send us our health care problems. These aren't Japanese hospitals, Japanese doctors, Japanese insurance companies, Japanese lawyers.

Japan did not give us our bureaucracy at every level of government or make it keep growing and growing at a stultifying rate. It was not Japan who abused the Savings & Loan system. Milken was not from the Land of the Rising Sun.

Japan did not export racial bigotry to America. It didn't create our slums. It didn't make us more materialistic than altruistic. Japan didn't pollute the air and tear up the land and dump in the rivers.

We did all this to ourselves. This was Made in America. The Japanese didn't have anything to do with it.

February 11, 1992

SOMETIME AGO I mentioned that the old names of farms and houses and places depended on what time you lived. When you move onto a place, it does not automatically become your place. Your neighbors will know it as the immediate past owner's place, not yours. If you are Kennedy and the people who lived here before you are Harvey, it is the Harvey place for some time afterward. But where did Harvey go? They went to the Luderman place which did not become the Harvey place until the Flitners bought it.

The other day some of us were talking about Lower Shell and the Garnett place. Howard McNulty said he lived near the Garnett place when he was a little kid.

"Where was your house compared to where Butch Denzin lives?" we asked.

Howard said he didn't know that place.

"Frank Norris, Sr. owned it in the Fifties," we said.

No, didn't ring a bell.

Russell Kimbro said, "Howard, it's the old Heller place."

"Oh, of course, I know that place," Howard said.

The rest of us were just in the wrong time frame.

February 18, 1992

THE LADIES at the Cody driver's license office do not ask you to say "CHEESE" when you step in front of the camera. They tell you to say "MEETEETSE." If you can say "Meeteetse" without grinning, you deserve to have a sourpuss on your license.

THE ICE has gone out of the Big Horn river at Greybull – on Feb. 14 – nearly a month ahead of time. That's a good sign of warm winter days.

March 3, 1992

SOME PEOPLE go south for the winter. And some people stay home. Those in the south usually are warm. Those up north are usually cold. Those who come home in March from the southwest usually talk about how warm it was. People who stayed in Wyoming all winter normally never talk about the winter at all. When the folks at home greet a returning snowbird in normal years, wintertalk is brief and passed over quickly, hopefully forgotten. The snowbird likes to talk about the weather because it has been warm and sunshiny and full of snowless days where he was. The Wyoming homebird has been wet and cold and had to unthaw pipes. These are miserable thoughts.

But this winter is different. It is the Wyoming people who want to keep talking about the winter. If the snowbird hears it once, he will hear it twenty times how we "suffered" through the snowless weeks and warm days and clear skies. Twenty times someone will say to him, "This was the winter to stay home." He must weary of our bad manners. But we can't help it. We're still giddy from the heat.

March 10, 1992

I'VE SPENT a great deal of time looking at my thumb these last couple of months. That's about all you can do with a broken thumb, just look at it. It was a victim of a slipping crowbar and a solid piece of wood. That's a threesome with a loser in between.

But it got well by itself, just like everyone said it would. And though I spent hours watching, I never did discover the miracle of the human body healing itself. It is a wonderful mystery that something which can be so beat up can eventually return to almost normal and even, once again, push buttons through a buttonhole.

That old scar from my boyhood, I noticed, is still visible. I hadn't thought about it in years. Who looks at a well thumb? I would have thought in over 50 years a scar would eventually fade away with a lot of other things! But it's still there.

I can tell you the exact day that thumb wound up in the car door. Armistice Day, Nov. 11, 1938. No, I didn't remember it. I looked it up in the 1938 Greybull Standard file. That was the afternoon Basin and Greybull played football in the old block, big, vacant lot in the south end of town. It wasn't near the school. But it was big enough to hold the crowd of cars that lined all sides. The Basin-Greybull rivalry, always intense, probably more so in those years, took a city block to hold everyone.

I was one of those little kids who talked their folks into letting me and Billy Zane sit on top of the car to watch the game.

The field was just gravel. They scraped off what rocks they could. Football was played that way in those days. I often think of that. Hard ground and those old thin helmets. Old days football. The end of it really. Green grass and hard plastic helmets were just over a decade away. But no one dreamed of that in 1938.

I don't remember anything about the game except Jerry Henderson running the ball. I idolized Jerry Henderson. I loved the way he ran the ball, one of those quick, 140-pound backs which high school football is meant for. I thought he was the biggest man on the field. I saw nobody else.

The score was 38 to 0, all Basin, a lot of Jerry Henderson. Basin would go on to win the Big Horn Basin championship, for the first and only time. That, too, must be a record of some sort.

Just before the game ended, Mother opened the car door to tell us they were backing up and to hold on. Good advice, but a careless kid. The thumb and the car door. Who knows what I was thinking about? I spent a while looking at that thumb then, too. My mother must have thought, as with all boys, "Will I ever get him raised up?"

Two sore thumbs. I don't mind that they were 50 years apart.

March 24, 1992

IT IS NOT hard to recognize paradise. But the trouble with all paradise eventually, is that paradise is not home. Hawaii may be paradise, but Wyoming is home. Paradise is where you forget everything and frolic in the sun and see beautiful sights. But home is where all those things you still want to do are waiting; where the iris is coming with promises of great color; where new foals are to arrive so very soon; where all the old friends are who listen to your old stories and are comfortable with you and forgive you and laugh with you.

Home is where the kids are and their kids and all those shared joys and shared lives. And there are still miles to go in all directions.

And you think about all of this with the sand between your toes and the sun warm on your shoulders and you can't help but wonder, which one is really the paradise?

April 7, 1992

BILL MAULDIN is putting up his cartoonist pen. At 70 he says it's time to quit. It is hard to believe he must have been barely 20 years old when he created his memorable GI's, Willie and Joe in World War II. But then that was a war of young boys, as all wars are. At the time they seemed so much older.

But Mauldin was old for his years in understanding life. He could "see" life as it happened around him. He had "the eye," as the old time photographers always said, the ability to visualize the picture before it was captured on film or paper. Taking pictures or drawing cartoons has first to do with life, not the mechanics of shooting or drawing. You have to first see the humor or irony or the pathos in front of you. Then it can be put on film or paper. It is not the other way around.

Mauldin's cartoon the day after John Kennedy was shot, showing Lincoln's marble statue at the Lincoln Memorial with a single tear under one eye, was a classic.

When Mauldin retires an era ends, and it is a constant reminder that there is no such thing as status quo. Nothing ever stays the same no matter how much you will it so. Just when you are comfortable with a part of life, then life changes. The river keeps flowing past all that life on the riverbank, and try as you will, you cannot go back up stream to experience it again.

That Mauldin cartoon of the GI's liberating the French town had a very odd-looking guy sitting on top of the truck. He had a very long nose and a big Adam's apple and funny hair. He was looking at the French name on the town sign. He says to his GI companion: "I think this is the town my father liberated in the First World War." And all the people hanging out of the windows, and waving from the sidewalks, or shouting from rooftops, all of them had very long noses and big Adam's apples and funny-looking hair!

April 28, 1992

WHEN BEN JOHNSON, the great old cowboy actor, received an Oscar for Best Supporting Actor in "The Last Picture Show," he said he didn't know what he was going to say when he got up on the stage.

"I wasn't prepared and I realized I'd been standing up on the stage for a long time, so I said, 'I don't know how you will take this,' and my wife slid down in her chair because she thought I was going to say something about the hippies. But I said, 'This couldn't happen to a nicer fella.'"

I SPENT one glorious November afternoon with Garry McLean. He was a halfback, an Evanston senior then, and he had come to Greybull to play for the 1960 Class A state championship. Evanston ran out of a single wing that day, an offense that was still around sometimes, and for sure if you had a tailback like McLean. He would crank up out of the backfield and everyone knew the ball was coming around end. But those long legs with the long, long stride would take off and oh, gosh he piled up the yards.

He was a great kid to watch, even when he was about to beat you. Only a Tom Wilkinson call in the fourth down huddle, changing the coach's punt to a fake pass, broke the game for Greybull. You could outrun Tommy Wilkinson but you had to work hard to outthink him. McLean's Evanston team that day was a great team, maybe even the best on the field, and he made a sensational contribution to it.

Funny how that unseasonably bright, shirtsleeve day stays in the memory. That's a small-town trait, to remember so many kids on so many playing fields. I always thought very warm thoughts about Garry McLean. I saw him afterward, even watched him catch a Tom Wilkinson pass in a University of Wyoming win at once, an ironic, that's-Wyoming turn.

And I never saw his name again without thinking of that youngster with a very long stride dominating a football afternoon.

He was only 49 when he died last week in Rock Springs. The youngster on the field should not have to go before the old fan in the stands.

May 5, 1992

THE VERY FIRST mourning dove I ever heard was in the morning and 20 years went by before I lost a bet to someone in Lander who said it was "mourning" and not "morning." I was so positive I would have bet the farm. These past mornings when it is still cool and the day is just beginning, the doves sing back and forth to each other. It is such a pleasant, beautiful sound, so soft and gentle. It is a new day, a new morning, and it's not sad at all. But I still lose the bet.

May 12, 1992

IT'S BEEN YEARS since I ran into Ben Minter at the post office and I asked him "what was new in his neighborhood."

"Well, actually," Ben said, "there was something last night. A car wreck. Sounded like a couple of blocks away. I woke up and all you could hear was screeching metal and brakes, and I said, 'Oh, oh, there goes Bill Wilkinson's brand new steel fence.'"

It wasn't 15 minutes later I ran into Bill Wilkinson. I said, "I hear you had a car wreck down by your house."

"We did. A terrible noise. Lots of scraping metal. And I said, 'Ruby, there goes our brand new fence.'"

Actually the fence did escape. The wreck was nearby but it missed the Wilkinson front lawn. What it didn't miss is how small towns are and what it's like to know the neighborhood!

SPEAKING OF things small towns do, I notice in the files it was just 29 years ago this week that the Burlington brought back an old steam engine for a final, nostalgic run. It came down from Billings and made an excursion trip back and forth to Frannie.

Quite a crowd turned out at the depot to see it. I can remember the whistle sounded marvelous, but I'd forgotten the old steam engine had to have a pull by a diesel, a humiliation often suffered by the elderly.

I ran into Irv Wilkinson at the train. (That's more "neighborhood." He was Bill's dad.) And Irv reminded me he had come down to see this "last steam engine" because "I saw the first one that ever came to Greybull."

Irv's wife was Johnny Borner's daughter. She was just a girl when the family arrived at what was to be Greybull in a wagon from Lander. The widowed Borner and his kids were the town's first citizens. She'd never seen a train before so when the first train came into Greybull in 1907, Irv took her over on the bluff east of the river and they watched the train come in.

May 19, 1992

WE DON'T have a new bucket on our entire place. Nothing but old buckets. We've been using old buckets for so long, I can't remember when we had a new one.

These old pails had to be new once. But that was a long time ago. Old buckets, like a good old coat, just aren't thrown away. They can always hold something. One that leaks water won't leak oats. One that's bent and beat up still carries something. Even the leaking ones – if you go fast enough – can carry some water. If you bail out of the ditch, leaks won't matter so much anyway. If you load them with dirt or trash or pulled weeds, who worries about how bent or beat up they are?

The other day I looked at that old bucket in the grain bin and I couldn't remember when it was ever new. Maybe we didn't buy it. We could have inherited it. I wouldn't be surprised if that bucket is older than the place is.

But all the rest of the half dozen old buckets around here are just as ancient. If they don't have leaks and holes and been stepped on a couple of times, we don't have much use for them. We wouldn't know what to do with a new one.

IN 1963 the Big Horn County jail was leaking prisoners faster than the county could keep them in. A typical old bucket. They poured a new concrete floor and George Warfel observed at the time (all this from the old Greybull Standard files) that if they would run out the remaining prisoners and let them stand in the concrete while it hardened, "at least we'd know where they were!"

May 26, 1992

JOHNNY CARSON could have been president. Fifty-five million people stayed up to say goodbye to him the other night. You don't need the electoral college to figure out that popularity. I don't know that he would have run the country all that wonderfully, but oh, the laughs we would have had. As Perot supporters keep saying, why not Ross? Why not Johnny? What we got is working?

I SAW Johnny Carson on a Lincoln, Nebr. stage in 1949, an undergraduate, emceeing a college show. He was so far above all the rest, you should have known he was already off and running.

THE WAY I have this Man and Woman Thing of the present day figured out is that we men aren't half as good as we think we are. But then we aren't half as bad as you women think we are either.

June 3, 1992

MEL Christler of Greybull couldn't make up his mind whether to renew his medical and his pilot instructor's license or not. Then he talked to the guy who had soloed him. That guy had just renewed both. So Mel renewed. He's 75. They guy who soloed him on Mar. 2, 1937 is 85. That's many, many years of flying for those two since flying began with the Wright brothers' solo of 1903.

June 9, 1992

THAT OLD, OLD yellow rose bush is blooming now in many places. Call this the Month of the Yellow Rose in Wyoming, the time when that faithful early settler of the state is gloriously bright yellow.

I wonder if it wasn't one of Wyoming's earliest domestic flowers. Many of the old farm houses still have a bush somewhere in the yard. You can also find them on the streets just off the main street in several towns. These were the first settled parts of town and the old roses are still there. In one yard in Thermopolis' old part of town, the yellow roses have grown up along a fence.

It must be nearly 30 feet of bright, bright yellow this week. There's a magnificent bush of yellow roses on Beck Avenue in Cody. Another one is blooming just off Greybull's main street and one long forgotten one is in bloom now in back of Murdoch's Service station, a splash of yellow amid the garbage can and old tires. It was once in the backyard of the old Braden place.

The one in our backyard can't be as old as the Braden one, but Randa Harvey planted it at least 50 years ago.

Luella Clement said her family called it "the Perkins rose" but she doesn't know why.

You won't find them in the newer parts of town. Or on "modernized" farms. This old Wyoming yellow rose did not make the jump into these newer times.

In those early years of Wyoming, it seemed like a family planted a lilac, a yellow rose and two cottonwoods.

In a couple of decades people would plant more evergreens and elms, more "town trees" and things like spirea and hedges. From the Fifties through the Seventies it was Russian Olives and flowering crab trees, Lombardy poplars and fancier shrubs. In the next 20 years you grew honey locusts, gold drop shrubs and anything with a purple leaf.

And all the while that old yellow rose, where people left it alone, kept on being bright yellow during these days in May and June.

I always think of Wyoming as indestructible. I feel like it's been here forever, with not much change, not much of the outside pushing in, not even the remotest chance of one town melding into another like it is back east or out in California. I look on its old trees and flowers the same way. You have to admire the way they've hung on.

This year on Memorial Day one of the flowers on Mother's grave was an iris bloom from one of her plants she put out in the 1930's in Basin. I dug up the last of her plants and brought them over to our place years ago. One of them bloomed in time for Memorial Day and there was only one place it should have been on that day.

I don't know where Mother got those plants, probably from someone else's garden. Maybe old Fred Pauley who lived a few blocks away and who loved to grow iris. They were probably several years old when she moved them. And they moved twice since. They sure don't look like much alongside the modern iris. Neither does the old rose or the old cottonwood. But they just keep on going, bless them, same as always, same as Wyoming.

AS I FLIPPED BY the PBS station the other morning, Fred Rogers was just signing off on "Mr. Neighborhood" and he was saying, "I like you just exactly the way you are."

And that, my friends, is the key to human relations. I don't want you to be anything or anybody but you and I don't want you to think I should change. I like you "just the way you are."

Pages from an Editor's Notebook

By Bruce M. Kennedy

August 2, 1962

Most of us who came to Greybull to live, particularly those of us in this generation, drove here in a modern car or came on modern trains. And we searched for (and eventually found) up-to-date places to move our furniture and begin our work.

But men like Ira Sherard didn't. Civilization was waiting for us. Ira had to help start his own, and he did, here in Greybull back in the days before there was a town.

The CB&Q rails didn't reach to Greybull yet when Ira arrived and his home was at the Rogers ranch, those old log buildings still standing down near Magnet Cove. Up here where Greybull flourishes now, was just a sagebrush flat.

But Ira probably told you all about this, too, for he had a wealth of stories of those old days, nearly sixty years ago.

Sixty years is a pioneer's length of time in any town. You and I walk by Probst Western or remember the bank before the modern facade of brick covered up the stone work underneath and we think nothing of it. But Ira helped blast the blocks off the big sandstone bluff north of town and haul them here for those first stone buildings in town. And that's what he remembered when he walked by.

Everywhere he went there must have been memories like those. Sagebrush in the streets, the railroad coming in, houses being built. Over a half century of life and progress went by his doorstep in Greybull. And through all these years he was among the few who could look back and remember when it wasn't even here.

The world doesn't raise many pioneers. Most of us, either by choice or circumstance, take the soft life civilization offers.

But there wasn't much civilization when Ira Sherard came here those sixty years ago, and started saying hello to the rest of us who came afterward to live in this town, too.

He was a personal friend of mine and many others. And now he's gone and the rest of us are still here . . . and we'll miss him.

August 30, 1962

Sports fans never forget.

"They're just like elephants," Red Lindsey believes. Take what happened to Red at the Riverton softball tournament a couple of weeks ago as an example.

You should know first that Red's a heckler of the highest degree. If you've heard him at sports events you know what we mean. All the clever things you think of saying after you're home in bed, Red's already said out on the floor or the field or the ball diamond. His barbed comments travel further, sink in deeper, cut sharper than anyone else's. In the heckler class, he's par excellence.

Ask any of the Riverton softball fans, for instance, who took the sharp ends of some of those caustic comments when the tournament was held down there two years ago. And they're still smarting from them.

And like we said, they haven't forgotten.

So when Red sauntered out on the field to coach third base during Jim's Texaco's first game, he's recognized immediately. And all the crowd in that side of the bleachers stands up and boos and boos and boos.

The Bronx cheers fairly roll out across the field. They give it all they got and Red stands there letting his thick hide absorb it all. Then he turns around and doffs his cap to show them he appreciates their good judgment and to let them know there's no hard feelings.

After all, to an old campaigner like Red, what a gratifying welcome that was!

September 13, 1962

The Floyd Patterson-Sonny Liston heavyweight bout at our place is the running skirmish between our tail-wagging dog and a long-eared cottontail.

Right now the cottontail is about two-up on the dog. And if you count the old man as a worthy opponent, also, he's one-up on us, too. We "lost" at least one important battle and worse, lost face in front of our seven-year-old who started the whole deal by running to us with:

"The dog's got a rabbit in the culvert pipe and the water's coming."

"Well," we told him after we'd peeked in one end of the pipe and confirmed it, "you are just about to witness what happens when rabbits don't watch where they're going and get into the wrong places. Like little boys sometimes."

"How do you mean?"

"I mean the rabbit has no choice but to get away from the water and if you want to get a good look at this particular Peter Rabbit, all you have to do is walk to this lower end of the pipe and wait for the water to shoo him out."

"What about the dog?"

"Let him watch, too; he hasn't caught old cottontail yet and he'll be as surprised as the rabbit when the water comes through."

So the three of us tiptoed over to the end of the pipe and waited for the water.

And we waited . . . and waited. Finally a little trickle of water.

"It'll be soon now," we whispered. And then we waited and waited . . . and waited some more. Water was gushing out now.

"Where's the rabbit." Both the boy and dog were looking at me reprovingly.

"He'll be coming in a minute. He can't stand much of that."

"Hey, Daddy, he's behind us, at the other end!"

Sure enough there sat Brer Rabbit at the upper end instead of the lower, wet and bedraggled and dripping water all over. But out on the bank. And with a good 10-yard headstart on the dumbfounded dog.

"He came out that end while we were watching here, Daddy."

"I see that."

"He went the other way and fooled you."

"I guess you could say that."

"He's wet but he got out. And we never saw him."

"That's true."

"He must be laughing at you."

"Probably."

And Brer Rabbit was, too. You couldn't miss that grin from one long, floppy ear to the other. Sort of a sarcastic, know-it-all type of grin, as we recall it.

September 20, 1962

The funeral procession to the Shell cemetery was going slow, too slow for the guy in the Sheridan car, apparently, for he whipped around the slow-paced cars and floorboarded it on towards the mountain.

Because the incident is common in these hurry-hurry days, Cleo McKinney didn't think much about it.

But a few days later, driving back from Manderson, an incident with another funeral procession made him remember the guy in the Sheridan car, and his disregard for the long line of cars.

And it gave Cleo pause to think (as it did us when he relayed the story) about the times and the present sense of values people practice. And "old country" habits new countries sometimes lose in the transition.

Cleo had pulled over to the side of the road as the Manderson funeral procession went by.

From his parking spot he could see three Mexican nationals working in the adjoining field. And as he watched one of them straightened up and noticed the line of cars. He nudged his companions, who stopped work, too, and looked at the procession coming toward them.

Then, each one took off his hat, and heads uncovered, stood there in the field quietly and respectfully as the hearse and cars moved past them and on down the road and out of sight.

October 4, 1962

Blame an "accident" for not allowing the Homecoming Parade to start on time.

It was the crepe-hidden driver of the senior float who didn't see the Slow School sign on North Sixth street. And he rammed that first place float smack into it.

But fortunately dents in crepe paper can be smoothed out easier than those in chrome and metal. So a few pieces of paper in the appropriate places, a little padding here and there and the float moved serenely on down the street as if nothing had got in its way.

But sabotage threatened the freshman entry, "Skunk 'Em" showing a jaunty black-and-white striped animal. Sometime Thursday night pranksters (or jealous competition) poured tar on the float. But the show goes on, even if you're on a freshman level, and the class spent extra hours repairing the damage before the parade time.

It was a good Homecoming. Maybe it was the Indian summer afternoon – perfect football weather trying to steal the show that made it easier to remember all the little details. Or because it was just plain Homecoming instead of just another high school football weekend.

It was a first night, too, for the PA system and announcer Frank Norris, Jr. who ably supplied the names and statistical information to the crowd.

And another "first" for an original composition by Band Director Charles Rutherford which the band played in honor of Queen Linda Buchanan. The band's performance was a halftime highlight, as it always is, and it especially bowled over those Codyites on the far side who hadn't seen the band perform before.

John Kosich, who has seen many Greybull homecomings from the coach's bench, was on hand to watch the game from the bleacher seats.

That night the floats made their rounds of the field and then lumbered to the "float graveyard" in the northwest corner where the kids demolished them in less time than it takes to write it.

The biggest laugh was watching the senior stork in its flight away from the crowd. The senior behind the wheel, once he was in back of the west side stands, took off in high gear and Mr. Stork stretched out in the ensuing gale, weaving and bobbing, his "bundle" streaming behind, and looking very much like storks must sometimes do when they get in a hurry!

October 18, 1962

"Quite a load you got here in the trunk," the service station man in Casper pointed out to us.

It was last Sunday and we were hurrying home from a Nebraska trip, stiff in the joints, anxious to get off the road, weary of miles of asphalt.

"Sh, not so loud. The wife'll hear. She doesn't need to be reminded of this stuff back here."

The guy poked and prodded with his foot. "Looks like steel fence posts to me," he said.

"Strange that you'd say that just that way. That's what the wife said when she saw them for the first time. You're both right. They are."

"What are you doing with fence posts?"

"It's a long story. But I went to a farm auction in Verdigre, Nebraska and I couldn't resist the bargain."

"Verdigre. Where's that?"

"About 500 miles back down the road."

"Quite a ways back to be buying fence posts."

"I've heard that a couple of times today, too. It isn't exactly shopping at home, I'll admit. But it was a good buy. And I couldn't resist the urge to bid. It isn't so bad. They almost fit in the trunk."

"Only a foot or so sticking out. Rattle any?"

"Just on the bumps. But with the trunk up the wife's afraid the rain'll get everything wet inside."

"Well, it won't hurt the posts."

"That's what I told her."

"And you saved the freight."

"That's right. I'll point that out to her."

"Tell her it could have been worse. You could have bid on a horse. Then what would you've done?"

"It would have been a long ride, mister, a long ride."

December 27, 1962

You have . . .

. . . a four-year-old, named Morris Smith

. . . and his mother, Mrs. Gladys Smith who was driving the car.

. . . the Beaver creek road

. . . a field of the Michelena's

. . . and eight buck deer of various size and horn racks grazing in it.

Mind you now, it's Christmas time – Friday, the 21st to be exact – and everyone's been talking of Santa Claus and toy trucks and candy canes. And you've heard every Christmas carol a hundred times.

Now you suddenly see eight deer grazing out in the field. What would be your first thought?

No, don't answer. Let us relate to you what Morris excitedly told his mother. They weren't deer out in the field but reindeer, just as Santa had left them. Feeding and resting, Morris explained, before that important Monday evening spin over Shell town and the rest of the world.

Feeding and resting on Beaver creek pasture, taking on some good Big Horn mountain air. It's no wonder, Morris, that old Santa gets around so well.

January 31, 1963

Every morning at the breakfast table our family talks about Dan Martin.

Usually it's "Can you see Dan Martin yet?"

And sometimes you can, far-off down the road, his big yellow bus stopping to pick up the first kids on Lower Shell, the exhaust on the cold mornings billowing up behind and if he's turned just right, the lights blinking on and off, on and off.

Mostly, though, the kids are too early, too afraid they'll miss the bus –

especially the middling one who doesn't have the nonchalant air yet of kids who've ridden miles and miles in their little lifetimes. So usually they begin watching minutes too soon.

"Can you see Dan Martin yet?"

On snowy days and sunshiny days and just plain days, on the days when they ride their bikes instead of the bus, and on the days when a sleepy voice calls out from beneath tousled hair:

"Tell Dan Martin I'm sick today."

"Can you see Dan Martin yet?"

"There he is – over by Smith's." – Or, "He's just on the hill."

And on some days: "Hurry, Dan's waiting. We're late, we're late." And then panic and flight and little feet flying and little hearts pounding. What a catastrophe, that missing the bus!

"Can you see Dan Martin yet?"

Of course, every morning you can. Every morning, same roads, same time, same kids, same stops, same Dan.

May 30, 1963

This Birmingham thing is spreading.

Right this week at our place it's threatening to upset the segregation we've instilled for years on the mice in the basement and the Kennedys upstairs. It's tradition that the mice can have part of the basement and half of the rolled oats we keep in the corner of the garage. We get the house.

But since Friday night they've been pushing for more, and now it's this business of staging sit-ins smack dab in the middle of the wastebaskets.

Frankly we're not for it at all. The kids, who don't understand this integration bit are intrigued with mice showing up in the wastebaskets and not being able to get out. But it's bugging us.

Friday night we discovered our first one, small but defiant, trapped in the bottom of the boys' wastebasket.

"Look, Daddy, he can't get out."

"I see that – what shall we do with him?"

"Oh you can't do anything to him – not like this. I'll take it tomorrow morning and give it some cheese, and then turn it loose. Okay?"

"Fine, I'm whipped. Just this one mouse."

But the next night, another mouse. Same wastebasket.

"Are you sure you turned him loose?"

"Of course, Daddy. He just likes it there."

"Oh, sure!"

Same routine the next morning. More Velveeta. Turn him loose. Kids happy. The old man apprehensive.

Sunday night . . . honest . . . same thing. Mouse winds up in same wastebasket amid much hand-clapping and fond greetings. This guy's a pro.

Monday night . . . a dry hole . . . not a mouse in sight. The bottom of the lucrative wastebasket in the boys' room is mouse-clean. We've beaten the sit-in.

But from their sister's room: "Daddy, he's in my wastebasket."

Sure enough, there he is snuggled down among the bubble gum wrappers and the mountain of Kleenex.

"It's my mouse tonight," she tells the crestfallen boys.

Four straight nights of this non-violence stuff! Our mice segregation policy is in tatters.

July 25, 1963

Sunshine reservoir was calm, the day was clear, the sky blue and the boat was running fine.

And Bill Ford (at the helm) and Passenger Willie Grisham were enjoying it all.

They'd made a couple of tight turns and had spent some time sending the boat skimming out over the lake.

Then they spotted the seagull.

It was low down in the water, apparently enjoying the day too, and it made a perfect sitting-duck-of-a-target.

And Bill said, "Let's get that seagull."

So he set the boat on a collision course, straight for the old bird out there in the water and ramming speed increased and the boat went faster and the water and waves whistled by.

Closer and closer came the seagull and it never moved a feather. The boat, never varying an inch off course, sped right at the bird. Just a few more feet were left . . .

And then . . .

WHAM!

Mr. Seagull was sitting on a submerged tree!

Up flipped the boat into the air. Down it came with a wet crash.

The hot motor went under water and exploded. The two men were spilled out and had to swim to an island where another boater from Meeteetse picked them up. The boat had some damage and the motor will cost $50 to fix up.

But Mr. Seagull, smoothing its ruffled feathers, settled back down on his underwater tree perch and went on enjoying the blue sky and the clear day and the calm, calm water.

October 24, 1963

It was the Big City's finest Chinese restaurant and everything about the place looked the part. Big reed baskets hanging around, lanterns, kimonoed waitresses, superb service, Oriental art, bamboo curtains. And so dark you needed a flashlight to see the menu.

The little Chinese girl served a rice and meat and noodle concoction of which I remember not the name. It heaped on the platter and there was some oriental music going all the time and the bamboo curtain rattled. The atmosphere was perfect. And so was the tea! My what tea! If you tend toward ulcers and can't drink coffee this Chinese blend of tea was superb. It tasted straight out of Old China. Not very dark, but strong. And yet not too strong. And served in those delicate cups, so tiny they disappeared in your hand. What wonderful tea!

It made the entire meal.

"This is marvelous tea," I asked the girl. "What kind of Chinese blend is it? Can I get some?"

"You must ask Ah Fong?"

"Who is Ah Fong?"

She giggled behind her hand. "The cook. In the kitchen."

"How do I get there? I would like to ask him."

She pointed to a solemn Chinese by the door. I went over to him. I felt very expansive and very contented. Like you do when you are about to praise someone. All life seems good. And I was full of food and that very, very hot Chinese tea.

"I would like to see Ah Fong. To ask about the tea. It is so . . . delicious, I must ask . . ."

"In the kitchen. There." He pointed to a door. I went through it and saw another man in a white suit.

"Ah Fong?" I asked.

He shook his head and pointed to another door.

Inside this one it seemed to me the tea smell was stronger than any of the other kitchen smells. I felt drawn to it.

"Where is Ah Fong?" I said to the first Chinese girl I saw. She stopped scurrying to look at me, a stranger in the kitchen.

"I wish to ask him about the tea. What kind is it? I want to take some home."

She looked at me again and pointed to the back of the kitchen. I could see several men working feverishly, concentrating on steaming kettles and pans of cooking food.

"Where is Ah Fong?" I said loudly.

Heads turned my way. Someone repeated my call: "Ah Fong, Ah Fong." Blank faces regarded me curiously. At once an old man padded over to me. He looked wizened and wrinkled. He was very polite. I tried to explain about the tea.

"It's marvelous. I wondered what kind it could be. Maybe I could buy some somewhere? What kind of an old Chinese blend is it?"

He motioned for me to come with him. I didn't know whether he had understood me or not. I followed him over to a big shelf. Boxes and cans were everywhere. Ah Fong took down a big box, with the top torn open.

"Ah the tea," he said in a high-pitched almost falsetto voice. "It is very good." He pointed to the red and yellow label and the big white letters.

They read: Lipton's.

December 12, 1963

If anyone in your family put down they want a puppy for Christmas, we can help you out.

There's five out at our house and while they're a little too big to fit into a Christmas stocking, they'll snuggle just right into a little boy's or girl's arms.

Yes, they're male and if you didn't know it any other way, you could tell by the way they fight amongst themselves. Just like all little boys do.

And they're free, no charge, no strings attached, but sorry no merchandise returned.

We know who their mammy was and have a very good idea who their pappy was. But the genealogy ends right there. Their grandpappy is a mystery and his pappy and the pappy before him. They might have been gray or brown or black (their descendants are anyway) or black-brown or brown-gray or gray-black. And of course white wherever the rest of the colors aren't.

In fact, you could close your eyes and call "Spot" and they should all come running. They come running anyway, whether you call or not, but they do have their own names. Which you can change of course. No papers on these pooches.

There's Snowball (white naturally) and Rascal. And there's a Jocko and a Tip. And Brownie (guess what color he is) who got changed to Mick who got changed to Toby.

We've lost track how old they're supposed to be now, but their tails wag joyously, they can bark in their squeaky voices and can set up a forlorn howl which sort of peters out at the end. They end up much of the time on their noses or flopped over on their backs. But they take it good-naturedly. And you can't stay down-hearted around them for very long.

Each member of our family has its own pup it likes best and we've agreed to keep one but not which one. Maybe you can help us decide.

May 14, 1964

Our family had waited all week for word about the spelling pin and when it finally came, when the word was brought dejectedly home from school, none of us wanted to hear it.

But the little feller piped up anyway and told us as manfully as he could that he'd missed a word on the last test of the year and he wouldn't get his pin after all.

The last test . . . and he was the only one left in the room with all 100's and that last list got him.

"I was awful nervous about it," he said by way of explaining.

But he didn't have to explain. We knew how he felt. It didn't really matter. It wasn't a tragedy and Life would go on and there'd be other pins to win, maybe, or things to get or achievements to make. But it meant a lot to him right at this time in his life and because of that it meant a lot to us "old people" too. And gosh it hurt to see him disappointed.

"The teacher said I was a good sport about it," he added.

Well, of course that's the lesson, not the 100 perfect words. But the old man wasn't a very good sport about it we're sorry to say. We moped around when he wasn't looking for a couple of hours and felt his hurt for him without his knowing.

No we can't say we were a good sport. But he was and he got over it, as all kids do whether it's something small like a little pin of brass and gold plate or, an important first team berth or a queen candidate.

And we got over it, too, as all parents have done through Life. And we saw for just an instant all the shared hurts and disappointments and the tough times ahead that parents spend without the kids ever knowing. We realized in that brief revelation that it's Life and that's the way It is and always has been. Your kids are everything. You rejoice when they excel; you cry with them when they don't quite make it. Your parents did the same before you and theirs before them. You feel their hurts and their bad times as much as they do. But they never really know, your kids don't, they shouldn't know it. Not until they grow up, too, and have their kids and have spelling words that are missed and a pin that doesn't get to come home.

And they'll know then how much you cared.

July 2, 1964

West Thumb in Yellowstone Park has a pedestrian traffic that crosses the road or walks alongside of it in a constant stream down to the boat docks and the lake's edge. We've never come along there yet and you probably haven't either without almost running over a half dozen people on foot. There's just no hurrying through the place. People are everywhere usually.

Like they were this past weekend when we went through. In fact we almost ran into a bunch of girls, apparently Park "savages" who were walking together down the road. As we got by them, they all started yelling: "Flat tire, flat tire," and pointing at our right front wheel.

"What did they say," our kids asked in unison.

"Something about the tire being flat."

"Daddy, do you have a flat tire?"

"No, they were just acting silly. Still, the car has been steering harder."

We drove along a little ways.

"You don't suppose it is flat, do you?" we asked the wife.

"Of course not. That's the oldest game there is."

"Well I don't know, the car's acting funny, Can't you feel it? Very sluggish. And that's a bad tire, too, you know."

"Daddy, I hear something going ssssss. Like that." The other two kids said they heard it too.

"My gosh I think it is flat. Feel the way it handles. Don't you think it's flat?"

The wife didn't. Not at all. In fact she was very emphatic about it. "How could five girls all say the same thing at the same time and all point to the same tire."

"It's flat I can tell. You're not driving. It's pulling over to that one side. It must just be going down. Look! There's other people looking at us, too, now!"

"Daddy, you'd better stop."

"I'm going to. Right now. The tire'll be ruined if I keep on arguing about it."

I picked out a level spot and pulled off to the side where the road was wider.

The kids all wanted to get out too. "How about you," I asked the wife.

"No," she said. "I'll stay inside." The rest of us piled out on the road. I walked around to the tire. It looked like a perfectly normal 32 pounds of pressure. Not even pancaked a little. I kicked it . . . hard. It kicked back . . . hard.

We all got back in the car.

"What's the verdict?" the wife wanted to know.

"Sure pretty up here in the Park this time of year. Isn't it?"

December 10, 1964

The first thing we said to Tom Hubbard when we called him to report our lights were off was: "We're going to change to natural gas."

"Well, that's fine," Tom replied, "see if you can get hooked up in the next hour or two."

Always quick with the answer, that Tom. But he agreed to come right out on the Heights and see if he couldn't get the Pacific Power and Light back into the light business.

And we turned to the job of locating the emergency supplies again.

Like the candles. They haven't burned since the last time the lights went off.

And the Coleman lantern which sputtered and took off and smelled the place up because the old man spilled the fuel all over.

And we had to build a fire in the fireplace 'cause the heat went off with the power, but any excuse is a good one to build a fire.

And we had to start rationing the water since the pressure pump quit, too.

But on the other hand there's compensation when the power's gone.

"I don't have to do my homework, you know," the fourth grader shouted gleefully.

And half-cooked hamburgers still taste good in front of a fire.

And there's immense fun burning candles. But it's hard on the candle supply. For the record our family is now poorer by four large candles, two medium-sized ones and 31 birthday candles, most of them burned up in dark corners and very few out where the lights were really needed.

But candlelight! It's almost worth having the lights go off! And just when we finally got the kids and the candles all down to the dinnertable at the same time . . . and the fire was going perfect! . . . and you got used to the smell of the Coleman lantern . . . and one of the kids had pointed out to her daddy that maybe "you won't have to go to the Council meeting after all" . . . and the candlelight started dancing on the walls . . . and one of the kids sighed: "Isn't this the real life" . . . and everything was going just fine . . . and right then . . . the lights went back on.

What a jolt!

And everybody wailed: "Oh, no."

But the lights were on, as bright as ever.

"Oh, let's turn them off and have fun again," pleaded our little girl. "Please, Daddy, let's turn them off."

Well, what are you going to do with the fire going and the candles burning and everyone looking at you? Of course you are.

So we turned them off. Every light in the house. OFF. Every blasted light.

Sorry, Tom.

February 4, 1965

"How was school today?" we asked all the kids as soon as we got home.

"Fine," said the girl.

"Fine," said the fourth grader.

"Fine," said the little boy who goes to kindergarten.

It happens every night. Same question. Same answer. Is that the way in your house, too? We adults ask some dull questions and kids in their infinite wisdom have found that the best answer to a dull question is just to say, "Fine, Dad, fine."

"How was the show?" we ask.

"Fine," chorus the kids.

"How are you feeling tonight?"

"Fine," they say.

"Good morning. How did you sleep?"

"Fine," they yawn.

One day I walked in the front room, and just raised my eyebrows at the oldest boy. "Fine," he quickly said.

What a dull parent, I thought, not to be able to come up with a decent question to stimulate little minds, to make them think, to get them away from this everlasting "fine" this and "fine" that and "just fine" everything.

So the other night I switched questions, made a new rule about not saying "fine" and the conversation just flowed. I learned, among other things, that Friday is the best day for the school lunch because that's the day for chocolate milk; that so and so wore a yellow dress "just like mine;" that there were three 100 marked papers, two B's and one "terrible" grade; and a wealth of other information.

"Now isn't this better," I asked everyone. "Isn't this better than just saying fine?"
"Yes, Daddy."
"Well, let's remember if it we can. No more "fine." Now let me read the paper."
"Daddy, will you put the paper down, so I can ask you a question?"
"Go ahead. I'm listening."
"Daddy, how was the office today?"
"Mmmm?"
"I said how was the office today?" A little louder.
"Oh, fine," I said, "just fine. Everything was fine."
Silence. Everywhere.
That's odd, I thought. I lowered the paper. Three solemn little faces. All turned in my direction.
"Now what did I do?"

June 17, 1965

Vonnie Harnden is an advertising salesman for the Greybull Standard and a regular columnist, an exceptional columnist really who has what we call in the trade as "the touch" for column writing. She is widely read and has a great following everywhere the Standard goes.

She is also energetic and enthusiastic and doesn't mind the hard work it takes to build a float for the Days of '49 parade.

But when she asked us if the Standard was going to have a float in the parade, we said we didn't think so. Too much rodeo week, too much work, too little time. Forty pages of Jubilee paper had added 40 years and we couldn't face the crepe paper and an empty flatbed truck.

So we said "no", let's wait for next year which is what we have been saying every year.

But we reckoned without Vonnie Harnden's energy and high spirits. After finishing up the Boy Scout float, she enlisted the aid of husband Chuck, the Boy Scouts and went ahead to see that the Standard was represented.

So unbeknownst to us until the afternoon of the parade, the Greybull Standard did have a float after all, although we saw it about the same time as all the rest of the people along main street did.

As the Boy Scout float came by, one of the Scouts who had helped Vonnie, hollered over to us behind our camera. "I like your float!" And he grinned as big as he could.

Well, we liked it too, and thank you, Vonnie.

June 24, 1965

What are you going to say this week in your "notebook column," the family wanted to know?

What can you say when you've got a pen with stage fright?

Saturday night the National Editorial Association judges said this Editor's Notebook was the best one topic column in the United States, among both weeklies and dailies.

And this week you've got a pen that's dried up in a panic.

This week of all weeks, what does an editor writing in his notebook say? But what can you write with a cotton-mouthed pen?

This week of the curious eyes, the wondering what will be said, the waiting to be convinced, the week of the "reputation" . . . and a ball point goes bashful.

Your quivering knees are showing, pen. Where's all this memorable stuff? This first-place calibre?

Don't worry about the "crowd." Don't be nervous and tongue-tied. Just be yourself. Forget those judges.

And write something clever, pen, something deathless.

Stop your shaking, pen, stop this stage fright.

You just can't leave this paralyzed editor out here all alone!

February 10, 1966

Little kids who go through print shops are usually very gracious in saying thank you and sometimes, like Mrs. Mary Brooks' third grade did last week, they sit down afterward and send us all letters.

The letters prove one thing:

You see a print shop a lot different when you're only three feet high.

Our old press will be crushed to know it hardly scored in the "My favorite thing . . ." category. But its companion, the folder, was a big hit. Something about that paper being folded and cut and trimmed all up into a finished product fascinated the little kids . . . and grown ups, too for that matter.

The darkroom was second in the list of attractions. "I think the darkroom was exciting" little Diana Collingwood wrote to us. And that summed up many of her classmates.

"Exciting" must be a third grade word these days. It found its way into many of the letters. So is "neat" apparently. "The way you print and fould the paper is neat," wrote one boy. Neat and exciting. Oh, to be eight again.

And the same little girl who asked how we "put the paper to bed" wrote that she'd learned how we did it now. She doesn't know . . . and we didn't tell her . . . that "putting the paper to bed" is more Hollywood than Greybull, Wyoming. And we don't stand at the doorway on a Wednesday afternoon and shout, "Let's put 'er to bed." Instead it comes out something like: "Let's just get the darn thing out." But putting it to bed technically happens and now she knows.

When you're barely tall enough to see on top of a printer's stone, you call things by the best names you can. "The stamper . . . the metal piece (we gave each one the usual Linotype slug with their name on it) . . . "the machine that put the print on the paper" . . . "the folding machine . . . the instruments . . ."

Almost everyone signed it "Love, . . . or With Love," but one boy signed off with "Your visitor . . ."

"I enjoyed every moment of the trip," Marilyn Molaskey was nice enough to write. And Ricky Bryant invited us to "come and see us some time."

Steve Allard had one complaint though. "I liked the darkroom, but it wasn't dark!" he wrote.

July 21, 1966

The Basin high school class of 1947 (as class members reminded themselves in a short reunion Friday) didn't leave much to the posterity of BHS.

But it did leave one mark still untouched: It gave the most gosh-awful junior play dress rehearsal in the school's history. And when you take all the gosh-awful junior class plays given in the world every year, that's quite a record. But "Girl Shy" topped them all.

Miscues, wrong entrances, missed lines, it was all there in that production before the grade school kids.

Marjorie Knapp walked on the stage to give her lines once and to her dismay found the place empty. Utter silence! Everyone on stage had walked off. So she did, too! When everyone did come back on, they all came back at once. Utter pandemonium!

Freddie Clements and I were discoursing in a forced monotone on the stage in the next act and I blanked out completely. In desperation I brightly said: "Well, it sure's going to be a good dance." And Freddie, whose eyes were showing his sheer terror at being cast adrift on stage, replied in similar desperation: "Yes, it sure is."

Such spirited conversation went on for hours and hours it seemed until one of us recognized a cue and struggled back on to the script again.

And then there was the incident of the new dress in the box that Freddie and Carolyn Bratton were supposed to admire. Carolyn was to reach in the dress box, pull out the dress and hold it up. This she did. But it was a two piece outfit and someone had forgotten to pin it together. So only the top part came out. Freddie's line was: (And he didn't know what to do but go ahead and say it as Carolyn stood clutching this dinky blouse by the neck) "Gosh, I can't wait to see you in THAT!"

How the kids roared at that one!

But if those little tykes knew how awful the whole thing was, they graciously never said anything, bless them. And after this shattering shakedown, the next night's main performance went off without a hitch. It could be classified as only normal-Junior-Class-play-awful. Not gosh-awful!

Such is the stuff junior class plays are made of.

And reunions, too.

July 28, 1966

The thought that school was just barely a month away panicked our kids a few days ago and sent them in a flurry of pencils and paper to the table where they could "practice a little" and "see if I remember."

Our fourth grader girl even made the supreme sacrifice and took an extra glass of "that awful" milk so she could "get used to it before the school lunch starts again."

But mostly it was writing and figuring and trying to make "r's" look like "r's". And writing all the alphabet.

And that's an all night task sometimes.

The fact that as a nation we're not as good writers as our forefathers isn't the fault of the schools. It's the times. Even killing out the old Palmer method of teaching writing can't be the cause. For there's a lot of us around who did the ovals and the push and pulls and made all the proper hooks and curley ques and moved our arms, who can't write a sentence so you could read it.

Palmer method and straight pens. Pen points and ink wells on the desk. Now that brings back a few years doesn't it?

L.C. Sheppard had the classic story on ink wells and kids. (He's down at Worland now after serving as Basin's superintendent in the 1940's) When he was a kid dipping a pen out of an ink well, the boys got to pestering a shy little girl in the room. Every time she'd try to take the cork out of her ink bottle, one of the boys would stick his finger inside his cheek and snap it quick out of his mouth. You know how that's done (or ask your kids to show you!) Pop! it goes.

So every time the little girl would attack that cork POP, it would make a noise.

The exasperated teacher would call over gently as possible, Mary, you don't have to make a noise with your ink cork. And the little girl would color all up and be too embarrassed to try to explain.

Next day. Same thing. POP! Finally the teacher strode over to Mary's desk, picked up the bottle and said: Let me show you how to do this without making any noise.

And he proceeded to carefully work the cork out of the bottle, giving an exaggerated demonstration of how the cork comes out smoothly, without noise, etc.

"Now, see" he said and he pulled the cork out.

POP! from the back of the room. The boys couldn't let that chance go by!

February 16, 1967

Surely you recognized Pepper in Core's Used Car ad in two week's ago Standard.

You may have wondered about the mechanics of getting a dog to clamp a cigar in his mouth, put spectacles on his nose and smile for the camera.

It was a snap actually. You have to reckon with that dog's acting abilities. But we still approached the task of photographing a cigar-smoking dog with an animal photographer's wariness.

We have had to nearly tie a Santa Claus hat on to the family boxer to get a Christmas shot.

Margaret Knudson struggled alongside of us for 35 minutes trying to get her pet rabbit to keep on a pair of earmuffs one Easter.

We've browbeat cats into standing still, pleaded with horses to put their ears forward. We've cajoled calves, lambs, chipmunks, chickens, puppies, and even a marauding bobcat one time to pose for the camera.

But never a dog with a cigar!

"What kind of a cigar do you think she would like?" we asked Jim Core.

"Get something I can smoke."

So we bought a single Roi Tan Perfecto (fatter and rounder to show up better) loaded our pockets with flashbulbs and extra film, and stripped off our coat for the struggle ahead.

But old Pro Pepper was ready.

"Hold this" Jim said to her and gave her the cigar. The jaws open and clamp down.

"Keep these on!" The glasses are added. Nothing moves. Just her eyeballs follow Jim around.

"Now look here!" Pow, a picture. "Look over here!" Pow, another.

"Do you suppose she'd smile," we asked facetiously.

"Smile," commanded Jim.

We swear she did. Just a trifle. What an old pro!

I wonder if she ever flies after the Red Baron.

April 13, 1967

I wanted that cheeseburger in the worst way. A cheeseburger and milk, the cheeseburger in a gob of ketchup and the milk in a tall, tall glass. A regular feast, a Wednesday night's feast that winds up that long press day.

So I stopped at the first Cody cafe I came to, went in and ordered the cheese and the burger and the ketchup and the tall, tall glass of milk and went to with gusto.

It was every bit as good as I thought it would be.

Except about three-fourths way through I remembered I was flat broke, not even a parking meter nickel. The usual I-left-my-wallet-in-my-other-pants-pocket routine.

That old cheeseburger wilted a little right then. The thought of washing dishes always takes away my appetite.

Besides it's embarrassing to be away from friends and check cashing buddies and people who might even let you sign your name to the old chit.

Well, I thought, as I forced down that last bit of cheeseburger, you can always try the cash-a-check route. So I broached the subject as delicately as I could to the waitress who kindly said yes she'd take a check "if it was for just the amount of the dinner." I got the 60 cents scribbled out okay and handed it over with as much savoir faire as I could muster and she said: "Oh, you're from Greybull. You should go back and say hello to Mary Bradford."

"Is she here?"

"She cooks right in back."

I went back and hollered through the swinging door: "Anyone around here ever been to Birdie's Cafe?"

"I sure have," Mary hollered back and came out to see who remembered that little place with the horseshoe counter and the friendly banter. I thought I'd recognized that good cheeseburger.

"By Gosh, while you're here, I'll just pay you for my paper. The one I'm sending to my daughter. Save me sending it down. Still $4.50 for out of state?"

"Still four and a half."

So I scribbled her out a receipt on the back of a piece of scratch paper, and she gave me $4.50 in cash.

The old editor wasn't broke after all.

April 27, 1967

When Dr. Lewis Hay and I used to see each other nearly every Thursday night at the Norris Cafe, while he had his late dinner and I took a break from putting the paper down, our conversation was usually about politics. Because Doc Hay liked politics; he was a student of them, really, as everyone seems to be who's lived in Cheyenne. The interest in the state government, in what's going on in the political parties becomes a pleasant habit among Cheyennites.

He still kept track of what was going on, he knew some interesting political history which he invariably shared.

He also had a continuing interest in literature, in fine words and the art of expression. This is a fading interest, I sometimes think. You see less of it in today's "modern" world, it's stressed less in schools. One time I went to see him in his room and he was killing time with a book of Shakespeare's plays. That's a habit from another generation, surely not ours.

His move to the Thermopolis Pioneer Home years ago ended our weekly conversations of literature and politics. But when he moved back to the Basin Sanitarium, he sent word for "us to get together again." I promised I would.

But we members of the younger generations live too much in our own present. We're too busy with today, too rushed to think of the tomorrows.

There're dollars we think we must chase, hours we're sure need stretching. We never take the time to do things we ought to do. There always seems to be enough time "some other day."

But there's fallacy in the thinking about that "some other day." It seldom comes. It's usually too late before it does. Like with Doc Hay, now. I waited too long. I should have gone over to see him at least one more time.

And I've been guilty before of not sharing these days of the present with friends, especially older friends who do not have as many tomorrows as I.

I renew a promise: There cannot be any rush so important, any task so pressing that it couldn't spare a half hour.

October 12, 1967

For no reason at all except that possibly I'm getting older and more sentimental (and maybe the senility is setting in early) I started thinking about the old dog the John Cowan family had in Basin years ago.

I haven't thought of that dog for 25 years, but I can see her right now waddling across the room on her short legs, all stomach and nothing else. What a pet she was to the Cowan boys and all the boys in the neighborhood. Spotty was a feisty thing when she was young, a fox terrier belligerence far bigger than her size. But the steam went out of her as the years passed, like it does out of us "old" people, too, and she ended up pampered and weary and barely able to scoot around. I think that was the first dog I ever saw grow old.

Thoughts of Spotty led me to other dogs in Basin in those "old" days. T.K. Bishop had a bulldog, the likes of which I've never seen since. Maybe he was bigger only in my grade school eyes, but he was the biggest bulldog I can ever remember. And just about the ugliest. What a face!

He was forever getting into fights, as I remember it, and the Bishops would paint him up with iodine which only added to his terrifying appearance, a pug-nosed, daubed up witch doctor straddling the sidewalks. I don't know how many miles I walked on those grade school legs of mine, detouring around the Bishop home.

And there was Jerry, the Doc Walker's police dog, who was by far the best dog I have ever known. He had been trained on the West Coast before he came to the Walkers and if you wanted him to mind, he did. Right then. He was completely gentle, quiet and even dispositioned unlike most of the other police dogs in town. He was bigger, too, with a rich thick coat, a beautiful dog. He adopted me when Myron Walker went off to school and I was overjoyed. For years we were companions though we lived in different next-door houses. He had one trick (although to him it was serious business) of pulling you to shore if you acted like you were drowning. He'd swim with us in the wide spot of the Big Horn canal in back of where all the new homes are built now. If we'd thrash around in the water and "go under", he'd get excited and grab your arm in his teeth and pull you to shore. He was strong enough to do it and he didn't care if his teeth made big deep marks as long as he dragged you to the bank. A fine old dog, another one out of those old days.

We had a dog of our own for awhile, a little toy shepherd named Wimpy who took to liking fresh chickens more than he did the hamburgers. He apparently started raiding Mrs. Alexander's chicken house and Mrs. Alexander walked all the way up from her home where Dr. Fallon is now, to complain to mother about our dog.

Mother, of course, was indignant and protesting, and in the end she convinced Mrs. Alexander that some other dog, not ours was doing the killing. As Mrs. Alexander turned to go, there was Wimpy on the step behind her, tail wagging and happy, a white leghorn in his mouth, the hunter home with the kill.

And that was the end of Wimpy!

January 4, 1968

No Pied Piper's flute ever drew as many little kids as one camera taken into the school playground does. They don't need much encouragement to have their picture taken. They crowd around, a cluster of fur collars and red noses and stocking caps, all wanting, in a dozen different voices to "have my picture taken" until you feel that if you would lead them out onto the street they'd follow you on downtown.

So I was standing among them, trying to think of pictures, trying to listen to what they had to say, feeling good about all the little tykes around me, when someone hit me right alongside the head with a big snowball.

Kapow! A direct hit.

No one said anything. But as I turned around at this crowd on the playground the little kid with the biggest grin on his face was my own third grader son. It didn't take much parental insight to know that I'd just been hit alongside the head with a snowball fashioned by those tender little fingers of my very own son!

What a great joke on Dad!

I took a half step towards him but I stopped. I haven't been able to catch him since both he and I got older.

Instead I put a stern look on my face and scolded: "Listen here, Buster. You do that again and I'll bend you over right here on the snow."

A couple of little kids who didn't know who I was or who I was to him, looked at me with wide eyes and probably thought to themselves, "What an old grouch he is." But my little mischievous Bob wasn't fazed at all. He's lived with me too long. All he did was dart away to a safe distance and grin that grin of his. And enjoy himself hugely.

What a great joke on Dad!

November 28, 1968

It was just 20 years ago this fall that Bud Jones got the old football used in Greybull's 26 to 6 victory over Powell.

And it was just the other day that Bud, rummaging around in his closet at his Sacramento, Calif. home, found the ball again.

"It's still good," he told me over the phone the other night. After he'd found the ball, he started thinking about Greybull and football and the Standard and he decided he'd just call back home again. "We pumped it up and my boy and I have been throwing it around this evening," he reported over the phone.

"It's a lot bigger than the footballs are nowadays," he said. "Hard to get a grip. But it still holds air."

J.C. Quigg gave him the ball. And signed it. Greybull had beaten Powell that year and topped Thermopolis. But these were the only two wins.

Jones thought it might have been the Homecoming game. But the old Standard files showed that it was Lovell who played on Homecoming and soundly thrashed the Buffs that evening. The football Jones has at least was a winning football even though it wasn't a Homecoming football!

Jones is in Sacramento now, an associate inspector for the county of Sacramento. His father, the late Billy Jones, was one of Greybull's best-liked citizens. His mother lives in Thermopolis but recently visited her son on the coast.

Jones played with William Coakley, Dave Pearson, James Hill, Ted Peterson, Ken Greene, Leon Sanders, Duane Hankins, Bill Wilkinson, Wayne Yorgason, Junior Phillips, William Clifton, Larry Bullinger, Glen Mowell, John Pearson and Don Bristow.

The team was coached by Cooper.

All of which brought up a lot of memories and talk of old times.

And it just goes to prove again that old footballs . . . and old fans . . . take a long time to fade away.

Index of Names

A

Adam, Rev. Thomas 34, 41
Adamy, Charlotte . 56, 74, 186, 273
Adamy, Fred 56
Adkins, Kenneth 63
Aggers, Jack 351
Allard, Steve 500
Allen, Harry 449
Allen, John 60
Alexander, "Pinky" 477
Alexander, "Speck" 477
Anders, Gary 390, 425
Anderson, David 25
Anderson, Rev. Jack 25
Anderson, John 75
Anderson, John Sr. and Eleanor . . . 95, 172, 425
Anderson, Nancy 279
Anderson, Press 112, 210, 266, 411
Anderson, Skip 33, 52, 66, 84, 110, 235
Anderson, Ted 39, 62, 69, 80, 209, 252
Anderson, Ted Sr. 279
Ankrum, Dorothy 37
Arnett, Joe 118
Arney, Scott 111
Atwood, Del 207
Auckenback, Joe 26
Avery, Bob 255
Avery, Jim 47
Avery, Mildred 40
Avery, Morris and Plet 31, 58, 60, 92, 237, 293, 374

B

Back, Joe 217
Bailey, Don 474
Baker, K.C. 90
Balfour, LeRoy 129
Balison, Jeff 259
Bama, James 164
Barbee, Bob 397
Barkell, Charla 271
Barnett, Mr. and Mrs. Harry . . . 71, 255
Barnett, Jama Leigh 71
Barnett, Paul 242
Barnett, Stacy 71
Barnett, Wayne 342
Bass, Ann 35
Bass, John 28, 36, 58
Batenhorst, Lucy 156
Batenhorst, Mary 86
Baugh, Art and Gladys 76, 237, 270, 389
Baugh, Randy 207
Baugh, Richard 76
Beach, Otis 125
Beach, Percy 282
Beaver, Billie 181
Beaver, Cecil 181
Beaver, Raymond 181
Bechtold, Carl 320
Beck, Jode 200
Becker, Randy 252
Befus, Everett 66
Beirith, Tony 85
Bellamy, Frank 29, 83, 388
Bentley, Alan 270
Bentley, Bartie 347
Bentley, Bob 250
Bentley, Mark 251, 329
Berger, Elsie 271
Bergstrom Bo 270
Bergstrom, Bruce 331
Bernard, Dorothy 308
Bernard, Sonja 367
Berry, Pitt 26
Bickford, George 331
Birnbaum, Louis 269
Bishop, T.K. 504
Black, Bill 266
Black, Don 66
Black, Jess 68, 252

Black, Tom and Del 308, 475
Blackburn, Randy 440
Blackwood, Jim 115
Blakesley, Anna 56
Blakesley, Charles 73
Blakesley, Lois 402
Blank, Lester 271
Bloom, Keith 181
Bluejacket, Bonnie 63
Bluejacket, Jim 405
Boelens, Vic 179
Bohl, Jim 52
Bond, Henry 271
Bond, Russell 61, 71, 449
Booth, Randy 270
Borders, J.T. 114
Borner, Johnny 48, 83, 482
Bosnic, Jock 181
Boson, Mike 401
Boyd, John 38, 56, 129, 281
Boyd, Pappy 249
Boylan, Cash 334
Boyle, Bill 82, 128
Braden, Bill 252
Bradford, Mary 503
Bratton, Carolyn 500
Brewer, Slim 12, 85, 94, 95,
  118, 120, 129, 221, 237, 250, 269,
  367, 380, 401, 449, 474
Bricker, Dutch 35
Brinkerhoff, Bob 86
Bristow, Don 506
Bristow, Ray 28, 31, 60, 70, 75
Bristow, Steve 73
Brome, Chuck 205
Brooks, Mary 499
Brown, Almira 331
Brown, Art and Rose 330,
  371, 449
Brown, Barnum 468
Brown, DeAnna 10
Brown, Mrs. E. 45
Brown, M.J. 402
Brown, Pat 135, 385

Brown, Red 48
Browne, Don 331
Bruce, Bill and Alma 222, 252
Bryant, Mr. and Mrs. Jim 71
Bryant, Ken 71, 308, 330
Bryant, Rick 71, 308, 330, 500
Buchanan, Linda 489
Buchanan, Millie 162
Buchmeier, Roy 425
Budd, Bertel 10
Bullinger, Larry and Roberta ... 19,
  95, 250, 389, 448, 506
Bullinger, Lynn 93
Bullinger, Matt 389
Bullinger, Nan 389
Bunch, Eddie 351
Burkhart, Bruce 286
Burkhart, Dick 32, 67, 73
Burkhart, Jay 286
Burroughs, E.C. 461
Burrows, Darren 89
Bush, Bill 71, 181, 351
Bush, Joe 351

C

Cabre, Hank 351
Caffeen, Johnny 284
Call, Mildred 15
Campbell, Bruce 252
Cannady, Steve 368
Carey, Joe and Claire 124,
  251, 255
Carne, David 271
Carney, Maurice 449
Carothers, Bob 419, 447
Carrell, R.W. 402
Carrico, David 425
Carroll, Loree 366
Casey, Frank 53, 83, 89,
  117, 159, 175, 251
Casey, Ken 46, 58
Castro, Alvin 286
Castro, Joe 271

Cathcart, Leland 235
Chamberlain, Dale 17
Chambers, Doc 30, 31, 42, 43, 66, 170, 474
Chapman, Bob and Daisy 328, 366, 424
Cheatham, Carrie 309, 401
Christ, Gerald 449
Christianson, Mike 280
Christler, Mel 34, 242, 252, 308, 402, 449, 483
Christler, Tony 125
Chroninger, Pete 46
Clapper, Roger 252
Clark, John 74
Clark, Paul 237, 367
Clark, Randy 12
Clark, Rich 12
Clarke, Tom 123
Clause, Larry 12, 53, 113, 119
Clause, Marvin 53
Clavier, Paul 271
Claycomb, Dick 86, 88
Clement, George and Luella . . . 40, 484
Clements, Freddie 393, 500
Cleveland, Terry 109
Clifton, Bill 249, 308, 425, 506
Clifton, Earl 249
Clifton, Elva 83
Clifton, Jim and Dee . . 42, 237, 368
Clifton, Mike 374
Cline, Bud 271
Close, Dan 270, 401
Clucas, Jack and Mary . . . 448, 476
Clucas, Joe 428
Clucas, Tom 330, 425
Coakley, William 506
Cochrane, Boots 22
Cockins, Sim 55, 262
Coleman, Max 36
Coleman, Roy and Florence . . 156, 272, 375
Collingwood, Art 53, 173
Collingwood, Bill 425
Collingwood, Bud and Connie 246, 249
Collingwood, Cub . . 68, 87, 88, 89, 105, 226, 341
Collingwood, Diana 499
Collingwood, Don and Charlene . . 45, 236, 330, 386, 448
Collingwood, Floyd 384
Collingwood, Gary 108
Collingwood, John 60, 82
Collingwood, Larry 45
Collingwood, Linda 45
Collingwood, Norman 474
Collingwood, Paul 308, 474
Collingwood, Renee 251
Collingwood, Wee and Ina 13, 34, 45, 308, 385, 406
Collopy, Jim 251
Conners, Fred 55, 130, 366
Coons, A.W. 59, 124
Copenhaver, John 8, 11
Copp, Frank 113, 122, 129
Core, Clint 4, 19, 35, 54, 62, 124, 304
Core, Mrs. Jack 251
Core, Jim and Ginny 27, 47, 89, 95, 331, 502
Cortez, Eloise 308
Cortez, Frank and Grace . . 331, 367
Cowan, Bill 207, 321
Cowan, John 504
Cowan, Leonard 164
Coxen, Glenn 14, 32, 129, 333
Coyne, J.J. 271, 331
Coyne, John 402
Craft, Connie 148
Crain, Hap and Lucille 15, 32, 331, 332, 374
Crandell, Delbert 392
Crawford, Jamie 401
Crawford, Jerry 252
Crawford, Jim and Mary . . . 43, 65, 73, 98, 110

Crawford, Judy 65
Crawford, Lee 65, 309
Cropsey, Dan 130
Cropsey, Linn 367
Crosby, Ross 346, 394
Crouch, Phil 71, 351
Crumrine, Patty 402
Cummings, Dixie . . . 251, 308, 367
Cummings, Tim 329
Cyrus, Kenny 245, 421

D

Dalbey, Wally 43
Daley, Rick 43
Dalin, Brad and Lisa 425
Dalin, Robb 401
Dalin, Ron and Donna 73, 271
Dalrymple, Glen 401
Darr, Harold 252
Davidson, James 51
Davis, Mr. and Mrs. Bill 89
Davis, Corky 123
Davis, Irv 68, 95, 166
Davis, J.G. 58
Davis, Jonathan 14, 30, 51, 67, 448
Davis, Stan 123, 271, 273
Davis, Terry 89
Denny, Al 363
Denzin, Butch 249, 270, 402, 424, 459, 478
DeRoche, Steve 36
DeSomber, Anthony 271
DeSomber, Ray 30, 68, 388-90, 401
Despain, Roy 66
Deveraux, Gary 21
Deveraux, O.J. and Ruth . . 22, 108, 262, 357, 402, 448, 477
Deveraux, Phyllis 357
Dewitt, Brett 110
Diener, Frank 271
Dill, Owen and Bessie . . . 259, 344

Dillon, Annette 447
Dillon, Kay 279
Dillon, Russ 279
Dobbins, Gene 139, 338, 448
Dockery, Larry 235, 403
Doerr, Bob 182
Donovan, Rev. Herb 27
Doornbos, Al 270, 330
Dorn, Cy 57
Douglas, Dean . . 308, 330, 367, 384
Douglass, Clyde . . 74, 235, 363, 367
Douglass, Jack . . 18, 45, 82, 90, 100
Douglass, Rich 42, 43, 52
Dunn, "Red" 477
Dunning, Frank 66, 129
Dunning, Lew 424
Dunning, Steve 66
Durfey, Truman 328
Durkee, Carroll 12, 15, 39, 474

E

Early, Terry 270
Eaton, Lloyd 37
Eckhardt, Terry 181
Eckroth, Buck 17, 20, 41, 82, 119, 233, 235
Edeler, Del 237, 270, 385
Edeler, Melanie 271
Elgin, John 213
Elliot, Ron 111
Ellis, Fred 90
Ellison, Barbara 367
Ellison, Rev. Floyd 237, 321
Emert, Billie 425
Emrich, Joe 60
Erlich, Gretel 368, 388, 401
Ernst, Art 236
Evans, Afton 425
Evans, Bobby 10, 123
Evans, Kathy 425, 447
Ewen, Jerry 27, 76
Ewen, Maxson 27

F

Farr, Floyd 45, 62
Fees, Paul 265
Fenwick, Red 145
Fiene, Henry 14
Fiene, Martin 14, 59
Fiene, Ron 425
Fink, John Jr. 4
Fisk, Walter 39
Fletcher, Cullen 14, 25, 59
Fletcher, Nellie 233
Flitner, Dave and Sue 260, 270
Flitner, John 17
Flitner, Stan and Mary . . . 326, 331, 332, 386, 404
Flitner, Tim 367
Flon, Mary 271
Foe, Bob and Wanda . . 44, 47, 228, 253, 418
Foe, Dale 124, 404
Foe, E.T. and Karen . . 210, 265, 368
Foe, Tom 39, 74, 402
Forbes, Clyde 366
Forbes, Gertie 56
Ford, Bill 8, 492
Forsyth, Betty 18
Fowler, Mrs. Pete 425
Francisco, Clyde 389
Franklin, Frosty 98
Franscell, Ashley 302, 341, 391, 441
Franscell, Matt 421
French, John 271, 402
Friesen, Ed 118

G

Gahley, John 39
Garland, Bob 110, 425
Gebhart, Jerry 96
George, Dick 254
Gernant, Dwayne 449
Gernant, Otto 331
Gernant, Renea 402
Gibler, Shelby 227
Gifford, Eric 437
Gillett, Harry 17, 63, 348
Gillis, Mr. and Mrs. Ed 23
Gilmore, Pat 401
Gipson, Merl 356
Golden, Barbara 60
Good, Mr. and Mrs. Albert 89
Good, Frankie 448
Good, Gary and Pat . . 78, 237, 266, 331, 385, 425
Good, Harry 331
Good, Hector 75, 80, 95, 249, 331, 363
Good, John 73, 77, 80
Good, Lawrence 84
Good, Lee 448
Good, Leonard 73
Good, Marjorie 385
Good, Myrtle 56
Good, Sam 270
Good, Scott 474
Good, Tony 89
Good, Vera 270
Goodwin, Allen 298
Goodwin, Greg 366
Gormley, Mary 19
Gormley, Richard 252, 369, 440, 448
Goton, Tom 318
Gould, Don 328
Gould, Fred 93, 112, 139, 338, 448
Grabbert, Dave 118
Graham, Stan 270
Graham, Tim (Tilman L.) 33
Graham, Tim 251
Grammar, Jim 147
Grant, Bill 309
Grant, Cora 474
Graunke, Dave 237
Green, Mel 81
Green, Mike 309
Greene, George 214, 224

Greene, Ken 506
Greene, "Red" 477
Greene, Tammy 385
Greer, Bill 413
Gregg, David and Betty 18, 25
Grenier, Lee 385
Griffith, Jim 69, 353
Grisham, Bertha 331
Grisham, Willie 492
Groseclose, Gary 286
Groseclose, Gordon . . . 97, 115, 117
Groseclose, Guffy 49, 68, 73
Groseclose, Jerry 160, 286, 309, 322
Groseclose, Lloyd 4, 25, 50, 63, 83, 88, 94
Groseclose, Loidene 94
Groseclose, Lora Jean 4
Gruden, Dorothy 232

H

Haddenhorst, Mrs. George 309
Haddenhorst, Mary Lee . . 329, 385
Hageman, Debbie 148
Hageman, Fred 114
Haiman, Marvin 96
Haley, Jillray 25
Haley, Mr. and Mrs. John 74, 78-80, 87, 183, 251, 402
Haley, Ralph 25
Hallcroft, Bob 95, 271
Haller, David 77
Halstead, Lyle 328
Hamilton, F.L. 199, 270
Hammond, Frank 380
Hand, Darby 298
Hankins, Duane 506
Hankins, Lewis 389
Hankins, Marge 214
Hankins, Marvin and Beverly . . 19, 72, 331, 448-49
Hansen, Cliff 185
Hansen, Esther 74

Hanson, Ann 367
Hanson, Bill 55
Hanson, Bruce 86, 112
Hanson, Chris 287
Hanson, Darrel 35
Hanson, Kent 271, 287
Hanson, Lawrence 360, 401
Hanson, Steve 270, 290
Harbaugh, Bill 24, 48, 59, 124
Harnden, Chuck and Vonnie . . . 34, 50, 130, 459, 498
Harnden, Wayne 79
Harper, Elmer 4
Harper, Thad 474
Harrington, Tom 236
Harris, Bert 145, 226, 241
Harris, Chester 59
Harrison, B.L. 29
Harrison, Pat 474
Hart, Avalon 371
Hart, D'Arcy 326
Hart, Marie 236, 350
Hartman, Daphne 271
Hartman, Gary 210, 270, 308, 402
Hartsock, Paul 214
Harvey, Bob 90, 101, 123, 291, 365
Harvey, Oral and Randa . . 32, 190, 392, 478, 484
Haun, George 36
Hawkins, Bob 207
Hawkins, Dan 145
Hay, Lewis 32, 503
Haycock, Jim 124
Hayes, Bill and Pat 271, 308
Hein, Jesse 68
Henan, Benny Earl 181
Henderson, Jerry 255, 367, 479
Henderson, Vernon 270, 384
Heinzen, Ray 237, 251
Herman, Wes 368
Hershberger, Ernie 25
Hesco, John and Vera 330, 404, 447

Heywood, Oscar and Gladys . . . 35, 46, 125, 156
Hibbert, Mr. and Mrs. Guy 69
Hickman, Jerry 17
Higdon, Mark 66
Hill, Mr. and Mrs. Dale . . . 37, 308, 327, 384
Hill, James 506
Hill, Mike 49
Hinckley, Charlotte 437
Hinckley, Frank and Mike . . 237-38, 306, 308, 325-26, 330-31, 385, 420, 449
Hinckley, Mart 384
Hindorf, Julie Ann 31
Hinman, Scotty 250, 332
Hirsch, Gabe 50
Hiser, Jean 475
Hoback, Oscar 9
Hoff, Johnny 425
Hoffman, George 42, 178, 194, 216, 475
Hoffman, Mary 372
Hoflund, Leo 58
Hogue, Rachel 309
Holcomb, Kent 437
Holland, Kurt 12, 16
Holm, Clifford 389
Holtz, Russell 77
Hoover, Logan 27
Horn, Jim 60, 227, 402, 449
Horton, Bernadene 271
Horton, Nina 372
Horton, Russell 440, 448
Horton, Stan 78
Houk, Frank 368, 401
House, Jim 129, 249, 281
Howe, Amos 281
Howe, Barker 468
Howe, Charlie 56
Howe, Martin 71
Hubbard, Pat 121, 286
Hubbard, Tom 28, 49, 60, 496
Huddleston, Eddie . . . 41, 124, 308, 311, 385
Huffman, Peewee 249
Huffman, Roger 425
Hughes, Del 29
Hughes, George 129
Hughes, Jerry 475
Hunsaker, Myrtle 404, 441
Hunt, Bill 286
Hunt, Bob 402
Hunt, Brenda 385
Hunter, Barry 113, 331
Hunter, Dan 12
Hurst, Andy 22
Hurst, Thurman 430
Hutt, Ralf 271

I

Ingalls, Jim 309
Isbell, Debbie 475

J

Jackins, Bob 309
Jackson, Arlene 394
Jackson, "Sandy" 477
Jenkins, Walt 366
Jenks, George 381
Jennings, Henry 10
Jennings, Leonard 23
Jennings, Max 58
Jennings, Steve 58
Jensen, Earl 236
Jensen, Earl Sr 402
Johnson, Bob 380
Johnson, Carol 43
Johnson, George 5, 14
Johnson, Lois 330, 402
Johnson, Paul 282
Johnson, Reginald 79
Johnstone, George 351
Jolley, Fred and Pam 271
Jones, Bud 506

Jones, Ken 16, 53, 67
Jones, Spud 440
Jones, W.J. 42, 506
Judy, Kent and Doris 204, 308
Jurovich, Tritz 71, 351

K

Kapas, Steve 252
Karhu, Dick 252, 308, 367
Karhu, Jack 36
Kawulok, Don 113
Keisel, Lane 425
Keller, Kay 59
Kelly, A.J. and Bonnie 37, 237, 249, 402
Kelly, Chris 52
Kelly, Jim 388
Kelly, Raelene 47
Kelly, Sean 61, 75, 77
Kennedy, Ann 6, 31, 49, 58, 67, 72, 81, 99, 103, 154, 204, 307, 322, 421, 501
Kennedy, Bob and Jeanna . . 17, 43, 44, 47, 48, 53, 54, 56, 60, 62, 66, 70-72, 75, 77, 81, 99, 103, 107, 149, 168, 218, 228, 263, 275, 297, 418, 469, 505
Kennedy, Brian and Carol 3, 5, 8, 10, 18, 22, 24, 25, 32, 33, 44, 47, 50, 56, 63, 99, 115, 152, 305, 318, 351, 355, 415, 460, 476, 487, 494
Kennedy, Gib and Leila 156, 205-7, 266, 328, 340, 347, 353, 355, 372, 380, 395, 420, 434
Kennedy, Jim . . . 311, 350, 451, 461
Kennedy, Justin 375, 438, 476
Kennedy, Kevin 469
Kennedy, Tia 391
Kent, Scott 270
Kershner, Al 365
Kershner, George 38
Kimbell, Harry 473
Kimbro, K.K. 130

Kimbro, Russell and Dorothy 59, 402, 478
King, Bill 17
King, Jack 71, 181, 351
Kingery, LeRoy 308
Kinghorn, Curt 72
Kinghorn, Jack 347
Kinnaird, Paul . . . 70, 113, 124, 127
Klitzke, Earl 366
Klitzke, LeRoy 366
Knapp, Marjorie 500
Knowlton, Buck 366
Knudson, Leo 46
Knudson, Margaret 502
Koch, Lonnie 96, 308, 450
Koller, John 448
Kosich, John 233, 474, 489
Kost, David 475
Kost, Ned 207, 251, 324, 425
Kost, Reynolds and Thelma 256, 448
Kovacs, Mrs. Ernie 30
Krueger, Aaron 309
Krusee, Larry 235
Kulow, Herb and Diana . . 271, 368
Kunkle, Bill 17
Kunkle, Lee 232, 270, 385
Kunkle, Terry 368
Kuroki, Ben 92
Kurtz, Don 116
Kvale, Debbie 68
Kvale, Jack 38

L

Larchick, Gale 339, 346, 387, 425, 448
Larson, Oscar 4
Larson, Vic 21, 40, 48
Lassiter, Turk 191
Lawson, Floss 22, 232
Lawton, Cal 196
Lazaros, Cleo 25
Leavitt, Andy 367, 474
Leavitt, Betty 252

Leavitt, Brenton . . 32, 368, 425, 474
Leavitt, Richard W. "Red" 477
Leavitt, Rich 43
Leavitt, Virginia 60
LeDuc, Kris 72
LeDuc, Mabel Jean 270
Lenninger, Cliff 451
Leonard, Bert 388
Lesser, Beryl 402
Lester, Jack 16, 108, 252, 285
Letellier, Hank 402
Leveraus, Leonard 309
Lewis, Gerald 425
Lewis, Monte 219
Lilja, Axel 210, 266
Lindell, Al 26
Lindsey, Dave 97
Lindsey, Ethel 118
Lindsey, "Red" and Esther . . 35, 89, 237, 306, 331, 477, 486
Linn, Mr. and Mrs. Frank 252, 331, 425
Linn, John 466
Linse, Derb 331, 367
Linse, Jack 367
Lipp, Betty 270
Little, Joe and Laura 308, 314, 348, 422, 425
Lockard, E.F. 402
Lockard, Harold 209, 237, 252, 330
Logan, Maurie 23
Long, Andy 20
Loran, Glenn 474
Love, Iver 474
Loveland, John 36, 56, 64, 130, 389
Lundbert, Bob 309
Lynam, Bill 87
Lynam, Walter 73

M

MacAdams, Bill 235
MacKenzie, C.F. 42
Madsen, Earl 111, 129, 271, 364, 470
Madsen, John 235
Maller, Hugh 230
Malmberg, J.T. 387, 445
Marcus, Mrs. Gottlieb . . . 10, 16, 62
Marcus, Jake 62
Markos, Nicky 270
Martin, Dan 322, 490
Martin, John 142
Maser, Hank 285
Massey, Paul and Sally 128
Maxon, Bruce 449
Maxon, Ivy 249, 308
May, Blondie 108
Mayland, Herman . . . 208, 227, 271, 329, 368, 456
Mayland, Wally 324
Mayville, Mike 402, 448
McAdams, Milton 235
McBride, Father 318
McColloch, Scott 373
McCracken, Harold 118
McGough, John 384, 425
McGuffey, Jay 4
McHale, Byron 453
McHugh, James 369, 449
McIntosh, "Red" and Jill 58, 69, 388, 390, 402, 477
McKenzie, George and Ida 357
McKethen, Joe 71, 351
McKinney, Cleo 23, 26, 27, 35, 50, 82, 261, 488
McLean, Garry 481
McLean, Ron 251
McMillan, Rev. Michael and Christine 304, 475
McNulty, Howard 478
Mead, Eddie 430
Meadows, Maxine 29
Meeker, Mr. and Mrs. Bob . . 70, 96
Meeker, Jody 70, 113
Meier, Doug 385

Meier, Heinie and Ruth 7, 124, 219, 237, 360, 385
Meloney, Con 259
Menzel, Ben 474
Menzel, Mr. and Mrs. John 56
Menzel, Paul 386
Mercer, Chester 55
Merriot, Lew 100
Meyer, Linda 447
Michaelis, Barry 90
Michaelis, Bill 218, 323, 449
Michaelis, Dan 74, 90
Michaelis, Dick 323
Michaelis, Jim 90, 323
Michaelis, Kelly 86
Michaelis, Mike 323
Michaelis, "Red" 3, 23, 65, 76, 90, 92, 149, 202, 225, 270, 287, 323, 325, 331, 424, 477
Michaelis, Sandy 204, 369, 401, 475
Michaels, George 331
Michelena, Connie 369
Michelena, Martin 122
Miller, Barbara 309
Miller, Doug 330
Miller, Marc 402
Miller, Tim 449, 475
Mills, Dr. Benjamin 474
Mills, Merritt 49
Minnis, Henry 127
Minnis, John and Allie 15, 475
Minter, Ben 124, 237, 385, 482
Minter, Rick 43, 235, 242, 424
Minter, Willie 124, 385
Mitchell, Nowles 345
Moberly, Bill 108
Moberly, Harry and Donna . 19, 20
Moberly, Jim 106, 188
Moberly, John 425
Mobley, Dave 68
Mohr, Mandy 33, 65, 74, 75, 105, 126
Molaskey, Joe 73

Molaskey, Marilyn 500
Moon, Brad 69
Moore, Hervey 449
Morris, Jean 386
Morris, Kane 424
Mowell, Glen 506
Murdoch, Bill and Dawn 129, 237, 331, 367, 425, 431, 475
Murdoch, Paul and Claudine .. 374, 424
Murphy, Bill 236, 308
Murphy, Patrick 367
Murray, Frank 448, 474

N

Nance, Jess 58
Nau, Harriet 425
Neeley, Harry 17
Neeley, Roy 115
Neiman, John 356
Nelson, Betty 252, 309
Nelson, George 32
Nelson, Julius 4
NiCastro, Jeanne 474
Nichols, Orpha 475
Nielsen, Billie 237
Nielsen, Bob 252, 331, 384
Nielsen, Roger 226
Nielsen, Slim 16, 90, 100, 226, 251, 401, 428, 432
Nisselius, Jack 145
Nittinger, Tony 449
Nolan, Beth 401
Nolan, Tim 308
Norman, Lewis 309
Norris, Frankie 31, 33, 39, 51, 118, 121, 122, 170, 385, 428, 489
Norris, Julie 42
Norskog, Howard 75
North, J.L. 386
Noyes, Colonel 31
Noyes, Linda 474

O

Oleson, Orin 369
Oliver, Mike 235
Olney, Tom 127
Olson, Barry 252
Olson, Don 47
Olson, George 32
Olson, O.E. 19
Olson, Orvie 63
Olson, Steve 330
Olson, Ted 18, 333
Ondracek, Mrs. Charles 309
O'Neill, "Red" and Eleanor 90, 331, 477
Ortman, Clarence 14, 337, 448
Overgaag, Terry 465
Oxarart, Greg 198

P

Palmer, Jeanie 100
Palmer, May 22
Paris, DeLane 313
Paris, John and Leota . . . 3, 67, 313
Paris, Tim 52
Paris, Wayne 309, 384
Parker, Doris 402
Patterson, Jerry 13
Patterson, Jim 359
Patterson, Liz 330
Patterson, Lorna 331
Patterson, Peyton 14
Pauley, Fred 484
Paustian, Chris 103, 385
Paustian, Debbie 8
Pavlus, Joe 309, 386
Pavlus, Matt 76
Pearce, Frank 356
Pearson, Dave 506
Pearson, John 506
Peavler, Mrs. Carl 56
Peck, Bob 355
Peck, Roy and Margaret . . 355, 427

Perkins, Dee 120
Perkins, J.D. 73, 464
Perkins, Jess 430
Perry, Anna 271
Peters, Bill 329, 367, 384
Peterson, Art 15, 53
Peterson, Chuck 15, 57, 63, 64, 69, 284, 404, 441, 476
Peterson, Paul 77, 78, 107, 430
Peterson, Ted 506
Phillips, Junior 506
Picton, John 17
Pierce, Jack 265
Piercy, Jake 26, 54, 87, 106
Porter, Frank 73
Porter, Jerry 419, 424, 473
Porter, Jim and Connie 65, 270, 286
Porter, John 286
Porter, Joyce 271
Powers, Duane 252
Powers, Fred 237
Powers, Gene and Louise 241, 424, 449
Powers, Mark 87, 113
Powers, Wilbur 235, 271
Preator, Joe 380
Preator, Roy 309
Preis, Adam 171
Preis, John 81
Preis, Walt 315, 330, 372
Presgrove, Don and Linda 327, 330
Presgrove, Shirley 384
Preston, Clint 318
Preston, Randy 69, 75
Prindle, Ade 362
Probst, Kevin 73
Probst, Larry and Ora . . . 2, 40, 42, 48, 124, 222, 424
Probst, Nan 447
Pruett, Mel and Martha 22
Prugh, Myrtle 369, 475

Q

Quigg, Jim and Dorothy 118, 232-4, 506

R

Radovich, Moe 71, 351
Raffl, Mary 331
Rainey, Lawana 463
Ramsey, Frank 464
Randolph, Wayne 444, 475
Rannells, Mid 474
Rath, Dorothy 441
Rech, Ed 75, 249
Rech, Jock 286
Reed, Bob 113, 125
Reed, Dick 72, 309
Reeg, Mary 55
Reifschneider, Reuben 65, 81, 116, 121, 169-70
Reilly, Earl 59, 237, 329, 402, 447, 466, 473
Reilly, Jim 80
Ressler, Don 386
Reynolds, Adrian and Helen .. 267, 470
Rice, Mr. and Mrs. Ernie .. 35, 221
Rice, Jeanine 449
Rice, Larry 221
Rice, Vern 49
Ridenour, Bud 76
Ridley, Luke 398
Riley, Tom 4
Rimer, Butch 308
Riopelle, Rosalind 43
Robb, Will 344
Roberts, Charley 182
Roberts, Vaughn 82
Robertson, Jim 305, 368
Rodman, Shannon 110, 123
Rodman, Tom 73
Roe, Harry 18
Roehrkasse, Laurence 101
Roehrkasse, Lennie 101
Rogers, Dr. A.S. and Betty .. 18, 33, 52, 77, 80, 237-38, 250, 273, 274, 330, 331, 385, 448
Rogers, Dan 42
Rogers, Steve 37, 235
Rohloff, Ed 248
Roice, Judi 237
Roush, Denny 143
Ruder, Mel 355
Ruhl, Donald 221
Rutherford, Chuck 56, 233, 474, 489

S

Saban, Helen 308, 385, 449
Saban, Vera 367
Sackett, Mary 308, 347
Sanders, Elden and Belle .. 85, 235
Sanders, Leon 506
Sanders, Pat 183
Sanders, Paul 235
Sanders, Peg 475
Saul, Elvin 88, 90, 121, 322
Saunders, Lula Green 365
Sawyer, Ron 235
Schafer, Mr. and Mrs. Harry . 34, 56
Schaffer, John 68
Schaffer, Melville Roy 68
Scharen, Mr. and Mrs. Bud 40
Scharen, Dolan .. 330, 402, 424, 474
Scharen, Joe 443, 448
Scharen, Linda 314
Schmer, John 79, 218
Schmidt, Andy 64
Schmidt, Bill 4
Schmidt, Don 137
Schmidt, Pat 235
Schmoldt, Irma 424
Schoeggle, Reba Williamson 46
Schroll, Ann 113
Schubert, Paul 144, 355
Schultz, Don 7
Schutte, Art and Idell .. 95, 198, 236

Schutte, Diana 470
Schutte, Mike 12, 368
Schutte, Tim 88
Schuyler, Don 78, 369
Schuyler, Jim 12, 66, 78, 283
Schuyler, Skip and Edna 78, 124, 385, 449
Schuyler, Tom 78
Scott, Doug 270
Scott, Edith 45, 118
Scott, Emerson 385, 448
Scott, George Conoco 8, 29, 44, 49, 91, 95, 183, 216
Scott, Mike 79
Scurlock, George 101
Sehorn, Tom 12
Sellars, Elaine 385, 425, 474
Selvidge, Florence 309
Senift, Ralph 451
Senstad, L.J. 29
Severance, Lynn 112, 126, 130, 209-10, 231, 264, 266, 361, 453
Severy, Bob 74
Sharp, Bill 182
Shell, Dick 122
Shelledy, Bill 85, 237, 250, 331, 368, 379, 385
Shelledy, Bill Jr. 48
Shelledy, Pat 204, 237, 322
Shepard, Larry 126
Shepard, Rob 97
Sheppard, L.C. 501
Sherard, Ira and Edythe 22, 309, 486
Sherman, Leigh 331
Shirran, Chuck 121, 327
Shoemaker, Ed 366
Shoemaker, Oscar 23, 51, 73, 88, 112, 124, 129, 136, 235, 451
Shores, Anita 61
Shores, Forrest 38, 40, 61
Shores, Glen 45
Shortt, Lavern and Lois .. 16, 20, 33
Shortt, Linda 8

Shotton, Gary 249
Shotwell, Gertrude 55
Siekierski, John 252
Sills, Pat 12, 331
Sims, Lessie 26, 30, 34, 59
Simpson, Al 113, 202, 211-12, 468
Simpson, Bill 17, 28, 385
Simpson, Milward 430
Simpson, Russell 252, 425
Small, Amos 13, 330, 354, 367
Small, Homer 20, 82, 235
Small, Ralph 394
Smith, Andy and Kathy 447
Smith, Art 76
Smith, Charlie 327
Smith, Chot and Gladys 122, 237, 490
Smith, Cub 381
Smith, Don 65, 390
Smith, Elwood 181
Smith, George and Dailiah 329
Smith, Gil and Jade 360, 379
Smith, Herb 38, 51, 130
Smith, Marcel 65, 309
Smith, Metz and Thelma 27, 81, 129, 208, 237, 241, 249, 270, 278, 385
Smith, Morris 109, 490
Smith, Nick 11
Smith, Paul 65
Smith, Robert 65
Smith, Robin 341
Smith, Rod 308
Smith, Roland 113, 252, 330
Smith, Scott and LaRae (Kinghorn) 249, 252, 289, 367, 424
Smith, Slim 40
Smith, Sylva 81
Smith, Vern 14
Smith, Zeva 331
Snell, Doug 235
Snell, Hillman 44
Sniffen, Bill 145

Snyder, Chuck 49
Snyder, Del 409, 420, 424, 447
Sommerville, Butch . . . 12, 40, 235
Spangler, Dan 12
Spargur, John 65
Spence, Bud and Opal 474
Spencer, Mr. and Mrs. Claude . . 10
Spencer, Mike 42
Spencer, Ruth 357
Spragg, Tina 425
St. Jermain, Mr. and Mrs. Frank . . . 46, 51
St. Jermain, Griff 63
St. John, Bert 181
Stadtfeld, Lon and Louise . 270, 375
Staggs, Henry 10
Staudt, Josh 449
Stearns, Clair 101, 129, 281, 326, 330, 365, 366, 449
Stephens, Press 401, 404, 449
Stickley, Elizabeth (Kennedy) . . 56, 260, 314, 332, 346, 352, 358, 393
Stickley, Glen 302
Stockert, Dean 449
Stockhouse, Axel and Janet . . . 251, 447, 475
Stockwell, Greg 330
Stockwell, Jack 37, 61, 242
Stockwell, Jim 242
Stockwell, Ken 292
Stockwell, Orville 43, 85, 129
Stoddard, Morris 236
Stoffer, Betty 474
Stolcis, Ron 236
Storeim, Jerry and Alberta 369, 474
Stott, Ells 385
Stout, Asa 475
Stout, Willie 330, 442, 447
Straight, Dan 47, 49
Stratton, Britt 416
Strickland, George 118, 429
Strohman, Jake 235
Strube, Victor 402
Suiter, J.B. 345
Sullivan, Mike 426
Sullivan, Randy 207, 368, 384
Sylvester, Art 72, 76, 251, 309, 350, 368, 454

T

Tarter, John 270, 390, 401, 464
Tatlock, Pauline 448
Temme, Rev. and Mrs. Ralph . . 449
Tew, Don 22
Tew, Merrill 22
Thayer, Mrs. A.L 386
Thompson, Maurice 127
Thorley, Dick 235
Thorley, Tom 45
Thorley, Wes 40
Thorn, Neal 63
Thorp, Judy 270
Tillard, John 118
Tisdale, Tom 326
Tolman, Bob and Freda . 19, 47, 122
Tolman, Jeff 73, 401, 405
Tolman, Mary 90
Tomlinson, Becky 86
Tomlinson, Pat and Sheila 80, 100, 389
Tonn, Terry 41
Tracy, Dwight 360
Trout, John "Fishy" 321
Turner, Helen 91
Turner, Robert 252, 401
Turner, Warren 386
Twomey, Albert 235, 283
Twomey, Jack 381

U

Unterzuber, Chuck 19, 109, 233, 448
Unterzuber, Howard 30, 42
Unterzuber, W.F. 42, 231, 294
Urbach, Debbie 474

V

Valasek, Paul 401
Valasek, Susan 425
Van Gelder, Dave 474
Van Gelder, Tom and Arlene . . 237, 326
Vannoy, Spike 351
Vaught, Betty 389
Vickerman, Doug 270
Vinnola, Tony 36
Vukelich, Mike 265

W

Waddell, Jack 240
Waddell, Randy 447
Walker, Doc and Olive . . . 199, 504
Walker, Myron 504
Wallace, Margaret 87
Waller, Bill 182
Wallin, Bob 330, 331, 402
Wallop, Malcolm 132
Walton, Bob 109, 120, 208
Walton, Clarence 63, 78, 129
Walton, Dave and Brenda 418, 454, 474
Wamhoff, Arnold 38
Wamhoff, Tom and Stephanie . 300
Ward, Hugo 346
Warfel, George and Mildred . . . 53, 82, 88, 144, 330, 469, 483
Warren, Slim 164
Waterworth, Doyal 252
Webb, Mabel 449
Welch, John 17
Welch, Mary 29, 42
Welling, Blaine 81
Welton, Dorothy 425
Wendling, Ron 474
Werbelow, Bill 42, 235
Werbelow, Irvin 35
Werbelow, Rick 400, 401, 425
Wesnitzer, Bill 394

Whaley, Alice 252
Whaley, Chester 40, 106
Whaley, Jim 331, 386, 428
Whaley, Jolene 326
Whaley, Richard and Ruth 273, 424
Whipps, Fritz and Ellen . . 112, 348, 475
Whipps, Jim 79
White, Helen 98
Whitney, Fred 122
Wilcox, Liesa 60
Wilcox, Oren 60
Wiley, Red 447
Wilkerson, Blanche and Babe . . . 32
Wilkerson, Harley 123
Wilkinson, Bill (W.M.) 80, 237, 482, 506
Wilkinson, Bill 386, 405, 424
Wilkinson, Brandy 425
Wilkinson, Guy 237, 251, 270
Wilkinson, Irvin 48, 361, 482
Wilkinson, Jay 83, 402
Wilkinson, Jim 32, 405
Wilkinson, Tom 12, 16, 52, 53, 66, 119, 128, 234-35, 252, 481
Williams, Buck 235
Williams, Corky 10
Williams, Gerald 40
Williams, Jack 6, 11, 51, 52, 53, 84, 88, 177, 237, 271, 331, 336, 360, 421, 450
Williams, John 11, 37, 177
Williamson, Chuck 73, 86, 368
Williamson, Dave and Kelly 196, 474
Williamson, Lynn 309
Willson, Howard 195, 207, 302
Wilson, Larry 469
Wilson, Riley 18, 22, 433
Winkler, Gary 301
Winsor, Dwight and Gerry 237, 252, 425
Winzenreid, Fritz 38
Wood, Bill 46
Wood, Charles 252

Wood, Jim 46
Wood, Will 110
Woodring, Minnie 91
Woodruff, J.D. 122
Woodward, R.S. 34, 265
Wright, Brad . . . 271, 386, 399, 474
Wright, Carolyn and Dale 77, 217, 236, 399
Wright, George 30
Wright, Jack 77
Wright, Orville 115
Wright, Ron and Patricia 237, 251, 308, 331, 384, 447
Wright, Wayne 81

Y

Yates, Darwin and Cecil . . 250, 251, 442, 443, 448
Yates, Rowe 378
Yeager, Pat 207
Yorgason, Wayne 506
Young, Shirley 449

Z

Zane, Billy 246, 479
Zaring, Jim 195
Zellner, Adolph "Ox" 11, 12, 84, 161